CHAUCER'S DREAM VISION AND SHORTER POEMS

BASIC READINGS IN CHAUCER AND HIS TIME
VOLUME 2
GARLAND REFERENCE LIBRARY OF THE HUMANITIES
VOLUME 2105

BASIC READINGS IN CHAUCER AND HIS TIME

CHRISTIAN K. ZACHER AND PAUL E. SZARMACH, *Series Editors*

WRITING AFTER CHAUCER
*Essential Readings in Chaucer
and the Fifteenth Century*
edited by Daniel J. Pinti

CHAUCER'S DREAM VISIONS AND
SHORTER POEMS
edited by William A. Quinn

CHAUCER'S DREAM VISIONS AND SHORTER POEMS

EDITED BY

WILLIAM A. QUINN

GARLAND PUBLISHING, INC.
A MEMBER OF THE TAYLOR & FRANCIS GROUP
NEW YORK AND LONDON
1999

Published in 1999 by
Garland Publishing Inc.
A Member of the Taylor & Francis Group
19 Union Square West
New York, NY 10003

10   9   8   7   6   5   4   3   2   1

Library of Congress Cataloging-in-Publication Data
Chaucer's dream visions and shorter poems / edited by William A. Quinn.
      p.   cm. — (Garland reference library of the humanities ; v. 2105.
Basic readings in Chaucer and his time ; v. 2.)
    Includes bibliographical references and index.
    ISBN 0–8153–3100–2 (alk. paper)
    1. Chaucer, Geoffrey, d 1400 — Criticism and interpretation. 2. Visions
in literature. 3. Dreams in Literature. I. Quinn, William A., 1951–.   II.
Series: Garland reference library of the humanities ; vol. 2105. III. Series:
Garland reference library of the humanities. Basic readings in Chaucer and
his time ; v. 2.
PR1924.C48 1999
821'.1–dc21
                                                                   99–35 726
                                                                    CIP

Printed on acid-free, 250-year-life paper
Manufactured in the United States of America

To Catherine Mary and to William Reed

CONTENTS

IV. *The Parliament of Fowls*

V. *The Legend of Good Women*

VI. The Short Poems

VII. Conclusion

SERIES EDITORS' PREFACE

Basic Readings in Chaucer and His Time is a series of volumes that offers reprints of significant essays in the field, written mainly after 1950, along with some new essays as commissioned by editors of the individual volumes. The series is designed so that each volume may serve as a "first book" on the subject within the area of Chaucer studies treated, thus offering students easy access to major landmarks in the subject. There are three main branches within the series: collected essays organized according to Chaucer's work or works, essays collected from other fields that support an understanding of Chaucer in his time (e.g., art history, philosophy, or comparative literature) and special volumes addressing specific problem areas in the study of Chaucer. Each volume editor has the autonomy to select essays that reflect the current state of knowledge and that point toward future directions. Chaucer remains the major pre-modern author in English and has become a center-point where the history of literature intersects with contemporary methodologies. Basic Readings in Chaucer and His Time aims to offer an authoritative entry through its several volumes to this lively, engaging, and perduring area of study. The series is part of the remarkable flowering of Chaucer studies that has marked the last few decades, reflected in the growth of the New Chaucer Society, including its conference and publications programs; the Chaucer sessions at Kalamazoo; and the sustained activity of the Chaucer group at the Modern Language Association. At the same time, Basic Readings in Chaucer and His Time seeks to compensate for new publications patterns and changed library acquisitions policies in serials and retrospective titles by providing affordable access to significant scholarship in the field.

Chaucer's Dream Visions and Short Poems gathers seventeen essays (previously published between 1959 and 1994) which have significantly influenced our current comprehension of *The Book of the Duchess, The*

House of Fame, The Parliament of Fowls, The Legend of Good Women,
and Chaucer's lyrics. As a compilation, this volume exemplifies a variety of critical approaches, both traditional and new, including: source studies, allegorical exegesis, rhetorical and formalist analyses, as well as psychoanalytic, post-structuralist,feminist, Marxist, New Historical and performance-based theories of interpretation. Quite different, but complementary introductory essays by A. C. Spearing and Robert R. Edwards provide overviews of Chaucer's dream visions as a cohesive subset of the poet's canon. Reprints of explications of each dream vision and of the short poems considered discretely represent the highly influential studies of R. M. Lumiansky, D. W. Robertson, Jr., and Bernard Huppé, Phillippa Hardman,Robert O. Payne, Sheila Delany, Larry D. Benson, Bertrand H. Bronson, Paul A. Olson, David Aers, Robert Worth Frank, Jr., Lisa J. Kiser, Carolyn Dinshaw, Richard F. Green, Lee Patterson and James I. Wimsatt. An entirely new essay by John Ganim, which serves as the volume's conclusion, discloses the somewhat surprising critical importance of the study of Chaucer's reputedly "minor poetry" to Chaucerian criticism in particular and to contemporary literary theory in general.

The series editors thank William A. Quinn for compiling this collection.

Christian K. Zacher
Ohio State University

Paul E. Szarmach
Western Michigan University

ACKNOWLEDGMENTS

I would first like to thank Paul E. Szarmach and Christian K. Zacher, the general editors of the Garland Series of *Basic Readings in Chaucer and His Times*, for this opportunity. I am especially grateful to John Ganim who so generously contributed his new essay "Chaucer's Dreams: Chaucer's Early Poems, Literary Criticism and Literary Theory" to this volume.

I must also thank Bernie Madison, Dean of the Fulbright College of Arts and Sciences of the University of Arkansas, and Charles Adams, Chair of the Department of English, for their generous financial support of this research project. I am no less indebted to Beth Juhl, Head Reference Librarian of Mullins Library, and Lyna Lee Montgomery, Associate Chair of English, for their expert and selfless assistance. I am likewise grateful to the editorial staff of the Garland Press for their care and patience.

Finally, I would like to thank my wife and children for not shuffling all the papers too much or too often. And, most of all, I need to thank Chad Andrews without whose technical expertise and selfless dedication this project could simply have never come to fruition.

LIST OF ABBREVIATIONS

Chaucer's Works

ABC	"An ABC"
BD	*The Book of the Duchess*
ClT	"The Clerk's Tale"
CT	*The Canterbury Tales*
Form Age	"The Former Age"
FranklT	"The Franklin's Tale"
HF	*The House of Fame*
KnT	"The Knight's Tale"
LGW	*The Legend of Good Women*
MerchT	"The Merchant's Tale"
MLT	"The Man of Law's Tale"
PF	*The Parliament of Fowls*
Purse	"The Complaint of Chaucer to His Purse"
Romaunt	*The Romaunt of the Rose*
Sted	"Lak of Stedfastnesse"
Tr(oilus)	*Troilus and Criseyde*
T&C	*Troilus and Criseyde*

Journals, Series, Reference and Other Primary Works

AHDLMA	*Archives d'Histoire Doctrinale et Littérair du Moyen Age*
BJRL	*Bulletin of the John Rylands Library*
ChR	*Chaucer Review*
ChauR	*Chaucer Review*
CL	*Comparative Literature*
EETS e.s.	*Early English Text Society*, Extra Series
EETS o.s.	*Early English Text Society*, Original Series
ELH	*ELH* (English Literary History)
JEGP	*Journal of English and Germanic Philology*
JWCI	*Journal of the Warburg and Courtland Institute*
L&H	*Literature and History*

MED	*Middle English Dictionary*
M&H	*Medievalia et Humanistica*
MLN	*Modern Language Notes*
MP	*Modern Philology*
N&Q	*Notes and Queries*
NED	*New English Dictionary*
NLH	*New Literary History*
OED	*Oxford English Dictionary*
PL	*Patrologia Latina* (ed. J. P. Migne)
PMLA	*PMLA* (Publications of the Modern Language Association)
Purg.	*Purgatorio*
RES	*Review of English Studies*
Rose	*Le roman de la rose*
SAC	*Studies in the Age of Chaucer*
Spec(ulum)	*Speculum: A Journal of Medieval Studies*
Tes.	*Teseide*
TLL	Thesaurus Linguae Latinae
YES	*Yearbook of English Studies*

Chaucer's Dream Visions and Shorter Poems

I. CATEGORICAL CONCERNS

As part of the Garland Series of *Basic Readings in Chaucer and His Time*, this compilation of essays about *Chaucer's Dream Visions and Short Poems* is meant to provide advanced undergraduates and graduate students with a common core of exemplary and influential studies. This volume is intended to enhance class discussions, to highlight certain major issues currently under consideration, and to enable young scholar-critics to join the ongoing conversation as quickly as possible. On a more mundane level, it alleviates some of the anxiety that waiting for recalled books or for interlibrary loans can cause. But it is not meant to be thought of as an all-inclusive collection of "the best articles to date"—a promotional blurb that would prove both pretentious and contentious.

All citations of Chaucer's own works (unless otherwise noted in the reprints themselves) are taken from Larry Benson, *et al.*, eds., *The Riverside Chaucer* (1987). I have tacitly corrected the few, minor and obvious typographical errors that I noted in the original articles. I apologize for any new errors that I may have introduced during the reprinting process; I hope my own mistakes will prove equally obvious and correctable.

This particular collection of *Basic Readings*, unlike other volumes in this series, lacks the inherent cohesiveness that focusing on a single text or a single topic provides. Perhaps the only feature that all the articles reprinted herein have in common is that each demonstrates how to achieve a major critical statement regarding some of Chaucer's reputedly less significant compositions. Each of the essays included in this volume proposes some basic insight that affects our view of an entire work and often, therefore, of Chaucer's entire career. Each essay is also exemplary in that it offers a paradigm for either a significant school of interpretation or for some distinct critical methodology. Furthermore, each essay remains stimulating, to be valued as much for the contrary statements as for the complementary studies it has provoked.

Another criterion for inclusion in this volume is each essay's individuality, which is not to say its uniqueness. Each exemplifies how criticism can be both convincingly new and true without seeming utterly idiosyncratic. Collectively, the variety of different strategies assumed by these seventeen critics also indicates the increasing diversity of Chaucerian studies. Some contemporary critics have convinced themselves that the notion of a permanent or even perdurable critical record is quaintly passé. But the majority of Chaucerians refuse to consider an article out-of-date merely because it is more than a decade old. The enduring usefulness of Richard J. Schoeck and Jerome Taylor's *Chaucer Criticism II: Troilus and Criseyde and the Minor Poems* (1961) or of Edward Wagenknecht's *Chaucer: Modern Essays in Criticism* (1959) testifies to the still vital currency of several time-honored studies. So, too, the value of printing together such a colloquy of various critical opinions has been more recently demonstrated by C. David Benson's *Critical Essays on Chaucer's Troilus and Criseyde and His Major Early Poems* (1991). I think each article included in this volume should likewise be considered both timely and timeless.

Though no essay included in this volume needs any further apology, I do heartily repent my sins of exclusion. The more successful this book is at accelerating the student-scholar's awareness of the current critical scene, the more acutely aware he or she will become of this collection's shortcomings. But the apparent contrariness of several articles that are included in this volume represents a less readily correctable challenge (for novice and experienced Chaucerians alike) than my mere omissions. This particular choir of *Basic Readings* makes what seems an intensifying cacophony among Chaucerians readily apparent. In 1987, Robert M. Jordan anticipated that his *Chaucer's Poetics and the Modern Reader* would meet resistance "from many quarters—such as the old philology and the New Criticism" (p. 5). Critical sects continue to divide and then subdivide interminably, "Thus jangle they, and demen, and devyse . . ." (*CT* 5. 261). In the aftermath of such publications as *The New Medievalism* (Brownlee 1991) and the appearance (even in the hallowed pages of *Speculum*) of such issues as "The New Philology" (Nichols 1990) or "Studying Medieval Women: Sex, Gender, Feminism" (Partner 1993), it has become impossible to tell what radical revisionisms remain new enough and which will soon be attacked themselves as yesterday's orthodoxies, what critical assumptions will need no further apology and which will be given no further attention.

Some Chaucerians dread the complete Balkanization of Chaucer studies. It can be all very daunting for the novice critic who feels compelled to walk some uncharted *via media* between the

Strengewissenschaft of yore and the hippest patois of contemporary theory. Try to do so, and run the risk of being wishboned for straddling an unforeseen critical boundary. I hope that this collection of *Basic Readings* will, nevertheless, testify to two of the strongest critical trends in Chaucer studies: first, that there still exists a dynamic collaboration among all these diverse inquiries; and, second, that there endures a continuity between the allegedly old questions and the reputedly new answers:

> For out of olde feldes, as men seyth,
> Cometh al this newe corn from yer to yere,
> And out of olde bokes, in good feyth,
> Cometh al this newe science that men lere. (*PF* 22-25)

In fact, one of the least new points of contention among Chaucerians today is a grey-haired grumbling about the loss of some once-upon-a-time gentleman's agreement regarding what the critical agenda should be.

In 1960, Bertrand H. Bronson rather wryly reminisced about a time when "one did not affront one's equals by pointing out literary qualities or values" (*In Search of Chaucer*, p. 7). At the time, some historians, linguists, and textual editors perceived the New Critics as the new threat. But the real donnybrooks among Chaucerians in the Sixties and the Seventies took place between those who identified themselves as "pro-" or "anti-Robertsonians." It is difficult to convey to young Chaucerians the intensity of controversy triggered by D. W. Robertson, Jr., and Bernard Huppé, whose *Fruyt and Chaf* is excerpted below. A frequently vehement and haughty and mutual dismissiveness still divides realist readers of Chaucer from the disciples of a Robertsonian School.[1] The primary objection that many anti-Robertsonians made was not that this allegorical method generates invalid (though perhaps anachronistic) readings, but that it need not be promoted as an exclusively valid filter for the interpretation of all medieval texts.

By the time Chaucerians had exhausted their own internecine squabbles, the rest of English literary studies had already become accustomed to forgetting the controversial novelty of New Criticism, post-structuralism, deconstruction, gender studies, queer theory, New Historicism, and so on. But, as John Ganim details in the concluding essay to this volume, "The Interpretation of Dreams: Chaucer's Early Poems, Literary Criticism and Literary Theory," the sometimes seemingly marginal study of Chaucer's dream-visions and short poems has paralleled and often anticipated several of the most significant developments in contemporary critical theory.

All the resulting competition for attention among various interpretive camps ignites new, yet not newly intense oppositions, a contrariness which remains no longer simply binary as in the good old days. And, again, mutual dismissiveness on an *a priori* basis—not diversity *per se*, nor even divisiveness—remains the only real threat to the further advancement of Chaucer studies. I hardly expect all Chaucerians to sit down to tea. Yet, recollection of the more profound compromises (as well as the mere fatigue) generated by the Robertsonian vs. realist debates should suggest how seemingly opposed critical dispositions can richly complement one another—eventually.

By definition, no basic reading can be considered completely irrelevant to any other basic reading; nor can any critical perspective that generates such a basic reading be dismissed as outdated. For example, a question regarding the sources of one of Chaucer's dream visions might have once upon a time started simply enough as a seemingly objective inquiry into its possible Latin or French or, more problematically, Italian and Spanish precedents.[2] But most such detailed text-to-source comparative studies tend finally to emphasize the originality of Chaucer's borrowings (*i.e.*, to applaud his departures from putative sources) and, therefore, tend to affirm the intrinsic superiority of his art. Certain New Critical assumptions regarding an achronic or ontological conception of poetic excellence have fallen into recent disfavor. To achieve a more historicized appreciation of Chaucer's own *ars poetica*, however, Chaucerians have long referenced the various medieval *artes* (the *ars dictaminis, ars praedicandi, ars grammatica, ars dictandi, ars versificandi, ars longa*, etc.). Such journals as *Assays, Exemplaria*, and *Envoy* foster enhancing the use of this received medieval terminology (both formal and exegetical) with the often highly eclectic lexicon of modern theory. Conversely, the critical premises of the medieval lexicon have been made readily accessible to modern theorists by such landmark studies as Judson Boyce Allen's *The Friar as Critic* (1971) and *The Ethical Poetic of the Later Middle Ages* (1982), as well as A.J. Minnis's *Medieval Theory of Authorship* (1988).

Chaucerians today are every bit as engaged with the theory of history as with the history of theory. Once upon a time, it seemed simple enough to praise Chaucer as inventor of the pentameter couplet and rime royal. Recent reconsiderations of Chaucer's place in England's literary history and the Western canon have proven especially provocative, however. While clarifying Chaucer's pivotal role as exemplar of the socio-political forces that contributed to the end of a medieval "channel culture" and to the establishment of a modern, national tradition, these more historicized assessments also seem to debunk any romanticized portrayals of Chaucer's unique status as the "Father of English Poetry."[3] Nevertheless, many Chaucerians still actively produce formalist analyses for their own sake. And retro-designating Chaucer the first poet laureate of England remains a curiously popular and persistent critical habit. Stylistics, especially prosody and issues of pronunciation, preserve the currency of linguistics, the "old philology." The study of Chaucer's short poems, including the lyrics embedded in his longer narratives, is being particularly enhanced by research into medieval musicology and performing arts.

Yet another kind of controversy emerges, however, whenever a seemingly objective (because simply formalist) critic quite unconsciously uses the adjective "Chaucerian" to applaud some uniquely brilliant as opposed to conventionally "medieval" feature of Chaucer's craft. To Chaucerians, "Chaucerian" conventionally suggests several positive, secular, humanist, ironic, modernist, and/or post-modernist connotations. Any disappointingly sincere, pious, didactic, or merely medieval composition in Chaucer's canon can *ipso facto* be disregarded as "un- Chaucerian." Although this sort of aesthetic judgment seldom undermines the authenticity of a Chaucerian piece that has been judged genuine by textual scholars, critically dismissing one of Chaucer's non-masterpieces as anomalous, or juvenile, or artistically negligible for whatever reason, has much the same impact on future readers as calling it apocryphal.[4] So stylistic analysis translates itself into reader-response criticism and then circles back to ambush the tacit assumptions of canon studies.

It has long been proposed that certain historical events actually occasioned several of Chaucer's dream visions and short poems. Hard as it is to imagine reconstructing Chaucer's own autographs (which his scribe Adam apparently contaminated almost immediately), a cluster of oral theories contending that Chaucer once himself performed several compositions has generated yet another entirely different and entirely relevant set of controversies regarding the retrieval of authorial intent. Conceptualizing the specific occasions of Chaucer's original recitations offers a premise for discussing the original reception contexts of his extant texts. New Historicism joins oral theory to illuminate the interpretive milieu of each hypothetical performance's first audience(s).[5]

But the critical implications of the fundamental idea that Chaucer occasionally wrote for performance occasions neither mandates nor needs to be restricted to retrieval of an actual *mise en scène* for any particular text. Laura Kendrick's *Chaucerian Play* (1988), Leonard Koff's *Chaucer and the Art of Storytelling* (1988), and John Ganim's *Chaucer's Theatricality* (1990) all extend critical consideration of Chaucer's role as proto-reciter to include his authorial expectations regarding the dramatically engaged responses of a familiar, contemporary readership and then of posterity.

Critical dissension is, of course, most intense whenever Chaucer's themes can be addressed as pertinent to some modern controversy. To call Geoffrey Chaucer a misogynist[6] or a latent homophobe or an anti-Semite or a Lollard or Pelagian or Laodicean, for that matter, can spark a number of interpretive firestorms. In these most heated debates, Chaucerians frequently find themselves forced to translate an interpretive lexicon derived from Marx and Freud and Lacan and Foucault and Bahktin and Derrida, *et al.*, into the idiom of the *Middle English Dictionary* and Migne's *Patrologia*.

In the headnote to each section below, I briefly try to indicate both the longstanding critical issues and the most current controversies that are driving discussions of each dream vision and the short poems considered discretely. But one last, largely unresolved issue that requires the mutually illuminating perspectives of all Chaucerians is how to divide the poet's canon into meaningful subsets. The study of Chaucer's dream visions and short poems as a unified field of inquiry has produced some of the most insightful and provocative reassessments of the poet's entire corpus. But the rubric "dream visions and short poems" designates no simply defined category. Indeed, the plots of Chaucer's four dream visions have almost nothing in common (except the dreamer, of course), and not one is simply a dream vision. Furthermore, Chaucer's short poems range from as few as seven lines ("Wordes Unto Adam") to as many as two hundred ninety-eight (the "Complaint of Mars").

Alternative, conventional labels for this rather protean subset of Chaucer's works include: his "Early Poetry," or his "Minor Poetry," or the compositions of his "French Period," or his "Occasional Poems," or his "Shorter Poems." Yet, none of these familiar headings names a category both adequately inclusive and generically significant for all the works to be considered by this volume of *Basic Readings*. It might as readily have been entitled *Chaucerian Et Cetera* or *Not Troilus and Criseyde, Not The Canterbury Tales, and Not Prose* or—most problematically—*Chaucer's Non-Masterpieces*.

The two essays that I have chosen to initiate this volume both address (and thereby legitimize) Chaucer's dream visions as a critically significant grouping. A.C. Spearing reads Chaucer's dream visions against the panorama of their literary background. Robert B. Edwards foregrounds those elements of these same texts that comprise Chaucer's own critical theory. Spearing's analyses of Chaucer's dreams explicate their archetypal timelessness; Edwards retrieves Chaucer's contribution to our contemporary critical discourse.

A BIBLIOGRAPHIC NOTE

There are no valid shortcuts to professional expertise for the novice Chaucerian. But there are a number of highways. *The Riverside Chaucer* (1987) edited by Larry Benson, *et al.*, now supersedes F.N. Robinson's Second Cambridge Edition of *The Works of Geoffrey Chaucer* (1957) as the definitive critical edition to be cited in publications. The Riverside edition's introductions and notes, both "Explanatory" and "Textual," provide judicial synopses of the current consensus among Chaucerians regarding most issues. Its "General Bibliography" (pp. 771-778) also provides numerous, excellent recommendations for critical introductions and overviews, to which may be added several excellent studies published subsequently, including: Piero Boitani and Jill Mann, eds., *The Cambridge Chaucer Companion* (1986); Dieter Mehl, *Geoffrey Chaucer: An Introduction to his Narrative Poetry* (1973; trans. 1986); J. Stephen Russell's *The English Dream Vision; Anatomy of a Form* (1988); and Stephen F. Kruger's *Dreaming in the Middle Ages* (1992).

Donald R. Howard's *Chaucer: His Life, His Works, His World* (1987) and Derek Pearsall's *The Life of Geoffrey Chaucer* (1992) now supplement the standard biographies recommended in the Riverside edition. Martin M. Crow and Clair C. Olson's *Chaucer Life-Records* (1966) provides succinct commentaries as well as transcripts of the contemporary records pertaining to Chaucer's life.[7]

The *Oxford Guide to Chaucer: The Shorter Poems* (1995) offers not only a scholarly precis of each work's provenance, style, sources, themes, and critical heritage, and excellent selective bibliographies but also A.J. Minnis's own significant readings of each work. Like Minnis, the contributors to Beryl Rowland's *Companion to Chaucer Studies* (1968; rev. 1979) offered strong and strongly opinionated overviews; still mandatory reading are the comments of Rossell Hope Robbins on "The Lyrics," D.W. Robertson, Jr., on "*The Book of the Duchess*,"

Laurence Shook on "The *House of Fame*," Donald Baker on "The *Parliament of Fowls*," and John H. Fisher on "The *Legend of Good Women*." To conduct a full bibliographic survey of secondary materials (including early editions) in chronological sequence, consult Eleanor P. Hammond's *Chaucer: A Bibliographic Manual* (1908; facs. rpt. 1994), Dudley D. Griffith's *Bibliography of Chaucer, 1908-1953*, then William R. Crawford's *Bibliography of Chaucer 1954-1963* (rev. 1967), then Lorrayne Y. Baird's *Bibliography of Chaucer, 1964-1973*, then Lorrayne Y. Baird-Lange's *A Bibliography of Chaucer, 1974-1985*. To begin research into the "Chaucerian Apocrypha," see Rossell Hope Robbins' contribution to Albert E. Hartung, gen. ed., *A Manual of the Writings in Middle English 1050-1500*, Vol. 4 (1973).

Russell A. Peck's *Chaucer's Lyrics and "Anelida and Arcite"*: *An Annotated Bibliography 1900-1980* (1983) is extremely helpful. The annual Annotated Bibliographies provided by *Studies in the Age of Chaucer*—also available on-line at <telnet://libcat.utsa.utsa.edu>—now expedite the Chaucerian's need to keep up to date; formerly, annual reference to the *Chaucer Review* and *Neuphilogische Mitteilungen* was required. A Supplement to the *Chaucer Review* (Vol 31. No. 2) provides a "Bibliography of the First Thirty Years of the *Chaucer Review*," edited by Peter G. Beidler and Martha A. Kalnan, available on-line at <http:www.baylor.edu/~Chaucer_Bibliography>.   The Modern Humanities Research Association's *Annual Bibliography of English Literature and Language* (1920-), the *Modern Language Association of America's International Bibliography* (1921-), as well as the descriptive essays of the *Year's Work in English Studies* also provide annual updates.

Retrospective analyses of critical trends in Chaucer studies most conveniently start with Derek Brewer, ed., *Chaucer: The Critical Heritage*, 2 Vols. (1978) and Caroline Spurgeon's *Five Hundred years of Chaucer Criticism and Allusion, 1357-1900*, 3 Vols. (1925). Twelve essays about the twelve most significant editors of Chaucer (*i.e.*, from William Caxton to F.N. Robinson) are gathered in Paul G. Ruggiers, ed., *Editing Chaucer: The Great Tradition* (1984).

The on-line MLA Bibliography is especially convenient for quick topic searches and for accessing the most recent publications. Both the Medieval Academy of America <http://www.georgetown.edu/Medieval Academy/> and the New Chaucer Society <http://ncs.rutgers.edu> maintain home-pages on the Worldwide Web, and one link leads to another. Chaucer-Net <CHAUCER@LISTSERV.UIC.EDU> now serves very much as a sort of cyber-*Notes and Queries*.

For semantic studies, John S.P. Tatlock and Arthur G.
Kennedy's *Concordance to the Complete Works of Geoffrey Chaucer and to the
Romaunt of the Rose* (1927) remains a convenient single-volume
reference (even though it is keyed to the Globe edition). Akio Oizumi's
twelve-volume, computer-generated *Complete Concordance to the
Works of Geoffrey Chaucer* (1991-1994) is more exhaustive, is keyed
to the Riverside edition and provides rhyme indices.

Norman Davis' *A Chaucer Glossary* (1979) provides a handy and
affordable dictionary available in paperback. To pursue more detailed
lexical inquiries, consult Hans Kurath, *et al.*, eds., *The Middle English
Dictionary* (1954-) as well as J.A. Simpson, *et al.*, eds., *The Oxford
English Dictionary*, 2nd Ed. (1989). If it is necessary to gloss
Chaucer's loan words or to analyze his translations as such, consult as
appropriate: P.G.W. Glare's *Oxford Latin Dictionary* (1982) and J.F.
Niermeyer's *Mediae Latinitatis Lexicon Minus* (1976), Frederic
Godefroy's *Dictionnaire de l'ancienne langue francaise* (1881-1902;
rpt. 1965), or Salvatore Battaglia's *Grande dizionario della lingua
italiana* (1961- [1998]).

Several phrases in Chaucer's poetry still require literal explication,
and often such passages require alternative editing. A.J. Minnis's *Guide*
(pp. 6-7) provides a convenient list of facsimiles and of the major
editions to be consulted, including *A Variorum Edition of the Works of
Geoffrey Chaucer, Vol. V: The Minor Poems, Pt. 1* (1982), edited by
Alfred David and George B. Pace. M.C. Seymour has also provided *A
Catalogue of Chaucer's Manuscripts, Volume I: Works Before The
Canterbury Tales* (1995).

NOTES

1. A.J. Minnis, for example, has most recently seconded Maureen
Quilligan's rejection of the "invasive" force of Robertsonian exegesis
when applied to the "vulnerable" *Parliament of Fowls* (*Guide*, p. 276).

2. Two extremely useful reference tools for beginning such
research are Robert P. Miller, ed., *Chaucer: Sources and Backgrounds*
(1977), and Lynn King Morris' *Chaucer Source and Analogue
Criticism: A Cross Referenced Guide* (1985). Ernst Curtius's
European Literature and the Latin Middle Ages (1953) remains a
magisterial introduction to the classical heritage of literary topoi.
Charles Muscatine's *Chaucer and the French Tradition* (1957) and
John P. McCall's *Chaucer Among the Gods* (1979) likewise offer still
authoritative analyses of Chaucer's stylistic and thematic indebtedness

to French and classical literature. A.J. Minnis's *Chaucer and Pagan Antiquity* (1982) investigates Chaucer's imaginative constructs of the non-Christian outlook.

3. See, for example, Seth Lerer's *Chaucer and His Readers* (1993) and Christopher Cannon's "The Myth of Origin and the Making of Chaucer's English" (1996).

4. John M. Bowers, ed., *The Canterbury Tales: Fifteenth Century Continuations and Additions* (1992) offers a very available and affordable introduction to the study of the Chaucerian apocrypha and the concomitant determination of the poet's canon.

5. See, for example, Joyce Coleman's recent study of *Public Reading and the Reading Public in Late Medieval England and France* (1996).

6. In addition to Carolyn Dinshaw's *Chaucer's Sexual Poetics* (1989), excerpted below, see Jill Mann's *Chaucer* (1991) and Elaine Tuttle Hansen's *Chaucer and the Fictions of Gender* (1992). Fran Utley's *The Crooked Rib* (1944; rpt. 1970) provides a primary bibliography of medieval England's misogynist literary tradition.

A.J. Minnis offers a provocative analysis of the homosocial sensibilities implied by the dialogue between the Black Knight and Chaucer-the-dreamer in the *Book of the Duchess* (*Guide*, pp. 100-122); this reading marries contemporary gender theory to traditional source studies (*i.e.*, of Machaut's *Jugement dou Roy de Behaigne*).

7. See too Christopher Cannon's "*Raptus* in the Chaumpaigne Release and a Newly Discovered Document Concerning the Life of Geoffrey Chaucer," *Speculum* 68 (1993); 74-94.

CHAUCER

by A.C. Spearing

My chief purpose in this chapter will be to offer detailed studies of each of Chaucer's four dream-poems, but I begin with some brief general remarks about Chaucer as a dream-poet. The first is that, being widely read, he was familiar with many of the visionary works, dream-poems, and *dits amoreux* already mentioned. He had certainly read the *Aeneid*, the *Somnium Scipionis* with Macrobius's commentary, the *De Consolatione Philosophiae* the Biblical and apocryphal visions, Alanus, the *Roman de la Rose,* several of the poems of Machaut and Froissart, and, after the middle 1370s, Dante. Some, though not all, of this wide reading is likely to have been shared by his own readers and listeners.

Second, Chaucer wrote a comparatively large number of dream-poems. Though he may be thought of nowadays chiefly as the poet of *The Canterbury Tales* and *Troilus and Criseyde* (and I do not dispute that these remain his major works), he also wrote four dream-poems, or five, if we include his translation of the *Roman de la Rose.* Only Dunbar, whose poems are very much shorter, has more dream-poems attributed to him than that. Part of my argument will be that, although each of these poems has an independent existence as a work of art, they also form an intelligible sequence, in which certain leading themes are carried from one poem to another, and are not merely repeated but developed. The existence of this series of related dream-poems is of great help in our understanding of any one of them, because each throws light on the others. Although there is no reason to suppose that the poems reflect a real series of Chaucer's dreams, they are like dreams in being the most personal and intimate of his works, and it may be that a series of dream-poems gives the literary critic the same kind of advantage as a series of dreams gives the dream-analyst. The point has been made by Jung:

Every interpretation is hypothetical, for it is a mere attempt to read an unfamiliar text. An obscure dream, taken by itself, can rarely be interpreted with any certainty, so that I attach little importance to the interpretation of single dreams. With a series of dreams we can have more confidence in our interpretations, for the later dreams correct the mistakes we have made in handling those that went before. We are also better able, in a dream series, to recognize the important contents and basic themes . . .[1]

Jung is of course aware of the analogy between dream-interpretation and literary interpretation, as his reference to reading an unfamiliar text makes clear.

Third, Chaucer, more than any other dream-poet known to me, was interested in dreams as they really are. The existence of four dream-poems is only part of the evidence for this: he includes dreams and their interpretations in several of his other poems, and also several elaborate discussions of the significance and validity of dreams. One such is the sceptical statement about the validity of dreams made by Pandarus in book v of *Troilus and Criseyde*, followed shortly by Cassandra's serious interpretation of one of Troilus's dreams.[2] Another is the comically solemn discussion between Chauntecleer and Pertelote in *The Nun's Priest's Tale* about the significance of Chauntecleer's dream of the fox. In looking at Chaucer's dream-poems, we shall see again and again that he is making use of his understanding of real dreams, in producing works which are dreamlike, not only in superficial details, but in matters of method and structure.

'The Book of the Duchess'

Chaucer's earliest dream-poem, *The Book of the Duchess*, in one way looks like another example of a type of work already familiar to us. It is apparently a vision of the other world, in which the visionary not only visits another place, but learns a truth from an authoritative person whom he meets and questions there. The narrator falls asleep, and dreams that he wakes up in his bed on a May morning. He has been awakened by birds, singing 'the moste solempne servise' (302), as harmoniously as if 'hyt had be a thyng of heven' (308). This is the paradisal world we have come to expect in religious visions and their courtly imitations; and there is the usual reference back to a literary tradition of visions when the Dreamer tells us that the walls of his dream-bedroom were painted with 'al the Romaunce of the Rose'

(334). When he goes outside, he finds the sun shining, but it is neither too hot nor too cold—this avoidance of extremes of temperature is another common feature of medieval conceptions of paradise. He hears and sees men hunting, and follows them into the forest; they lose track of the hart they are pursuing; then a little puppy comes up to him in a friendly way, and he follows it deeper into the forest, along a path which is still paradisal, for it has as many flowers

> As thogh the erthe envye wolde
> To be gayer than the heven. (406-7)
> *envye* desire

There are also the usual shady trees, and many living creatures running about beneath them. Suddenly, beneath one tree, the Dreamer sees sitting a 'man in blak' (445), a knightly figure in a state of profound melancholy. They have a long conversation, a major theme of which recalls Boethius's *De Consolatione*: the power of Fortune over human life, and the attitude men should adopt towards it. The Black Knight explains that he has played at chess with Fortune, and she has captured his queen; the Dreamer begs him to

> Remembre yow of Socrates,
> For he ne counted nat thre strees
> Of noght that Fortune koude doo. (717-19)
> *stroes* straws

The Dreamer fails to understand the metaphor of the game of chess, and the knight has to tell him the story of his love for a beautiful lady, herself an almost heavenly being, a 'goddesse' (1040). The Dreamer persists in trying to find the cause of the knight's depression; it finally emerges that it is that his lady is dead. With this the dream ends, and the Dreamer finds himself lying once more in his bed. All this seems thoroughly familiar; and if one is startled at first, as one is probably meant to be, by the appearance of mourning and death in the midst of an earthly paradise, one may reflect that it is perfectly usual, from Homer onwards, for otherworld visions to bring news of the dead.

But two aspects of this courtly vision demand further comment. The first is that *The Book of the Duchess* appears to be written for an occasion, and to allude to an event in real life. Most scholars would agree that the 'man in blak' in the dream represents John of Gaunt, Duke of Lancaster, and that the lady he has lost, whom he calls 'goode faire White' (948), represents his first wife Blanche, who died in 1369.

We know that from 1374 onwards Chaucer received a pension from John of Gaunt, for services which may have included the writing of this poem. Chaucer himself refers to the poem as 'the Deeth of Blaunche the Duchesse' in the *Prologue to The Legend of Good Women*, and the odd name 'White' is obviously an anglicized version of Blanche. Towards the end of the poem, there are also certain cryptographic allusions to John of Gaunt: within two lines we find a 'long castel' (Lancaster), a 'ryche hill' (Richmond, of which John was Earl), and 'seynt Johan' (1318-19). There is widespread agreement that the poem was written to commemorate the death of Blanche and to console her husband, though some would deny that the Black Knight is to be identified with the Duke. One scholar, for example, sees the whole poem as having a Boethian meaning, and takes the Black Knight to represent unreasonable grief and the Dreamer to stand for reason.[3] This seems unlikely, because, in view of the cryptograms and the real-life situation, the courtly circle which formed the poem's original public could hardly have failed to identify the Black Knight with the bereaved Duke; and it is hard to believe that Chaucer was in a position to lecture him on the unreasonable nature of his grief. Besides, it would be highly abnormal in a medieval dream-poem for the dreamer and not an authority he meets in his dream to be the source of doctrine. An interpretation in terms of historical allegory seems the obvious one, though the transmutation of the Duke and Duchess into 'man in blak' and 'goode faire White', as if they were pieces in Fortune's game of chess, gives them a generality of significance beyond their historical identities. Where the poem differs from the tradition of otherworld visions is in the fact that the Dreamer sees not the dead person living a life after death, whether of reward or punishment, but the bereaved survivor. The dead lady is brought back to life in imagination only, through the knight's mere words in recalling the course of his devotion to her and the happiness it brought him. The dream brings no supernatural revelation: what the Dreamer learns is not the state of the lady's soul after death, but the bare fact that 'She ys ded' (1309). Once the knight has admitted that, there is no more to say: he can ride 'homwardes' (1315) to a castle where a bell marks the completion of a phase of experience by striking 'houres twelve' (1323), and the vision can come to an end. We shall see that a fundamental theme of Chaucer's later dream-poems is the validity and limitations of poetic imagination, frequently symbolized by the dream itself. Already in the dream of *The Book of the Duchess*, it is imagination—the knight's imagination, and the 'sorwful ymagynacioun' (14) of the poet who

created the knight—that brings the dead back to life, and that only
momentarily: the poem offers no assurance of any other life after death.
The second aspect of *The Book of the Duchess*, considered as a
traditional vision, which demands further comment is that the actual
dream forms only part of the poem. The *Book* has 1333 lines,[4] but it is
not until line 291 that the narrator falls asleep. In the long introduction
to the dream, the narrator begins by explaining that he is suffering from
insomnia. This has been caused by a mysterious sickness, referred to in
such a way that most readers (especially if aware of such precedents as
the love-sickness of the narrator at the beginning of Machaut's *Dit dou
Vergier)* gather that love-sickness is meant. There is but one physician
who could heal him,

> but that is don.
> Passe we over untill eft;
> That wil not be mot nede be left. (40-2)
> *eft* later

If the sickness is love-sickness, the one physician is presumably the
lady who refuses to respond to his love. Some scholars see the sickness
rather as spiritual, and the physician as God;[5] but in that case why is the
narrator so sure that the physician will not heal him? Moreover, as we
shall see later, love-sickness would help to provide a psychological
explanation for certain aspects of the dream which follows. In any case,
the narrator takes a book one night to read himself asleep, a collection
of pagan stories written 'While men loved the lawe of kinde' (56), and
in it he finds the story of Ceyx and Alcyone. These details identify the
book as Ovid's *Metamorphoses*, but Chaucer never mentions its author;
and indeed he followed what was to be a common practice in his poetry
by comparing different versions of the same story, taking as his source
not only Ovid's version but a retelling of it by Machaut in his *Dit de la
Fonteinne Amoreuse*. The story is repeated, of how King Ceyx was
drowned at sea, and how his wife Alcyone bitterly mourned his
absence, and prayed to Juno to send her in a dream definite information
about his fate. We learn how Juno responded by sending a messenger to
Morpheus, the god of sleep, to order him to convey a dream-image of
Ceyx to Alcyone. The messenger had difficulty in waking Morpheus
and his assistant deities—naturally enough, they were sleeping—but
eventually he succeeded by blowing his horn loudly, and the necessary
dream was sent to Alcyone, who almost at once died of grief. Here
Chaucer cuts the story short, with the favourite excuse that 'Hyt were to
longe for to dwelle' (217). But the abridgment is a matter of the poet's

design rather than his audience's convenience, because it means that he silently omits the metamorphosis in Ovid's version, which has both husband and wife transformed into seabirds and thus reunited beyond death. Instead, the narrator explains that from the story he got the idea of praying to Morpheus, Juno, 'Or som wight elles, I ne roghte who' (244) (or some other being, I did not care who)—he does not really believe in these pagan gods—and vowing that he will give him a magnificent feather-bed if he will send him to sleep. No sooner has he pronounced this vow than sleep descends on him, and he dreams a dream so 'wonderful' (277) that it could not be interpreted by either Joseph or Macrobius. The rest of the poem, except for the last eleven lines, describing his awakening, consists of the dream itself.

What is to be made of this highly elaborate introduction to the dream? I believe that interpretations of a number of different kinds are possible, and, because they are on different planes, they do not necessarily clash. One thing they have in common, though, is that they see the function of the preliminary material as an extension or support of the dream itself; it is not by accident that Chaucer has brought together in the same poem (and, as we shall see, in his later dream-poems too) a dream and an elaborate introduction. The most general kind of interpretation would relate the introduction to late-medieval aesthetic principles, and it would apply as much to *dits amoreux* (such as Machaut's *Jugement dou Roy de Navarre*, with its long introductory account of the events of 1348-9) as to dream-poems proper. Much recent work on Chaucer makes us aware that it is not enough to think of him simply as a medieval poet; he is more specifically a late-medieval poet, who reflects in his work many tendencies of style and structure found in other arts of the late Middle Ages. The *Roman de la Rose* belongs to an earlier phase of medieval style, in which a basically simple outline is still visible beneath the elaborately acentric surface. But already in Chaucer's earliest poetry, as in the French poetry of the mid-fourteenth century, we can recognize at least the outward signs of what Huizinga sensationally called 'the Waning of the Middle Ages'. Wolfgang Clemen was among the first to recognize this, and he writes, in connection with *The Book of the Duchess*, that 'The liking for an indirect method of presentation, for shrouding the theme in exuberant ornament and disguise, corresponds to the *gout des complications* illustrated in the flamboyant style of late Gothic art'.[6]

A more recent art-historian, George Henderson, finds a tendency towards ambivalence in late-Gothic architecture, which provides a suggestive parallel to the introductory technique of *The Book of the Duchess*:

> The ambivalence of late-Gothic architecture is immediately obvious in the silhouette of buildings. Long since conditioned not to commit themselves to any formal accent unless they can balance it by its opposite, Gothic architects even attempted a fantastic and ingenious compromise between the two poles of being and non-being. A Gothic building cannot simply stop, it has to fade away. Hence the familiar flurry of curves and spikes, by which the physical presence is gradually withdrawn and the dense material mass is dissolved into the empty air.[7]

Henderson speaks of the building as 'dissolving' rather than 'stopping'; one might equally reverse the image, and speak of it as 'condensing' rather than 'starting'. It would then apply well to *The Book of the Duchess*: the introduction gets the poem started almost imperceptibly, as if it were condensing out of the empty air; it forms that 'familiar flurry of curves and spikes' with which late-medieval artists felt it necessary to mediate between the everyday world and the work of art. It can now be seen that the setting of the poem in a dream is, from one point of view, a means to the same end, for the dream is neither being nor non-being, but a compromise between the two. And from the same point of view, the first part of the contents of the dream serves the same purpose of meditation between everyday reality and the world of imagination. The Dreamer leaves his dream-bedroom, goes first into a field and then into a forest, and penetrates to the very depths of the forest before he finally comes to the true subject of his poem, the encounter with the Black Knight. Thus the dream-poem, as developed in fourteenth-century France and England, is an ideal expression of late-Gothic taste.

Secondly, this very process of elaborate introduction can be seen to relate to the poem's specific social occasion. The encounter between the Dreamer and the Black Knight appears to represent, in symbolic form, an imaginary encounter between Chaucer and the Duke of Lancaster. But these two were persons of very different social standing. The poet was a wine-merchant's son who had married into the aristocracy, and who was making his way in courtly circles by his own gifts and skills. The Duke was King Edward III's fourth son, and was one of the wealthiest and most powerful men of his time. We should not exaggerate the rigidity of the class-system in fourteenth-century England, but surely the only setting in which these two could chat together on such a delicate subject, even in fiction, was one made studiously remote from everyday reality. Now the sense of remoteness is given partly, of course, by the dream-setting itself. Things can happen in dreams which cannot happen in real life; but some things cannot happen even in dreams unless they are translated into a symbolic form—put into code, as Freud sees it, in order to deceive the internal censor. It was presumably something analogous to this—a social rather than psychological censorship—which made it impossible for Chaucer to begin his poem more directly by saying that he, Geoffrey Chaucer, met the Duke of Lancaster and had a chat with him about his recent sad bereavement. I am not suggesting that *The Book of the Duchess* would have been a better poem if Chaucer had felt able to write in that way. On the contrary, the translation into symbolic form has a generalizing and enriching effect, and is indeed creative. Similarly, much post-Freudian work on dreams, beginning with Jung, has insisted that the symbolism of dreams cannot be simply interpreted away, but has its own validity as being the best way of expressing something that could not be fully expressed in other terms.[8] The introduction to the dream has a similar effect. The preliminary section of the poem gives the feeling of passing through one anteroom after another until we reach the work's inner sanctum. And that inner sanctum is, for the Duke, a place of intimate feeling—the feeling of bereavement, loss, desolation, even though within this is encapsulated the recollection of the happy past. This is not to imply that the poem necessarily articulates the Duke's, or indeed Chaucer's, real feelings at Blanche's death. We have no means of knowing what those were. It is rather that *The Book of the Duchess*, like other public elegies of the Middle Ages or the Renaissance, expresses the feeling appropriate to a death. Such feelings are made both more special and more tolerable when they are set within an elaborate fiction which enacts its own remoteness from the mundane and the quotidian.

Thirdly, and for our purposes most importantly, the introductory part of *The Book of the Duchess* serves to provide a psychological explanation for the dream that follows; and this is where Chaucer's originality as a dream-poet shows itself most strikingly. Throughout the introductory section there is a clear linkage of cause and effect on the psychological plane. Because the narrator is sick, he cannot sleep; because he cannot sleep, he reads a book; because the book tells a story of a sleep brought on by a vow to a god, he makes a similar vow; because of this he falls asleep; and, above all, because of the state of mind he was in and the effect on his mind of the contents of the book he read, he has a dream of a certain kind. The content of the dream, that is, can be accounted for not only externally, as the reflection of a real-life situation, but also internally, as a reflection of the Dreamer's psychological state. There is nothing similar to this psychological causation in the poem's French sources, and I must now digress somewhat in order to explain the theories underlying it.

We have seen that, according to Macrobius, there are two basic types of dream—those with natural and those with supernatural causes—which are then divided into a number of sub-types. Dream-classifications of this kind went on being made throughout the Middle Ages, and, though they differed considerably in detail, often according to the special interests of the classifier as a theologian, doctor, astrologer, or whatever he might be, they usually went back to Macrobius, and retained a similar basic distinction. W.C. Curry, for example, has shown how physicians, with their greater interest in the natural than in the supernatural, tended towards a threefold classification into *somnia naturalia, somnia animalia,* and *somnia coelestia.*[9] There is no evidence that Chaucer knew this specific terminology, but he certainly shows a knowledge of these three categories of dream, and they prove to be convenient for discussion of his dream-poetry. The *somnium naturale* is the dream of purely physical origin. According to medieval physiology, the most fundamental cause of illness is a disturbance of the balance of the four bodily humours—blood, phlegm, choler and melancholy—and this disturbance will tend to be reflected in the image-making part of the patient's mind in the form of a dream. Because the content of the dream will indicate the nature of the disturbance giving rise to it, *somnia naturalia* can be used by doctors for diagnostic purposes. Chaucer shows his knowledge of this category of dream in *The Nun's Priest's Tale.* There Pertelote explains to Chauntecleer that when people have an excess of choler (which is red) in their bodies, they dream of red things; when they have an excess of melancholy (which is black), they dream of black things; Chauntecleer has dreamed of a red doglike creature with black tips to its tail and ears, therefore he has an excess of both humours, and needs to 'taak som laxatyf'. The *somnium animale,* the second category, is the dream of mental origin, caused by the preoccupations of the waking mind, and reflecting these in its content. This is the type described by Chaucer in a passage in *The Parliament of Fowls* (lines 99-105) where the hunter is said to dream of hunting, the knight of fighting, the lover of success in love, and so on. The third category, the *somnium coeleste,* comes from outside the mind, being produced, as the theologians see it, by God or by angels or devils, or, as astrologers see it, indirectly through planetary influences. The doctors naturally have little to say about the *somnium coeleste,* because it is the speciality of experts in other fields. Chaucer shows his knowledge of it when he makes Pandarus, the sceptical pagan, describe it as the speciality of priests:

> For prestes of the temple tellen this,
> That dremes ben the revelaciouns
> Of goddes, and as wel they telle, ywis,
> That they ben infernals illusiouns.
>
> (*Troilus and Criseyde* v. 365-8)

In the same passage, Pandarus goes on to summarize the other types of dream I have been listing, describing each as the product of the thought of particular groups of men: doctors see dreams as caused by physical disease, others see them as resulting from mental preoccupations, others again as varying according to the seasons of the year and phases of the moon.

Similar kinds of dream-classification, often using different terminology, can be found in many medieval writers. Some of the sources used by Curry to illustrate medieval dreamlore are later than Chaucer's time, but I add one further illustration of the kind of discussion that Chaucer himself could have read. In the *Liber de Modo Bene Vivendi*, which in Chaucer's time was wrongly attributed to St Bernard, we find:

> Certain dreams occur through eating too much or too little; . . . certain again arise from preceding thought [*ex proposita cogitatione*], for often we meet again during the night the things we have been thinking of during the day; many dreams occur through the illusions of impure spirits . . . ; sometimes however there occur visions in the true sense of the word, that is, visions concerning the mystery of revelation . . . And sometimes there occur visions of a mixed kind . . .[10]

As it happens, this particular classification would have been available to Chaucer and his audience in English, because this section of the *Liber* had been translated, with certain modifications, by Richard Rolle in his widely-read treatise, *The Form of Living*.[11] But Chaucer's interest in dreams no doubt led him to read widely about them in Latin and French as well as English, and I am not trying to identify specific sources, but to illustrate the range of ideas about the causes of dreams that was available in Chaucer's time.

Having glanced at this range of ideas, we can form a clearer picture of the links between the waking section at the beginning of *The Book of the Duchess* and the dream itself. With remarkable ingenuity,

Chaucer has made it possible to see the dream as linked to the narrator's waking life in all three of the ways indicated as alternatives in the theories we have been considering. The dream can be seen as a *somnium naturale* or a *somnium animale* or a *somnium coeleste*. Chauntecleer's dream as seen by his wife offers a clear analogy to the view of the *Book of the Duchess* dream as a *somnium naturale*. An excess of melancholy causes one to dream of black things; the narrator at the beginning of the *Book* is plainly dominated by the humour of melancholy, and indeed tells us that 'melancolye / And drede I have for to dye' (23-4); it is therefore natural that his sickness should cause him to dream of a 'man in blak'. It is also suggested, though it is not clear how seriously we should take the suggestion, that the dream could be seen as a *somnium coeleste*. The dream sent to Alcyone in the tale from Ovid, as a result of her prayer to Juno, is a vision of supernatural origin which discloses a truth to her. The narrator is stimulated by this story to make his own prayer to the gods, even though he does not really believe in them; what he prays for is sleep, and sleep is immediately granted to him. Perhaps his dream too may come from some supernatural source, pagan or Christian? Certainly, in just the same way as Alcyone's dream, it discloses the truth that someone is dead; and, in introducing the narrative of the dream, the narrator compares it with two celestial visions, one scriptural and one pagan—the dreams of Pharaoh interpreted by Joseph, and Scipio's dream. But there is an ambiguity here: the story of Alcyone's dream can be taken, from one viewpoint, as providing authoritative 'proof' that dreams give access to truth, but from another viewpoint it could be said that the fact of reading this story was itself the psychological cause of the following dream, which was in fact a *somnium animale*.

The *somnium animale* explanation is worth more detailed comment, for the poem's introductory section provides two separate elements of psychological causation for the dream, which, taken together, supply psychological links of a complexity commensurate with the richness and suggestiveness of the dream itself. The two elements are the Dreamer's predominant thoughts, and his reading of the story from Ovid. I take the latter first. The *somnium animale* is the category of dream in which the psychoanalysts have been particularly interested, and indeed they have tended to see all dreams as belonging to that category—a professional prejudice which would not have surprised Pandarus. Freud assures us that 'in every dream it is possible to find a point of contact with the experiences of the previous day', and he adds that that 'point of contact' is to be found in the manifest content of the dream as opposed to its latent content (which, in Freud's theory, will derive from childhood experiences).[12] Now Chaucer's major innovation in the tradition of medieval dream-poetry was to identify this point of contact in the experiences of the previous day with the reading of a book. There are one or two examples of the reading of a book in fourteenth-century French poems (Machaut's *Voir Dit* and Froissart's *Espinette Amoureuse*), but there is never that detailed connection between the contents of the book and the contents of a following dream which we find not only in *The Book of the Duchess* but in *The Parliament of Fowls* and in some dream-poems influenced by Chaucer.[13] In *The Book of the Duchess* the connection is ingenious and psychologically plausible. The narrator reads a story of a wife's loss of her husband by death, and in his dream the same situation reappears, but in a mirror-image: now it is the husband who has lost his wife by death. And Chaucer has been careful to make the story and the dream fit each other exactly. The purpose of the dream is not to offer the Black Knight the promise of a reunion beyond death, but to encourage him to adjust himself to the fact of the lady's death, and in doing so to celebrate her life. Hence Chaucer omits the part of the Ovidian story which has the couple reunited as seabirds, so that it will correspond more exactly to the dream it is to motivate. There are other, smaller reflections of the book in the dream, too; for example, the horn blown by Juno's messenger to awaken the sleeping Morpheus reappears in the dream as the horns blown by the huntsmen. The effect of such parallels is not only to gain psychological plausibility (for dreams do reflect details from our lives and reading in just such strange ways), but to achieve an artistic ordering of the poem's diverse material. Such diversity had been present in a merely sectional way in the French poems which lie behind Chaucer's, but now Chaucer, through his interest in dream-psychology, has begun to find a way of linking together the separate parts of the poem by the recurrence and development of certain themes and images.

The other element of psychological causation is the Dreamer's general state of mind. His 'sicknesse' (36) has psychological as well as purely physical symptoms; if, as seems likely, it is love-sickness, then it is natural that in his dream his troubled mind should frame the image of a melancholy lover. Thus the Black Knight has a double significance. From an external point of view, he stands for John of Gaunt; but from an internal point of view he is a projection of the narrator himself, though of course on a far grander and more aristocratic scale.[14] It need not surprise us to find the central figure of a dream thus possessing two distinct meanings. Freud explains that 'the dream-work is under some kind of necessity to combine all the sources which have acted as stimuli for the dream into a single unity in the dream itself'. This necessary element in the work carried out by dreams he calls 'condensation', and he shows, with numerous examples, that 'The construction of collective and composite figures is one of the chief methods by which condensation operates in dreams'.[15] There are many parallels between the narrator and the Black Knight. For example, the narrator tells us at the beginning of the poem that it is a wonder he is still alive,

> For Nature wolde nat suffyse
> To noon erthly creature
> Nat longe tyme to endure
> Withoute slep and be in sorwe. (18-21)
> *suffyse* permit

When he meets the Black Knight, his first thought is of a very similar kind:

> Hit was gret wonder that Nature
> Myght suffre any creature
> To have such sorwe, and be not ded. (467-9)

Again, the narrator hints that his sickness can be cured by one doctor only (presumably the lady who scorns him); and similarly the Black Knight describes his lady as 'my lyves leche' (920) and later says that when he first saw her she cured him of all his grief (1104). Admittedly such parallels are somewhat conventional in content, but they still serve to bring the two figures close together.

Moreover, the implicit contradiction between the two meanings of the Black Knight seems to move towards explicitness within the poem. Inasmuch as the dream is a *somnium coeleste,* which in symbolic form reveals a truth to the Dreamer and to us, it has an autonomous existence, independent of the Dreamer and perhaps outside his previous range of experience. This reflects a situation in which, as the poem tactfully implies, Gaunt has known a true cause for noble grief, but Geoffrey Chaucer has not: his petty sorrow can be brushed aside with a 'Passe we over untill eft'. But inasmuch as the dream is a *somnium animale*, it must reflect the Dreamer's own experiences and preoccupations, which he naturally tends to impose on the figure in his dream. This is to be seen in the central question of the cause of the Black Knight's sorrow. This is precisely what the Dreamer is trying to find out as he questions the knight, and he evidently begins from the assumption that the cause must be the same as that of his own sorrow—rejection by the lady he loves. For this reason, he persistently fails to grasp the point of the knight's statements; this has the effect of drawing out the knight still further, in the effort to convey his meaning to the Dreamer; and it is not until almost the end of the poem that the Dreamer makes explicit his initial assumption, and is thus able to learn the truth. The Dreamer is eager to know how the knight made his love known to his lady, perhaps in the hope of getting a hint about how to approach his own unresponsive mistress. Then he naively goes on to ask what it is that the knight has lost and, if it is the lady herself, what he did to offend her:

> 'But wolde ye tel me the manere
> To hire which was your firste speche,
> Therof I wolde yow beseche;
> And how she knewe first your thoght,
> Whether ye loved hir or noght.
> And telleth me eke what ye have lore,
> I herde yow telle herebefore.'
> 'Yee!' seyde he, 'thow nost what thow menest;
> I have lost more than thou wenest.'
> 'What los ys that?' quod I thoo;
> 'Nyl she not love yow? ys hyt soo?
> Or have ye oght doon amys,
> That she hath left yow? ys hyt this?
> For Goddes love, telle me al.' (1130-43)
> *lore* lost; *nost* knowest not; *thoo* then

In response to this, the knight tells how when he first declared his love his lady rejected him, but then later he tried again and was more successful. Once more the Dreamer interposes a question based on his own self-reflecting assumption, and now at last he hears and grasps the truth: 'She ys ded'. The nakedness of the statement, coming after so much amplifying description of the lady's beauty and virtue, is irresistibly touching; and so is the simplicity of the Dreamer's response, as the truth at last breaks through his self-projection:

> 'Sir,' quod I, 'where is she now?'
> 'Now?' quod he, and stynte anoon.
> Therwith he wax as ded as stoon,
> And seyde, 'Allas, that I was bore!
> That was the los that here-before
> I tolde the that I hadde lorn.

Bethenke how I seyde here-beforn,
"Thow wost ful lytel what thow menest;
I have lost more than thow wenest"—
God wot, allas! ryght that was she!'
'Allas, sir, how? what may that be?'
'She ys ded!' 'Nay!' 'Yis, be my trouthe!'
'Is that youre los? Be God, hyt ys routhe!' (1298-310)
stynte anoon ceased at once; *wax* became; *bore* born; *routhe* a
pity

The dream in *The Book of the Duchess,* then, could be classified as
a *somnium naturale,* a *somnium animale,* or a *somnium coeleste.* One
significance of this uncertainty as to how it should be classified is that
it is part of the tact with which it fulfils its social function. Seen in one
way, the dream is a heavenly vision, conveying the truth in a symbolic
form: Blanche is dead, and death is a fact which can only be accepted.
But on the other hand, who is Chaucer to claim visionary powers,
which would seem to place him in a superior role, priestly or prophetic,
in relation to his patron? Surely it would be better for the poet to hedge
his bets, by hinting at the visionary possibilities of the dream, but
claiming explicitly no more than that it is 'wonderful' and hard to
interpret? In this way he could leave open the possibility that the dream
was merely one of the 'fantasies' (28) in the head of a melancholiac, or
the product of mental indigestion caused by too much reading in pagan
books. At the same time, the merely psychological explanation of the
dream would provide suggestions for the organization of the dream-
poem as an intricate late-medieval work of art. In later dream-poems
Chaucer will make these issues explicit and generalize them, so that the
uncertainty about the status of dreams can be used as a way of
discussing the status of the poem as such. For the moment, in *The Book
of the Duchess,* he is only feeling his way towards this, and the
importance of the treatment of the dream as a *somnium animale* lies
chiefly in the model it provides for a new kind of poetic structure.

Many people, both in the Middle Ages and now, have seen dreams
as incoherent fantasies. One of the commonest medieval sayings about
dreams is *somnia ne cures,* or, as Pertelote translates it, 'Ne do no fors
of dremes' (*Nun's Priest's Tale* 2941). More recently, James Winny
has written that 'We should now regard a dream, with its curious
linking together of seemingly unrelated ideas, as differing
fundamentally from the creative activity of imagination', while George
Kane has said of dream-poems that 'the reported dream must surpass
any actual dream in organization, coherence, and circumstantial

character'.[16] Chaucer from time to time made use of this low view of
dreams in his poems (as in the case of Pandarus), but I do not believe
that it was his own view, nor do I believe that it is a correct view. Freud
frequently calls attention to the similarity between the 'dream work'
and the methods by which literature shapes experience, and he points
out in particular that, just as dreams demand a multiple interpretation if
they are to be fully understood, so 'all genuinely creative writings are
the product of more than a single motive and more than a single
impulse in the poet's mind, and are open to more than a single
interpretation'.[17] There is an obvious parallel, for example, between the
unity which the imagination attempts to impose on all the component
parts of a poem and the unity which dreams seek to achieve by
'condensation'. A standard Freudian work on dreams claims that 'the
dream is the matrix from which art is developed', and draws many
parallels between the stylistic devices of literature and the methods of
communication (which, in the Freudian view, are also methods of
concealment) used by dreams.[18] Jung, too, is much aware of this
parallel, and argues that Freud gives insufficient weight to the
genuinely creative and exploratory nature of dream-symbolism.[19]
Dreams surely *are* works of art, though, since they are inescapably
private experiences, they can never be fully open to criticism. Perhaps
they are the only kind of work of art which most of us go on producing
throughout our lives. All children can draw and paint, and, given the
materials, do; most of us stop doing these things when we grow up, but
we go on dreaming. I believe that one of Chaucer's greatest
achievements in his early poems was to make use in consciously
contrived works of literature of the creative and constructive methods
employed by the unconscious mind to make dreams. This does not
mean, of course, that his dream-poems are surrealist productions, the
direct expressions of his unconscious mind. Nor does it mean that they
are always dreamlike in their surface effect (though they sometimes
are).[20] The dream-poems *make use* of the methods of dreams. One of
the most striking characteristics of dreams is that on a superficial level
(that of their 'manifest content') they are mysteriously disordered and
often unintelligible, and in particular that they involve abrupt
transitions from one sequence of events to another, with a lack of any
connecting links. And yet on a deeper level (that of their 'latent
content') they can be shown to be intricately ordered and fully
intelligible. This characteristic is shared by the dream in *The Book of
the Duchess*, as I hope to show.

The narrator of the *Book* finds himself, in his dream, in bed, where
he has apparently been awakened by birdsong. As he lies there, he

hears another noise, a horn blowing, and then others still, all indicative of a hunt going on outside. Men are talking of hunting the hart; at this, the Dreamer is glad, and he immediately takes his horse and leaves his bedroom. The horse, we must suppose, was in his bedroom—a typical makeshift device of the kind used by real dreams to cover a transition from one setting or sequence to another. He overtakes the huntsmen, learns from one of them that it is 'th'emperour Octovyen' (368) who is going hunting, and himself joins the hunt. Who is the emperor Octavian?[21] Why should the Dreamer take it upon himself to join his hunt uninvited? Is he suitably dressed for hunting? (He told us that he was 'in my bed al naked' (293), and he has said nothing about putting his clothes on, unlike the narrator of the *Roman de la Rose*, who carefully washes and dresses before walking out into his dream-world.) If we pause for a reply to such questions, we are likely to pause for a long time. In dreams, such questions do not arise, and this is surely a part of the poem which is thoroughly dreamlike in its effect. The hunt finds the hart, then loses it again, and the Dreamer is left by himself. But a puppy comes up to him and makes itself pleasant, in a charmingly doglike way—

> Hyt com and crepte to me as lowe
> Ryght as hyt hadde me yknowe,
> Helde doun hys hed and joyned his eres,
> And leyde al smothe doun hys heres. (391-4)

The puppy leads the Dreamer deeper into the forest, and there, quite suddenly, he notices the 'man in blak' sitting with his back to a huge oak. He observes how pale and melancholy he is, overhears him speaking a lay in which he laments that his lady is dead, and finally goes right up to him. At first the knight fails to notice him, but eventually the Dreamer strikes up conversation, and the rest of the poem consists of their conversation, which begins at line 519 and ends only 24 lines before the end of the poem.

It is an obvious question to ask why the scenes of the hunt and the puppy are in the poem at all. One kind of answer to this question would relate them to the late-medieval aesthetic of transitions, of 'fading' in and out, discussed earlier. Another kind of answer, somewhat more specific, would say that hunting was a characteristic pastime of the medieval aristocracy, and one which is habitually described in terms of joy and energy. Its place in the poem would then be to establish a contrast between the present melancholy of the Black Knight and the gaiety and vitality of the mode of existence which would be normal for

him, but which he is wearily allowing to pass him by. And a third kind
of answer, more specific still, would suggest a metaphoric relationship
between the hunt and the encounter with the Black Knight. Once the
literal hunt has disappeared, its place is taken by a metaphorical hunt,
and the transition between them is provided by the scene with the
puppy.[22] The puppy is a kind of miniature hunting hound, and he leads
the Dreamer on a quest into the forest, where he comes upon an
unexpected quarry, the Black Knight, whom the Dreamer 'stalks' (this
is the very word used in line 458) before addressing him. The ensuing
dialogue with the knight takes the form of a psychological hunt, in
which the Dreamer's questions press him to disclose more and more of
what lies at his heart, until he eventually admits that his lady is dead. At
this point the hunt is over; and, to confirm the metaphoric relationship,
the moment we learn that 'She ys ded' we are told that the literal
huntsmen sound the call for returning home (*strake forth*), because their
hart- hunting is finished:

> 'She ys ded! '' Nay! '' Yis, be my trouthe!'
> 'Is that youre los? Be God, hyt ys routhe!'
> And with that word ryght anoon
> They gan to strake forth; al was doon,
> For that tyme, the hert-huntyng. (1309-13)

We may even take the equivalence between the two hunts a little
further, because, if the huntsmen are in pursuit of a *hart*, so the
Dreamer, as metaphorical huntsman, has the *heart* of the Black Knight
as his quarry. It is no accident that the word *hert*, which means both
'hart' and 'heart', occurs nearly thirty times in the poem, sometimes
referring to the animal, sometimes to the organ of the body, sometimes
(as a term of endearment) to the lady, sometimes to the knight's
feelings for her. One of the first things the Dreamer notices about the
knight is the pallor of his face, and he explains at some length that all
the blood had rushed to comfort his injured heart.[23]

It must be added that a medieval audience would have been
prepared to see a poetic hunt as metaphorical even if it did not occur in
a dream. In *Sir Gawain and the Green Knight*, just as in Chaucer's
poem, there are hunting scenes which frame scenes of conversation, in
such a way that we understand that what is happening in Gawain's
bedroom is also a kind of hunt, perhaps to the death. In both poems,
scenes of hunting and of conversation are superficially contrasted but at
a deeper level parallel. In *Sir Gawain*, however, the relationship
between the hunting and bedroom scenes is conveyed by a threefold

repetition of the same formal pattern (hunt begins, bedroom scene, hunt ends); in *The Book of the Duchess* the aesthetic patterning is less marked and has more of the obscurity of a dream. Freud points out that if dreams form a language, it is a language without a syntax, that is to say without any explicit means of indicating the relationships among its juxtaposed elements. It may be impossible for the dream to represent directly 'those parts of speech which indicate thought-relations, e.g. "because," "therefore," "but," and so on', but instead

> . . . the dream-work succeeds in expressing much of the content of the latent thoughts by means of peculiarities in the *form* of the manifest dream, by its distinctness or obscurity, its division into various parts, etc. The number of parts into which a dream is divided corresponds as a rule with the number of its main themes, the successive trains of thought in the latent dream; a short preliminary dream often stands in an introductory or causal relation to the subsequent detailed main dream; whilst a subordinate dream-thought is represented by the interpolation into the manifest dream of a change of scene, and so on. The form of dreams, then, is by no means unimportant in itself, and itself demands interpretation.[24]

This doctrine can of course be applied to poems generally: Freud's work on dreams represents a major contribution to literary criticism. For Chaucer, it seems likely that the study of dreams suggested ways of giving unity and richness of meaning to structures which in his literary models were merely sectional and episodic. In *The Book of the Duchess*, the formal juxtaposition of hunt and human encounter is a way of indicating the link in meaning between those two elements. Moreover, Freud's theories even provide for the pun on *hert*, as an example of that central principle of the dream-work, condensation, which we also found in the double meaning of the Black Knight. As Freud puts it, 'the dream-work . . . strives to condense two different thoughts by selecting, after the manner of wit, an ambiguous word which can suggest both thoughts'.[25]

I must now mention another way in which *The Book of the Duchess* organizes its meaning by using the methods of dreams. The *Book* is a poem about death, but it is also a poem about sleep, and it persistently works in such a way as to identify these two similar states. It is surprising, the narrator remarks at the beginning, that he can remain alive despite his sleeplessness. Insomnia has 'sleyn my spirit of quyknesse' (26), and 'melancolye / And drede I have for to dye' (23-4).

In the story from Ovid, after Alcyone has prayed to Juno, she is seized by 'the dede slep' (127), and in her sleep she dreams of death. In Morpheus's dark valley, streams falling from the cliffs make 'a dedly slepynge soun' (162). After all this, we ought not to be surprised that when the narrator himself falls asleep, he does not thereby merely escape from the death he fears, but comes upon death in a different form—that of a knight, dressed in black, who looks as if he were about to die of grief, and whose grief is caused by the death of his lady. 'She is dead' is a message being delivered by the poem long before it reaches its end. This repetition of the same message in different forms is strongly characteristic of dreams: 'A dream will state and restate the same theme until the solution is reached'[26]—the 'solution' in *The Book of the Duchess* being an acknowledgment of the unchangeable fact of death.

It is interesting that recent work on the structure of myths has indicated that they too work in this way, repeating certain motifs which are their means of conveying latent significances. Moreover, in at least some myths there is a tendency for the manifest meaning to come gradually closer and closer to the latent meaning as the latter is repeated, until eventually the two are identified. Claude Lévi-Strauss, for example, writes of a Canadian Indian myth: 'Everything seems to suggest that, as it draws to its close, the obvious narrative . . . tends to approach the latent content of the myth . . . ; a convergence which is not unlike that which the listener discovers in the final chords of a symphony'.[27] *The Book of the Duchess*, at once like a dream and like a myth, conforms to this pattern: the final 'She is dead", understood at last by both participants in the encounter, comes as the confirmation of a whole series of earlier hints, in the form of metaphor, analogy, and half-understood statement.

I now turn from the structure of *The Book of the Duchess* to consider another aspect, which is closely connected with its nature as a dream-poem, and which raises some important general issues about medieval literature. This is the role in the poem of the character called 'I', who is first the narrator and then, once asleep, the Dreamer. Many medieval poems, not only dream-poems, include figures of this kind, but they are of special importance in dream-poems, because a dream can only be a first-person experience. There has been much discussion of the part played in medieval poems by such first-person dreamer-narrators. The simplest view of the matter would be that, being 'I', the Dreamer is identical with the writer of the poem. Even if we rejected the naive supposition that Chaucer really had the dream described in his poem, there would still be the fact that the poem itself asserts by its conclusion that the narrator is in some sense the same as the poet. The narrator wakes from his dream, to find himself in bed, with the book containing the story of Ceyx and Alcyone in his hand:

> Thoghte I, 'Thys ys so queynte a sweven
> That I wol, be processe of tyme,
> Fonde to put this sweven in ryme
> As I kan best, and that anoon.'
> This was my sweven; now hit ys doon. (1330-4)
> *queynte* strange; *sweven* dream; *Fonde* attempt

And so the poem ends. Yet on the other hand the narrator is represented in the poem as something of a simpleton. He is extremely kind-hearted, it is true: when he merely reads of Alcyone's sorrow, his sympathy flows as freely as a child's:

> Such sorowe this lady to her tok,
> That trewly I, which made this book,
> Had such pittee and such rowthe
> To rede hir sorwe that, by my trowthe,
> I ferde the worse al the morwe
> Aftir, to thenken on hir sorwe. (95-100)
> *ferde* fared

The same reaction occurs when he dreams of the Black Knight's sorrow; and he seems anxious to give him what comfort he can, as when he tells him,

> Me thynketh in gret sorowe I yow see.
> But certes, sire, yif that yee
> Wolde ought discure me youre woo,
> I wolde, as wys God helpe me soo,
> Amende hyt, yif I kan or may. (547-51)
> *ought . . . me* reveal to me anything of; *as . . . soo* as sure as God may help me

Yet he apparently fails to grasp much of what the knight says. He does not understand the extended metaphor by which he speaks of his loss as that of a queen in a game of chess with Fortune; he makes lukewarm comments which are bound to seem inadequate to the bereaved lover; and, above all, he reports that before addressing the knight he overheard him speaking a lay in which he disclosed that his lady was dead—and yet, once the conversation has started, he appears not to have understood this, or to have forgotten it. Surely this stupid Dreamer cannot be the real Chaucer? The point was made many years ago by G.L. Kittredge. The Dreamer, he wrote, is 'a purely imaginary figure, to whom certain purely imaginary things happen, in a purely imaginary dream'. And he went on:

> This childlike Dreamer, who never reasons, but only feels and gets impressions, who never knows what anything means until he is told in the plainest language, is not Geoffrey Chaucer, the humorist and man of the world. He is a creature of the imagination, and his childlikeness is part of his dramatic character.[28]

The essential question for our purposes is not whether the Dreamer is the real Chaucer (because 'the real Chaucer' can be no more than a hypothesis); the essential question is how, and how far, is the Dreamer characterized? We have seen that fourteenth-century French poets, whose works formed the main sources of *The Book of the Duchess*, had developed the convention of a narrator who was in some sense identified with the poet, but who was characterized as naive and socially inferior. It seems likely enough that Chaucer should have adopted a similar literary solution to a similar social problem. But how consistently does he characterize himself as narrator and Dreamer? L.D. Benson has suggested that it was the existence of the dream-poem convention which made possible the development in fourteenth-century poems of 'a fully developed and consistently maintained personal, dramatic point of view'. This may be an exaggeration, because a growing interest in 'point of view' can be observed in the fourteenth-century arts generally—for example, in the development of perspective in painting. But at least the existence of the dream-poem convention must have made it easier for fourteenth-century poets to explore the possibilities of a 'personal, dramatic point of view'; and that was surely one reason for the continuing interest in dream-poetry. Benson goes on to contrast the dream-poem with the romance:

> A romance always takes place in some remote past, and its narrator is always a clerk, depending on written authority and transmitting, ostensibly unchanged, the ancient story 'as the book tells'. The dream or vision, on the other hand, is always a contemporary event, a personal experience related by a narrator who, so he asserts, saw everything with his own eyes.

Such a narrator is necessarily naive rather than omniscient, for the 'eyewitness' convention requires that he report only what he has personally seen or heard.[29]

There may be some exaggeration here, too, in respect of the 'eyewitness convention'. We have seen that in the *Roman de la Rose* there are occasions when the narrator has to tell us about something of which, as Dreamer, he was unaware. There are similar moments in Machaut's *dits amoreux*, though he has begun to be more conscious of problems of point of view.[30] Perhaps the situation for Chaucer about 1370 was that, while the dream-poem exerted a distinct pull towards a 'personal, dramatic point of view', it did not yet demand that such a point of view should be maintained with complete consistency.

Kittredge and others have seen the Dreamer of the *Book* as child-like; but a different school of commentators has seen him quite differently.[31] They find it difficult to believe in a Dreamer so dull-witted that he fails to understand the lay which he himself reports the Black Knight as speaking, and they argue that he is not really childlike, but displays a sophisticated tact. He does not really fail to understand the knight's statement that 'my lady bryght . . . Is fro me ded and ys agoon' (477-9); he only pretends not to have overheard it. His whole purpose is to encourage the knight to relieve his sorrow by giving utterance to it, and that is why he pretends not to know its cause and not to understand the chess metaphor, and why he makes remarks which can only have the effect of arousing the knight's indignation and thus inciting him to recall the past more fully:

> 'By oure Lord,' quod I, 'y trowe yow wel!
> Hardely, your love was wel beset!
> I not how ye myghte have do bet!'
> 'Bet? ne no wyght so wel,' quod he.
> 'Y trowe hyt, sir,'quod I, 'parde!'
> 'Nay, leve hyt wel!' 'Sire, so do I;
> I leve yow wel, that trewely
> Yow thoghte that she was the beste,
> And to beholde the alderfayreste,
> Whoso had loked hir with your eyen!'
> 'With myn? nay, alle that hir seyen
> Seyde and sworen hyt was soo . . .' (1042-53)
> *Hardely* certainly; *beset* bestowed; *not* know not; *bet* better; *leve* believe; *Yow thoghte* it seemed to you; *alderfayreste* fairest of all; *Whoso* if one; *seyen* saw

And off he goes again, to explain in more detail just how he would
have loved his lady whoever he had been, and what it was that made
her so irresistibly loveable. The Dreamer, after all, having no religious
consolation to offer, can do no better than to encourage the knight to
come to terms with his earthly situation, both his past happiness and his
present bereavement.

　　Yet a tactful Dreamer may be more difficult to believe in than a
naive Dreamer, and it is possible that those who have seen him as
tactful have confused the nature of the Dreamer with the nature of the
poem. *The Book of the Duchess* is certainly a supremely tactful poem.
It is not a private poem; delivering it must have been a public act. It
would not do for Chaucer to lecture his noble patron on what his
attitude should be towards his wife's death, still less to promise a
heavenly reunion—for all we know, Gaunt may have been planning his
second marriage by the time the poem was read. It would be better to
contrive some way in which Gaunt himself would be the central figure
of the poem, noble and glamorous in the depth of his grief, and the
dead lady would live on only in his memory. Even in the licensed
setting of a dream, Chaucer would surely be tactful not by presenting
himself as tactful, managing his patron and drawing him out with
admirable skill, but by establishing a contrast between his patron's
transcendent grief and his own clumsy and uncomprehending attempts
to grasp its nature. The Black Knight is thoroughly at home in the ideal
world of Chaucer's dream; it is Chaucer himself who is ill at ease in it,
and fails to understand what would be obvious to any 'gentil herte'.
The Dreamer is kind-hearted but slow on the uptake, innocent and
inexperienced, because he, unlike the knight, knows nothing of the
fulfilled love which is, in courtly theory, the peculiar property of the
truly noble.[32] On the other hand, we do not have to believe that he is so
stupid as not to understand the knight's lay when he hears it. The lay
must be in the poem so that we, the audience, shall know all along what
is the cause of the knight's sorrow, and shall thus be able to feel with
him more deeply than the Dreamer does, and to recognize the full
extent of the Dreamer's failure to gauge the depth of his sorrow. But
the convention of the dream-poem does not demand that we should be
conscious of the Dreamer as the witness of every event in his dream.
We have to imagine ourselves among the original listeners to the poem,
when it was first read aloud to a courtly circle. In those circumstances,
we should inevitably always be aware of the *poet*, as narrator of
everything in the poem; but we should only be aware of the poet *as*

Dreamer when Chaucer gave him something of a noticeably personal kind to say.

Through quite large sections of the poem, we have no reason to be conscious of the Dreamer at all. For example, when the Black Knight is delivering one of his longer speeches, the speech itself is conveyed directly, and insofar as the poet is doing any dramatic impersonation in his reading, it must be of the knight, not of the Dreamer listening to him. Our attention will be focused on what the knight himself is saying, and it would only be in pursuit of a theory, not in response to the words of the poem, or any imaginable recitation of them, that we could be thinking of it as being transmitted to us through the consciousness of the Dreamer. This is not to apply to *The Book of the Duchess* McLuhan's remark that 'The "I" of medieval narrative did not provide a point of view so much as immediacy of effect.'[33] That is too sweeping: what I want to suggest is that the 'I' of this narrative provides a point of view only intermittently, and that there are times when the poet employs the ambiguity or instability of his 'I' to allow the Dreamer as such to fade away. There would be an obvious parallel in the visual arts of Chaucer's time, where there is a growing interest in the perspective effects that derive from Italian painting, but, as yet, no conviction that the whole of a picture must form a single three-dimensional space, seen from a single point of view. Perspective is still a local, partial effect, in competition with older methods of organizing a picture; and so it is with Chaucer's poem. This helps to explain what happens in the case of the knight's lay. Its words are presented to us immediately, in the form of direct, not reported, speech; it is on them that we concentrate, and for the moment we cease to be aware of the Dreamer at all. We hear them without noticing that, theoretically, he must be hearing them too.

I end with a brief consideration of the effect of the narrator on the tone of *The Book of the Duchess*. Like most other aspects of the poem, this is one about which widely differing views have been held. C.S. Lewis, for example, wrote of 'comic effects which are disastrous, and which were certainly not intended', while P.M. Kean has described the poem as 'Chaucer's longest and most successful essay in pure urbanity'.[34] Certainly in the dream itself there is a recurrent comedy which radiates from the Dreamer in his innocently clumsy attempts to understand something outside the range of his possible experience; and he in turn strikes comic sparks from the Black Knight. I suggested earlier that sometimes in French dream-poems and *dits amoreux* 'the simplicity of the dreamer encourages us to think critically about the validity of the authorities he encounters in his dream'. There is surely some sign of this in lines 1042-53 of *The Book of the Duchess* (quoted above), where the knight becomes indignant and even irritable to have his total idealization of the dead lady submitted to questioning and measurement, brought down to earth. This part of the dialogue brings us back to the question of point of view, for what the Dreamer is saying is that the lady was the best and fairest of all ladies if seen from the viewpoint of her lover—'Whoso had loked hir with your eyen'—whereas the knight is asserting that she was the best and fairest from anyone's viewpoint—'alle that hir seyen / Seyde and sworen hyt was soo'. The Dreamer is a relativist, the knight an absolutist. The dialogue between them articulates a contradiction latent at the heart of the dream-poem as a medieval literary form. Insofar as the dream is a vision, a *somnium coeleste,* it claims to convey absolute truth, unmodified by the personal consciousness of the visionary; insofar as it is a psychological product, a *somnium animale*, it must inevitably reflect the relativism of the dreamer's personal point of view. As we shall see, fourteenth-century dream-poems show a strong tendency to develop conflicts between absolutist and relativist conceptions of reality; and this ambivalent nature of the dream itself will be treated more explicitly and more prominently in Chaucer's subsequent dream-poems.

In *The Book of the Duchess*—and this is inevitable in view of the poem's personal occasion—the balance is tilted in favour of the Black Knight's absolute claims for his idealization of the lady herself and of his love for her. Much of what he has to say is in the form of set-pieces for which recipes could be found in textbooks of medieval rhetoric. Here I have not discussed these parts of the poem; they would include the elaborate description of the lady's appearance (816ff.), the extended paradox in which he states that each of his qualities has been transformed by grief into its opposite (599ff.), the description of the goddess Fortune in similarly paradoxical terms (620ff.), and the passage in which he asserts that he would still have loved the lady if he had been as beautiful as Alcibiades, as strong as Hercules, as excellent as Alexander, and so on (1056ff.). The Dreamer's interjections may express a natural human unwillingness to believe that reality could truly correspond to such ideal patterns, but, with him, we have eventually to be convinced that it could. Perhaps, as twentieth-century readers, natural sceptics and relativists, we cannot always be convinced, and we may well find some parts of the knight's discourse tedious. But in most cases one is carried forward by the poem's enthusiasm, and perhaps particularly by the knight's insistence that the lady did *not* always conform to what might be expected of a courtly

mistress. She did not deceive men, or play hard to get, or set a suitor
some impossible task as the test of his worthiness:

> And byd hym faste anoon that he
> Goo hoodles to the Drye Se
> And come hom by the Carrenar,
> And seye, 'Sir, be now ryght war
> That I may of yow here seyn
> Worshyp, or that ye come ageyn!'
> She ne used no suche knakkes smale. (1027-33)
> *faste anoon* straight away; *Drye Se* Gobi Desert; *Carrenar*
> Black Lake; *war* careful; *here seyn* hear spoken; *Worshyp*
> honour; *or that* before; *knakkes smale* petty tricks

There is no contradiction between the knight's joyful recollection of the
past and the comedy associated with the Dreamer, for this is ultimately
not a poem of mourning but of celebration. It is partly for this reason
that elements of comedy are also introduced into the introductory
section, so that in tone as well as content it will prepare the way for the
main part. The narrator's love-sickness cannot be taken quite seriously,
and his promise of a feather-bed to Morpheus if he will cure his
insomnia displays just the literal-mindedness or materialism that is also
part of his character as Dreamer. Even the sad tale of Ceyx and
Alcyone is enlivened by the vigorous action of Juno's messenger in
waking the inhabitants of the cave of Morpheus by blowing his horn
'ryght in here eere' (182), and by the way that even then the god of
sleep can get only one eye open. We may find it difficult to adjust
ourselves to the flexibility of tone of *The Book of the Duchess*, but I
believe that that is as much under Chaucer's control as the poem's
complex associative structure.

'The House of Fame'

The date of *The House of Fame* is uncertain, but it was probably
written in the middle or late 1370s, and is thus Chaucer's second
dream-poem. It is the most boldly experimental of his dream-poems,
and this, added to the fact that it has come down to us in an unfinished
form, makes it peculiarly resistant to interpretation and analysis. Most
readers would agree that, though its energy and vivacity make it
inexhaustibly interesting, it is not a perfect work, in the sense that
Chaucer's underlying intentions are not fully embodied in the poem as

it stands. Some of the creative work is left for us to do; and this was no doubt part of the attraction the *House* had for subsequent poets such as Lydgate, Skelton and Douglas. Skelton and Douglas at least wrote poems which do not merely imitate it but rework the material Chaucer left to create new poetic wholes. This is what Chaucer's poem seems to demand, and the commentator who is not a poet approaches this do-it-yourself poem-kit at his peril. In what follows I have tried not to rewrite *The House of Fame*, but I have found it impossible to pin down for rational analysis a work which seems ready to fly apart when touched, but in which also everything comes to seem connected with everything else. I have had to content myself with a series of approaches to the poem from different angles, none of them complete in itself.

The House of Fame begins with a proem of 65 lines, which consists largely of a discussion of the causes and validity of dreams. This comes closer to raising explicitly questions of a kind that were only hinted at in *The Book of the Duchess*. Discussions of the fundamental issue of the relationship between dream and truth come to form a regular part of the medieval English dream-poem, and the case of *The House of Fame* makes it particularly clear why this should be so. We have seen that the Middle Ages possessed a variety of elaborate methods of classifying dreams according to their causes and their value or lack of value as guides to truth. These systems of classification were highly ingenious, but they had one fundamental drawback: there was almost never any way of telling from a dream itself which category it belonged to. It might look and feel like a true vision of the future caused by divine or planetary influence, when really it was a mere fantasy caused by indigestion or drunkenness or melancholy or the influence of books or even by diabolic means. Only subsequent events would tell whether or not it was really prophetic. This drawback was much to be lamented by doctors or theologians, but for poets it could prove a distinct advantage. Dreams and poems are both types of fiction; and one thing that was lacking to medieval culture, whose intellectual roots were theological, was an adequate theory of fiction, and particularly a way of allowing some intrinsic value to the works of the human imagination. A fiction might be seen as an allegory or parable, in which case it could be said to convey the truth in a veiled form; a favourite medieval image for this is that of the sweet kernel of truth hidden inside the worthless shell of the fable. But nutshells, once cracked, are thrown away, and so this is not really a defence of fiction. Or again a fiction might claim to be a true history, an account of what really happened as set down in authentic sources. But there was no way of saying that a fiction possessed an imaginative truth or validity even though it did not correspond to any literal truth; in that case it was merely a lie, and there was no way of justifying its delightfulness. In these circumstances, to present a literary fiction as a dream—one imaginative product as an analogue or metaphor for another imaginative product—offered a medieval poet an extremely useful way out of his dilemma.[35] Precisely because it was almost impossible to tell from any individual dream whether it was a reflection of a truth outside itself, the dream in general was felt to be a highly ambivalent phenomenon. There is an amusing image of this situation in the *Nun's Priest's Tale*, where Chauntecleer thinks his dream must foretell the future because he believes that all dreams are 'significaciouns' of what is to come, while Pertelote thinks the same dream is 'vanitee' because she believes that all dreams are the product of bodily disorders.

Some scholars have argued that the main use of the dream-framework was to provide an assurance of authenticity: 'It is perhaps hard today to think of the dream framework as an authenticating device, but . . . For much of the past it served to suspend disbelief and to obtain credence. The dream may be fantastic, but it really happened.'[36] One purpose of the dream-framework is no doubt to define an area within which the poem, as it were, 'has permission to exist', a purpose which can be seen at its simplest in the closing line of *The Book of the Duchess*: 'This was my sweven; now hit ys doon'. But within this area the medieval reader or listener was not necessarily called on to suspend his disbelief. The use of the dream-framework is frequently to evade the whole question of authenticity, of belief or disbelief. What the dream-poet implicitly says is not, 'This is true—I know, because I dreamed it—and therefore you must believe it'. It is, 'I truly dreamed it; but there can be no guarantee that a dream corresponds to the truth. You had better give it whatever credence you usually give to dreams.' This is precisely the implication of the opening proem of *The House of Fame*. It begins by praying,'God turne us every drem to goode!'—not 'May all our dreams come true', but 'May God make every dream profitable for us'. And it goes on at once to say that to the narrator it is a wonder what causes dreams and why some come true but others do not. He then lists the elaborate technical terminology of medieval dreamlore—*avisioun, revelacioun, drem, sweven, fantome, oracle*—not defining the terms, but saying that he does not know why dreams belong to these categories. Next, at greater length, and with enormous relish, he goes through all the possible causes of dreams: the bodily humours, or illness, or hardship, or overwork, or melancholy, or religious devotion, or the hopes and fears of lovers, or spirits, or the prophetic powers of the soul itself. Finally, when we are burning with impatience to learn which of all these is the true cause, he concludes with a teasing profession of ignorance:

> But why the cause is, noght wot I.
> Wel worthe, of this thyng, grete clerkys,
> That trete of this and other werkes;
> For I of noon opinion
> Nyl as now make mensyon,
> But oonly that the holy roode
> Turne us every drem to goode! (51-7)
> *Wei worthe . . . clerkys* Let great scholars concern themselves with this matter; *Nyl* will not

And that leaves us exactly where we started. All he will say about the dream which follows, and which contains the rest of the poem, is that it is 'wonderful' (62), which is what the narrator said about the dream in The *Book of the Duchess*: not true, or false, but wonderful. The dream is indeed full of wonders, which Chaucer describes with fine energy, though, as many readers have felt, with a bewildering uncertainty of direction. We saw, from the opening stages of the *Book of the Duchess* dream, that one possibility of the dream-framework for Chaucer was that, like a real dream, it could liberate the mind from the demands of causal and rational coherence, so as to open creative opportunities of a different kind. It is conceivable that in *The House of Fame* he experimentally pushed still further in that direction, but was unable to develop alternative principles of structure.

If we stand far enough back from the wonders seen by the Dreamer, we can easily recognize in *The House of Fame* the outlines of a *somnium coeleste*. I set aside for the moment book I, in which the Dreamer finds himself in a temple of Venus decorated with a pictorial version of the *Aeneid*; but from the moment a great eagle swoops down from the heavens at the end of book I, he seems embarked on a religious vision. The eagle itself is derived most immediately from Dante's *Purgatorio* IX, one of the few parts of the *Divine Comedy* which is explicitly in the form of a dream or vision. Dante falls asleep, and has a dream in the morning, the time when, as he says, 'la mente nostra . . . alle sue vision quasi è divina' (IX. 16-18) (our mind is almost divine in its power of vision). He dreams of being carried by a golden eagle up to the sun, and there consumed. The eagle was often used in the Middle Ages as a symbol of the flight of contemplation or of thought.[37] Indeed, when the Dreamer is in mid-flight, he remembers

a passage from the *De Consolatione*, which we noted earlier, and which
seems to confirm that this is the significance of the eagle here:

> And thoo thoughte y upon Boece,
> That writ, 'A thought may flee so hye,
> Wyth fetheres of Philosophye,
> To passen everych element;
> And whan he hath so fer ywent,
> Than may be seen, byhynde hys bak,
> Cloude' . . . (972-8)
> *Boece* Boethius; *flee* fly

Philosophy had told Boethius,

> I have . . . swifte fetheris that surmounten the heighte of the
> hevene. Whanne the swifte thoght hath clothid itself in tho
> fetheris, it despiseth the hateful erthes, and surmounteth the
> rowndnesse of the gret ayr; and it seth the clowdes byhynde
> his bak . . . (IV, m. 1. 1-6)

The eagle, then, is a personification of philosophical thought itself,
carrying the Dreamer on a journey through the heavens, a vantage point
from which 'al the world, as to myn yë, / No more semed than a prikke
[point]' (906-7); or, as Philosophy puts it to Boethius, 'al the
envyrounynge of the erthe aboute ne halt but the resoun of a prykke at
regard of the gretnesse of hevene' (II, pr. 7. 24-6) (the whole surface of
the earth is of no more consideration than a point in comparison with
the greatness of heaven). It is all very like a real dream, both in the
common dream-sensation of flying, and in the transformation of
Boethius's metaphor of feathers into the dream-reality of an eagle.

There are numerous other indications that the dream is a *visio* or
somnium coeleste. The eagle explains that he has been sent by Jupiter
of 'his grace' (661, 2007) (the eagle being Jupiter's bird in classical
mythology), to reward the Dreamer for his 'great humblesse, / And
vertu eke' (630-1); and the Jupiter of a dream could no doubt stand for
the Christian God. He tells the Dreamer that he is being carried higher
than

> Daun Scipio,
> That saw in drem, at poynt devys,
> Helle and erthe and paradys. (916-18)
> *at poynt devys* with exactitude

The Dreamer even repeats on his own part some of the words of St Paul
which allude to his vision of paradise, and which came to suggest the
Apocalypse of St Paul and to be considered typical of mystical
experience:

> Thoo gan y wexen in a were,
> And seyde, 'Y wot wel y am here;
> But wher in body or in gost
> I not, ywys; but God, thou wost!'   (979-82)
> *waxen in a were* fall into doubt; *wher* whether; *not* know not

And although, as we shall see, the goddess Fame is a somewhat
dubious theme for a *somnium coeleste*, she is compared with what St
John saw in his vision—

> For as feele eyen hadde she
> As fetheres upon foules be,
> Or weren on the bestes foure
> That Goddis trone gunne honoure
> As John writ in th'Apocalips   (1381-5)
> *feele* many; *gunne honoure* honoured

—and, like Boethius's Philosophy, she sometimes seems small and
sometimes to touch the heavens. Finally, at the point where the poem
breaks off, it appears about to declare itself as a Macrobian *oraculum*,
in which one who 'semed for to be / A man of gret auctorite' (2157-8)
is going to deliver some important doctrine to the Dreamer—the
'tydynges' that he has been promised as the goal of his vision.

We can discern then, in *The House of Fame*, the outline of a
somnium coeleste, and the more convincingly, perhaps, because the
whole poem except for the introductory sections to each book, is
included in the dream. It has the same basic structural divisions as *The
Book of the Duchess*: first a section which repeats a story from a
classical poet, second a journey in which the Dreamer has an animal as
his guide, and third the arrival at what appears to be the main subject of
the poem, a section in which the Dreamer is searching for some piece
of information. But in the *Book* the classical story (from Ovid) is read
by the narrator before he falls asleep, and thus becomes a likely
influence on his dream, considered as a *somnium animale* while in the
House the classical story (from Virgil) is itself part of the dream, and
no natural cause of the dream is suggested. When we look at the *House*

more closely, however, the conception of it as a *somnium coeleste* has
to be modified. One kind of modification is already familiar to us from
the *Roman de la Rose* and its tradition. The religious vision is
secularized and applied to the purposes of human love. The eagle tells
the Dreamer that his vision comes as a reward for his services not to
Jupiter himself but to 'Hys blynde nevew Cupido, / And faire Venus
also' (617-18). Like the narrator of the *Book*, the Dreamer here has had
no success in the practice of love, but that has not stopped him from
writing poems 'in reverence / Of Love, and of hys servantes eke'(624-
5). He is so devoted to his books that he has 'no tydynges / Of Loves
folk yf they be glade' (644-5), and his reward will be to be carried
where he can learn 'of Loves folk moo tydynges' (675). The theme of
love helps us to see the relevance of book I to the remainder of the
poem. The Dreamer recognizes the temple in which he finds himself as
being dedicated to Venus, and in it he sees carved or engraved the
opening lines of the *Aeneid*, followed by the rest of the story in
pictures. A retelling of the story through a description of the pictures
makes up the substance of book I, and it is a retelling which, in the
medieval way, presents it as centring in the love-affair of Aeneas and
Dido. It is Venus who commands Aeneas, her son, to flee from Troy,
who implores Jupiter to save his ship in the storm, who appears in order
to comfort him when he lands at Carthage, and who

> made Eneas so in grace
> Of Dido, quene of that contree,
> That, shortly for to tellen, she
> Becam hys love, and let him doo
> Al that weddynge longeth too. (240-4)
> *weddynge . . . too* appertains to marriage

The love-affair itself is recounted at length, with great emphasis on
Dido's sufferings, and at the end of the story the part played by Venus
is once more stressed and is related to the lives of the poet and his
audience:

> For Jupiter took of hym cure
> At the prayer of Venus,—
> The whiche I preye alwey save us,
> And us ay of oure sorwes lyghte! (464-7)
> *cure* care; *lyghte* relieve

But the expectations that may have been aroused by book I and by
the eagle's promises in book II, that the poem will be a secular *visio* of

love, are not fulfilled by the remainder. Much of book II consists of an exposition by the eagle of the theory of sound, in explanation of how all that men say is transmitted to the house of Fame.[38] And when the Dreamer reaches his destination, he finds in book III little that corresponds to the love-tidings he has been promised as his reward. There are entertainers, but 'love-daunces' (1235) are only one of the pleasures they offer. There are poets, but only one of them, 'Venus clerk, Ovide' (1487), is a love-poet. There are many groups of suppliants to the goddess for renown or oblivion, but only 'the sexte companye' (1727) refer specifically to love in their requests, asking that they may be reputed to be great lovers though they are not so really. The Dreamer himself begins to be dissatisfied with the lack of what he has been led to expect, and when an unnamed person asks if he has come there to gain fame himself, he answers that he has not, that he has been promised 'Tydynges, other this or that, / Of love, or suche thynges glade' (1888-9), but that 'these be no suche tydynges' (1894). His interlocutor therefore invites him to go elsewhere to find 'What thou desirest for to here' (1911), and leads him to the house of Rumour instead. There he once more finds the eagle, who repeats Jupiter's wish that the Dreamer should be rewarded for his sufferings, though now those sufferings are not explicitly associated with love, nor are the tidings which are to be his reward. There is a scene of violent confusion, as various tidings struggle to get out of the windows and make their way to Fame. At last the Dreamer hears a great noise 'In a corner of the halle, / Ther men of love-tydynges tolde' (2142-3). He sees the man of 'gret auctorite' amid the bustle, and it seems that his and our expectations are to be fulfilled at last—but at this point the poem breaks off. Various suggestions have been made as to what the man might have said: perhaps, for example, he was going to deliver a 'love-tiding' that related to some court love-affair, and for that very reason the end of the poem has been suppressed. But there is absolutely no evidence for this, and in any case it is impossible to imagine any 'love-tiding' that could by now make the poem cohere as a love-vision. If that is its intended purpose, it has long ago begun to disintegrate, and we must agree with Muscatine that *The House of Fame* has 'the elaborateness and pointlessness' of much poetry of the following century, and that it belongs to the 'decadence of late Gothic art'.[39]

Chaucer himself called his poem 'the book of Fame' (*Canterbury Tales* X. 1085), but we have not yet seen how far fame can be defined as the true theme of the vision. Certainly it could be argued that Fame has almost as good a claim as Venus to be the presiding goddess of book I. Dido laments that every man would have three wives if he could, for 'of oon he wolde have fame / In magnyfyinge of hys name' (305-6), and she later invokes Fame herself, as she apostrophizes the absent Aeneas:

> For thorgh yow is my name lorn,
> And alle myn actes red and songe
> Over al thys lond, on every tonge.
> O wikke Fame! for ther nys
> Nothing so swift, lo, as she is!
> O, soth ys, every thing ys wyst,
> Though hit be kevered with the myst. (346-52)
> *name lorn* reputation lost; *wyst* known; *kevered* covered

This passage suggests a way in which the whole conception of book I is relevant to the theme of fame, for it was by means of Virgil's poem that Dido's acts were 'red and songe', and came to be known in Chaucer's time. Further, as we discover from book III, there is a special unreliability about Fame, exemplified in the case of those who have the reputation of being great lovers and even prefer the name to the reality: 'Sufficeth that we han the fame' (1762). In retrospect, then, it would be possible to see the lengthy complaints of Dido and the Dreamer about the deceptiveness of men as illustrating this aspect of fame: the 'apparence' (265) which may be the very opposite of the reality of things. In retrospect, too, we shall notice perhaps that Aeolus, the 'god of wyndes' (203), who plays a part in the story of Aeneas by blowing up the storm which endangers the Trojan ships, reappears in book III as the messenger of Fame, with two trumpets called 'Clere Laude' (noble praise) and 'Sklaundre' (1575-80). And if fame, whether good or bad, is 'Bot wind inflat in uther mennis eiris',[40] then we can also see the relevance to this theme of the Dreamer's journey through the heavens in book II, and the eagle's discourse on sound.[41] We begin to recognize in the poem just that dreamlike recurrence and development of themes and images that we found in *The Book of the Duchess*, though here it is still further removed from the claims of logical discourse.

The central idea of book III, the imaginative evocation of the nature of an abstract conception such as 'Fame' by means of a description of the palace or house which the personified abstraction is said to inhabit, is thoroughly traditional. An ultimate source is Ovid's description of Fame's dwelling in *Metamorphoses* XII; more immediate sources are probably the descriptions of the dwelling of Fortune in two French dream-poems, the *Roman de la Rose* and Nicole de Margival's *Panthère d'Amours*. The similarity between Fame and Fortune is noted by the Dreamer when he says that Fame treats her suppliants arbitrarily, 'Ryght as her suster, dame Fortune' (1547); and it seems likely that Chaucer's picture of Fame was influenced by the depiction of 'Fortune as arbiter of Fame'[42] in the *Mirour de l'Omme* of his friend John Gower. Many of the details of the description in Chaucer's poem are symbolic, though none obscurely so. The placing of Fame's castle on a rock of ice illustrates the time-honoured idea that the ascent to fame is slippery and insecure; at the same time, the fact that some of the names written in the ice have melted away, while others are still fresh and legible, indicates the arbitrariness with which some people are remembered and others forgotten. Further, the castle itself has walls of beryl, a precious stone which is said to have a magnifying effect: they

> made wel more than hit was
> To semen every thing, ywis,
> As kynde thyng of Fames is. (1290-2)
> *kynde thyng* natural attribute

Thus, as in dreams, thoughts are translated into images; moreover, the whole description of Fame's dwelling is not presented as a formal set-piece, as in Ovid, but is conveyed bit by bit, as seen through the eyes of the Dreamer as he moves about, noticing first one thing and then another.[43] In *The House of Fame*, far more than in *The Book of the Duchess*, we feel the effect of that pull towards the 'personal, dramatic point of view' which is characteristic of dream-poetry. Always at the centre of the poem is the figure of the Dreamer, bewildered by the strange experiences of his dream.

We have already seen, in Watriquet de Couvin's *Dis des Quatre Sieges*, an example of the adaptation of the religious vision to claim glory in heaven for those who have achieved fame on earth. The vision is only pseudo-religious, in the sense that it presents heavenly glory as a mere reflection of earthly fame; but on the other hand the poem conceives of fame, whether earthly or heavenly, as genuine and deserved. In *The House of Fame*, however, the goddess is arbitrary and unreliable in her gifts. Some of her suppliants have done good, some evil, and some nothing at all; some seek fame, some oblivion; but she grants them good, bad or no reputation entirely according to her own whims, without regard to their deeds. Further, it emerges that Fame is dependent on Rumour: Rumour's enormous revolving house of twigs is full of tidings on every possible topic, which have to escape through the windows before Fame can decide what their fates shall be, and pass them on to Aeolus to be spread abroad. The whole atmosphere of book III is one of hilariously contradictory movement and noise, verging on hysteria, and far removed from that of religious vision, or the solemn seats of state in Watriquet's poem. Chaucer's poem, indeed, seems to embody a humorous critique or exposure of the notion of fame as a positive value. It may perhaps be significant that both the allusions to the *De Consolatione* noted above come from contexts which reflect unfavourably on earthly fame. The passage on the smallness of the earth compared with heaven occurs in the course of Philosophy's demonstration of the unimportance of that earthly fame that men strive for so eagerly: 'And ye thanne, that ben envyrouned and closed withynne the leeste prykke of thilke prykke, thynken ye to manyfesten or publisschen your renoun and doon yowr name for to be born forth?' (II, pr. 7. 41-5). Chaucer in his translation of this section uses the words *renoun, glorie,* and *fame* with little if any difference in meaning. And the passage on the feathers of philosophy comes immediately after a statement by philosophy that in the kingdom of God 'blisfulnesses [blessings] comen alwey to goode folk, and infortune comith alwey to wikkide folk' (IV, pr. 1. 54-6). The order of the heavenly kingdom is thus described as the very opposite of the disorder of earthly affairs, ruled by the sisters Fortune and Fame. There is nothing heavenly about Fame's kingdom; and, just as the *Roman de la Rose* was, among other things, a mock-*visio* set in a pseudo-paradise, so *The House of Fame* might be seen as a mock-*oraculum*, setting forth the full meaninglessness of earthly renown and leading up to the non-delivery of doctrinal truth by one who only '*semed* for to be / A man of gret auctorite'. Fame's world is one of seeming, of *apparence*, where reality and truth are not to be found.

Such a view of the poem, though relating it intelligibly (as it demands to be related) to the complex tradition of visionary writing and dream- poetry, still over-simplifies it, in that it does not relate the

theme of fame to that of love. I suggest that the link between the two is
to be found in the Dreamer himself. We have seen that the Dreamer of
The House of Fame is conceived not only as an unsuccessful lover but
as a love-poet. *In The Book of the Duchess*, the Dreamer, as 'I, which
made this book' (96), was a poet too, but merely in a formal sense; the
House is the first of Chaucer's poems in which the narrator is realized
in the specific role of poet. There is good reason why this could not
have happened earlier in Chaucer's work; it is surely not that 'The idea
of making [the narrator] a hopeful but untalented poet seems not to
have occurred to Chaucer until he came to write ne *Hous of Fame*',[44]
but that Chaucer could not have presented himself as one who had done
his incompetent best to write poems 'in reverence / Of Love, and of hys
servantes eke' (624-5) until he was known as a love-poet to his
audience. Once the Dreamer is characterized at all, his biography must
he based on that of the poet. To be a poet, in the courtly circle for
which Chaucer wrote, was the same as to be a love-poet; it was taken
for granted that love was the inspiration of poetry, and that is why
Chaucer, in the proem to book II, invokes the aid of Venus (*Cipris*,
518) ahead of that of the Muses in his poetic enterprise. But he is a poet
quite without experience of the main subject of his art, and thus,
although he retells the *Aeneid* as a love-story, when he comes to speak
of the sexual relations between Aeneas and Dido, he draws modestly
back:

> What shulde I speke more queynte,
> And peyne me my wordes peynte
> To speke of love? Hyt wol not be;
> I kan not of that faculte. (245-8)

(Why should I speak more elaborately, labouring to decorate my words
in speaking of love? It cannot be; I know nothing of that branch of
study.)

It is for this reason that he needs to be rewarded with tidings of love in
the house of Fame.

The connection between poetry and love, then, is clear, and we
now need to consider the connection between poetry and fame. They
are associated in more than one way. Poetry is a chief means by which
fame is conferred and transmitted: we saw that this was so in book I, in
Dido's prediction that her deeds would be 'red and songe', and indeed

one function of book I is to present the *Aeneid* as an example of this power of poetry. In book III we learn that the permanent inhabitants of Fame's palace are minstrels, harpers, musicians, magicians, poets, and historians. With the exception of magicians, all these groups of people can be seen as conveying fame through words. The greatest detail is given in the case of poets: Statius, 'That bar of Thebes up the fame' (1461); Homer, Dares, Dictys, Guido de Columpnis, Geoffrey of Monmouth, and the mysterious 'Lollius' (the supposed source of *Troilus and* Cr*iseyde),* all of whom bore up the 'hevy . . . fame' (1473) of Troy; 'Venus clerk, Ovide' (1487), who raised the fame of the God of Love; Virgil (another link with book I); Lucan and other poets who 'writen of Romes myghty werkes' (1504); and Claudian who in his *De Raptu Proserpinae* 'bar up al the fame of helle' (1510). For Chaucer, words were the chief means by which fame was created, and above all words in their most memorable and lasting form, as poetry; and in his list of poets he is naming many of the major sources of his own works, past and future. But to say this is to suggest another aspect of the matter; Chaucer as poet does not merely transmit fame, he is dependent upon fame for his subject-matter. As a modern writing about the classical past, he is inevitably stepping outside the bounds of his personal experience, and he has to rely on what has been written by others. And as a love-poet with no experience of love, he is in the same position, and can only pass on 'love-tydynges', whispers originating in rumour and half-heard amid the hubbub of Fame's palace. In book II we learn that such fame is 'noght but eyr ybroken' (765), and in book II we see how impossible it is to rely on any correspondence between fame and the reality of human experience. The narratorial method of *Troilus and Criseyde* is founded on Chaucer's sense of this dilemma for the poet: relying on the dubious 'Lollius' for his information about the Trojan war, and on what 'men say' for his understanding of love, how can he do anything but withdraw from judgment? His position is precisely that dramatized in book I of the *House*: a man seeing a story of profound historical and emotional significance not directly, but only through the images of art. This dependence on secondary sources is conveyed pervasively throughout the Dreamer's visit to the temple, by the constant repetitions of 'Ther saugh I . . .' and the relegation of the actual events of the story to subordinate clauses. The main verbs in book I belong to the Dreamer as he sees and tries to understand the 'queynte manere of figures / Of olde werk' (126-7). As he leaves the temple, it is still not the events themselves that hold his attention (for there is inevitably the barrier of art between him and them), but the artistic means by which they are conveyed, the 'noblesse / Of ymages' (471-2).

Thus it is the situation of the Dreamer as poet that lies at the heart of *The House of Fame*. The first proem, as we have seen, is concerned with the uncertainty of the relation between dreams and truth, and it will now be more apparent, perhaps, that this is a way of approaching the uncertainty of the relation between poetry and truth. Poetry can be inspired and prophetic, and in both the second and third proems Chaucer for the first time, under the impact of his reading of Dante and Boccaccio, indicates the possibility of this high role for the poet. In the second proem, after describing the dream confidently as a 'sely . . . avisyon' (513) (blessed vision) like that of Isaiah or Scipio, he invokes the aid of Venus and the Muses, and invites men to judge the 'engyn and myght'(528) (skill and power) of the 'Thought' (memory) (523) that fixed this vision in the treasury of his brain.[45] Thus he presents himself as the dedicated recorder of an inspired truth. And in the third proem he invokes the guidance of Apollo, the 'god of science [knowledge] and of lyght' (1091) and the 'devyne vertu' (1101), in expressing the 'sentence . . . That in myn hed ymarked ys' (1100-3) (meaning that is *imprinted* in my brain).[46] The dream has come to him on the tenth of December, a date which may have some astronomical significance, but which also suggests the sterility and deadness of winter, and hence the poet's need for some quickening inspiration. In the temple of Venus, the Dreamer confronts his own situation as poet: a mere onlooker, a tourist in the shrine of love, repeating a story that comes to him at second hand. When he leaves the temple, he finds himself in a landscape of terrifying desolation, related, as I suggested earlier, to the hell that forms part of traditional visions of the other world:

> Then sawgh I but a large feld,
> As fer as that I myghte see,
> Withouten toun, or hous, or tree,
> Or bush, or gras, or eryd lond;
> For al the feld nas but of sond
> As smal as man may se yet lye
> In the desert of Lybye;
> Ne no maner creature
> That ys yformed be Nature
> Ne sawgh I, me to rede or wisse.
> 'O Crist!' thoughte I, 'that art in blysse,
> Fro fantome and illusion

> Me save!'and with devocion
> Myn eyen to the hevene I caste. (482-95)
> *eryd* ploughed; *rede* advise; *wisse* guide

Thus, when the poet leaves his secondhand dealings with love, he finds himself in a state of frightening emptiness, with nothing whatever to say. Not for the last time, one senses a certain personal resonance in this passage: the landscape conveys a sense of the failure of creative power, reinforcing the wintry date of the dream. The poet needs heavenly inspiration to rescue him; and as he looks up, it appears to be coming, in the shape of the swooping eagle.

We have seen that the eagle can be a symbol of the flight of contemplation or philosophical thought; and in this context of secularized vision, in which the visionary has become a courtly poet of love, it is easily transformed into a symbol of poetic inspiration. Certainly, the whole experience the Dreamer now undergoes, of being 'carried away' by a force outside himself, seems to relate to that of inspiration, whether philosophical, religious, or poetic. We have seen that in the distant past these distinctions were not made, and the poet and the religious prophet were one and the same. But at the same time, the experience is irresistibly comic, in a way which is analogous to the encounter between Dreamer and Black Knight in *The Book of the Duchess*. The Dreamer remains earthbound in spirit, and does not wish to be carried to the heavens. First he faints and then he wriggles, and the eagle complains that he is 'noyous for to carye' (574). He fears that he is going to be 'stellified', turned into a star like the prophets and heroes of old, and he protests that

> I neyther am Ennok, ne Elye,
> Ne Romulus, ne Ganymede,
> That was ybore up, as men rede,
> To hevene with daun Jupiter,
> And mad the goddys botiller. (588-92)
> *Ennok* Enoch; *Elye* Elijah; *daun* lord

Since Chaucer's father had been the king's deputy butler, the court audience might recognize a personal reference here, and be amused at how firmly the Dreamer's thoughts were attached to earthly things. Well might he repeat in a lower key Dante's 'Io non Enea, io non Paolo sono', and with far greater truth: rather, he is a kind of J. Alfred Prufrock of the fourteenth century, who is not Prince Hamlet, nor was meant to be:

> Deferential, glad to be of use,
> Politic, cautious, and meticulous;
> Full of high sentence, but a bit obtuse;
> At times, indeed, almost ridiculous—
> Almost, at times, the Fool.[47]

He does not wish to take this unique opportunity of learning about the stars:

> 'Wilt thou lere of the sterres aught?'
> 'Nay, certeynly,'quod y, 'ryght naught'. (993-4)
> *aught* anything

He gives two reasons for this reluctance: first that he is too old, and second, most significantly, that he does not need this firsthand knowledge, because he believes what he reads in books:

> 'No fors,' quod y, 'hyt is no nede.
> I leve as wel, so God me spede,
> Hem that write of this matere,
> As though I knew her places here;
> And eke they shynen here so bryghte,
> Hyt shulde shenden al my syghte,
> To loke on hem.' 'That may wel be,'
> Quod he . . . (1101-17)
> *fors* matter; *shenden* damage

The Dreamer is content with his books after all; he feels no need for reality, and is afraid it might shine so brightly as to hurt his eyes. The eagle, whose eye can gaze on the sun unharmed, sadly agrees, and immediately deposits him at Fame's dwelling, where he will be untroubled by direct experience, and will at best receive no more than 'tydynges' of love.

    Chaucer's portrait of himself as a poet whose timidity makes him positively resistant to inspiration, and the use he makes of this portrait to explore the whole question of the relationship of art to experience, is a brilliant achievement, the more so in view of the fact that the poem in which it is conveyed is itself deeply indebted to literary tradition and yet generates a strong sense of the occasionally uneasy working out of a personal problem. Equally brilliant is the portrait of the eagle; and in *The House of Fame*, far more than in *The Book of the Duchess*, the comic treatment of the Dreamer infects the presentation of his dream-authority. The eagle does not hold the privileged position in the poem that must necessarily be granted to a figure representing Gaunt. He is no genuinely authoritative figure, whose words the Dreamer is too simple and inexperienced to understand, but rather a garrulous and complacent pedant, whom the Dreamer has good reason not to wish to understand. Hence the comedy is broader than in the earlier poem: on one side we find verbose self-congratulation, on the other monosyllabic sullenness. 'Have y not preved,' asks the eagle,

> 'Have y not preved thus symply,
> Withoute any subtilite
> Of speche, or gret prolixite
> Of termes of philosophie,
> Of figures of poetrie,
> Of colours of rethorike?
> Pardee, hit oughte the to lyke!
> For hard langage and hard matere
> Ys encombrous for to here
> Attones; wost thou not wel this?'
> And y answered and seyde, 'Yis.'
> 'A ha!' quod he, 'lo, so I can
> Lewedly to a lewed man
> Speke, and shewe hym swyche skiles
> That he may shake hem by the biles,
> So palpable they shulden be.' (834-69)
> *the to lyke* to please you; *encombrous* burdensome; *Attones* at the same time; *Lewedly* unlearnedly; *skiles* arguments; *biles* beaks

The eagle, even at his most schoolmasterly, remains imprisoned within his avian nature, and thinks of even arguments as having beaks.

The poem is incomplete, almost certainly because Chaucer did not finish it, rather than because part has been lost in transmission.[48] It can plausibly be guessed that Chaucer was unable to complete it, not because it was 'pointless' (as Muscatine suggests), but because it had too painful a point, in its exploration of problems concerning Chaucer's own life as a poet, problems which he was unable to resolve. It seems to have been a matter of bearable pain, rather than of the unbalancing *Angst* from which more recent artists have suffered; and when the Dreamer is asked, near the end, whether he has come to Fame's house to seek fame for himself, he answers, with a nice blend of modesty and sturdy self-reliance,

> I cam noght hyder, graunt mercy,
> For no such cause, by my hed!
> Sufficeth me, as I were ded,
> That no wight have my name in honde.
> I wot myself best how y stonde;
> For what I drye, or what I thynke,
> I wil myselven al hyt drynke,
> Gerteyn, for the more part,
> As fer forth as I kan myn art. (1874-82)
>
> *as . . . ded* i.e. by my life; *drye* suffer; *drynke* swallow; *fer forth* far; *kan* have knowledge of

Chaucer evidently felt, rightly, that he had inner resources that would enable him to move forward, even if at present he could not see exactly in what direction, and was therefore forced to leave his poem incomplete. It is rather unlikely that the incompleteness was a planned part of the poem's effect, and that Chaucer had intended all along that the 'man of gret auctorite' would have nothing to say. On the other hand, he evidently put it into circulation in its incomplete form, and, at least for subsequent readers, its incompleteness may make it all the more telling. I have suggested that this may have been part of its attraction for later medieval poets; and modern readers, with the benefit of hindsight, can see the final appearance of a bustling crowd including 'shipmen and pilgrimes' (2122) and 'pardoners' (2127) as pointing towards *The Canterbury Tales*[49] where Chaucer was to find in the framed narrative a final solution to the problem of the validity of fiction. What is more, the artistic effect of *The House of Fame*, with its dynamic restlessness, is positively enhanced by incompleteness. Some words of Arnold Hauser about Gothic architecture might have been written with this poem in mind:

> A Gothic church . . . seems to be in process of development, as if it were rising up before our very eyes; it expresses a process, not a result. The resolution of the whole mass into a number of forces, the dissolution of all that is rigid and at rest by means of a dialectic of functions and subordinations, this ebb and flood, circulation and transformation of energy, gives us the impression of a dramatic conflict working up to a decision before our eyes. And this dynamic effect is so overwhelming that beside it all else seems a mere means to this end. So it

comes about that the effect of such a building is not merely
not impaired when it is left uncompleted; its appeal and its
power is actually increased. The inconclusiveness of the
forms, which is characteristic of every dynamic style, gives
emphasis to one's impression of endless, restless movement
for which any stationary equilibrium is merely provisional.[50]

'*The Parliament of Fowls*'

Chaucer's third dream-poem was *The Parliament of Fowls*, which
probably dates from 1382. In style, it is considerably more settled and
composed than the two earlier dream-poems. Italian influences, which
had affected only the content of the *House*, have now been absorbed
stylistically too, and it is written not in the octosyllabic couplets of the
two earlier poems, but in rime royal stanzas. The effect is less of rapid
movement, whether gay or nervous, than in the earlier poems, and more
of 'a grave sweetness and a poised serenity';[51] though colloquial
touches are by no means excluded, and indeed stand out more sharply
in this more dignified setting. Here more than ever Chaucer shows his
awareness of the long and complex tradition of visionary writing, but it
is now as much a matter of deft and pervasive allusion as of explicit
reference. In structure, however, Chaucer remains very close to *The
Book of the Duchess*. Indeed, one might guess that, after *The House of
Fame*, where, under the impact of insoluble personal problems, he had
pushed the use of dream-methods for literary creation so far as to make
the poem unfinishable, he now decided to follow more exactly the
causal sequence that had proved so successful in his first dream-poem.
As in the *Book* there is a long introductory section, in which the
narrator is still awake and reads a book about a dream, which then
provides motivation for his own dream. As in the *House*, the narrator is
a devotee of love but only in books, not through experience:

> For al be that I knowe nat Love in dede,
> Ne wot how that he quiteth folk here hyre,
> Yit happeth me ful ofte in bokes rede
> Of his myrakles, and his crewel yre. (8-11)
> *quiteth* pays; *hyre* wages

But, in laying its emphasis on the narrator as would-be lover rather than
poet of love, the *Parliament* is nearer to the *Book* than it is to the
House. However, the distinction is not very clear-cut; there are one or

two explicit references to the narrator as poet, and there is also a pervasive suggestion that love and poetry can be seen in the same terms, as creative experiences, which are highly desirable and yet difficult of achievement.[52] It is significant that the narrator invokes Venus not only as the cause of his dream, but also for help 'to ryme and ek t'endyte' (119) when he comes to set it down.

The narrator is introduced as reading one particular book, 'a certeyn thing to lerne' (20). What that thing is, we are never explicitly told, and at the end of the poem he resumes his search in 'othere bokes' (695); but here perhaps the poem is truly dreamlike, in that it solves the Dreamer's problems (at least for us) in the very act of reflecting them. The thing sought is surely found in the dream itself, without the Dreamer being aware of it, though if asked to define it one could only say that it is the meaning of the whole poem, which cannot properly be expressed in other terms. To put it more crudely than the poem does, what the narrator is seeking is presumably the meaning of that love which is the major subject of medieval courtly poetry, but which he sees chiefly as a cause of suffering; what he finds in the dream is a subtle placing of love in the larger context of the social order and of the relationship between the natural and the human, nature and culture. But to put it like that *is* to put it crudely, for the poem itself is deliberately enigmatic; it holds back from direct statements and conceptual formulations, and prefers to explore and order experience in the way dreams actually do, through images. Perhaps it would be better to say, through symbols, using 'symbol' in its Jungian sense as 'the expression of an intuitive perception which can as yet, neither be apprehended better, nor expressed differently'.[53]

The book the narrator of the *Parliament* is reading is the *Somnium Scipionis* itself, 'Tullyus of the drem of Scipioun' (31), of which he proceeds to give a compact summary. It is seen as a threefold vision of judgment, according to the traditional formula embodied in the *Divine Comedy*, except that earth takes the place of purgatory between heaven and hell:

> Chapiteris sevene it hadde, of hevene and helle
> And erthe, and soules that therinne dwelle. (32-3)

In the summary the emphasis is on heaven, that 'blysful place' which is the reward of the good; and the word 'blysse' is repeated three times, and the phrase 'blysful place' twice, in this brief passage. Another repeated phrase is 'commune profit': heavenly bliss is the reward above all of those who have pursued the welfare of the community rather than private profit or even personal salvation. Finally the narrator, as it gets dark, puts the book down, dissatisfied with its teaching,

> For both I hadde thyng which that I nolde,
> And eke I nadde that thyng that I wolde. (90-1)
> *nolde* did not wish; *nadde* did not have

That is enigmatic indeed, but similar statements are made elsewhere in Chaucer's poems, for example in *The Complaint unto Pity* and *The Complaint to his Lady*, and they always refer to the situation of the unrequited lover, who has the suffering that he does not wish but lacks his lady's mercy, which he does desire.[54] So in one way these lines probably refer to what we already know, the narrator's role as one who has had no success in love. But a similar phrase is also used by Philosophy in the *De Consolatione*, to refer to the general state of man, who seeks mistaken means to arrive at that ultimate good which is his goal, and therefore suffers from a perpetual anxiety, because 'the lakkide somwhat that thow woldest nat han lakkid, or elles thou haddest that thow noldest nat han had' (III, pr. 3. 33-6). Thinking of *The House of Fame*, we might feel inclined to see the dissatisfaction as that of the medieval courtly poet, conscious of lacking the 'love-tidings' he needs if he is to produce the expected kind of poetry, and finding in the *Somnium Scipionis* a philosophical doctrine which seems to be of no use to him, because it contains nothing about love (except, significantly, in the phrase 'that lovede commune profyt' (47)). The dream will reconcile these contradictions, and will provide the poet with 'mater of to wryte' (168); but in its immediate context the statement is mysterious, used to express a state in which the mind is dissatisfied for an undefinable cause, weary as night falls, but still seeking for a truth that will answer its longings.

The narrator falls asleep, and dreams that Scipio Africanus stands at his bedside, just as Scipio the younger saw him in the book he has been reading. As in the two earlier dream-poems, there is an ambiguity concerning the status of the dream, which implies an ambiguity in the status of the poem itself, and by extension of imaginative fiction in general. The only theory about the causation of dreams which is stated in this poem occurs in a stanza I have mentioned before, which sees all dreams as reflecting states of body or mind: the hunter dreams of hunting, the sick man of drinking, the lover of success in love, and so on. And the narrator seems to assume the truth of this theory at the very end of the poem, where, after his awakening, he goes on reading more books in the hope that they will so affect his mind that one day he will have a dream that will do him good:

> I hope, ywis, to rede so som day
> That I shal mete som thyng for to fare
> The bet, and thus to rede I nyl nat spare. (697-9)

(Indeed I hope [or expect] some day to read in such a way that I shall dream some thing that will bring me greater success, and thus I will not refrain from reading.)

But he has already expressed doubt—

> Can I not seyn if that the cause were
> For I hadde red of Affrican byforn,
> That made me to mete that he stod there (106-8)

—and, as we have seen, he goes on to say that it was Venus who made him dream as he did. Taken literally, this would imply that the dream was a *somnium coeleste,* inspired by the goddess of love in her planetary form; taken metaphorically, it would indicate that it was a *somnium animale,* inspired by the narrator's waking thoughts of love. Then again, a dream which introduces a venerable figure such as Scipio Africanus the elder would count, according to Macrobius, as an *oraculum,* like the younger Scipio's own dream. If this were true, then the *Parliament* would be the kind of vision that *The House of Fame* stopped short of being; on the other hand, as J.A.W. Bennett has remarked, Chaucer 'reduces to a minimum Africanus' oracular function: the latter becomes a benevolent compère rather than the embodiment of divine wisdoms'.[55] Are we to see the dream which follows as offering supernatural guidance, or as a fantasy woven by the Dreamer's mind out of his waking preoccupations and his reading? Chaucer does not commit himself to any answer to this question, nor to the question which by implication follows from it: are we to see a poem like this as a mere deceptive fiction, or does it offer access, through imagination, to truth?

Like the waking section, the dream in the *Parliament* follows closely the pattern of *The Book of the Duchess.* A preliminary section describes the dream-place (forest or garden), and then comes what appears to be the real subject of the poem (meeting with Black Knight or gathering of birds). We shall find in the *Parliament* as much in the *Book* that what may seem merely a preliminary diversion is in fact related to the main subject through the kind of linkage that belongs to dreams. Africanus leads the Dreamer to the gate of a walled park, reminiscent of the walled garden of the *Roman de la Rose.* Over it are written two inscriptions 'of ful gret difference' (125), one at each side. These derive from the single inscription over the mouth of bell in Dante's *Inferno*, which promises grief and despair to all who enter. But Chaucer's inscriptions are, characteristically, more ambiguous. One promises:

> Thorgh me men gon into that blysful place
> Of hertes hele and dedly woundes cure;
> Thorgh me men gon unto the welle of grace,
> There grene and lusty May shal evere endure.
> This is the wey to al good aventure.
> Be glad, thow redere, and thy sorwe of-caste;
> Al open am I—passe in, and sped thee faste! (127-33)
> *hele* health; *lusty* joyful

Then the other:

> 'Thorgh me men gon,' than spak that other side,
> 'Unto the mortal strokes of the spere
> Of which Disdayn and Daunger is the gyde,
> Ther nevere tre shal fruyt ne leves bere.
> This strem yow ledeth to the sorweful were
> There as the fish in prysoun is al drye;
> Th'eschewing is only the remedye!' (134-40)
> *Daunger* resistance; *were* weir

The Dreamer is paralysed by the contradiction between the two inscriptions, but Africanus tells him that they are meant to refer only to one who is 'Loves servaunt' (159), and therefore not to him. And so he 'shof' (shoved) the Dreamer in through the gate, telling him that he can only be an onlooker, not a participant, but that he will at least gain material for his poetry.

What is behind the gate is evidently a garden of love, like that in the *Roman de la Rose* and its successors, and the inscriptions are saying that love is both heaven and hell. It is the 'blysful place' promised to the good in the *Somnium Scipionis,* with imagery of health, flowing water, and greenness; it is also a place of dryness, sterility and death, which can be avoided only by never entering the garden in the first place. The dream of a heaven and a hell is explicable psychologically through the influence of the vision of judgment read about in the *Somnium Scipionis;* but now the heaven and the hell are the same place—an original variant on the traditional pattern of visions. So far as

the dream is to be thought of as providing material for poetry, one
might also suggest that two contrary states of the imagination are
indicated by the double inscription. The imagery of dryness and
sterility recalls the desert outside the temple of Venus in book I of *The
House of Fame*, which I suggested was a symbol, among other things,
of the failure of inspiration; the imagery of growth and flowing water,
on the other hand, suggests a renewal of creativity. Love, as the subject
for poetry, can provide either or both of these.

The Dreamer enters the garden, and it proves to be a typical
paradise-landscape, with a meadow and a river, a temperate climate,
leaves that are always green, day that lasts for ever, birds singing like
angels, and harmonious music sweeter than was ever heard by God
'that makere is of al and lord' (199). It contains the whole variety of
natural species, instanced by lists of trees and of animals. But it soon
becomes clear that this seeming paradise, as in the *Roman de la Rose,* is
really a pseudo-paradise of idealized desire. In it 'Cupide, oure lord'
(212) sharpens his arrows, 'Some for to sle, and some to wounde and
kerve' (217), and his bow lies ready at his feet. The Dreamer sees
personifications of pleasing qualities such as Pleasure, Courtesy and
Beauty, but also others less pleasing, such as Foolhardiness, Flattery
and Bribery, and, most forcefully described, with a real shudder in the
rhythm of the last line, Cunning:

> . . . the Craft that can and hath the myght
> To don by force a wyght to don folye—
> Disfigurat was she, I nyl nat lye. (220-2)
> *can* knows how; *don by force* compel

Now he presses further into the garden, and comes upon a temple of
brass, the atmosphere of which is at once exotic and sinister. It may
have Patience and Peace sitting at the door, but inside the air is hot with
lovers' sighs, which make the altar flames burn more fiercely, and
which he sees are incited by 'the bittere goddesse Jelosye' (252). The
description of this temple is based on that of the temple of Venus in
Boccaccio's *Teseida*; but in the *Parliament*, unlike book I of *The House
of Fame*, we are not told to whom the temple is dedicated. Chaucer tells
us that the 'sovereyn place' in it is held by Priapus, and leaves us to
guess that it is his temple rather than Venus's. Priapus is the god of the
phallus as well as of gardens, and a recent scholar has suggested that
'Chaucer's direct reference to the story in Ovid's *Fasti* of Priapus'
thwarted attempt to make love to the nymph Lotis clearly marks the

temple as a place of sexual frustration'.[56] Moreover, the Dreamer tells us that

> Ful besyly men gonne assaye and fonde
> Upon his hed to sette, of sondry hewe,
> Garlondes ful of freshe floures newe. (257-9)

(People were eagerly attempting and endeavouring to set on his head garlands full of fresh new flowers, of various colours.)

The emphasis on *attempting* to do this is not in Boccaccio, who says merely that there were garlands of flowers about the temple; and, though the modern reader may think of a notorious incident in chapter 15 of *Lady Chatterley's Lover*, the suggestion Chaucer intends is probably that the cult of sexuality cannot be so easily prettified, however 'besyly men gonne assaye and fonde'. In a dim corner, the Dreamer finds Venus performing a kind of striptease act, which draws an approving snigger from him. The temple is hung with broken bows, symbolizing the lost virginities of those who 'here tymes waste / In hyre servyse' (283-4), and it is decorated with paintings of famous figures from myth and legend who died for love.

From this hothouse atmosphere, the Dreamer re-emerges into the garden 'that was so sote [sweet] and grene' (296), and walks about to recover from his insight into obsessive sexuality. There he sees another goddess, contrasting with Venus. This is Nature,

> . . . a queene,
> That, as of lyght the somer sonne shene
> Passeth the sterre, right so over mesure
> She fayrer was than any creature. (298-301)
> *shene* bright; *over* beyond

Chaucer does not describe her in detail, but, with another of the poem's allusions to the visionary tradition, simply says that she looked just as Alanus described her in the *De Planctu Naturae*. Now, however, the birds of different species, which in Alanus were pictured on her garments, have come alive, and they are all crowded round her, awaiting her judgment. The day, we learn, is that of St Valentine, when the birds choose their mates; and it is likely that the *Parliament* was composed to form part of the St Valentine's day celebrations in Richard II's court. 1382 was the year of Richard's marriage, at the age of fifteen, to Anne of Bohemia. Nature is later described as God's deputy, 'vicaire of the almyghty Lord' (379), but there is little emphasis on her subordination to some higher realm of values. By contrast with the *Roman de la Rose*, this poem lays its stress not on the limitation of Nature's realm but on its extensiveness, though it is also concerned with the intricate relationships between the natural and the human. Nature is so surrounded with birds, the Dreamer says, that 'unethe was there space / For me to stonde, so ful was al the place' (314-15); and indeed, from this point on, the Dreamer drops almost completely out of sight, as if the birds had squeezed him out of the poem; and so does Africanus, his guide. This is one way in which the *Parliament* is very different from both of Chaucer's earlier dream-poems: the subject-matter of the dream itself becomes so solid and energetic that it elbows the Dreamer aside, and instead of a contrast of points of view between Dreamer and guide there is a contrast *within* what the Dreamer sees. There may be a connection between this disappearance of the Dreamer's point of view and the poem's lack of emphasis on the Dreamer as poet; here it is what is seen that is important, not the role of the person who sees it.

The first things seen are all the species of birds, described in five stanzas, each bird with its own epithet or attribute, which serves to humanize it or to align it with some aspect of human life—the noble falcon, the meek-eyed dove, the thieving crow, the gluttonous cormorant, the wise raven, and so on. These are traditional epithets, evidence of the longstanding human tendency to think of birds as constituting a society parallel to human society. We may compare this list with the earlier list of trees in the garden. Both are concerned not simply with description of the natural world, but with the interaction of the natural and the human. The epithets in the list of trees call attention to the usefulness of the different species to men: the oak for building, the box for making pipes, the fir for ships' masts, the yew for bows, and so on. The list of birds, on the other hand, presents them as independent of human beings but parallel to them. The anthropologist Claude Lévi-Strauss has suggested some reasons for this attitude towards birds, which

> can be permitted to resemble men for the very reason that they are so different. They are feathered, winged, oviparous and they are also physically separated from human society by the element in which it is their privilege to move. As a result of

this fact, they form a community which is independent of our own but, precisely because of this independence, appears to us like another society, homologous to that in which we live: birds love freedom; they build themselves homes in which they live a family life and nurture their young; they often engage in social relations with other members of their species; and they communicate with them by acoustic means recalling articulated language. Consequently everything objective conspires to make us think of the bird world as a metaphorical human society: is it not after all literally parallel to it on another level? There are countless examples in mythology and folklore to indicate the frequency of this mode of representation.[57]

There are also countless examples in medieval literature, among them Clanvowe's *Cuckoo and the Nightingale*, which we shall consider later, and the earlier English poem *The Owl and the Nightingale*, in which the two birds are used to articulate a whole range of binary contrasts among human attitudes.

In *The Parliament of Fowls*, under Nature's arbitration, the birds are choosing their mates. Like men in medieval society, they are divided into several broad classes: the birds of prey, those that live on worms, those that live on seeds, and water-fowl. Fittingly, in terms of the human hierarchy of the Middle Ages, Nature begins with the noblest, the birds of prey, and among these with the highest, the royal eagle. But here there is a difficulty, for there are three candidates for the hand—or wing—of the beautiful female eagle, the formel, whom Nature herself is holding on her hand. They are, naturally, three male eagles, or tercels. Each speaks in turn to stake his claim to her: the first rests his claim essentially on the total humility of his devotion, the second on the length of his service as her admirer, the third on his exclusive loyalty. The statement of these claims, in a style of appropriately courtly amplitude, occupies some time, but meanwhile the other classes of birds are anxious to express their own views. Their attitudes are often less courtly than those of the aristocratic birds, and the poem echoes with cries of 'kokkow' and 'quek quek'; indeed, our last reminder of the Dreamer's presence as an observer occurs just here, when he complains that 'thourgh myne eres the noyse wente tho' (500). Nature determines that each class of birds shall select its own spokesman to offer a solution to the dilemma. The falcon, for the birds of prey, says that there is no further possibility of discussion, and the three tercels must fight to the death, unless the formel can choose among them herself. The goose, for water-fowl, offers the simple solution that any of the tercels who is not loved by the formel should choose another female as his mate—an uncourtly view, which is treated with ridicule by the sparrowhawk and the other 'gentil foules alle' (573). The turtledove, on behalf of the seed-fowl, claims that each of the tercels must show his loyalty to the formel by loving no-one else until he dies, even if she should die first—a *reductio ad absurdum* of courtly claims for the transcendent value of personal emotion, in which we are perhaps intended to see a touch of bourgeois sentimentality. The duck agrees with the goose: there are other fish in the sea, other stars in the sky:

> 'Ye quek!' yit seyde the doke, ful wel and fayre,
> 'There been mo sterres, God wot, than a payre!' (594-5)

The last verdict is that of the cuckoo, for the lowly worm-fowl, the *vylayns* of bird-society: since the eagles cannot agree, let them remain solitary all their lives. Another *gentil* bird, the small falcon called a merlin, protests against this in most *ungentil* language, calling the cuckoo 'wormes corupcioun' (614); but at this point Nature intervenes again.

In the paralleling of different types of bird with the attitudes supposed to be appropriate to different social classes, there is a close resemblance to the way in which primitive men use the categories built into nature as means of thinking about their own lives as part of human culture. In many areas of life such habits of thought have been retained by civilized societies too, so that, as Lévi-Strauss puts it, 'The differences between animals, which man can extract from nature and transfer to culture, . . . are adopted as emblems by groups of men in order to do away with their own resemblances'.[58] In the *Parliament* the poet of a highly civilized society to some extent reverses the original process: the already existing human groupings, and the attitudes which accompany them, are transferred to the realm of the birds, a realm which remains under the dominion of Nature. There are objectively and permanently different species of birds; but they are only birds, after all. One consequence of this is that we can think about their differences of attitude, even towards so central a subject as love, with amused tolerance. The irreducible birdlikeness of the eagle in *The House of*

Fame had a similar function, in preventing us from being able to take him too seriously as a figure of authority. This part of the poem, the actual parliament of the birds, is very funny, not least as a parody of the unruly parliament of Chaucer's own time. Its amusing aspects, indeed, have perhaps tended to overshadow the rest of the poem. A second consequence of the way in which the birds remain birds is that Nature, the mother of them all, can call them to order, if necessary somewhat sharply: 'Holde youre tonges there!' (521) or '"Now pes!" quod Nature, "I commaunde here!"' (617). Their different degrees of *worthinesse* are not conceived as a merely historical phenomenon, but are ratified as part of Nature's 'ryhtful ordenaunce' (390). And she is in a position to insist that their mating must be by mutual agreement, by *eleccioun* (621) rather than by the force that the earlier temple of brass seemed to imply.

Finally, towards the end of the dream, a provisional solution to the dilemma of who shall mate with the formel is achieved by moving out of the realm of birds and back into that of men and women. Nature allows the formel to make her own choice—which was what the falcon had originally urged. Nature herself, it appears, is on the side of the *gentil*, even though she 'alwey hadde an ere / To murmur of the lewednesse [coarseness] behynde' (519-20). She advises the formel, saying that were she not Nature but Reason she would counsel her to choose the first of the tercels; but the actual choice she leaves to the bird herself. The formel, however, declines to choose; she does not yet wish to serve Venus or Cupid, and she needs more time to make up her mind. This too Nature grants. She allows her until the next St Valentine's day to make her choice, and meantime the three tercels have a year to prove their devotion to her. With this problem removed for the time being, all the other birds can now choose their mates. They choose immediately, and before their departure they sing a roundel in honour of Nature, the exquisite lyric 'Now welcome, somer, with thy sonne softe' (680). The noise of the birds' 'shoutyng' when the song is finished awakens the Dreamer from his sleep, and the poem ends with him reading still more books, in the hope of one day having a dream that will do him good.

There is a striking contrast between the evident dissatisfaction of the Dreamer with his dream, which he thinks has not given him what he was seeking in his books, and the satisfying completeness which most readers find in the poem that contains the dream. The difference is that between the conscious mind, always seeking for rational solutions to life's problems on the 'bookish' level of philosophy, and the unconscious mind, which achieves mastery over problems by enacting them in the form of concrete images rather than through rational analysis. One scholar writes of all Chaucer's dream-poems that 'The great originality of these poems is in their attempt to exploit the possibilities of *dispositio*—over-all structural arrangement—in ways more complex and meaningful than anything the [rhetorical] manuals suggest in their perfunctory treatments of it.'[59] This is particularly true of *The Parliament of Fowls*: the meaning of the poem is conveyed through certain contrasts embodied rather than stated in the dream-experience, and it was surely his sensitive understanding of dreams that enabled Chaucer to go beyond the inadequate treatment of *dispositio* in the *artes poeticae*. There is, for example, the contrast between the temple of Priapus and Venus and the garden of Nature, between love conceived as enslaving obsession and love conceived as natural impulse, operating within the orderly hierarchy of Nature; then there is the further contrast, within the natural order, now seen as mirroring the human order, between different attitudes towards love. We *feel* the contrast between the enclosure of Venus and Priapus and the freedom of Nature (and we may note that the temple is set within Nature's garden: Nature is more inclusive than sexuality). This freedom, always combined with order, is enacted in the parliament, where every attitude is allowed freedom of expression. This is how the 'commune profit' of the *Somnium Scipionis* is achieved in Nature's realm, which in one way encloses and in another way is homologous with the realm of human society. The cuckoo even uses the phrase 'comune spede' (507), which means the same as 'commune profit'. And the freedom of speech and choice includes a freedom not to choose, or at least to defer choosing. The poem ends unexpectedly, so far as the suitors are concerned: this mating season for them brings not the achievement of love but its deferment. This has the advantage of finally transferring the freedom of discussion to the poem's audience. As some scholars have suggested, *The Parliament of Fowls* leads up to a *demande d'amour*, a love-question to be settled by the courtly listeners as *they* think fit. Whom should the formel choose next St Valentine's day? It is for us to decide. Moreover, the deferment of die choice implies a richer civilization than merely seasonal activities might lead us to expect. Human love, the poem implies, involves not merely the gods of sex and their temple of illicit passions, but the possibility of resisting Nature, or at least of gaining a certain margin of freedom within which to choose the time and manner of one's submission. No doubt, as Jean de Meun's La Vielle puts it, quoting Horace,

> qui voudroit une forche prandre
> por soi de Nature deffandre
> et la bouteroit hors de sai,
> revandroit ele, bien le sai (13991-4)

(if anyone wanted to take up a pitchfork to protect himself against Nature and shove her out of himself, she would come back, I know well).

But human beings, though they may not be able to overcome Nature completely, at least are not like birds in being so absolutely dominated by natural impulse that they cannot resist the mating season. The subject of the poem, as I have argued, is that central subject of anthropological study, the relation between nature and culture. The dream, then, though it does not satisfy the Dreamer, does weave the thoughts that had been preoccupying him, both from books and from life, into a new and more richly significant pattern. Love, heaven, hell, the 'commune profit': all these appear, transmuted, in the dream, which offers, like myth, an imaginative mastery over the problems of human life.

The mastery is only imaginative, of course, and that is one meaning of the poem's dream-framework. Once the dream is over, the Dreamer may still be troubled by problems so fundamental to human nature that they cannot be abolished. Moreover, the poem in its texture, its 'feel', is genuinely like a dream. It may make use of conceptual thought, but it does so in the most tentative way, with conceptual oppositions largely replaced by concrete contrasts, and one contrast merging dreamlike into another. Such a delicate structure could not have been created by a poet who was truly in the dreamlike state in which he represents himself. A superb intelligence is at work in *The Parliament of Fowls*, and some words written about a great poet of the twentieth century would apply equally well to this poem of Chaucer's:

> The poet's magnificent intelligence is devoted to keeping as close as possible to the concrete of sensation, emotion and perception. Though this poetry is plainly metaphysical in preoccupation, it belongs as purely to the realm of sensibility,

and has in it as little of the abstract and general of discursive
prose, as any poetry that was ever written.[60]

The 'Prologue' to 'The Legend of Good Women'

The *Prologue* to *The Legend of Good Women* is the last of Chaucer's
dream-poems, and it stands alone in his work in existing in two distinct
versions, F, dating from about 1385-6 and G, a revised version which
probably dates from 1394 or later. This brings us to the period of
Chaucer's most mature work. The *Prologue* is certainly later than
Troilus and Criseyde, the translation of Boethius, and the first versions
of *The Knight's Tale* and *The Second Nun's Tale*, because all of these
are mentioned in it; and yet Chaucer is still using and further
developing the dream-poem. For him, contrary to the common
assumption, the dream-poem cannot have been a mere literary artifice
which appealled to him only in his early, imitative period. The
Prologue is perhaps the most puzzling and enigmatic of Chaucer's
dream-poems, although it is the shortest, and is comparatively simple in
outline. It begins with a discussion by the narrator of the relative values
of personal experience and of the authority of old books—a topic
familiar from *The House of Fame*. He is himself a devotee of books,
but in May at least he leaves them behind and goes out into the
meadows to perform his devotions to his favourite flower, the daisy.
This he praises at some length, and then explains that one May morning
he went out in this way, listened to the birds singing in praise of spring
and love, and adored the daisy all day long. Then, at night, he slept in
the garden and had a dream. In it the God of Love appears to him,
accompanied by a beautiful lady who in appearance is like a
transfigured daisy. The God and his company of ladies themselves
worship the daisy, and then the God notices the Dreamer. What, he
asks, is *he* doing so near the God's own flower? It would be better for a
worm to be near it than for the Dreamer to do so, because the Dreamer
has written works which are heresies against the religion of love, and
which persuade wise men not to believe in women's
trustworthiness—namely, the *Romance of the Rose* and *Troilus and
Criseyde*. (The G text inserts at this point a list of books possessed by
the Dreamer from which he could have drawn stories of the faithfulness
of women.) But the beautiful daisy-like lady defends the Dreamer
against the angry God, arguing that his works were translations, that he
had not noticed that they were heretical, that he may have been writing

under the orders of some patron, and that in any case he is now repentant. The God of Love, as a just ruler, ought to be merciful, not harsh. And she mentions a whole string of works which the Dreamer has also written, 'Al be hit that he kan nat wel endite' (F 414): *The House of Fame, The Book of the Duchess, The Parliament of Fowls*, the story which later became *The Knight's Tale*, and many lyrics. She adds that he has also written works of 'other holynesse' (F 424)—belonging, that is, not to the religion of love but to Christianity—and she mentions some of these. She proposes that the Dreamer should be forgiven if he agrees to write in future about women 'trewe in lovyng' (F 438). The God magnanimously consents, and the Dreamer thanks the lady, explaining that, whatever his sources intended, his own purpose was only to blame false lovers. The lady tells him that he must henceforward spend his time writing of good women and false men, and that, even though not a lover himself, he must 'speke wel of love' (F 491). The God of Love now identifies the lady by reminding the Dreamer that he has at home a book which tells how Alcestis, who died to save her husband from death, was afterwards transformed into a daisy. That is who the lady is, and the Dreamer must write of her too. Lastly, the God returns to his home in paradise, and the Dreamer is left to proceed with his task. Only in G is his awakening mentioned. There follow nine stories of 'good women', mostly taken from Ovid. The last is unfinished, and the work as a whole is incomplete, since the *Prologue* has mentioned nineteen legends to be recounted.

In many ways the *Prologue* to *The Legend of Good Women* belongs to the category established by Chaucer's earlier dream-poems, and indeed it further develops certain possibilities inherent in that category. For example, the opening discussion of experience and the authority of books is from one point of view a generalization of issues raised in the earlier poems. Each of them had begun with a story from a book by 'these olde wyse' (F 19)—Ovid, Virgil, Cicero—and each of them had gone on to counterpoint the adventures of an inexperienced dreamer against the authority encountered in his dream. In the *Prologue*, moreover, the discussion begins with the example of 'joy in hevene and peyne in helle' (F 2), of which we know only from books, since no man has been there and returned; and yet each of the dream-poems, including the *Prologue* itself, claims to be a record of experience of a kind of heaven; though, yet again, each of them is no more than a book. The confident affirmation with which this section of the *Prologue* concludes—

> Wel ought us thanne honouren and beleve
> These bokes, there we han noon other preve (F 27-8)
>   *preve* experiential proof

—dissolves into ambiguity as one thinks about it. To take another example, we saw that in *The Parliament of Fowls* the existence of the poem was justified by the fact that the dream had been sent to the poet in order to provide him with material for poetry. In the *Prologue*, this justificatory function of the dream is taken further, and the commands received in the dream justify the existence not just of the dream-poem itself but of the sequence of other poems attached to it. This conception of the dream-prologue proved to be highly influential on subsequent writers, particularly in Scotland, and I shall return to it later.

Like *The Book of the Duchess* and *The Parliament of Fowls*, the *Prologue* appears to be associated with some courtly occasion. In it, Chaucer twice refers to the courtly cult of the flower and the leaf, a kind of game at the court of Richard II, in which the courtiers divided into two parties or mock-chivalric orders, in order to provide a framework for the discussion of questions of love.[61] Chaucer refers to this cult only to assert that the cult of the daisy which is a central theme of his poem does not imply that he supports the party of the flower against that of the leaf. His poem, when he reaches the actual legends, is going to be concerned with stories dating from long before the flower and leaf game was invented:

> Ne I not who serveth leef, ne who the flour;
> Wel browken they her service or labour;
> For this thing is al of another tonne,
> Of olde storye, er swich stryf was begonne. (F 193-6)
>   *not* know not; *browken they* may they enjoy; *of . . . tonne*
>   drawn from a different barrel

The cult of the daisy, too, was not an invention of Chaucer's, but has a courtly background in a number of French 'marguerite' poems, especially by Machaut and Deschamps.[62] Both cults seem to have been associated with the courtly May games, which were probably aristocratic imitations of popular seasonal festivities. The dream in the *Prologue* takes place on the night of May the first in the F-text, and 'Whan passed was almost the month of May' (G 89) in G; possibly these two dates indicate occasions on which the poem was read aloud.

The birds and their celebration of the mating season are repeated from the *Parliament*, and the *Prologue* also has the birds referring to St Valentine's day. The F-text refers specifically to the queen, when the God of Love instructs the Dreamer to send his book of good women, once complete, to 'the quene, / On my byhalf, at Eltham or at Sheene' (F 496-7). The queen in question is Anne of Bohemia, and the G-text must date from after her death in 1394, because it deletes this reference to her and the palaces; indeed, Richard II, in his passionate grief, had ordered the palace at Sheen to be destroyed. The strength of these bonds linking the *Prologue* to its setting in court life is an important source of the poem's puzzling quality. One cannot help suspecting that crucial elements in its meaning may relate to some situation outside itself, to which we no longer have the key. However that may be, the conception of Chaucer as court-poet is familiar to us from his other dream-poems.

The *Prologue* employs the dream for a purpose which we can now easily recognize. It is a secularized version of an otherworld vision, in which an authoritative figure appears to the Dreamer and conveys to him commands and teaching beyond those available to him in his waking life in this world. As in the *House* and the *Parliament*, the content of the vision relates to Chaucer's role as a courtly poet of love. As in the *Parliament*, the narrator is presented from the beginning as a devoted student of 'olde bokes' (F 25)—those very 'olde bokes' from which he is eventually to draw the legends of good women. He has no personal experience of love, and in this he is much inferior to the courtiers who form his audience, whom he addresses as 'lovers that kan make of sentement' (F 69) (lovers who are able to write poetry based on their own feelings). They are the reapers of the harvest of poetry, and he comes behind gleaning 'any goodly word that ye han left' (F 77); he has to apologise to them for merely repeating what 'ye han in youre fresshe songes sayd' (F 79). Just as in the *Parliament*, then, the vision comes to him as a way of providing matter for his poetry; only now it is not, as it was in both the *Parliament* and the *House*, a reward for his devoted service, and a new inspiration to him, but a penance for what he has done wrong, and he remains uninspired, nothing but a humble translator. It is true that the vision concludes with a doctrinal assurance of a more general kind, of exactly the sort that earlier visionaries had brought back from the world beyond death. The God of Love tells him,

> But er I goo, thus muche I wol the telle:
> Ne shal no trewe lover come in helle. (F 552-3)

(There is of course an intentional ambiguity in that message, which
might refer either to Christian truth or to a secular parody of it, such as
is enunciated by Genius in the *Roman de la Rose.)* But the main body
of the vision focuses more distinctly than any of Chaucer's earlier
dream-poems on poetry itself, and it throws fascinating light on
Chaucer's role as a poet.

The Dreamer is even more firmly identified with Chaucer as poet
than he was in *The House of Fame.* He has written all of Chaucer's
works, and the list of them, which Chaucer modestly puts in Alcestis's
mouth rather than his own, acts as a form of self-advertisement.
Chaucer can evidently assume, as Machaut could in writing the
Jugement dou Roy de Navarre, that some of his earlier work is
sufficiently well known to his audience, and perhaps sufficiently
controversial, for a contradiction of it to be a plausible starting-point
for a new poem. Yet the Dreamer evidently wrote Chaucer's work in
total unawareness of what he was doing—while dreaming, as it were.
He was only translating, and *Troilus and Criseyde* was as simply a
translation as *The Romaunt of the Rose. Troilus* indeed offers itself as
being not just the story of Troilus and Criseyde, but the story of how a
naive and incompetent court-poet, a mere servant of the servants of the
God of Love, performed the task of translating it. The *Prologue* goes
even further than this. It argues not just that *Troilus and Criseyde* is
only a translation, but that it is a translation by a writer who did not
grasp the meaning of his source. The defence Alcestis suggests against
the God of Love's angry accusation is not that *Troilus* is really a poem
in praise of the love of women, despite Criseyde's unfortunate lapse,
but that Chaucer had failed to understand that the story was directed
against the love of women:

> Therfore he wrot the Rose, and ek Crisseyde,
> Of innocence, and nyste what he seyde. (G 344-5)
> *nyste* knew not

Later, Chaucer as Dreamer hesitantly suggests a slightly different
explanation: it is true that he failed to understand what his sources
meant, but he thought he was telling the story as an *exemplum* warning
against falseness in love, and therefore in favour of true love:

> what so myn auctour mente,
> Algate, God woot, yt was myn entente
> To forthren trouthe in love and yt cheryce,
> And to ben war fro falsnesse and fro vice
> By swich ensample; this was my menynge. (F 470-4)
> *what so* whatever; *Algate* nevertheless; *cheryce* cherish; *ben war* beware

But Alcestis quickly tells him to hold his tongue; the God of Love has been remarkably merciful to him, and he had better not argue about the matter, or presume to have theories about his own work:

> And she answerde, 'Lat be thyn arguynge,
> For Love ne wol nat countrepleted be
> In ryght ne wrong; and lerne that at me!
> Thow hast thy grace, and hold the ryght therto.' (F 475-8)
> *countrepleted* argued against; *at* from

Instead let him proceed with his penitential task of writing about women who were true in love, and about men who betrayed them in the way which is so sadly typical of the earthly world in which the Dreamer leads his waking life:

> And telle of false men that hem bytraien,
> That al hir lyf ne do nat but assayen
> How many women they may doon a shame;
> For in youre world that is now holde a game. (F 486-9)
> *ne do nat* do nothing

This abrupt treatment of the Dreamer is also similar to what we have seen in earlier dream-poems. He is a person of no importance in his own dream, fiercely rebuked by the authoritative figure who confronts him, and unable even to think of an excuse for his misdoings until one is suggested for him by Alcestis; and then rapped over the knuckles by Alcestis herself for attempting to explain what he thought he was doing in his own poetry. The Dreamer says very little indeed: he is a comically inadequate figure, far more at home diligently reading and translating old books in his earthly life than when he is transported to the presence of the God who defines the doctrine of all true love poetry. But, somewhat as in the encounter between the Dreamer and the Black Knight in *The Book of the Duchess*, the meeting of the simple Dreamer with the princely figure in his dream sets up ironic reverberations which also affect that princely figure. We all know that Chaucer really understood what he was doing when he wrote his poems, that his task as 'translator' of *Troilus and Criseyde* was really of a quite different order from his task as translator of the *Roman de la Rose*, and that, after all, the Chaucer who cuts such a poor figure in his dream is also the Chaucer who wrote the poem in which the dream occurs, the creator of the God of Love as well as the trembling poetaster who thankfully accepts penance from him. The God, we are prepared to believe (and in this we have Alcestis's encouragement too), is a literary tyrant, a censor who insists that reality shall be presented only in a certain light; and the poet, in his simplicity, may have stumbled into a more truthful picture of things. This profound ambiguity about the status of Chaucer as court-poet is developed, as usual, out of the essential ambiguity in the status of dreams.

From one point of view, the dream in the *Prologue* is obviously a distorted reflection of the Dreamer's waking life, a *somnium animale*. In his dream he finds himself in the same meadow into which he had gone earlier to do his devotions to the daisy; indeed, in the G-text the point at which he falls asleep is moved forward in the poem, and part of F's description of the real meadow becomes in G a description of the dream-meadow. In his waking life he has been entirely preoccupied with the daisy; in his dream he sees a lady who is, as it were, a daisy personified and transfigured, and he at once recognizes the similarity:

> And she was clad in real habit grene.
> A fret of gold she hadde next her heer,
> And upon that a whit corowne she beer
> With flourouns smale, and I shal nat lye;
> For al the world, ryght as a dayesye
> Ycorouned ys with white leves lyte,
> So were the flowrouns of hire coroune white.
> For of o perle fyn, oriental,
> Hire white coroune was ymaked al;
> For which the white coroune above the grene
> Made hire lyk a daysie for to sene,
> Considered eke hir fret of gold above. (F 214-25)

real royal; *fret* ornament; *beer* wore; *fluorouns* petals; *and* (1. 217) if; *leves lyte* small petals; *o* one

The French 'marguerite' poems provide a link between the flower and the pearl, because in French *marguerite* means both 'pearl' and 'daisy'. Obviously enough, this dream-lady is a projection of the Dreamer's waking thoughts; but beyond this we do not find in the *Prologue* any of the complex psychological motivation for the dream which is part of Chaucer's other dream-poems, and above all of *The Book of the Duchess*, nor do we find much sign of adaptation of the constructive methods of dreams to provide imaginative linkings within the poem. The drama of the dream is self-sufficient; its outlines are strongly drawn, and there seems to be no network of hidden correspondences beneath them. This might suggest that the poem is better considered in its other aspect, as a vision coming from outside the Dreamer's mind, under supernatural influences, a *somnium coeleste*.

The standing of the dream as a *somnium coeleste* is indicated in a number of ways. The poem begins with a reflection on heaven and hell, and on the fact that we get all our information about those interesting places from books, written by men who have never been there. But the dream itself is presented as a vision of heaven, imagined as a paradisal landscape of the usual kind. It is a flowery meadow, evidently a kind of outskirt of paradise itself, which the God of Love and his company are visiting temporarily. 'I moot goon hom,' the God says, '—the sonne draweth west — / To paradys, with al this companye' (F 563-4).[63] The God has 'aungelyke' wings (F 236), and the whole situation is like that inside the garden at the beginning of the *Roman de la Rose*: a secular version of the religious vision of the other world, based on a pseudo-theology of sexual love. The relation between the religion of love and Christianity is never clarified; as we have seen, the God of Love is able to promise that no true lover will go to hell. The world of the dream is also the world beyond death: Alcestis, the nineteen ladies immediately attendant on the God, and the multitude of other women who were true in love, are all apparently people who have lived and died on earth, and whose stories (like that of Blanche in *The Book of the Duchess*) are to be given a more lasting life in Chaucer's poetry. The God reminds the Dreamer of the story of Alcestis, and thus, as in other dream-poems, the theme of hell is touched on in this literary heaven. Alcestis is

> She that for hire housbonde chees to dye,
> And eke to goon to helle, rather than he,
> And Ercules rescowed hire, parde,
> And broght hir out of helle agayn to blys. (F 513-16)
> *chees* chose

Her story is completed with an Ovidian metamorphosis: Alcestis was turned into a daisy, and this emerges as the apparent justification for Chaucer's initial devotion to the daisy. Thus the flower is a symbol of love itself, a human love which can conquer even death. That is why the God of Love refers to it as 'my flour' (F 318) and even 'my relyke, digne and delytable' (F 321). It is, we may suppose, the depth of the narrator's devotion to the daisy which opens the way to the revelation in his dream of the flower's heavenly meaning and the course of action to which it directs him—the writing in future of legends of good women. Medieval devotional writers sometimes recognize a type of dream which is halfway between a *somnium animale* and a *somnium coeleste*, a type in which previous devotion leads on to supernatural revelation. Richard Rolle, for example, mentions a kind of dream which derives from 'thoghtes before that falles to Criste or hali kyrk, revelacion comand after'.[64] Perhaps in the *Prologue* we might recognize a secular equivalent to this type of religious vision. There is, however, one difficulty in this view of the poem. It is that there is not really any book Chaucer could have possessed that would have told of the metamorphosis of Alcestis into a daisy, because this event in the myth seems to have been invented by Chaucer himself. Thus the link between the daisy and Alcestis is apparently fictional, and completely arbitrary; if we are to accept it at all, it will have to be on the assumption that the dream is really an inspired revelation.

We seem to be thrown back on the acknowledgment that the poem contains an enigma. The devotion to the daisy expressed in the waking section has a peculiar fervour, which feels almost genuinely religious:

> She is the clernesse and the verray lyght
> That in this derke world me wynt and ledeth.
> The hert in-with my sorwfull brest yow dredeth
> And loveth so sore that ye ben verrayly
> The maistresse of my wit, and nothing I.
> My word, my werk ys knyt so in youre bond
> That, as an harpe obeieth to the hond

And maketh it soune after his fyngerynge,
Ryght so mowe ye oute of myn herte bringe
Swich vois, ryght as yow lyst, to laughe or pleyne.
Be ye my gide and lady sovereyne!
As to myn erthly god to yow I calle,
Bothe in this werk and in my sorwes alle. (F 84-96)
wynt directs; *sore* ardently; *nothing* not at all, *it soune* its
sound; *after* according to; *mowe* may; *pleyne* lament

A recent scholar has written of this passage that 'It is possible . . . to
read the praise of the daisy both as a beguiling tribute to a modest,
charming flower and as a sly and cheeky mockery of the worshipful
lover and the worship of love'.[65] But my own impression is that the
emotional temperature of the passage is higher than 'beguiling tribute'
suggests, nor can I detect any 'sly and cheeky mockery' in it. If the
passage is serious, it might be possible to explain it as alluding to the
source of poetic inspiration itself. The mistress of the poet's wit is
surely his muse; and if we could understand the vision of this 'white
goddess' as being one of the power that makes Chaucer a poet, then it
would be possible to see the *Prologue* as a culmination of the tendency
that has been developing through Chaucer's dream-poems, the
tendency to use the dream as a way of writing about imaginative fiction
itself. The legends that follow are to bring back to life ladies who died
ages ago; insofar as they succeed, it is the power of the poet's
imagination that enables them to transcend death; what could be more
appropriate than that this power should be embodied in his dream in the
person of Alcestis, who herself overcame the power of death? But the
question would still arise, why Chaucer should have attached the vision
of Alcestis to the existing tradition of 'marguerite' poems. What
relation was there between his inspiration as a poet and the real or
imaginary lady—perhaps called Margaret?—who is alluded to in the
daisy-imagery? Behind the poem must surely lie some courtly situation
which would clarify its obscurities. There have been attempts to
identify the lady symbolized by the flower, none of them conclusive;
and I think we shall have to resign ourselves to ignorance.

NOTES

1. C.G. Jung, *Modern Man in Search of a Soul* (London, 1933), p.16.

2. The statement is provoked by Troilus's nightmares, which are realistically described at V. 246-59 in a passage added by Chaucer to his sources. I have discussed another dream in *Troilus and Criseyde*, that of Criseyde in book II, in *Criticism and Medieval Poetry*, 2nd edn (London, 1972), pp. 139-47.

3. D.W. Robertson, 'The Historical Setting of Chaucer's *Book of the* Duchess', in *Medieval Studies in Honor of U.T. Holmes* (Chapel Hill, 1965), pp. 169-95.

4. Though most editors, believing a line to have been omitted after 479, give a total of 1334.

5. E.g. J.B. Severs, 'Chaucer's Self-Portrait in the *Book of the Duchess*', *Philological Quarterly*, vol. XLIII (1964), pp. 27-39.

6. *Chaucer's Early Poetry* (London, 1963), p. 30. Clemen had offered a similar view of Chaucer in the earlier version of this book, *Der junge Chaucer* (Köln, 1938).

7. *Gothic* (Harmondsworth, 1968), p. 115.

8. Cf. Jung's definition of 'genuine symbols' (in the arts as much as in dreams) as 'the best possible expressions of something as yet unknown—bridges thrown out towards an invisible shore' (*Contributions to Analytical Psychology* (London, 1928), p. 239).

9. *Chaucer and the Mediaeval Sciences*, 2nd edn (London, 1960), chapter 8.

10. Latin original in *Patrologia Latina*, vol. CLXXXIV, col. 1300.

11. *English Writings of Richard Rolle*, ed. H.E. Allen (Oxford, 1931), p. 93.

12. *The Interpretation of Dreams*, pp. 165 and 218.

13. For discussion, see W.O. Sypherd, *Studies in Chaucer's Hous of Fame* (London, 1907), p. 10; M.W. Stearns, 'Chaucer Mentions a Book', *Modern Language Notes*, vol. LVII (1942), 28-31; Wimsatt, *Chaucer and the French Love Poets*, pp. 84-5.

14. Suggested by B.H. Bronson, '*The Book of the Duchess* Reopened', *Publications of the Modern Language Association of America*, vol. LXVII (1952), pp. 863-81.

15. *The Interpretation of Dreams*, pp. 179, 293.

16. Winny, *Chaucer's Dream Poems*, p.35; Kane, *The Autobiographical Fallacy*, p. 13.

17. *The Interpretation of Dreams*, p. 266.

18. Ella Freeman Sharpe, *Dream Analysis* (London, 1937), p. 59.

19. E.g. in his essay 'On the Relation of Analytical Psychology to Poetic Art', in *Contributions to Analytical Psychology*.

20. D.W. Robertson writes that 'the dream vision as a poetic form . . . is . . . certainly not conducive to dream "realism"' (in *Companion to Chaucer Studies*, ed. Beryl Rowland (Toronto, 1968), p. 338). But the presence of elements of 'dream realism' in medieval dream-poems has been studied, though without much penetration, by Constance B. Hieatt, *The Realism of Dream Visions* (The Hague, 1967).

21. Numerous attempts have been made to solve this riddle, ranging from Skeat's suggestion that it is a compliment to Edward III to the assertion that 'Octovyen' is a numerological pun, meaning 'Christ coming' (B.F. Huppé and D.W. Robertson, *Fruyt and Chaf* (Princeton, 1963), p. 49, developed further by R.A. Peck, 'Theme and Number in Chaucer's *Book of the Duchess*', in *Silent Poetry*, ed. Alastair Fowler (London, 1970), p. 100).

22. Chaucer's description of the puppy is derived from two of Machaut's poems, the *Jugement dou Roy de Navarre* and the *Dit dou Lyon*. The puppy itself has been variously interpreted as symbolic of marital infidelity, the priesthood, flattery, and dialectic. J.B. Friedman sensibly remarks that 'Like many familiar objects recurrent in the literature of the Middle Ages, the dog appears in so many different ways that there cannot accurately be said to be a "tradition of the dog" to cast symbolic light upon his every appearance in medieval literature' ('The Dreamer, the Whelp and Consolation in the *Book of the Duchess*', *Chaucer Review*, vol. III (1968-9), pp. 145-62; at p. 149). My remarks relate simply to the part the puppy plays in the action of this poem.

23. Several scholars, and notably J.E. Grennen, '*Hert-huntyng* in the *Book of the Duchess*,' *Modern Language Quarterly*, vol. XXV (1964), pp. 131-9, have suggested that the hunt has a symbolic significance, and have noticed the pun on *hert*, though they have arrived at very diverse conclusions as to the meaning of these elements in the poem as a whole.

24. *Introductory Lectures on Psycho-Analysis*, trans. Joan Riviere, 2nd edn (London, 1929), pp. 148-9.

25. Ibid. p. 145.

26. Sharpe, *Dream Analysis*, p. 157.

27. 'The Story of Asdiwal', in *The Structural Study of Myth and Totemisim*, ed. Edmund Leach (London, 1967), p. 21.

28. *Chaucer and His Poetry* (Cambridge, Mass., 1915), pp. 48, 50.

29. *Art and Tradition in Sir Gawain and the Green Knight* (New Brunswick, 1965), pp. 180-1.

30. For example, in the *Jugement dou Roy de Navarre* Machaut as participant is so absorbed in hunting that he fails to notice the lady who wishes to complain about the judgement given in his earlier poem, and yet as narrator he is able to tell us what the lady and her squire were saying to each other. Later in the same poem, however, with a certain self-consciousness, he explains that he is able to report what the king and his advisers said when they left him to consider their verdict, because a friend informed him.

31. E.g., J.R. Kreuzer, 'The Dreamer in *The Book of the Duchess*', *Publications of the Modern Language Association of America*, vol. LXVI (1951), pp. 543-7, and Bronson, in *Publications of the Modern Language Association of America*, vol. LXVII.

32. Cf. John Lawlor, 'The Pattern of Consolation in *The Book of the Duchess*', *Speculum*, vol. XXXI (1956), 626-48, and *Chaucer* (London, 1968), pp. 21-6.

33. Marshall McLuhan, *The Gutenberg Galaxy* (London, 1962), p. 136.

34. *The Allegory of Love*, p. 170; *Chaucer and the Making of English Poetry*, vol. I, p. 45.

35. Cf. Sheila M. Delany, *Chaucer's House of Fame* (Chicago, 1972), p. 44: 'That the Narrator's position as dreamer and as poet is the same suggests that the dream is not only analogous to the composition but may be a metaphor for it—or, more accurately, for the poetic conception embodied in the work. The process of dreaming becomes nearly synonymous with the creative act.' Also Winny, *Chaucer's Dream-Poems*, p. 35: 'The . . . contemporary interest in dreams encouraged the poet to relate his imaginative experiences as if he had dreamt them, and to use conventional figures of the dream-poem to embody his imaginative awareness.'

36. M.W. Bloomfield, *Essays and Explorations* (Cambridge, Mass., 1970), p. 184.

37. See J.M. Steadman, 'Chaucer's Eagle: a Contemplative Symbol', *Publications of the Modern Language Association of America*, vol. LXXV (1960), pp. 153-9. The eagle has been the subject of much scholarly comment, not all of it relevant to the poem; but for

some ingenious suggestions, see J. Leyerle, 'Chaucer's Windy Eagle', *University of Toronto Quarterly*, vol. XL (1971), pp. 247-65.

38. Lying behind this may perhaps be discerned the explanation of the music of the spheres in the *Somnium Scipionis*.

39. C.A. Muscatine, *Chaucer and the French Tradition* (Berkeley, 1957), p. 246.

40. Robert Henryson, *The Testament of Cresseid*, ed. Denton Fox (London, 1968), line 463.

41. This point is made by J.A.W. Bennett, *Chaucer's Book of Fame* (Oxford, 1968), p. 150.

42. Ibid. p. 153.

43. See Clemen, *Chaucer's Early Poetry*, pp. 114-16.

44. Winny, *Chaucer's Dream-Poems*, p. 149.

45. The chief source is Dante, *Inferno* II. 7-9, which confirms that by 'Thought' Chaucer means memory. Winny, *Chaucer's Dream-Poems*, pp. 33-4, is entirely mistaken in asserting that 'Thought' here means imagination and that 'Chaucer seems to reject firmly the idea that the dream has been impressed on his mind from outside by some kind of supernatural agency, and asserts that it has been produced by the purposeful workings of his own mental forces.'

46. Closely based on Dante, *Paradiso* I. 13-27.

47. T.S. Eliot, *The Love Song of J. Alfred Prufrock*.

48. As suggested by D.M. Bevington, 'The Obtuse Narrator in Chaucer's *House of Fame*', *Speculum*, vol. XXXVI (1961), pp. 288-98.

49. Suggested by Bennett, *Chaucer's Book of Fame*, p. 187.

50. *The Social History of Art* (London, 1951), vol. I, p. 220.

51. J.L. Lowes, *Geoffrey Chaucer* (Oxford, 1934), p. 117.

52. In this Chaucer is continuing a tradition that goes far back in medieval courtly poetry, though it rarely achieved conscious realization. Cf. E.I. Condren, 'The Troubadour and his Labor of Love', *Mediaeval Studies*, vol. XXXIV (1972), pp. 174-95: 'Many troubadour lyrics seem indeed to speak about a new and rarefied concept of love—about *fin' amors*. But several of them also use the language of love to describe the poet's search for poetry. Similarly, the poet's anguish and frustration in love are frequently co-subjects with his inability to create songs' (p. 175).

53. *Contributions to Analytical Psychology*, p. 232.

54. Noted by D.S. Brewer, ed., *The Parlement of Foulys* (London, 1960), p. 103.

55. *The Parlement of Foules: An Interpretation* (Oxford, 1957), p. 54.

56. G.D. Economou, *The Goddess Natura in Medieval Literature* (Cambridge, Mass., 1972), p. 136.

57. *The Savage Mind* (London, 1966), p. 204.

58. Ibid. p. 107.

59. R.O. Payne, *The Key of Remembrance* (New Haven, 1963), p. 145.

60. F.R. Leavis, 'T.S. Eliot's Later Poetry', in *Education and the University*, 2nd edn (London, 1948), p. 88.

61. It is interestingly similar to totemism as seen by Lévi-Strauss, though in play, not in earnest; cf. *The Savage Mind*, pp. 75-6.

62. See James Wimsatt, *The Marguerite Poetry of Guillaume de Machaut* (Chapel Hill, 1970).

63. Or perhaps we ought to imagine the scene of the dream as being the earthly meadow in which the Dreamer falls asleep, and to which the God and his company have come on a visit from paradise. The earthly setting is so paradisal that it scarcely matters.

64. See note 11, above.

65. Frank, *Chaucer and the Legend of Good Women*, p. 22.

THE PRACTICE OF THEORY

by Robert R. Edwards

Chaucer was by no means the first sophisticated or self-conscious poet to write in English, but he was the first to present himself consistently as such to his audience and readers. By dramatizing his poetic office and making that dramatization an essential part of his work, he inevitably raises questions about the aesthetic conceptions underlying his art. Although we have from Chaucer no strictly discursive statements about his poetics, the poetry speaks continually to the critical questions this self-presentation evokes. These are always embedded, however, in the contexts of narrative action and characterization.

Here the contrast with Dante is instructive: there is no formal treatise of vernacular poetics like the *De vulgari eloquentia*; no analyses of specific poems, as in the *Convivio* and *Vita Nuova*; and nothing comparable to the conceptual exposition of the *Commedia* given in Dante's "Letter to Can Grande della Scala." The closest point of comparison is the extended treatment of reading, aesthetic creation, and artistic succession in *Purgatorio* 21-26. It is not until Sidney's *Apologie for Poetrie* (1580) that a major English poet will undertake a direct commentary on the theory and practice of his craft. And yet the conscious artistry and literary allusions of Chaucer's poetry make it apparent that he thought deeply and abstractly about his art, that he adapted the conceptual models of medieval culture to examine the assumptions and possibilities of poetic creation, and that formal traditions of aesthetic speculation figure large in his conception of what poetry is and is about. Although Chaucer wrote no discursive account of literary theory, he has left an extensive practice of aesthetic reflection.

This practice is a constant feature of Chaucer's writing, and, as Joerg Fichte concludes in a recent review of modern approaches to Chaucer's poetry, "we have to use the clues implicitly contained in Chaucer's poetry" to understand his poetics (18). In some essential way for Chaucer, thinking about poetry is inseparable from writing poetry; reflection is inscribed in creation. In his early narrative poems

Chaucer's practice of theorizing takes two important forms: reference
to his own works and the use of poetic emblems. I want in this chapter
to describe Chaucer's autocitation and his reliance on emblems in the
dream visions. The extent of his intertextual and self-reflexive
references will demonstrate that the dream visions are a body of closely
linked works that both represent narrative action and offer a reflection
on the nature of poetry. Then I want to set this practice in a broader
literary context showing the relation of Chaucer's aesthetic reflections
to medieval poetic theory and theories of translation.

Chaucer's Autocitation

Chaucer's narrative poetry begins with a conscious intertextual citation.
The opening lines of the *Book of Duchess* quote the beginning of Jehan
de Froissart's *Paradys d'Amours*, and throughout his work Chaucer
refers to classical and vernacular writers. At the same time Chaucer
alludes to his own writing through verbal repetitions, shared motifs,
and common themes. His allusions and echoes suggest the unity of his
artistic vision and the coherence of the poetic assumptions behind his
works. The dream visions in particular set out a network of intertextual
references that offer a way of understanding the artistic project that the
early narratives represent and of tracing the development of Chaucer's
concerns in later works.

   In the *Book of the Duchess*, where Chaucer is clearly writing
within a courtly context, his poem naturally evokes the kind of lyric
that courtier-poets composed within a literature of polite entertainment.
Though Chaucer begins the *Duchess* by signaling his debt to Froissart,
he adds to Froissart's motif of insomnia his own remark that "agaynes
kynde / Hyt were to lyven in thys wyse" (*BD* 16-17). The same motif,
with the distinguishing reference to natural law (*kynde*), appears in the
first lines of the early experimental poem "A Complaint to His Lady,"
which is generally associated with the conventions of contemporary
French lyricism.

> The longe nightes, whan every creature
> Shulde have hir rest in somwhat as by kynde,
> Or elles ne may hir lif nat longe endure,
> Hit falleth most into my woful mynde
> How I so fer have broght myself behynde
> That, sauf the deeth, ther may nothyng me lisse,
> Se desespaired I am from alle blisse. (1-7)

Chaucer will return to this motif and phrasing in Anelida's complaint in
Anelida and Arcite (written between 1378 and 1382), yet the
resemblances between "Lady" and the *Book of the Duchess* are telling
on several points. The speakers in these two poems begin by focusing
on their inner lives; each is obsessed with the mental world of "thoght,"
which stands as a term for poetic imagination. In "Lady" the work of
imagination is consuming: "This same thoght me lasteth til the morwe /
And from the morwe forth til hit be eve" (8-9). In the *Book of the
Duchess*, the narrator is consumed by "so many an ydel thoght / Purely
for defaute of slep" (4-5) that his other powers of discrimination fail.
Anelida, by contrast, is kept awake by the image of a repentant Arcite
which she projects on her own and by the tears "this wonder sight"
(333) elicits from her.

The "Complaint of Venus," adapted in the mid-1380s from three
ballades by the French poet Oton de Grandson, elaborates on the
predicament of the narrator in the *Book of the Duchess* while
substituting a female voice for the conventional male speaker of the
lyric complaint. Venus's description of the allegorical figure Jelosie
serves to explain the effect on sensation produced by the narrator's
"sorwful ymaginacioun" (14) in the *Book of the Duchess*. Love, says
Venus, often gives "withouten ordynaunce, / As sorwe ynogh and litil
of plesaunce, / Al the revers of any glad felyng" (38-40). The
Duchess's narrator, in lines which again have no counterpart in
Froissart's *Paradys*, complains, "Al is ylyche good to me— / Joye or
sorowe, wherso hyt be— / For I have felynge in nothyng" (9-11). In
addition Venus's account of how one behaves under the influence of
Love's "nobil thing" (26) resonates with the man in black's highly
figurative account in the *Duchess* of what he experiences when "fals
Fortune hath pleyd a game / Atte ches with me" (*BD* 618-19).

> As wake abedde and fasten at the table,
> Wepinge to laughe and singe in compleynyng,
> And doun to caste visage and lokyng,
> Often to chaunge hewe and contenaunce, . . .
>   ("The Complaint of Venus" 27-30)

The same vocabulary and the same figures of antithesis express, in the
one case, the lover's infatuation and, in the other, the knight's loss of
his lady to death.

In the ballade "Womanly Noblesse," which may date from the
mid-1370s, we can find enumerated the qualities that the man in black

ascribes to White, who is the locus of ethical values in the *Book of the Duchess*. The "stidefast governaunce" (2,32) and "trewe perséveraunce" (8) that the lyric speaker celebrates echo the knight's recollection of White's "stedefast perseveraunce / And esy, atempre governaunce" (1007-08), lines that Chaucer adds to the passages he borrows from Guillaume de Machaut. It is this notion of erotic "governaunce" that also describes Venus's beneficent effects on Mars in "The Complaint of Mars": "Who regneth now in blysse but Venus, / That hath thys worthy knyght in governaunce?" (43-44).

I mention these links between the lyrics and Chaucer's first narrative poem not merely to suggest sources. The chronology of Chaucer's lyrics is, if anything, probably more vexed than the dating of the narrative poems. Nevertheless, the lyrics reflect the literary conventions of the court environment for which, as Alceste says, Chaucer "useth thynges for to make" (*LGW* F 364), and we know he wrote lyrics throughout his career. The lyrics serve in many respects as a poetic commentary on the narratives. What is especially interesting about the citations of the *Duchess* that Chaucer makes in these poems is that they point to the central aesthetic issues of his narrative. In the *Duchess*, as in "Lady," the narrator initially defines the workings of imagination through the dialectic of thought and absent sensation. But his definition, which is repeated by the man in black's description of himself as a young lover, lacks an object and a direction. It is the social and moral virtue ascribed to White that confers, as the lyrics reiterate, an ethical dimension to the imaginative powers that love and poetry share.

I shall argue later that the *Book of Duchess* is a work of poetic beginnings that consciously rewrites authors like Ovid, Froissart, and Machaut. In a number of ways the *House of Fame* and the *Parliament of Fowls*, like the lyrics, refer back to this inaugural poem. The glass temple of Venus in Book I of the *House of Fame*, which conserves the text and illustrations of Vergil's *Aeneid*, recalls the luxuriously decorated chamber in the *Book of the Duchess*, which is covered with the text and glosses of the *Roman de la rose* and the Troy Book. The narrator of the *Duchess* and Creusa in the *House of Fame* lose their way "at a turnynge of a wente" (*HF* 182; cf. *BD* 398), and the narrators of both poems awaken to their dreams. The desert which the narrator enters after leaving the temple of Venus is a counterpart to the barren, dark valley of the underworld that Juno's messenger visits in the *Book of the Duchess*. Both poems make a point of explicitly discounting the reliability of biblical and classical authorities to interpret the narrator's dreams. "Thoght," "wonder," and "fantasy" stand at the core of perception in the two poems, and constitute both the poet's material and the language for understanding his craft. They are the terms that describe the operations of imagination and memory.

The *Parliament of Fowls* continues the pattern of intertextual references, citing the *Book of Duchess* and the *House of Fame* by repeating their language and themes. The *Parliament* opens with an elegant transposition of the craft of poetry and the art of love: "The lyf so short, the craft so long to lerne" (*PF* 1). The conceit harkens back to the man in black's definition of himself: "I ches love to my firste craft" (*BD* 791). The lovesick narrator of the *Duchess* says to himself, "I have felynge in nothyng" (*BD* 11); in the *Parliament*, the power of love is overwhelming, and "my felynge," the narrator says, "Astonyeth with his wonderful wekynge" (*PF* 4-5).

In the *Book of Duchess*, "ydel thoght" had rendered the narrator "a mased thyng, / Alway in poynt to fall a-doun" (*BD* 12-13); and in the *Parliament* the effect of love is so great, he says, that "whan I on hym thynke, / Nat wot I wel wher that I flete or synke" (*PF* 6-7). The narrator hears birds singing in the *Parliament*'s love garden "with voys of aungel in here armonye," and he listens to the "ravyshyng swetnesse" of instrumental strings playing "in acord" (*PF* 191, 197-98). The general source for the description is Boccaccio's *Teseida* (7.51-53), but Chaucer's phrasing goes back to Boccaccio's own source in the *Roman de la rose*, which is also the source for the description of the chamber and garden in the *Book of the Duchess* where the "swetnesse" of the birds' song, "al of oon acord" (*BD* 305), makes the narrator think "hyt had be a thyng of heven,— / So mery a soun, so swete entewnes" (*BD* 308-9).[1]

The dreamer's painted chamber in the *Book of the Duchess* is "ful attempre . . . / For nother to cold nor hoot yt nas" (*BD* 341-42). The *Parliament*'s narrator finds the same environment in the paradisiacal garden: "Th'air of that place so attempre was / That nevere was grevaunce of hot ne cold" (*PF* 204-5). White, whom the lamenting knight in the *Book of Duchess* describes as the social objectification of "mesure" (881), "resoun" (922), and "governaunce" (1286), is an adumbration of her maker, the goddess Nature in the *Parliament*, who embodies divine order and works through "mesure" (300), "governaunce" (387), and "ryghtful ordenaunce" (390).

A comparable network of citation and allusion links the *Parliament of Fowls* to the *House of Fame*. In a sense, the *Parliament* redeems the truncated ending of the *House of Fame* by introducing its own figure of authority, Scipio Africanus. Scipio, like the docent eagle, sees the poem's narrator as a bookish drudge who is untouched by love yet still deserving of some recompense to "quyte" him (*HF* 670, *PF* 112) for his "labour" (*HF* 666, *PF* 112). Writing is a cause for the eagle's comic diminution of "Geffrey" in the *House of Fame* (614-71), and it becomes the purpose of the dream vision in the *Parliament*. Scipio tells the narrator, "And if thow haddest connyng for t'endite, / I shal the shewe mater of to wryte" (167-68).

Venus's temple reappears in the *Parliament*, changed from the historiated text of Vergil's *Aeneid* in Book I of the *House of Fame* to Boccaccio's brass temple supported by "pilers greete of jasper longe" (*PF* 230), which recall the pillars of Fame's palace. The message about the disastrous conclusions of love remains the same as in the retelling of Dido's story. Inside the temple the narrator sees "peynted overal / Ful many a story, of which I touche shal / A fewe, as of Calyxte and Athalante" (*PF* 284-86). Here, too, are present the acoustical images of sound, no longer scattered capriciously as they had been by Fame but now driven purposively by Jelosye: "of sykes hoote as fyr / I herde a swogh that gan aboute renne, / Whiche sikes were engendered with desyr" (*PF* 246-48). The barrenness that lies outside Venus's temple in *House of Fame* (482-91) lends the compelling motif of sterility to the warning carved above the gate to the love garden (*PF* 137-39). Chaucer had used the term "sond" to pun on the barrenness of the desert and the empty sounds of speech reduced to a physical property (*HF* 486); it is specifically added in the *Parliament* to Boccaccio's description of the "Pazienza palida" sitting with the allegorical figure of Peace at the entrance to the temple: "Dame Pacience syttynge there I fond, / With face pale, upon an hil of sond" (*PF* 242-43).

The narrator of the *Parliament* apostrophizes Venus in the role of Cythera as a source of poetic inspiration. "So yif me myght to ryme, and endyte!" (119), he asks. Earlier, "Geffrey" had invoked Cipris's help "to endite and ryme" (520) at the beginning of Book II of the *House of Fame*. The celestial journey that the narrators of both poems undertake in imitation of "Daun Scipio" shows them "helle and erthe and paradys" (*HF* 918, *PF* 32-33: "hevene and helle / And erthe"). It also joins them in the common error of supposing that Cicero's mention of the "infernal regions" (1.11.5) refers to the divisions of a Christian cosmology. J.A.W. Bennett observes that the two poems vary considerable in tone: "Whereas the lesson of the *Somnium*, as Chaucer construes it in the *Parelement*, is that we should not in the world delight, the *House of Fame* is flooded with ecstatic pleasure in the visible universe" ("[Some] Second Thoughts [on The *Parlement of Foules*]" [in E. Vasta and Z.P. Thundy eds., *Chaucerian Problems and Perspectives*, Notre dame, Ind.: Notre Dame University Press, 1979]

136). Whatever the differences in outlook, the poems share the same quandary about dreams. The Proem to the *House of Fame* shows the irrelevance of Macrobius's categories for deciding the causes of dreams, and the narrator of the *Parliament* admits at length that the reasons for his dreaming are still indeterminate: "Can I not seyn if that the cause were / For I hadde red of Affrican byforn" (*PF* 106-7).

It might be argued that the close verbal echoes merely reflect Chaucer's rich and allusive language, his characteristic diction and style of speech. Alternatively, his reliance on imaginative devices such as the dream vision or the love garden might entail certain lexical choices that are bound to recur in successive poems, much as the choice of certain rhetorical commonplaces determined the linguistic register of many medieval lyrics. Cogent arguments have been made, too, for seeing similarities in poetic structure, and these may have an influence on language. A.C. Spearing (89) notes that the *Parliament* and the *Book of the Duchess* each have a preliminary section describing a dreamplace and then come to the real subject of the poem. He sees a larger resemblance between the *Parliament* and the *House of Fame* in their presenting a long introductory section with the narrator awake. All three poems are constructed so that each successive structural unit is longer than the one that precedes it.

If we study the patterns of citation and allusion, it becomes clear, however, that the poems are linked not simply by a common set of lexical choices dictated either by authorial style or literary conventions, nor again are they joined principally by resemblances in structure. Rather, the intertextual patterns reveal a sustained engagement with several key issues: the nature of love and art, the poet's relation to his work, the problematic grounds for his knowing the interpreting experience. These are Chaucer's principal poetic concerns, and they inform his narrative poems as poetic themes and sources of aesthetic theorizing.

Poetic Emblems

Poetic emblems are narrative elements of the text—often visual or iconic images—that function as parts of the story but present at the same time a self-reflexive statement about poetic art. Robert W. Hanning ("Poetic Emblems [in Medieval Narrative Texts]"[in *Vernacular Poetics*, ed. Lois Ebin, 1-32. Kalamazoo, Mich.: Medieval Institute Publications, 1984]) has shown that emblems are important devices in medieval vernacular literature, where in the absence of a formalized poetics they provide a means for poets to comment on their art. I have discussed in the Introduction how Chaucer situates one such emblem at the very outset of his storytelling. That is the figure of the dreamer's chamber in which the narrative action of the *Book of the Duchess* begins; it is this figure which he evokes and then modifies with the icon of the desert of "sond" in the *House of Fame*. Later in the *House of Fame* Chaucer presents another emblem of poetic art. He places Fame's palace on a rock of ice. Names are chiseled in the ice, but some of them, warmed by the sun, have melted into illegibility. Here the image makes a dual statement. It expresses at one level the transience of fame; at another, it shows the impermanence of writing and by extension the fragility of art works as a source of knowledge and memory. The narrator observes in a remark that applies equally to the story and his own efforts to tell the story, "This were a feble fundament / To bilden on a place hye" (1132-33).

Poetic emblems operate as parts of the text, parts of its imaginative economy, and our understanding of them depends, as elsewhere, on interpretive reading. What they have to say abstractly about poetics grows out of concrete literary symbolism and poetic language. Architectural structures in particular lend themselves to symbolically representing the artifice of poetry. The insomniac narrator of the *Book of Duchess* playfully promises the gods, Morpheus above all, everything appropriate to a chamber: "and al hys halles / I wol do peynte with pure gold" (258-59) and cover with matching tapestries. Immediately thereafter he awakens in the room which embodies the *Roman de la rose* and the Troy Book. In "The Complaint of Mars" the emblem reappears as the site of erotic consummation and the place where Phoebus violently intrudes to part Venus and Mars: "The chambre ther as ley this fresshe quene [Venus] / Depeynted was with white boles grete" (85-86). The image of Taurus, which depicts Jupiter's ravishing Europa, conveys the mingling of desire and violence that animates the poem. The *House of Fame* is organized around a succession of emblems—the glass temple, the chiseled rock, Fame's palace—which culminates in the labyrinthine House of Rumor. In the *Parliament*, the temple of Venus, imported from the *Teseida*, is an emblem that demonstrates the profound ambivalence of passionate love, and thus it stands as a representation of the conflicts that underlie Chaucer's office as a love poet.

One of the most versatile emblems of poetic art is the figure of Morpheus. In retelling the story of Ceyx and Alcyone, Chaucer uses him to thematize the problem of representation, and Morpheus serves as the transition to the poet's own dream. In the *House of Fame*, the first of the poem's three invocations addresses the god of sleep through a highly nuanced reference of Morpheus that again calls forth the powers of poetic representation: "Prey I that he wol me spede / My sweven for the telle aryght, / Yf every drem stonde in his myght" (78-80). Later in the poem the eagle reveals that words have the power to take the shape of their speakers (1068-83). Though it has parallels in Boethius, Dante, and Vincent of Beauvais, the eagle's revelation describes the same kind of scene as the one in which Morpheus appears before Alcyone in imitation of Ceyx.

Finally, the dream itself is the most powerful emblem for poetic creation. In classical antiquity it served Plato and Cicero as a structure for symbolic action and philosophical speculation. The Bible, too, offers a network of dreams and visions and draws attention to the problem of interpreting symbolic content. For the Middle Ages the most important authority—and the one whom Chaucer cites even before he reads him—is the fourth-century Latin writer Macrobius, whose Neoplatonic commentary on the dream of Scipio Africanus, which appeared at the end of Cicero's *De re publica*, set out the essential protocols for distinguishing categories of dreams.

Macrobius, drawing on the Greek writer Artemidorus, classifies five main types of dreams—enigmatic, prophetic, oracular, nightmare, and apparition—but the fundamental difference is between prophetic dreams (the first three) and those without significance (the last two). There are abiding contradictions in Macrobius's taxonomy, however, and medieval commentators on his commentary were sensitive to the difficulties of distinguishing types of dreams. The enigmatic dream, for instance, is "one that conceals with strange shapes and veils with ambiguity the true meaning of the information being offered, and requires an interpretation for its understanding" ([William H.] Stahl [trans., *Commentary on the Dream of Scipio*. New York: Columbia University Press, 1952] 90). The definition succeeds, of course, in reproducing the difference that Macrobius intends to explain, and the subdivisions that he appends to it continue in a steady logical regression.

Despite these contradictions, Macrobius's categories remained highly influential. We shall see later that Guillaume de Lorris's adaptation of Macrobius at the beginning of the *Roman de la rose* is something like an originary text for Chaucer. In the high and late Middle Ages, attention focuses on the categories of dream that Macrobius dismisses as "not worth interpreting." Medieval Latin poets, the Neoplatonic theorists of the school of Chartres, Guillaume, Jean de Meun, and Chaucer employ these sorts of dreams as a way of talking about the status of poetry, the truth value of artistic representation, and the place of subjective experience as a form of knowledge. The cognitive model of the dream vision becomes a model of aesthetic perception.

Medieval Poets

The evolution of Chaucer's poetics can be traced through the evidence of the poems, but it is embedded at the same time in a complex literary-historical context. A native tradition of narrative poetry preceded Chaucer and found an audience in the aristocracy and merchants outside court circles. Elements of that tradition remain visible in Chaucer's writing, as for example in the metrics and some of the diction of the early narrative poems and the battle descriptions of the Knight's Tale (I.2601-16) and the *Legend of Good Women* (629-53); they are visible, too, in parodies like Sir Thopas and the Parson's protest, "I kan nat geeste 'rum, ram, ruf,' by lettre" (X. 43). But the tradition itself was largely isolated from the main stream of medieval poetic theory and especially from the much-debated question of vernacular literature. The latter was an important element in theorizing about poetry and fiction form the twelfth century onwards.

The question, briefly stated, was whether the European vernaculars were adequate vehicles for serious poetry. Of course, the issue was decided almost as soon as the question could be formulated. Chrétien de Troyes and Marie de France established the cultural prestige of chivalric literature; earlier the *romans d'antiquité* had created a vernacular equivalent to classical epic. Dante's focus on lyric poetry in the *De vulgari eloquentia* extolls the achievement of writers in the "illustrious vernacular," and the *Roman de la rose* and the *Commedia* are beyond doubt the central literary texts of the high Middle Ages.

The debate continued throughout the fourteenth century, however, and some of its most notable disputants—Petrarch, for one—judged wrongly, believing that Latin would endure as the principal vehicle of literary composition. That Chaucer's early poems earned him a place within the continental vernacular tradition is clear from Eustache Deschamps's ballade in 1386 praising Chaucer as the "grant translateur." And Chaucer's engagement with Latin, French, and Italian writers throughout his career offers strong evidence of his commitment to defining a body of poetic work within the vernacular tradition. Elizabeth Salter observes: "It is as if the situation of the English poet had to be seen to be broadly comparable with that of the greatest

European vernacular writers: a relationship between a chosen language and the Latin of tradition—which was enhancing rather than exact in its implications" ([*Fourteenth-Century English Poetry*. Oxford: Clarendon Press, 1983] 126).

The aesthetic reflections that emerge from within Chaucer's practice take shape, then, in the foreground of his own writing and the middle distance of European literary tradition. The substructure of these reflections is to be found in the *artes poeticae*, which were compiled by Latin theorists in the twelfth and thirteenth centuries from the teachings of ancient grammar and rhetoric. The poetics they formulated offered medieval writers the procedures to invent, order, and adorn a literary work in fitting style. The doctrine was centered on the three internal parts of classical rhetoric, relegating the two external parts (memorization and delivery) to second position.

Chaucer's allusions to the thirteenth-century rhetorician Geoffrey of Vinsauf in *Troilus and Criseyde* (1.1065-71) and the Nun's Priest's Tale (VII.3347-52) are evidence of his familiarity with the standard doctrines of composition. The ironies and dislocations of his allusions demonstrate, however, that Chaucer views established poetic doctrine as an unstable body of precepts open to change and new formations. His reference in the *Troilus* associates poetic invention with the project of seduction, and "Gaufred, deer maister soverayn" (VII.3347) is apostrophized in the Nun's Priest's Tale to witness his own exaggerated lament on King Richard's death and the poet's satiric employment of the devices of amplification that Geoffrey taught. Chaucer's acknowledgment of poetic theory thus points to a creative tension and revision rather than a simple assimilation of its doctrine.

The poetics to which Chaucer alludes in these passages is, as James J. Murphy (*Rhetoric [in the Middle Ages*. Berkeley: University of California Press, 1974]) remarks, highly prescriptive, and it generally reflected the aesthetic values of Latin high culture in the universities. The texts that transmitted the doctrines of composition answered the needs of specific audiences and the demands of pedagogical systems. No theorist before Dante wrote of poetics in general. Tough they claim to be a general theory of discourse, the precepts embody a particular compositional slant, and they are constrained by the social contexts of the works.[2] Generalizing from the *artes*, Edmond Faral held that medieval poetics was largely given over to concerns with stylistic ornamentation. Though Faral's view has subsequently been modified by later scholars who object that he accorded a privileged place to style within a broader domain of aesthetic issues, the teachings of medieval poetics remained overwhelmingly technical rather than speculative.[3] Dorothy Everett ("[Chaucer's]Love Visions [,with Particular Reference to the *Parlement of Foules*]" [in *Essays on Middle English Literature*, ed. Patricia Kean, 97-114. London: Oxford University Press, 1959]) among others, has placed great emphasis on Chaucer's rhetorical dexterity and especially his use of technical devices such as *digressio, sententia, repetitio,* and *contentio* (antithesis).

Although it fails to render a full account of artistic creation, medieval poetic theory nonetheless offered a vocabulary for defining the process of creation. Beyond showing which figures to use in composition, the doctrine described the means for setting out the imaginary architecture of a work. In particular, discussions of rhetorical invention offered techniques for discovering and selecting the conceptual order of the poet's materials, and it is within the domain of invention that poetic theory attains its fullest conceptual expression in the Middle Ages.

The procedure of invention depend on what Matthew of Vendôme in his *Ars versificatoria* (c. 1175) terms the "inner meaning" (*interior sententia*) and "the conceptual realization of the meaning" (*sententiae conceptio*) of a work. The most celebrated figure for this process is the architectural metaphor that Geoffrey of Vinsauf introduces at the beginning of the *Poetria nova* (43-48), which compares the poet to the builder of a house who first plans the work in his imagination and then executes it.

> Si quis habet fundare domum, non currit ad actum
> Impetuosa manus: intrinseca linea cordis
> Praemetitur opus, seriemque sub ordine certo
> Interior praescribit homo, totamque figurat
> Ante manus cordis quam corporis; et status ejus
> Est prius archetypus quam sensilis.

> If a man has a house to build, his impetuous hand does not rush into action. The measuring line of his mind first lays out the work, and he mentally outlines the successive steps in a definite order. The mind's hand shapes the entire house beforethe body's hand builds it. Its mode of being is archetypal beforeit is actual.[4]

Peter Dronke finds in this passage an "insistence on the organic nature of a work of art" ("[Mediaeval] Rhetoric" [in *Literature and Western Civilization, Vol. 2,* ed. D. Daiches and A. Thorlby, 315-45. London: Aldine, 1973] 327). A fourteenth-century commentary on the *Poetria nova* explains that this description of invention is what is meant by *poesis*, "the art of the poets" ([Marjorie] Woods [ed., *An Early Commentary on the Poetria Nova of Geoffrey of Vinsauf.* New York: Garland, 1985] 16).

In addition to these general precepts, medieval literary theory envisioned two practical approaches to invention. Poets could find their sources, it was said, in materials that had already been versified (*materia exsecuta* or *pertractata*), or they could find new subject matter (*materia illibata* or *remota*). In setting out this distinction the theorists followed and amplified Horace's admonition, "Aut famam sequere aut sibi convenientia finge" (Either follow tradition or invent what is self-consistent, *Ars poetica* 119). Either choice involved the practice of topical invention, by which the poet would devise his work according to the commonplaces (topoi) that were connected with the materials. It was thus that the primary act of conceiving a work took place not only within the imagination but also within a closed discourse. The world of the poem is set out within the limits of the topoi, and these—as in the highly differentiated symbols for persons, places, and implements imaged by devices like the wheel of Vergil ([Edmond] Faral [*Les arts poétiques du XIIᵉ et du XIIIᵉ siècle.* Paris: Champion, 1924] 86-89)—are associated with genre (epic, comedy, and pastoral).

When poets choose to use previous sources, as Chaucer does in most of his writing, the strictures are explicit. "Ne sequamur vestigia verborum," Geoffrey of Vinsauf exhorts in his *Documentum*, a school manual devoted to elaborating verse from existing materials: "let us not trace the footsteps of the words" (Faral 309). He goes on to counsel that writers, looking over the imaginative world of their source (*universitatem materiae speculantes*) want to speak where the earlier authors are silent and rearrange the order of the work: "ibi dicamus aliquid ubi dixerunt nihil, et ubi dixerunt aliquid, nos nihil; quod etiam prius, nos posterius, et e converso" (let us say something where they have said nothing, and where they have said something, let us say nothing; what they put first, let us put last, and vice versa, Faral 309-10). A process of creative elaboration and restructuring is thus already contained in the techniques of medieval poetic composition. In the Monk's Tale the retelling of Ugolino's tragic story, for example, suppresses the dream and cannibalism that Dante records in *Inferno 33* and emphasizes the pathos of the situation. When we turn in subsequent chapters to a detailed examination of the dream visions, we will see that Chaucer plots the action of his narrative and signals his meaning by exploiting the possibilities of what remains implicit in his sources.

Later vernacular writers recognized that, in addition to an abstract
plan of composition against which the fitness of topoi and figures of
speech could be measured, the process of invention involved chance,
the discovery of what is already virtual and immanent in perception
though not yet articulated, the indeterminant and perhaps always
elusive constituent of artistic creation. Much as Aristotle had to admit
chance as a supplement to his theory of causality, a fourteenth-century
poet schooled in the posthistory of the *artes* confronted chance within
the compositional archetypes that were held to precede and enable his
execution of a work. When he retells the tale of Ceyx and Alcyone
early in the *Book of the Duchess*, for example, Chaucer finds in
Alcyone's dilemma a complex analogy to his own situation and the
distress of the man in black. His omission of the ending of Ovid's story
shifts the accent to the emotions of pity and dread. The account of the
Aeneid in the *House of Fame* dwells on Dido rather than on Vergil's
epic themes. Similarly, Cicero's "Dream of Scipio" is given new
emphasis in the summary presented in the *Parliament of Fowls*. In
Anelida and Arcite Chaucer begins with an imitation of Boccaccio's
epic style but finds that his subject is not military prowess but the "slye
wey" (48) of Arcite, which he began writing about even before he
realized it.

For Chaucer, as Donald Howard ("[Chaucer's] Idea [of an Idea]"
[in E. T. Donaldson, ed. *Essays and Studies 1976*, 39-55, n.s. 29.
London: John Murray, 1976] 42-43) points out, "The act of planning in
his original becomes something much closer to a lucky accident,
'winning'—as we would say, 'getting' or 'catching'—something. And
the thing caught is not the *archetypus* of his original but a
'purpose'—as we would say, an 'intention.'" The text that emerges has
a double bond to this process: it is both an artifact of intention and a
trace of the informing intelligence that "wins" its purpose. But Chaucer
goes a step further, especially in the dream visions. By dramatizing his
narrator he places a figure of this intelligence within the text. The
poems stand as both the creations of a writer's imaginative process and
the site of the "accidents" that attend his writing. They, more than any
set of abstract principles, are the evidence of his theories and attitudes.

I have mentioned that Chaucer tends to work from *materia
exsecuta*, materials that other poets have already used and that he gives
a new configuration. Medieval poetic theory makes it clear that this
kind of transformation depends on an understanding of the antecedent
text. It follows, then, that Chaucer's poetic invention occurs in relation
to entire texts and not as an isolated reworking of parts. Writers make
their choices informed by the full scope of the original; they survey its

conceptual order and set out a new disposition of its parts. The essential dialectic, as Geoffrey of Vinsauf explains it, is between speech and silence. Such a dialectic is possible, though, only to the extent that writers engage the source as a complete text. There remains, of course, a difference between the prescriptions of the *artes*, which are directed to exercises in composition, and the practice of an accomplished poet like Chaucer. But the habit of engaging the antecedent text rather than extracts is a consciously articulated principle of medieval poetics, and it is consistent with the practice of compositional modeling that Chaucer acknowledges in his poetry.

The protocols of invention described in the *artes* necessarily influenced Chaucer's view of poetic creation, and they ought to influence as well our historical understanding of the process underlying his poetry. The exhaustive source studies carried on since the nineteenth century have shown the wide range of Chaucer's reading and the diverse patterns in which he adapts other texts by allusion, citation, and reworking. Although few critics now debate whether Chaucer is imitative or innovative in these adaptations, the general assumption remains that the borrowings are limited and local, that Chaucer takes parts of other works which are distinctive and attractive and therefore offer him heightened possibilities of expression within his own poems.

For the dream visions the question of textual influence is deeply implicated in the practice and theory of poetic composition. B.A. Windeatt holds that Chaucer selectively and combinatively borrows parts of his sources, incorporating passages rather than whole texts or even the whole idea of a text ([ed. and trans., *Chaucer's*] *Dream Poetry* [Totowa, N.J.: D.S. Brewer/ Rowman and Littlefield, 1982] ix). Windeatt sees the effects of such borrowing in Chaucer's coordinating new structures, and in this view he accepts Wolfgang Clemen's description of Chaucer's relation to literary tradition. Clemen writes of Chaucer, "He sets free much of what he borrows from the past by turning it to new uses. He disregards what had previously been the function of certain themes, and gives them a new connotation which often produces an ironic contrast between their former overtones and what they now imply and signify. With light-hearted dexterity he simply reverses the plus and minus signs in front of these traditionally conditioned themes, and fits them into a context which is the very opposite of their previous one" ([*Chaucer's Early Poetry*, trans. C. Sym. London: Methuen, 1963] 3-4).

On this view, isolated borrowings and a pattern of aesthetic innovation can be accounted for simultaneously. However, Chaucer's adaptations cannot be both isolated borrowings and elements of a textual restructuring that takes its meaning at least in part from its divergence from the sources. The arguments are flatly at cross-purposes with each other. Windeatt's belief that meaning arises from deploying the sources in new settings, like Clemen's assertion that a "new connotation" arises from contrast with the original texts, indicates instead Chaucer's deep and thoroughgoing engagement with his sources. Like all great poets Chaucer makes informed and resonant use of other writers. Behind the selective borrowings and his reversals of themes implicitly stands a practice of critical reading, one that involves both antecedent texts and literary tradition.

We shall see in later discussion that the dream visions use earlier works not only as sources but also as symbols of meaning, which Chaucer contrasts and modifies in the course of his own narrative. Perhaps the most complex example of his critical reading occurs later in his career, in *Troilus and Criseyde*. Winthrop Wetherbee ([*Chaucer and the*] *Poets* [Ithaca, N.Y.: Cornell University Press, 1985]) contends that in *Troilus* Chaucer comes to the material of his courtly and pagan love story through the cultural reading of antiquity that was furnished by Dante and Dante's Statius. As Wetherbee explains, the radical extension of a tragic love story set in the pagan past requires the historical framework of an authoritative Christian poet before Chaucer in turn can transcend the attractions of the materials and see them or himself in their full dimensions. Like the works Chaucer reads for his earlier narrative poems, Baccaccio's *Filostrato* serves two facets of invention in *Troilus*—as a material source for Chaucer's poem and coevally as a text interpreted in the light of literary hermeneutics.

In its large dimensions the gesture of appropriating sources, as the theorists recommended, is not directed merely toward a collection of separate antecedent texts, each of them engaged independently as a source of composition, but rather toward literary tradition as a whole. Chaucer's adaptation of his predecessors revives their work at the same time that it places his own writing within the context of serious writing. Much like Dante, whose installation in the *bella scuola* is recalled comically in the envoi to the book in *Troilus and Criseyde* ("kis the steppes where as thow seest pace / Virgile, Ovide, Omer, Lucan, and Stace," 5.1791-92), Chaucer wants to join the community of poets by placing his work among theirs—and theirs within his. He does so while claiming a status for his own vernacular writing that associates it with the other developed vernacular traditions. His ambitions, measured against the achievements of Dante and Petrarch, require both a distinguished body of work and a theory of poetry to define its nature.

"Grant Translateur"

The techniques of poetic invention that Chaucer follows in his early narrative are closely connected to the practice of translation. Although some critics argue for making a distinction between literary adaptation and translation, both activities exist on a spectrum defined by invention. Translation, like topical invention, uses strategies of embellishment, preservation, and intertextuality ([Gerald] Bruns ["The Originality of Texts in a Manuscript Culture," *Comparative Literature* 32 (1980):113- 29]). [Barry A.]Windeatt in his study of *Troilus* finds that Chaucer uses at least three separate techniques of translation: rendering yet re-expressing the original, small additions of phrases and lines, and larger interpolated passages ([ed.,]*Troilus [and Criseyde.* New York: Longman, 1984] 4). The effect is a transvaluation of Boccaccio's *Filostrato* that both conveys the sense of the original and registers the poet's distinctive response to the poem. Chaucer's earlier narratives employ the same techniques to a greater or lesser degree, and they operate within the rhetorical conventions that evolved from antiquity and the rise of Christian culture.

The governing strategy of medieval translation is given in Saint Jerome's dictum (*Epistula* 72.5.2) "non uerbum e uerbo, sed sensum exprimere e sensu" (interpret not word by word but sense by sense, 1:508). Jerome draws on Horace ("nec verbo verbum curabis reddere fidus / interpres," *Ars poetica* 133-34) and on the practice that Cicero describes in his approach to rendering Greek texts into Latin. Cicero intends to keep the same ideas and forms (or figures of thought) as in the originals, while observing the usage of his own language. "I did not hold it necessary to render word for word," he says, "but I preserved the general style and force of the language" (*De optimo genere oratorum* 5.14). Jerome's admonition is perhaps more a commonplace than a practical guide, and he makes an important exception by insisting on the need for literal translation in the case of Scripture.[5] For vernacular writers in the Middle Ages a crucial development is the assimilation of the rhetorical functions of invention and interpretation within translation. Rita Copeland has proposed that, in addition to training the writer in the resources of his own language (the pedagogical aim of Roman literary education in Cicero and Quintilian), translation serves as a means for discovering materials and establishing their meaning through a literary hermeneutics.

In Chaucer's translations modern scholars have seen the practical application of these principles. The A-fragment of the *Romaunt of the*

Rose and *Boece* remain close to the original texts from which Chaucer worked, and Chaucer's literary achievement can be measured by his success in appropriating the models. Caroline Eckhardt says, "The *Roman* has thus been transformed into an English near-equivalent that still carries with it the prestige, sophistication, and courtliness associated with its original, along with much (if we can hear it) of the actual sound of the original words" (["The Art of Translation in *The Romaunt of the Rose*," *Studies in the Age of Chaucer* 6 (1984): 41-63] 50). Tim William Machan believes that "writing *Boece* was in part a way for Chaucer to examine language as language" ([*Techniques of Translation*. Norman, Ok.: Pilgrim Books, 1985] 127) and not just an exercise in refining his compositional skills. The translation of the "lyf of Seynt Cecile" in the Second Nun's Tale offers a clear case in which translation and invention have reciprocal functions. The tale combines two sources, the *Legenda Aurea* of Jacobus de Voragine and a Latin life of the saint, and switches from one to the other approximately midway in the story. The effect of manipulating the sources, Sharon [Sherry L.] Reames ["The Cecilia Legend as Chaucer Inherited It and Retold It; The Disappearance of an Augustinian Ideal," *Speculum* 55 (1980): 38-57] observes, is to offer a more pessimistic vision of divine power and man's free will than was portrayed in earlier versions. The strategy of translation, like that of rhetorical invention, depends on an interpretive reading of the sources.

Moreover, for Chaucer translation serves the aim of cultural appropriation and definition that it had earlier achieved for Roman writers. Salter regards translation as a decisive gesture in the poetic project that Chaucer's poetry represents: "Chaucer's very deliberate act of beginning his poetic career by training his skill as a translator of French shows a freshly awakened preoccupation with English as a fit vehicle for the major works of European literature. It is impossible that Chaucer should not have been familiar with the theory, and the practice, of the fourteenth-century Italians, such as Dante and Petrarch, on this question of the use of the vernacular" (*op. cit.*, 123).

The key text in this regard is undoubtedly the *Romaunt*. Chaucer's translation of the *Rose* is the cause of Deschamps's extravagant praise of Chaucer as the "grant translateur." For Deschamps translation means both the rendering of the text and the cultural transference implied by the text. It is *translatio* in the sense that Chrétien de Troyes (*Cligés* 24-42) portrays the passing of chivalry from Greece to Rome and then to France, the difference lies in the subject matter—love rather than war. Deschamps's praise is not for Chaucer's fidelity to the original or his refinements of his own diction and style. Deschamps sees Chaucer as the figure who has transplanted the *Rose* to English soil and made it flourish there. The major metaphor is insemination.

> Aigles treshaulz, qui par ta theorique
> Enlumines le regne d'Eneas,
> L'Isle aux Geans, ceuls de Bruth, et qu'i as
> Semé les fleurs et planté le rosier
> Aux ignorans do la langue pandras,
> Grant translateur, noble Geffroy Chaucier.

> Lofty eagle, who by they science
> Dost illumine the kingdom of Aeneas,
> The isle of giants (those of Brutus), and who there hast
> Sown the flowers and planted the rose-tree;
> Thou wilt enlighten those ignorant (of French),
> O great translator, noble Geoffrey Chaucer.[6]

In succeeding stanzas Deschamps expands the metaphor so that Chaucer's translation becomes itself another version of the garden and then an authentic source to other writers. He says, with encomiastic exaggeration, "Et un vergier, où du plant demandas / De ceuls qui font pour eulx auctorisier, / A ja long temps que tu edifias" (And a garden, for which thou hast asked plants / From those who poetize to win them fame, / Now for a long time thou hast been constructiong, 17-19). It is from this distant source rather than the original that Deschamps, the literary successor of Machaut and others inspired by the *Rose*, ostensibly takes his inspiration: "Requier avoir un buvraige autentique, / Dont la doys est du tout en ta baillie" (I ask to have an authentic draught, / For the spring is entirely in thy keeping, 22-23).

In a sense Deschamps's compliment to Chaucer's skill as an appropriator of literary tradition veils a claim to reassert the power of the original and the national tradition that created it in the first place. Chaucer may have carried off the rosebush and recreated the garden in Brutus's Albion, but lineage and priority, hence the literary authority of the original, are not seriously in doubt. For Chaucer the *Rose* is as close as anything to an originary text. By that I mean it is the mythological ground where he first discovers the condition of authorship already determined and the materials of invention ready for deployment. In a later chapter we will see how the *Book of the Duchess* functions as a work of conscious poetic beginnings for Chaucer's narrative art, a declaration of self-inauguration that breaks from its sources even while using them. By contrast, the *Rose* remains a source that cannot be

abandoned by the poet's self-conscious historical breaks. It is the text
he shares with Machaut and Froissart, even as he vies with them to
establish the place of his own work. More important, he finds in the
Rose—and shows in his translation of it—the aesthetic issues that
inform his own early narrative poetry.

The essential issue for Chaucer concerns the truth value of poetry,
the capacity of a fictional work to represent reality. This issue is the
opening topic of the *Rose*, and Guillame de Lorris remarks at some
length on the reliability of dreams. Dreams are a figure for all poetic
fictions, and the case Guillaume makes for them establishes by analogy
the rationale for poetic representation. Guillaume finds his "garant"
("warraunt" in the *Romaunt*) in Macrobius but gives a notably
incomplete account of Macrobius's doctrine, saying that he "halt nat
dremes false ne lees" (*Romaunt* 8) when he sharply distinguished
prophetic from unprophetic dreams. In fact Macrobius's discussion of
the categories of dreams begins, "The last two, the nightmare and the
apparition, are not worth interpreting since they have no prophetic
significance" (Stahl 88).

In some measure Guillaume's misreading is a response to the
problem of Macrobius's categories. Macrobius, as we have seen,
differentiates dreams according to their truth value by separating those
which prove prophetic form those that do not. The difficulty is that
their truth can be established only afterwards, and so the categories and
subdivisions he expounds are circular. This is the problem that Chaucer
brilliantly anatomizes in the Proem to the *House of Fame* and makes
the source of irony in the Nun's Priest's Tale. Guillaume rewrites the
circularity of Macrobius's taxonomy into a flawed argument. He
concedes that many people dismiss dreams as mere fables and lies but
contends that some dreams can be dreamed which are not lies because
they afterwards appear to be true.

> Aucunes genz dient qu'en songes
> n'a se fables non et mençonges;
> mes l'en puet tex songes songier
> qui ne sont mie mençongier,
> ainz sont aprés bien aparant. . . .

> Many men sayn that in sweveninges
> Ther nys but fables and lesynges;
> But men may some sweven[es] sen
> Which hardely that false ne ben,
> But afterward ben apparaunt. (*Romaunt* 1-5)

Guillaume therefore asserts, against those who doubt dreams, that he is confident of the significance of dreams as signs of the good and evil that will befall men: "quar endroit moi ai ge fiance / que songes est senefiance / des biens as genz e des anuiz" (15-17). Thus he concludes that most people dream many things symbolically (*covertement*) which they later see openly (*apertement*): "que li plusor songent de nuiz / maintes choses convertement / que l'en voit puis apertement" (18-20).

Guillaume's argument is invalid, and the final conclusion he reaches is false. For an argument to be valid the truth of the premises must force the truth of the conclusion. What Guillaume does is to construct two related subarguments of which the first employs valid reasoning but the second does not; he thus gives the appearance of deductive rigor without being able to sustain it. The first subargument properly employs what medieval logicians called contradictories: the premise "some dreams are not false" forces the conclusion that is not the case that all dreams are false. In the second subargument he tries, however, to relate opposing propositions that have no necessary logical relation to each other. The premise "some dreams are not false," does not force the truth of the conclusion "all dreams are not false," which is to say, "no dream is false." Quite apart from its logical structure, Guillaume's argument fails as a piece of informal reasoning. As in Macrobius the truth of the conclusion falters because there is no reliable way to distinguish false from prophetic dreaming.

Chaucer's translation makes it clear that he recognized precisely where Guillaume's argument turns form valid to invalid reasoning. Guillaume attempts to move from the acceptably true statement that not all dreams can be reckoned false to the general claim that (all) dreams are predictive of what will happen: "songes est senefiance / des biens as genz e des anuiz" (16-17). Chaucer translates the passage, however, so as to suggest that he sees the impossibility of making universal assertions from particular and merely probable statements. Following the line of Guillaume's argument and anticipating its next step, which is to conclude that most people have some significant dreams, Chaucer corrects the reasoning to emphasize the experience of many people ("many wightes") but not all people ("as genz").[7]

> For this trowe I, and say for me,
> That dremes signifiaunce be
> Of good and harm to *many* wightes
> That dremen in her slep a-nyghtes

Ful many thynges covertly
That fallen after al openly.
(15-20; emphasis added)

Chaucer's translation is faithful to the diction and style of the *Rose*, but we can see that it also involves a critical reading of the text, which recognizes its inconsistencies. Translation serves a hermeneutic function and at the same time serves the purpose of poetic invention. Chaucer discovers in the logical weakness of Guillaume's argument an imaginative space for situating poetic fiction. Guillaume's confusion of the particular and the universal, the many and the all, defines the territory of the counterfactual and hypothetical. Chaucer in effect rejects the global theorizing Guillaume wants to impose on psychological and aesthetic processes. His translation of Guillaume's defense of visionary experience emphasizes what is not universal about dreaming, what remains idiosyncratic, though still accessible to understanding.

In this respect the *Romaunt* lays the aesthetic groundwork of the early narrative poetry. All the dream visions will reject the kind of determinate meaning that Guillaume wants to claim as a justification for his poem. Instead, they locate their materials and their poetic discourse in "wonder thinges" that fall outside systematic meaning. This choice entails other kinds of aesthetic problems, for the decisive tension in the early narrative poetry is between the particular and the general, but it is a choice that Chaucer makes clearly and consistently.

Chaucer's translation of the *Rose* discovers a second aesthetic issue in the theme of desire and in the relation of desire to poetry. The first narrative told within the framework of the narrator's dream is the story of Narcissus. Guillaume's handling of the story links the erotic and the aesthetic. His dreamer in fact reenacts the story he has recited, for he lets himself down beside the well to gaze at the water and the shimmering gravel. In the dreamer's story Narcissus is drawn to the well by thirst after a day of hunting; these two facets of appetite are ironically combined to represent self-infatuation as a search for an inner desire that cannot be satisfied. For the dreamer, who thinks to escape "scatheles, full sykerly" (*Romaunt* 1550), desire has to do specifically with representation. The "merveilous cristall" (1579) is a "mirrour perilous" (1601) that depicts the garden in full and accurate detail.

For ther is noon so litil thyng
So hid, ne closid with shittyng,

> That is ne is sene, as though it were
> Peyntid in the cristall there. (1597-1600)

The crystal is an emblem of the poem and of the art that conceives the poem, and it has the same power of representation that Guillaume ascribes to dreams. Just as dreams represent "ful many thynges covertly / That fallen after al openly" (19-20), the crystal creates images with unambiguous meaning.

> Ryght as a myrrour openly
> Shewith all thing that stondith therby,
> As well the colour as the figure,
> Withouten ony coverture, . . . (1585-88)

Chaucer signals that he recognizes Guillaume's references when he embellishes the couplet "et as cristaus, qui me mostroient / mil choses qui entor estoient" (1603-4) by translating it with the additional allusion to seeing openly: "the cristall in the welle / That shewide me full openly / A thousand thinges faste by" (1636-38).

The *Rose* elaborates the parallels between desire and representation in order to suggest that the erotic is constituted through the aesthetic. In the mirror provided by the well and the crystals, the dreamer sees a rosebush surrounded by a hedge, and he is seized by the "lust and envie" to look more closely and to pull a bud from it. The "rage" that overtakes him is not caused, however, by the object of desire but by the act of figuration; he sees the rosebush depicted in the mirror, and it is then that desire appears. In addition, the object of desire is itself remarkably indeterminate. Though he praises the particular rosebud above the others, the essential gesture is arbitrary: "Among the knoppes I ches oon / So fair that of the remenaunt noon / Ne preise I half so well as it" (1691-93). The rosebud cannot be differentiated by its intrinsic qualities, only by the dreamer's response to it; its value is a function of the dreamer's projection.

The scene thus contains a number of themes that will emerge in Chaucer's own writings—the arbitrary and solipsistic nature of desire, the role of artistic representation in constructing erotic attachments. The story of Narcissus, perhaps like the tale of Ceyx and Alcyone, stands as an example of Chaucer's first narrative. Its importance as a work of translation lies both in the technical skill it allowed Chaucer to develop and in the materials it helped him invent.

Chaucer's speculations about his art are written into his poems. His early narratives are self-conscious literary texts that are also conscious of one another as works that explore the nature of poetry. Within the poems Chaucer's practice of theory turns around autocitation and poetic emblems. But these devices are not isolated gestures of artistic definition. Rather, they draw on the resources of poetic invention and translation to locate the matter and manner of writing. Though his contemporaries and Renaissance successors admired Chaucer for his style, his larger contribution lay in establishing the claims of English vernacular poetry to be a self-conscious art with a capacity for critical reflection. That achievement grows out of his creative dialogue with his own works and with his literary predecessors.

NOTES

1. [James I.] Wimsatt ("[The *Book of the Duchess*: Secular] Elegy [or Religious Vision?]" in *Signs and Symbols in Chaucer's Poetry*, ed. John P, Hermann and John J. Burke, Jr., 113-29. University: University of Alabama Press, 1981] 119) uses the passage to argue for a spiritual meaning that balances the secular meaning of the *Book of the Duchess* by analogy to the double genres and twin meanings of the Canticles and Apocalypse in the Bible. The point of the line, however, is to emphasize the aesthetic effect of harmony rather than the spiritual meaning.

2. [Lawrence A.] Gushee ["Questions of Genre in Medieval Treatises on Music" in *Gattungen der Musik in Einzeldarstellungen (Gedenkschrift Leo Schrade)*, ed. Wulf Art, *et al.*,, 365-433. Munich, Francke Verlag, 1973] points out that the theory contained in musical treatises is determined by audience as well as critical doctrine. Gushee's observation applies as well to medieval literary theory. I contend (*Ratio* [*and Invention*. Nashville, Tenn.: Vanderbilt University Press, 1989]) that the precepts of literary criticism vary according to the author's view of his audience and that medieval literary theory is therefore not determinate; rather, it represents a literary thematic, a set of categories and topoi for discussing poetry, many of which become subject matter in their own right. [A. J.] Minnis [*Medieval Theory of Authorship*. London: Scolar Press, 1984] takes an opposite view.

3. [Douglas] Kelly ("[The] Scope [of the Treatment of Composition in the Twelfth- and the Thirteenth-Century Arts of Poetry]" [*Speculum* 41 (1966):261-78] and "Theory [of Composition in Medieval Narrative Poetry and Geoffrey of Vinsauf's *Poetria Nova*, *Mediaeval Studies* 31 (1969): 117-48]") corrects [Edmond] Faral's [*Les*

arts poétiques du XIIe et du XIIIe siècle. Paris: Champion, 1924]
overemphasis on the place of ornamentation in medieval poetics.
[Peter] Dronke ("[Mediaeval] Rhetoric" in *Literature and Western
Civilization, Vol. 2*, ed. D. Daiches and A. Thorlby, 315-45. London:
Aldine, 1973) argues for the conceptual sophistication of medieval
poetic theory, especially Geoffrey of Vinsauf's theory of invention.
[Edgar] De Bruyne (*Études d'eststhétique médiévale*, 3 vols., 1946; rpt.
Geneva: Slatkine, 1975] 2:26-27) notes that Geoffrey's architectural
image borrows Platonic terminology and has an aesthetic rapport with
the Victorines and Cistercians; the comparison itself recurs throughout
Aquinas's remarks on art. See [Ernest] Gallo [*The Poetria Nova and Its
Sources in Early Rhetorical Doctrine*. The Hague: Mouton, 1971]and
[Robert M.] Jordan ([*Chaucer and the*] *Shape* [*of Creation*. Cambridge,
Mass.: Harvard University Press, 1967]) for discussion of the aesthetic
and rhetorical implications.

    4. [Winthrop] Wetherbee observes that "Chaucer has significantly
altered the emphasis of his original. Geoffrey's equivalent to the 'hertes
line' of 1068, 'intrinseca linea cordis,' is a wholly inner resource, a
faculty of the 'interior man,' which traces in its archetypal form what is
then, by a secondary process—the 'hand of the heart' giving place to
that of the body—translated in an outward imitation. In Pandarus's
case, by contrast, the 'hertes line' is sent '*out* from withinne' as the first
stage of the creative process, which thus becomes a process not of
preconception, but of reconnaissance. The point, I think, is that
Pandarus has little or no inner life in the sense that Geoffrey's example
implies and no archetypal preconception of what he seeks to realize"
([*Chaucer and the*] *Poets* [Ithaca, N.Y.: Cornell University Press, 1985]
78-79). [James J.] Murphy ("[A New] Look [at Chaucer and the
Rhetoricians,]" *Review of English Studies* 15 (1964): 1-20]) disputes
whether Chaucer had firsthand knowledge of Geoffrey of Vinsauf, but
see [Peter] Dronke ("[Chaucer and the] Medieval Latin [Poets]" [in
Geoffrey Chaucer, ed. D.S. Brewer, 137-54, Athens: Ohio University
Press, 1975] 170) for an alternate view.

    5. Boethius makes a claim for verbatim translation in the opening
remarks in the second edition of the commentary on the *Isagoge* of
Porphyry: "This second task of exposition, which I have undertaken,
will clarify the course of my translation, for I am afraid I have fallen
victim in my translation to the fault of the faithful interpreter, in that I
have rendered every word, expressed or implied, with a word. The
reason for the present undertaking is that in these writing, in which
knowledge of things is sought, there must be expressed, not a charm of
translucent style, but the uncorrupted truth [*non luculentae orationis*

lepos, sed incorrupta ueritas]." He goes on to say, "It seems to be me
that I shall have accomplished a great deal to this end if books of
philosophy should be composed in the latin language by painstaking
and complete translation, until nothing more were missing from the
literature of the Greeks" ([Richard] McKeon [*Selections from Medieval
Philosophers*, 2 Vols. New York: Charles Scribner's Sons, 1929]1:70).
His remarks make it clear that fullness (*per integerrimae translationis
sinceritatem*) is somehow essential to the task of matching the Greek
sources. The phrasing consciously reverses the emphasis in Horace.
Horace's *fidus interpres* does not strive for word-by-word translation,
whereas Boethius is obviously content to bear the *fidi interpretis
culpam* of rendering the passage *uerbum uerbo.*

6. I have emended Jenkin's text with the revisions proposed by
Wimsatt ("[Chaucer and] French Poetry [in *Geoffrey Chaucer*, ed. D.S.
Brewer, 109-36, Athens: Ohio University Press, 1975]" 109-10) and
[John H.] Fisher ([ed., *The Complete Poetry and Prose of Geoffrey*]
Chaucer, 197 7 [New York: Holt, Rinehart and Winston, 1977] 952-
53). The passage is discussed by Glending Olson ("[Deschamps'] *Art
[de dictier* and Chaucer's Literary Environment]" [*Speculum* 48 (1973):
714- 23]).

7. There is a great deal of commentary on Guillaume's apology for
dreams at the beginning of the *Roman de la rose* (see recent discussion
in [David F.] Hult [*Self-Fulfilling Prophecies.* Cambridge: Cambridge
University Press, 1986] 114-37). My analysis reads the passage in
terms of the medieval Square of Opposition, a set of logical relations in
syllogistic logic. Guillaume's propositions can be located within the
following array:

Universal

A All dreams are false   contraries   E No dreams are false

Affirmative   *Negative*

I   Some dreams are false subcontraries   O Some dreams are not
                                                                                            false

Particular

A and E are universal propositions; I and O are particular. A and I are affirmative propositions; E and O are negative. According to the Square of Opposition, A and E are contraries, and I-O are subcontraries (the former pair cannot both be true and the latter pair cannot both be false). A-O and I-E are contradictories: the truth of one member of a pair of forces the falsity of the other. For example, if the O proposition (some dreams are not false) is true, then the A proposition (all dreams are false) cannot be true. Guillaume's first subargument is valid: if the O proposition is true, then it follows that the corresponding A proposition cannot be true. Guillaume then tries to argue that if the O proposition is true, the E proposition must also be true. Here the reasoning can work only one way: if the E proposition is true, then the O proposition must be true (the truth of the universal proposition determines the truth of the particular proposition). But the reverse does not hold: the truth of the O proposition does not determine anything about the E proposition. It is at the point where Guillaume tries to go from the O proposition to the E proposition that Chaucer's translation emphasizes the force of Guillaume's asseveration ("moi ai ge fiance" 15) by doubling it: "For this trowe I, *and say for me*" (15, italics added) as if to mark the character of its special pleading.

II. *THE BOOK OF THE DUCHESS*

Criticism of *The Book of the Duchess* recurrently focuses on a number of interrelated issues including the circumstances of its composition, Chaucer's appropriation of Latin and French sources, the regularity of this poem's tetrameters and their place in the history of English prosody, the narrator's rhetorical sophistication, the dream's allegorical significance, the characterization of the dreamer himself, the nature of his dialogue with the Black Knight, and the poem's affective success as a *consolatio*. Furthermore, this rich matrix of critical inquiries has generated some of the most fundamental remarks about how *Chaucer* should be read.

A note attributed to John Stowe in the Fairfax MS. indicates that Chaucer was commissioned by John of Gaunt, Duke of Lancaster, to compose *The Book of the Duchess* as a lament "pitously complaynynge" the death of Duchess Blanche. Though the limiting legitimacy of this footnote is deniable, *The Book of the Duchess* remains most tempting to read as a *roman à clef* with real referentiality to Chaucer's personal acquaintances. Whether historical or fictional, *The Book of the Duchess* presents a sort of *tableau vivant* of Chaucer's relationship to John of Gaunt. The biographical as well as socio-political implications that readers attribute to the *Book*'s occasion, therefore, become inextricably connected to our comprehension of the poet's intent and the poem's effects.

However, specifying just one significant date for Chaucer's presentation of the *Book of the Duchess* remains tentative at best. Blanche died of the plague on September 12 in 1368 or in 1369, but John of Gaunt was abroad until November 3, 1369, and could not himself attend one of the annual services in her honor until 1374. Edward Condren has suggested that the occasion for dating *The Book of the Duchess* might be a memorial service as late as 1377.

Whether the *Book of the Duchess* should itself be considered a work of Chaucer's juvenilia or no—"In youthe he made of Ceys and Alcione" (*CT* 2. 57)—its footnotes comprise a sort of medieval *paideuma*. Chaucer obviously loved his lore, and the rich trivia of the *Book of the Duchess* greatly enhances our general view of the Lancastrian scene. On the other hand, the intermittently obscure quality of several passages in the *Book of the Duchess* can also be attributed to its elusive occasionality; many esoteric details (the tenors of which are no longer decodable) may once have been self-evident to Chaucer's familiar audience.

Some readers find that critical attempts to specify the occasional significance of such details in the *Book of the Duchess* only diminish its thematic import. Various more generalized interpretive filters have been proposed in order to amplify the poem's otherwise restricted significance. But one reader's abstraction often proves to be another's distraction. D.W. Robertson, Jr., for example, rejected outright any appeal to the "modern fantasy" of courtly love as a significant context of interpretation. Robertson preferred reading the poem essentially as a *psychomachia* (*Companion*, pp. 407-408; cf. Robertson's "Historical Setting").

Whether or not allegoresis be taken as normative medieval reading, the method of interpretation itself, like archetypal criticism, can claim universal applicability. Nevertheless, the specific relevance of *The Book of the Duchess* to John of Gaunt and the Duchess Blanche is still its most widely accepted context of interpretation even though such a realist reading can be held somewhat to blame for postponing recognition of what now seems Chaucer's quite obvious fabrication of the dreamer-narrator as a fully fictionalized voice. Displacing George Lyman Kittredge's conception (1915) of the "naive" dreamer in *The Book of the Duchess*, James R. Kreuzer (1951) and Bertrand H. Bronson (1952) persuaded most Chaucerians that the persona's pose is a rather clever rhetorical tactic. Chaucer's apparent obtuseness actually serves as an ironic strategy to bring the verbose Black Knight to a self-realization. It should be remembered that E. Talbot Donaldson's landmark study of "Chaucer the Narrator" did not appear in *PMLA* until 1954.

The dreamer's reticence in the *Book of Duchess* is, however, still often interpreted as a fictive dramatization of the poet-Chaucer's own anxieties about the remedial power of rhetoric facing the *wanhope* of a Black Knight or Troilus or, perhaps, his own. The *Book of the Duchess* rewards the scrutiny of readings based upon both modern psychoanalysis and post-modernist conceptions of the narrative. Chaucer's self-consciousness, for example, is recurrently foregrounded when the narrator reports his reading experience within the writing process. The dream vision's apparent false starts also seem highly self-reflexive. The author/narrator/character boundaries are often indiscernible. And, at the text's conclusion, Chaucer announces his intent to report the dream that has just been reported. Some

Chaucerians, however, dismiss the attribution of so much self-reflexivity to Chaucer's *Book* as the rather matter-of-fact and conventional idiom of the dream-vision's genre. The *Book of the Duchess* has, therefore, despite its surface simplicity, proven to be quite a critical gadfly for modern Chaucerians: "Remembre yow of Socrates" (*BD* 717). The *Book of the Duchess* is almost universally conceded to be an exercise in consolation, although readers disagree regarding who receives how much consolation and for what. R.M. Lumiansky sees in the real sympathy of "The Bereaved Narrator" of Chaucer's dream vision the key to the poem's dramatic coherence. But D.W. Robertson and Bernard Huppé's chapter renounces any straightforward identification of the Black Knight with John of Gaunt and reads the dream vision as Chaucer's allegorical encounter with the alter-ego of his own melancholy. Philippa Hardman (by employing the very Robertsonian strategy of referencing the visual arts) suggests the complementary interdependence of the poem's universal and particular significance.

THE BEREAVED NARRATOR IN CHAUCER'S
THE BOOK OF THE DUCHESS

R.M. Lumiansky

There is little room for doubt that Chaucer wrote *The Book of the Duchess* as consolation for John of Gaunt shortly after the death of his wife Blanche. Most criticism of this poem finds it occasionally delightful but generally immature, highly conventional and dependent upon French models, tedious, poorly connected, and ill-proportioned.[1] More recently, however, several critics have stressed the poem's unity, subtlety, and technical skill.[2] The present article, an effort in support of the latter view, will treat three aspects of the poem, which together seem to me to suggest a unified approach to its thought and method, and which have not to my knowledge been fully considered by earlier commentators. My three chief contentions will be (1) that the Narrator presents himself as suffering bereavement rather than love-longing; (2) that there is a major movement of the poem toward a way of consolation for this bereaved Narrator, as well as for the Black Knight; and (3) that fundamental to Chaucer's presentation of the thought pattern of this poem—consolation in the face of bereavement—is a functional treatment of Fortune, on the one hand, and Nature, on the other. Let us look first at the situation of the Narrator.

One of the best known Chaucerian puzzles is found in the following lines spoken by the Narrator near the beginning of the poem:

> But men myght axe me why soo
> I may not sleepe, and what me is.
> But natheles, who aske this
> Leseth his asking trewely.
> Myselven can not telle why
> The sothe; but trewly, as I gesse,
> I holde hit be a sicknesse
> That I have suffred this eight yeer,

> And yet my boote is never the ner;
> For there is physicien but oon
> That may me hele; but that is don.
> Passe we over untill eft;
> That will not be mot nede by left. . . . (30-42)

A number of explanations have been offered for this passage.[3] Most early commentators—Furnivall and ten Brink, for example—assumed a connection with Chaucer's personal experience, whereby he here makes reference to his rejection by a lady with whom he was actually in love, though Fleay in 1877 argued that Chaucer referred here to his unhappy married life. In 1905, however, W. O. Sypherd showed that in love poems of the thirteenth and fourteenth centuries poets often described themselves as suffering from unrequited love; he argued therefore that Chaucer's statement in *The Book of the Duchess* is simply his adoption of a conventional pose. Since 1905 most writings about this poem accept this "conventional" view, as in the recent essays by Kreuzer, Bronson, Lawlor, Manning, and Donaldson. Loomis is even more specific when he claims that Chaucer in an effort to be conventional took the idea of eight years' sickness from a line in Machaut's *Jugement dou Roy de Behaingne*. But there is still some support for the theory of autobiographical connection: Margaret Galway asserts that this passage, like other similar passages in Chaucer's works, points to his unrequited love for Princess Joan. Finally, we have the view advanced fifteen years ago by M.W. Stearns that the mention of eight years' sickness is the poet Chaucer's courtly compliment to the dead Blanche of Lancaster, implying his own love-longing for that lady.

No one of these explanations is without difficulties. To assume that the "I" of the passage quoted above, and of the whole poem, is the real-life Geoffrey Chaucer reporting on an actual experience seems unwarranted. Rather, as in many of Chaucer's poems, the Narrator here is a fictional character, invented to play a leading part in the action and effect of the poem, who uses this passage to introduce himself for his role. He states here that he is not sure why he cannot sleep, but that he supposes the sleeplessness results from a sickness he has suffered for eight years. The remaining lines of this passage—as I understand them—suggest, not that the cause of his eight-year sickness is conventional love-longing for a lady who does not return his affection—as most commentators have assumed—but rather that the cause is grief for a loved one who has died. My reading is supported by several parallels in the Narrator's and the Black Knight's phraseology. The Narrator's "But that is done . . . what will not be must needs be left"—lines 38-42 of the passage quoted above—is strikingly similar to the Black Knight's statement later in the poem "For that ys doon is not to come" (708), which of course refers to the death of his beloved Lady.

There are three other passages concerning the grieving Narrator which are strikingly similar to passages related to the bereaved Black Knight.[4] First, the Dreamer expresses surprise that grief has not killed him:

> For Nature wolde nat suffyse
> To noon erthly creature
> Nat longe tyme to endure
> Withoute slep and be in sorwe. (18-21)

We are later told, with reference to the Black Knight's situation:

> Hit was gret wonder that Nature
> Myght suffre any creature
> To have such sorwe, and be not ded. (467-469)

Second, grief has deadened the Narrator's spirit; he says,

> Defaute of slep and heavynesse
> Hath sleyn my spirit of quyknesse; (25-26)

and the Black Knight's experience is exactly the same:

> His spirites wexen dede;
> The blood was fled for pure drede
> Doun to hys herte, to make hyrn warm—
> For wel hyt feled the herte had harm. (489-492)

Third, grief has affected the Narrator's mental powers:

> I take no kep
> Of nothing, how hyt cometh or gooth . . .
> For I have felynge in nothyng,
> But, as yt were, a mased thyng,
> Alway in poynt to falle a-doun. (6-13)

And the Black Knight exhibits the same difficulty:

> Throgh hys sorwe and hevy thoght,
> Made hym that he herde me noght;

For he had wel nygh lost hys mynde. (509-511)

My point, therefore, is that since we have four passages concerning the Narrator's grief which practically match four passages concerning the Black Knight's grief, we may reasonably suppose that the cause in the Narrator's case matches the cause in the Black Knight's case; namely, the death of a beloved Lady.

These similarities of phraseology are certainly not conclusive proof that the Narrator is grieving over the death of a loved one; and I have no better explanation as to why the period is "eight years" than have those who consider his "sicknesse" love-longing for a haughty courtly lady. However, there is a structural and thematic relationship which seems to offer strong support for the reading I espouse.

The Book of the Duchess consists of three main parts: first, the Narrator's statement of his sorrowful situation, which we have been examining; second, the story of Ceyx and Alcyone, which the Narrator reads before going to sleep; and third, the account of the Black Knight's grief for his dead Lady, which of course furnishes the heart of the dream and the main reason for the poem. As has often been observed,[5] the second part is a highly appropriate prelude for the Black Knight's forlorn situation, in that it stresses Alcyone's grief for her drowned husband Ceyx. It becomes immediately apparent that if in the first part of the poem the Narrator is telling us that he cannot sleep because of grief for the death of a loved one—presumably a Lady—we find for the whole poem a structural principle which rests upon the three parallel situations: the Narrator's grief over the death of his Lady, Alcyone's grief over Ceyx' death, and the Black Knight's grief over Good Fair White's death. Such parallelism would place the Narrator in a far better position to accomplish his main function in the poem—namely, consolation of the Black Knight—than if he is suffering only love-longing for a courtly mistress. Further, we may consequently observe in *The Book of the Duchess* a deeper subtlety of design than it is usually granted, in that the situation of Alcyone and the Black Knight bear precise relationship not only to each other but also to the situation of the Narrator.

In urging this more exact parallelism among the three structural situations in *The Book of the Duchess*, I do not mean to claim that a poem with such parallelism is more effective than one without it, or that Chaucer—or any other poet—should be judged by rules borrowed from mechanical drawing. But I do maintain that certain aspects of this particular poem are more readily acceptable if we assume that the Narrator's grief—like that of Alcyone and the Black Knight—arises from the death of a loved one. There is the passage reporting the Narrator's violent reaction to Alcyone's lament over the possibility of Ceyx' being dead. He says:

> Such sorwe this lady to her tok
> That trewly I, which made this book,
> Had such pittee and such rowthe
> To rede hir sorwe, that, by my trowthe,
> I ferde the worse al the morwe
> Aftir, to thenken on hir sorwe. (95-100)

Surely, these lines and this deep sympathy are more easily understandable from a Narrator who has himself experienced the death of a loved one than if he is simply melancholy because of his rejection by a haughty courtly lady.

Similarly, we have the often-debated question of the behavior of the Narrator-Dreamer toward the grieving Black Knight. Of late, several commentators have emphasized the delicate tact with which the Narrator-Dreamer conducts a cathartic process which enables the Black Knight to talk out his grief. Such tact is far less surprising from an individual who has experienced a similar loss by death than from a rejected courtly lover. In sum—although it is certainly true that when the Narrator says "For there is physician but oon / That may me hele" (39), he is using a stock figure for a haughty courtly lady—I nevertheless contend that an assumption of bereavement rather than rejection as cause for his grief seems the more likely reading of the Narrator's situation in *The Book of the Duchess*.

If we make this assumption of a bereaved Narrator we are able to see—perhaps more clearly than otherwise—that a major aim of the poem is to establish a means of consolation for the Narrator, as well as for the Black Knight. Certainly, until the latter is led to recount the story of his winning and losing of Good Fair White, the focus of the poem is almost wholly upon the character designated as "I". And, although a number of critics have pointed to the considerable differences between the Narrator and the Dreamer as characters—or between the Dreamer's waking and sleeping states—I find that this movement in the earlier parts of the poem toward consolation for the bereaved Narrator well accounts for his behavior when he presents himself as Dreamer.

In the second of the poem's three successive situations presenting bereaved persons—that of Alcyone—we encounter death from grief as the reaction to bereavement: "'Alas!' quod she for sorwe, / And deyede

within the thridde morwe" (213-214). It is important to notice that
Alcyone's death is reported just after the vision of Ceyx has urged upon
her a philosophical acceptance of her loss. Ceyx tells her:

> My swete wyf,
> Awake! let be your sorwful lyf!
> For in your sorwe there lyth no red.
> For, certes, swete, I nam but ded;
> Ye shul me never on lyve yse.
> But, goode swete herte, that ye
> Bury my body, for such a tyde
> Ye mowe hyt fynde the see besyde;
> And farewel swete, my worldes blysse!
> I praye God yowre sorwe lysse.
> To lytel while oure blysse lasteth! (201-211)

But Alcyone is unable to profit from her husband's advice.

After telling of Alcyone's death, Chaucer does not consider it
appropriate to include the remainder of Ovid's story, in which Ceyx
and Alcyone are reunited as birds: "Hyt were to longe for to dwelle"
(217). Ovid's ending is not pertinent to Chaucer's purpose, since
Alcyone's reaction to her bereavement—the chief reason for the
inclusion of her story in *The Book of the Duchess*—has already been
shown. We should also note that because of this same lack of
pertinence Chaucer does not include the early part of Ovid's story,
which gives the reason—to consult an oracle of Apollo—for Ceyx'
undertaking the sea-journey. As is his habit in later poems, Chaucer
here uses only that part of his borrowed story which is to his purpose,
the preparation for and presentation of Alcyone's reaction to Ceyx'
death. B.H. Bronson has pointed out that the climax in the third section
of *The Book of the Duchess* comes when the Black Knight seems to
realize the wisdom in philosophical acceptance of his bereavement.[6]
And certainly a main function of the story of Ceyx and Alcyone, with
its emphasis on the latter's death because of bereavement, is to stand in
sharp contrast to the Black Knight's being led later in the poem toward
a wiser reaction, philosophical acceptance of White's death. But it is
the Narrator, not the Black Knight, who reads the story of Ceyx and
Alcyone. Consequently, the negative moral of Alcyone's death from
grief not only prepares the Narrator as Dreamer to suggest the positive
reaction when the bereaved Black Knight longs for death, it also
simultaneously offers the Narrator an example of what not to do in the
face of his own bereavement. In this fashion the story of Ceyx and

Alcyone, presenting the second of the three bereaved situations, must first point backward for the instruction of the Narrator before it can move ahead for the instruction of the Black Knight through the efforts of the Narrator-Dreamer.

That Chaucer intends Ceyx' advice to apply more widely than to Alcyone's bereavement only, is suggested by the tense of "lasteth" in line 211. Ceyx does not say "Our [his and Alcyone's] happiness *lasted* for too brief a time"; rather he says "our [mankind's] happiness *lasts* for too brief a time." Thus the Narrator as reader of this story can easily apply Ceyx' words to his own unhappy situation.

By noticing the Narrator's attitude in two passages in the poem which I think have been too seldom considered, we may observe more fully Chaucer's presentation of the Narrator's movement toward consolation. First, in the passage concerning the Narrator's "sicknesse," there are the lines "Passe we over *untill eft*; / That will not be mot nede by left" (41-42). According to my reading of the Narrator's situation, the first of these lines means, "Let us leave *for the time being* the matter of my great sorrow because of the death of my loved one." But the clear implication of *untill eft* is that the Narrator plans to return to the question of his grief later in the poem. Accordingly, after recounting the story of Ceyx and Alcyone, to introduce his dream the Narrator says:

> ryght upon my book
> Y fil aslepe, and therwith even
> Me mette so ynly swete a sweven
> So wonderful, that never yit
> Y trowe no man had the wyt
> To konne wel my sweven rede. . . . (274-279)

In commenting on this passage, James R. Kreuzer suggested that the Narrator's dream cannot be interpreted "because to do so would violate the initial purpose of the poem—to pay tribute to Blanche, Duchess of Lancaster, and console the bereaved John of Gaunt."[7] Perhaps so; but such a comment does not make clear why the Narrator calls a dream treating Blanche's death and her husband's grief "so ynly swete" and "so wonderful." In my opinion this appreciative view of the dream is to be understood in connection with the Narrator's own situation: He has been suffering terribly from sorrow over the death of his loved one; and he has just read an account in which the bereaved Alcyone died of such sorrow. But the dream which he dreamt "this other night" (45), was a great comfort to him (was "so ynly swete") because it gave him opportunity to observe the enjoyment of life possible for him, despite his bereavement, should he be able to accept the advice set forth in Ceyx' words to Alcyone. The *untill eft* of line 41 is fulfilled by the Narrator's appreciative comment in line 274 as to his dream's beneficent application to his own circumstances.

Further, the end of the poem connects with these two passages. There the Narrator, awakened from his dream by the striking of the bell, says:

> And the book that I hadde red,
> Of Alcione and Seys the kyng,
> And of the goddes of slepyng,
> I fond hyt in myn hond ful even.
> Thoghte I, "Thys ys so queynt a sweven
> That I wol, be processe of tyme
> Fonde to put this sweven in ryme. . . ." (1326-32)

In this passage the mention of the book and the story recalls for us the Narrator's sorrowful situation at the beginning of the poem, and the comment in line 1330 upon the quality of the dream recalls its earlier description as "so ynly swete" and "so wonderful." Probably the most frequent meaning of "queynt" in Middle English is "strange, curious, unusual"; but this word also meant "having some attractive or agreeable feature."[8] This latter meaning would seem to me to apply here and to reinforce the idea of the opportunity that the dream has afforded the Narrator to see the beneficent possibilities in applying Ceyx' advice to his own bereaved situation.

So far I have maintained that the Narrator presents himself as bereaved, and that a major movement of *The Book of the Duchess* is toward a means of consolation for the Narrator, as well as for the Black Knight. We move now to a consideration of Chaucer's inclusion in the poem of a functional treatment of Fortune and Nature, which supports and illustrates the possibility for consolation despite bereavement set forth in Ceyx' advice to Alcyone.

It is in the Black Knight's well-known metaphor of his unsuccessful game of chess that we find extended treatment of Fortune: "For fals Fortune hath pleyed a game / Atte ches with me, allas the while" (618-619). The Black Knight then devotes thirty lines (620-649) to bitter castigation of Fortune's deception and fickleness. These lines lead to his statement of his great loss in the game:

> At the ches with me she gan to pleye;
> With hir false draughts dyvers
> She staal on me, and *tok my fers*. (652-654)

Perhaps he could have kept his "fers," the Black Knight thinks, had he
been a more skilful chess player; but then he concludes that even skill
would not have helped, "For Fortune kan so many a wyle, / Ther be but
fewe kan hir begile" (673-674).

The upshot of the Black Knight's lengthy speech is that because of
false Fortune only grief and death are left for him. To counter this
argument the sympathetic Narrator-Dreamer calls Nature to the Black
Knight's attention:

> And whan I herde hym tel thys tale
> Thus pitously, as I yow tell,
> Unnethe myght y lenger dwelle,
> Hyt dyde myn herte so moche woe.
> "A, goode sir," quod I, "say not soo!
> Have som pitee on your *Nature*
> That formed yow to creature.
> Remember yow of Socrates,
> For he ne counted nat thre strees
> Of noght that Fortune koude doo." (710-719)

To the Black Knight's insistence upon Fortune's leading him to Death,
the Narrator-Dreamer presents Nature as Life. After further admonition
against suicide (721-741), the Narrator-Dreamer's effort seems to be
succeeding, for he is able to lead the Black Knight into giving an
account of his devotion to Love and his wooing and winning of White.
We see very clearly that the Black Knight views Love as an aspect of
Nature (761, 778). At one point in this account he briefly reiterates his
bitter view of Fortune, because it was she who first caused him to look
upon White:

> Hit happed that I cam on a day
> Into a place ther that I say,
> Trewly, the fayrest companye
> Of laydes that evere man with ye
> Had seen togedres in oo place.
> Shal I clepe hyt hap other grace
> That broght me there? Nay but Fortune,
> That ys to lyen ful comune,
> The false trayteresse pervers!

God wolde I koude clepe hir wers!
For now she worcheth me ful woo. (805-815)

But in his adulatory description of White, he emphasizes in three
passages that she was wholly Nature's creature (871, 908, 1195). Such
consideration of the blessings he has received from Nature in the
person of White brings him to a firm rejection of the regret he earlier
expressed that Fortune had led him to fall in love with White (1115-
1125). It would thus seem from the pattern which we have just traced
that Chaucer has the Narrator-Dreamer suggest for the Black Knight a
means of consolation by opposing Nature's beneficence to Fortune's
falsity. That such is the case, is clearly indicated in the earlier parts of
The Book of the Duchess by Chaucer's preparing the Narrator for this
role. There we find frequent emphasis upon the opposition represented
by Nature as Life to excessive grief.

As soon as the Narrator has stated, at the opening of the poem, his
sorrowful condition, he makes known his awareness that excessive
grief is contrary to Nature's law:

> For sorwful ymagynacioun
> Ys always hooly in my mynde.
> And wel ye woot, *agaynes kynde*
> Hyt were to lyven in thys wyse;
> For *Nature* wolde nat suffyse
> To non erthly creature
> Nat longe to endure
> Without slep and be in sorwe. (14-21)

Then, because of his awareness of his breach of Nature's law, in
seeking to pass away the sleepless night he requests a particular sort of
book:

> And in this bok were written fables
> That clerkes had in olde tyme,
> And other poets, put in rime
> To rede, and for to be in minde,
> While men loved the *lawe of kind.* (52-66)

The Narrator has requested this particular book because in it are stories
from the period when men followed Nature's law, stories which he
thinks will prove helpful to him because his excessive sorrow violates
Nature's law.

In *The Parliament of Fowls* the Narrator does not find what he is seeking in the book which he selects.[9] But in *The Book of the Duchess* the Narrator's choice of reading material is successful. He tells us that he would have died "Yf I ne had red and take kep / Of this tale next before" (224-225). His death because of grief resulting from bereavement would have matched Alcyone's reaction. However, he specially states here that he paid attention to ("take kep of") the meaning of the story. It would consequently seem that because he knows that his excessive grief from bereavement violates Nature's law of Life he is able to appreciate the wisdom of Ceyx' counsel.

Having taken to heart Ceyx' emphasis upon philosophical acceptance of death, the Narrator is able as Dreamer to observe and take pleasure in the joyful aspects of the natural world: the singing of the birds which awakens him (294-320); the physical appeal of his bedchamber with the sun shining upon it and the weather perfect (321-343); the noise and bustle of the hunt in which he takes part (344-386); and the beauty of the "floury grene" to which the little dog leads him (387-442). This exuberant joy in Nature as Life, made possible for the formerly sorrowful Narrator-Dreamer by his awareness of Nature's law against excessive grief and by Ovid's story, is in such contrast to the extreme sorrow of the Black Knight, whom he observes and overhears, that he wonders, "that *Nature* / Myght suffre any creature / To have such sorwe, and be not ded" (467-469). And that the Black Knight's heart should be frightened "by kynde" (494) seems to the Narrator-Dreamer a terrible situation. Also, he remarks that the Black Knight had almost lost his mind with grief, even though Pan, "that men clepe god of kynde, / Were for hys sorwes never so wroth" (512-513).

These numerous references to the Narrator-Dreamer's understanding of the law which Nature as Life holds forth against excessive sorrow resulting from bereavement make plain, when taken together, the functional opposition within the poem between this concept and the concept of Fortune as Death in the Black Knight's metaphor of the chess game. This pattern in the presentation of Nature shows the bereaved Narrator-Dreamer a means of consolation stemming from Ceyx' words to Alcyone, and puts him in position to lead the bereaved Black Knight into a similar line of thought.

It remains to consider how the picture presented above of a bereaved Narrator-Dreamer who visualizes the consolation inherent in Ceyx' advice and Nature's law, and who by his attitude and words extends this conception to the bereaved Black Knight, fits into the historical context surrounding *The Book of the Duchess*. For, however one sees the inner workings of the poem, he must bear steadily in mind that Chaucer wrote it for John of Gaunt shortly after the death of Blanche, Duchess of Lancaster, and that in such a situation extreme tact was required of the poet. In the last analysis, the chief goal of the poem, from Chaucer's point of view, was not consolation for the bereaved Black Knight, but consolation for the bereaved and presumably grief-stricken John of Gaunt.

It is consequently necessary to have in mind the considerable difference in situation for these two individuals. The Black Knight does not read or hear Ovid's story of Ceyx and Alcyone, nor is he able to take into consideration most of the words the Narrator speaks in the poem. But John of Gaunt does hear Ovid's story and is in position to consider the whole poem, including the bereaved Narrator and the symbolic Black Knight. Accordingly, it seems to me that Chaucer means the opening lines of the poem to indicate a situation parallel to that of the bereaved and grief-stricken John of Gaunt whom Chaucer must visualize as recipient of the poem. Whether or not John of Gaunt was actually grief-stricken had to be beside the point for Chaucer. Then, after first presenting his sorrowful state, the Narrator says:

> Such fantasies ben in myn hede,
> So I not what is best to do. (28-29)

The remainder of the poem thus becomes the answer to the question of what one should do in such a situation. And the exquisite tact on Chaucer's part resides largely in the fact that this answer—accept bereavement philosophically and find whatever enjoyment Nature makes possible—is not directed in labored fashion at John of Gaunt, but is rather made evident to him through the attitude and behavior of the Narrator as Dreamer, through Ceyx' counsel, and through the Black Knight's reflective account. Not the least aspect of this tactful presentation is that the Narrator stands in the position of one who knows what he should do in the face of his bereavement, but who has not yet been able to put theory into practice.

In summary, the reading of *The Book of the Duchess* here presented—with its greater emphasis than usual upon the first section of the poem—visualizes a Narrator suffering excessive grief resulting from bereavement, who within the poem moves toward a means of consolation, based chiefly upon the conception of Nature as Life, and whose experience is thus tactfully placed as object lesson before the bereaved John of Gaunt.[10]

NOTES

1. See, for example, B. ten Brink, *History of English Literature*, vol. II (1893), pp. 42-48; G.L. Kittredge, *Chaucer and His Poetry* (1915), pp. 37-72; R. K. Root, *The Poetry of Chaucer* (1922), pp. 59-63; J. L. Lowes, *Geoffrey Chaucer* (1934), pp. 116-128; R.D. French, *A Chaucer Handbook* (1947), pp. 86-90; N. Coghill, *The Poet Chaucer* (1949), pp. 22-35; J. S. P. Tatlock, *The Mind and Art of Chaucer* (1950), pp. 26-32; and K. Malone, *Chapters on Chaucer* (1951), pp. 19-41.

2. See W. Clemen, *Der junge Chaucer* (1938) ; J.R. Kreuzer, "The Drearner in *The Book of the Duchess,*" *PMLA,* LXVI (1951), 543-547; B.H. Bronson, *"The Book of the Duchess Reopened,"* *PMLA*, LXVII (1952), 863-881; and E.T. Donaldson, *Chaucer's Poetry* (1958), pp. 951- 953.

3. See F.J. Furnivall, *Trial Forwards* (1877), pp. 34-36; ten Brink, *History*, vol. II; p. 45; F.G. Fleay, *A Guide to Chaucer and Spenser* (1877), pp. 36-37' W.O. Sypherd, "Chaucer's Eight Years' Sickness," *MLN*, XX (1905), 240-243; Kreuzer, Bronson, and Donaldson, as in Note 2 above; John Lawlor, "The Pattern of Consolation In *The Book of the Duchess,*" *Speculum*, XXXI (1956), 636; Stephen Manning, "Chaucer's Good Fair White: Woman and Symbol," *Comparative Literature*, X (1958), 97; R.S. Loomis, "Chaucer's Eight Years' sickness " *MLN*, LIX (1944), 178; M. Galway, "Chaucer's Hopeless Love," *MLN*, LX (1945), 431-439, M.W. Stearns, "A Note on Chaucer's Attitude toward Love," *Speculum*, XVII (1942), 570-574.

4. See pp. 871-872 of the article by Bronson cited in Note 2 above.

5. See the articles by Kreuzer and Bronson cited in Note 2 above, and D.C. Baker "The Dreamer Again in *The Book of the Duchess,*" *PMLA*, LXX (1965), 279-282.

6. Bronson, pp. 880-881.

7. Kreuzer, p. 544.

8. *NED*, "*Quaint,*" A, 1, 8.

9. *Parliament of Fowls*, lines 90-91 and 695-699.

10. Since this article was written, Dorothy Bethurum has presented the same view of a lovelorn Narrator which B.H. Bronson set forth in the article cited in Note 2 above; see *PMLA*, LXXIV (1959), 512-514.

THE BOOK OF THE DUCHESS

by Bernard F. Huppé
and D.W. Robertson, Jr.

The Book of the Duchess begins with an elaborate picture of a man
made sleepless through unfulfilled desire. His loss of sleep makes him
idle, indifferent to good or evil, and above all full of sorrowful
imaginings. Death, he thinks, will soon result from his unnatural state,
for the spirit of life is dead within him. In his "mased" or irrational
condition,[1] he is so confused by phantasies that he is unable to decide
"what is best to do" or to determine the cause of his sleeplessness. In
Froissart's *Paradys d'Amours,* from which Chaucer probably
developed the introduction to *The Book of the Duchess,* the speaker
specifically declares himself to be a lover languishing for his mistress;[2]
but Chaucer's speaker says that if men ask him why he is sleepless, he
will be unable to answer. He knows merely that one physician can cure
him, and that the physician seems impossibly beyond his reach:

> I holde hit be a sicknesse
> That I have suffred this eight yeer,
> And yet my boote is never the ner;
> For ther is phisicien but oon
> That may me hele; but that is don. (36-40)

The professed ignorance of the speaker presents a problem to the
reader, particularly about the identification of the one physician. On the
one hand, the image of the lady as the only physician to her lover's
discomfort is traditional. On the other hand, the image of Christ the
Physician represents an even earlier and more pervasive tradition. A
similar ambiguous clue is afforded by the eight years' malady, which
may simply indicate the temporal extent of the lover's suffering, or,
with reference to the Physician, Christ, it may be a specific reflection of
an eight years' malady found in the New Testament, that of Aeneas in
the Acts of the Apostles. The eight years' malady of Aeneas is
elaborately glossed. Aeneas himself is taken to represent humanity; his
malady of eight years symbolizes earthly delight which is cured in the

name of Christ, the Physician.[3] In the biblical figure of the Physician,
the audience is given one way of understanding the portrait of the
sleepless man. He is one who knows that there is but one Physician, but
he has lost access to Him because he has been so overcome by a
temporal loss that he has almost fallen into despair. He sees, for the
moment, no way to the "sleep" or quiet of life which he knows that
God alone can give him.[4] In short, the reader is made aware that the
temporal loss suffered by the poet is very great, a measure of the worth
of the subject of eulogy, Blanche the Duchess, so sorely mourned by
one of her followers.

In his imaginary self-portrait, Chaucer stresses his idleness. He
suggests thereby that for one who, like himself, has lovingly served
Blanche, her loss may lead to an almost inconsolable bereavement, that
is, to the condition of *tristitia*,[5] the nature of which may be suggested
by John the Scot's definition of Hades as "tristitia vel deliciarum
privatio."[6] *Tristitia* prevents the speaker from performing any good
works and even from desiring to do so. To him, as well as to her other
mourners, Blanche had presumably been a source of spiritual
inspiration, one among those who, with Queen Philippa, helped to instil
ideals of courtesy and chivalry in Edward's court, which, for a time,
was the most brilliant in Europe. But just as love for Blanche in life
inspired noble action in her friends and admirers, so also that love may
be turned toward even greater inspiration at her death. The problem of
the poem is to show how this "conversion" may be effected. And the
solution is suggested at the opening by the eight years' malady and by
the play on the idea of the physician.

Continuing in his "mased" search for consolation, the speaker,
lacking sleep, considers various kinds of slothful distraction. A French
book, or "romance," seems better game than chess or tables. It is an
ancient book, translated and rhymed by poets who wrote "while men
loved the lawe of kinde," or, that is, while they respected Nature,
whose precepts are violated by the speaker's slothful condition. He
finds in the book stories about kings and queens which seem irrelevant
to his condition and hence trivial. But one story seems "a wonder
thing," perhaps because it is relevant to him in mirroring and
commenting upon his own grief. It reveals one possible consequence of
his despairing grief, which he has, in fact, already considered, that is,
self-destruction. When her husband, Seys, is lost at sea, Alcyone
laments for him inordinately. She vows to her god that she will never
eat bread until she hears from Seys. In answer to her prayer, Juno sends
a messenger to Morpheus, who lives in a dark, barren cave, demanding

that he bring the body of Seys to Alcyone in a dream. When Seys comes to her through Morpheus, he tells her that her sorrow is futile:

> My swete wyf,
> Awake! let be your sorwful lyf!
> For in your sorwe there lyth no red.
> For, certes, swete, I nam but ded;
> Ye shul me never on lyve yse.
> But, goode swete herte, that ye
> Bury my body, for such a tyde
> Ye mowe hyt fynde the see besyde;
> And farewell swete, my worldes blysse!
> I praye God youre sorwe lysse.
> To lytel while oure blysse lasteth! (201-211)

The message is essentially philosophical; it urges Alcyone to awaken from worldly concern and to act as a true widow should, realizing herself to be "bereft of every aid except that of God alone."[7] But Alcyone, who is blind to truth of this kind, cannot understand him:

> With that hir eyen up she casteth
> And saw noght. (212-213)

She continues to lament, and dies on the third day. The selection of this story from among the others in his book may indicate that the speaker is in a parallel situation of bereavement. If he too had a vision, would he be able to understand a message like that of Seys?

At the point where Alcyone is unaware of the fate of her husband, saying that she will not eat bread until she hears certainly of him, the speaker pauses to attest his sympathetic grief for her:

> Such sorwe this lady to her tok
> That trewly I, which made this book,
> Had such pitee and such rowthe
> To rede hir sorwe, that, by my trowthe,
> I ferde the worse al the morwe. (95-100)

Alcyone's grief was at first like that of David before he knew certainly the fate of his first son by Bathsheba. He mourned and refused to eat before the boy died, but afterward, unlike Alcyone, when he knew that his son was dead, he threw off his mourning and broke bread, declaring to his servants the futility of further lament. His statement is not unlike that of Seys in its import (2 Kings 12. 22-23): "And he said: While the child was yet alive, I fasted and wept for him: for I said: Who knoweth whether the Lord may not give him to me, and the child may live? But now that he is dead, why should I fast? Shall I be able to bring him back any more? I shall go to him rather: but he shall not return to me." Death has effectively removed all justification for further show of grief.

Alcyone, on the contrary, continues to lament after she has learned the truth, refusing consolation. At first glance, for the speaker to fare the worse "al the morwe after" in thinking of her sorrow seems inconsistent. Since the morrow would be after he had awakened from the dream which he recounts in his own poem, he betrays inordinate sympathy for an irrational grief, and he appears to be left sorrowful rather for Alcyone than for the lamented Blanche. These inconsistencies disappear if we remember that one should not grieve for a true Christian who has gone to his reward, although one may grieve, but not inordinately, over the lamentable fate of a misled sinner. As St. Jerome explains in one of his consolatory epistles, "David, justly lamented the death of his son who was a parricide; but afterward, when he could not bring it about that his other son might live, he did not lament his death because he knew that he had not sinned."[8] Chaucer's statement of grief over Alcyone can represent a foreshadowing of the consolation he attains at the end of the poem. Seys brings a philosophic message of comfort which that other "mased" creature, Alcyone, chooses not to hear; in consequence, it is her sorrow which is lamentable, not the death of Seys, the occasion for her grief. The application of the *sentence* of her fate to the plight of the grieving poet is clear. He must regard his own loss as something other than a blow of adverse Fortune, and he must learn to understand the relevance of Seys' message to his own situation.

In spite of his statement that he grieved for Alcyone "al the morwe aftir," the poet indicates no immediate, overwhelming concern for Alcyone's plight. He merely wonders about any god who can cause a man to sleep, and speaks in "game," though his mood is not playful. When he has read his Ovidian story, he makes a joking vow to Morpheus or to Juno or to "som wight elles," and falls immediately to sleep. The fact that he prays to Morpheus "in game" and at the same time asserts that he knows only one God shows that he does not take the personages to whom he prays seriously as deities. Whatever power they have to "make men sleep" is not their own, but God's. Their power is illusion. The sleep of the poet, if it is to provide rest from his torment, must result from a deeper understanding of the story of Seys and Alcyone, which he had read "wel" and "overloked everydel."

Alcyone prays to Juno for help:

> Helpe me out of thys distresse,
> And yeve me grace my lord to see.
> Soone, or wite wher-so he be,
> Or how he fareth, or in what wise,
> And I shal make you sacrifise,
> And hooly youres become I shal
> With good wille, body, herte, and al. (110-116)

Whatever meaning Juno may have in this context, it is clear that Alcyone is interested only in what she may see or hear and not in the intangible but nevertheless real virtues which Seys may have had. In Christian terms, her prayer is in substance idolatrous.[9] In terms of pagan wisdom like that found, for example, in Cicero's *De amicitia*, a work which Dante praised for its efficacy in consolation, it is unreasonable. Alcyone is subject to "fantasye" in her solicitude and is therefore not in a position to heed any reasonable counsel her vision may suggest to her.[10] As a result of her plea to Juno she falls into a "ded slepe," a sleep of spiritual torpor, reflected in the details of the dark vision of the rocky cave of Morpheus.[11] If his habitation suggests the mind, it suggests one darkened by loss of the guiding light of reason. The approach to the cave is a valley between two rocks where nothing grows. The cave is dark as "helle-pit," it contains Lethean streams, and the figures within it are asleep.[12]

Morpheus is awakened rudely by Juno's messenger, who cries "'Awake,' wonder hie." Morpheus provides that an image of Seys be brought to the dreaming Alcyone. Seys reveals the truth of his condition, and thus of her own, if she will awaken:

> My swete wyf,
> Awake! let be your sorwful lyf!
> For in your sorwe there lyeth no red
> For, certes, swete, I nam but ded. (201-204)

Seys is dead and thus, like Troilus as he ascends through the spheres, beyond illusion and beyond remedy. Thus Seys is able to reveal a truth which would have been available even to pagans like Cicero; but Alcyone, whose mind is darkened by grief, does not respond to her husband's message. Seeing nothing but her temporal loss, she does not hear the wisdom he has to offer.

To the speaker, who knows "phisicien but oon"—"I ne knew never god but oon"—and can thus see in Alcyone's vision the wisdom which she is unable to perceive—"Ne she koude no rede but oon"—the story could suggest a solution to his own difficulties. If he desired the truth and was prepared to heed it, he would be able to receive a vision which would bring the peace of mind he desires. Alcyone received without understanding a message that the speaker would like to find again for himself. Thus he vows to give Morpheus or Juno, or "som wight elles," a bed. The vow of the bed is elaborately developed. It is to be of dove's feathers, white within, adorned with gold, and covered in black satin. More than this, the feather-bed will be ensconced in a magnificent chamber with surrounding halls. These rooms will be painted entirely in gold and adorned with tapestry "of oo sute." Someone up there takes this vow seriously so that the poet falls asleep over his book, and dreams a dream.

The poet's splendid offer and its unexpectedly sudden soporific result are so happily ludicrous as not to need comment. On the other hand, the elaborateness of the vow does open up the possibility of highly appropriate symbolic values which provide another level of transition from wakefulness to dream. The bed is a traditional symbol for contemplation; so too are the feathers, the gold, the black cover, and the pillows.[13] The rooms which he vows also suggest contemplation. The manner of their decoration is reminiscent of that of Solomon's Temple, traditional symbol of the inner mind adorned to receive the Truth in prayer and contemplation.[14]

If the possibility of such fairly obvious symbolic values is granted, behind the humor of the transitional passage rests a further signification; the poet has responded sufficiently to the story of Seys and Alcyone to recognize that he must order his own mind if he is to find the comfort in his bereavement which the true Physician alone can give. Alanus says, in defining the symbolic sense of a bed, "just as in bed the sick man labors, the healthy man is at peace: so in the conscience the sinner labors, the just man is at peace."[15] On the symbolic level, the transition to the dream suggests that the poet finds sleep because his reading has prepared him to dream dreams purposefully. The transition also suggests that the dream will have a curative effect.

When the speaker has expressed his proper intentions, the contemplation he desires comes to him "sodeynly"; he falls asleep "ryght upon" his book. Chaucer comments that the dream he saw was so "ynly" sweet and so "wonderful" that no one—not even Joseph or Macrobius—could interpret it correctly. The exaggerated surface humor of the preceding passage is maintained, but obviously Chaucer is not saying that there is no use listening to the dream because any attempt at interpretation will be futile. What he does instead is to hint that the wonder and inward sweetness of the dream make it well worth interpreting. The statement is a humorous admonition to go beyond the sense to the doctrine within.

The dream begins (290-293) with a definite indication of time of year, May, and the time of day, dawn. The dreamer is awakened by the singing of birds (294-320), sitting on his "chambre roof" and singing a "solempne servise," that

> But hyt had be a thyng of heven—
> So mery a soun, so swete entewnes,
> That certes, for the town of Tewnes
> I nolde but I had herde hem synge. (308-311)

He discovers that his chamber is windowed with painted glass, depicting the "story of Troye," and the walls are "peynted" with "both text and glose of al the Romaunce of the Rose" (321-334). Through the windows the sun is shining. It is a cloudless, temperate day (335-343).

Are these details merely empty "convention," borrowed purely imitatively by Chaucer, or do they have significance? A leading question, for the great poet (our assumption) will not merely dress up conventions; he will use them meaningfully. And what is meaningful in the details which open the dream is not hard to come by, even for the modern reader if he is willing to make use of the obvious.

Most obviously, staying within the poem itself, the beginning of the dream contrasts sharply with the details of the story which put the poet to sleep. The temporal setting of the story of Alcyone is not given, except for the fact that Seys appears to Alcyone in her swoon, "a quarter before day," that is, in the dark or the false dawn in contrast to the poet's awakening in the bright, full dawn of a May day. Other details are contrasted: Morpheus' rocky cave, dark "as helle-pit," filled with "a dedly slepynge sown," the difficult awakening of Morpheus, as against the brightly painted, radiantly lighted room filled with the "solempne servise" of the birds which seemed "a thyng of hevene," and, finally, the poet's pleasant awakening. If the details of the story of Seys and Alcyone had relevant symbolic values, so should the contrasting details of the dream.

The transition from story-reading to dreaming is stressed by triple repetition:

> Loo, thus hyt was, thys was my sweven,
> Me thoghte thus: that hyt was May,

> And in the dawenynge I lay
> (Me mette thus) in my bed al naked. (290-293)

Emphasis is thus given to the details of the dream which must not be left unexamined as merely suggestive of Spring or as merely conventional or as providing merely a poetic parallel to the dawn in the Alcyone story. In interpreting the symbols in the dream we must posit its locale as the mind of a poet, darkened by loss, but incipiently lightened if he has understood the story of Seys and Alcyone, that he may sleep and in a dream perhaps hear and heed the message of the one Physician. To put the matter simply, the poet is suffering because Blanche the Duchess has died; his comfort must come f rom Christ, who died and was resurrected. And the Spring is the season of the Resurrection. In the annual calendar of his memory the Resurrection is a recent event, a reminder of the source of comfort. The dawn, too, is a conventional symbol not only of the Resurrection, but of the *lux divinae cognitionis* in the individual.[16]

The birds, in singing the "solempne servise" which awakens the dreamer, are performing what appears to be a symbolic action. The harmony of the bird's song is a conventional reflection of the heavenly harmony,[17] but the "solempne servise" would appear to have specific relevance to the subject of bereavement. The song of heavenly harmony provides an appropriate device for awakening the dreamer to the May dawn and the sun, with its omnipresent symbolic value, perhaps here of the *lux divinae cognitionis*. Suggesting, as it does, the service of Lauds and the Resurrection, the song provides very different awakening from the rude awakening of Morpheus in the unillumined cave.

Whatever one's reluctance to add to the number of Chaucer's puns, here he does appear to play with words in such a way as to enforce the symbolism of "solempne servise":

> So mery a sown, so swete entewnes,
> That certes, for the town of Tewnes
> I nolde but I had herd hem synge. (309-311)

Literally as "town of Tunis," the phrase has no apparent value except to provide a rhyme. But "town of tewnes," allowing for the usual flexibility of vocalic shifting common to word play, may also be read as "tune of tunes," i.e., song of songs, or "Town of Towns," i.e. the New Jerusalem. The Song of Songs is the song of love between Christ and His Church, or between Christ and the soul of the faithful which seeks union with Him in the New Jerusalem. The dreamer's awakening has placed before him the possibility of peace for his unquiet heart. And immediately he notes the sun illuminating his painted windows, with their Aeneid-like story, and lighting the painted walls, with their story and gloss of the *Romaunce of the Rose*. No reader of Dante will need to be reminded that the medieval reader considered that the *Aeneid* was illumined through Christian understanding, which saw in Aeneas' search for the new city the pilgrimage of the human spirit. Similarly in the light of doctrine, the gloss on the *Romaunce of the Rose* would serve as a warning against the idolatry of the lover who enters the garden of amorous delight.[18] "Late, this other night," presumably by candlelight, the poet had read the story of Seys and Alcyone in a collection,

> That clerks had in olde tyme,
> And other poets, put in rime.

Now other stories are presented to him, dreaming, in the light of the sun shining through or illuminating them. Perhaps only coincidentally, but none the less aptly, it was another Aeneas who was cured of his eight years' illness by the one Physician, and in the description of the poet's illness at the beginning of the poem, one possible diagnosis was love-sickness, the illness of the lover of the Rose.

At all events, the sun illumines the bed of the dreamer, as it does the atmosphere outside the room. The air is temperate, and the sky is without any clouds. In the *Miscellanea* attributed in Migne to Hugh of St. Victor is a passage which may help to explain the significance of these details and their relation to the dreamer. Heaven is described as a place of light without clouds, "lux sine nubes." It is filled with the praise of God sung by the bands of the blessed. This Heaven cannot be seen with the eyes, but only through the mind guided by the Church. Perhaps this is why the dreamer can see the sun only as it shines through painted windows or as it is reflected on the painted walls. In his mind alone may the dreamer catch a glimpse of the heaven he may attain by faithful attention to the teachings of the Church.[19] In his dream the poet may find curative peace by seeing the experience of his grief in the light of the truth of God's heaven. It is not enough, however, to contemplate; action is required, and the dreamer is called from his bed.

As Morpheus was aroused by a horn to provide Alcyone with the image of her husband, the dreamer is aroused to activity by hearing a hunting horn blow and the sounds of hunters speaking of hunting the hart, and of how the hart has become "embosed," exhausted. The dreamer declares:

> I was ryght glad, and up anoon
> Took my hors, and forth I wente
> Out of my chambre. (356-358)

He meets with a "route" of hunters and learns from one, leading a dog, that it is "th' emperour Octovyen" who will be hunting. Again the dreamer is pleased.

> "A Goddes half, in good tyme!" quod I,
> "Go we faste! " and gan to ryde. (370-371)

The hunt begins in earnest. The hart is discovered, chased, and then,

> This hert rused, and staal away
> Fro alle the houndes a privy way. (381-382)

The "forloyn" is blown.

There is in all this, at least on the surface, a dream-like air of inconsequence. When the dreamer hears of the hart it is "embosed," but the hunt begins in earnest later, and only then does the hart steal away. The dreamer apparently mounts his horse inside his chamber.[20] He is utterly unsurprised, but he is delighted first to hear that the hunt has begun and then to hear that the hunter is the "Emperor Octovyen." The symbolic level may provide a consistent meaning for these details.

The exposition of this symbolism may well begin with the double meaning of "hert," *hart* and *heart,* and the commonplace allegorization of God as the Hunter-King hunting after the human soul.[21] In addition, the name of the King, "Octovyen," may contain an etymological pun: *octo,* "eight," and *vyen* "coming." The number *eight* signifies Christ's Resurrection, the recollection of which has already been suggested by the song of the birds in the May dawn, or the resurrection of the faithful on the Day of Judgment. Again, it suggests the kind of inner resurrection implied by the end of the eight years' malady.[22] The mounting of the horse may be used to suggest the proper intention of the dreamer.[23] The apparent inconsequence of the "embosed" hart, for whom the hunt begins in earnest only after the dreamer joins the hunt, but who later escapes, has relation to the two states of mind of the dreaming poet. On the one hand, he is a "mased" creature like Alcyone, insensible to comfort; the "hart" who steals away is like the heart of the poet, too overcome by grief to heed the message of wisdom. On the other hand, the poet, because he is aware of the Physician who can cure his malady, vaguely realizes the solution to his problem. There are, as it were, two parts of the poet's mind, one grieving at the loss of what appears to have been a gift of Fortune, and another aware of the sources of rational consolation. Medieval readers were familiar with inner divisions of this kind, most obviously, perhaps, in the *Consolation* of Boethius, where, as glosses like Trivet's explained, a dialogue takes place between two aspects of a single person, one wise and knowing, the other confused by the whims of Lady Fortune. We should understand that inner divisions of this kind in medieval texts are not aspects of "psychology" in the modern sense, but of moral philosophy.

This division in the mind of the dreamer may suggest an important clue to the meaning of the ensuing action. Suddenly, after he hears the "forloyn," the dreamer says,

> I was go walked fro my tree,
> And as I wente, ther cam by mee
> A whelp, that fauned me as I stood,
> That hadde yfolowed, and koude no good. (387-390)

He, in turn, follows the whelp along a flowery path in a shady wood, until he comes to a "man in blak" with his back to an old oak tree. The remainder of the dream reports the conversation between the dreamer, who had left his tree, and the grieving Black Knight, who is found leaning against a tree. The Black Knight, is commonly identified as John of Gaunt, but beyond the reasonable assurance that the poem is about his deceased Duchess, there is little basis for this identification, which has not gone unchallenged. There are reasons to distrust it. The Black Knight's age is given very specifically as twenty-four; John was twenty-nine when Blanche died—a small discrepancy, but the argument for the identification must take it into account. There is no evidence to suggest—as with Richard II—any extravagant grief over the loss of his wife; indeed he remarried very soon, although for purely political reasons. This fact supplies no evidence either way, but does raise the question of whether Chaucer was writing to console the Duke or to eulogize the Duchess, two matters not necessarily the same. At any event, would not Chaucer in picturing the Alcyone-like violence of the Black Knight's grief have been treading on potentially tactless ground? Would the Duke have been flattered? Further, the line of description, "upon hys berd but lytel her" (456), seems hardly designed to flatter. John may not have been vain, or, at best, vain about his beard. But the beard was considered the "ornament of a man's face," and a sign of masculinity.[24] To say that John's beard had "little hair" would hardly have been tactful. Finally, how pleased might John have been with Chaucer's picture of himself as the Black Knight under the tutelage of Blanche, so that, in effect, he overcame his youthful folly through her?

Such arguments as these have convinced us that the Black Knight was not intended as the dream representative of John of Gaunt, but rather as a sorrowing alter ego of the speaker in the poem, like the poet himself representative of all those who have honored and loved Blanche and lost her in death. However, the biographical question is not central to our reading of the dream dialogue. We find it more consonant with what is in the poem and with historical probability to assume that the Black Knight is not John of Gaunt. For us the importance of the Black Knight in the poem rests in the fact of his being Alcyone-like in his grief. He *is*, in effect, grief itself. Whether the dreamer learns the nature of his own sorrow from observing a simulacrum or the dream representative of an historical person is not too material; those who feel strongly that the Black Knight is John of Gaunt can replace the general with the particular. For them the dreamer will discover the truth of his own sorrow through observation of John's grief; for us he discovers the truth in an alter ego, representative of his own grief. In what follows we assume that the Black Knight is *not* John of Gaunt.

The situation in the dream very possibly suggests the story which inspired the poet to dream in the first place. At the heart of his dream he finds a "mased" Alcyone-like person. Just as Seys came to Alcyone, so he as a rational being confronts a creature like that part of him which is immersed in irrational grief because of an act of Fortune. Here is the significance of the dreamer leaving his tree to find the Knight in mourning leaning against a tree.[25] In effect, the point is a fairly simple one, however devious the allegorical vehicle may seem to be. Grace is available to man, but only if he prepares himself to receive it. The sorrowing Poet must search his own heart for understanding, and this is the "hunt" with which the remainder of the poem is concerned. The loss of Blanche must be seen not as a loss of a gift of Fortune but as an inspiration. It is important, moreover, not that the dreamer specifically be led to see this, but that the audience of the poem be led to understand it. The subject of the poem is not the poet, but the Duchess whom it eulogizes.

The details of the poet's discovery of his mourning self through facing its simulacrum are perhaps symbolic. The whelp, for example, may have a fairly specific significance in relation to the hounds from whom the hart had stolen away. In the symbolism of the hunt, the hounds have a traditional role as preachers. But the hart has escaped the hounds, and it is the whelp, who could not thrive in the hunt, who leads the dreamer to the vision of his "mased" inner self. What is intended here is perhaps suggested by the symbolic distinction between dogs and whelps in the *De bestiis et aliis rebus*, a commonplace book. After discussing the various functions of hounds, the author describes the curative functions of hounds and whelps considered symbolically as priests. Hounds with their tongues represent priests who heal sins which are revealed at confession. Whelps represent priests in their function of curing both by word and by example sins unwittingly retained in the mind and thus not confessed.[26] The cure "in opere vel sermone" is much the same as that which succeeded with Aeneas after his eight years' malady.[27] The poet, as he is pictured at the beginning of the poem, is unrepentant, but the words and examples of those who seek to console him nevertheless bring him to a realization that only a part of him is lost.

The hart, as we recall, escaped the hounds "a privy way," which may imply that he separated himself from his fellows by retiring into his private sorrows where no external ministrations could reach him. To help him find himself, the whelp leads the dreamer down a flowery path through the woods.[28] The grove is so flowery that the earth seemed to wish to be "gayer than the heven." It is a typical earthly paradise whose delights are transitory. The branches shade the grass and flowers so as to form a sort of "via tenebrosa" whose shadows indicate oblivion. Finally the dreamer finds an, image of his grief-stricken self in the black of tribulation, leaning against an oak, the tree of despair, perhaps the same symbolic tree from which he in rationality had walked.[29]

Whatever the meaning of the whelp, the dreamer has walked from his tree, through a wooded path, to find his own suffering, but now viewed in another person. In his grief the poet had lost sight of the only source of comfort, God. The true reason for his sorrow is error; the speaker had been temporarily misled to believe that the loss of another human was the cause of his grief. In Christian fact there can be no sorrow except that arising in separation from God. A man's love has two sides, one false (cupidity) the other true (charity) ; his grief has two sides, one *tristitia*, false grief caused by the loss of an object of desire, the other a true grief caused by his enforced bodily separation from God. What the speaker had taken as grief was itself false worldly vanity. It is to understand this that the dreamer, representing the released rationality of the poet, is led to view in another person the false sorrow into which he had chosen to fall. Therefore, the recognition of the man in black by the dreamer is not immediate, but follows only, as it were, his awakening to the realization of the sober truth about himself.

As he approaches, the dreamer sees that the man in black seems by his manner to be "A wonder wel-farynge knyght." The knightly status need not be either literally autobiographical or indicative of "historical allegory." All Christians became knights spiritually at Confirmation. Symbolically all who live are in battle either as knights of God or as knights of the world.[30] His age of twenty-four may have an incidental symbolic value. It would place the Black Knight in the period of adolescence, which extended from fourteen to twenty-eight. It is the period when man should be informed by precepts and ruled by counsel, so that he may learn to conquer himself.[31]

The dreamer takes up a position behind the Black Knight and hears him complain piteously:

> Hit was gret wonder that Nature
> Myght suffre any creature
> To have such sorwe, and be not ded. (467-468)

In this detail and in the subsequent description of the Knight's condition, it becomes clear that he is exactly in the same situation as the speaker at the beginning of the poem whose mode of life was "ageynes kynde." In contrast to the song of the birds, which had reminded the dreamer of the "toun of Tewnes," the song of the Black Knight is "withoute noote, withoute song." The song that the birds sang was one of joy in God. The Black Knight's song is without melodious joy; it is a song of sorrow for an earthly object.[32] The song itself states explicitly the desperate sorrow of the poet's heart. He will never be joyful again because his lady is dead and gone from him. She is good beyond compare. He should himself have died because only his lady can bring him joy. When the Knight has finished his song, the blood rushes to his heart, where the internal wound lies. He falls into a state parallel with that described in the opening lines of the poem. He is oblivious to outward circumstances, wonders how he may live, and lapses into a state contrary to Nature.

Finally the Knight sees the dreamer, and the two exchange courtesies, during which the Knight impresses the dreamer as being strikingly amiable. He spoke

> As hyt had be another wyght. (530)

Perhaps this line means that the Knight is pleasant in spite of his sorrow. He acts like any other man, even though he seems bound in despair. At all events, he is "tretable" even in sorrow. At this point the dreamer has observed the Black Knight closely and overheard his joyless song. He has all the facts at hand to recognize his despair. The questions which he asks, as Professor Kittredge observed, cannot be asked in ignorance but must be part of a deliberate plan. This attitude is supported by the dreamer's statement,

> I gan fynde a tale
> To hym, to loke wher I myght ought
> Have more knowynge of hys thought. (536-538)

By causing the alter ego of his grieving self to make a sort of confession, the dreamer, symbolizing the poet's own rational self, may indicate the way to the solace of truth to the poet, or at least to the reader. The Knight is unconcerned that the hart has escaped:

> Y do no fors therof, quod he;
> My thought ys theron never a del.

> By oure Lord, quod I, y trow yow wel;
> Ryght so me thinketh by youre chere. (542-545)

If the hunt for the hart is significant, then the Knight's statement is indicative of his despairing state. The dreamer promises that if the Black Knight will tell his woe to him, he may be able to amend it. But the despairing one is unable to believe in this possibility of comfort:

> No man may my sorwe glade,
> That maketh my hewe to falle and fade,
> And hath myn understondynge lorn,
> That me ys wo that I was born! (563-566)

The sorrow upon which he is wilfully fixed has deprived him of understanding, which the intellect alone can supply. He demonstrates that he has lost his understanding in his list of impossible cures. Ovid cannot cure him of his love. Orpheus with his melody may not raise his spirits. Dedalus with his magic may not divert him. The speaker at the beginning of the poem knows that there is one Physician who may cure him, but the despairing Black Knight feels that there is no cure because the lady has died. When he speaks of the impossibility of any physician curing him, he refers to the founders of medicine:

> Ne hele me may no phisicien,
> Noght Ypocras ne Galyen.
> Me ys wo that I lyve houres twelve. (571-573)

Because his lady has died, it is painful to him even that he must live for twelve hours. But in rejecting the twelve hours, perhaps the Knight inadvertently reveals the cause of his sorrow. There are twelve hours in the day, and he who walks in the day walks under the protection of the Physician.[33] His complete abandonment to sorrow is also indicated in his unavailing desire for death and his considerable self-pity. His pains are greater than those of "Cesiphus"; indeed, he exclaims,

> For y am sorwe and sorwe ys y. (597)

Sisyphus was a thief whose futile task was thought to represent, not, as some would now have it, the Fate of Man, but the punishment of those who persist in their iniquity.[34] If the Knight's sorrow is, as he says, greater than that of Sisyphus, he has indeed created for himself a Hades of *tristitia*.

The Knight's worldly virtues and comforts, as he explains at some length, have become vices and discomforts. As a result, among other things, he is sorrowful, idle, wrathful, ill, fearful, foolish, wakeful, and at strife. This change from his apparently happy former state he attributes to the hypocritical falseness of Fortune, the idol of false portraiture, as he calls her. She promises all, but keeps no promise. She seems to walk upright in integrity, but actually she is halt. She seems fair, but is inwardly foul, and so on. There is a direct relation between the doubleness of Fortune and the abrupt change in all that has been dear to him. Actually, he has been defeated by Fortune because he has relied on her in too great love for one of her gifts, so that his life partakes of the instability of Fortune. His complaint against false Fortune is another indication of his blindness. Not Fortune but he himself is at fault, for he has relied upon her completely.[35] Figuratively, the Knight ventured to play chess with her in setting his love on things subject to Fortune. The figure is itself a delusion because it implies that a man may win in a game with Fortune. If he had known the truth, the Knight would have realized that when Fortune took his "fers" she was acting in accordance with her nature. His virtues and comforts were dependent on Fortune's external well-seeming. When her true nature becomes apparent, he loses the object of his love, and his comforts and virtues vanish.

The figure of the chess game is used to emphasize the element of Fortune in the Knight's loss and his own lack of reason. It is based on the account of Fortune given by Reason in *The Romance of the Rose*, where King Manfred of Sicily, flaunting the Church, subjects himself to Fortune but is mated by a "paonet errant," losing his "fierce" on the first day of battle. Having told this story, Reason admonishes:

> Veiz ci genz qui granz eneurs tindrent,
> Or sez a quel chief il en vindrent:
> N'est donc bien Fortune seüre;
> N'est bien fos qui s'i asseüre,
> Quant ceus qu'el veaut par devant oindre
> Seaut ainsinc par darriere poindre?
> E tu, qui la rose baisas,

> Par quei de deul si grant fais as
> Que tu ne t'en sez apaisier,
> Cuidaies tu toujourz baisier,
> Toujourz aveir aise e delices?
> Par mon chief, tu iés fos e nices. (6741-6752)

The Black Knight had unreasonably expected to maintain "aise e delices," a wish, like Manfred's proud ambition, "Contre la fei de sainte iglise." The only way that he conceives to contend with Fortune is to be more skillful at the "jeupardies," or problems of the game. He is aware that hope of overcoming Fortune by skill is deceiving, but he does not really understand why, except in terms of his blind adoration for his lost lady. He says that if he had been in Fortune's place, or if he had been God who controls Fortune, he would have taken the Queen too, because of her great worth. The Black Knight sees that there is a power which governs Fortune, but he does not see that only by trusting in this power may he triumph over Fortune. In short, the chess game reveals the Black Knight as one who believes in God but must be shown that he must turn to God for comfort.

The contrast between the Black Knight and the dreamer is made explicit. The latter not only knows his Physician but knows also that his Physician may easily be approached, since He is seeking him. Morally, the situation is uniquely that of the will and the intellect. The will must be guided in its love by the knowledge furnished it by the intellect. Not seeing beyond Fortune, the self-willed Knight is reduced to desperation. Since he has lost his bliss, he has no recourse but to end his life:

> But through that draughte I have lorn
> My blysse—allas! that I was born!—
> For evermore y trowe trewely;
> For al my wille, my lust holly
> Ys turned; but yet, what to doone?
> Be oure Lord, hyt ys to deye soone. (685-690)

What follows is an explanation from the Black Knight's point of view of why death is the only recourse for him. He is determined not to abandon his sorrow over the loss of his lady. Since he lives for the lady, he must either find her or die. He looks to the sky and the earth, but cannot find her, so that the world brings him only weeping. But his sorrow brings him nothing; that is, he owes it nothing for anything gained from it. No gladness may refresh him, and he has lost the sufficiency that makes life possible. Thus only death is left. Like Tantalus (709), who, as Trivet explains in his commentary on Boethius, was too avaricious to supply himself with necessities,[36] the Knight is too much concerned for his loss to take any care for his own needs.

When the dreamer hears the lament of the Knight, he remarks,

> Unnethe myght y lenger dwelle,
> Hyt dyde myn herte so moche woo. (712-713)

The woe of his own "heart," the rused "hart" of Christ's hunt, is almost unbearable to him. Intellectually, he strives to correct the false basis of the Black Knight's despair, asking the Knight to pity his "nature" that formed him "to creature." This request suggests that the Image of God, in which he is made, is distorted in the idolatry of the will.[37] He reminds the Knight of Socrates, who cared nothing for Fortune, just as Reason in *The Romance of the Rose* reminded the dreamer of the same example.[38] This the Knight refuses to heed.

The Black Knight blinds himself to the truth, in part by means of the simile of the chess game. The dreamer is aware of this self-deception and knows that the truth must be acknowledged plainly if the cure for sorrow is to be effective. He takes up the figure that the Black Knight has suggested, but in such a way as to indicate that he understands it figuratively. Literally, there is only one "fers"; yet the dreamer says that even if the Black Knight had lost the "ferses twelve," he would not be justified in committing suicide. Actually, since he has overheard the Black Knight's opening complaint, the dreamer knows that he is elegantly alluding to his lady in the figure of the "fers." But he knows that the plain statement of the loss must preface the acknowledgement, to paraphrase Seys, that in

> sorwe there lyth no red
> For, certes . . . [she is] but ded.

The Black Knight had said only "I have lorn my blysse." For his own purposes the dreamer accepts this statement, later saying,

> Good sir, telle me al hooly

> In what wyse, how, why, and wherfore
> That ye have thus youre blysse lore. (746-748)

By the loss of the "fers" the dreamer pretends to understand the only loss acknowledged by the Knight, the loss of his bliss.[39] The dreamer now demolishes the Black Knight's argument that the only course open to him is suicide. First of all, he shows that the amount of the loss has no bearing on the issue, for even if the Black Knight had lost not only bliss but the other fruits of the spirit as well, and had committed suicide, he would be as guilty of homicide as was Medea; for Phyllis, Dido, and Echo, who had committed suicide or died in sorrow, were like Medea, damned for the folly they had done because of earthly grief. The four women also have in common a self-deception caused by idolatry of a gift of Fortune. His last illustration is Samson:

> And for Dalida died Sampson,
> That slough hymself with a piler. (738-739)

Samson's death, however, is significantly different from the others since he did not die "for Dalida," at least in the context of the dreamer's examples. Rather he died in sorrow for his sins, obedient to God's purpose. Moreover, his death was universally taken as prefiguring Christ's sacrifice on the cross. The other suicides are wickedly idolatrous; Samson's death is one of self-sacrifice, of repentance, following God's wishes:[40]

> But ther is no man alyve her
> Wolde for a fers make this woo! (740-741)

Samson, prefiguring the Redeemer, may be said to have given his life for a "fers," the supreme act of charity, but no man may throw away his life because he has made his earthly good another human creature.

But the Black Knight does not understand why he should not lament over the loss of an earthly object, and he does not learn the lesson which the dreamer implies. Rather, he continues in his belief that the greatness of his loss is sufficient reason for his unnatural grief:

> Thou wost ful lytel what thou menest;
> I have lost more than thow wenest. (743-744)

These lines become something of a refrain for the remainder of the dialogue as the dreamer, through pretended misunderstanding, draws the Knight into a full confession. The dreamer knows that the Black Knight has lost an earthly object of surpassing worth, but the Black Knight believes that he has lost more than he actually has, for he fails to see his loss in the light of God's Providence. Acknowledging its loss and accepting it as coming from God is the end to which the will must be directed. The dreamer now asks the Black Knight the circumstances of his loss of bliss. The terms of his question are those of the confessional, suggesting that the succeeding dialogue will take the form of a confession in which the true state of the Black Knight will be revealed. Specifically, the dreamer asks two of the traditional circumstantial questions: How? and Why?[41] Before beginning his confession of love, the Black Knight has the dreamer swear to listen attentively. The swearing of the oath is humorously formal, indicative of his patient willingness to hear out the Black Knight. The Knight in being so earnestly insistent that the dreamer realize the seriousness of the situation appears from the outset a little ridiculous. He demands

> That thou shalt hooly, with al thy wyt,
> Doo thyn entent to herkene hit. (751-752)

When we remember that the Knight is simply asking the dreamer to be attentive, his pertinacious solemnity seems humorously childish, and witless. The simple reply of the dreamer, "Yis, syr," dissatisfies him. "Swere thy trouthe therto," he insists. "Gladly," replies the dreamer, but this is not enough for the Knight: "Do thanne holde therto." Patiently, the dreamer makes his formal vow:

> I shal ryght blythely, so God me save,
> Hooly, with al the wit I have,
> Here you, as wel as I kan. (755-757)

Except for one important detail the dreamer's vow recalls that which Alcyone made to Juno:

> And hooly youres becom I shal
> With goode wille, body, herte, and al. (115-116)

The contrast is that the dreamer's vow significantly involves only his wit. The roles played by the Knight and the dreamer in their dialogue seem to be those of will and wit, roles suggested not only by the contrast between the wording of the dreamer's vow and that of Alcyone, but more strongly by the Knight's self-reported vow to love, which is almost identical with that of Alcyone. He vowed to Love that he would

> hooly with good entente
> And through plesaunce become his thral
> With good wille, body, hert, and al. (766-768)

A parallel between the Knight and Alcyone is suggested, as well as their difference from the dreamer. As they are associated with the will, he is associated with the wit.

The confession begins with due solemnity, "A Goddes half." For the Black Knight, however, what ensues is not a confession but an act of self-justification for the extremity of his grief. His basic position is that the greatness of his loss excuses the greatness of his sorrow. He explains why he was susceptible to such a great loss, disclaiming in this way any responsibility. First he explains that it was "kyndely" understanding and his "owne wyt" that led him to do homage to love,

> That hyt plesance to hym were,
> And worship to my lady dere. (773-774)

However, at the time he made the vow to serve his lady, he had not met her.

> And this was longe, and many a yer,
> Or that myn herte was set owher,
> That I dide thus, and nyste why;
> I trowe hit cam me kyndely. (775-778)

The Knight seems to say that he has the will's natural propensity to love so that his service to love was in accord with nature and thus justified. What is more, he continues, offering still another explanation, his mind when he came to love was "as a whit wal or a table" (780) prepared to receive any kind of impression. Any impressions he received were not his responsibility; his thought, or wit, put love there. Since love was there first, he chose it, and since he chose it first, it has been there ever since. This happened before too much knowledge had turned his heart to malice, which stands in opposition to love. As a final explanation, he says that love came to him in early youth when man is naturally idle and when his thoughts are uncontrolled.[42]

On the surface, these hasty and inconsistent explanations, however typical of the earthly lover, are not reasonable. Considered on the level of *sentence* they involve an unwitting confession of lost innocence, but not a very good confession. The Knight's sorrow is not the sorrow of true repentance,[43] but sorrow arising directly from his error. Moreover, he disavows responsibility, thus repeating the sin of Adam in blaming Eve for his fall.[44] Specifically, he blames his wit for his own wilful irrationality in paying homage to Love as the abstract of his desire. He blames nature, saying that his tendency to earthly love came to him "kyndely." This was evidently a favorite device. A typical warning against it in a standard handbook of penance runs: "He [the penitent] should know the sin to be his own, nor should he wish to excuse himself lest he make his crime greater, as Adam did."[45] The "white table" he mentions is a symbol of innocence, so that the description of its dedication to earthly love is an unwitting description of lost innocence.[46] In youth he was governed by idleness, the sin which leads to cupidity; his works were not the works of charity, but "flyttynge"; and everything was "ylyche good" to him. He was thus exactly in the same confused condition as Alcyone or as the speaker at the beginning of the poem. It is a condition which he should long since have overcome, since the age of adolescence is one in which one subjects oneself to discipline, is informed by precept, and is ruled by counsel.[47] In short, the Knight reveals that through wilfulness he has lost his innocence in youth because he was governed by idleness.

Continuing his apologia, the Knight tells of his first encounter with his lady. He was introduced to a fair company, not by "hap or grace," but by Fortune, "false trayteresse pervers" (813). Among the ladies in the company, one was much fairer than the others, excelling them in beauty, in manner, and in every way. The Knight was caught so suddenly that he took "no maner counseyl but at hir lok" and at his own heart (840-841). Fortune, as Boethius shows, has control under God only over that which happens externally to man. It has no control over his heart unless he wills his service to Fortune by loving too much one of its gifts and thus abandoning reason. To complain of Fortune is thus irrational; it is a false way of shifting responsibility. He complains of Fortune,

> For now she worcheth me ful woo. (813)

Fortune is appointed by God as a trial to the just in prosperity and grief, leading man to turn from God either in the delights of the world or in the world's adversity. The Black Knight has succumbed to both temptations, as his complaint against Fortune reveals. In admitting that it was in answer to his plea that Love brought the lady into his thought and that he took counsel only at her look and at his heart, the Knight implies that the wit was responsible:

> That purely tho myn owne thoght
> Seyde hit were beter serve hir for noght
> Than with another to be wel. (843-845)

He irrationally shifts the blame to wit in the very act of disregarding wit. Actually, as we begin to discover, both Fortune and wit have benefitted the will, revealing to him a lady so virtuous that through her example he is led into good action. In the description that follows, we are shown how the lady leads him to virtuous love through the love of her virtues. She brings him out of his wilful childishness and governs him in his first youth. Like Dante's Beatrice, she serves as a model and guide.

As we shall see, in the description of the lady, the details are contrived so as to suggest not only the beauty of the flesh which the Knight sees, but also the true beauty of the spirit. Her beauty is like that of the sun; she surpasses others in beauty as the sun surpasses the moon or the seven stars. That is, she surpasses others as Christ surpasses the church and the saints and yields them the brightness of his own light. Rabanus gives the key to the comparison: "For the sun expresses the idea of the Savior in that just as it exceeds the other sidereal bodies, that is, the moon and the stars, in brilliance . . . so also Christ, radiant with His own virtue and needing assistance from no one, lends the radiance of virtue and wisdom to holy Church and to its saints."[48] The luminosity here suggested is also the light of charity, which is most intense in Christ. This light may radiate from the human heart throughout the whole body, producing an incomparable beauty. St. Bernard's account of this process suggests several of the features of the Black Knight's description:

"But when the splendor of that charity fills the depths of the heart more abundantly, it is necessary that it shine forth without, like a light hidden under a bushel [cf. Mark 4. 21-22, Luke 8. 16-17], or, more appropriately, like a light which shines in the darkness and does not know how to be hidden [cf. John 1. 5]. Then the body, the image of the mind, receives it shining and throwing forth its rays, and diffuses it through its members and senses, until it appears in its actions, its words, its looks, its gait, its laughter (if there is laughter) mingled with gravity and full of dignity. Then when the movements, actions, and functions of the members and senses are grave, pure, modest, free from all insolence and effrontery, foreign to both levity and listlessness, but disposed in equity and devoted to piety, the beauty of the soul will become manifest, provided that no hypocrisy lurks within it. For these things may all be simulated and may not be derived from an overflowing heart. And that this beauty of the spirit may be understood more clearly, that virtue in which we find it may perhaps be defined: it is that noble demeanor of the mind solicitous to preserve with a good conscience the integrity of reputation. Or, according to the Apostle [2 Cor. 8. 21], *we forecast what may be good not only before God, but also before men.* Blessed is the spirit which invests itself with that chaste beauty, as if with the whiteness of celestial innocence through which it achieves for itself a glorious conformity not with the world but with the Word, whence it is said that it is [Wisdom 7. 26] *the brightness* [candor] *of eternal life,* and [Heb. 1. 3] *the brightness of his glory and the figure of his substance.*"[49]

The lady's serious yet joyful demeanor, her radiance, her "whiteness," all arise from charity. The white radiance of Blanche is a reflection and a promise of the white radiance of the celestial city.

The theme of the description of the lady is set in the opening lines:

> I sawgh hyr daunce so comlily,
> Carole and synge so swetely,
> Laughe and pleye so womanly,
> And loke so debonairly,
> So goodly speke and so frendly,
> That, certes, y trowe that evermor

> Nas seyn so blysful a tresor.
> For every heer on hir hed,
> Soth to seyne, hyt was not red,
> Ne nouther yelowe, ne broun hyt nas,
> Me thoghte most lyk gold hyt was. (848-858)

These attractions serve as a summary of the lady's beauty, in act and word. The attributes of singing and dancing on the level of sense are social graces appropriately put first on the list of those things which attracted the Black Knight to the lady. If these actions are truly beautiful by medieval standards, they are performed in the worship of God, the source of all beauty.[50] Otherwise they are delusory and false. Singing, as we have suggested, is a typical expression of man's highest activity, praise of God. Beautiful dancing signifies the devotion of a generous heart manifested in good works. Her laughter and play express her spiritual joy. Her eyes, the light of the body, reveal her charitable intention, and her speech is the "goodly" and "friendly" speech of faith. These virtues are crowned by her golden hair, symbolic of the beauty of the virtues in the faithful soul.[51] In these terms the lady is a treasure which thieves may not steal nor moths corrupt, since her virtues are above Fortune. At the very opening of his description, therefore, the Knight indicates the true remedy for his own sorrow. He has been lamenting over the loss of a physical being, although the virtues which inspire his love are not subject to earthly corruption. He must realize this fact if he is to be cured. The remainder of the description, to the dreamer's first interruption, is concerned with the development of detail.

The lady's eyes, expressing the intention of her heart, are not only gentle and good; they are also "glade and sadde." Although the last two attributes seem to be contradictory, they do not appear so when one considers that the joy is the joy of charity and the seriousness is the seriousness of charitable purpose. Her eyes are also "symple," or without hypocrisy,[52] of great good, and not too wide or staring. Not as in the description of Envy in *The Romance of the Rose*, or commonly in the visual arts, with eyes looking aside, the lady Blanche looked directly, "not asyde ne overthwert," at the object of her attention, seeing it wholly and steadily. The impression of her eyes, because of the charity they expressed, was that "anon she wolde have mercy." Fools, seeing her as an object of desire, mistook this look for what in

The Romance of the Rose is called "franchise," the generosity of the submissive coquette. But the temperateness of her glance, expressive of temperance within, was completely natural. She never feigned a foolish interest in anyone, even in play. In spite of his understanding of the virtue revealed in the lady's eyes, the Knight, pledged to the God of Love, saw the mercy that fools thought they saw:

> But ever, me thoght, hir eyen seyde,
> Be God, my wrathe ys al foryive! (876-877)

Her eyes reveal the spiritual joy which illumines her so that "dulnesse was of hir adrad" (879). With spiritual wisdom, *sapientia*, she lives without dulness or *taedium* that accompanies immersion in the world.[53] The steadiness of her eyes reveals her "mesure," temperance. In temperance she follows the middle way: *medium tenuere beati*. She is familiar with none, but equal to all. Her eyes do harm, but as we have seen, only to fools who desire her carnally. These persons she does not suffer gladly, but in temperance does not chide them.[54] Those foremost in pursuing her with earthly desire were always farthest from her love:

> The formest was alway behynde. (890)

Finally, she has charity, loving her neighbors, "goode folk" who are just, above all others.[55] She loves prudently, turning her affection only to those who deserve it. To sum up, the intention of the lady's heart was the intention of charity, the source of true beauty and the opposite of the amorous desire with which the Knight first approached her.

The themes already set are carried out in the description of the lady's face, indicative of the nature of her soul.[56] The Knight speaks concerning it with more truth than he knows:

> I have no wit that kan suffise
> To comprehenden hir beaute. (902-903)

The red and white of her complexion, as applied to the soul, imply her imitation of Christ, continuously renewed in charity.[57] Among her attractions, the face is thus especially beautiful. Its radiance, which is wisdom,[58] shines for the Knight "be hyt never so derk." That is, the example of her wisdom is a beacon to him in tribulation. Her face without "a wikked sygne" symbolizes an innocent soul without spot, "sad, symple, and benygne." The beauty of the lady is thus the beauty of charity, wisdom, and innocence, virtues which for the Knight in his grief have become temporarily submerged. Her speech, sweet, friendly, and founded on reason, reveals the goodness of her soul, since in speech the spirit is attested.[59] She was true of tongue in faith and never used speech to harm others; she never flattered nor chided but always adhered to the truth.

The Knight refers briefly to the other features of the lady's body. Her neck was white and round, like the tower of ivory in Cant. 7.4. The reference indicates that she was an example to others, beautifying those around her. The whiteness of ivory, symbolizing chastity or innocence,[60] is emphasized in the lady's name:

> And goode faire White she het;
> That was my lady name ryght.
> She was bothe fair and bryght;
> She hadde not hir name wrong. (948-951)

Finally, her other physical features were harmonious with these virtues. The description of the lady's eyes was followed by an account of the spiritual truth they reveal; the description of her face by an account of the virtue of her speech. The description of her person is now followed by an account of her actions, her "play." She was like a torch of inexhaustible brightness, furnishing a perpetual example to all others.[61] From such good example every man

> Myght cacche ynogh, yif that he wolde,
> Yif he had eyen hir to beholde. (969-970)

As the chief mirror of the feast, the lady is preeminent in good example.[62] Without her, any company would be as a crown without jewels, and without her the Black Knight is without a guide.[63] The Knight concludes by comparing his lady to the Phenix. To the Christian the resurrection of the Phenix was a symbol of hope in the Resurrection.[64] In the same way the death of Blanche should be a source of hope rather than despair to the Knight. The comparison should remind him that his lady has not died, but lives.

From the physical description of his lady, the Knight turns to an account of her virtues. In this account, the qualities which have been symbolized in the preceding description are summarized, so that the passage serves as a fitting conclusion to the description. He considers first her goodness. She was as debonair as Hester, who symbolizes mercy and humility.[65] Her intellect was directed wholly toward the good, so that she was always cheerful. In action, she was innocent, harming no one, although this innocence did not spring from ignorance. She knew the evils she avoided. Next, the Knight describes her truthfulness. In truth she was so perfect

> That Trouthe hymself, over al and al
> Had chose hys maner principal
> In hir, that was his restyng place. (1003-1005)

That is, in terms of the dreamer's vision, she had prepared her Temple well. As a "maner principal" she resembled the Virgin Mary in whose imitation she lived. She was steadfast and temperate, never deviating from the truth,

> So pure suffraunt was hir wyt. (1010)

Since she was wise in truth, her goodness followed naturally, and she did well gladly. Then, too, her will was guided by her intellect so that her heart was turned toward justice. She wronged no one, and through her righteousness prevented anyone from shaming her. She was no tyrant to her admirers, since she had no desire to enslave anyone. Nor did she deceive them with suggestions and half-truths. Finally, she made no unreasonable and unnatural demands on them,

> Ne sende men into Walakye,
> To Pruyse, and into Tartarye,
> To Alysaundre, ne into Turkye,
> And byd hym faste anoon that he
> Goohoodles to the Drye Se
> And come hom by the Carrenar;
> And seye Sir, be now ryght war
> That I may of yow here seyn
> Worshyp, or that ye come ageyn.
> She ne used no such knakkes smale. (1024-1032)

She served as a good example and as a worthy object of love, but did not take it upon herself to send men on vain crusades. Overcome by his own recollection, the Knight exclaims that all his love was set on her. She was everything to him, and he was entirely hers. In view of what he has just said, it is clear that his bondage is self-imposed.

The Black Knight in his youth was blind to the true character of his lady, which his description has revealed. Because he saw Blanche only as an object of desire she was his "worldes welfare," and his "godesse." The dreamer, who has perceived the implications of the description, exclaims,

> Hardely, your love was wel besete;
> I not how ye myghte have do bet. (1043-1044)

But the Knight insists on the uniqueness which the lady has for him as the object of his desire.

> Bet? ne no wyght so wel, quod he. (1045)

The dreamer corrects him mildly, pointing out that he can think she is the fairest only because she seems so to him. The implication is that the judgment is predicated upon a false value derived from a self-centered love. But the Knight's failure to understand this implication is shown in his reply: Everyone said she was most beautiful, and his love for her was independent of his own beauty, strength, worth, wealth, bravery, or wisdom (1052-1074). It is significant that the virtues the Knight lists are worldly virtues associated with pagan exemplars: he says nothing of such virtues as humility or innocence.[66] His love, he implies, was destined; he "moste nede" love Blanche (1074). This again is an excuse for sinning. He is not responsible; destiny forced him to do what he did.[67] Realizing the foolishness of this extreme excuse, the Knight hastily amends it, and in doing so admits the truth of the matter. He loves Blanche because his heart "hyt wolde" (1077). He turned to her of his own free will, for she was as good as Penelope or as Lucrece and so overcame him with her virtue. However, the Knight does not elaborate this hasty admission of responsibility. Instead he returns to further excuses. When he first saw his lady, he was young and had much to learn. Again he holds his wit responsible:

> After my yonge childly wyt,
> Withoute drede, I besette hyt
> To love hir in my beste wyse,
> To do hir worship and the servise
> That I koude thoo, by my trouthe,
> Withoute feynynge outher slouthe. (1095-1100)

The very sight of Blanche in the morning was enough to make his whole day a happy one. She has such a firm place in his heart that he would not cease to think of her for anything. In his present despair the Knight has forgotten that the virtues of Blanche, which he revealed in his description of her, were the features of her character which actually gave rise to his happiness. With his will turned to her in frustrated longing, he can only despair. Like Alcyone, he keeps the memory of his loved one as an earthly object in his heart. He cannot see that what he loved in her is immortal and that it is only as an earthly being that she is "but ded."

The dreamer interrupts for the first time with direct reference to the Knight's desperate situation:

> Now, by my trouthe, sir! quod I,
> Me thynketh ye have such a chaunce
> As shryfte wythoute repentaunce. (1112-1114)

Or, as Skeat paraphrases it, "You are like one who confesses but does not repent." As we have said, in explaining his sorrow the Knight is actually confessing. Excuses aside, he has admitted his own responsibility. If he continues to mirror in his soul only the earthly love of his lady, his confession will be worthless and false, so that no absolution may follow to bring him peace of mind. In searching his heart, the Knight must learn to place the loss of his lady in the perspective of God's Providence. He must learn to love his lady's virtues, which endure, rather than her presence, which has gone. But the Knight still understands only the suggestion that he cease to adore his lady, and he refuses to accept the suggestion:

> Repentaunce! nay, fy! quod he,
> Shulde y now repente me

> To love? nay, certes, than were I wel
> Wers than was Achitofel,
> Or Anthenor, so have I joye,
> The traytor that betraysed Troye,
> Or the false Genelloun,
> He that purchased the tresoun
> Of Rowland and of Olyver.
> Nay, while I am alyve her,
> I nyl foryete hir never moo. (1115-1125)

The dreamer has not suggested that he forget her, but only that he repent his misdirected love which has led him to desperate grief. The Knight's assertion that he is not like Achitophel is ironic, since Achitophel represented heresy, or turning away from God,[68] and it is precisely in turning away from the Hunter that the Knight has brought himself into despair.

The dreamer, recognizing that the Black Knight merely continues in his blindness, takes up the theme of the confession, again utilizing the terminology of circumstances. Having learned "how" and "where," he wishes to know the manner of the Knight's first address to his lady, and the circumstances under which she first knew of his love. Since the virtues of the lady as the Black Knight has described them are imperishable, he has suffered no enduring spiritual loss. To imply that the loss was merely physical, the dreamer asks again what the Knight has lost. The Knight replies somewhat impatiently, almost with the identical words that he used when the dreamer pointed out that the amount of his loss did not entitle him to immoderate grief:

> Yee! seyde he, thow nost what thow menest;
> I have lost more than thou wenest. (1137-1138)

The dreamer replies, deliberately skirting the true situation, of which he is aware. He asks whether the lady does not return the Knight's love, or whether he has offended her. By stating these alternatives directly he forces the Knight ultimately to make a direct statement of his loss. Further, the two alternatives place the Knight's loss in perspective. Both are remediable. The Knight can perhaps do something to be worthy of his lady's love, or to restore himself in her grace. There would be some point in grief over a loss which might be remedied. But if the lady is dead, grief is pointless. The only action possible is to turn to God.

The Knight answers the questions about the manner and circumstances of his revelation of love to his lady. At first she knew nothing of his love, and she remained in ignorance of it for a long time. The Knight dared not tell her, for fear of angering her. She controlled him, for

> She was lady
> Of the body; she had the herte,
> And who hath that may not asterte. (1152-1155)

When a man is in such a situation he may not escape. He wished his will to be at one with hers, so that he did not wish to express a desire that was not hers. He could not deny her will any more than he could his own. On the level of the Knight's understanding, the statement is pure idolatry. Since the lady was obviously not responsible for his capture, and since, as the Knight has explained, she had no wish to enslave anyone, it is clear that he was enslaved by his own desire. The complex image involved is that of the hunt—in the false hunt of earthly love, desire itself ensnares the heart, so that perversely it escapes from the true Hunter from whom by nature it should not desire to escape. When Blanche is admired for her virtues, the love involved is charity. This love is alone eternal and thus ultimately inescapable. But in his despair the Knight's love is earthly, since he longs for her physical presence. Thus he escapes from his Physician.

In recognition of his lady's example, the Knight did attempt to abandon his former mistress, idleness (797-798). But in his blindness, he succeeded only in going from one kind of idleness to another. He spent his time making idle songs. The references to Lamech and Tubal (*sc.* Jubal) are again revealing, for Lamech's three sons and one daughter, Noema, whose name is said to mean "voluptas," complete the generation of Cain which is figuratively the generation of the wicked.[69] Tubalcain wrought images in metal, and the sound of his labors at the anvil was thought to have inspired his brother Jubal, or Tubal as he was frequently called, to invent the art of music.[70] If the Knight's melodies were like Tubal's they were in all likelihood not derived from the melody which is said in *The Parliament of Fowls* (60 ff.) to come from the "speres thryes thre" but were instead harmonious with the melodies of Venus or amorous pleasure. The Knight's first song, which he quotes, has only one significant detail: the lady is "semly on to see." At this point he sees only the external beauty of the lady.

One day the Knight thought of his sorrow and of the dilemma in which he found himself:

> Allas, thoghte I, y kan no red;
> And but I telle hir, I nam but ded;
> And yif I telle hyr, to seye ryght soth,
> I am adred she wol be wroth.
> Allas! what shal I thanne do? (1187-1191)

This rather foolish dilemma ironically reflects that of the Knight after he has lost his lady. The alternatives are absurd. Unless he tells her, he is "but ded"; yet he is afraid to tell her. In his present plight, unless he finds her, he is "but ded"; yet he cannot find her in any physical sense. Thus, he rightly says he knows "no red." The solution to the dilemma in both instances is obvious: he must speak out, facing the truth as it is. The Knight now describes the woe he suffered because of this "debat." Finally, he remembers that Nature is not deceiving, so that a lady as beautiful as Blanche must also be merciful. But he is asking for a wrongful mercy which in fact signifies surrender to desire. For this reason he speaks in worldly shame and distress of spirit, making a most ludicrous figure of himself:

> Bowynge to hir, I heng the hed;
> I durste nat ones loke hir on,
> For wit, maner, and al was goon.
> I seyde "mercy!" and no more.
> Hyt nas no game, hyt sat me sore. (1216-1220)

His "wit" was indeed gone. After this false beginning, the Knight found that his "hert was come ageyn." He has just said that "she had the herte," so that it becomes obvious that in order to speak to her, he has to get it back. Then with "hool herte" he beseeches and swears and "hertely" promises

> Ever to be stedfast and trewe
> And love her alwey fresshly newe. (1227-1228)

His heart is now within him, yet he calls his lady his "herte swete." The empty word-play on *heart* emphasizes the inherent fatuousness of his love. Although his conduct gives little promise of steadfastness, he swears it none the less. The Knight swears, moreover, that he will never be false to his lady unless he dreams, but he dreams amorously at the very moment he swears. Although he has indicated the lady's dislike of enslaving her admirers, he says to her,

> For youres is alle that ever ther ys
> For evermore, myn herte swete! (1232-1233)

She recognizes him as one hurt by her look, of whom "she ne roughte a stree" (887). The lady, whose wisdom has been attested, answers him in some detail, but he has forgotten the details because his wit was gone, and he could not comprehend them. He knew only enough to understand that "she sayde 'nay.'" At this, the Knight was thrown into sorrowful despair. "For pure fere" he "stal away," and for many a day he suffered in sorrow in his bed. In his present despair over the loss of his lady he has come full circle back to sorrow.

However, in his sorrow over his rejection by the lady, he did not abandon himself completely to despair. In another year, evidently after time for meditation on the lady's virtue and a recognition that the steadfastness of his love was more than mere desire, the Knight recovered from his callow wilfulness. There was a marked change in the heart which he wished to disclose to her. The foolish vows had disappeared, and the lady understood

> That I ne wilned thyng but god,
> And worship, and to kepe her name
> Over alle thyng, and drede hir shame,
> And was so besy hyr to serve;
> And pitee were I shulde sterve,
> Syth that I wilned noon harm, ywis. (1262-1267)

The reason for this change of heart is not made explicit, but it is clear from the earlier description of the lady. In his enforced separation from her, when the desires of the flesh have been refused, he has learned to love her for her virtue; he has come to a realization of the nature of true love; he is no longer moved by simple natural desire, but has made a rational selection of an object worthy of love.[71] This temporary earthly separation with its beneficent results could serve as a model of the greater separation of her death. As the former served to teach him the lesson of true love, so the separation occasioned by death should bring his heart to a realization of the ultimate love of which true love is but a mirror, the love of God. In being apart from her he learned to love what was true and everlasting in her. In the separation of death, the lesson should be made even clearer. Instead of his earlier foolishness, the Knight wished now to defend the lady's name, to keep her from shame, and to serve her. The relationship he desired was not physical worship but spiritual direction. He wished her to become his spiritual overlord. Seeing that he meant no harm, the lady granted his wish, allowing him to serve her. The ring she gave him is a token of faith to her and to the virtues she represents, an investiture which grants him the advantage of her company in return for faithful good works.[72] To his joy, the lady took him "in her governaunce," directing his youthful waywardness. He learned to share her joys and her sorrows without strife. And thus he lived guided by her virtue "ful many a yere." The example of the lady brought him from a state of childishness to a condition reflecting her own virtues.

The Knight has reached the point where the consolation open to him is clear from the context of what he himself has said. The dreamer has brought him to admit that his love for his fair White was a love for her virtues. If that is true, it follows that her death, although it is grievous, is not a cause for despair. The virtues of the lady have not died with her. The grief the poet feels in his heart is sufficiently great so that it is not easily to be assuaged, but its nature has been exposed to the intellect. He has lost nothing in comparison to that which still lives in his memory, the example of the virtue of the lady. His true love for her has been a medicine for his foolish youth. She was his physician under Christ while she was alive. In death her memory should lead him to seek the true Physician:

> Pon giú il seme del piangere, e ascolta:
> sì udirai come in contraria parte
> mover dovieti mia carne sepolta. (*Purg.*, 31, 46-48)

His dream began in the time of the promise of the Resurrection. The Hunter Octovyen and his hunt also afford the promise that Blanche is dead only in the body. To remind the Knight of these things, and to force him to speak plainly, the dreamer asks, "Sir, where is she now?" The Knight has already eliminated the alternative possibilities suggested in the dreamer's earlier question; the lady did not refuse him, and he did not offend her. They lived together in peace and harmony. Only one further possibility remains, but even now the Knight cannot quite make the direct statement. He says simply what he is forced to say:

> Allas, that I was bore!
> That was the los that her-before
> I tolde the that I hadde lorn.
> Bethenke how I seyde here-beforn,
> Thow wost ful lytel what thow menest;
> I have lost more than thow wenest—
> God wot, allas! ryght that was she! (1301-1307)

The meaning is unmistakable, but the dreamer persists and the Knight speaks the truth, simply, without equivocation,

> She ys ded!

The dreamer attempts no consolation,

> Is that youre los? Be God, hyt ys routhe! (1310)

The loss is a pity; that is all. The natural grief of affection is inevitable, but it is not a cause for despair. And the grief itself should vanish in time before the memory of a lady as good and virtuous as was Blanche. The important thing is to face the truth rationally in the promise of Christian comfort. In Blanche the speaker had found a guide to his Physician. In his memory, even though she has died, she remains his guide. Just as her first refusal brought him to reject false love, so her death, after a temporary lapse, should bring him even closer to his Physician.[73]

In the Seys and Alcyone story, Seys says to Alcyone in her vision:

> My swete wyf,
> Awake! let be your sorwful lyf!

For in your sorwe there lyth no red.
For, certes, swete, I nam but ded;
Ye shul me never on lyve yse.
But, goode swete herte, that ye
Bury my body, for such a tyde
Ye mowe hyt fynde the see besyde;
And farwel, swete, my worldes blysse!
I praye God youre sorwe lysse.
To lytel while oure blysse lasteth! (201-211)

Alcyone refused to recognize the implications of the statement, "I nam but ded." Immersed in her sorrow, she could not accept the idea of death, so that there was no remedy for her. When she looked up, she "saw noght." The speaker in the poem, through contemplation, has acquired intellectual instruction which enables him to see more than Alcyone saw. He has looked within himself for the image of God there, in search of his Physician. He has been reminded of the Resurrection of Christ in token of man's salvation, of the joy of the faithful in praising God, of the emptiness of false desire which leads to despair, and of the lightening of man's search by the hunt of Octovyen. Moreover, in his memory of Blanche he has seen not only her physical beauty but her virtue as well. And he has learned the nature of true love which is a step toward the Physician. In short, he has been prepared to make the admission which Alcyone refused to make.

Thus, with the simple admission that the lady has died, the search for the hart has come to an end. The rest remains simply in the healing hands of time if the bereaved turns to Christ, his Hunter:

And with that word ryght anon
They gan to strake forth; al was doon,
For that tyme, the hert-huntyng. (1311-1313)

The symbolic hunt ends. Significantly, the dreamer and the Knight see the King, Octovyen, returning home to his long castle with white walls on a rich hill. The punning reference to Lancaster and to Richmond is only a small part of what is here implied:

With that me thoghte that this kyng
Gan homwardes for to ryde

> Unto a place, was there besyde,
> Which was from us but a lyte.
> A long castel with walles white,
> Be seynt Johan! on a ryche hil. (1314-1319)

The King is returning to his Heavenly Home, the white City of Jerusalem, on the rich hill of Sion, which Saint John described. Through the dialogue with grief, his alter ego, the dreamer, who is the poet's rational self, has turned toward his true Physician. He watches the Savior return to His home. The action which he observes symbolizes the Ascension, with its promise of the Resurrection of the just. The references to Lancaster and to Richmond, fixing at this point the historical allusion to Blanche, the Duchess of Lancaster, suggest that Blanche is among the just, and that the speaker must turn to her in memory not as an earthly figure but as a follower of Christ in the New Jerusalem. In the manner of Dante's Beatrice or Petrarch's Laura she is now at one with the Physician. As he sees the vision of Christ returning to the Heavenly City, the castle bell tolls twelve, the vesper hour which signifies the time of reward for the just in the heavenly kingdom. The sound is a promise of comfort in loss and of hope of future joy. Moreover, it brings the dream to a rounded conclusion, since the dream itself began in the "dawenynge." That is, it began at Lauds when Christ is praised for His light. There are twelve hours in the day, which is Christ, the day which begins with Lauds, the promise of the Resurrection, and ends with Vespers, the promise of the reward of the just.[74] The dream itself, which is concerned with Christ's hunt, is thus in its true structure a symbol of the Physician the poet seeks. Through it he finds the approach to the Physician he had lost at the beginning. The one physician who was his lady and the one Physician who can cure him are now united. The poet has found them both.

The poet wakes at the sound of the Vesper bells of his dream:

> Therwyth I awook myselve. (1324)

He finds himself with the book in his hand

> Of Alcione and Seys the kyng,
> And of the goddes of slepyng. (1327-1328)

Since he is now in a position, through illumination, to understand the
sentence of the story, the reference to the Seys and Alcyone story at
this point is not irrelevant. Alcyone did not heed Seys' warning,
"Awake!" but continued in spiritual torpor. But through his
contemplative vision the speaker has awakened himself from slumber.
The story provided the key to his own release from sorrow when he
consulted "the goddes of slepyng" within himself. Having recovered
from despair and inaction, he determined "to put this sweven in ryme."
At the beginning of the poem, he was alienated from his
Physician—"but that is don" (40). Now his problem has been solved:
"now hit is doon" (1334).

The progression here outlined finds a clear parallel in the progress
of Dante's love for Beatrice as pictured in the *Vita Nuova*. As Professor
C.S. Singleton has shown, Dante first moved from earthly love to a
love of Beatrice's virtues, then to a love of God through the inspiration
of Beatrice. The stages are identified by Singleton with the three
degrees of spiritual ascent: "This itinerary of the mind to God, as
Augustine had conceived it, began, at its first level, outside of man. It
turned *inward* at its second level or degree. And in its third and last
stage, it rose above man. St. Bonaventura, in Dante's own century, is
still tracing much the same pattern. In his *Itinerarium mentis in Deum*
the stages, as with Augustine, bear the names of *extra nos, intra nos,*
and *supra nos*."[75] Like Dante, the Black Knight first looked outside of
himself at Blanche's physical attractions. Being repulsed, he turned to
his memory to learn the love of Blanche's virtues. Finally, like Dante,
after the death of Blanche, he looks above toward the Physician whose
creature Blanche is.

In *The Book of the Duchess* Chaucer celebrated the virtues of a
great feudal lady with whom he was connected, either directly or
indirectly. Specifically, he wrote an elegy extolling the virtues of the
deceased lady, portraying the grief of the bereaved, and offering
consolation. The great danger of the elegy as a type is that it becomes
too complimentary for belief, or becomes trite beyond endurance,
stating the timeworn obvious truths which are too general to be
specifically consoling, or becomes a statement of truths which have
only casual connection with the avowed elegiac purpose. In *The Book
of the Duchess*, through deft use of the allegorical method with its
demand that the readers or hearers heed the *sentence*, Chaucer has
managed to convey a sense of personal grief over the loss of a virtuous

woman and at the same time to present the great consoling truths of the Christian faith in such a way as to make them fresh and new. Above all, the poem is a graceful tribute to one of the most widely admired ladies of the English court. It is an achievement in its kind almost without parallel in English literature. However much one may be willing to admit of oversubtlety in this poem, it is difficult, once one has grasped what Chaucer is saying, to continue to patronize the book for the "something of his vivid imagination" which lies in "this relatively crude work." It is a work of imagination making fresh, vigorous use of traditional symbol and truth. Its structural excellence is attested in its subtle use of repetition and in the use, for example, of the illustrative story of Seys and Alcyone as a counter-theme to the main theme of Christian consolation. The poem is thoroughly coherent. Once the symbolic context is established, the rest unfolds clearly. The problem, especially for the modern reader, is to find the one key. This found, the understanding of the poem ceases to be an exercise in ingenuity and becomes a stimulating discovery of new relationships and unexpected correspondences, of the clear and inevitable unfolding of the truths of Christian consolation.

The opening lines present the key to the poem by means of an ambiguity which, when resolved, leads to only one conclusion. The speaker is distracted to a degree that death seems a likely outcome of his grief. The portrait points on the one hand to a distracted lover, but in the figure of the one Physician who can cure the eight years' malady, the truth is shown. The speaker is one who is lost in the cares of the world. At the same time the nature of these cares is indicated by the suggestion of the lover's malady. The griefs are those of a bereaved lover who knows though darkly that his comfort cannot ultimately come from his lady. Since the circumstances of the poem were clear to Chaucer's audience, the tenor of this portrait was also clear. The speaker is suffering from his grief caused by the death of the Duchess. He is lost in worldly cares since she is gone, as was Dante after the death of Beatrice:

> Piangendo dissi: "Le presenti cosi
> col falso lor piacer volser miei passi
> tosto che gl vostro viso si nascose." (*Purg.*, 31, 34-36)

He must learn that the physician who was his lady derived her curative powers from the Physician. Although the beginning of the poem seems to be chiefly concerned with the sorrow of the poet, the heart of the poem is the description of the lady. This difference between the parts of the poem, when the structure of the whole is realized, is not the result of patchwork, but of subtle craftsmanship. In the introduction a climate of belief for the eulogistic portrait is prepared through the picture of a grief which almost transcends consolation.

The desperation of the poet leads him to one of the comforts of physical sleeplessness, reading, and his reacting to a story of one whose grief refused consolation. Although her grief was for an object of infinitely less intrinsic worth than Blanche, it was to a certain extent more justified than was the poet's. Unlike Blanche, Seys did not provide a perfect example. Alcyone's despair led to the supreme folly of self-destruction over the loss of an earthly joy. Although Alcyone did not succeed in overcoming her grief, her story does suggest the proper mode of Christian conduct. The poet has an inkling of the true meaning of the tale.

The Seys and Alcyone story has significance not only as a skillful introduction to the ensuing sleep and as a foreshadowing of the theme, but also as an indication of the process by which the grieving heart may find peace. The perception of this meaning brings a kind of gaiety to the speaker, who, in spite of the heaviness of his heart, joyfully vows gifts to the "goddes of slep," for him symbolizing the faculties which give contemplative understanding. But, as in effective penance, the speaker must have the intention of effective action. His vow symbolically affords the promise that he will aspire to God. If he is granted understanding, he will effectively act to implement this understanding. The sleep and the dream ensue after a mock-serious warning that even Joseph would be nonplussed to interpret the vision.

Skillfully contrived as to atmosphere, the dream opens with several definite symbolic indications of its purport. The room of the mind where the dreamer awakes suggests contemplation. To the ears of his mind are given the sounds of the praise of God and to its awakened eyes are shown pictures illuminated with Truth. The intellect of the speaker awakens in faith at the symbolic season of the Resurrection. He hears the horn of hope sounding the call of the hunt of Christ and His Church for the human soul. Taking his horse in preparation for spiritual battle, he encounters the hunt of Octovyen, Christ coming for the salvation of man. But the hart escapes from the effort to take the heart by strength. That is, the will of the speaker is too overwhelmed to accept at once the formal consolation of the Church. It is necessary that the hunt be pursued within the mind of the speaker, that his will be made to recognize the truth, accepting the truth for itself. The little dog, perhaps symbolic of the elucidation of the hidden cares of the human soul through example, leads the dreamer to the place of worldly concern where his will has escaped. His wilful grief is epitomized in the Black Knight, who is found leaning against the tree of despair. Through the course of a patient questioning, the dreamer brings the Knight to reveal the true nature of his grief. In doing this he reveals the spiritual grace of Blanche and demonstrates how she effectively cured him of his youthful idleness and led him into the paths of virtue.

The poet in the person of the dreamer receives a reminder of the significant facts of the faith: the Resurrection, the Resurrection of the just, the necessity to praise God, the necessity to look toward the light of charity, and the necessity to seek Christ the Hunter. Only in the light of faith may the true virtue of Blanche be seen and the implications of her death be appreciated.

Thus instructed, the dreamer is led to regard his own despairing will objectively. The condition of the Knight is unworthy of Blanche's memory. As a woman pre-eminent in virtue, she would have been shamed to be the cause of an unrighteous sorrow. For this reason, the grief of the Knight is treated with some humor. He is at times amusingly obstinate, but by means of a skillful interrogation he is led from a desperate attack on Fortune to the recollection of Blanche's real virtue. The portrait of the lady is itself motivated by the desire of the will to excuse itself for its temporal grief. But with this spiritual portrait as a background, we can understand his account of his own transformation under her influence from youthful cupidity to true *amicitia*. Again, with the virtues of the lady and the character of the Knight's actual love assumed, the implications of his final confession—"she is dead"—became clear. In this simple statement Chaucer achieves an extraordinary resolution of apparently conflicting elements: an appreciation of the beauty of the lady, and thus of the greatness of her loss, along with the understanding that her death was not cause for grief but for a resolution to take comfort and joy in her memory. The memory of Blanche can be revered only by turning to the Physician, the source of her virtues and exemplar of the kind of love

she encouraged. The poet recovers and finds the true memory of
Blanche as he sees the Redeemer returning at the vesper hour of Hope
to the Heavenly Jerusalem. Blanche is dead, but in the image of
Christ's Ascension rests the complementary truth that she has not died
in the spirit. The dreamer awakes with the determination to set forth his
vision, no longer so distraught as to be incapable of poetic activity.
Even the conclusion, for all its apparent haste, contains an externally
gracious compliment. The writing of the poem hinges on the poet's
discovery that Blanche the Duchess remains even in death a source of
inspiration.

Structurally, the dream operates on three symbolic time sequences.
With reference to the Black Knight it covers the period from his early
youth to maturity, a development from waywardness to responsibility.
The shadow of his loss of Blanche has reduced the poet to, the first of
these states, but in the course of the poem he regains the latter. With
reference to the ecclesiastical year, the dream develops from the period
immediately following Easter to the Ascension. That is, it begins with a
theme of promise, *mors Christi qua vivimus*, and ends with fulfillment.
In terms of the liturgical day, there is a parallel sequence from the first
hour of the day to the last, from Lauds to Vespers, from praise to final
reward. Within this triple framework the dream develops through the
reactions of the Black Knight as seen by the dreamer. At the outset, the
Knight's situation is almost an echo of the poet's situation at the
beginning of the poem, except that we are enabled through the dream to
evaluate his condition in the light of Christian truth. The portrait of the
lady, the central portion of the poem, serves not only its obvious
function of praise, but reveals the relationship between the lady and the
Physician. The beauty of the "goode faire White" springs from the
same light which the dreamer saw through his windows in the dawn.
Her whiteness sets off in contrast the blackness of the Knight's sorrow.
The process of the love affair reinforces the parallel between Blanche
and the Hunter. Through her radiance she attracts men to the truth,
hunts them for God. When the Black Knight, in misdirected desire for
her physical beauty, "ruses" in desire, he is lost in the temporary
despair which follows his repulse. When he looks for Blanche in his
own heart and comes to see her in her true light, he finds his heart and
wins the lady.

Finally, the Knight's realization of the actual nature of his love
makes any added moralizing after his last confession unnecessary. In

general, the technique of the poem is one in which certain truths are revealed first, and then events are described in the light of these truths. The implications, after due warning, are left to the reader or listener. Since the poem develops on the level of these implications, the ending is abrupt only on the surface. The implications which arise from what has been said in the body of the poem are more powerful than any direct statement of them could be. *The Book of the Duchess,* like all significant poetry, exists only partly in what it says. Its reality is a series of controlled developments touched off in the mind of the reader.

NOTES

1. In *The Harrowing of Hell,* 247, "mased" is an alliterative synonym of "madde."

2. Ed. Scheler, lines 1-12.

3. Acts 9.33-34. For the interpretation, see Bede, *PL,* 92, 965: "Aeneas iste genus significat humanum, infirmorum prius delectatione languescens, sed apostolorum opere et ore sanatum. Quia etenim mundus ipse quatuor plagis sublimatur, et cursus saeculi annuis quatuor temporibus variatur, quicunque praesentia labentiaque gaudia complectitur, quasi bis quaternario annorum numero, grabato sternitur enervis. Grabatum quippe est ipse segnities, ubi requiescit animus aeger et infirmus, id est, in voluptate corporis et omni delectatione saeculari. *Aenea, sanet te Dominus Jesus Christus. Surge et sterne tibi.* Quem de paralypsi curaverat, mox surgere et sternere sibi praecepit, spiritualiter insinuans ut quisque fidei solidamentum in corde perceperit, non solum torporem, in quo fessus jacuerat, discutiat, sed etiam bona opera, in quibus requiescere valeat, paret." This explanation is repeated in the *Glossa ordinaria, PL,* 114, 449. The figure of Christ the Physician is sufficiently commonplace. The number "eight" frequently suggests Christ, who brings about a cure for the languor described by Bede. See Isidore, *Liber numerorum, PL,* 83,189; or Bede, *Hexameron, PL,* 91, 149 and 162. For the idea that the sorrow of the *persona* at the opening of the poem is sorrow for Blanche, and not for some conjectural lost mistress, see Marshall W. Stearns, "A Note on Chaucer's Attitude Toward Love," *Speculum,* XVII (1942), pp. 570-574. R.S. Loomis, *MLN,* LIX (1944), pp. 178-180, thinks that Chaucer was simply being

conventional. Chaucer had probably read Henry of Lancaster's *Livre de Seyntz Medicines* and was thus thoroughly aware of the Scriptural connotations of figures like "malady," "physician," and so on.

4. *Quies vitae* is one of the standard allegorical meanings of sleep." E.g., see *Allegoriae in sacram scripturam, PL*, 112, 913. The fact that "sleep" has a number of other meanings equally commonplace need not be disturbing, since they do not fit the context of our poem. To indulge for a moment in an analogy, the fact that a word may have various meanings does not imply that it is useless for poetic purposes. The meaning intended is usually clear from the context. On the source of true rest, see St. Augustine, *De catechizandis radibus*, 16: "Nam et in hac vita homines magnis laborious requiem quaerunt et securitatem, sed pravis cupiditatibus non inveniunt. Volunt enim requiescere in rebus inquietis et non permanentibus; et quia illae tempore subtrahuntur et transeunt, timoribus et doloribus eos agitant, nec quietos esse permittunt." This is, of course, one of the lessons of Boethius in the *De consolatione*. The poet or speaker at the beginning of Chaucer's poem has been disturbed by a temporal loss.

5. See Chaucer's *Parson's Tale*, p. 297: "Now comth wanhope, that is despeir of the mercy of God, that comth somtyme of to muche outrageous sorwe. . . ."

6. *De div. nat., PL*, 122, 954. Hell involves the ultimate "despeir of the mercy of God."

7. Alanus, *Distinctiones, PL*, 210, 1002. Chaucer's version of the story should be contrasted with the original, where Ceyx says (*Met.* 11.669), "da lacrimas lugubriaque indue." In effect, the sense of the original is reversed.

8. *Epistolae*, ed. Hilberg (Vienna, 1910), Pars I, 301. See also Hugh of St. Victor, *PL*, 177, 495.

9. Cf. Chaucer's *Parson's Tale*, line 859: "Certes, be it wyf, be it child, or any worldly thyng that he loveth biforn God, it is his maumet, and he is an ydolastre."

10. On "phantasies," see St. Augustine, *Epistolae*, 7, to Nebridius. The most widely known interpretation of the story of Ceyx during Chaucer's maturity was probably that which appears in Holkot's commentary on Wisdom. W.A. Pantin, *The English Church in the Fourteenth Century* (Cambridge, 1955), p. 145, says, "Holkot on Wisdom was one of the best-sellers of the age, the sort of book you would be sure to find in every respectable late medieval library." The remarks on this story were incorporated by Berchorius in his

commentary on the *Metamorphoses*, with a reference to their source. Following Ovid's account in *Met.* 11.633 ff., Holkot explains, In librum *sapientiae* (Basel, 1586), pp. 632- 634, that there are three dream messengers: Morpheus, Icelos, and Phantasos. Morpheus appears to the dreamer in human form with human speech and gesture. Icelos assumes the shapes of beasts and birds, and Phantasos appears in the forms of inanimate objects. All three represent types of worldly solicitude. Chaucer's Alcyone is obviously suffering from solicitude of this kind over the loss of what is to her a gift of Fortune in human form, and it is clear that her dream originates within herself. On the other hand, it was widely held in the fourteenth century, even by such authorities as Bradwardine, that the substance of dreams frequently incorporates divine warnings. In Chaucer's poem, the dream results from solicitude, but the message it contains may be thought of as Providential, even though Alcyone is unable to understand it.

11. For this variety of "sleep" as distinguished from that referred to above in note 4, see Rom. 13.11-13, 1 Cor. 15-34, Eph. 5-14, 1 Thess. 5.4-8. The awakening here urged is sometimes celebrated in the medieval *aube*.

12. For the streams see the *Ovide moralisé*, 10.258-269.

13. The meaning of the bed is fairly obvious. However, see, for example, Rabanus, *De universo*, *PL*, 111, 79; Peter Lombard on Ps. 6.6, *PL*, 191, 107. For feathers, see Alanus, *Distinctiones*, *PL*, 210, 897. Although gold is usually associated with wisdom, it may also suggest contemplation; see *ibid.*, 714. The black cover probably suggests outward tribulation or penance. See *Allegoriae*, *PL*, 112, 1006. Cf. the epithet "Black Prince" adopted by Edward of Woodstock. For pillows, see Bede on Mark 4.38, *PL*, 92, 174. These references do not imply that Chaucer had specific Scriptural verses in mind as sources for the details. Rather, the context of the details is so arranged as to suggest certain commonplace associations.

14. See Bede, *De templo Salomonis liber*, *PL*, 91, 757-758. For the gold, see col. 752, and tapestry, col. 770.

15. *PL*, 210, 843.

16. *Ibid.*, 770.

17. *Ibid.*, 1009. Cf. St. Ambrose, *Hexameron*, *PL*, 14, 237-238; Gregory, *Moralia*, *PL*, 76, 97. It may be significant that in Bede's account of the Temple of Solomon, *PL*, 91, 751, the roof is made up of *tabulata* on three levels where the three types of faithful in the Church sing in praise of God.

18. For Chaucer's attitude toward the meaning of the *Roman*, see *LGW*, Prologue (G) 458ff. His use of the poem suggests that his

attitude toward it must have resembled that taken later by Pierre Col, rather than that taken by Christine de Pisan and Jean Gerson. Cf. D.W. Robertson, Jr., *A Preface to Chaucer* (Princeton, 1962), pp. 91-104.

19. Cf. *PL*, 177, 702.

20. This inconsequence has been noted, and in one case has seemed sufficiently inexplicable to warrant an unsupported emendation of the text. See Robinson's notes on lines 357-358 and 368.

21. See Ps. 41.1 and Lombard, *PL*, 191, 415-416. The idea is taken up in Bede's *Soliloquium*, *AH*, 50.114-115. Cf. 3 Kings 4.23, and Rabanus, *PL*, 109, 131. The idea is reflected in *The Besitary of Guillaume le Clerc*, trans., G.C. Druce (Ashford, Kent, 1936), 11. 2815-2816. See also *Gesta romanorum*, *EETS*, LXIX, p. 320.

22. On "eight," see Rabanus, *De universo*, *PL*, 111, 491 ; Bede, *De templo Salomonis*, *PL*, 91, 806; Gregory, *PL*, 76, 1341, 1391; Lombard, introduction to Ps. 6, *PL*, 191, 103. Cf. the meaning of the octave in St. Augustine, *De trinitate*, 4.3, and, for some notion of the pervasiveness of the idea, Richard Krautheimer, "Introduction to an 'Iconography of Mediaeval Architecture.'" *JWCI*, V (1942), p. 11. The Resurrection was celebrated on the eighth day (Sunday), and late medieval baptismal fonts commonly had eight sides to suggest the resurrection of the baptized Christian with Christ. See Berchorius, *Reductorium morale*, Book XIII, xxviii, "octonarius signat beatitudinem et tempus future resurrectionis." Cf. Robertson, *Preface*, pp. 122-124.

23. For the horse and horn see Alanus, *Distinctiones*, *PL*, 210, 780 and 949.

24. Berchorius, Reductorium morale, II, xiii. Berchorius cites Chaucer's "daun Constantyn." He equates the beard with virtue, and states that three types of persons are lacking in beards, women, *castrati* and boys, types of the effeminate, those cut off from virtue, and the ignorant. See also Alanus, *PL*, 210, 826.

25. If other precedents are wanted in addition to the *D e consolatione* for the kind of inner dialogue suggested here, cf. St. Augustine's *Soliloquium*, Dante's *Vita nuova*, or Petrarch's *Secretum*.

26. That the whelp "koude no good" (390) suggests in context his wordless, humble role of teaching by example rather than by preaching. Further, the hart is symbolically complex. The "defaute" (389) of the hunters does not represent their inability but the lost state of the mourner. The whelp, too, may reflect this state.

27. See above, note 3.

28. One of the traditional meanings of *semita* is *cogitatio*. See Alanus, *Distinctiones*, *PL*, 210, 940. The "privy" way suggests solitude

which, *ibid.*, 948, may represent "separatio ab Ecclesia." Cf. *Gregorianum, PL,* 193, 269-270.

29. The scenery in general resembles that of the garden of Deduit in the *Roman de la rose.* For the blackness of the knight and the oak, see *Allegoriae, PL,* 112, 1006, 1036. Cf . the oak under which Delyt stands alone in *The Parliament of Fowls,* discussed below, Ch. III.

30. Gregory, *Moralia, PL,* 76, 618, 1079.

31. On adolescence, see above, Ch. 1, note 19.

32. A "song without song" is probably one that does not reflect celestial harmony. Cf. Ch. III, note 5, below.

33. John 11.9. Cf. Bruno Astensis, *PL,* 165, 541-542: "Si quis autem hunc diem sequatur, si quis in eo ambulaverit, si quis mihi crediderit, non offendet. Cur? *Quia lucem huius mundi videt. Ego sum lux mundi. Si vero in nocte ambulaverit,* si errorem et tenebrarum principem secutus fuerit (hoc est enim in nocte ambulare), offendet et cadet. Cur? *Quia lux non est in eo."*

34. G.H. Bode, *Scriptores rerum mythicarum* (Cellis, 1834), p. 177. This work, attributed variously to Alexander Neckam and Albericus of London, was extremely popular. Petrarch had a copy made for his library.

35. See Boethius, *De cons.,* 2, Pr. 1.

36. London, British Museum MS Burney 131, fol. 49 verso.

37. See our *"Piers Plowman" and Scriptural Tradition* (Princeton, 1951), pp. 107-109.

38. *RR,* 5847-5856. It is significant that Reason in the *Roman* and the dreamer in Chaucer's poem play very similar parts. The lines are from the same discourse on Fortune which suggested the figure of the chess game.

39. Note that "bliss" may have a double meaning: the Knight's false view of it, and the true. Peter Lombard, *PL,* 192, 160, explains *gaudium* as "puritas conscientiae et elatio animi super his quae digna sunt exsultationis." According to Alanus, *PL,* 210, 138-139, *gaudium* frees the mind of care. It is like the garden of Paradise and is a sure protection against the whims of Fortune. Again, it is like the Temple of Solomon.

40. For Samson as a figure of Christ, see *Glossa ordinaria, PL,* 113, 532. The idea is, of course, a commonplace in medieval art.

41. For the "circumstances," see *Parson's Tale,* pp. 309-310. For Chaucer's use of confession as a symbolic device in a secular poem, W.A. Pantin's comment on Gower's *Confessio amantis* is to the point, *op.cit.,* p. 227: "Here we have in fact an elegant, moral parody of the contemporary treatises on confession. At first sign it sounds like a piece

of profanity, but it is simply an example of the medieval love of allegory; men were as ready to make moral allegory out of the technique of confession as they were to make a moral allegory out of Noah's Ark or Ovid's *Metamorphoses.*"

42. On *pueritia,* see above, Ch. I, note 19.

43. On true contrition, see *Parson's Tale,* p. 310.

44. Cf. St. Augustine, Sermo xx, *PL,* 38, 139.

45. *De vera et falsa poenitentia, PL,* 40, 1126.

46. The table, like most of the other details in this passage, is from Machaut's *Remede de Fortune.* Lines 2.6-28 (ed. Hoeppfner) read, "Car le droit estat d'innocence / Ressamble proprement la table / Blanche. . . ." Innocence is necessary for a place in the New Jerusalem.

47. See above, Ch. 1, note 19.

48. De *universo, PL,* 111, 268.

49. *Sermones in cantica, PL,* 183, 1193, or *Opera* (Rome, 1957 ff.), II, pp. 314-315. Cf. E. de Bruyne, *Etudes d'esthétique médiévale* (Bruges, 1946), I, p. 9.

50. Cf. Peter of Blois, *De amicitia Christiana,* ed. Davy (Paris, 1932), p. 146.

51. For singing, see Gregory, *Hom. in Ezech., PL,* 76, 885, or *Allegoriae, PL,* 112, 887. The significance of dancing is explained by Bede on Luke 7.32, *P L,* 92, 422, and by St. Bonaventura, *Opera* (Quaracchi, 1895), VII, p. 181. Singing and dancing are popular themes in fourteenth-century art. For an example, see the Bohun Psalter in the Nationalbibliothek at Vienna (Cod. 1826*), fol. 85 verso, where Moses and his followers sing and dance after crossing the Red Sea. Cf. Robertson, *Preface,* pp. 130-132, and Fig. 37. On laughter, see *Allegoriae, PL,* 112, 1040 or Alanus, *Anticlaudianus, PL,* 210, 551. Rabanus explains, *De universo, PL,* 111, 149, that the eyes indicate the intention of the heart. For the hair, see *ibid.,* 145. The details in the description show no indication of being "realistic" reflections of the appearance and demeanor of the Duchess of Lancaster. They are, rather, conventional figurative devices designed to indicate her character.

52. Cf. Gilbert de Hoyland, *Sermones in Canticum, PL,* 184, 114-115: "Prudenter quidem, quoniam si simplex oculus fuerit, totum corpus lucidum erit. . . . Bona enim est oculata simplicitas, ita simulationem excludens, ut non caliget in veritate."

53. See Wisdom 2.1, 8.16, 11-13.

54. Cf. Alanus, *Summa de arte praedicatoria, PL,* 210, 161.

55. For the meaning of these "good folk," see Alanus, *Distinctiones,* PL, 210, 913.

56. Cf. Rabanus, *De universo, PL*, 111, 147: "Vultus autem animorum qualitatem significat."

57. Cf. Gilbert de Hoyland, *Sermones in Canticum, PL*, 184, 252: "Si sponsa es, aemulare misturam gemini coloris hujus a sponso tuo, ut similiter candida et rubicunda sis, id est sincera et succensa."

58. Cf. Eccl. 8.1.

59. Cf. Alanus, *Summa de arte praedicatoria, PL*, 210, 163: "Qualis sermo ostenditur, talis etiam animus comprobatur."

60. *Glossa ordinaria, PL*, 113, 1161; Bede, *PL*, 91, 1192; Alanus, *PL*, 210, 99; *Allegoriae, PL*, 112, 882.

61. Cf. Matt. 13.13, and *Allegoriae, PL*, 112, 921, and 981; Alanus, *In cantica, PL*, 210, 106.

62. *Allegoriae, PL*, 112, 1050: "Per speculum exempla bona. . . ."

63. On the crown, cf. Alanus, *Distinctiones, PL*, 210, 830.

64. The symbol of the Phenix became a commonplace because of the influence of the *De ave phenice* of Lactantius. See *De bestiis, PL*, 177, 48-49.

65. See Rabanus, *In Esther, PL*, 109, 646. Cf. Machaut, *Remede de Fortune*, pp. 123-124.

66. Cf. the corresponding list of virtues in Machaut, *Remede de Fortune*, pp. 109 ff., where Solomon, Job, Judith, Esther, and Abraham appear along with Alexander and the rest. Chaucer has deliberately avoided Christian virtues here.

67. See note 45 above.

68. See Rabanus, *PL*, 109, 107. Peter of Blois, p. 156, cites the followers of Absalom, such as Achitophel, as examples of false lovers, that is, fleshly lovers who abuse love.

69. *Glossa ordinaria, PL*, 113, 101.

70. See Paul E. Beichner. C.S.C., *The Medieval Representative of Music, Jubal or Tubalcain?* (Notre Dame, Indiana, 1954), esp. pp. 5-13.

71. Love taken simply is an appetitive force. True love, or *amicitia*, involves a rational choice of a human object. See Peter of Blois, *op.cit.*, p. 108. *Amicitia* is highly desirable, *ibid.*, p. 116: "In rebus humanis nihil dulcius amicitia invenitur, nihil sanctius appetitur, nihil fructuosius custoditur; habet enim fructum vitae quac nune est et futurae. Ipsa propria suavitate virtutes alias condit, adversa temperat, prospera componit, tristitiaque jucundat." Finally, this love is a step toward God, *ibid.*, p. 120: "Amicitia quidam gradus est hominibus ad Deum. Dilectione enim mediante, hamo Deo approximat, dum ex hominis amico Dei amicus efficitur."

72. The ceremony of the ring is not, of course, a marriage ceremony, which we should expect if John of Gaunt were the Black Knight. Rather, the ceremony in the poem suggests feudal investiture.

73. A similar attitude toward physical death appears in Boccaccio's letter "A Francesco da Brossano" on the death of Petrarch, *Opere latine minori*, pp. 222ff.

74. On the morning hours of worship and their symbolism see Honorius, *Gemma animae*, *PL*, 172, 625-626: "A mane autem dicitur matutina, quasi laus Deo pro luce exhibita. . . . Hac hora Christus victor a morte resurrexit, et diem nobis ab inferis revexit, et populum sanguine suo redemptum a regno tyranni reduxit, et hostes eorum barathro immersit." For Vespers, see *ibid.*, 637: "Duodecima hora dies clauditur, et operariis jam peracto opere denarius dabitur (Matt. 20). Finis autem uniuscujusque intelligitur, cum pro transacta vita merces cuique reditur." Cf. Alanus, *PL*, 210, 812.

75. *An Essay on the Vita Nuova* (Cambridge, Mass., 1949), pp. 105-106.

THE *BOOK OF THE DUCHESS* AS A MEMORIAL MONUMENT

by Phillipa Hardman

Chaucer's presentation of the lady White in the *Book of the Duchess* has long been seen as a conventional idealization of feminine beauty and grace,[1] while the portrayal of the Man in Black has recently been rightly called a "Symbolic picture of grief."[2] The poem can thus be read as a universal statement about beauty, love, and loss. On the other hand, the *Book of the Duchess* has been aptly described as an occasional or commemorative poem presented by Chaucer to John of Gaunt, as a "poetic monument to his grief."[3] Clearly these two readings are not exclusive; on the contrary, I should like to suggest an interesting interdependence between them.

There is little real dispute with the assumption that the personae of the Man in Black and the lady White are related in some way to the historical persons of John of Gaunt and Blanche of Lancaster; the question is, in what way? The most favored theory for the last half century has been that some variety of consolation or therapy is offered to John of Gaunt by Chaucer, through the surrogate figures of the Black Knight and the dreamer, together with a eulogy of the dead duchess. Many readers have pointed out the unsatisfactoriness of these consolation theories. David Lawton has proposed an alternative interpretation of the relation between the fictional characters and the real-life persons in terms of Chaucer's poetic vocation, and (although I do not entirely concur with his reading) I am wholly in agreement with his conclusion:

> It has always seemed puzzling, on grounds of social as much as literary structures, that Chaucer should have tried in this way to console one of the most powerful members of the royal family for the loss of his wife, especially as the poem appears to have been composed some considerable time after Blanche's death and there is no strong sense of occasion in the poem. On my reading, Chaucer does not presume to console Gaunt for his loss but presents him with a poetic monument to

his grief. The *Book of the Duchess* is . . . a tribute to both the
living husband and the dead Wife.[4]

The fact that modern critics have been so divided about the way in
which the poem is supposed to function in relation to the real-life
persons with whom it has always been associated is perhaps to be
attributed to the originality and indirectness that have been observed in
Chaucer's approach when compared with other medieval elegies and
laments for the dead.[5] Indeed, in seeking to understand Chaucer's
design in creating the *Book of the Duchess* as a "poetic monument," it
may be that a better model than the French love visions or the Boethian
literature of consolation to which it is often compared is to be found in
a completely different branch of the arts: in monumental tomb
sculpture.

   Closely connected with the critical debate about the historical
grounding of the poem is the question of its date. The *Book of the
Duchess* has usually been assumed to have been composed between the
date of Blanche of Lancaster's death in 1368 or 1369 and John of
Gaunt's remarriage in 1372, on the grounds that it would be
inappropriate thereafter to represent him as grieving for his first wife,
and that the riddling reference at the end of the poem to a rich hill
refers to a title—Earl of Richmond—which he no longer held after
1372. Against these objections, however, can be placed the evidence
provided by the documents relating to the double tomb for himself and
Blanche which John of Gaunt commissioned in 1374;[6] and some critics
have seen good reason to prefer this date for the poem.[7] As for the
allusion to the Richmond title, it may he relevant to compare the use of
heraldic displays at funerals as "matters of record," which "do not
affect the way a man would bear arms in his lifetime": a similarly
commemorative purpose may be intended here.[8] It seems reasonable to
consider a date for the poem close to the commissioning and building
of the tomb in 1374-75, when John of Gaunt was in England to specify
the alabaster from his quarries at Tutbury for the tomb effigies, and to
attend the annual memorial service at St Paul's and the anniversary
supper at the Savoy.[9]

   In his biography of the mason Henry Yevele, John H. Harvey quite
naturally assumes that "while Yevele was engaged on the Duchess's
tomb, Chaucer was writing the Book of the Duchesse as a tribute to her
memory."[10] If we follow this line of reasoning, and suppose that
Chaucer had finished his book by the time the tomb was complete, we
might have a date—1376—which would make sense of the vexed
reference to the sickness that the narrator says he has been suffering for

"this eight yeer" (37). Chaucer could be indicating delicately the subject of his poem by representing in the highly detailed and clinically accurate, but strangely unattributed sorrow of his narrator the irremediable grief of those who mourned the memory of the young duchess, who had died eight years before. However, this suggestion does not necessarily presume a date as late as 1376 for the composition of the whole poem: it is not impossible that the number of years specified could have been altered had Chaucer undertaken a revision of his poem, perhaps to suit a new occasion, at a date later than that of original composition. For example, the numbers two, three, four, five, or six would all fit the metre in place of eight, so that an elegy originally written in any year between 1370 and 1374 could easily have been adapted in 1376 to produce a "new version" coinciding with the completion of the duchess's tomb.[11]

There is no documentation to support suggestions that the poem was formally presented or recited to John of Gaunt on any particular occasion. Nor do I wish to suggest that Chaucer's purpose in writing the poem was to celebrate the erection of the tomb; though it is an attractive and not implausible thought that the idea of constructing a poem to commemorate the death of Blanche of Lancaster might have been provoked in part by the plans for her monument. My interest lies rather in a comparison of the structure and function of a memorial tomb such as that planned for Blanche with the structure and function of Chaucer's contemporary poem, read as a "poetic monument" to a dead duchess and her surviving husband.

At the time of Blanche's death the fashion for elaborate sculptural monuments with life-sized portrait effigies, architecturally designed tomb chests and canopies, and rows of weepers representing mourning friends and relatives, was at its height. Impressive church monuments commemorating the dead and displaying their family connections with heraldic tomb embellishments had become common in the late thirteenth century; and the earliest English example of the arcaded weeper tomb, in which heraldic shields were replaced by a "pictorial representation of the funeral cortège," is that of Thomas de Cantelupe at Hereford, dated 1282-84.[12] Tomb effigies in alabaster grew in popularity in the fourteenth century, enabling sculptors to achieve more delicate and finely detailed effects, though for the most part the images they produced were of idealized standard types rather than individuals.[13] However, a kind of imitation of life exists in the structure and disposition of the elements of the tomb, which preserve in stylized form the ceremonial mourning observed on the occasion of the burial.[14]

The splendid tomb built by Henry Yevele in 1374 for Blanche of Lancaster and John of Gaunt in Old St Paul's was unhappily destroyed in the Great Fire of London, but it is possible to get an idea of how it looked from an engraving made in the seventeenth century by Wenceslaus Hollar.[15] (*Plate 1*) In the canopied arcading along the side of the tomb chest there are pairs of niches clearly of considerable depth, where presumably weepers once stood. The tomb of Queen Philippa in Westminster Abbey, which provided Yevele with a model, certainly once had weepers in its niches: there were originally thirty, of which only two now remain; and the monument which Yevele designed for her husband, Edward III, still has portrait figures of their sons and daughters as weepers on one side of the tomb. (Among those now lost from the other side was the figure of John of Gaunt.)[16]

Chaucer thus had many easily available models of an art form intended to have a multiple memorial function: to record the death of an individual with an idealized portrait image, to be a witness to the bereavement of family and friends in the figures of the weepers, and to make a statement to posterity about the memorable worth of the family and its connections through heraldic devices and through the very magnificence of the tomb. The *Book of the Duchess*, part lament, part eulogy, elaborately constructed, and with clear family allusions, may be said to have a structure and function similar to those of such a tomb.

Before the Man in Black voices his long description of his lady's virtues, the centerpiece of the poem (817-1033), he gives an elaborate account of his grief in which he explicitly presents himself as an image of sorrow (560-709).[17] Similarly, he now presents White as an image of beauty, goodness, and truth. His purpose is obvious: to make the dreamer understand the nature of his loss by creating for him a facsimile of the image of his lady which is constantly present and visible to him, "for be hyt never so derk, / Me thynketh I se hir ever moo" (912-13); an image which imposes on him the response of continual grief and faithful remembrance.

If the *Book of the Duchess* does figure a relationship between Chaucer and John of Gaunt and the dead duchess Blanche, it surely operates through this process of image-making. While the narrator identifies himself as the poet at the outset, "I, that made this book" (96), the responsibility for the accuracy of the image thus preserved "in ryme" is shared between the dreamer and the Man in Black. The Man in Black endeavors to convey to the dreamer the image of the lady White and of the relationship he shared with her; he is in possession of all the factual details which the dreamer/poet needs to acquire before he can undertake the act of representation which the poem becomes.[18] The elaborately repetitive arrangement between the Man in Black and the dreamer, one to tell and the other to listen (746-58), sounds like a contractual agreement: the patron to describe in great detail the image which the artist is to reproduce. The persona of the dreamer, therefore, may be seen as figuring Chaucer's role as poetic image-maker.

For Chaucer and his contemporary readers, the reality of Blanche of Lancaster could be metamorphosed into an image of goodness, truth, and beauty made timeless by death, and the person of John of Gaunt into an eternally grieving image of sorrow: verbal equivalents for the images sculpted on aristocratic funeral monuments. The Man in Black functions like a weeper: a stylized mourning figure incorporated into the structure of the tomb; and the image of "goode faire White" is like an idealized alabaster effigy, freshly colored in imitation of life.[19] At the conclusion of the Man in Black's portrait of his lady, Chaucer addresses directly the question of the relation between the idealized portrait likeness and the living subject in a passage for which he had no known model (1042-53). The dreamer suggests that the Black Knight's image of his lady's superlative qualities is, understandably, an exaggeration of reality: "Yow *thoghte* that she was the beste" (1049); to which the knight vehemently replies that her real perfections were well attested: "Nay, alle that hir seyen / Seyde and sworen hyt was soo" (1052-53).

Helen Phillips has commented on the *descriptio* of the lady White that its "rhetorical stylization" gives it a "sense of hieratic stiffness—an icon-like quality" that "renders it aesthetically more fit to stand as a memorial, transmuted already into something beyond the world of change."[20] The impression of changeless stillness is heightened by Chaucer's emphasis on certain attributes traditionally associated with the ideal woman: a "stedfast countenaunce" (833), a "lokynge . . . not foly sprad" (874), a face "sad, symple, and benygne" (918); but above all by the sustained contrast drawn between the lady and Fortune. The lady is presented as an embodiment of moderation: "In alle thynges more mesure / Had never, I trowe, creature" (881-82); and of truth: "Trouthe hymself . . . / Had chose hys maner principal / In hir" (1003-05); whereas immoderate Fortune glories in lying, "for that ys hyr nature; / Withoute feythe, lawe, or mesure" (631-32). By opposing his lady to Fortune in this way the Man in Black claims immutability of a specific kind for her: freedom from the power of changeable Fortune, won not by death but in life by the lady's own virtue.

A different kind of immutability afflicts the Man in Black: he suffers an irremediable grief, so that no matter what aspect of him we see—mysterious mourner, courteous interlocutor, personification of sorrow, victim of Fortune, lover—it is always his unalterably grief-stricken condition of which we are made aware. His lay of complaint opens with the assertion that his sorrow is so great "that joye gete I never non" (476), and he gently refuses the dreamer's offer of help with the same absolute certainty that "hyt may never the rather be doo. / No man may my sorwe glade" (562-63). He identifies his very existence with his sorrow: "For y am sorwe, and sorwe ys y" (597), and fatalistically accepts the loss of his "fers" to Fortune as an inevitable result of her power, which, had he been in her place, he would have exercised in the same way (665-84). The whole of his discourse is structured by his frequent repetition of the simple, conventional ejaculation of sorrow, "alas!".

Every section of his complaint—the overheard song, the definition of his pains, the denunciation of Fortune, the explanation of his unchangeable state—is punctuated by this word. It also occurs repeatedly at three other significant points in the narrative: first in the story of Alcione, the fiction-within-the-fictional counterpart of the Man in Black, to express her grief at the death of her husband: "Ful ofte she swouned, and sayed 'Alas!' / For sorwe ful nygh wood she was" (103-04; and see 90, 213); then in the Black Knight's own account of the sorrow of unrequited love from which his lady later rescued him: "Allas! that day / The sorowe I suffred, and the woo" (1244-45; and see 1187, 1191); finally in anticipation of the stated fact of his lady's death, when the Man in Black and the dreamer join in their expression of sorrow and concern: "'allas! Ryght that was she!' / 'Allas, sir, how?'" (1307-08; and see 1301).

There are more than these simply verbal echoes of the Man in Black's grief: telling similarities of appearance and deportment also link the sorrowful figures in all sections of the narrative. Alcione, the Man in Black, and the picture of the Black Knight when young all share the distinctive bodily gesture of the bowed head (122, 461, 1216); the Man in Black describes himself as he was in his youth, with his "sorweful herte and woundes dede" and his "hewe al pale" on account of love (1211-14), echoing the heart-sick pallor of his appearance now (488-99); Alcione, like the Man in Black, is described as if transformed by grief into cold, lifeless stone (123, 1300); and the dreamer sees and sympathizes with a reflection of his own life-suspending sorrow in the behavior and appearance of the Man in Black (1-29, 503-13). A deliberately limited repertoire of verbal and physical signals ensures that the reader perceives all these figures in a single serial pattern of repetitions.

Like the weepers round a tomb, then, the different sorrowful episodes of the poem—Alcione's bereavement; the Man in Black's loss with his thrice repeated, emphatic statement "I have lost more than thow wenest" (744, 1138, 1306); the prefigurative sorrow of the young Black Knight, and the sympathetic sorrow of the dreamer—all are juxtaposed in varied, but complementary images of grief.

An interesting visual parallel to Chaucer's symbolic treatment of the Man in Black may be seen in a miniature in the Catalogue of Benefactors of St Albans Abbey which shows John of Gaunt in an attitude much like that of a weeper.[21] (*Plate 2*) Unlike all the other portraits of royal donors in the book who are depicted seated, in square frames, he is shown kneeling under an architectural niche resembling part of the arcading on the side of a tomb chest. His hand-on-heart gesture is found frequently among weepers on tombs dating from the thirteenth to the sixteenth centuries, and is a stylized indication of grief.[22] The text makes clear that John of Gaunt's donation of the cloth of gold that appears draped over a monument beside him is intended to commemorate the fact that the body of Blanche lay at the abbey one night on its way to burial in London (recalling the erection of the Eleanor crosses to mark the resting places of his grandmother's body on a similar journey). It would appear, then, that the artist responsible for this little portrait of John of Gaunt was well aware of the emotional significance of the commemorative act which it records, and expressed it by using the same symbolic gesture of grief that appears so frequently in the design of weepers on fashionable tombs.

The tomb of Blanche of Lancaster and John of Gaunt was presumably meant to express the same meaning as the contemporary monument at St Mary's, Warwick, to Thomas and Katharine Beauchamp. Husband and wife lie side by side, hand in hand, in serene harmony, while the weepers all around express their grief in a variety of stylized gestures, and a series of heraldic shields in a frieze surrounding the base of the tomb declares the family's genealogical connections. (*Plate 3*) Precisely the same effect is achieved at the end of the *Book of the Duchess*.

The Man in Black concludes his story with a picture of the ideally harmonious union that he and his lady enjoyed:

> Oure hertes wern so evene a payre
> That never nas that oon contrayre
> To that other for no woo.
> . . . .
> Al was us oon, withoute were. (1289-91, 95)

But as soon as the dreamer's question "where is she now?" returns him to the present, the Man in Black becomes "as ded as stoon," and repeatedly bewails his loss: "Allas, that I was bore!" "allas! Ryght that was she!" (1298, 1307). Compassionate fellow feeling converts the dreamer from interrogator to fellow mourner: "Allas!" "Is that youre los? Be God, hyt ys routhe!" (1308, 1310). This moment of illumination and compassion is the climax and conclusion of the dreamer's interview with the Man in Black, and it leaves the reader with a final image of the two silenced speakers, united in sorrow for the loss of that ideal love relationship, for an unforgettable past happiness that cannot be recovered. Looking back towards the Man in Black's celebration of that mutual love, the two mourning figures complete a tableau which is scenically comparable to that presented to the viewer of the serene, idealized effigies and the grief-stricken weepers on the tomb. It is immediately followed by the riddling references to the long castle with white walls on a rich hill, and the exclamation "be Seynt Johan," which invite the reader to recognize in the Black Knight and the lady White the historical persons of Blanche of Lancaster and John, Earl of Richmond; and which at the same time record their titles and ancestry, in the manner of the punning or "canting" charges frequently used in heraldic coats of arms.[23]

The tomb of Blanche and John of Gaunt shares another conventional feature with the Beauchamp monument: in both the effigies rest their feet upon stylized stone beasts. The most typical choice of beasts seen on English tombs (unless they have special heraldic family significance as do the bears on the Beauchamp monument) is for a lion at the knight's feet and a dog at the lady's. Traditional heraldic and bestiary symbolism determines their appropriate meaning: the lion stands for valor and nobility and the dog for loyalty, expressive of the virtues proper to man and wife. The tomb of Blanche and John of Gaunt does indeed show a lion at the feet of the husband; the space beneath the wife's feet is obscured by a pillar in Hollar's engraving, but the conventional expectation is that her feet would be resting on a dog. John M. Steadman suggested long ago that the whelp which leads the dreamer to the Man in Black, in common with the dogs sculpted on funerary monuments, might symbolize marital fidelity.[24] The whelp would therefore be a particularly appropriate choice as the guide leading the dreamer towards an epitome of married loyalty in the grieving Man in Black and his faithful lady. If we may suppose that Chaucer and his contemporary readers were well aware of the customary use and significance of dogs on tombs, then this detail could be seen as contributing to a sustained poetic device in which every characteristic figural element of a fashionable double tomb such as that erected by John of Gaunt for Blanche and himself is brought to life in the poem. The poet animates a funerary monument and makes it "speke"—much as Morpheus is instructed to do with the body of Ceyx (136-52).

When the dreamer awakes to find his book of Ceyx and Alcione still in his hand, and resolves, "be processe of tyme, / . . . to put this sweven in ryme" (1331-32), he implicitly takes on the role of the "clerkes" and other poets of the past who "put in rime" such stories "of quenes lives, and of kinges" (58) in order to preserve their memory for posterity: "for to be in minde" (55). The invocation to Polymya in *Anelida and Arcite*, praying her to assist the poet with her "vois memorial" (15-18) to save the story of Anelida from oblivion, is a more elaborate announcement of essentially the same motive.[25] Chaucer is to record for future generations the story of Blanche and John of Gaunt so that it will never be "devoured out of oure memorie" (*Anelida*, 14), and to preserve the image of the young duchess so that readers of the poem, like the Man in Black, will "se hir ever moo" (913) and will "foryete hir never moo" (1125). In this sense, then, I would argue that the poem functions as a verbal equivalent of the tomb erected by John of Gaunt as a memorial to Blanche and to his own grief: it presents us with a beautiful, idealized image of the dead duchess, a monumental effigy showing her as she appeared in life, supported by repeated images of the inconsolable sorrow of her surviving husband, frozen like a sculpted stone weeper in an attitude of grief. Chaucer, like the sculptor of effigies on a tomb, has created images that both memorialize the beauty of the life that is lost, and symbolize the sorrow of death.

NOTES

Research on this article was assisted by a travel grant from the Research Board of the University of Reading.

All quotations from Chaucer's works are taken from *The Riverside Chaucer,* ed. Larry D. Benson (Oxford, 1988).

1. J.I. Wimsatt, "The Apotheosis of Blanche in *The Book of the Duchess," JEGP* 66 (1967):26-44.

2. W.A. Davenport, *Chaucer, Complaint and Narrative* (Cambridge, Engl., 1988).

3. David Lawton, *Chaucer's Narrators* (Cambridge, Engl., 1985), 56.

4. Lawton, 56. For his full discussion, see 48-57. He argues that the Black Knight is a lover-poet who teaches the inexperienced dreamer how to write poetry: a characterization that he bases on the belief that Chaucer presents this "figure of John of Gaunt" in "an Orphic role," as a "master-poet lamenting his irrevocably lost wife" (55), in a setting for which "by far the nearest analogue" is "Ovid's description of Orpheus in a grove leaning against a great tree and singing his heart-rending lament" in *Metamorphoses* X (56). Lawton here misrepresents Ovid in a way that makes the scenic parallel sound far more significant than it really is. For an opposing view of the poetic roles of the dreamer and the Black Knight in relation to Chaucer and John of Gaunt, see Phillipa Hardman, "'Ars Celare Artem': Interpreting the Black Knight's 'Lay' in Chaucer's *Book of the Duchess*," *Poetica* 37 (1993): 49-57.

5. Helen Phillips, *Chaucer: The Book of the Duchess*, Durham and St Andrews Medieval Texts, 3 (Durham, 1982), 49.

6. There is nothing unusual in a patron's ordering his tomb in his own lifetime, nor in the construction of a tomb for his wife some years after her death; see Lawrence Stone, Sculpture in Britain: *The Middle Ages* (Harmondsworth, 1955), 114. As an estimate of the time it might take to complete such a tomb, Richard II ordered a double tomb for himself and Anne of Bohemia in 1394, which was to be ready by 1397 (Stone, 193).

7. John M. Hill, "The *Book of the Duchess*, Melancholy, and that Eight-Year Sickness," *ChauR* 9 (1974): 35-50 (46). Edward I. Condren argues for a date of composition in 1377 in "The Historical Context of the *Book of the Duchess*," *ChauR* 5 (1971): 195-212.

8. Thomas Woodcock and John Martin Robinson, *The Oxford Guide to Heraldry* (Oxford, 1988),123.

9. See N.B. Lewis, "The Anniversary Service for Blanche, Duchess of Lancaster, 12th September 1374," *Bulletin of the John Rylands Library* 21 (1937): 176-92. Records of the commissioning of the tomb and of payments to Yevele are printed in Sydney Armitage-Smith, *John of Gaunt's Register II*, Camden Society 3rd series, 21 (1911), nos. 1394 and 1659, dated 18 June 1374 (ordering the alabaster for the two images) and 26 January 1375 (payment to "Henry Yeveley mason . . . pur un toumbe affaire deinz l'eglise de Saint Poul de Londres pour nostre tres cher et tres ame compaigne, Blaunche").

10. *Henry Yevele: The Life of an English Architect* (London, 1944), 30. It was not until some years later that Chaucer's appointment as Clerk of the King's Works (1389-91) brought him into contact with Yevele; but he could scarcely have failed to be aware of John of Gaunt's plans for the double tomb, and his continuing interest in its execution.

11. The reference to "eight yeer" occurs in that part of the text for which the only evidence is Thynne's printed edition of 1532.

12. Stone, 133, 146.

13. Joan Evans, *English Art: 1307-1461* (Oxford, 1949), 153-55. Stone remarks: "It was family status not individual personality whose record these tombs were intended to secure, and in consequence the art of portraiture remained unsought by all but royalty" (179).

14. The relation between the art of the sculptural tomb and reality can most strikingly be seen by comparing weeper-tombs with miniature paintings depicting royal funerals: the weepers, the tomb chest, and the effigy replicate in stone the mourners, the coffin, and the life-sized wooden model of the dead king, robed as in life, that was carried in the funeral procession. See, for example, a miniature showing the funeral of a king, from an English Coronation Order *c.* 1380 (Pamplona, Archivo General de Navarra, MS. 197, fol. 22v), reproduced in L.F. Sandler, *Gothic Manuscripts, 1285-1385*, A Survey of MSS Illuminated in the British Isles, Volume 5 (London, 1986), plate 418. See also W.H. St J. Hope, "On the Funeral Effigies of the Kings and Queens of England," *Archaeologia* 60 (1907): 517.

15. In William Dugdale, *The History of St Paul's Cathedral in London* (London, 1658), 90. Hollar seems to have misinterpreted the duchess's costume for she appears to be wearing a stiff, armor-like, hip-length tunic over a gathered skirt, whereas the original effigy no doubt showed her in the costume of her day, wearing a dress with close-fitting bodice, and a hip-level belt.

16. Also lost is the monumental brass from the tomb of John's brother, Thomas of Woodstock, though a seventeenth-century drawing fortunately survives and shows the central figure surrounded by his wife and other family weepers, including John of Gaunt, standing in rows of architectural niches. The marble slab from the tomb of Thomas of Woodstock (d. 1397) survives in St Edmund's chapel, Westminster Abbey. The brass is illustrated in F. Sandford, *Genealogical History of the Kings and Queens of* England (1677); reproduced in John Page-Phillips, *Children on Brasses* (London, 1970), figure 6.

17. See my discussion of the Man in Black's self-portrait in "Chaucer's Man of Sorrows: Secular Images of Pity in the *Book of the*

Duchess, the *Squire's Tale* and *Troilus and Criseyde*," *JEGP*, forthcoming.

18. For a fuller discussion of this cooperative relationship between the dreamer/poet and the Man in Black, see Hardman, "Ars Celare Artem" (note 4 above).

19. The description of her face is particularly interesting: "she / Was whit, rody, fressh, and lyvely hewed" (904-05)—a formulation that actually seems to suit a complexion painted to imitate the colors of life rather better than the natural coloring of a living face. Contemporary effigies of ladies are illustrated in Arthur Gardner, "Alabaster Tombs of the Gothic Period," *Archaeological Journal* 80 (1923): 1, plate 44.

20. Chaucer: *The Book of the Duchess*, 39.

21. MS BL Cotton Nero D vii, fol. 7, c. 1380.

22. Examples may be seen on the tombs of Thomas de Cantelupe (1282-84) in Hereford Cathedral; Edmund Crouchback (1296) and John of Eltham (1340) in Westminster Abbey; Thomas, Earl of Warwick (1375-80) in St Mary's, Warwick. A late example from the tomb of Sir John Blount (d. 1531) at Kinlet, Shropshire (Gardner, "Alabaster Tombs", plate 11), shows the gesture very strikingly repeated three times in a group of weepers who "pose in mimic attitudes of grief" (Gardner, *English Medieval Sculpture* (Cambridge, Engl., 1951), 319). The same gesture is sometimes used in Crucifixion scenes: although St John at the foot of the Cross is usually shown in a sorrowful pose with his hand pressed to his check, he is sometimes represented with his hand on his heart to express his grief (see, for example, a leaf from a French Book of Hours, c. 1290-95 (Washington, National Gallery of Art B-15, 390), reproduced in *Medieval and Renaissance Miniatures from the National Gallery of Art*, ed. Gary Vikan (Washington, 1975), plate VIII). An identical gesture appears in a secular context in an Italian manuscript from the mid-fourteenth century, which shows an abandoned bride, "her left hand raised to her breast in a gesture of mourning" (Vikan, 50; figure 15a). This is an illustration to the *Novella* of Johannes Andreae (Washington, Nat. Gall. Art B-22, 225).

23. Woodcock and Robinson, *Oxford Guide to Heraldry*, 63.

24. John M. Steadman, "Chaucer's 'Whelp': A Symbol of Marital Fidelity?" *N&Q* n.s. 3 (1956): 374-75.

25. See Phillipa Hardman, "Chaucer's Muses and his 'Art Poetical'," *RES* 37 (1986): 478-94 (480).

Tomb of John of Guant and
Blanche of Lancaster in Old St
Paul's Cathedral from an
engraving by Wenceslaus
Hollar.

Portrait miniature of John of
Guant in an attitude of grief
from BL MS Cotton Nero D
vii, fol. 7. By permission of the
British Library.

Tomb of Thomas and Katherine Beauchamp in St Mary's, Warwick showing (a) the effigies, (b) the weepers and shields. Photgraph (a) courtesy of Courtauld and Fred H. Crossley and Maurice H. Ridgeway. Photgraph (b) Author's photograph.

III. *THE HOUSE OF FAME*

It remains uncertain whether Chaucer composed the *House of Fame* before the *Parliament of Fowls*, or vice versa. John Fyler (*Benson*, p. 978) prudently judges that the preponderance of evidence supports the priority of the *House of Fame*. Nevertheless, many Chaucerians still find John Fisher's alternative ordering very appealing.[1] The editorial placement of these two works in Chaucer's "large volume" (*CT* 2. 60) thus itself becomes a significant interpretive gesture. The sequencing and titling and architectonic formatting of a critical edition of *Chaucer*, not to mention the choice of a base text, the inclusion or omission of variant readings, the degree of regularization and punctuation provided, and so on, are all important—and therefore hotly contested—issues precisely because they lack any record of authorial intent and yet so affect the readers' predisposition towards the text in hand.

But, when the controversy calms, all Chaucerians agree that the *House of Fame* and the *Parliament of Fowls* were composed and probably presented in close proximity to each other. There endures a longstanding critical habit of interpreting the two as a pair, which more recent studies subsume under the rubric of intertextuality. A shift in Chaucer's satirical register is difficult to specify and necessary to feel. The *Parliament* seems to portray the foibles of Nature's court with a certain Horatian politeness. The *House* mocks with more Juvenalian acidity the fickleness of Fama, the fantasies of her courtiers, and the folly of *Geffrey* himself as an arriviste. The titles of both works reinforce the notion that they shared a similar performance/publication milieu. The "Retractions" do refer to "the book of Seint Valentynes day of the *Parlement* of Briddes." Though the *House of Fame* is therein referred to only as "the book also of Fame," the use of *house* in the title does have strong manuscript authority, and it can be invested with the same potential for verbal play as *foules*. After all, the "house" setting of the poem is the *camera* of Fama's "parlement."

Both dream visions end with frustrated expectations. Both dream visions provoke consideration of Chaucer's self-consciousness as an author, his discomfort as an *auctor*—his anxiety towards tradition (*i.e.*, his books), his anticipation of an audience's immediate response, and/or his expectations of being read by posterity.

Laurence K. Shook (in Rowland's *Companion,* 1979) argued that a modern reader's appreciation of the *House of Fame*'s true sophistication depends upon recognition of its significance as Chaucer's *ars poetica*: "the subject of the *House of Fame* is the art of Poetry itself" (*Companion,* p. 417). This extremely influential interpretive premise, as Shook himself noted, has been confirmed by the complementary readings of J.A.W. Bennett, Sheila Delany, and P.M. Kean (*Companion,* pp. 423-4); it also harmonizes well with F.O. Payne's reading of the Prologue to the *Legend of Good Women* in *The Key of Remembrance* (1973). Despite the almost thirty years which separate Rowland's *Companion* from Minnis's *Oxford Guide,* this fundamental conception of the *House of Fame* as one of Chaucer's crucial self-assessments of his role as public poet endures—in numerous permutations.

The formalist implications of reading the *House of Fame* as an *ars poetica* are also especially intriguing. Its division into three books, for example, has challenged Chaucerians to reexamine their most fundamental assumptions regarding the protocols of *unity* and the notion of *the book* itself. Paul Ruggiers (1953) suggested that a sequence of topics (Love, Order, Wisdom) gave the *House of Fame* its thematic unity. A number of other readings of the *House of Fame* construct alternative scaffoldings. In his chapter on the "The First Structural Stereotype" (1963) excerpted below, Robert O. Payne provides an interpretive key to the significant ordering of Chaucer's "combinative structures" (including the *House of Fame,* the *Book of the Duchess* and the *Legend*'s Prologue) as distinguished from his "inclusive single narratives" or "framed collections" (*Key,* p. 115).

Sheila Delany's close analysis of "Chaucer's *House of Fame* and the *Ovide moralisé*" (1968) reprinted below exemplifies a rather straightforward sort of source study, one that hardly seems to anticipate her innovative and provocative studies of the *House of Fame* (1972) and of the *Legend of Good Women* (1994)—except as a highly particularized and convincing reevaluation of Chaucer's text in terms of its pre-texts. Larry Benson's immediately and admittedly controversial study (1986) of the "love tydynges" referenced at the conclusion of the *House of Fame* reads this particular dream vision in terms of its presumed performance's courtly subtext.

NOTES

1. In *The Complete Poetry and Prose of Geoffrey Chaucer, 2nd Ed.* (1989), Fisher suggests that the *House of Fame* was composed after the *Parliament* because it "appears to be a more appropriate transition to *Troylus and Criseyde*" (p. 564) and *The Canterbury Tales* project "upon which his true fame rests" (p. 582).

EXCERPT FROM
"THE FIRST STRUCTURAL STEREOTYPE"

by Robert O. Payne

. . . The *House of Fame* takes the problems latent in the unresolved ironies of the Narrator's situation in the *Book of the Duchess*, and those buried in the formulation about old poets and the "lawe of kynde," and makes them the central motif of the poem, insofar as it has one. Consequently, the not fully developed irony of the poet's personal situation vis-à-vis the situation in his poem becomes a deliberately double point of view, maintaining unresolvable ambiguities all through the poem. In Book III these are translated into the very structure of the allegory. In Book II they remain matters of viewpoint, reflected principally in the dialogue and in stylistic exaggeration. In Book I, where the poet is alone, they must be managed as they are in the Prologue to the *Legend of Good Women*, by a style and a juxtaposition of topics. In one way, that means of handling ambiguity carries right through the poem, in its over-formal, overblown rhetorical paraphernalia of proems, invocations, etc., which suggest pretensions to high art at the same time that the parodic tendencies of the style and the content of the poem deny them.[31]

In the *House of Fame's* version of this structural stereotype, the salient characteristic of the alignment of books, dreams, and experience (aside from the fact that they so patently fail to corroborate each other) is the absence of that careful blocking of each into its own structural area which characterizes the structure of the *Book of the Duchess*. The dream is this time very nearly a complete framing device. The old book—the retelling of the Aeneas-Dido story—comes within it, in Book I, and the poet's experience is, in Book II, introduced within the dream by the attribution of it to the dreamer as a life outside the dream but relevant to its character and purposes. The Proem, however, and the Invocation to Book I do come outside the dream, and they raise questions about books and dreams which send us into this particular dream (which contains much about old books) in a very carefully prepared frame of mind.

In a manner akin to that of the discussion of books and experience which opens the Prologue to the *Legend of Good Women*, Chaucer opens with a Proem discussing dreams in terms of the variety of opinions about them available in the old books. These opinions are so at variance ". . . that oure flessh ne hath no myght / To understonde hyt aryght, / For hyt is warned to derkly" (49-51). Whether this is the fault of the books or the dreams there is no way to say, but the net effect is that each makes us distrust the other, and this just as we are about to hear of a wonderful dream in which the poet is to be told that a vision will correct him where books had led him wrong and experience had yielded him nothing at all. Furthermore, all this ought to result in some improvement in Geffrey's poetry, as we learn from the Eagle, first in the long speech from line 605 to line 699,[32] again as the Eagle leaves him at the end of Book II ("And God of heven sende the grace / Some good to lernen in this place"), and finally in another long speech near the end of the poem (lines 2000-26), concluding with the reminder that Jove

> ". . . yaf expres commaundement,
> To which I am obedient
> To further the with al my myght,
> And wisse and teche the aryght
> Where thou maist most tidynges here,
> Shaltow here anoon many oon lere."[33]

The conclusion of the Invocation (lines 81-110) gives still another twist to the knot of uncertainties tied up in the Proem. The reader is dragged into the problem too, so the poet's problem is now not only what to believe, how to find out, and how to put it into verse, but also what the audience will make of it. And this time, contrary to his usual attitude, Chaucer charges his readers directly with the responsibility for understanding him, and in the curse delivered upon those who do not understand, gives negative recognition to the possibility that poetry may fail not through its own fault, but through that of its readers. He evidently had less faith in the infallibility of his audience than do some modern critics, who would make it the standard of critical judgment.[34] Altogether, by the time we reach the first line of the vision story proper, learned tradition, visionary revelation, individual perception, and the *concensus gentium* have all been cast into doubt, though nothing has been denied outright. After that start, it is little wonder that Geffrey comments, only about 250 lines from where the poem breaks off, that so far he hasn't learned anything he didn't know before he started, except for the mere mechanics of the house of Fame:

> "For certeynly, he that me made
> To comen hyder, seyde me,
> Y shulde bothe here and se,
> In this place, wonder thynges;
> But these be no suche tydynges
> As I mene of." "Noo?" quod he.
> And I answered, "Noo, parde!
> For wel y wiste ever yit,
> Sith that first y hadde wit,
> That somme folk han desired fame
> Diversly, and loos, and name." (1890-1900)[35]

The organization of materials within the three-part structure is also indication of the concern with books, dreams, and experience, although the baffling result in this poem is that as structural materials they seem to have almost no connection with each other. Technically, the vision spans all three parts. Actually, most of Book I is the retelling of an old story, and while the story is going on, we lose almost all awareness of the dream. True, at line 314 he insists that he dreamed the whole thing; but digressions on the difficulty of writing poetry (245-52), moral apostrophes to the reader (265-92), and the long digression proving the moral by collecting book authorities (283-426) certainly counter that insistence by establishing a clear and direct poet-to-reader relationship, very much of the sort that will subsequently characterize *Troilus and Criseyde*. It would be all but impossible to guess that Book I had been part of a longer poem, if the manuscript had happened to come down to us separately and with the beginning and ending destroyed. But the real point is that stylistically as well as structurally, Book I (excluding the Proem and Invocation) has a completely separate existence; it does not suggest anything which follows, and critics have been able to correlate its "sentence" with the rest of the poem only by abstracting to so great a degree as to vitiate comparison.

After all the interpretations and arguments are in, the same assertion remains true of Book II: it also has its own self-contained existence, with the exception that its ending leaves a logical (though not necessarily poetic) link to Book III. The Eagle has brought Geffrey to Fame's house, but Geffrey hasn't yet told us about what happened there. This is the Book which contains all we are to get of "experience" in this poem. Although this time we are unmistakably in the dream all the while, the humor depends largely on a style which presents the extraordinary in very commonplace colors; and either directly or by implication the constant topic of conversation is Geffrey's experience outside this dream. It is summarized, criticized, corrected, and various offers are made to supplement it; it is, in fact, what had brought on the vision. But Book I had not even mentioned it, and Book III scarcely does. Again, Book II has a style all its own, which it shares with neither of the others, although much of its over-celebrated humor[36] derives from parodying by one means or another the rhetorically decorated styles of the other two. The mode of operation of that humorous style is foreshadowed in the opening of Book II: a short but almost pretentiously high-serious Proem introduces a Book which within thirty lines has dropped into simple farce and tired jokes about a nagging wife and a swelling waistline.

Yet Book II does clearly define some issues, so that it is possible (most critics have agreed about the *House of Fame* to this extent) to say fairly easily what it is about, and to see that its "statement" quite closely parallels that of the Proem to Book I. The problem is, as the Eagle makes clear, one of reliable sources of knowledge to make the poetic services which Geffrey had been offering to the God of Love more rewarding to all concerned. Equally clearly, in this case neither books nor experience had done the job (at least in the opinion of Jove and the Eagle), so the vision now had to take over. But as the Proem to Book I had left us able finally to trust neither book nor dream, so again does Book II, adding a dimension to the uncertainty by suggesting the extent to which experience shares their limitations.

A good deal of earlier criticism to the contrary notwithstanding, there simply cannot be any question here of a "turning from books to life as the model for art." First, as much of the satiric wit of Book II is at pains to point out, one is always too close to life to see it either broadly or very clearly; thus even the Eagle takes whatever help Aristotle can give him, and Jove's gift to Geffrey was not (as it might appropriately have been) an affair with the lady next door, but a visionary expedition to another world. Second, and I think more important and more noticeable, what the Eagle promises Geffrey as aid and comfort is a completely indigestable mass of "tydynges" —information.[37] If the Eagle's "demonstration" is correct, then what Geffrey will find for his profit and delight at the house of Fame will be everything that anyone has ever said. And all this will be not only without any sorting of true from false, or useful from useless, but rather with the prior assurance that the nature of the place will guarantee that no such sorting can occur.

> ". . . The grete soun,"
> Quod he, "the rumbleth up and doun
> In Fames Hous, full of tydynges,
> Bothe of feir speche and chidynges,
> And of fals and soth compouned.
> Herke wel; hyt is not rouned.
> Herestow now the grete swogh?" (1025-31)

This is surely an *embarras de richesses* for a poet who has been accused of lack of knowledge of life, and it just as surely undercuts the stiff and tiresome allegory of Book III, as well as theories which maintain that Geffrey's voyage with the Eagle taught him a proto-naturalistic theory of art.

In Book III, finally, we reach the otherworldly destination and the whole Book is devoted to its description. As Book I had concentrated largely on an old book and Book II on Geffrey's experience, Book III devotes its stylistic energies to the elaboration of the banal marvels of this dreamland. It is a good example of Chaucer's ability to produce exactly the kind of poetry which some critics believe the rhetorical poetic produced inevitably: exaggerated elaboration of the obvious without any illumination. If the Eagle were the narrator of Book III, we might take the whole thing as rather overextended parody. But he is not, and the style—elaborate but not certainly overelaborated—gives us no clear warrant to take it as such anyway. What we do know is what Book II led us to expect and Geffrey himself remarks (lines 1890-1900), that the pageantry of the House of Fame was neither very new nor particularly useful to him.[38] Whatever ending may have been intended or written and then canceled could not change that impression. The House of Rumor is after all only a kind of de-allegorization of Eolus' clarions, and even less likely (if that is possible) than the House of Fame to provide him "tydynges" which can be of any use.

The *House of Fame* was nearly impossible to end, or perhaps any ending would be as good or bad as any other, because the poem is not about any particular tidings, and it has already said what it has to say about tidings in general. I wonder, in fact, if an important reason for the high incidence of unfinished work among Chaucer's poems might not be that, in accord with the aesthetic tradition behind him, he sought in his poetry to make his statement by formal arrangement rather than in a particular substance or by abstract declaration. This approach to his art left him with a particularly acute version of two classical problems of the poet: a formal arrangement has to be an arrangement of something, so that the substance itself may come to make demands (such as narrative completeness) which the poet wasn't originally much interested in; and the formal arrangement may just not work out, as it clearly did not with the relation of most of Book I to the rest of the *House of Fame*. Further, when the end is to raise questions, and the means chosen are contrast and irony, the problems of reaching a "conclusion" are greatly complicated. In the *Parliament of Fowls*, Chaucer brings off a splendid illusion of termination with the purely technical device of the roundel of the birds, and it is a little surprising that he did not experiment more with that kind of illusion. But the *Parliament of Fowls* is also, like most of the rest of his poetry, work in which the problems of art and the truths it is to contain occur simultaneously and almost inseparably. For instance, Love can (usually) be explored, questioned, analyzed through a medium (poetry) which is necessary to the process, but which itself shares the limitations and uncertainties it is trying to explore in the "subject."

The *House of Fame*, however, has no such "subject." It is certainly not a discussion of Love, nor of Fame, although it contains an example of one and a description of the other. All it has is the manner—the attempt to twist around the arrangement of books, dreams, and experience so as to produce some ironies which could illuminate the problem of art, knowledge, and illusion. After a start in Book I which no one has yet explained satisfactorily, the poem returns to the ironies of the Proem and Invocation and develops them to a point of paralysis by the end of Book II—a paralysis of exactly balanced uncertainties about books, dreams, and life which is in itself the principal "meaning" of the poem as it stands. Book III translates those ironies into the overt, cumbersome, and mathematically precise allegory of the palace of Fame, and as soon as they are separately embodied in so rationalistic a set of conventions, they are no longer instructive ironies at all, but only jejune platitudes which do not even seem to apply to the kind of artistic problem Book II had left us with. I think Book III is an attempt to illuminate the problems by reclothing them in a different set of amplificatory figures; but the Book is repetitious, in the end, rather than recapitulatory, because, as Chaucer himself realizes late in Book III, the new figures do not amplify anything. Even within Book III, the repetition of part of the mechanics of Fame, in the slightly altered figure of the House of Rumor, shows the same futile struggle toward a different image, one which will turn the ironic balance a bit so we can see it differently and more completely. Perhaps this is the point at which Chaucer really learned his distrust of formal allegory.

NOTES

31. Robert J. Allen, "A Recurring Motif in Chaucer's 'Hous of Fame'," *JEGP*, 55 (1956), 393-405, is the only critic, to my knowledge, who defines the problem of the poet as a "motif" in the poem, although Miss Bethurum recognizes its presence: "The implication is, I think, that the tidings of love he is to hear will furnish more material for his poems, for certainly mere tidings of how other people fare would not be the reward a lover looked for" ([Dorothy] Bethurum, ["Chaucer's Point of View as Narrator in the Love Poems," *PMLA* 74 (1959), 511-20] p. 514). It will become apparent, however, that I consider the "poetic problem" rather more than a "recurring motif" in *HF*, and that I do not agree with Professor Allen about the contrasting attitudes toward experience in the scholar and the literary artist.

32. It seems to me that the statement of the poem is simply contrary to Sypherd's assertation that ". . . the purpose of the journey, which is the purpose of the poem, is not to provide Chaucer with new poetic material." See "The Completeness of Chaucer's Hous of Fame," *MLN*, 30 (1915), 67.

33. This passage does not seem to me properly punctuated in Robinson's text. There almost certainly needs to be heavier punctuation than a comma after "here," or quite possibly a stop after "aryght."

34. Cf., among others, A.C. Baugh's remark, ". . . I do not care to look too far below the surface of Chaucer's poetry to discern a meaning that few in the audience for which he wrote would have grasped," in "Fifty Years of Chaucer Scholarship," *Speculum*, 26 (1951), 665.

35. This passage by itself, even discounting all arguments from the structure of the poem, seems to me to invalidate claims that *HF* has an over-all unity in some continuous "education" of the poet or "progressively universalizing impulse." See particularly David M. Bevington, "The Obtuse Narrator in Chaucer's *House of Fame*," *Speculum*, 36 (1961), 288-98; and Paul G. Ruggiers, "The Unity of Chaucer's *House of Fame*," *SP*, 50 (1953), 16-29.

36. "Over-celebrated" because here and elsewhere in his works, Chaucer's great skill with humorous dialogue has drawn so much critical attention that it has made us much too slow too see other, more important things in his art.

37. Again, it seems that rather careless reading has led to and supported some untenable theories about the nature of *HF*. The "tydynges" Geffrey is to get are, from their first mention in line 644 to their last in line 2143, unmistakably plural; and especially in Book II.

672-99 and Book III. 1960-76, long passages pile up *frequentatio* and
polysyndeton specifically to exaggerate the plurality (and
unmanageability?) of the "tydynges." Certainly no interpretation
—occasional or otherwise— which insists on a single final piece of
news can be made to square with the rest of the poem, although
probably the opposite extreme of arguing a series of tales to complete it
is defensible only through lack of evidence to the contrary.

   38. Cf. [Paull F.] Baum, "Chaucer's 'The House of Fame'," [*ELH*,
8 (1941), 248-56] p. 255: "While we are not suppose that Chaucer had
planned a complete hoax and ended deliberately in the middle of a
sentence, still there can have been little to add . . . In such a state of
uproar and tumult, men trampled under foot and climbing over one
another, no item of serious news could be expected. The whole tenor of
the second and third books is against such a possibility."

CHAUCER'S *HOUSE OF FAME*
AND THE *OVIDE MORALISÉ*

by Sheila Delany

Chaucer's portrait of his "variant goddess" has long been recognized as unique in that it presents Fame not merely as the goddess of rumor and report (a figure derived from *Aeneid*, IV, 173-192), nor as a personification of worldly glory, but as a judge whose function is to assign men to their places in history.

The iconographical tradition of Fame is strikingly devoid of anything that might have served Chaucer as inspiration. Fame was not among the usual medieval personified abstractions, and does not appear in art until the later middle ages.[1] Even then there is little to suggest the idea of Fame as arbiter. Early illustrations of Petrarch's *Trionfi* show Fama, like the other abstract figures, mounted on a chariot in procession rather than stationed in court.[2] Much of Chaucer's description of the Houses of Fame and Rumor is drawn from Ovid's version of Fama's dwelling in *Metamorphoses*, XII, 39-63; but in illuminated manuscripts of the *Ovide moralisé*, the early fourteenth-century translation and allegorization of the *Metamorphoses*, we find no illustration of this passage which strikes the modern reader as an ideal set piece for illustration. No doubt the reason for this is that the passage on Fame as it occurs in Ovid and in the medieval translation is nothing more than an "allegory" in the classical sense; that is, it does not form part of the narrative proper but is instead an extended rhetorical ornament, a figure of thought, a lively and concrete way of expressing the statement that news of the impending invasion reached Troy before the Greek fleet itself had arrived. It is probably for the same reason that Pierre Berçuire in the "Ovidius moralizatus" makes no reference to Fame in his summary of Ovid's account of the Trojan War.[3]

The generally accepted theory about the origin of Chaucer's conception of Fame remains that of W. O. Sypherd, who traced it to medieval iconographical and literary traditions of Love and Fortune.[4] Many details of the Fame figure are found here: the rock of ice on which her palace is built, the two trumpets, the goddess' alternating nature. However, Fortune herself is not represented specifically as a judge, but rather as proprietress of her wheel, or occasionally as a queen. Her power, moreover, is to assign material goods and social position, not to determine anyone's place in history; her realm is strictly the mundane, the temporal, and the temporary. There is, nevertheless, a medieval text which does connect Fame with the act of judgment, and which raises as well a problem central to the *House of Fame*: that of conflicting literary authorities. This is precisely the *Ovide moralisé*, a popular text known to have been used by Chaucer elsewhere but not discussed as a possible source for the *House of Fame*.

Chaucer's use of the *Ovide moralisé* was noticed long ago, particularly in connection with his most obviously Ovidian work, the *Legend of Good Women*. John L. Lowes found that Chaucer's version of the legend of Philomela, though based on the classical narrative in *Metamorphoses*, VI, 424 ff., was supplemented with details from the vernacular account,[5] and Karl Young suggested that the reference to Platonic doctrine in the first three lines of this legend could also have been derived from the *Ovide moralisé*.[6] Several details in the Legend of Ariadne have been traced to the *Ovide moralisé* by Professor Meech, who suggests that the legend of Thisbe may have been influenced as well by the French poem.[7] Finally, James A. Work has noted that the story of "li corbiaus" (*OM,* II, 2130-2548) is "remarkably close" to Chaucer's *Manciple's Tale* "in spirit, and occasionally in phraseology."[8]

A verbal comparison of the three texts involved shows, like most of the studies mentioned above, no evidence of exclusive reliance on either the original or the translation, but indicates rather that Chaucer worked primarily from the classical narrative with some details of description and style adapted from the vernacular. A breakdown of the most pertinent results follows, together with the relevant passages from the sources.

> Orbe locus medio est inter terrasque fretumque
> caelestesque plagas, triplicis confinia mundi;
> unde quod est usquam, quamvis regionibus absit,
> inspicitur, penetratque cavas vox omnis ad aures:
> Fama tenet summaque domum sibi legit in arce,
> innumerosque aditus ac mille foramina tectis
> addidit et nullis inclusit limina portis;
> nocte dieque patet; tota est ex aere sonanti,
> tota fremit vocesque refert iteratque quod audit;
> nulla quies intus nullaque silentia parte,

nec tamen est clamor, sed parvae murmura vocis,
qualia de pelagi, siquis procul audiat, undis
esse solent, qualemve sonum, cum Iuppiter atras
increpuit nubes, extrema tonitrua reddunt.
atria turba tenet: veniunt, leve vulgas, euntque
mixtaque cum veris passim commenta vagantur
milia rumorum confusaque verba volutant;
e quibus hi vacuas inplent sermonibus aures,
hi narrata ferunt alio, mensuraque ficti
crescit, et auditis aliquid novus adicit auctor.
illic Credulitas, illic temerarius Error
vanaque Laetitia est consternatique Timores
Seditioque recens dubioque auctore Susurri;
ipsa, quid in caelo rerum pelagoque geratur
et tellure, videt totumque inquirit in orbem.

(*Metamorphoses*, XII, 39-63)

Uns leus fu entre ciel et terre
Et mer qui seoit droitement
Ou milieu dou monde egalment.
De là voit l'en à la reonde
Quanque l'en fet par tout le monde.
Là set l'en toutes les nouveles,
Touz les diz, toutes les faveles
Qu'en dit en toutes regions.
C'est li leus, c'est la mancions
Ou Renommee est demorant.
Là vont les noveles corant
De tout le monde. En la maison
D'arain, qui plaine est de raison,
Puet l'en par plus de mil pertuis
Entrer sans porte et sans huis.
Jor et nuit œuvre la maison
Sans fermeture et sans cloison,
Et sans repos et sans silence
Les voiz repere et recomence,
Sans criërece, à bas murmure,
De voir et de controveüre.
Y vient nul manieres de jour.
Là vont et vienent sans sejor
Cil qui nouveles vont trouvent,
Si ne font que pastre le vent

Et les oreilles des oians,
Si font mains vainement joians.
Li autres recorde et recite
La parole que l'en a dite.
Li un tesmoignent verité.
Li autre dient vanité.
De mançonge et en racontant
Croissent la fable et vont mentant.
Toutes arrivent à ce port:
Vaine leësce et vain deport,
Vaine error et vaine creance,
Vaine doute et vaine esperance,
Vaine paour, vaine discorde
Et vain murmure, qui recorde
Ce qu'il ot aus autres retraire.
L'en ne puet riens au siecle faire,
En ciel, en terre, en mer, en monde,
Que tout ne l'oye à la reonde
Renommee, qui là demore.
            (*Ovide moralisé*, XII, 1588-1631)

(1) Some features of Chaucer's description are independent of both Ovid and the *Ovide moralisé*. Chaucer omits, for instance, the information that from Fame's house everything can be seen as well as heard. He also omits the list of abstract qualities cited in the other two texts as inhabitants of the place. Whereas both earlier texts specify brass to be the material of Fame's dwelling, Chaucer claims the House of Fame to be built of beryl (1184) and the House of Rumor of twigs (1936). Both of the Ovidian texts state that the noise at Fame's house is a soft one ("nec tamen est clamor"; "sans criërece"), but Chaucer writes that the House of Rumor is filled with "tydynges, / Other loude, or of whisprynges" (1958). Finally, Chaucer is unique in making the ascent of sound to the House of Fame a necessary process of nature (729 ff.).

(2) In a few instances Chaucer includes details which are found in Ovid but not in the translation. The two most important are the mountain top on which Fame's house is built (*HF*, 1116), and the comparison of the sound of the place to that of the sea heard from afar and to distant thunder (*HF*, 1034-42).

(3) Finally there are some details in which both the *Ovide moralisé* and the *House of Fame* differ from Ovid and resemble one another. In Ovid, for example, Fama searches the world ("inquirit in orbem") for news; in the other two texts the goddess is receptive only and does not

move outside her palace. Ovid writes that within Fame's house there is no quiet ("nulla quies"). It is clear from the context of this phrase, which describes the peculiar quality of sound in the place, that the word "quies" means silence rather than rest or the absence of motion. The French writer nevertheless translates "quies" as "repos"—a possible meaning for the word, but wrong in this context. Chaucer repeats the mistake; his word is "rest" (1956). In Ovid the location of Fame's house is given as "inter terrasque fretumque / caelestesque plagas" ; the translation gives the order of places as "entre ciel et terre / Et mer," and so does Chaucer: "Betwixen hevene, erthe, and see" (715). In the classical description of the palace architectural details precede the statement of material, while in both later versions the reverse is true.

Lastly, it is possible that Chaucer took inspiration from the *Ovide moralisé* for his enormously effective amplification of the nine lines in which Ovid describes the activities at Fame's house. In these lines (53-61) Ovid relies mainly on the rhetorical device of alliteration to convey the sense of continual sound. He uses homoteleuton as well in 60-61, the repeated ending "-que" formally representing the accumulation of persons being named. In the *Ovide moralisé* this section is expanded to eighteen lines (1610-27). The octosyllabic couplet is too brief to make effective use of sustained alliteration; only a few examples of it occur, and the translator substitutes anaphora as a characteristic device in this passage. He repeats the definite article and the adjective "vaine," using both words at the head of a line and also to begin phrases within the line. Chaucer's amplification of the Ovidian passage also occupies eighteen lines (1959-76), and he, too, relies primarily on anaphora. So wholeheartedly does he take up the stylistic suggestion that sixteen of his eighteen lines begin with the same word, "Of," and fifteen contain the word at the beginning of an internal phrase. This is a daring display of virtuosity, for extended anaphora is one of the easiest figures of speech to reproduce, and runs the risk of monotony through repetition of clause structure. Chaucer handles the technique far more skillfully than does the French poet, using antithesis to set up balanced pairs of prepositional phrases, and occasional subtle alliteration throughout the passage. He also varies the number of phrases per line from one ("Of divers transmutaciouns") to four ("Of love, of hate, acord, of stryfe"), providing a continually varied syntactic rhythm within the couplet structure.

If it is true, as these verbal parallels imply, that Chaucer consulted the *Ovide moralisé* as well as the *Metamorphoses* in composing his *House of Fame*, he would have found in the French text more to interest him than merely a translation of the classical material. He would have found as well an interpretation of this material according to Christian doctrine. This interpretation of Fame and her dwelling may, I suggest, have had some influence in shaping Chaucer's conception of the goddess as a judge over men. The exegesis begins as follows:

> Par la maison de Renomee
> Où toute est dite et recitee
> La chose qui au monde avient
> Puet l'en entendre, si devient,
> L'Escripture, qui tout retrait
> Ce qu'est à faire et qui est fait.
> C'est cele qui certainement
> Fait assavoir l'avenement
> Dou Dieu des olz qui doit venir . . . (XII, 1657-65)

Inclusiveness is the basis of this analogy: as Fame's house includes all that is said or done in the world, so Scripture contains the entire Christian past and future: that is, all of Christian history and all that pertains to salvation. Further, just as Fame's palace is a vantage point from which all may be seen, so Scripture is the central text in which the coming of God is revealed, at which time all shall be seen. The exegete now develops the retributive aspects of Scriptural revelation:

> A grant honte et à grant damage
> Puet torner as presumcieuz,
> Aus gloutons, aus luxurieuz,
> S'il ne vienent à repentance
> Ains que viegne au jor de vengance,
> Quant Diex vendra por vengier s'ire
> En son celestial empire. (Lines 1674-80)

This description of the sinful who are to be judged recalls the earlier lines in which the inhabitants of Fame's house are characterized one after the other as "vaine"; again anaphora is used, and what was previously stated to be vain (false, deceptive) is here shown to be so. In the thirty lines of his doctrinal interpretation, the poet devotes himself to an enthusiastic account of the horrors that await the sinful, forgetting to anchor his interpretation to the Ovidian material that evoked it. Thus the allegory is neither thorough nor particularly subtle here, and there is no exegesis of specific details of the goddess' nature or palace. The passage concludes with a contrast between the followers of Antichrist and "the friends of God":

> Et cil qui sor touz sera pire,
> Fiers et plains d'indignacion,
> Li princes de perdicion,
> Antecris, qui lors regnera
> Sor la gent Dieu, forsenera,
> Et cil qui premiers aparront
> Pour la loi Dieu le comperront,
> Qui lor espandra les boëles,
> Les entrailles et les cervelles,
> Et pluiseurs iront damagent
> Des amis Dieu, lui et sa gent. (Lines 1698-1708)

Despite the inferiority of exegetical analysis in this section of the *Ovide moralisé*,[9] we nevertheless find in it several features of Chaucer's goddess which are absent from the traditional iconography of Love and Fortune. Most importantly, Fame is associated with the act of judgment, albeit indirectly through the intermediary of a doctrinal analogy which compares her house to Scripture. As controlling figure in the place, Fame herself implicitly assumes the role of judge—though this extension of the analogy is not specifically made in the *Ovide moralisé*—and she acquires an aura of authority which Virgil's and Ovid's portraits lack, but which is present in Chaucer's. Also implied in the doctrinal interpretation is the scene of the *dies irae*: a great assembly of persons whose deeds in life cause them to be assigned to one or another place in the hierarchy of salvation. This, too, may have played a part in Chaucer's presentation of the judgment scene at Fame's court, for in Ovid no process of cause and effect is acted out; it is supplied only in the medieval exegesis. These common traits suggest that Chaucer's portrait of Fame was influenced, in part at least, by his reading of the French text.

A third area of possible influence remains to be explored. Immediately following the description and interpretation of Fame, the French poet raises another subject with which Chaucer is concerned in the *House of Fame*, that is, the problem of estimating the truth in conflicting but equally authoritative traditions. Chaucer's most obvious reference to this problem appears in the brief passage describing the various *auctores* who support the fame of Troy:

> And by him [Statius] stood, withouten les,
> Ful wonder hy on a piler
> Of yren, he, the gret Omer;

> And with him Dares and Tytus
> Before, and eke he Lollius,
> And Guydo eke de Columpnis,
> And Englyssh Gaufride eke, ywis . . .
> But yet I gan ful wel espie,
> Betwex hem was a litil envye.
> Oon seyde that Omer made lyes,
> Feynynge in hys poetries,
> And was to Grekes favorable;
> Therfor held he hyt but fable. (Lines 1464-80)

The question of conflicting sources is also suggested in the plethora of contradictory dream lore in the Proem to the *House of Fame*, and in the presentation of both Virgilian and Ovidian material in Chaucer's version of the Dido and Aeneas story (Book I). These sections of the work indicate that Chaucer's method of handling contradictory traditions is simply to present the material in all its ambiguity, without comment or choice between several alternatives.

The French poet is less subtle in his treatment of the ambiguity of literary tradition. After his analysis of Fame, he resumes the Trojan narrative, and this leads him to consider the problem of sources:

> A quelque paine ont Grieu port pris.
> Achilles, li vaillant de pris,
> Est ja venus à la bataille.
> Des or comenceront, sans faille,
> L'ocision et le martire,
> Que traist li clers de Saint More
> De Darès . . . (Lines 1709-15)

Benoît de Sainte-Maure's *Roman de Troie*, the earliest extant vernacular account of the matter of Troy, is based largely on the *De Excidio Troiae Historia*, a sixth century translation of a forged Greek "eyewitness" version of the Trojan War which purported to be the work of one Dares Phrygius, a Trojan soldier. Benoit also made some use of *De Bello Trojano*, another translation, dating from about the fourth century, of another Greek forgery which claimed to be the military diary of a Greek soldier, Dictys Cretensis.[10] These two sources drew on and perpetuated a long-standing anti-Homeric tradition which, largely through their efforts, became a medieval tradition as well. They and others rejected the authenticity of Homer on the grounds that he was naturally partial to his countrymen, that he shows the gods in combat with mortals, and shows them to be of bad character.[11] In Dares and Dictys the techniques of criticism are mainly implicit, i.e., both exalt characters whom Homer treats as minor, deprecate or minimize the roles of the great Homeric heroes, and omit or provide alternate explanations for various supernatural interventions. In addition, the Dares document includes a prefatory letter in which the putative discoverer and translator writes that his readers may

> judge for themselves whether Dares the Phrygian or Homer wrote more truthfully—Dares, who lived and fought at the time the Greeks fought Troy, or Homer, who was born long after the War was over.[12]

Thus the accuracy of sources for the matter of Troy was in question from the very beginning. Benoît, like a proper modern twelfth-century skeptic, comes down firmly on the side of the "eye-witness" version (*Troie*, 45- 128) ; but it is an interesting comment on the nature of some medieval critical skepticism that while Benoît felt free to doubt Homer he did not doubt both sources; one truth at least was required.

The *Ovide* poet, unlike Benoît, refuses to exalt one authority at the expense of another; he finds each writer to be worthy in his fashion:

> Moult fu li clers bons rimoierres,
> Cortois partiers et biaus faigtierres,
> Et moult fu bien ses romans fais,
> Mes nequedent, sauve sa pais,
> Il ne dist pas en touz leuz voir,
> Si ne fist mie grant savoir
> Dont il Homers osa desdire
> Ne desmentir ne contredire
> Ne blasmer œuvre qu'il feïst.
> Ne cuit c'onques Homers deïst
> Chose que dire ne deüst
> Et que de verté ne seüst.
> Ja nel deüst avoir repris,
> Quar trop iert Homers de grant pris,
> Mes il parla par metaphors.
> Por ce li clers de Sainte More,
> Que n'entendoit qu'il voloit dire,
> Li redargua sa matire. (Lines 1719-36)

Benoît, he writes, is a fine craftsman, but he does not always speak the truth. Homer is authoritative but has been misunderstood because-that great panacea for reconciling discordant texts—"il parla par metaphore." Most startling assertion of all, the poet claims to know from his own reading that Dares contradicts Homer in nothing:

> Neïs Darès, de quoi fu fais
> Li romans Beneois et trais,
> N'est de riens contraires à lui,
> Quar l'un et l'autre livre lui,
> Fors tant que plus prolixement
> Dist Darès le demenement . . . (Lines 1743-48)

The claim seems absurd unless we assume that by "Darès" the French poet meant a text other than that which we designate by the name. It was shown by Robert K. Root that Chaucer's "Dares" was in fact the late twelfth-century *De Bello Trojano* of Joseph of Exeter, which is named in all extant manuscripts as "frigii daretis yliados liber."[13] Thus the apparent paradoxes in the critical evaluations of the *Ovide* poet may be due to his having known a version of the Dares material which omitted the pejorative introductory letter and perhaps some of the details more obviously divergent from Homer.[14] Another possibility, supported by the tendency of many medieval writers to invoke the authority of fictitious sources or of sources not actually known to them, is that the poet's assertion of personal acquaintance with "Dares" is simply untrue. Chaucer himself provides an example of the latter practice with his references to "Lollius" in *Troilus and Criseyde*.[15]

Having posed and in his own way resolved the problem of conflicting authorities, the poet hastens to conclude his literary digression. The last three lines of this section indicate, however, that the reconciliation of sources is not fully satisfactory even to the writer, for he abandons his justification of authors and leaves the matter to the reader's own preference:

> Ne sai que plus vous en diroie,
> Mes cil qui l'un et l'autre orra
> Croie celui qui miex vaudra. (Lines 1752-54)

Obviously Chaucer did not depend exclusively on the *Ovide moralisé* for his awareness of the complexities involved in the matter of Troy. His own reading of Virgil and Ovid would have sufficed to bring to his attention the discrepant versions of Aeneas; and if Chaucer read

Benoît, the *Roman de Troie* would have alerted him to similar discrepancies in connection with the war itself. Nevertheless we know enough of Chaucer's reading habits to assume that when working from a medieval or classical Latin source he would take advantage of a translation if one were available. This was his practice in a number of works, among them the *Clerk's*, *Physician's*, *Monk's* and *Manciple's Tales*, the *Tale of Melibée*, the *Legend of Good Women*, and possibly the translation of *Boethius*.[16] It would therefore have been typical for Chaucer to reach for the *Ovide moralisé* when considering Ovid's version of Fame as possible material for his own writing, and it would have been virtually impossible for him not to have noted there the allegorized interpretation of the Ovidian Fame material. In the light of the verbal and thematic parallels here discussed, it seems likely that the *Ovide moralisé* deserves to be included among Chaucer's sources for the *House of Fame*.

NOTES

1. See Raimond van Marle, *Iconographie de l'art profane au moyen âge et à la Renaissance* (The Hague, 1932), II, 111 ff.

2. Only Amor was specifically so described by Petrarch, but the chariot motif was used by illustrators for all of the triumphal figures. For discussion of this motif see Victor d'Essling and Eugène Muntz, *Pétrarque* (Paris, 1902).

3. Berçuire, or Berchorius, a friend of Petrarch, died in 1362. The "Ovidius moralizatus" is Book 15 of his encyclopedic *Reductorium morale*. It is omitted from all early printed editions of the *Reductorium* and was printed separately as the work of Thomas Walys. The "Ovidus moralizatus" has been published in *Werkmateriel (2) uitgegeven door het Institut voor Laat Latijn der Rijksuniversiteit* (Utrecht, 1962).

4. W. O. Sypherd, *Studies in Chaucer's Hous of Fame* (London, 1907), pp. 17, 114-118. See also Howard R. Patch, *The Goddess Fortuna* (Cambridge, Mass., 1927), p. 110. F.N. Robinson considers Sypherd's suggestion to be "the most probable'; see *The Works of Geoffrey Chaucer*, 2nd ed. (Boston, 1957), p. 784, note 1130. I have used Robinson's edition for all quotations from Chaucer in my text.

5. John L. Lowes, "Chaucer and the *Ovide Moralisé*," *PMLA*, XXXIII (1918). The legend as it appears in the *Ovide moralisé* is an incorporated fragment by Chrétien de Troyes, which has been edited separately by C. de Boer (Paris, 1909). All quotations from the *Ovide moralisé* in my text are from de Boer's edition (Amsterdam, 1915-38).

6. Karl Young, "Chaucer's Appeal to the Platonic Deity," *Speculum*, XIX (1944).

7. Sanford B. Meech, "Chaucer and an Italian Translation of the *Heroides*," *PMLA*, XLV (1930); "Chaucer and the *Ovide Moralisé*—a Further Study," *PMLA*, XLVI (1931).

8. In *Sources and Analogues of Chaucer's Canterbury Tales*, ed. W.F. Bryan and Germaine Dempster (New York, 1958), pp. 702-703.

9. This is by no means a typical allegoresis, however. The story of Orpheus (Book X) is extensively analyzed from an historical, a moral, and a doctrinal point of view. Again, the brevity of treatment here is probably due to the status of the Fame passage as merely rhetorical ornament.

10. Benoît de Sainte-Maure, *Le Roman de Troie*, ed. Léopold Constans (Paris, 1904); *Dictys Cretensis et Dares Phrygius*, ed. A. Valpy (London, 1825). The two Latin documents have been translated by R.M. Frazer in *The Trojan War* (Bloomington, 1966). For additional information, see Nathaniel E. Griffin, *Dares and Dictys* (Baltimore, 1907).

11. Another manifestation of this last objection to Homer was the Greek exegetical movement, which explained supernatural events in Homer and other poets in terms of moral or philosophical allegory.

12. Frazer, p. 133.

13. Robert K. Root, "Chaucer's Dares," *MP*, XV (1917). The text of Joseph's poem is included in Valpy's Dares and Dictys.

14. Constans interprets the remark that Dares is "plus prolixe" than Homer as evidence that the *Ovide* poet knew an expanded version (*Troie*, VI, 263).

15. *Troilus*, I, 394 and V, 1653. That these references to Lollius are errors, not deliberate fictions, was suggested by G.L. Kittredge, "Chaucer's Lollius," in *Harvard Studies in Classical Philology*, XXVIII (Cambridge, Mass., 1917). This opinion is supported by the findings of R.A. Pratt, "A Note on Chaucer's Lollius," *MLN*, LXV (1950). As Kittredge notes, Chaucer's fiction is not in citing Lollius, but in claiming the *Troilus* to be a direct translation from the Latin (II, 12-14).

16. *Sources and Analogues*, pp. 289, 563, 398 ff., 615, 699; J.L. Lowes, "Chaucer's *Boethius* and Jean de Meun," *RR*, VIII (1917) ; and Sanford B. Meech, "Chaucer and an Italian Translation of the *Heroides*," *PMLA*, XLV (1930).

THE "LOVE-TYDYNGES"
IN CHAUCER'S *HOUSE OF FAME*

by Larry D. Benson

Doctor Johnson's judgment of *Paradise Lost*—"no man ever wished it longer"—applies to a large number of literary works but not to Chaucer's *House of Fame*, which many readers wish had been longer if only by a few lines. Caxton and Thynne did make it longer.[1] They supplied the conclusion the work seems so sorely to lack, but even they failed to include the information that many readers hope for—the identity of the "man of gret auctorite" and the "love-tydynges" we expect him to bring. In recent years an increasing number of readers have become convinced that Chaucer intended the poem to end as it does now, with the abrupt, unexplained appearance of the "man of gret auctorite," and probably even more agree with F.N. Robinson that the identity of that man and the nature of his tidings are now beyond conjecture.[2] Yet the problem remains to tease and in some ways to delight the reader. Kittredge wrote, "I am glad the *House of Fame* is unfinished, for this gives me a chance to guess at the story that should conclude it."[3] He added that he had a very pretty theory of his own, which he prudently refused to reveal. I too am glad that the *House of Fame* is unfinished, and I too have a theory, which, lacking Kittredge's prudence, I here reveal: the *House of Fame* is unfinished because that is what Chaucer intended; he fails to identify the "man of gret auctorite" and to specify the "love-tydynges" that he brings because his audience already knew what those tidings were, and that must have been part of the fun in Chaucer's most fun-filled poem.

These tidings are but a minor part of the poem. Beginning with Book II, the promise of "love-tydynges" provides the "plot," the occasion for the eagle's lecture on elementary acoustics and for the journey to the houses of Fame and Rumor. These in turn supply the framework for the thematic concerns—the problems of poetry, love, fame, authority, and experience—that engage Chaucer's and the reader's main interest. Not knowing what the "love-tydynges" are has not notably affected our understanding of the poem, though bad guesses about the identity of the "man of gret auctorite" have. It may even be

that the "plot" involving the "love-tydynges" was added at the last
stage of the poem's composition, when an occasion at court suggested
this means of controlling the materials of this lively, nearly
uncontrolled, but brilliant work.

However that may be, the prospect of learning what the "love-
tydynges" will be draws on both Geoffrey and the reader, as Chaucer
repeatedly hints that we will learn something of great importance. What
that will be is not at all clear at the beginning of Book II. We only
know that it will be news from the real world rather than from books, in
which Geoffrey has been immersed so long that he knows nothing
"noght oonly fro fer contree . . . but of thy verray neyghebores" (647-
49). The eagle, with characteristic expansiveness, promises Geoffrey
that in recompense for this devotion to books about love, he will hear
every possible sort of love-tidings at the House of Fame:

> Mo wonder thynges, dar I leye,
> And of Loves folk moo tydynges,
> Both sothe sawes and lesinges;
> And moo loves newe begonne
> And longe yserved loves wonne,
> And moo loves casuelly
> That ben betyd, no man wot why . . . (674-81)

The catalogue continues for eighteen lines, and it seems to break off not
because the eagle has exhausted his list of promised tidings but because
he detects a trace of incredulity in his auditor:

> And eke of loves moo eschaunges
> Then ever cornes were in graunges,—
> Unnethe maistow trowen this? (697-99)

Yet in Book III, when Geoffrey finally arrives at the House of Fame, he
hears nothing of the sort—no tidings at all. When he complains to his
unknown interlocutor that what he has seen and heard at the House of
Fame "be no suche tydynges / As I mene of" (1894-95), he is asked:

> Which than be, loo, these tydynges,
> That thou now [thus] hider brynges
> That thou hast herd? (1907-1909)

The nature of the tidings has changed. Geoffrey is apparently now
seeking not news of just any sort but some particular tidings,

confirmation perhaps of some rumor that he has heard. And so he is taken to the House of Rumor, where again the eagle promises him tidings "many oon" (2026).

The House of Rumor, we soon learn, is concerned mainly with news from foreign parts, for it is populated solely by travellers—shipmen, pilgrims, pardoners, couriers, and messengers (2122-30). Geoffrey, nearing the end of his quest for tidings, goes eagerly about seeking to hear a particular piece of foreign news, presumably the same that his interlocutor implied had brought him to the House of Fame:

> And as I alther-fastest wente
> About, and dide al myn entente
> Me for to pleyen and for to lere,
> And eke a tydynge for to here
> That I had herd of som contre
> That shal nat now be told for me—
> For hit no nede is, redely;
> Folk kan synge hit bet than I;
> For al mot out, other late or rathe,
> Alle the sheves in the lathe— (2131-40)

It is typical of the comic reversals and anti-climaxes that characterize the *House of Fame* that Geoffrey, who started out at the beginning of Book II apparently seeking any sort of "love-tydynges," is now seeking one very particular piece of information and that he who began as a hapless outsider, whom the eagle (and reader) can patronize because he is so busy with his reckonings that he knows nothing of the real world of affairs, has now become the insider. He knows something, from "som contre," that we do not know, and we now realize that Geoffrey, the bookish and unworldly (so he would have us believe) reckoner of Customs, is also Chaucer, the discreet diplomat, privy to news from "som contre." We are now the outsiders, eager for the tidings that Chaucer teasingly refuses to tell us.

At that moment a great uproar arises in a corner of the hall, where men "of love-tydynges tolde" (2143). By now we are almost as eager to hear those tidings as those who rush to that corner:

> And whan they were alle on an hepe,
> Tho behynde begunne up lepe
> And clamben up on other faste

> And up the nose and yёn kaste,
> And troden fast on others heles
> And stampen, as men don after eles.
> Atte last y saugh a man,
> Which that y [nevene] nat ne kan;
> But he semed for to be
> A man of gret auctorite . . . (2149-58)

Here the poem ends abruptly. We are never told what the tidings are. Yet, we have been given broad hints about their nature: they are tidings of love from the real world rather than from the world of books; they come from abroad, from "som contre" known to Chaucer; and they are of sufficient importance to be announced by one who seemed—not necessarily was—of great authority. Some news of national concern, some alliance sealed by marriage—something "Of werres, of pes, of mariages, (1961)—is clearly implied. Consequently, scholars have argued that the news was an announcement in late 1380 of the betrothal of Richard II to Anne of Bohemia (Imelmann's theory) or (according to Brusendorff) an announcement in 1381 of Anne's imminent arrival in England.[4] Koch believed the poem was written in 1384 to announce the expected betrothal of John of Gaunt's daughter to Charles VI of France.[5] Baugh suggests, cautiously, that the *House of Fame* may have been written in anticipation of the expected betrothal of Richard to a French Princess (little Marie), while negotiations for this alliance were in progress in 1377.[6] The "man of gret auctorite" has been identified as of the same high stature as these "tydynges": John of Gaunt, Thomas of Gloucester, even Richard II himself.[7]

The main objection to such theories is that the setting in which this "man of gret auctorite" appears is pure slapstick comedy, a raucous scene in which everyone is leaping up and down, stomping on one another's feet, and climbing on backs in riotous disorder. It is a setting in which a man who appears to be "of gret auctorite" can only seem ridiculous, like a dignitary in top hat and tails suddenly appearing in a similar scene in a Marx Brothers comedy. Our sense of the ridiculous is heightened by Chaucer's revelation that he already knows the news: whatever tidings this dignitary may bring will be, at least slightly, anti-climactic. Moreover, the whole third book has cast doubt on the validity of any tidings that might emerge from the House of Rumor, and the entire poem has comically deflated the whole idea of "auctoritee." If even the great "auctors" cannot be trusted, squabbling as they are while trying to hold up the fame of Troy, and with even Virgil having been shown in Book I to be untrustworthy, what real authority can there be in such a figure? One can hardly imagine that either Richard II, who insisted on being treated with elaborately ceremonial respect, or John of Gaunt, would-be "King of Castile," would have been pleased to have been placed in so indecorous a setting.

The theories of Imelmann, Brusendorff, and Koch have therefore been rejected by most scholars not so much because of the weaknesses of their arguments—Brusendorff makes a good case for his theory—but because of what is regarded as the improbability of an announcement of serious and important news in so indecorous a context.[8] I suspect that the unsuitability of the setting has been somewhat overemphasized. The tone is festive—boisterous and comic—but never overtly satiric. Though it is difficult to imagine King Richard or John of Gaunt in such a role, some lesser—but still authoritative—dignitary could be imagined in this setting. Some good-natured official with a lively sense of humor might even have relished the momentary deflation of dignity this role would have produced.[9] It does seem, however, that the comic treatment of the news—the fact that it comes from the House of Rumor from which the whole truth never emerges—renders it unlikely that the announcement of some definitely settled betrothal or marriage was intended. Yet, this is a poem of comic reversals, in which almost anything is possible.

Though the comic tone of the setting may not completely rule out tidings of some important engagement or wedding, it does seem to me to rule out the possibility that the tidings concerned some shocking court scandal. Bertrand H. Bronson, arguing that the setting rendered an announcement of a wedding or betrothal unlikely, concluded that the poem must have been written to retail some scandalous bit of court gossip—so shocking that Chaucer, on sober reconsideration, decided to destroy the conclusion he had written.[10] Frederick C. Reidel, on somewhat different grounds, argued that the scandal to be announced was John of Gaunt's appearance in court with his mistress, Katherine Swynford, in 1378.[11] Given the good-natured, spoofing tone of the final scene, this seems unlikely. Some scandalous bit of news is not out of the range of possibility, but one would expect something more trifling than shocking. To fit the tone of the final scene, the "tydynges," like the "man of gret auctorite" himself, must be at least slightly anti-climactic and therefore a trifle comic—or, at the very least, news that can be made to seem so.

Such considerations seem to me to rule out the various literary, philosophical, and religious figures whom critics in recent years suggested as the man of great authority. A number of scholars have argued that he was to be Boccaccio or Boethius; Donald C. Baker has suggested Virgil; and B.G. Koonce, most daring of all, believes he was to be Jesus Christ.[12] Though J.A.W. Bennett holds that the word "auctorite" shows that the man of authority is necessarily an author, it seems unlikely that Virgil, Boethius, or Boccaccio could have been intended.[13] Chaucer often uses "auctorite(e)" in non-literary senses—in *Troilus*, for example, Calkas is called a "lord of greet auctoritee"[14]—and the eagle has promised Geoffrey news from the real world instead of the world of books. The theory that the final scene is intended to introduce Christ depends on an abstemiously ironic reading, which yields so dreary a theological interpretation that, if valid, it would lead many readers to wish not that Chaucer had finished the poem but that he had never started it.

Perhaps partly because of the unsatisfactory nature of the solutions offered to the problems posed by the "man of gret auctorite," critics in recent years have tended to set that problem aside and to consider the *House of Fame* finished as it stands, satisfactory even without the promised tidings. There is much to recommend this position, since obviously the poem has given pleasure over the centuries despite its failure to reveal the love-tidings Geoffrey seeks. Much of its fun is in its contradictions, its sudden shifts of focus, and its creation of significant tensions, and part of its peculiar pleasure lies in the fact that it ends, as Kay Stevenson has observed, with these tensions intact and unresolved.[15] Donald K. Fry—at a previous celebration of Chaucer at Albany—reconstructed the original ending in a way that takes account of the qualities that Stevenson admires in the final lines of the poem. Fry notes that Chaucer builds toward the appearance of the "man of gret auctorite" by comically undercutting the whole idea of "auctoritee":

> Since nothing this character says can have any validity, he abruptly cuts him off. I picture the first reading of this poem to the court ending something like this. Chaucer reads the closing lines: "Atte laste y saugh a man, Which that y nevene not ne kan; But he semed for to be A man of gret auctorite," closes his manuscript volume, and sits down smiling to a rising crescendo of shocked surprise, laughter, understanding, and finally applause.[16]

Yet the teasing about tidings from "som contre" remains. Part of the laughter must have been because the "man of gret auctorite" has little or no authority at all, but part must also have been because of the realization of what the news was, tidings that Chaucer knew and that his audience must also have known but perhaps until this moment did not realize that this was the "tydynges" the man of "gret auctorite" was to bring. If this is the case, this would be the last of the comic reversals: Chaucer, who began as an outsider and has now apparently become an insider, privy to some secret he will not divulge, turns out to have no secret at all; the news that "will not be told for me" is news his audience already knows.

If we could be sure when the *House of Fame* was first read, we would be in a somewhat better position to learn what those tidings are. Clearly they are news of some sort, and stale news is no news, so it is reasonable to assume that the first reading came not too long after news arrived in London from "som contre." Since they are to be "love-tydynges," "of werres, of pes, of mariages," they likely concern some international alliance sealed by marriage. And since Chaucer makes so much of December 10, an unusual time for a dream-vision, and insists that it is not just any December 10 but this present tenth of December—"the tenth day now of Decembre" (63; cf. 111)—it seems reasonable to assume that the poem was first read not too long after some particular December 10 when there was some bit of international love-tidings. I say "first read" rather than "composed," for, as I have noted, it is possible that Chaucer had been working on this poem for some time and simply adapted it for this particular occasion.

If this occasion was connected with a particular December tenth, the problem becomes: December tenth of which year? Since Chaucer refers to his laboring over his accounts (653), the date most probably falls during those years when he was controller of the Customs—between 8 June 1374, when he was appointed to the post with the stipulation that he keep the accounts with his own hand ("manu sua propria"), and most likely 23 June 1383, when he was allowed to appoint a deputy because he was so busy ("si grandement occupez") or, at the latest, after 1386, when Chaucer ceased having anything to do with the office.[17] Though in the nineteenth century it was generally believed that the *House of Fame* was the "comedye" promised at the end of *Troilus*, in 1905 John Livingston Lowes demonstrated that the *House of Fame* definitely preceded *Troilus*, and he argued that its most likely date was "around 1379."[18] This is the date accepted by Robinson ("1379-80") and many others, but agreement is not complete. Albert C. Baugh assigns the poem to 1377; John Fisher places it in 1380-81; Reidel, to fit his theory about the "tydynges,"

argues it was written in 1384; and George Williamson spans the entire
period, placing the dream on the night of 10 December 1372 and the
poem itself sometime between 1386 and 1389.[19] We must therefore
consider in some detail the evidence for the dating of the *House of
Fame*.

Lowes's main reason for placing the *House of Fame* before the
1380's was that beginning around 1380 Chaucer was so deeply
influenced by the *Teseida* which he apparently first read on his journey
to Italy in 1378. Boccaccio's *Teseida*, Lowes wrote, was a work with
which Chaucer was fascinated, with which he "played almost as a child
with a new toy . . . In the *Ariadne*, in the *Anelida*, within the
Parliament of Fowls, in the *Troilus*, and in the two forms of the
Knight's Tale itself, its material appears, as if its appeal had been so
irresistible that Chaucer found it hard to keep his hands off it, whatever
he commenced."[20] Chaucer knew the *Teseida* when he wrote the *House
of Fame:* from that work he may have acquired his erroneous belief that
Helicon was a well rather than a mountain peak ("Be Elicon, the clere
welle," 522); but it is only in such ornamental touches that he shows
that he has read the *Teseida*, and Lowes concluded that the *House of
Fame* was written when Chaucer was first becoming acquainted with
the work, after 1378 but before the works of the 1380s which show him
so deeply involved with the challenges and fascinations of Boccaccio's
poem.[21]

In more recent years scholars have found confirmation for Lowes's
belief in a number of small but significant bits of evidence. Lowes's
idea that the *House of Fame* must have been written after rather than
before the journey to Italy in 1378 depends on the assumption that
Chaucer first encountered the *Teseida* on that journey and it is of
course possible that Chaucer learned of that work on his first journey or
acquired it from some traveller or Italian merchant in the years between
his first and second journeys. However, Lowes's assumption that the
poem must have been written after the journey of 1378 is strengthened
by J. S. P. Tatlock's observation that Fame's trumpets, "Clere Laude"
and "Sclaundre" (1572-82), bear a striking resemblance to Fortune's
trumpets, "Remonee" and "Desfame," in Gower's *Mirour de l'Omme*
(22129-52).[22] Howard R. Patch suggested the existence of a common
source, but none has ever been found, and the two texts most likely
have a direct relation.[23] Tatlock thought Gower was the borrower, but J.
A. W. Bennett offers grounds for regarding Chaucer rather than Gower
as the debtor.[24]

Gower's *Mirour*, according to John H. Fisher, was composed in
the years 1376-78, and if Tatlock was right in his study of the *Mirour*,

the section dealing with Fortune's trumpets came later than earlier in this period—probably quite late in 1378 (Tatlock thought 1379), since Gower refers to the Great Schism, which did not begin until September of that year.[25] Chaucer, of course, could have known Gower's work while it was in progress, and the *House of Fame* does not necessarily date after Gower's work was "published." Nevertheless, the probable debt to Gower's *Mirour* lends support to Lowes' belief that the *House of Fame* could not have been finished earlier than the later part of 1378.

There is also evidence supporting Lowes' belief that the *House of Fame* must have been written before the *Parliament of Fowls*, which is among the earliest of the works showing the heavy influence of *Il Teseida*. Robert A. Pratt has shown that in the *Parliament* Chaucer "borrowed from himself"; in the invocation to Venus (113-16) Chaucer drew on lines that first appeared in the *House Of Fame*.[26] Years earlier, in 1916, Martha H. Shackford had noted that in the *Romaunt of the Rose* (7-10), in the *Book of the Duchess* (284-89), and in the *House of Fame* (916-18), Chaucer consistently refers to Scipio (in the *Somnium Scipionis*) as "kyng Cipioun."[27] This is an error that Chaucer apparently inherited from Guillaume de Lorris, who refers to "roi Scipion" in the *Roman de la rose* (12). Chaucer knew of Macrobius (from the *Roman de la rose*, if not from other sources), and in the opening lines of the *House of Fame* he shows knowledge of Macrobius' classification of dreams, but he apparently knew of Macrobius only at second hand or in excerpt, and at this stage of his career, he had not yet read the *Somnium Scipionis*. By the time he wrote the *Parliament of Fowls*, he clearly had read that work, since the *Parliament* opens with a full and accurate summary of "Tullyus of the dreme of Scipio" (31). Derek Brewer, in his edition of the *Parliament*, concludes that the mistaken reference to "kyng Scipioun" "points to the *House of Fame* being earlier than the *Parliament*," and almost all scholars agree with this order of composition.[28]

Brewer dates Chaucer's beginning the writing of the *Parliament* in May, 1382, as do many scholars, because of the apparent astronomical reference in v. 117, where Venus is said to be visible in the "north-north-west."[29] Hamilton Smyser questioned this dating; he notes that the astronomical reference fits May of 1380 as well as May of 1382, and he regarded 1380 as "a more plausible date" than 1382.[30] However, Smyser also notes that there is a legitimate doubt that an astronomical reference is intended. Leaving that problem aside, as well as my own conviction that the *Parliament* was written in 1380, most scholars believe that the *Parliament* was begun in 1382 at the very latest.[31] Given the probability that the *House of Fame* was written before the

Parliament, December of 1381 seems a reasonable *terminus ad quem* for the earlier work.

There is a possibility that the poem may be placed even more precisely within its probable limits of December 1378 and December 1381. In his study of the *House of Fame*, John F. Leyerle addressed himself to the problem of why Chaucer so emphasized the "tenthe day now of Decembre": "The December date has puzzled readers of the poem because they have missed a relatively simple fact: in December, as the sun moves through its annual path in the ecliptic, it approaches close to Aquila, the constellation of the eagle."[32] Leyerle notes that Chaucer's golden eagle appears "faste be the sonne, as hye / As kenne myghte I with myn eye" (497-98), unlike the eagle that is merely in the sky ("nel cielo") in the passage in the *Purgatorio* (ix. 20), on which this passage is based. When Geoffrey first sees the eagle, his immediate reaction is the fear that "Joves wol me stellyfye" (586), that he himself will be turned into a constellation. Chaucer's eagle is, Leyerle concludes, like that other eagle in Dante (*Paradiso*, xviii-xx), the constellation Aquila, near the sun in the December skies.

Leyerle also notes that the eagle says he dwells with Jove, and, conceding that the eagle is traditionally associated with Jove, Leyerle suggests that this means that Aquila is not only near the sun but close to the planet Jupiter. This corresponds to the actual condition of the skies in December of 1379, 1380, and 1381, but it corresponds most closely to the skies on December 10, 1379, and Leyerle concludes that "the poem can be dated, with some hesitation, as December, 1379."[33]

Hesitation is clearly appropriate in such matters. The dating of Chaucer's poems is, at best, an inexact science. I have gone into this problem in such detail, because the usual way of dating the *House of Fame* by those who want to prove what the tidings were has been first to find one's tidings and then to date the poem accordingly—1377, 1380, 1381, 1384. Save for those scholars with a special interest in the tidings, no one has seriously challenged Lowes's date of "about 1379," and all the evidence uncovered since Lowes wrote tends to confirm his findings. Although no one piece of that evidence is in itself conclusive, the convergence of the various types of evidence on this date allows us to conclude, with appropriate hesitation but with more confidence than we can usually feel in assigning dates to Chaucer's works, that it is most probable that the final version and first public reading of the *House of Fame* came some time around December 10, 1379.

The question is, then, whether there were in December of 1379 tidings from "som contre," some news of international consequence—"of werres, of pes, of mariages" (1961), among many other possible topics—that was yet suitable for Chaucer's lightly comic treatment of that news and the man of great authority who delivered it.

There was such news on 10 December 1379. It concerned a matter in which Chaucer had a personal interest and about which he probably had a good deal of inside information: the projected marriage of Richard II to Caterina Visconti, daughter of Bernabò, lord of Milan.

By December of 1379 the search for a suitable wife for Richard had been going on for almost three years. The Emperor Charles IV had offered his daughter, Anne of Bohemia, as a wife for young Richard in 1377, but this was brusquely rejected.[34] Instead there was hope for a marriage with a princess of France, and Chaucer played a prominent part in the negotiations of 1376 and 1377 that were intended to lead to that marriage. However, that infant princess, Marie, died in 1378, and the search had to begin anew.[35]

Attention then turned from the old enemy France to the rich and powerful state of Milan, located strategically on the enemy's borders—actually within it, since Gian Galeazzo, Bernabò's nephew, was Count of Virtú. In October of 1377 an embassy had come from Milan proposing negotiations. The proposal was well received, and in May of 1378 Chaucer and Edward de Berkeley were sent to Milan to negotiate with Bernabò and Sir John Hawkwood "for certain affairs touching the expedition of the king's war." Among the affairs touched upon was an alliance between England and Milan and, apparently, a marriage between Richard and Caterina. When Chaucer and Edward de Berkeley returned to London in September, 1378, they were accompanied by two Milanese ambassadors, "from which London would hear the most seductive offers of alliance. As a pledge of their promises, they offered to Richard the hand of the young Caterina, along with a large fortune."[36] The fortune—fifty thousand florins—was not all that large but was perhaps attractive, since Richard's government was badly in need of funds.

There was great interest in the matter. "At this season," Froissart writes, "there were many councils held in England by the uncles of the king, the prelates, and barons relative to the marrying of young king Richard."[37] John of Gaunt, Froissart reports, wanted Richard to marry his daughter, but this was rejected by the people, not only because they were too closely related but because "they wished the king to choose a queen from beyond the sea, in order to gain stronger alliances." Bernabò's offer satisfied all; England would have its alliance, Caterina's rich dowry would provide the funds the government needed, and Richard would have his queen. The matter was therefore settled; in March of 1379 a delegation consisting of Michael de la Pole, John Burley, and George Felbrigge was dispatched to Milan with full power to sign the marriage contract.[38] Chaucer had reason to be proud of the outcome of his second Italian journey, as he and the court settled down to await the happy news that the contract had been signed and that the long search for a queen had finally ended.

That news was never to come. The delegation began discussions in Milan. Felbrigge returned to England on 10 June 1379 (with what news is not known, though apparently things were going smoothly enough when he left), and Michael de la Pole and John Burley went on to Rome to engage in other negotiations. "There it was," wrote Edouard Perroy, "that the Milanese project was definitely buried."[39] The Great Schism had begun in the preceding year, and the Roman Curia—more particularly Pileo da Prato, Cardinal of Ravenna, who was the architect and executor of the policy—saw a chance to drive a wedge between France, which supported Pope Clement in Avignon, and its old ally, the House of Luxembourg, whose head, Wenceslas, had just been elected to succeed his father as Holy Roman Emperor and was a supporter of Pope Urban in Rome. Milan was already securely in the Roman camp; an alliance between England and the Empire would effectively surround France with enemies. Bernabò's disappointment at the collapse of his plan to marry Caterina to Richard would be allayed by a papal dispensation allowing him to marry his daughter Caterina to his brother's son, Gian Galeazzo.[40] Though a trifle irregular from the standpoint of canon law, the incestuous union had for Bernabò the obvious advantage of keeping Caterina's dowry in the family and, for the Vatican, the hope of increasing pressure on the Clementists' southern flank, since, as I have noted, Gian Galeazzo was count of Virtú as well as heir to Milan.

Perroy reconstructed the events in Rome during the summer of 1379 as follows:

> La Pole and Burley, arriving from Milan, were quickly convinced; they were shown that, for the glory of England and the Church, Richard could contract a more brilliant marriage. Germany had adhered enthusiastically to the legitimate Pope: the union between the houses of Valois and Luxembourg was crumbling. If the Plantagenets succeeded in concluding a new alliance with the King of the Romans [the Emperor Wenceslas] there would be for England the hope of a victorious war against Charles V [of France] and, for the

Church, a prompt crushing of the Schism. They were advised, though they had no official authorization, to go to Germany to open negotiations with the court of Bohemia.[41]

They did so. Richard and his Council probably received some word of what was going on in Rome from the priors of the Franciscan provinces of England and Ireland, who returned to London from Rome in August carrying letters from both Pope Urban and Emperor Wenceslas. Wenceslas's letter has survived; it proposes an alliance between England and the Empire to crush the Schism, though it makes no mention of a marriage.[42]

Michael de la Pole and John Burley set off from Rome to Germany in September 1379. They apparently received new instructions from Sir Richard Stury, who was sent to Germany about this time "pro certis negociis regis."[43] But the matter remained in doubt, and one suspects that the talk about Richard's marriage that Froissart reports in the early months of the year increased in the following months, as England waited for news from Milan. None came: the project for the marriage of Richard to Caterina could not be completely ruled out until England could be sure that the mission of Michael de la Pole and John Burley to Germany showed promise of a successful outcome. There was apparently some indecision about whether to pursue the prospect of the marriage to Anne, and in September, about the same time the mission to Germany received new instructions, an embassy was sent to France to discuss the possibilities of a French marriage .[44] Insiders at the court—including, in all probability, Chaucer—must have known what was happening and must have been pretty sure that the marriage with Caterina Visconti would not take place. But even they could not be certain, and others had to make do with rumors and guesses.

Finally the official news arrived. On 10 December 1379, gifts were made to two ambassadors from Milan: "Johannes Lisle milite et Roger Cane armigero, nunciis Barnabonis domini de Melan, venientibus ex parte eiusdem Barnabonis in nuncium domino regis."[45] On the very same day payment was made to an even more important messenger from Pileo da Prato, Cardinal of Ravenna, who was overseeing the negotiations between the English delegation and Wenceslas. On December 10, 1379, ten pounds was paid to: "Nicolus, Vrsyn de fferrario Armigero sanctissimi patris pape veniente ex parte Candinalis de Ravenii in Nuncius cum lettris directis domino Regi."[46] The long-awaited news had finally arrived: the brilliant match with Caterina Visconti would not take place. The marriage was off, and the tedious task of arranging for Richard's marriage would start all over again, back where it had been in 1377, when England had abruptly rejected an offer to marry Richard to Anne of Bohemia and thus ally itself with the impoverished House of Luxembourg.

If the chroniclers of the time are any indication, there was a good deal of indignation at this turn of events. The loss of Caterina's dowry was keenly felt, especially later when it became clear that Richard not only received no dowry from Anne but had to pay Wenceslas ten thousand pounds, plus expenses, for the privilege of marrying her. The Westminster Chronicler wrote, with some indelicacy, that Anne was not given in marriage but rather bought. "Nam non modica pecunia refundebat rex Angliae pro tantilla carnis portione."[47] Even those who were not indignant must have been a bit put off by the manner in which the Cardinal of Ravenna, a notoriously corrupt churchman, had taken on himself the authority of directing English foreign policy.

If Chaucer was either shocked or disappointed by these turns of events, he did not show it. His reaction was rather the *House of Fame* as we have it. His motto seems always to have been to "maken virtu of necessitee / And take it weel that we may nat eschue" (*KT* 3042-43). He chose to regard the whole business as slightly comic, by playing up the uncertain nature of such affairs and the anti- climactic turn that events had taken. It was, under the circumstances, the most tactful way of dealing with the news. Treating the whole affair as slightly comic deflated the importance of the projected match by assigning it to the uncertain realm of Fame and Rumor, thus effectively disarming possible critics concerned about the loss of those fifty thousand florins. Moreover, by the device of the "man of gret auctorite," this treatment deflected any possible blame for this development from Richard's council and his ambassadors and directed it toward a better target, the man who came on the authority of Cardinal Pileo, whose own authority, because of the Great Schism, was open to serious question.[48] The whole matter, the comic treatment implies, should not be taken too seriously. Take it for the best; the tidings, though comically anti-climactic so far as Caterina is concerned, are nevertheless glad tidings, for now there can be no hope of a match with Anne. Those who were annoyed at the long delay in arranging Richard's marriage or vexed at the turn of events could, at least for the moment, "take it weel," with good humor. Even the Cardinal's nuncio (who probably could not understand English anyway) could hardly have taken offense.

The "love-tydynges" Chaucer hints at were, then, the tidings that arrived around December 10, 1379. This was the news brought by Nicolò, a man who seemed "of gret auctoritee," since he came on the authority of Cardinal Pileo. The news he brought was that there was no news, so far as the marriage with Caterina was concerned, and that the Imperial Eagle was in the ascendant. If John Leyerle is right in his argument that Chaucer's eagle is, in some sense, the constellation Aquila, it is possible that Chaucer was led to think about that constellation and to consult his tables about it (as he would have had to, since it is not visible in December), because of the heraldic associations of the eagle (not yet invariably double-headed) with the Empire.

However that may be, it is very likely that the *House of Fame* was first read not too long after December 10, 1379, long enough after Nicolò's arrival for Chaucer to adapt his poem for the occasion and for the news from Cardinal Pileo to become well known, at least in courtly circles. That, I believe, is why the poem ends as it does. There was no need to tell the news; Chaucer's audience already knew it. If any were so dull as not to understand Chaucer's hints, they must have realized what was intended when Chaucer got to the last line.

Of course, none of this can be proven. Barring the unlikely discovery of some direct contemporary testimony, we must make do with whatever theory best fits the probabilities and the facts: the probabilities are that the *House of Fame* was first read not long after 10 December 1379, and that it concerns some anticlimactic and therefore slightly comic tidings of war, peace, and marriage from abroad; the facts are that some particular December tenth is important to the poem, and Cardinal Pileo's nuncio arrived at the English court on or before 10 December 1379, with the news that Richard's marriage to Caterina Visconti would not take place and that a new set of negotiations would have to begin.

To move beyond probabilities and facts to the realm of sheer speculation is too tempting to resist. I would like to think that the *House of Fame* was first read to some courtly gathering in the way that Donald Fry reconstructed the performance, but with one change: when

Chaucer got to the final lines about the one who "semed for to be / A man of gret auctorite," he paused, turned, and slightly bowed in the direction of Cardinal Pileo's nuncio. Poor Nicolò, puzzled but pleased after sitting through over two thousand lines of verse in a language he probably could not understand, politely acknowledged the unexpected honor, and smiling, bowed in return. And then, as Fry puts it, Chaucer "pauses, closes his manuscript volume, and sits down to a rising crescendo of shocked surprise, laughter, understanding, and finally applause."[49]

NOTES

1. The endings are printed in the textual notes to F.N. Robinson, ed., *The Works of Geoffrey Chaucer*, 2nd ed. (Boston: Houghton Mifflin, 1957), p. 901, All quotations from Chaucer in what follows are from this edition. Caxton composed the twelve-line conclusion. Thynne reprinted it but altered the first three lines. Thynne's version also appears in MS Fairfax 16, added by the same seventeenth-century hand that wrote in lines 31-96 of the *Book of the Duchess*: see the facsimile edition of *Bodleian Library MS Fairfax 16*, intr. John Norton-Smith (London: Scolar Press, 1979) which incorrectly identifies the source as Caxton (p. xvii).

2. Robinson, *The Works of Geoffrey Chaucer*, p. 779.

3. G. L. Kittredge, *Chaucer and His Poetry*, intro. B.J. Whiting, Fifty-fifth Anniversary Edition (Cambridge, Mass.: Harvard University Press, 1970), p. 107.

4. Rudolf Imelmann, "Chaucer's *Haus der Fama*," *Englische Studien* 45 (1912), 397-431; Aage Brusendorff, *The Chaucer Tradition* (London: Oxford University Press, 1925), pp. 148-66. Brusendorff's theory is adopted by John H. Fisher in his edition, *Complete Poetry and Prose of Geoffrey Chaucer* (New York: Holt, Rinehart, and Winston, 1977), p. 564.

5. John Koch, "Nachmals: Die Bedeutung von *Chaucer's Hous of Fame*," *Englische Studien* 50 (1916): 359-82.

6. A.C. Baugh, ed., *Chaucer's Major Poetry* (New York: Prentice-Hall, 1963), pp. 27-28, Baugh follows Haldeen Braddy, *Three Chaucer Studies*, but see Manly's review, "Three Recent Chaucer Studies,"

Review of English Studies 10 (1934): 257, 262-73, and *Review of English Studies* 11 (1935): 209-13.

7. For John of Gaunt see Reidel, note 11 below; for Thomas of Gloucester see F.P. von Westenholz, "Nachträgliche Spähne zum Chaucer-gedenkentag," *Beiblatt zur Anglia* 12 (1901): 169-72; for Richard see F. J. Snell, *The Age of Chaucer* (London: Bell, 1901), p. 185 (Snell sees the *House of Fame* as a "begging poem").

8. Robinson, *The Works of Geoffrey Chaucer*, p. 779. "The poem seems at best inappropriate to the celebration of a wedding or betrothal."

9. See B.J. Whiting's delightful "conclusion" to the *House of Fame* (*Speculum* 49 (1974), 591-92), which was read at the dinner honoring Frederick H. Burkhardt on the occasion of his retirement from the presidency of the American Council of Learned Societies. Mr. Burkhardt was delighted to learn that the "tydynges" concerned him.

10. "Chaucer's *House of Fame*: Another Hypothesis," *University of California Publications in English* 3 (1934): 171-92.

11. "The Meaning of Chaucer's *House of Fame*," *JEGP* 27 (1928): 441-69.

12. R.C. Goffin, "Quitting by 'Tydynges' in the *House of Fame*," *Medium Aevum* 12 (1943): 40-44; Robert J. Allen, "A Recurring Motif in Chaucer's *House of Fame*," *JEGP* 55 (1956): 393-405; Donald C. Baker, "Recent Interpretations of the *House of Fame*: A New Suggestion," *Studies in English* (University of Mississippi) 1 (1960): 97- 104: Paul Ruggiers, "The Unity of Chaucer's *House of Fame*," *Studies in Philology*, 50 (1953): 16-29; B.J. Koonce, *Chaucer and the Tradition of Fame: Symbolism in the House of Fame* (Princeton, New Jersey: Princeton University Press, 1966). A full bibliography and review of scholarship is provided by L.K. Shook in *Companion to Chaucer Studies*, ed. Beryl Rowland, Revised Edition (New York: Oxford University Press, 1979), pp. 414-27.

13. J. A. W. Bennett, *Chaucer's Book of Fame: An Exposition of the House of Fame* (Oxford: Clarendon, 1968), p. xii.

14. *TC* I, 65; see also *Boece* I. pr. 1.78, *CT* IV. 1597, VI. 387-88, VIII. 471, X. 931.

15. Kay Stevenson, "The Endings of Chaucer's *House of Fame*," *English Studies* 59 (1978): 10-26; many years ago Wilbur O. Sypherd,

on much different grounds, also argued for "The Completeness of Chaucer's *House of Fame,*" *MLN* 30 (1915): 65-68.

16. Fry, "The Ending of the *House of Fame,*" in *Chaucer at Albany*, ed. Rossell Hope Robbins (New York: Burt Franklin, 1975), pp. 27-40.

17. Martin M. Crow and Clair C. Olson, *Chaucer Life Records*, ed. Martin M. Crow and Clair C. Olson (Oxford: Clarendon, 1966), pp. 148, 165. The stipulation was repeated—"manu sua propria scribat"—when Chaucer was reappointed in 1377. He was given a deputy for the Petty Customs shortly after he was appointed to that post in 1382 (p. 160). Chaucer was still associated with the office in 1386; see *Chaucer Life Records*, p. 246.

18. "The Prologue to the Legend of Good Women Considered in its Chronological Relationships," *PMLA* 20 (1905): 794-864.

19. See Baugh's edition, p. 28; Fisher's edition, p. 564: Reidet. note 11 above: George Williams, *A New View of Chaucer* (Durham, N.C.: Duke University Press, 1965), p. 123. Williams explains the reference to "rekynynges" by assuming that Chaucer was employed as an auditor or accountant for either Richard II or John of Gaunt. The earlier scholarship on this problem is conveniently summarized by H. Lloyd Jones, Jr., "The Date of Chaucer's *House of Fame,*"*Delaware Notes*, Nineteenth Series (1946): 47-55.

20. Lowes, note 18 above, 850-51.

21. Robert A. Pratt, "Chaucer's Use of the *Teseida,*" *PMLA* 62 (1947): 604, finds only the slightest use of the *Teseida* (*HF* 518-22, drawing on *Tes.* I.1 and IX.63) and notes that at this stage Chaucer is interested mainly in the "classical decorations" Boccaccio offered. He seems to have been particularly struck by the opening stanzas of the *Teseida* (I.1- 3) and by the similar passage in *Tes.* XI.63, which seem to have been combined in his mind with reminiscences of Dante: the cluster of reminiscences appears here (*HF* 518-22), in the first three stanzas of *Anelida*, and yet again in *Troilus*, III, 1807-10. See John Livingston Lowes, "Chaucer and Dante," *Modern Philology* 14 (1917): 705-35, Lowes notes that the idea that Helicon is a well rather than a mountain-peak is suggested by Dante, *Purgatorio* xxix.40: "Or convien chi Elicona per mi versi" and by a similar phrase in Guido della Colonna ("imbibens Elicona," quoted by Robinson, p. 782), but Chaucer's "Elicon the clere welle" seems directly based on Boccaccio's

"Elicon fonte" (*Tes.* XI.63); Lowes concludes, "The *immediate* source of this particular error is not Dante but Boccaccio" (p. 733).

22. *The Development and Chronology of Chaucer's Works*, Chaucer Society (1907), pp. 34-40.

23. *The Goddess Fortuna in Medieval Literature* (Cambridge, Mass.: Harvard University Press, 1927), pp. 11-12. For discussion see Bennett, *Chaucer's Book of Fame*, pp. 150-53,

24. *Chaucer's Book of Fame*, pp. 153-54.

25. John H. Fisher, *John Gower: Moral Philosopher and Friend of Chaucer* (New York: New York University Press, 1964), p. 99; Tatlock, *Development and Chronology*, Appendix A.

26. "Chaucer Borrowing From Himself," *Modern Language Quarterly* 7 (1946): 259-64.

27. Martha H. Shackford, "The Date of Chaucer's *House of Fame*," *MLN* 31 (1916): 507-08.

28. *The Parlement of Foulys* (London: Nelson, 1960), p. 2. Only Fisher puts the Parliament before the *House of Fame* (see his edition, p. 564). Fisher reads line 916 of the *House of Fame* as "Kynge; ne of Rome daun Scipio," as in Caxton and Thynne's editions, rather than "Ne the kynge, daun Scipio," the reading of the MSS adopted by all other editors.

29. *Parlement of Foulys*, p. 3 and note to lines 117-18, p. 104.

30. "Chaucer's View of Astronomy," *Speculum* 45 (1970): 364.

31. Most scholars agree with this dating of the *Parliament* in the early 1380's. Robinson places the poem first in the period 1380-86 and adds "possibly a little earlier" (p. xxix); Wolfgang Clemens, *Chaucer's Early Poetry*, tr. C.A.M. Sym (London: Methuen, 1963), p. 32, accepts the assignment "by most modern critics to a year near 1380." There are those who disagree: Fisher assigns the poem to 1377 (see his edition, p. 564); J.D. North, " 'Kalenderes Enlumyed Ben They,' "*Review of English Studies* 20 (1969): 270-74, dates the poem in 1393, though his assumptions are questionable (see the discussion by Smyser in the article cited in note 27); George Williams (note 19 above) would place it in 1359, when Chaucer was in his middle teens.

32. "Chaucer's Windy Eagle," *University of Toronto Quarterly* 40 (1971): 249.

33. *Ibid.*, p. 251. It should be noted that Smyser (note 30 above) believes Chaucer had little interest in astronomy when he wrote the *House of Fame*, and Leyerle's argument implies considerable interest.

34. Edouard Perroy, *l'Angleterre et le Grand Schisme d'Occident* (Paris: J. Monnier, 1933), p. 136. The following discussion is heavily dependent on Perroy's work.

35. *Chaucer Life Records*, 49; the *Records* quote Froissart on the identity of this princess, though with a warning from Manly on Froissart's doubtful reliability (p. 51, n. 1). Prof. Virginia Leland kindly draws my attention to the papers in *Froissart: Historian*, J.J.N. Palmer ed., 1981, which clearly show "Froissart was writing literature, not history."

36. Perroy, *l'Angleterre*, p. 138.

37. *Chronicles*, tr. Thomas Johnes (London, 1868), I. 592. The "season" to which Froissart refers is the time of the death of the Emperor Charles IV, in November, 1378. Froissart goes on to relate this talk to the marriage of Richard to Anne of Bohemia rather than to Caterina Visconti (about whom he knows nothing). Possibly Froissart is telescoping the events, since his account of the general interest in the problem of Richard's marriage would fit late 1379 and early 1380 as well as late 1378 and early 1379. On Froissart's unreliability, see n. 35 above.

38. Thomas Rymer, *Foedera* (London, 1869), IV.60.

39. *L'Angleterre et le Grande Schisme*, p. 139. Professor Virginia Leland points out to me that when Caterina's cousin Violante married Prince Lionel the dowry amounted to two million florins. The pro-Lancastrian chroniclers (see note 47 below) apparently exaggerated the size of the dowry for their own purposes.

40. *Ibid.*, p. 139; the dispensation was granted in September, 1380.

41. *Ibid.*, p. 139.

42. *Ibid.*, p. 140.

43. *Idem.*

44. Rymer, *Foedera*, IV, 70-71; an embassy was sent for the same purpose as late as April 1, 1380 (IV, 83).

45. Perroy, *l'Angleterre*, p. 139.

46. *Ibid.*, p. 141. I quote, however, from the transcription kindly made for me from Public Record Office E. 403/475, m. 10, by Prof.

Richard F. Greene of Bishop's University, Lennoxville, Québec. It is not clear when the gift was made.

47. *Ranulphi Higden Polychronicon*, ed. Joseph H. Lumby, Rolls Series (London, 1-86), TX, 12.

48. England unhesitatingly supported Rome, but this was a purely political decision, and some Englishmen, such as John Gower, were seriously troubled by the Schism; see *Mirour de l'Omme*, vv.188125-40, and *Confessio Amantis*, Prologue, 328-41.

49. See note 16 above.

IV. *THE PARLIAMENT OF FOWLS*

Chaucer's *Parliament of Fowls* is charming. Almost nothing more can be said about it with unanimous certainty. Most Chaucerians concur that the *Parliament* mildly pokes fun at the English estates in general and the Ricardian court in particular. The on-again off-again negotiations to arrange the betrothal of King Richard to Anne of Bohemia provide a most plausible set of circumstances to occasion Chaucer's composition of the dream vision (ca. 1381). This specific claim on the text's subtext has, however, been repeatedly challenged.

Rival readings (often based on alternative identifications of the formel and tercels) in turn destablize the dating of the poem. The safest determination of the *Parliament*'s date of composition remains sometime after 1375 and sometime before 1385—in other words, sometime before or after the *House of Fame*. Mutually contradictory efforts to identify the formel and the three tercels do, however, share a common conception of the *Parliament* as an actual reflection of Chaucer's courtly milieu—albeit in a fun-house mirror. Yet, "the meaning and the value of the poem do not depend," as Charles Muscatine has observed, "on its being read as an occasional poem" (*Benson*, p. 994).

The fictional annual occasion proposed by the poem itself is, of course, the feast of St. Valentine's Day. The *Parliament* is sometimes cited (not without cause, but not with any compelling proof) as the first literary reference to St. Valentine's day as a romantic festival. H.A. Kelly in *Chaucer and the Cult of Saint Valentine* (1986) has offered a most reasonable explanation for Chaucer's celebration of such an early May day in mid-February—there were two St. Valentine's days. A less resolvable puzzle posed by the *Parliament* is what, if anything, Chaucer actually has to say about the nature of love. Does his dream vision celebrate procreation or recreation, *cupiditas* or *caritas*, or —most difficult to define—*amors fin*?

The actual parliament of birds episode within the *Parliament* is obviously its most humorous section. The satiric ridicule that makes this part of the *Parliament* so enjoyable (and performable) is not a point of much contention. The effrontery of water-fowls is for modern readers, as it was for medieval listeners, as it is reported to be for the narrative's fictional audience of birds, laughable (575). But other targets of Chaucer's humor are more difficult to hit. Does Chaucer's caricature of upstart merchants (including, one assumes, the sons of vintners descended from shoemakers) valorize what seems (after the revolution) the hauteur of Richard's court? Or does "the parfit reson of a goos" (578) provide a pragmatic antidote to the extreme affec(ta)tion of the tercels? To answer such rhetical questions, it is crucial to imagine the affective implications of Chaucer's relations to his patrons and to his initial audience of readers or listeners.[1]

It is likewise tempting to study the initial part of the *Parliament* as Chaucer's fictionalized commentary on the nature of dreams, which, in turn, offers his interpretive metaphor for the imaginative experience of reading. The *Parliament* also teases some to read it as a sociological or psychological or anthropological if not ornithological document about the rites of spring. The literary topoi of medieval bestiaries and bird-debates provide less scientific but no less significant insights into the *Parliament*.

Formalist attempts to situate the *Parliament* in Chaucer's canon (arguing, for example, that the pentameters of the *Parliament*'s rime royal seem more prosodically mature than the tetrameters of the *House of Fame*) are extremely dubious. As a literary artifact, the *Parliament* seems a witty, perhaps hastily contrived piece of work, perhaps even a hodgepodged piecework. It begins with Chaucer's own rather idiosyncratic *accessus* to Macrobius and ends with his rehearsal of the birds' reverdie.

Various efforts to propose the poem's thematic unity or rhetorical strategies generally share the common conviction that the *Parliament* represents a significant step in Chaucer's maturation as a vernacular poet. The apparently haphazard flow (which suits so well the dreamer's lack of control over the scenes he merely observes) is unmasked as an evolving Chaucerian pose.

Chaucer the bookman drops a number of names in the *Parliament*. As usual, source studies disclose his highly provocative use of Latin and French precedents. And yet there seems to be some resistance to textual authority in Chaucer's voice—an incipient skepticism that Chaucer will later both mask and amplify *via* the persona of Alison of Bath.

The *Parliament*'s very traditional representation of Lady Natura as God's *vicus* can provoke much feminist commentary, though allegorical readings tend to diminish any significance attributable to her (grammatical) gender. The critical implications of Nature's decree granting the formel freedom of choice are particularly intriguing. But this seemingly crucial detail may have been merely occasional—a glitch in the negotiations to marry Richard.

Dramatically, the dream vision of the *Parliament* concludes with Chaucer's apparent presentation of a copy (678) of the roundel the birds sang as a recessional, "Now welcome somer." Chaucer can only vicariously join their celebration as its reporter. In the last stanza, Chaucer himself takes his leave with a hope (697) for better reading. Compared to Chaucer's two other reputed references to the feast of St. Valentine's day, even such muted optimism sounds remarkably upbeat.[2]

Bertrand Bronson's "revisiting" (1948) of the *Parliament of Fowls* starts by questioning the critical assumptions underlying the still generally accepted date for the poem's composition (ca. 1381-2). By emphasizing the significance of authorial revision, Bronson destabilizes (*sc.* makes "inconclusive") the tone and thematic import of Chaucer's narrative pose—the otherwise overlooked ironic subtleties that redeem the poem from frivolous occasionality. After Bronson, both Paul A. Olson (1980) and David Aers (1981) can presume a critical consensus that accepts the *Parliament*'s artistic success; both critics then proceed to address it as a significant political document as well. Whereas Olson reads the *Parliament* as heralding the English ideals of a parliamentary government enfranchised by Nature to moderate regal power, Aers reads the dream vision as a subversive (and as such incipiently Marxist) challenge to such dogmatic authority.

A.J. Minnis remarks that "What is remarkable" about the *Parliament* is "the wide unanimity of the intuition that one must go outside the poem to find some missing element" (*Guide*, p. 312). Linguists, biographers, Robertsonians, New Critics, New Historicists, Thomists, and Marxists are all welcome to the interpretive confabulation initiated by the *Parliament*. Yet, amidst their disorderly debate, there have also been several admonitions not to imagine too scholarly or too serious a Chaucer assimilating so much *philosophia* and *scientia* in search of a clear *sententia*.

NOTES

1. See Jill Mann's *Chaucer and the Medieval Estates Satire* (1973) that explicates the General Prologue's portraits of the Canterbury pilgrims in terms of the genre's conventions regarding form and content.

2. The hope for a better tomorrow voiced in the proem to "The Complaint of Mars" sounds rather desperate or, at best, "cheerfully coercive" (Minnis *Guide*, p. 473). In the last stanza of a "Complaynt D'Amours," the poet remarks that this "woful song and this compleynte I make" (88) on "Seint Valentynes day,/ Whan every foughel chosed shal his make" (85-86). This "make/make" rhyme/pun marries the act of imaginative creation (composing or, more probably, reciting in the present context) to the matching that precedes procreation. But the *complaint* proper is just that—a frustrated lament.

THE PARLEMENT OF FOULES REVISITED

by Bertrand H. Bronson

It is well to remind ourselves from time to time that the dates which most of us assign with unthinking confidence to plot the chronology of Chaucer's literary progress are for the most part grounded on nothing firmer than plausible conjecture. We find it all too easy to think of his French, Italian, and English "periods" as a series of suites inhabited in turn by the poet, each with a self-locking door that closed behind him, not to be re-opened; and like town councilmen we attach memorial plates with the dates of occupancy. It would be juster to think of him as having the run of the whole series in the last decade and a half of his life, and as passing back and forth from one to another as he saw fit.

There is certainly evidence enough that Chaucer himself did not feel that he had forever closed the door with each new advance on earlier practice; nor is there any indication that he felt he had outgrown his past achievements. If he began with "balades, roundels, virelayes" of love, he continued to write *jeux d'esprit* in the lighter lyric forms up to the last years, and most of what has survived in that kind from his hand is demonstrably late. Obviously, he was not prejudiced against the narratives that we suppose early, so much even as to feel that they were anomalous or inappropriate in the up-to-date Canterbury frame. We impute our "modern" responses to Chaucer when reading the more "archaic" tales; but he himself assigned them places in his greatest masterpiece-surely a critical judgment of his mature mind. He not only wrote the dream-vision Prologue to the *Legend of Good Women* after—so we believe—completing the *Troilus*, but took it up and re-worked it after the death of Queen Anne in June, 1394. This fact does not suggest either that he regarded the form as outmoded, or that he himself had lost active interest in it at a time when he was already engaged in the composition of his maturest work. Professor Tatlock may latterly have found few to agree with his opinion that the *Troilus* may probably antedate *The Hous of Fame*; nevertheless, he is right to insist that there is nothing inherently unnatural in such a sequence. And are we not naive to assume that Chaucer had to take a trip to Italy before the Italian influence could begin to be felt in his writing? We seem, in fact, to have fallen victims to the scholarly instinct for tidiness and neat arrangement in separate compartments.

To bring these generalizations to a head: what evidence supports the generally accepted view that *The Parlement of Foules* was written in 1881-82? It is limited, factually, to the following points. First, the poem is written in rime royal, not octosyllabics and not pentameter couplets, and reflects Chaucer's reading among the Italian as well as the French poets. Second, the famous stanza invoking Cytherea is believed to indicate a position of the planet Venus which was most closely approximated—though never reached for Londoners—in the Spring (April-May) of the years 1366, 1374, 1382, 1390, 1398. The first two dates are thought too early in Chaucer's literary career, the last two too late. On this simple basis all the scholarly hypotheses depend, and, although no convincing historical parallel has yet been discovered for the supposed allegory, these hypotheses by a circular influence react upon the dubious evidence just stated, to create an almost universal confidence that the date of composition has been, if roughly, yet securely established.

It is worth insisting, therefore, that nothing of the sort has been accomplished. If for the sake of immediate argument we accept the astronomical evidence as *bona fide*—an acceptance which we shall later have to withdraw—nothing in the sum of what we know of Chaucer would make it impossible for him to have written a poem like this in any of the years mentioned above, although probability is overstrained by a date as early as 1366, and the specific reference in the *LGW* seems to preclude so late a date as the last of the series. But by 1874, Chaucer was already thirty years old; he had already had an unusually wide and cosmopolitan experience of life; had been abroad several times, and was fresh from a fairly long sojourn in Italy. Can it fairly be imagined that his intellectual and artistic growth, although, favored by his own quickness, and by his opportunities for association with the most cultivated of his contemporaries of several countries, had been so retarded as to put the composition of this work beyond his powers at that date? If so, we should have cause to wonder. Or look at the opposite possibility. Supposing that an occasion had arisen for such a piece, what is there to have prevented Chaucer, with his facility, from reverting to a genre which he had mastered earlier, which contemporary poets were still practising as a vital and living form, and which future poets would not have discarded for another century and more? Short of arguing that he did write the work in 1398, we remember that in the *LGW* he was working in the love-vision tradition at least as late as

1394-95; and there is nothing in the literary, or social, or personal situation to preclude Chaucer from writing, or re-casting, a piece of this kind even up to the end of his life.

The possibility of revision must be faced, although it greatly complicates the question. Still allowing the invocation to Venus its face value, nothing, when we look at the context, is more obvious than that it may be an interpolation almost parenthetical. For consider: up to this point in the poem we have heard briefly, first, of the astonishing power of Love, conceived as a masculine tyrant, a lord and sire arbitrary and prone to cruel anger. Next, we have learned of the poet's reading the Dream of Scipio, which dealt above all with the merit of a life of public service and the rewards after death. Next, we have heard of Scipio's appearing in a dream to Chaucer himself, and saying:

> Thow hast the so wel born
> In lokynge of myn olde bok to-torn, . . .
> That somdel of thy labour wolde I quyte.

Remove the invocatory stanza, which immediately succeeds, and the poem continues without the slightest visible seam:

> This forseyde Affrican me hente anon,
> And forth with hym unto a gate broughte
> Ryght of a park walled with grene ston . . .

Henceforward, we learn no more about Cytherea, invoked only to be supplanted by the presiding divinity of the poem, the goddess Nature. To be sure, Venus appears later in the temple, but with little more prominence than the crowd of personified abstractions about her, and notably diminished by Chaucer from Boccaccio's voluptuous attention. Almost as much space goes to the god Priapus, who stands "in soverayn place" to receive votive garlands. After this, wrangling and debate supersede all other interests. At the end of the poem, the heroine of it repudiates service to Venus and Cupid; and the chorus of birds sings a little hymn, not to Venus, but to St. Valentine. Granted that the piece is about a love-suit, and that the other figures are ancillary to Love, we must yet admit that the overt role of the goddess is distinctly subordinate. Given other evidence of revision and change, it would be natural to infer that the invocatory stanza to Cytherea came in with such revision, and could therefore bear little weight as anchor for dating the poem as a whole.

It should be observed, moreover, that the past tenses of the stanza themselves suggest a belated inspiration. Instead of invoking Venus at the opening—'Thou who hast caused me to dream and whom I now see above me as I commence to write thy vision, be propitious, I pray thee, and favor my efforts!'—instead of so natural a prayer, the poet awkwardly indicates that he had begun his poem some while ago without any such appeal, although he had not failed at that time to observe the planet "north-north-west." This is surely very uncourtly, and looks like a lazy way of foisting in an invocation without re-writing, whether the idea occurred at first draft or later.

But the flimsiness of this clue to a date becomes more glaringly apparent when we scrutinize the stanza for its meaning, both in statement and in context. What Chaucer says is, first, that Venus caused him to dream this dream, and, secondly but indirectly, that she was visible to him north-north-west when he started to write it down. To the first assertion he adds a deprecatory phrase indicating that though he might seem an unlikely subject for her influence, she subdues with her firebrand whomsoever she pleases; thus glancing at his inability to be more than an observer in affairs of the heart:—a point made at the opening of the poem, and humorously resumed when a little later Scipio assures him in the dream that he need not fear to enter Love's park, since he has apparently lost the capacity of responding to Love's promptings. Scipio's reassurance goes far to cancel the assertion that Venus had caused the dream; and, moreover, the poet has already proposed an alternative suggestion, namely, that he may have dreamed of Scipio because he had been thinking so hard about him before falling asleep. These disclaimers are surely not to be ignored: the intention is clearly to suggest that Love and the poet are far apart; and we may take with reservations, therefore, the statement that his poem was written under the inspiration of Venus.

But we learn from the astronomers that for the meridian of London the planet Venus never, in 1382 or any other year, came within 22 degrees of the position NNW. In strict accuracy, Chaucer does not positively say he saw her there: he says, "Be my help as surely as I saw thee there"—a sufficiently ambiguous ejaculation, if we consider the context and the fact that to see Venus actually NNW he would have had to sail all the way to the Shetland Islands.[1] To suppose that he meant us to understand by this reference that he had made the voyage to the Shetlands in imagination, for reasons undeclared, is, however great a compliment to the auditor's intelligence, to our notion the very ecstasy of conjecture. We may agree, however, that, in view of the astronomical facts, he can hardly have meant to be understood literally.

And by this we would say, not that he intended us to understand that NNW, if not scientifically exact, was accurate enough for poetry, but that he meant something quite different.

That he meant something quite different I took occasion to propose some years ago, in an earlier paper on this poem.[2] I then suggested that he might be slyly implying an opposite sense, ironically indicating how far the poem really was from the conventional love-vision. Without abandoning that general point of view, I would now offer an alternative interpretation, the simplicity of which is perhaps the reason for its not having been, to my knowledge, at least, suggested long ago. When Chaucer refers to the positions of heavenly bodies, he plots them with reference to the celestial globe, in terms of zodiacal signs, arcs, degrees, and so forth. The reference to NNW, on the contrary, is not celestial, properly speaking, but terrestrial. NNW is, in fact, a compass indication,[3] a bearing on the earth's surface. Is it not probable, therefore, that the allusion here is geographical rather than astronomical? If so, we are to take Cytherea in her figurative sense. What Chaucer appears to be saying is that when he began his poem, Cytherea was exerting her influence in a particular quarter, which was the occasion of his writing. By a graceful and not too definite allusion, he means to suggest the locale of the event to be celebrated. Love, in other words, hovered over the park and palace of a certain highly placed personage whom the poet wished to compliment. If, for example, Chaucer wrote his poem at Greenwich, a line drawn thence due NNW would strike across Gaunt's palace of Richmond in Yorkshire, and a good many places of interest that lay between. It is idle to try to work out any identifications on this basis, because we do not know where Chaucer was at the time of writing, nor do we know when he began to write; and we do know that he was frequently on the move. But the present interpretation at least relieves us of the burden of astronomical calculation and conjecture.

Before we leave the invocation to Venus, we must consider its bearing on Manly's view of the poem as a conventional *demande d'amour*.[4] Manly, it will be recalled, took the allusion as a temporal clue, indicating the date of April-May, 1382. Now, if Chaucer were engaged upon a literary exercise for a festival, he would surely calculate his effects with that event in mind. The poem would have to be read at the celebration, not at another time of year in commemoration. If so, on Manly's hypothesis the poet was guilty here of a clumsy ineptitude. When Valentine's Day, 1383, arrived, he arose to tell the assembly, in this invocation, that he had commenced his composition some nine months before—a declaration entirely unnecessary. We should naturally suppose that a poet in such circumstances would do what he could to obliterate the time-table of effort, especially if prolonged, so as to create that air of spontaneity so helpful to the success of an occasional piece. But, by Manly's showing, Chaucer would seem to be infelicitously celebrating a dream deliberately dated in the previous year, at the same time gratuitously announcing that he began to labor on it soon after it occurred.

If there were no other obstacle than this in the way of Manly's hypothesis, this would perhaps be sufficient to dispose of it, unless he abandoned the temporal interpretation of the invocation. But of course there is the further sufficient objection that the poem proposes no topic for debate. Much of its humor lies in the fact that when all is clear and no room is left for uncertainty of rational decision, human (or avian) stupidity will still find matter for dispute. For here, even the principals would rather resort to force than submit to reason. The lesson is that every one's judgment is the slave of his ruling passion; no case is considered on its true merits; and most discussion is merely irrelevant.

Attention was earlier called to the curiously loose and detachable relation of the invocation to its context. It was suggested that herein we might find a possible hint of revision. We must now scan the poem for further evidences of change in scope or intention. Now, every reader has been struck, and captivated, by the surprisingly lively and irreverent wrangling of the lesser fowl in the central debate. Here, we say, Chaucer is completely himself, and inimitable. And it is generally recognized that the tone of this passage, in its farcical verve and complete informality, differs widely from the rest of the poem. To say the least, it is decidedly unconventional for a dream-vision. We should naturally, therefore, look here first for signs of reworking. The results of such a scrutiny are not such as we might have anticipated, but they are none the less extremely interesting.

If anything, we should expect, should we not, to find that the farce was a later inspiration? Let us consider this possibility. It is obvious that from the beginning there must have been some sort of discussion or debate. The very title would indicate as much. At least a part, therefore, of the rivalry between the tersel eagles would seem, at first glance, to be basically necessary to the scheme of the work. But when we review the debate, first and last, a strange anomaly appears which causes us to doubt that the original terms of the dispute were the same. For, with the exception of Nature, the only one of the speakers to pronounce upon the respective merits of the three eagles is the terselet of the falcon. Is it not clear that all the rest have a different, but identical, subject in view, which is, quite simply: Shall the formel accept the royal tersel or shall she not? On this point the answers are perfectly consistent, according to the several dispositions of the speakers. The goose pronounces: If she won't have him, let him love some one else. The duck, another water-fowl, agrees. The turtle-dove advises: Let him serve her faithfully till death, whether or no she reward him with acceptance. The cuckoo says: Who cares? So our own needs are satisfied, let each of them (which may more properly mean the royal tersel and the formel than it may the three rivals, since two of the latter would be left unprovided in any case) live solitary all their lives. The consistency of approach between all these answers is significant: it cannot be that Chaucer would charge the goose, the duck, the dove, and cuckoo with the same stupid inability to see the point at issue. That kind of muffin-headedness might do for the goose and the duck; but the cuckoo is selfish and sly, not stupid, and the turtle-dove, though tender-hearted and idealistic, is no fool. It looks, then, very much as if the debate of the lesser fowl were written for a version of the poem which had only the one royal suitor; and we are thus thrown back from the part of the poem where we expected to find revision to an earlier portion for further signs of change.

Such indications are not lacking. Nature says, opening the court, that all the kinds of birds shall choose in order of rank, from the royal tersel on down, with the proviso that every female shall make free acceptance. Though it might have been anticipated, no provision for a case of rivalry for the same female is introduced. Then, as soon as the royal tersel has spoken, the poet reports the formel's confusion, as if here were a climactic point in the narrative. Had the other tersels been part of the scheme from the start, we should have expected this stanza to follow the speech of the last contender, or else we should look to be notified of the formel's successive reactions to the others' speeches. But we are not; and no further use is made of the formel's initial embarrassment, which is left unintegrated with the conclusion and dramatically unexplained. After all points of view have been invited and expressed, Nature reverts to her original condition, which had been stated at the beginning with all possible clarity, and, as if the idea were new, offers the formel a free choice, thus rendering the whole debate an irrelevant interruption. Her resumption of the status quo looks like an effort to accommodate the old narrative sequence to unforeseen interpolations. If we cancel Nature's remarks, lines 624-37, which are adjustments in view of the rivalry and advice to take the best of the three, and similarly lines 659-65, which are summary advice to all the tercelets to wait a year, the frame of the debate still holds, and holds with better consistency:—assuming also, of course, that the second and third suitors' speeches, with the falcon's judgment, are dropped. Supposing a minimum of re-writing of the stanzas as they stand, there would be a gap, then, after line 658, which itself introduces a further speech of Nature to the other sorts of fowl. That gap would be adequately filled by inserting at this point lines 407-13, Nature's speech beginning "But natheles, in this condicioun [/] Mot be the choys of everich that is heere," which could properly be removed from its present position, since it now interrupts the train of thought. Lines 405-06,

> And therwithal the tersel gan she calle,
> And seyde " My sone, the choys is to the falle,"

would then be followed immediately by

> With hed enclyned and with ful humble cheere
> This royal tersel spak, &c.

And again, lines 666 ff. appropriately follow the content of lines 407-13 when the latter speech is removed to its new position. These shifts are not suggested as a necessary part of the argument for revision, but they show how little need have been done to accommodate the poem as a whole to the additional suitors. Lacking other drafts, the case will of course never be finally proved.

   Now if there was originally but one suitor, the very inconsequentiality of the basic plot would appear to be a strong argument for the poem's having been composed upon an historical event. Unless the allegory is to be tortured into a mode of symbolical abstraction alien to the medieval habit—making the formel, for example, an unnamed and unidentified political or religious symbol—it is reasonable to assume that its meaning is simply that a royal suitor, whom the poet obviously wishes to flatter, has applied for the hand of a lady, who has put him off, or at least postponed a decision. In view of Natures being the presiding genius, it is also natural to understand the reason for postponement in the simplest fashion, namely, that the lady was still too young to be interested (or so regarded by her guardians), and was not to be forced into a match:

> This formel egle spak in this degre:
> "Almyghty queen! unto this yer be gon,
> I axe respit for to avise me,
> And after that to have my choys al fre:

> This al and som that I wol speke and seye . . .
>
> I wol nat serve Venus ne Cupide,
> Forsothe as yit, by no manere weye."
> "Now, syn it may non otherwise betyde,"
> Quod tho Nature, " here is no more to seye."

Such a subject is surely unpromising, and that Chaucer has found so much to do with it is not only brilliant proof of his artistic resourcefulness, but also, I believe, a sign of the importance to him of achieving success. One would not suppose he would have undertaken it at all unless either he had been commissioned to do so, or had seen his account in it to win favor. The last three lines of the poem are in fact usually understood as a gracefully apologetic bid for tangible thanks; and it is most natural to suppose that those thanks would be expected from the object of his compliments.

Nor is it difficult to persuade oneself that the poet, until he gets into the farcical debate, is working against the grain of his disposition. Robert A. Pratt has recently pointed out[5] that Chaucer's use of the *Teseide* in this work shows evidence of haste and improvisation. It would appear that the garden in the *Roman de la Rose* gave him a running start that carried him over by associational processes to Boccaccio's kindred description, and that once there he saw the opportunity to amplify and pad with further borrowings. These were incorporated without too much care for consistency or a comprehensive plan, and the phraseology is relaxed in the manner of oral delivery: "I nyl nat lye," "I gesse." There are minor inaccuracies of translation, and contradictions unremoved, as that of the sun which was both too hot and yet never disagreeable, or that of the perpetual day which yet turns to night. The whole passage is introduced for decorative enrichment, and has little organic part in the total design.

We have already remarked the introductory disclaimers, Chaucer's insistence on his detachment and the incongruity of his position in writing a love-poem. It seems altogether clear, from this and other similar passages in Chaucer's work, that he could count on his audience's good-humored appreciation of the jest of his "unliklynesse," whatever its motivation. Since it is impossible to believe, in face of his cool, ironic temper, that he was always falling in love, and forestalling ridicule by making a joke of his characteristic and notorious weakness, we must suppose on the contrary that it was his detachment which was the object of amused and teasing remark in that passionate, sophisticated, and intrigue-loving circle within which he lived and worked; and that he was softening the jibes by anticipating them; holding it wiser, like Boswell, when about to be knocked down, to "lie down softly" of his own accord. Indeed, his language here is appropriate to a man who regards himself as incapacitated not so much by temperament as by advancing years for such amorous pursuit. For, as Scipio says,

> Thou of love hast lost thy taste, I gesse,
> As seek man hath of swete and bitternesse.
> But natheles, although that thou be dulle,
> Yit that thou canst not do, yit mayst thou see;
> For many a man that may not stonde a pulle,
> Yit lyketh him at the wrestling for to be,
> And demeth yet wher he do bet or he.

Many critics have been troubled by the inappropriateness of the Dream of Scipio in this context, and have felt it to be quite unnecessary for the poet to go to the length of outlining the contents, chapter on chapter, "as a curious traveller counts Stonehenge." Whilst I believe that these matters can nearly all be artistically justified, wholly or in part, it seems undeniable that Chaucer was exhibiting the *tours de force* of a virtuoso utilizing whatever lay nearest to hand, compelling it into service.

Had he been free to invent, he would surely have fashioned a more substantial plot, would not have submitted voluntarily to the handicap of so lame a conclusion. He managed to surmount the disadvantage not merely adequately, but with triumphant bravura. But if he did this once, how are we to explain his returning to the piece? Is it to be supposed that the same, or almost identical, circumstances would again arise, so that the same *jeu d'esprit* would serve once more for the new occasion and the new reward? Would no one in his circle recognize that this performance was a repeat? Or could the first attempt have succeeded so ill that it was suppressed without a hearing?

If only the signs of revision went the other way, tending to show that the bird-debate came in when the poem was revised, we might be able to believe that the revisal was so drastic as to be in effect a new work. But, unfortunately for the rule of right and the fitness of things, the evidence does not point in that direction. What seems possible in face of the evidence is that when for reasons of his own Chaucer chose to re-work his poem, he was motivated chiefly by artistic considerations. It seems altogether unlikely, considering his close relation to his audience, that the changes he introduced were for the purpose of bringing an old piece up to date; and I think we should surmise that what was done in revision tended to carry the poem farther away from correspondence with an actual event. It is obvious that a rivalry between three suitors, whether equal or unequal, is a livelier spectacle than one suitor left dangling in uncertainty. On grounds of mere narrative interest, then, the change would be justified. At the same time Chaucer has not robbed his hero of clear preeminence, but has reinforced that superiority. We need not, therefore, look too assiduously for the historical counterpart of three suitors pursuing the same lady. And likewise, it would appear that the importance of the type of story denominated "The Contending Lovers" by Professor Willard Farnham is diminished, so far as it relates to our poem.

It seems possible, furthermore—though proof is unattainable—that the grave irony and the underlying seriousness with which the introductory passages are charged may itself be a product of revision. For this is thoroughly mature writing. Throughout the decade of the eighties, Chaucer must have watched with growing anxiety the increasingly ominous posture of public affairs, the widening of the rift between the young king and his subjects, the ruthlessly selfish jockeying of rival factions for deadly advantage. In such an atmosphere, he might welcome the opportunity to urge that men can learn wisdom from the past, and find it desirable to reiterate the old truths about the service of the common weal. Assuredly the advice was "newe science" in Richard's reign, and Scipio's admonition,

> loke ay besyly thow werche and wysse
> To commune profit,

was never more timely. It might be indicative, also, that nowhere else is the emphasis of Chaucer's detachment in matters of love put so clearly in terms of age. For in *The Book of the Duchess* he complains of the lack of success, in the *Troilus* he wishes, though himself "unlikely," to further the success of others, in *The House of Fame* he is detached but observes with pity and humor, in the *Thopas* prologue he laughs outright at the notion of himself in love; but here alone he seems to say chiefly, "It's too late." I will not be so unwary as to commit myself to an opinion as to the year of his life at which a man may begin to voice this sentiment, and I am willing to allow much on the score of a humorous pose in the poet. But there seems to be a shift of emphasis in his various humorous references to the subject; and here the references coincide with other signs of growing sobriety.

It is obvious that the foregoing remarks have been quite as inconclusive as the poem which has occasioned them. The poem, however, has so often been employed as a mere charabanc for historical holiday excursions that there is little harm in calling back the attention of literary students to the terms of the work itself, to its actual stated content. In the end, to do so will certainly not damage the poem as a work of art, but will increase our appreciation of its subtlety, its ironic humor, the beauty of its verse, and the skill and virtuosity with which its creator has compelled his unlikely and disparate materials into an artistic and satisfying whole.

NOTES

1. There is a troublesome awkwardness in his syntax, however we punctuate. Robinson stops with an exclamation point after *best*, and Skeat with a semi-colon; but it might be better to use a comma at that point to indicate a closer relation between the adjacent clauses: "for thou mayst help me best, as surely as I saw thee" &c. Skeat understands the passage in another sense:" As wisly as . . . , when . . . , so yif me. . . ." And Robinson, though he prints a colon after *write*, appears to take the meaning in the same way.

2. *University of California Publications in English*, III (1935). 193-224.

3. I owe the recognition of this fact to Charles Polk, First Officer in the U.S. Merchant Marine, whilom a graduate student in the University of California.

4. J.M. Manly, "What is the *Parlement of Foules?*" *Studien zur Eng. Phil.*, L (1915). 229.

5. "Chaucer's Use of the *Teseide*," *PMLA*, LXII (1947). 605-08.

6. "The Source of *Chaucer's Parlement of Foules*," *PMLA*, XXXII (1917). 492-518; "The Fowls in Chaucer's *Parlement*," *Wisconsin Studies in Lang. and Lit.*, II (1918). 340.

ARISTOTLE'S *POLITICS* AND THE FOUNDATIONS OF HUMAN SOCIETY

by Paul A. Olson

Recent studies in *The Parlement of Foules* have made it fairly clear that the two fabulous places in the poem, Venus' hothouse and Nature's hill, are representations of contrasting systems of value or ways of loving. The primary emphasis of the criticism has been on the work as a "question d'amour" poem in which the debate concerns how human beings should conduct the amorous life or how love may be redirected toward the God of Nature and his glorious creation.[1] Without wishing to denigrate such interpretations, I want to urge an alternative view-one which sees the discussion of love between men and women primarily as vehicle for a discussion of the nature of the social and social love in general. Within this perspective, I would suggest that the inclusion of a "Parlement" is not fictional decoration, but a representation of that vehicle through which late medieval man found it most possible to develop his sense of sociability and conviviality.

I

The sources for my argument about Chaucer's *Parlement* are primarily late medieval neo-Aristotelian treatises on the nature of the political and social. As late medieval courts in northern Europe became somewhat more centralized, thinkers in those courts began to look at the nature of political conduct less from the perspective of single, personal loyalty between men located in a divinely arranged hierarchy—less from the perspective which makes the central political action of the disloyal follower Guenelon's remark to Charlemagne "I do not love you at all"—and more from the perspective of how groups of people acting in essentially corporate bodies work out problems of loyalty, goals, conflict of interest, and organization.[2] It should be recalled that a Christian frame allowed for no appeal to that selfishness or self-interest as the motor of society posited by Adam Smith, and the new thought had to deal with the question of how human beings in

society, in corporate bodies, are able to love one another *through* the
institutional forms of a more complex society.[3]

In the evolution of a tradition of thought which dealt with such
questions, Aristotle's *Politics* was particularly helpful in that Aristotle
provided a picture of how corporate institutions could support civic
charity. The concept of the existence in the civic world of equivalents
of cupidity and charity was conventional; natural law theory held that
the civic equivalent of cupidity was the quest for "private profit," or
what Chaucer calls "singular profit," and of charity was the quest for
"the common profit."[4] The quest for the common profit, insofar as it
was a natural instinct of man, could be seen as enlightened self-interest,
but nature itself, in the case of the beasts and redeemed men, was seen
as full of grace; and the human nature of redeemed men told them to
serve the commonwealth as an expression of love.

The usefulness of Aristotle's *Politics* was that it provided a picture
of how people can identify "the common profit." For Aristotle, what
makes man human is his capacity for speech—for speaking together to
identify species' interest. Thus, while bees and birds and other
collective creatures find out what they should do corporately by
listening to instinct, men find out what they should do by talking
together in assemblies until they recognize what the common interest
is.[5] It is not much of a step from this view of man to the medieval
institution of *parlement*—of speaking together. It is not the purpose of
this article to determine which came first, the practicing colloquia for
determining institutional direction called "parlements" or the idea of
such colloquia derived from Aristotle's thought. What is important is
that, in Northern Europe and particularly in England, Neo-Aristotelian
Christian thought having to do with the functions of civic speaking or
thinking together and the institution of formal "Parlements" converged.
The institution of speaking together was an important part of life on
rural estates, in guilds, universities, and the central royal
administrations. The importance of the tradition of thought which I am
investigating to Northern European courts, particularly to the English
and French courts, has not, so far as I know, been discussed. Walter
Burley, Sir Simon Burley's father, edited Aristotle's *Politics* for
Richard du Bury; Simon Burley, in turn, had Henry of Gauschi's
translation of Giles of Rome's *De Regimine Principum*, a
Christianization of the *Politics*, in his library, and Simon was Richard
II's tutor. Sir John Trevisa translated the whole of Giles into English
prose and Thomas Hoccleve translated part of it mingled with other
works into poetry while paying tribute to Chaucer in his *Regement of
Princes*. Aristotle's *Politics* was translated into French for Charles V of

France with commentary by Nicolas Oresme, and Giles appears prominently in Charles V's grand library.[6] Indeed, so far as I can discover, no other book about the conduct of political offices appears so often in Northern European libraries of men of affairs. It is not surprising that when Sir John Fortescue, Thomas Chaucer's lawyer, writes his *De Natura Legis Naturae*, he uses primarily St. Thomas' and Giles' arguments about the nature of the political and social, and when he praises the laws of England as opposed to France, he emphasizes the consultative parliamentary nature of British monarchy.[7]

Chaucer's *Parlement of Foules* is, I think, a picture of how people discover civic charity through institutions for "speaking together"; it is drawn to explore Aristotle's and Giles' thought, and the implications of those institutions for deliberation which existed in Chaucer's own time. The work opens, as do many of Chaucer's dream visions, with the poet reading the text for the dream. The piece of literature which inspires the revelation appropriate to Chaucer's day, which is also interpretive of the text read, is the passage from Macrobius where Scipio Africanus explains to Scipio the Younger the duties of citizenship, a text drawn out of Cicero's *Republic*—Cicero's version of Plato's *Republic*. It is important that Chaucer reads about republican senatorial Rome rather than imperial Rome; his guide to civic conduct is the Scipio who served the Roman republic, and not the Virgil, creator of the imperial myth, who is Dante's mentor.[8] The vision which Scipio offers defines civic charity as 'following the common profit' and living in harmony with the music of the spheres; it also marks for Scipio the Younger the Carthage which he must destroy and the Dido passion which he must avoid. However, it says almost nothing about how the common profit is to be found. This is the place of the dream.

In the dream, Chaucer passes through the gate which is split between the products of the quest for singular profit and the fruits of collective enterprise. He visits the temple of Venus and "Riches", which both embodies the values of the quest for private profit and sets the basic choice against the background of 'myth'. For Chaucer, rejecting Venus's house is rejecting Paris's choice and following better choices such as those of Hercules or Scipio, who went after the lives of action and contemplation (contemplation in that he dreams, and action in that he dreams of the active life).[9]

When Chaucer comes into the 'Parlement', he apparently has no guide. Scipio has disappeared, and no one is announced as a replacement, such as the Statius or Beatrice of Dante's *Comedy*. But the guide is here, I think, and she is Nature, that figure who can reveal the meaning and institutional form necessary to the quest for the common profit in the same way that Beatrice can reveal the theological meaning of history, of Hell and Purgatory, and pull together the meaning of the fragments of imperial and papal life which Dante has viewed in Hell and in the lower Purgatory. Nature is described as the vicar of God, and acts as an ordainer of statutes in this context. Whereas Nature is commonly described as the vicar of God in the tradition of Alanus' *De Planctu Naturae* and the *Romance of the Rose*, she is, I think, here the vicar of God *in a civic sense*; exactly the sense which makes the king the vicar of God in the language of medieval ruler-praise (or "ruler-worship" as Kantorowicz puts it). The king is the vicar of God in the sense that he translates natural law into positive law even as Nature translates eternal law into natural. The standard language makes the medieval ruler "the vicar of God" but this is a shorthand for the more extensive hierarchical relationship which is implicit in *The Parlement of Foules*: God/eternal law; Nature/natural law; King/positive law; people. This set of hierarchical relationships meant that a medieval king held his kingship in trust, and was a king to the degree that he interpreted natural law into positive law, enforcing "the idea of the species" through his legal ministrations and preventing Venus or "selfish impulse" from destroying man's basically social nature, his commonweal.

By looking at man's species nature (and also his fallen nature), a king was thought able to discern what natural law told him: i.e.,that man is a weak individual; that he is a collective species, requiring sustenance from special goods of the earth, and lengthy periods for the birth and rearing of children; that he is granted free will and the power of speech to solve problems, and, after the fall, possessed of a social nature which required defined social duties and roles if men were to serve one another in a continually constructive way.[10] If one were to write up the 'rules' of natural law as conceptualized by the ordinary late medieval thinker, they might read something like this:

(1) Man, by nature, has a right to meet in social assemblies and deliberate over—speak together about—the common good of the group assembled.
(2) Since the human species comes into the world as a "poor forked creature" and remains relatively helpless for many years, natural law requires something like a permanent relationship between the male and female of the species; since men are granted "freedom of will," marriage and other important contracts in life should be with the free assent of the parties.

(3) Since man is a creature who sustains himself from the soil, he needs soil to sustain himself—before the fall, common property, and after it private property held in trust from the emperor and God for the common good. (Richard II was found to be a tyrant for violating the precept in the case of John of Gaunt's estates.)

(4) Finally, since men after the fall are not given spontaneously to serving the collective good or interest of society, natural law requires the development of "roles"—like the divisions of a beehive—whereby the various sorts of service that men can give to each other are defined.[11]

This rule of nature is the foundation for late medieval estate theory. What Dame Nature does in calling the *Parlement* is to ask the creatures to behave as if they were somewhat stylized human beings whose species role demands what Nature's law demands: concern for the common profit, speaking together to realize what it is, permanent marriage and respect for freedom of choice, a conception of the collective and the individual in property and rights which does not jeopardize the group character, and a clear system of statutes which defines what men are to do for each other.

Dame Nature not only orders the *Parlement* according to natural laws as applied to the human sphere; she gives it a kind of symmetry reflective of the most orderly medieval conceptions of bird life in the natural spheres, and further orders that order. If one compares early medieval books cataloguing nature's creatures (such as *Physiologus*) with late medieval books, such as Bartholomaeus Anglicus' *De Proprietatibus Rerum*, one instantly recognizes that the perception of the creatures has changed sharply. In the *Physiologus*, no effort is made to classify; in Bartholomaeus, everything is classification, classification by anatomy, by surface physical characteristics, by habitat, by feeding characteristics, by social nature. And this obsession with classification (which stands at the head of the long tradition leading up to the Linnaeus) is the reflection of the growth of discipline in the art of reasoning and, to some extent, of induction fostered by the university studies in logic and science; it reflects an interest in taxonomy and detail which is essential in late medieval science and natural observation.[12] The scheme which Chaucer presents is a schematization of the scheme of that professional scheme- maker, Bartholomaeus Anglicus.[13] Instead of simply accepting Bartholomaeus' division of the birds (by habitat, by feeding habits, and by flocking habit), Chaucer puts the three divisions together. The categories go together as follows:

A. Habitat: mountains, field, forest, water.
B. Feeding habits: ravine, seed, worm, water plants.
C. Flocking habit: solitary, pairs, individual, flocks.
D. Speaker: eagle, turtle, cuckoo, duck, and goose.

The first three categorizations of creatures are clearly reflective of categories in Bartholomaeus; they are conflated to make a kind of stylized "Byzantium" of birdlife. The fourth category, the category of bird-class speakers, is a reflection of the habit of the British Parliament in Commons of having speakers after 1376.[14] It has been commonly argued that the debate which Dame Nature conducts has to do with the royal marriage; I am unable to find anything in the debate which anyone could trace to actual debates over the marriage of Richard to Anne of Bohemia or to Isabella of France. It would have been impolitic or foolish for Chaucer to have given political advice about a royal marriage through a dream-vision, ambiguous and subject to variant situational interpretations as it is. Indeed, when Philippe de Mézières gives advice to the identical court through dream-visions such as the *Epistre au Roi Richart II*, he specifies very clearly what he means and who he is talking about lest he be misunderstood. Rather, Chaucer's debate about love is a debate about how the estates should behave toward one another in all matters of life-concern, symbolized here by that first matter of life-concern, "Whom shall I marry when I grow up?" The conventional four-estate schemes identified the estates as lords spiritual, lords temporal, commoners, and, merchants. Other schemes identified lawyers or curial officials as the fourth estate.[15] While either of these interpretations may be satisfactory for the understanding of Chaucer's scheme, I am inclined to believe that in the context of the *Parlement*, lawyers or curial officials more likely constitute the fourth estate.

The fouls of ravine are interested in fighting to solve problems, and their symbolism is insistently martial, what one would expect of lords temporal or knights.[16] The speaker for the field foules is a turtle, which is a conventional symbol for the clergy or the contemplative[17]; the contemplative is married eternally to Christ, and can afford to urge endless unrequited fidelity in this world on the knights. The water fowl are pretty clearly common; the duck speaks for the commoners in Lydgate's, *The Horse, the Sheep and the Goose*.[18] And the cuckoo or worm foul seems to be a spokesman for selfish curial officials.[19]

The advice which each class gives about the conduct of love constitutes what wisdom the "class" (as opposed to Nature) has with respect to how civic affairs are to be conducted. The knights know that fighting solves problems and blood counts; the turtle knows that eternal values are to be kept eternal; the duck knows that for commoners the need to increase and multiply is more important than any particular values attached to curial protocol; and the cuckoo is concerned that the business get done. Each of these expressions is the expression of how, at one time or another, the class or "estate" was called upon to solve social problems. Knights fought wars to "solve problems"; they fought before the High Court of Chivalry to achieve justice. Clergy enforced their vows on one another to the same effect. Bureaucrats pursued efficiency in their jobs; and commoners such as the men of 1381 kept insisting that they could get their jobs as commoners done were it not for the interference of the gentry. But none of these bits of advice is necessarily appropriate to creating a love which must be freely willed or to the solution of social problems by a political vehicle which has to mediate the struggles of all classes of society.

Nature allows the Parlement to speak only what each class's concept of the social is; then she imposes her conception, that is, restraint for a year at the very top of society so that the rest of society, which can achieve its goals simply through a coming together under "nature" for a St. Valentine's "speaking together," can "marry". The song of love at the end, which reflects the feast at the conclusion of the annual Parlement, is surely one of the finest hymns to civic charity in existence:

> "Now welcome, somer, with thy sonne softe,
> That hast this wintres wedres overshake,
> And driven away the longe nyghtes blake!
>
> "Saynt Valentyn, that art ful hy on-lofte,
> Thus syngen smale foules for thy sake:
> Now welcome, somer, with thy sonne softe,
> That hast this wintres wedres overshake.
>
> "Wel han they cause for to gladen ofte,
> Sith ech of hem recovered hath hys make,
> Ful blissful mowe they synge when they wake:
> Now welcome, somer, with thy sonne softe,
> That hast this wintres wedres overshake,
> And driven away the longe nyghtes blake!" (*PF*, 680-95)

Thus it is that Venus, or the search for private profit, is overcome through a speaking leading into song, through self-abnegation on the part of the great, and through the application of nature's general reason rather than the strategies of any particular status to the solution of a total society's problem.

II

The *Parlement* has been seen as a reflection of the British parliament.[20] It certainly is a schematized version of that, but it is also a paradigm, in the classic sense of that word, for any speaking together among the estates in which the sense of the social—in which civic charity—is discovered, whether that speaking be in convocation, guild, city, university, or rural estate. Love is the business of every speaking together, and it should end in song as regards the *convivium* of our work together here.

It is possible to see *The Canterbury Tales* as another *Parlement*. But here the ending of the feast is different, because the poem opens on a wider horizon. Again, Nature begins the speaking together, and the speaking together of men and women is set against the speaking together of the April birds. The estates are present; the journey is a journey to the shrine of a saint who represents estate order in England because of his assertion of the authority of canon law in the face of Henry II's claims.[21] But whereas the *Parlement* is concerned only with how a "speaking together" and sacrifice on the part of the most noble in society can establish a form of civic charity under the laws of nature, *The Canterbury Tales* are concerned with this *a n d* with the transformation of the heart, of pride into love, which it is a function of penance to perform. Under the Bradshaw shift the first segment of *The Canterbury Tales* deals with the relation of lords temporal and peasants. It begins with an epic and ends with a prose tale of counsel for lords temporal, *The Tale of Melibee*. The second sequence begins with the false start of *The Monk's Tale* (a tragedy which leads to no penance, and ends as the knight objects to the sleepiness and heaviness of heart which it induces). It goes on to the Nun's Priest's "mock epic", which picks up the theme of civic charity developed in *The Knight's Tale's* conclusion. By mocking the epic temptation of pride for clergy and court, it prepares the way for the Parson's prose conclusion which deals with pride in all its manifestations. Between the tale of the Knight and the *Melibee*, many wayward bearers and would-be bearers of the temporal sword speak, and many who bear the marks of wayward bearing; between the Nun's Priest and the Parson, many would-be clerics who know of other ways and other "sectes" from that of St.

Thomas speak of wandering by the way (the Wife of Bath for instance).[22]

At the end, the Parson says he will knit up all the *feast* of tales with his penitential sermon. The "speaking together" of *The Canterbury Tales*, like a medieval parliament or the *Parlement* itself, is a "feast" knit up. But whereas the feast knit up of *The Parlement of Foules* is a feast of civic man seeking civic charity in the *convivium* of Nature and Nature's law, the feast of *The Canterbury Tales* ends in the Jerusalem which is above, which is an "infused charity", given to the human heart by an author beyond Nature. Chaucer in *The Parlement of Foules* recognized not only what was central in Aristotelian medieval *parlement* tradition—the importance of "speaking together" to civic love but—also elevated the consultative institution which Fortescue fifty years later was also to recognize as central to British governance—the parlement—as the most *natural* institution in the world.[23] That Chaucer did this is a tribute, not only to his percipience and to the profundity of his political understanding, but also to his courage, for he lived in an age torn between warhawk lords and a would-be imperial king, when men willing to listen to the give and take of the *parlement* so as to come to a picture of the common good (such as Shakespeare's John of Gaunt in his old age, or his Duke of York, or Chaucer's immediate circle) were all too few and too powerless. It would perhaps be useful to read Chaucer's *Parlement* not only as a beautifully crafted picture of the ways of love but as a political treatise as sophisticated and elegant in its way as Dante's *De Monarchia* and the political sections of the *Commedia*, and a good deal more useful. For whereas Dante looks for civic health to the centralization of power in the imperial see, and hopes for salvation for Italy from the single imperial figure, Chaucer writes as one of the first of a series of British political thinkers who recognize that in matters social and political the speaking together of many groups to discover what is right and natural for them to do has important functions that no civic savior-king, no matter how charismatic, can fulfill. Sir John Fortescue was to put the matter more succinctly some years later in another book praising the strength of British institutions, his *De Laudibus Legis Angliae;* after describing how authoritarian or royal monarchies like that in France began with a subjugation such as that which Nimrod compelled of the beast-men under him, after rehearsing how subjugation, long endured and valued for the protections it may bring, was eventually sanctioned by the people, Fortescue describes a wholly different kind of rule—political rule—which is based not on subjugation but on community of interest, which began with Brutus' band as it fled from Troy, and which is now established and organized through parliament:

> . . . a people wishing to erect itself into a kingdom or any other body politic must always set up one man for the government of all that body, who, by analogy with a kingdom, is, from "regendo", usually called a king. As in this way the physical body grows out of the embryo, regulated by one head, so the kingdom issues from the people, and exists as a body mystical, governed by one man as head. And just as in the body natural, as Aristotle said, the heart is the source of life, having in itself the blood which it transmits to all the members thereof, whereby they are quickened and live, so in the body politic the will of the people is the source of life, having in it the blood, namely, political forethought for the interest of the people, which it transmits to the head and all the members of the body, by which the body is maintained and quickened. . . . And just as the head of the body physical is unable to change its nerves, or to deny its members proper strength and due nourishment of blood, so a king who is head of the body politic is unable to change the laws of that body, or to deprive that same people of their own substance uninvited or against their wills. . . . Sometimes, also, by the negligence of such princes and the inertia of their counsellors, [the] statutes [of countries governed regally] are made so ill-advisedly that they deserve the name of corruptions rather than of laws. But the statutes of England cannot so arise, since they are made not only by the prince's will, but also by the assent of the whole realm, so they cannot be injurious to the people nor fail to secure their advantage. Furthermore, it must be supposed that they are necessarily replete with prudence and wisdom, since they are promulgated by the prudence not of one counsellor nor of a hundred only, but of more than three hundred chosen men—of

such a number as once the Senate of the Romans was ruled by—as those who know the form of the summons, the order, and the procedure of parliament can more clearly describe.[24]

From Giles of Rome, Fortescue knew the mystical body of society to be in many ways like a colloquium of birds, meeting, mating, and carrying ahead the functions required to maintain the species, but with this difference, that it has the gift of speech to discover community right reason:

> Also swalwes maken here nestes at the beste thei3 (though) they seie nevere other swalwes make nestes. . . . But a woman cannot helpe her self in traveile of childe but she be tau3t atte the flle by mydwifes. Thanne for man is not inclined at the fulle by kynde to do thewe werkes and dedes kynde 3eveth speche to mankynde so that by speche men mowe teche eche other and lerne of eche other and for that may not be but men lyve and dwelle ifere it is kyndelich to man to lyve with other and to be a companiable beist.[25]

I like to think that Chaucer understood the kind of tradition of thought represented by Giles, and that he to some degree anticipated what Fortescue wrote about in laying the foundations for a philosophic analysis of British political institutions. Chaucer made the *Parlement* a parliament of birds because the fundamental social relationships beyond the political community, created through speaking, posited by Aristotle and his successors, are those of dominance and sexuality *(Politics,* I, i, 5- 7). Dominance is represented by the hierarchy of the birds, sexuality by the presence of males and females choosing mates and establishing families. And birds in the order of nature are most "kyndelic", most natural and comely, in their mating and familial life:

> Among alle bestis þat ben in ordre of generacioun, briddes and foules [folwen] most honest[ee] of kynde. For by ordre of kynde males seche femalis wiþ bisynesse and loueþ hem whanne þey beþ ifounden and fi3tiþ and puttiþ ham to perile for ham and beþ ioyned to ham onliche, as it were by couenaunt

and loue weddynge, and norischiþ and fedeþ onliche briddes þat þey getyn. And so kyndeliche þey demeþ and knowiþ bytwene sext and sext, male and female. . . . And briddes and foules gendrynge kepiþ couenable tyme, for in springinge tyme whanne þe generacioun comeþ inne, briddes crien and singen. Males drawen to companye of females and preyen iche oþir of loue and wowiþ by beckes and voys, and makeþ nestis and leggiþ eyren and bryngiþ forþ briddes. And whanne þe briddes beþ igendrid þey fediþ and noirischiþ ham and bringiþ hem vp. But whanne þe offyce of generacioun is fulendid, þanne þey sesen of songe and departen atwynne and comeþ nouȝt togedres forto tyme of generacioun come aȝeyne.[26]

The Parlement of Foules is a very great civic poem, concerned not only with British institutions but also with the foundations of human community in its recognition of the weakness of our physical nature, which makes the interdependency of corporate groups necessary, and of the speech unique to our nature, which makes sacrifice meaningful and corporate action fruitful.

NOTES

1. J.A.W. Bennett, *The Parlement of Foules: An Interpretation* (Oxford: Clarendon Press, 1957); D.W. Robertson and Bernard F. Huppé, *Fruyt and Chaf* (Princeton: Princeton Univ. Press, 1963), pp. 101-48; D.S. Brewer, ed., *The Parlement of Foulys* (London: Thomas Nelson, 1960).

2. Compare, for example, the picture of social relations in Marc Bloch's *Feudal Society* (Chicago: Univ. of Chicago Press, 1961) with that in May McKissack's *The Fourteenth Century: 1307-1399* (Oxford: Clarendon Press, 1959). McKissack's remark that "when Edington became Chancellor in 1356 he found himself at the head of an elaborately organized bureaucracy" (p. 213) could be made about numerous fourteenth-century English figures.

3. Initially the economic contracts which made Smith's description possible, based on self-interest and usury, had to be concealed under the language of "chevisaunces" (achievements) and terms of friendship as in *The Shipman's Tale.*

4. For common profit and charity as analogues, see Nicolai Rubenstein, "Political Ideas in Sienese Art: The Frescoes by Ambrogio Lorenzetti and Taddeo di Bartolo in the Palazzo Publico,"*JWCI*, 21 (1958), 185-86; cf. John Bromyard, *Summa Praedicantium* (Venice: D. Nicolinum, 1586), I, 155; St. Bonaventura, "Commentary on the *Sentences* of Peter Lombard," I, 33; II, 35; Henri de Gauschi, *Li Livres du Gouvernement des Rois*, ed. S.P. Molenaer (New York: MacMillan, 1899), p. 25. An anonymous fourteenth-century commentator on Boethius says "ffor Governours shulde be as the sonne: or the more in vertuous brichtness; more to comune profit than to singuler . . ." Anon. comment on Boece, *West MS*. 2684, fol. 212. For Chaucer's use of singular profit, see *HF*, 1, 310. For definitions of "singular profit" and related concepts current in Chaucer's time, see Bromyard, II, 304v; Isidore, *Etymologiae*, V, 21, and for a summary statement, Ewart Lewis, *Medieval Political Ideas* (New York: Knopf, 1954), I, 210; cf. Rhoda H. Selvin, "Shades of Love in the Parlement of Foules," *SN*, 37 (1966), 146- 60.

5. Aristotle, *Politics*, I, 2; III, 1; IV, 14.

6. For Walter Burley's edition of Aristotle's *Politics*, see S. Harrison Thomson, "Walter Burley's Commentary of the *Politics* of Aristotle," *Melanges Auguste Pelzer* (Louvain: Bibliothèque de l'Université, 1947), pp. 557-78. For Simon Burley's library including Henri de Gauschi, see Maud Clarke, *Fourteenth Century Studies* (Oxford: Clarendon Press, 1937), pp. 120-21; Henri's version of Giles of Rome is *Li Livres du Gouvernement des Roi* cited *supra*, n. 4. Trevisa's translation of Giles is found in MS. Digby 233 (hereafter Trevisa). For Hoccleve, see "Regement of Princes" in Hoccleve's *Works*, ed. F.J. Furnivall, EETS, ES 72 (London, 1897). I cite Nicolas Oresme's translation of and commentary on Aristotle's politics, *Li Livres de Politiques de Aristote* in the 1489-93 edition, which does not indicate place or publisher.

7. Sir John Fortescue, *De Natura Legis Naturae*, ed. Lord Claremont (London: privately printed, 1864), dated 1461-62; for

Fortescue and Thomas Chaucer, see Martin B. Ruud, *Thomas Chaucer* (Minneapolis: Research Pub. of Univ. of Minnesota, 1926), p. 60. The contrast between regal or authoritarian and consultative or parliamentary government drawn in the *De Natura* is extended and applied to the French and English systems in the later (1468-71) *De Laudibus Legum Angliae* (cf. *infra*, n. 24).

8. For the medieval Scipio, see Aldo Bernardo, *Petrarch, Scipio, and the "Africa": The Birth of Humanism's Dream* (Oxford: Clarendon Press, 1962); cf. Bruce Kent Cowgill, "The Parlement of Foules and the Body Politic," *JEGP*, 74 (1975), pp. 316-19, *et passim*. Cowgill's comments on the garden of the *Parlement* as the purified active life, the paradigmatic temporal society, support my interpretation, and his arguments on natural law parallel mine partly because we worked together in the late 60's and the early 70's. The essential research for this essay was done in 1962-63 under a grant from the Guggenheim Foundation. I disagree with some of Cowgill's harsher judgements on the 'squabbles' of the birds, and his sense that the bird song ends in cacophony (*PF*, 693-95). *The Parlement* ends in the kind of harmony which the state and "nature" can give, which is not the same as what grace offers in the full overriding of lust and pride.

Fortescue emphasizes how much Rome declined when it went from a senatorial assembly system to an imperial autocratic system *(De Natura*, I, 16). It is not clear how Chaucer felt about Richard II's imperial ambitions or the increasingly unilateral character of his later reign, but his choice of Scipio Africanus as guide, and his placing of 'himself' in the dream in a role analogous to that of the Scipio the Younger of the *De Re Publica* may suggest a slant on the imperial dream which is also perhaps reflected in his condemnation of Nimrod (*Form Age*, 58), the archetype of regal or authoritarian rule, his urging Richard II to cherish his people and hate extortion, Nimrod's talent (*Sted*, 23), and his emphasis on Henry IV's achieving kingship by "free eleccion" as well as by conquest (*Purse*, 22 ff.). Two of Chaucer's noble leaders, Hector and Theseus, are careful to consult parliament in crucial state matters; and Chaucer reserves the imperial title for Nature herself in the *Parlement* (319) without suggesting that any of the tersel eagles are also imperial. The royal eagle is clearly under Nature.

I do not know how much weight to put on such evidence. Chaucer was obviously a faithful servant of the Richardian anti-warhawk party in the 1380's, and Thomas Chaucer quickly became an important force in the Lancastrian administration.

9. Boccaccio interprets his own House of Venus [*Teseida, della Nozze d' Emilia*, ed. Roncaglia (Bari: Laterza, 1941), p. 417], as the concupiscent rather than the irascible appetite, but the element of choice in Chaucer's dream draws it closer to Scipio's choice between the voluptuous, active, and contemplative, conventionally mythographized as the choice of Paris between Venus, Juno, and Minerva, a choice which appears in late fourteenth-century dream-vision in the *Eschecs Amoureaux*, B.N. 9197, fol. ciiiixxvii^r-ciiiixxxviii^r. The anonymous fifteenth-century commentary on the *Eschecs Amoureux* has been edited by Joan Jones, Diss. Univ. of Nebraska-Lincoln, 1968. The voluptuous life is unnatural in that it does not follow the rule of reason or the search for the common good: "Il convient que l'homme en ses concupiscences et en tous ses desires ensieue le Rieule de Raison ou il *desnature* (italics mine);" *Eschecs* gloss, B.N. 9197, fol. ciiiixxx-viii^v. Venus' loci are sometimes used to describe political situations as in the Burgundian satire on the putative adultery of Louis of Orleans and Isabella of France, which is located in the realm of Venus with the perilous fountain of Narcissus nearby; "Le Pastorelet," *Chroniques relatives à l'historie de la belgique sous la domination des Ducs de Bourgogne*, ed. Kervyn de Lettenhove (Bruxelles: Commission Royale d'Histoire, 1873), pp. 601, 606. A frequent complaint against younger courtiers in the 1380's and 90's was that they were followers of Venus rather than of more active military or statesmanlike pursuits.

10. For "Nature" as what translates eternal law or "divine providence" into natural law, see Philippe de Mézières, cited in Dora Bell, Étude sur le Songe du Vieux Pelerin de Philippe de Mézières (Geneva: Droz, 1955), pp. 189-90; Alain Chartier, *Les Oeuvres de Maistre Alain Chartier,* ed. Andre du Chesne Tourangeau (Paris: P. Le-Mur, 1617), p. 403. For Latin distinctions among eternal, natural, and positive (or enacted) laws, St. Thomas, *Summa*, I, ii, 91, 4; Trevisa, 150^r-63^v; Pierre d'Ailly, "Questio Eiusdem in Suis Vesperiis," *Fasciculum Rerum Expetendarum et Fugiendarum*, ed. Ortuin Gratius (London: R. Chiswell, 1690), II, 519; Fortescue, *Natura*, I, 5 and 43. In

calling Nature "the vicaire of the almighty Lord," Chaucer echoes both the *Romance of the Rose* and the language of civic ceremony, which makes the king who serves the common profit a *Rex Typus Christus* mediating between natural law and positive law; Ernst Kantorowicz, *The King's Two Bodies* (Princeton: Princeton Univ. Press, 1957), pp. 89, 134-35, *et passim*; actually, in medieval political theory, the king is move accurately *vicar naturae*. The King who uses his corporate body for private profit ("singular profit") is a tyrant by medieval definitions, one worthy of deposition (cf. Giles of Rome, *De Regimine Principum*, I, iii, 3).

    11. St. Thomas Aquinas, I, ii, 94, 2, says that natural law includes the species and individual interest in the preservation of its own being, sexual intercourse, engendering and education of offspring, the inclination to seek the species' good according to natural reason including living in society, shunning ignorance, avoiding offense etc; cf. Gratian, *Decretum*, I, i, 7. The ancient commonplaces from which medieval natural law theory develops are *Romans*, II, 12-14, Cicero, *De Re Publica*, II, 43-44; III, 22; and Augustine, *De Vera Religione*, XXXI, 58; *De Civitate Dei*, XV, 16; XIX, 21; *De Libero Arbitrio*, I, 5, 13, 31; VI, 15. The later history of natural law theory is well described in H.H. Chroust, "The Philosophy of Law from St. Augustine to St. Thomas," *New Scholasticism*, 20, (1946), pp. 61-62, developments which include the notion that natural law implies the golden rule, obedience to superiors, and a species of charity, ideas also reflected in Chaucer's *The Former Age and The Parson's Tale* (X, i, 755-74). The elaboration of the natural law or "kindly" functions of speaking together come after the revival of Aristotle in St. Thomas and Dante and in Oresme, sig. aiiii^v, and Giles (Trevisa, fol. 63^v and Henri de Gauschi, pp. 10, 145-48). The other clichés listed in the section are found in Augustine, Isidore, Ivo of Chartres, Giles of Rome, Roger Waltham, Gratian, Eustache Deschamps, "Le Songe De Vergier," Oresme, Trevisa, Jacobus' "Omne Bonum" and other sources too numerous to list. The notion that the estates or statuses are needed after the fall to define that character of man's service to man is set forth in Chaucer's *Parson's Tale* ("gilt disserveth thraldom but nat nature;" *ParsT*, X, 755); Fortescue, *Natura*, I, 16 and in Robert W. Carlyle and

H.J. Carlyle, *A History of Medieval Political Theory* (London: Blackwood, 1903-06), 11, 108, *et passim*.

12. Cf. Lynn Thorndike, "Bartholomew of England," *History of Magic and Experimental Science* (New York: Columbia, 1923), II, 401-35; cf. 528-42; Erwin Panofsky, *Gothic Architecture and Scholasticism* (Latrobe: Archabbey Press, 1951), *passim*. English philosophy after Ockham, including Strode, was much concerned to define the concepts of classification, species, and genus.

13. Bartholomaeus Anglicus presents the classes of birds by habitat, feeding habit, and flocking habit without conflating the classification schemes as Chaucer does; *On the Properties of Things: John Trevisa's translation of "Bartholomaeus Anglicus' De Proprietatibus Rerum"*, ed. M.C. Seymour, et al. (Oxford: Clarendon Press, 1975), I, 596-602 [hereafter Seymour]. Vincent of Beauvais' categories, including only feeding habit, not habitat or flocking habit, are not as close to Chaucer's as those of Bartholomaeus *pace* Brewer (pp. 114-15). Bartholomaeus is the main source of the common allegorical dictionaries which make the bird-classes into social estates.

Allegorized versions of Bartholomaeus' encyclopedia, which make the bird classes into statuses of society, include the New York Academy of Medicine Manuscript of Bartholomaeus (Ricci, II, 1312; fol. 92^v-93^r), Pierre Bersuire, *Opera Omnia* (Cologne: Antonium & Arnoldum Hieratos, 1631) II, 166-68; John of St. Geminiano, *Summa de Exemplis* (Basel: Froben and Petri), IV, lxxvii; and Bromyard, *Summa*, II, 109. These generally associate birds of prey with violent men and nobles; seed birds with preachers, prelates, or "religiosus"; water birds with worldly men involved in the active life; and woodland birds with seekers of luxury. The iconographic tradition is sufficiently inconsistent to require Chaucer's device of bird speakers who have clearer traditions to define the reference to conventional social statuses. The clearest reference to the estates as such and bird categories is found in Henri du Ferrieres' *Livre du Modus et Ratio* (1379):

> Si mist en livre des ois[i]aux de iii manieres et de iii estas aussi comme des gens de quoi les uns sont apeles clers, les autres nobles, les autres gens de labour; les oisiaux sont apeles les uns ois[i]aux de proie, les autres ois[i]aux marins, les autres ois[i]aux champestres et ches iii manieres dois[i]aux seuivent en diverses

manieres quer les oisiaus de proie seuivent des autres oisiaus et les
oisiaus champestres seuivent des fruis de la terre. . . . Et tieulz
oisiaus de proie sont lesgle, le faucon, le anier, le esequere, le
hobe, et pluseurs autres aux quieux sont atribues les clers du temps
present les quieux volent haut. . . . Autres oisiaux ia quant ils
veulent prendre leur proie que la chachent et prennent de randon
sans voler haut et la prennant par tost voler. Et tieux oisiaux sont
lostour, lespriner, lesmerillon, le gerfaut et mant dautres; iceulz
sont attribues aux nobles. . . . Autres ois[i]aus sont qui seuivent des
fruis de la terre comme coulomps, corneilles, oisiaux champestres
et oisiaus marins qui tous seuivent des fruis de la terre. Et yceulz
ois[i]aux sont attribues aus gens de labour qui du labour terrien
viennent de quoi les clers et les nobles sont sostenus." Henri of
Ferrieres, *Livre du Modus et Ratio*, B.N. Fr. 12, 399, fol. 102^r-02^v
(1379).

14. May McKissack, *The Fourteenth Century* (Oxford: Clarendon
Press, 1959), p. 388.

15. Brewer (p. 35) notes that the only class division known to
medieval theory was the three estate division into "Knights, clergy and
ploughmen," but that statement is far from accurate; for late medieval
men changed the plowman class into the more general laborers class as
the number of rural laboring toles proliferated, and, as urban groups
grew, a fourth estate, composed either generally of "merchants" (i.e.,
urban traders) or of "lawyers" or "curial and judicial officers"
reflecting the expanded royal bureaucracy, was often introduced into
the schemes of statuses. For lawyers or the king's judicial and curial
officers as the fourth estate, see William Stubbs, *Constitutional History
of England* (Oxford: Clarendon Press, 1891) II, 207-08; *The Complete
Works of John Gower*, ed. G.C. Macaulay (Oxford: Clarendon Press,
1901), IV, 230; Bromyard, *Summa*, II, 466^v; Philippe de Mézières,
Songe de Vieil Pelerin B.N. Fr. 22, 542, fol. 124^r-24^v; *Rotuli
Parliamentorum*, III, 100, 579. McKissack observes that separate kinds
of summons to Parliament went to these four classes in the late
fourteenth century (pp. 184-89), and reference appears to them in other
parliamentary documents, e.g., J.E.A. Jolliffe, *The Constitutional
History of Medieval England* (London: A. and C. Black, 1954), pp.
434-35. Merchants are described as the fourth estate in the writings of
Brinton, Bromyard, Philippe de Mézières and numerous other late
fourteenth-century writers, but they appear to be less appropriate as the
fourth estate in the context of this "parlement".

16. Most recent critics have accepted the fouls of ravine-eagles groups as representing lords temporal (e.g., Bennett, p. 169) on the basis of internal evidence in the poem, but this general iconology is confirmed in Deschamps, Lydgate, John of St. Geminiano, Bromyard, John of Sheppey, *Fleta*, Oton de Graunson, and in the conventional fourteenth- century treatises on heraldry such as Bishop John Trevour's, written for Anne of Bohemia, in *Medieval Heraldry*, ed. Evan John Jones (Cardiff: William Lewis, 1943), p. 119, a much neglected source of late medieval iconology.

17. For the turtle as clergy or contemplatives, see Alexander Neckham, *De Naturis Rerum* (London: Rolls series, 1858), p. 108; Johannes de Sancto Geminiano, IV, 56; Philippe de Thaun, "The Bestiary," *Popular Treatises on Science Written During the Middle Ages* (London: Historical Society of Science, 1841), p. 119; *Guillaume le Clerc, Das Thierbuc des Normanisschen Dicter Guillaume le Clerc*, ed. Robert Reinsch (Leipzig: O.R. Reisland, 1892), p. 340. The turtle of the *Song of Songs* whom January imitates when he calls May into his enclosed garden to be faithful to him, as he understands faith, was conventionally allegorized as the church or the faithful religious from the twelfth century through Luther. A fourteenth-century sermon on the three estates compares the turtle to "men of holy chirche" who are married to Christ, and to "holi Chirche" from the time of their taking on the "yok of chastitee." A.I. Doyle, "A Treatise of the Three Estates," *Dominican Studies,* 3 (1950), pp. 357-58.

18. The common medieval-Renaissance symbolism of the goose is as a symbol for simpletonism, a symbolism easy enough for a court poet to extend to the less lettered commons. The "goose-duck" class has commonly been associated with commons or a part of commons by modern critics (Bennett, p. 170; Brewer, p. 35; Robinson, p. 795) and explicitly in Lydgate's "The Horse, the Goose and the Sheep," *Minor Poems*, ed. H.N. MacCracken (London: Kegan Paul, 1911), II, 548-49; for additional documentation from Chaucer and the period, cf. David Lampe, "Lydgare's Laughter: Horse, Goose and Sheep as Social Satire," *Annuale Medievale.* 15 (1975), 154.

19. The cuckoo is commonly associated with greed, destruction of innocence, and feathering its own interests by laying its egg in other nests and pushing out the young of its host, a charge very like the common complaint that curial officials and advisors to the king usurped too much power and used the power to their own advantage. For the best characterizations of the cuckoo in the natural histories as a greedy usurper, see Neckham, *De Naturis Rerum*, p. 118; Lydgate, *Minor Poems*, II, 564; Jean de Condé, *Dits et Contes de Baudouin de Condé et*

son fils Jean de Condé, ed. August Scheler (Brussels: Devoux, 1866-67), III, 59; Roger of Waltham, *Compendium Morale*, Bodleian MS. Fairfax IV, fol. 138-39, makes the cuckoo, an ingrate who grows up in someone else's nest and destroys him, into "aliqua perversi et viles persone" who mix themselves in the good and noble society of magnates and later destroy them, or the familiars of the great who later show themselves to be "filii et sequaces Neronis."

20. Cf. W. Pieper, "Das Parliament in der m.e. literature" *Herrig's Archiv*, 146 (1923), 187-212, which should be supplemented by the works referring to estate conceptions of parliament cited *supra*, n. 15.

21. Lydgate, *Minor Poems*, I or II, pp. 140-43.

22. The Wife of Bath is the cleric of the voluptuous life, preached a sermon in its mode, and is addressed as a scholastic, teacher of clergy, and founder of a sect. Her church is like January's Song of Song's garden.

23. Fortescue, *De Natura*, I, 16, *et passim* for the view that consultative government is natural, and not simply a concession to evil as Nimrodic or royal government is.

24. Sir John Fortescue, *De Laudibus Legum Angliae*, ed. S.B. Chrimes (Cambridge: Cambridge Univ. Press, 1942), pp. 31, 33, 41.

25. Trevisa, fol. 63^v. Aside from Fortescue, one early political-regal commentator who may be usefully read in connection with *The Parlement of Foules* is John Rastell, who edited the *Parlement* in the 1520's. E.J. Devereux suggests the edition may have a connection with *Four Elements* and "with the recurrent theme of natural law in Rastell's legal prefaces and theological writings." See "John Rastell's Text of the Parliament of Foules," *Moreana*, 23-28 (1970), p. 116. As a matter of fact Rastell's conception of nature, natural law, human society, and "Sensuall Appetite," set forth in *Four Elements* (c. 1520) and in his *Exposition of the Termes of the Lawes of Englande* (1527), is identical with Chaucer's as explained in this article. Like Fortescue, Rastell was, first of all, a lawyer.

26. Seymour, I, 597-98; cf. St. Augustine, *De Nuptiis el Concupiscentia Carnis*, I, iv. Bird symbolism seems to have been used in actual marriage garments, as in the red vestment powdered with birds in which the Lady Joan, Countess of Kent, was married, listed in the 1384 inventory of the Royal Chapel at Windsor. See Maurice F. Bond, *The Inventories of St. George's Chapel: Windsor Castle* (Windsor: printed for the dean and canons of St. George's Chapel, 1947), p. 41.

THE PARLIAMENT OF FOWLS:
AUTHORITY, THE KNOWER AND THE KNOWN

by David Aers

In an important article published in *Chaucer Review*, H.M. Leicester maintained that the *Parliament of Fowls* manifests Chaucer's general awareness of "the multiplicity, richness and variety of the authoritative traditions" and that as these 'traditional and authoritative materials fail to cohere . . . the materials of the dream become meaningful primarily as projections of various elements of his consciousness.' Leicester argued that "the focus of the poem is on the disruptive force of individual personality," indeed on "the breakdown of order and communication produced by the very existence of differing individual styles.[1] With much of this stimulating essay I concur, however I may disagree with Leicester's identification of Chaucer's stance with the turtle's at lines 509-18, a counsel of 'self-limitation explicit in terms which apply as fully and precisely to the poem as a whole," a stance allegedly aiming to show readers "that culture can only be sustained in its traditional forms if individuals will agree, personally and collectively, to self-conscious self-limitation." I myself can find no such generalized commitment to what I presume Leicester means by 'traditional forms" of culture, although one of the difficulties with his article is its surprising lack of historical and cultural specificity even when claims are being made about general changes in society and culture to which Chaucer is supposedly responding.[2] What I wish to concentrate on here is the relationship between the knower and the known, and the bearing this relationship has on allegedly authoritative discourse, on texts treated as "auctoritees." I have recently written elsewhere about such preoccupation in the *Canterbury Tales*, about Chaucer's concerns with the *processes* by which authority is constructed, the presence of the speaker in his speech, however supposedly impersonal and objective, the ways in which the known is also at least partly contingent on the particular form of language and theory in which it is stated. These preoccupations bring the grounds and conditions of discourse and speculation into focus, making them problematic topics for reflection.[3]

They also inform the *Parliament of Fowls,* the poem in which the dream framework was both used and superseded within the vision itself.

During the opening stanzas the narrator tells us that he often reads books and that not long ago he came upon an old book which he read avidly:[4]

> For out of olde feldes, as men seyth,
> Cometh al this newe corn from yer to yere,
> And out of olde bokes, in good feyth,
> Cometh al this newe science that men lere. (22-25)

One of the striking facts about this image is that the agricultural processes are presented in a manner which quite deletes all human agents, their labor and social relations. A great human task, full of risks and, as Langland emphasized, full of conflicts among different social groups, is transformed into a closed and purely natural cycle.[5] In choosing this image to express his attitude to knowledge, authority, and tradition the narrator transfers precisely these features from the presentation of the agricultural realm to that of cognition and authority. He deletes the incarnate agents through whose contingent projects and practices the human world becomes known. The pursuit of knowledge is reified, "newe science" is envisaged as an entity with a life independent of that collective and historically changing human practice without which there would actually be no science, old or new. Stated in this way, the idea sounds bizarre, but the reification in question is a common enough trait, ancient and modern, of discourse which claims to present totally impersonal, timelessly valid knowledge, dogmatic discourse in which the presence of a contingent writer or speaker is systematically obscured. The "newe science that men lere" comes out of "olde bokes" without human mediations, new conceptual schemes simply emerge as by divine miracle, particular authors, readers, and circumstances disappear into a natural, nonhistorical cycle.

These lines exhibit in a compressed, almost emblematic form an attitude to knowledge and authority the poem will discredit. The processes through which such assumptions are undermined begin immediately. We now watch the narrator himself as reader of the particular old book he has mentioned. It is one of the standard authorities of the Middle Ages, Cicero's "Drem of Scipioun" preserved in Macrobius' Neoplatonizing commentary, one of the "olde bokes" out of which "newe science" may mysteriously emerge. But the poet has already begun to foreground the role of individual readers in bringing "olde bokes" into the present, of individuals in generating "newe science"; hermeneutical problems enter the poem.[6] The authoritative text instructs the reader "That he ne shulde hym in the world delyte" (66), yet the reader apparently takes immense "delite" (27) in the text. This encourages us to consider the active role of the human reader in the preservation and understanding of texts, the active, shaping aspects of learning from "olde bokes." It also encourages us to begin asking questions about just what kind of "delite" may emerge from encounters between readers and authoritative texts which overtly preach contempt of the world and its unequivocal transcendence. Even before we ourselves read far into Chaucer's poem and begin to "delite" in its concentration on very worldly energies, the poet shows us that he is interested in much that is problematic in the re-creation of authoritative metaphysical texts in the present.

The narrator-dreamer, however, presents the authoritative text in as unproblematic a way as possible, as befits his use of the reifying image in the stanza discussed above. He avoids any direct consideration of questions about the status of the dream in the text he reads, about his own presence in bringing the old work to new life, or about its relation to other versions of salvation and "the lawe" (36-84). But the poet follows this presentation with the narrator's report that he in turn dreamt how the visionary authority in his text visited him, and here he does raise questions about visionary knowledge. He now affirms that such experience is generated by the individual's daily preoccupations, wishes, and physical condition. For instance,

> The cartere dremeth how his cartes gon;
> The riche, of gold; the knyght fyght with his fon;
> The syke met he drynketh of the tonne;
> The lovere met he hath his lady wonne. (102-05)

This prompts us to wonder why we should exclude, as the narrator does, the dream of Scipio from such interpretation, one that, however well-founded, is at least potentially reductive of most claims to visionary knowledge. By juxtaposing the passages in this way the poet invites us to rehumanize official authority, to reflect on the processes through which it is produced and propagated, however complex these and the "cause" of dreams are acknowledged to be (106-08).

The human seer is Scipio, triumphant and patriotic Roman general, and he dreams of his grandfather, another triumphant and patriotic Roman general. He receives an oracular vision instructing him about the path to salvation. The instructor speaks with the dogmatic certainty associated with oracular dreams, for as the authoritative text itself proclaimed, "We call a dream oracular in which a parent, or a pious or revered man, or a priest, or even a god clearly reveals what will or will not transpire, and what action to take or to avoid." Macrobius states that Scipio's dream was oracular because the guides in it (Scipio the Elder and Aemilius Paulus) "were pious and revered men, and both were affiliated with the priesthood" and "revealed his future." It was also a prophetic vision since Scipio saw the regions of his abode after death and his future conditions. All this is presented as unambiguous and certain. True enough, Macrobius says it was "an enigmatic dream" since it "could not be comprehended without skillful interpretation," but this was of course provided by the skillful Neoplatonizing commentator, Macrobius himself.[7]

Yet the questions Chaucer is beginning to suggest around the narrator's reading and dreaming encourage some observations about this objectively reliable oracle. The text of the dream, the dream, and the celestial instruction all come from Roman politicians and patriots for whom service of the earthly city and empire comprised the highest vocation of man. This historically specific viewpoint emerges in the dream, and it commences most appropriately with African pointing out the Carthage his grandson is soon to destroy in the service of the Roman state.[8] For the authority here the total identification of Rome and "commune profyt" is a fundamental dogma which just could not be made a topic for reflection, let alone for critical investigation. But by turning the Latin text's _patriam_ and _rem publicam_ into English "commune profyt" in this context, Chaucer invites speculation concerning the relationship between self-righteous nationalistic war and "commune profyt," speculation concerning possibly _competing_ versions of "commune profyt." Such speculations would be relevant in his own society locked in the long, destructive war with France and, as the 1381 uprising made especially plain, composed of social groups whose interests were often antagonistic—whatever might be claimed in the dominant ideology which presented society as an organic body with hierarchical estates whose ends were mutual benefit and harmony.[9] When we reach the Parliament in his own poem precisely such issues are explicitly made topics for reflection; here they are _implicitly_ present, although neither reader, nor dreamer (Scipio), nor instructor (Scipio Africanus) raises them for meditation. Far from it, the generalized statement about public service is made the basis for confidently dogmatic claims about human salvation:

And seyde hym what men, lered other lewed

> That lovede commune profyt, wel ithewed,
> He shulde into a blysful place wende,
> There as joye is that last withouten ende.
>
> . . . .
>
>   "Know thyself first immortal,
> And loke ay besyly thow werche and wysse
> To commune profit, and thow shalt not mysse
> To comen swiftly to that place deere
> That ful of blysse is and of soules cleere." (46-49, 73-77)

Chaucer has already established a context which helps his own readers notice how little moral or psychological self-awareness there is in these assertions. They fail to register serious problems in the concept of "commune profyt" and they quite overlook the way it is being used by Roman militarists and nationalists to describe their own lives without any sense of even possible ambivalences. The assertions here also ignore the real difficulties in fusing a life of complete sociopolitical involvement with one of genuine contempt of the world, untouched by any "delyte" in worldly matters.[10] It should now cross our minds that as "The cartere dremeth how his cartes gon," so these Roman patriots and militarists may unself-consciously have generated grandiose metaphysical visions which are uncritical projections of their daily lives, unexamined sanctifications of the particular values of their own contingent and distinctly transient social group. As in the treatment of the great authorities on world history in the *House of Fame*,[11] the poet has encouraged us to focus on the individuals who create the authoritative discourse which offers itself as impersonal "science," old or new. As the poet retrieves the partial and particular viewpoints of speakers and authorities, the alleged impersonality and timeless, dogmatic objectivity of authoritative discourse are again challenged.

With his own direct knowledge of international and internal conflict, living in a period of the most lively political thought,[12] Chaucer had more reason to be impressed with St. Augustine's version of Roman rule and the problems of social justice than with the authority he paraphrases here. For Augustine was sharply aware of "how many great wars, how much slaughter and bloodshed' Roman rule rested on; and in the famous fourth chapter of the fourth book of *The City of God* he likened *all* earthly kingdoms to robber bands, the only difference being that states of the kind Scipio and his grandfather serve have far more impunity.[13] I am not, of course, claiming that Chaucer's views were the same as the mature Augustine's on such matters. My point is rather that he would have seen how Augustine's old book included a searching inquiry into the issues handled in the "Drem of Scipioun" which would unveil the partial, personal, and historically contingent grounds of its seemingly impersonal doctrine. Augustine's well-known inquiry could help one bring the grounds of Scipio's discourse into focus, help one see how unreflexive it is and how superficial its confident usage of the term "commune profyt."

Chaucer chose to emphasize this by selecting an authoritative text ostentatiously committed to a metaphysical doctrine directly incompatible with any version of Christianity, and his readers might well wonder what "newe science" will be made from this old book. Its instruction includes the Neoplatonic-Stoic doctrine of the great cycles of being, antithetical to the Judaeo-Christian version of a unique and linear history created and concluded by God; it includes the doctrine of universal salvation after an automatically granted purgatorial period, anathematized early in the history of Christian theology; it includes the doctrine of soul as self-moved and eternal, quite incompatible with orthodox Christian ideas; and it includes the assertion that salvation is achieved through service of the state, utterly alien to basic Christian ideas concerning salvation.[14] Even the psychological assumptions about the ability of the unaided human to do right and live virtuously are, in almost any Christian terms, an extreme kind of Pelagianism. It is not that the authoritative visionary text and commentary are reticent in areas Christians were concerned about, quite the opposite. Nor is it that here, as he definitely did elsewhere, Chaucer chose a non-Christian vision which freed him to examine areas dogmatically closed off from scrutiny within his own culture.[15] Africanus speaks with the most unreserved confidence, and Chaucer's paraphrase mirrors this quality of his source well, a feature nicely illustrated in Macrobius' commentary when he states, "Philosophers whose views are correct do not hesitate to agree that souls originate in the sky" as he begins a conventionally Neoplatonic description of how souls descend "from the sky to the infernal regions of this life."[16] In the poet's choice we are witnessing, I think, Chaucer's fascination with the recurrent human tendency to turn exploratory concepts and models, with the inquiries they make possible, into metaphysical dogma; to delete the human subjects and interpreters of all discovery; to transform contingent and inevitably exploratory discourse into an allegedly impersonal, unambiguous, and certain statement of "correct" views, the necessary basis for all the inquisitorial practices that pervaded medieval culture and continue to flourish in the different idioms of our own world.[17]

The reader within Chaucer's poem now falls asleep and has his own vision. He refuses any simply unicausal explanation for this vision and acknowledges the possible relevance of his individual psychological state and preoccupation to a vision which he could technically claim as oracular (92-119).[18] In his response to the Neoplatonising authority and its *contemptus mundi* he invokes Venus, "That with thy fyrbrond dauntest whom the lest, / And madest me this sweven for to mete" (114-16). This yokes the ascetic Africanus, stepping out of a Neoplatonic text, with the very earthly Venus. Such a move is quite clearly grounded in the narrator's multifaceted, rather unstable preoccupations which Chaucer has made evident from the poem's opening. Of course, the appeal to Venus is part of literary traditions in which Africanus, like later religious moralists, would find much to dislike. Yet it also casts further light on both the authoritative texts (of Scipio-Cicero-Macrobius) and fundamental hermeneutical issues Chaucer had also been examining in the *House of Fame*. Chaucer is implying that the lack of critical self- consciousness in the authoritative source, involving a basic failure to acknowledge the fully incarnate nature of humans, gives rise to grave distortions concerning the springs of human activity and aspiration. "Know thyself," indeed! From many points of view the text of Cicero-Macrobius would seem rather simpleminded in its untroubled classification of humanity into "rightful folk" and "likerous folk"—with the speaker unquestioningly aligning himself with the "rightful"! The more explicitly Christian the readers' viewpoint the more striking would be the text's Pelagian optimism about the abilities of man's unaided will and intellect to earn salvation. In fact, it would seem misguidedly optimistic in both theological and psychological terms. Chaucer certainly does not introduce any explicitly theological judgements, but with the narrator's uncertainty about the relative responsibility of Africanus (Cicero-Macrobius) for his dream he combines the fact that it is Africanus who leads him into an enclosed and very delightful, very worldly pleasure garden where Cupid is "oure lord" (212), and Boccaccio's realm of Venus the main literary source.[19] This combination points delicately to the inadequacies of the version of human motivation in the authoritative text and to its speaker's lack of self-reflexivity, his too easy claims about total transcendence of all that Venus represents. It hints at unacknowledged desires, or at least *interests*, in the celestial instructor. This feature was something Chaucer depicted elsewhere too in the form of moralists' self-deceiving relish for the materials and behavior they are obsessed, with condemning, so often sexual.[20] We can also take the combination of Venus and Africanus in terms of the reader-narrator's various personal needs and frustrations (1-21). This evokes considerations about the way texts may stimulate the very kind of imaginative activity they attempt, overtly, to negate. These two approaches are perfectly complementary, as the seemingly distorting and very subjective "delite" of the reader in a Neoplatonic text actually turns into a profound comment on its inadequacies. Chaucer thus makes the old authority contribute powerfully to its own supersession in a process which is thoroughly subversive of *all* forms of dogmatic thought, not just of those found in old Neoplatonizing authorities.

Once into the more recent vision, Chaucer continues to evolve a literary form which resists confident metaphysical assertions about "The wey to come into that hevene blisse" (72), presenting us with a dynamic world of conflicting interests and multiple viewpoints where no one can even claim access to an absolute and impersonal viewpoint, from which to issue timelessly valid "authoritative" statements. Instead of the simple and abstract dichotomy between "rightful folk" and "likerous folk" we now find no unequivocal dogmatically fixed moral boundaries. The transformation Chaucer effects to the portentous gates in Dante's *Inferno* is a small detail typical of the poem's development. Africanus and Venus, heaven and hell, are married, Scipio's dream now eroticized (46-48; 123-33) and joined with its counterpart, the frustrated lover's hell. The static schemes of abstract moralism and traditional allegorical imagery are put in solution.[21] Although Chaucerian scholars have tended to assume that Chaucer is moralizing unequivocally against Venus (239-94), in a recent close discussion of this passage and its source materials Elizabeth Salter has argued that Venus's temple is also an "ambiguous" place which does not function as a confirming *exemplum* for the "Drem of Scipioun." She demonstrates just what it meant for a fourteenth-century English poet to turn away from the "simple exemplary material" of northern European writers, such as Deguilleville, in whose *Pèlerinage de la vie humaine* Venus is "a woman defouled with dung and clay, riding on a fierce boar," and to use instead Boccaccio's version of Venus and her domain in the seventh book of his *Teseida*. Elizabeth Salter shows how Boccaccio's poetic text does not offer straightforward moral condemnation of Venus, focusing rather on real beauty, elegance, and wonderful sensuous delicacy, while acknowledging the psychological dangers of devotion to her (*Teseida*, VII. 53). Through her careful comparison of the treatment by Chaucer and Boccaccio with such conventional moralistic treatments of Venus as we find in Deguilleville and Lydgate, the reader is made aware that Chaucer's portrayal of lovers' experience is thoroughly complicated and combined with a relative suspension of conventional moral condemnations.[22] We come to suspect that even here Chaucer's poem makes it quite impossible for anyone within its ambience to claim access to an absolute, impersonally dogmatic viewpoint from which to launch unequivocal moral judgements.

With this we also see at least one reason for the total disappearance of traditionally "authoritative" instructors in Chaucer's works. The critique of the standpoint they aspire to and the kind of discourse they represent has been carried through so effectively that they themselves cease to have any further purpose, even as targets for satire. The ground has been quite taken from under their feet, and they disappear. Indeed, with the achievement of this critique and with the subversion of the authoritative guide and the absolute viewpoint habitually claimed through such figures, it seems the vision structure itself had served its purpose for Chaucer, both within the *Parliament of Fowls* and in the overall development of his poetic works. Having undermined claims to dogmatic knowledge and unreflexively impersonal discourse, having shown us the human mediations involved in all human knowledge, Chaucer now wanted to allow yet more voices, in more concrete settings, to enter his poetic works.[23]

Before going on to consider these developments in the remainder of the poem, I wish to make some brief comments on Alain of Lille, whom Chaucer acknowledges as one of his literary sources for the depiction of Nature and her realm (316-18). This acknowledgement should never be taken as licence for scholars to absorb Chaucer's text into the kind of twelfth-century Neoplatonizing Christian metaphysics informing Alain's "Pleynt of Kynde."[24] However interested Chaucer was in Alain, he was as interested in many other writers and traditions, and he and Alain are worlds apart intellectually and in their poetic practice. Although Alain and his Nature constantly reiterate how utterly degenerate and corrupt mankind has become, massively blind, unutterably vicious, the poet fails to see that this raises grave problems for himself as a human writer claiming visionary insight, knowledge, and moral credibility. His lack of self-reflexivity here is the very antithesis of Chaucer's style of thought and writing, and should remind us of his inquisitorial attacks on Cathars, Waldensians, Jews, and other non-Christians, of the unself-consciously circular arguments in his dogmatics which even Chaucer's eagle might have blushed to utter.[25] As for Alain's Nature, this is a source of authoritative law in an unquestioned metaphysical context and a sacramental universe which manifests specifically Neoplatonic harmonies and unity.[26] Chaucer, however, does not allow Nature the privileged place she has in Alain, as we shall see. In fact he is far more concerned with the conflicting reactions of the birds, and their conflicting forms of language, than with Neoplatonic metaphysics of Nature in "Chartrian" natural theology. Far from supporting Alain's metaphysical assumptions Chaucer suggests the absence of any metaphysical and authoritatively transcendental norms which could be known with certainty and could serve as stable guides leading us through a sacramental universe to either the Neoplatonic heaven or its completion and fulfilment in orthodox Christian theology. Instead of Alain's visionary narrator, so easily converted by the metaphysical authority he encounters, Chaucer's visionaries in the *Book of the Duchess*, the *House of Fame*, and the *Parliament of Fowls*, like the other participants, remain unillumined, unconverted, openly *absorbed* in history and its incorrigibly contingent forms of discourse. Nor are they condemned for this absorption from some absolute viewpoint or transcendental dogma, for the very availability of such objective, unmediated knowledge has been profoundly called into question.[27]

Chaucer's realm of Nature, with its Parliament, is also an image for his society, as scholars have long recognized.[28] It is neither a form of discourse nor a symbolic region designed to assert world-transcending metaphysics. Indeed, it proves quite as inimical to such transcendental enterprises as did the *House of Fame* or the earlier portion of the *Parliament*. Nature herself has very different attitudes and preoccupations to Alain's Neoplatonic Nature, with her complaints against humanity, her obsession with. "unchastity" and homosexual or bisexual forms of love, her careful acknowledgement of the still higher reality of the new Christian dispensation to which her own being allegedly conforms, her invocation of Genius, "her other self," followed by Truth, "sprung from the living kiss alone of Nature and her son, when the Eternal Mind greeted matter, as it was considering the reflection of forms, and kissed it by the intermediate agency and intervention of an image."[29] Such discourse is utterly alien to the discourse and outlook cultivated in the *Parliament of Fowls*.

Chaucer's Nature does assume that the fowls' society should be as unquestioningly hierarchic and fixed as it was in conventional and dominant social ideology.[30] Yet when it is patently not so, she does not even complain about her creation, let alone moralize against it in that self-righteous fusion of wrath and sadness so characteristic of Alain's Nature (and other moralists). As the birds assemble we actually find their society, their forms of discourse, and their knowledge are grounded in conflicts and violently egotistic behavior often presenting itself as a disinterested concern for the "commune profyt." The leading social groups are named first in a pointed enough manner:

> That is to seyn, the foules of ravyne
> Weere hyest set. . . .
> Ther was the tiraunt with his fetheres donne
> And grey, I mene the goshauk, that doth pyne
> To bryddes for his outrageous ravyne.
>
> . . . the merlioun, that payneth
> Hymself ful ofte the larke for to seke. . . .
>   (323-24, 334-36, 339-40)

Nature is dominated by predators, tyrants, and perpetrators of
"outrageous ravyne," and through his explicitly social categories, the
language the birds use, the form of a parliament, Chaucer plainly
enough invites the reader to take this as a simplified model of the
human society he inhabited.[31] Other, lower, social groups are also
imaged as having similar values. While they may include the "wedded
turtil, with hire herte trewe" (355), Chaucer emphasizes their continuity
with the upper class birds, from "the thef, the chough" and the "false
lapwynge, ful of trecherye" to the "swalwe, mortherere of the foules
smale / That maken hony," "the cukkow ever unkynde," and the
"drake, stroyere of his owene kynde" (345, 347, 353-54, 358, 360). In
fact Kynde (Nature) includes the "ever unkynde," the "stroyere of his
owene kynde," and also "Venus sone" (351). It would be a totally
unjustified dissolution of Chaucer's poetry to turn this into some
traditional reiteration of Neoplatonic-Christian commonplaces about
unity in diversity or dissonant consonance within an overall
metaphysical knot of concord and bond of peace.[32] No such
authoritative metaphysical perspective is established nor, as we have
seen, is it even compatible with Chaucer's exploratory and self-
reflexive poetic modes. To grasp contradictions and conflicting
interests, to notice the self-interested and partisan deployment of
notions like "commune profyt," both of which Chaucer does, is not at
all the same as imposing comforting and elevating metaphysical
harmonies, or as imposing generalized assertions about "commune
profyt," on "outrageous ravyne," tyranny, murder, and the presence of
both "Venus sone" and the "wedded turtil."

Having created this image of society and the natural world, Chaucer shows the members gathered together in Parliament. Three aristocratic birds monopolize the assembly for the whole day (414-90). Their pleas, as much sponsored by Nature as are the duck's comments, are phrased in a language Charles Muscatine called a "high-courtly idiom."[33] While they are differentiated, they share a fierce and unreflexive egotism in which neither the female's wishes nor the needs of other social groups ever enter into consideration. The "high-courtly idiom" is grounded in particular interests, and at last there is a spontaneous outburst in a very different language, expressing direct antagonism to the aristocrats (491-509). To imagine a language is to imagine a form of life, and Chaucer is quite clearly imagining conflicting forms of social life which involve conflicting perspectives and values.

> ... "Have don, and lat us wende!"
>
> "Com of!" they criede, "allas, ye wol us shendel!
> Whan shal youre cursed pletynge have an ende?
> How sholde a juge eyther parti leve
> For ye or nay, withouten any preve?"
>
> .... "Al this nys not worth a flye!"
> (492, 494-97, 501)

The way in which this outburst challenges the aristocratic monopoly of the Parliament and aristocratic forms of language may well serve as an image of what the historian Rodney Hilton has described as the "loss of plebeian respect for the traditional elites" in Chaucer's period, an image of energies we find refracted and re-created in *Piers Plowman*.[34] It is noteworthy that when Chaucer has the cuckoo invoke the notion of common welfare, made so much of by Africanus, he discloses the self-interest underlying the initial posture of charitable intervention (505-08; 605-06). Chaucer does not make the cuckoo out to be any worse, or better, than the aristocrats. Rather he shows us the inevitably competing versions of what is "commune profyt" in an increasingly differentiated and complex society such as his own. Delicately but consistently he unveils the very partial interests and perspectives informing talk about common welfare in a divided society. As with his exploration of metaphysical or moralistic dogmatism, he discloses the grounds of discourse, the contingent and historically specific "knower" and speaker.

Chaucer's depiction of appeals to *reason* works in a similar manner:

> And for these water-foules tho began
> The goos to speke, and in hire kakelynge
> She seyde, "Pes! now tak kep every man,
> And herkeneth which a resoun I shal forth bryuge!
> My wit is sharp, I love no taryinge;
> I seye I rede hym, though he were my brother,
> But she wol love hym, lat hym love another!" (561-67)

Reason turns out to be the pragmatic reasoning of a goose who assumes that "love" is an activity rather like going to market to purchase a commodity—if it has gone, get something else, for it will do as well. The sparrowhawk is fully justified in crying out, "Lo, here a parfit resoun of a goos!" (568). But Chaucer makes us realize that the sparrowhawk in turn fails to reflect that the perfect reason of an eagle or a sparrowhawk is as partial and lacking in self-critical awareness as the goose's. In fact the sparrowhawk's own discourse consists of repetitive and witless abuse (569-74) which is welcomed with appreciative laughter by the "*gentil* foules alle" (575), suggesting how class position and social antagonisms may exercise a determinating influence over the intellect and sensibility of aristocratic as well as plebeian speakers. In the same way the merlin responds to the cuckoo with a lack of self-reflexivity which Chaucer plainly holds up for our critical scrutiny. For when the merlin attacks the cuckoo as the ruthless "mortherere of the heysoge," the reader recalls the predatory pursuits of the aristocratic birds and the merlin's own hunting of the lark (610-16; 323-40). The participants in the Parliament manifest no self-reflexivity in their discourse nor any self-consciousness about its grounds in particular interests and egotism. And there is certainly no authoritative metaphysical instructor claiming an absolute and impersonal viewpoint from which to make dogmatic pronouncements about what "really" is transcendental reason, *sapientia*. The dialectical relations between partial, contingent incarnate "knowers" and the "known" cannot be superseded. Nature herself, "the vicaire of the almyghty Lord," is as ready to use the goose's idiom as the eagle's, and never prescribes any of the multiple and conflicting forms of language and life. Still less does Chaucer set her to construct or deploy metaphysics favored by Scipio-Macrobius or the twelfth-century author of the "Pleynt of Kynde." Her main aim is to preserve the rather precarious forms of social hierarchy still surviving (if not honored by the supposedly "lower" birds), and to further creatures' "ese" and their "nede" by encouraging their marriages "as I prike yow with plesaunce."[35] This leads to a release of "blisse and joye" which is sexual (as befits her claim, "I prike yow with plesaunce"), drawing readers into a celebration of a range of experience far removed from at least the conscious views propagated by Africanus:

> And, Lord, the blisse and joye that they make!
> For ech of hem gan other in wynges take,
> And with here nekkes ech gan other wynde,
> Thankynge alwey the noble goddesse of kynde. (669-72)

The unabashed release of sexual frustration that had undoubtedly exacerbated social antagonisms and individual aggression leads into a delicate courtly song, an English roundel allegedly set to music composed in France and sung by a chosen choir to celebrate the coming of very worldly, sensuous summer sunshine and sexual delight (673-92). This, Chaucer shows, is one way to do "honour and plesaunce" to "Nature, the vicaire of the almyghty Lord" (379). It is also a reminder that all versions of Nature are mediated in specific human discourse, through human forms created by specific individuals and groups in specific places and times.

   Only a reading, determined to dissolve the particulars of Chaucer's art and contexts would attempt to take this ending as an authoritative image of metaphysical and cosmic harmony coherently ordering apparent conflict into a unified totality accessible to natural reason.[36]

The poem, we have seen, has quite undermined such discourse and all claims to an impersonal and transcendental viewpoint, encouraging instead a continuous self-reflexivity combined with a marked epistemological modesty. Furthermore, the song celebrates a particular moment of sexual fulfillment in a particular season, a moment of release from the particular frustrations and antagonisms of the Parliament and, behind it, the "wintres wedres" (680-82). The last thing it can be made to serve is some grandiose and highly generalized natural theodicy. Any totalizing metaphysical stance is quite alien to a poetic process distinguished by its sustained and profound reflexivity about the grounds of discourse. Chaucer's mode is utterly subversive of all dogmatizing fixities and finalities, subversive of all attempts to substitute impersonal knowledge and an absolute viewpoint for the complex processes involving incarnate and historically specific "knowers." It is beautifully appropriate that Chaucer concludes his visionary poem with the narrator reaching out for more books in a quest which is clearly going to be open-ended, finely resistant to authoritative and dogmatic closures of all kinds.

NOTES

1. H.M. Leicester, "The Harmony of Chaucer's *Parlement*: a Dissonant Voice," *ChauR*, 9 (1974), 15-33, quotes here from pp. 18, 21, 25, 26.

2. Ibid., pp. 29, 32.

3. D. Aers, *Chaucer, Langland and the Creative Imagination* (London: Routledge and Kegan Paul, 1980), chapter 4, and for the social and cultural contexts also the pointers in chapters 1 and 2.

4. All quotations of Chaucer are from *The Works of Geoffrey Chaucer*, ed. F.N. Robinson, 2nd ed. (London: Oxford Univ. Press, 1968).

5. See Aers, *Chaucer, Langland*, chapter 1, especially *Piers Plowman* (B-version), VI.

6. See Macrobius, *Commentary on the Dream of Scipio*, trans. W.H. Stahl (New York: Columbia Univ. Press, 1952), and A.C.

Spearing, *Medieval Dream-Poetry* (Cambridge, Engl.: Cambridge Univ. Press, 1976), chapter 1.

7. Macrobius, *Commentary*, pp. 90-91; on p. 6 of his useful introduction Stahl justly describes Macrobius as "a devout follower of the Neoplatonists."

8. See Cicero, "Scipio's Dream," chapter 2 in Macrobius, *Commentary*, p. 70.

9. I have discussed and explained this, together with the grave problems encountered in Chaucer's period, in *Chaucer, Langland,* chapter I (and the foot-notes to that chapter, citing relevant historical studies of the period). J.A.W. Bennett notes the relevant change to the Latin text: *The Parlement of Foules* Oxford: Clarendon Press, 1965), p. 33. Unfortunately his whole book is a devotedly anti-historical attempt to impose a harmoniously untroubled Christian-Platonic universe (one which shares Bennett's unquestioning identification of the upper classes with spiritual values—for example p. 158) on to Chaucer's text, which is pulverized in the cause.

10. Macrobius himself *does* note the difficulty, I.8.

11. See *House of Fame*, 1419-1519 and the excellent discussion of this part of the poem in Sheila Delany, *Chaucer's House of Fame* (Chicago: Univ. of Chicago Press, 1972), chapter 8.

12. See note 9 above, and on the extraordinary fertility and diversity of political thought in the period see especially the following: Q. Skinner, *The Foundations of Modern Political Thought*, 2 vols. (Cambridge, Engl.: University Press, 1978), volume 1, passim, and volume 2, chapter 2; M. Wilks, *The Problem of Sovereignty in the Later Middle Ages* (Cambridge, Engl.: University Press, 1963); W. Ullmann, *A History of Political Thought: The Middle Ages* (Harmondsworth: Penguin, 1965); A.S. McGrade, *The Political Thought of William of Ockham*, Cambridge, Engl.: University Press, 1974).

13. *City of God*, XIX. 7 and IV. 4: on this see the helpful commentary by H.A. Deane, *The Political and Social Ideas of St Augustine* (New York: Columbia Univ. Press, 1963), chapter 4.

14. See lines 46-49, 67-84: on the soul, Cicero, chapters 8 and 9, and Macrobius I. 9-13, II. 13-17. For Bennett's commentary here, *Parlement of Foules*, pp. 41ff.

15. Examples of this are frequent in Chaucer; I have discussed two examples, *Troilus and Criseyde* and the *Franklin's Tale*, in *Chaucer, Langland*, chapters 5 and 6.

16. Macrobius, Commentary, pp. 124, 133.

17. For a specific illustration of inquisitorial discourse in the fourteenth century see my *Chaucer, Langland*, pp. 97, 98, 214, 216 (Bernard Gui).

18. See Spearing, *Medieval Dream-Poetry*, pp. 91-92; on the explicit acknowledgement of subjective psychological factors as one of the causes of dreams, in medieval theorizing, see Spearing and *The Parlement of Foulys*, ed. D.S. Brewer (London: Nelson, 1960), pp. 129-31.

19. Boccaccio's *Teseida* in *Opera Mincori in Volgare*, vol. 2 (Milan: Rizzoli, 1970), English translation by B. McCoy, *Book of Theseus* (Medieval Text Asssociation, 1974), book 7.

20. For one instance, Jankyn in the *Wife of Bath's Prologue*, D 733-39.

21. For some exemplification of traditional allegorical imagery and its implications, D. Aers, *Piers Plowman and Christian Allegory* (London: Arnold, 1975), chapters 2 and 3. My reading here obviously concurs with Leicester's as against Bennett's and the critical tradition Leicester opposes.

22. Here I refer to a chapter in Elizabeth Salter's unpublished study of Chaucer and traditions of European poetry, parts of which she most generously allowed me to read and use here. It is certainly unusual to refer to unpublished material for corroboration of a viewpoint, but I believe the importance and decisiveness of Elizabeth Salter's contribution in this area will be evident [as soon as her work is published]. Meanwhile, the questions around Venus are too relevant to my own argument to pass over in complete silence. (Elizabeth Salter died in May 1980. Her loss is desolating to all those who, like the present author, had the privilege of working with her and being sustained by her. The manuscripts are now being prepared for publication by Professor Derek Pearsall of the University of York and Nicky Zeeman.)

23. With regard to the *Parliament* itself, A.C. Spearing rightly observes that once the narrator-dreamer reaches Nature's "hil of

floures" (295-315), "the Dreamer drops almost completely out of sight, as if the birds had squeezed him out of the poem; and so does Africanus, his guide" *(Medieval Dream Poetry,* p. 96). My account of *why* this happens differs from Spearing's, who is rather reticent on this matter. On the "objectivism" of impersonal discourse mentioned here, see Aers, *Chaucer, Langland,* chapter 4, and A.W. Gouldner, *Dialectics of Ideology and Technology* (London: Macmillan, 1976).

24. *De Planctu Naturae,* ed. T. Wright in *Anglo-Latin Satirical Poets,* vol. 2 (London, 1872). I quote here from the translation by D. M. Moffat (New Haven: Yale Univ. Press, 1908; reprinted Archon, 1972), cited as *The Complaint of Nature*: all page references in the notes are to pages in this edition.

25. See *De fide catholica contra haereticos, PL* CCX; see *Heresies of the High Middle Ages,* ed. W.L. Wakefield and A.P. Evans (New York: Columbia Univ. Press, 1969), p. 218, for an example of the unreflexive circularity of dogmatic discourse I have in mind; for the crude abuse of the Waldensians, see pp. 218-20. In *The Complaint of Nature* see especially pp. 19, 31-33, 41-42, 65-66, 84-86, 93-95.

26. For example, pr. 3 (pp. 25-27), m.4 (pp. 32-33), pr. 4 (pp. 43ff.), pr. 6 (pp. 65-66); W. Wetherbee has an excellent discussion of Alain's metaphysics in *Platonism and Poetry in the Twelfth Century* (Princeton: Princeton Univ. Press, 1972), pp. 188ff.

27. Here Wetherbee offers an illuminating and relevant discussion of the decline of Chartrian philosophy as a symptom of deep changes during the Middle Ages (*Platonism and Poetry*, pp. 255ff.). Chaucer's deletion of Genius is also most significant and itself reflects a rejection of Alain's metaphysics. This is also well brought out by reference to Wetherbee's discussion of Genius in Alain and in Jean de Meun; the transformations involved in omitting Genius can be seen by comparing *Complaint of Nature*, pr. 9 (pp. 90-95) with Chaucer's text.

28. For example, see R.M. Lumiansky, "Chaucer's *Parlement of Foules*: A Philosophical Interpretation," *RES*, 24 (1948), 82; on the linguistic idioms, C. Muscatine, *Chaucer and the French Tradition* (Berkeley: Univ. of California Press, 1964), pp. 116ff.

29. Contrast the obsession with "unchastity" and with what convention judged as perverted sexuality, pr. 4 and pr. 5; the quotations are from pr. 8 and pr, 9 (pp. 85, 92).

30. See Aers, *Chaucer, Langland*, chapter 1, and *Parliament*, 319-29, 390-401.

31. I again concur with H.M. Leicester's arguments against conventional critical attempts to absorb this imagery into comforting assurances about unity and harmony. For an almost contemporary example of a preacherly allegorizing of birds to represent the most obnoxious and obvious forms of violence and exploitation perpetuated by dominant medieval social groups, see *Middle English Sermons*, ed. Woodburn Ross (London: Oxford Univ. Press, 1940), EETS, OS 209, pp. 238-39, 245; for striking images of class conflict see pp. 237, 311. Of course the preacher is quite unlike the court poet Chaucer's or Nature in the *Parliament*, in that he is sure the "birdes raveners" are bound for hell!

32. Compare, for example, Alain's *Complaint of Nature*, pr. 3 and m. 4 (pp. 25-26, 32-33).

33. *Chaucer and the French Tradition*, pp. 116ff.

34. The quotation is from R. Hilton, ed., *Peasants, Knights and Heretics* (Cambridge, Engl.: University Press, 1976), p. 8; also relevant here are Hilton's *English Peasantry in the later Middle Ages* (Oxford: Oxford Univ. Press, 1975), pp. 64-73, M. Mollat and P. Wolff, *Popular Revolutions in the later Middle Ages* (London: Allen and Unwin, 1973), pp. 242-70, and Aers, *Chaucer, Langland*, chapter 1. My own argument supports H. M. Leicester's views, especially pp. 23, 24, 26 of the article cited in note 1.

35. For an example of Nature's different idioms see lines 521 and 389; of her wish to preserve hierarchical forms, 390-401, 631-37; of her purposes, 383-88. The range of idiom is totally alien to Alain's Nature.

36. As I pointed out in *Chaucer, Langland*, chapter 4, the relationship between Chaucer's self-reflexivity, his concern with the grounds of discourse, and certain shifts in fourteenth-century philosophy and theology (*not* to be confused with epistemological "skepticism") is greatly in need of close investigation: see G. Leff, *Dissolution of the Medieval Outlook.*(New York: Harper and Row, 1976) and his *William of Ockham* (Manchester: Manchester Univ. Press, 1975).

V. *THE LEGEND OF GOOD WOMEN*

In the Prologue to the *Legend of Good Women*, Chaucer's dream dramatizes the text's own punitive premise. Cupid is so upset with Chaucer's misogynist slanders that he and Alceste condemn the poet to compose *vitae* of pagan female martyrs to Love—in perpetuity. There is no question that Chaucer wrote a *Legend of Good Women*. Textual controversy concerns primarily two discrete problems: we seem to have far too few legends proper and one too many Prologues.

The debate regarding both the legitimacy and the priority of the two extant Prologues did not begin until 1871 when the G (or A, the Cambridge MS. Gg. 4.27) version was first published. Biographical, codicological, stylistic, and especially source studies all contributed to this early and intense controversy regarding this version's relationship to the F (or B, the Fairfax MS.) version that heretofore had served by default as the base-text of the Prologue. John L. Lowes's studies of the *marguerite* (daisy, pearl) poetry of France were particularly influential and achieved a consensus in favor of reasserting the priority of the F-prologue. Reviewing this controversy itself offers an interesting exercise in assessing how a critical consensus is achieved and then institutionalized and then challenged again. If nothing else, the controversy proved that factual evidence and subjective impressions are often very hard to distinguish.

The publication of F.N. Robinson's Second Cambridge Edition in 1957 calmed the controversy for a while, but it seems to be intensifying again. Between 1994 and 1998, at least four publications resurrected the question: two privileged the F-version; two preferred G. This apparently interminable debate regarding the two Prologues also offers an exemplary case history of how Chaucerian scholarship can both drive and be driven by literary criticism. For one thing, it suggests why the New Critics' notion of "the text itself" was difficult for many Chaucerians to accommodate even when new.

Only the Prologue of the *Legend* can properly be termed a dream vision. Considered as an independent presentation, its length is comparable to the *Parliament of Fowls*. But, among Chaucer's dream-visions, the F-version of the Prologue is unique in that it neglects to mention that the dreamer-persona ever awakes; the G-version revises this apparent flaw, but whether the correction should be considered authorial or scribal or even a *corrigendum* for that matter remains in question.

Some very eminent Chaucerians have expressed some remarkably condescending opinions regarding the nine extant legends. F.O. Payne, for example, who so elevated critical opinion regarding the F-prologue, despised the relentless dullness of the legends. Paradoxically, the very liveliness of the Prologue makes the apparent drabness of the nine legends that much more conspicuous. The most fundamental critical question to be asked about the *Legend* remains: what is its artistic merit? All answers, positive or negative, necessitate several presuppositions regarding the *Legend*'s very *raison d'être*.

As a *compilatio*, the extant nine legends of the *Legend* surely look incomplete. The Prologue indicates that the commission originally inflicted upon Chaucer was for him to write about good (because victimized) women without end. In the "Retractions," Chaucer will revoke a "*book of the XXV. Ladies*" (*CT* 10. 1085). But the Man of Law recalled a somewhat shorter roll call for Chaucer's "Seintes Legende of Cupide" (*CT* 2. 61). And the *Legend*'s own "Balade" (F, 249-269) addresses still another somewhat different assembly of good women (with the occasional man). So, not one of these unstable checklists needs to be read as a definitive table of contents for *The Legend of Good Women*. In *Virtue of Necessity* (1984), Larry Sklute finds the *Legend of Good Women* "incomplete but conclusive" (p. 5) and not very appealing therefore. The indeterminant *Legend* provides, therefore, an important crux for any critical attempt to define Chaucer's more general conception of narrative closure.

To many modern readers, the extant *Legend*, albeit incomplete, seems much too long. Each individual legend, however, seems brutally short. The tonal implications of Chaucer's conspicuous *abbreviatio* is a recurrent point of discussion. In *Chaucer and the Legend of Good Women* (1966), Robert Worth Frank, Jr., was first to offer detailed critiques of the legends themselves as a series of (variously successful) experiments through which Chaucer mastered the short narrative form. Frank also most effectively discredited the "abandonment myth," the assumption that Chaucer began and then quit the misconceived project when he became actually "agroted" with it.

The longstanding critical suspicion that Chaucer's legendary is not only incomplete but poetically incompetent has proven especially hard to explain (or excuse) given the date of its composition (ca. 1387). It seems a unique mistake interrupting Chaucer's otherwise inevitable progress from *Troilus and Criseyde* to the *Canterbury Tales*. This dating of the *Legend* also disturbs an otherwise rather neat division of Chaucer's career into French, Italian, and English phases. And, since Chaucer derived the legends themselves primarily from Latin sources, the *Legend* also presents a most problematic test case for assessing Chaucer's proto-humanist classicism.

Finished or no, the *Legend* has provoked two irreconcilably opposed reader-responses throughout the twentieth century. In 1908, H.C. Goddard first proposed reading the pathetic melodrama the *Legend* as a "travesty"—a notion that Lowes dismissed to the satisfaction of most Chaucerians in 1909. But this parodic or subversive reading of the *Legend* just will not be silenced. So two utterly antithetical responses to the tone of the *Legend* now coexist among Chaucerians.

To some readers this affective debate is rather moot. The real appeal of the *Legend* does not depend upon an arbitrary perception of its being sad or funny, but upon the documentable fact that it is intellectually interesting. A.J. Minnis, for example, who provides an excellent excursus on feminist reponses to the *Legend*, claims himself content "to prove that the *Legend* is at once very medieval and very interesting" (*Guide*, p. 324). Minnis further argues that "Any reading of a medieval text which rests on a reconstruction of audience response and expectancy is on very shaky ground indeed" (*Guide*, p. 383). Here, again, a seemingly marginal controversy regarding Chaucer's minor poetry provides a major occasion for testing our own crises of faith as critics. One, nasty, "we-all-go-down-together" rhetorical gesture would be to deny the very concept that compelling interpretive validity can be attributed to historicized criticism of any ilk. Such incertitude, extrapolated to absurdity, would paralyze every reader's claim to linguistic competence. After all, the textual and philological groundings of the *Chaucer* we read are also (to varying degrees) reconstructions. And who, in the face of any abstractly absolute and absolutely dismissive skepticism, can claim to read Chaucer "in the original"?

On the other hand, I do not think that our confident contemplation of the idea(s) of the *Legend of Good Women* can be validly divorced from consideration of its emotional effects as well, even though such cerebral indifference to the affective success or failure of the *Legend* is a time- honored critical posture. John Fisher observed that until 1968 "Discussions of the *Legend* . . . turned upon various combinations and permutations of these two viewpoints: the *Legend* as an occasional poem motivated by royal command, and the *Legend* as a stage in Chaucer's poetic development" (in Rowland's *Companion*, p. 466). Neither of these "not mutually exclusive" propositions need consider whether the *Legend of Good Women* was or should be still considered simply entertaining, however. Feminist inquiries now find the ever elusive implications of the *Legend of Good Women* especially fascinating. The precise role of Queen Anne as Chaucer's immediate patron or anticipated audience or first reader seems both crucial and indeterminate.[1] But any acknowledgment that such occasionality provides a significant interpretive context makes two affective questions both inextricable and ineluctable: how did the Ricardian court respond to the *Legend*? and how should we?

Any attempt to read the *Legend* as either a sustained comic or a sincerely pathetic presentation cannot remain intellectually aloof and emotionally anaesthetized. Both readings require often highly speculative retrievals of the historicized responses of Chaucer's first audience and readers. In his essay (1975) reprinted below, Robert Worth Frank, Jr., addresses this fundamental issue of taste—the alterity of medieval and modern sensibilities regarding simple plot—that so affects our perception of the legends proper. Lisa J. Kiser's chapter excerpted from *Telling Classical Tales* (1983) addresses another fundamental question of alterity as it pertains to the *Legend*—the inherent antipathy between medieval hagiography and Chaucer's classical sources. Carolyn Dinshaw's chapter, excerpted here from her *Chaucer's Sexual Poetics* (1989), analyzes the *Legend* in terms of yet a third alterity—that between the sexes.

NOTES

1. See, for example, David J. Wallace's "Anne of Bohemia, Queen of England, and Chaucer's Emperice" (1995) and chapter 12 of his *Chaucerian Polity* (1997), Andrew Taylor's "Anne of Bohemia and the Making of Chaucer" (1997), and Alfred Thomas's *Anne's Bohemia* (1998).

THE *LEGEND OF GOOD WOMEN*: SOME IMPLICATIONS

by Robert Worth Frank, Jr.

The *Legend of Good Women*, if studied properly, can assist our understanding of Chaucer's art in several ways. One of the most important of these is that it forces on us an issue which, by our literary taste and training, we are reluctant to face or even unable to see. This is the fundamental importance of tale, of story, in the late Middle Ages and early Renaissance. Our passion today is all for other matters. If the modern novel is a cherished form, it is cherished as a rhetorical triumph. We admire it for style, for irony, for complexity of structure; we may also admire it for novelty of theme, for daring or outrageous material, even sometimes for truth or for subtlety of characterization, but not for story. Story is in some fashion necessary for the novel, but E. M. Forster's grudging, regretful acknowledgment of this necessity many years ago in *Aspects of the Novel*, his sigh, is ours also. "Oh, yes—oh, dear, yes—it tells a story." Story is the gross flesh that drags down and sometimes damns the bright soul of fiction.

But in the thirteenth, fourteenth, fifteenth, and sixteenth centuries a passion for story flamed up in the Western world. It is the period of great narrative collections. The explicitly religious or moral narrative collections that first come to mind are Caesar of Heisterbach's *Liber Miraculorum*, Jacobus de Voragine's *Legenda Aurea*, and the *Gesta Romanorum*. Italy is of course the home of the greatest secular collections. The first of these was probably that compilation of *novelle* of unknown authorship called the *Novellino*, first printed at Bologna in 1525 but probably collected around 1280. There were also Boccaccio's *Decamerone* (ca. 1350); Giovanni Fiorentino's *Pecorone*, fifty *novelle* exchanged by a friar and a nun, written between 1378 and 1385; Sercambi's *Novelliero*, *155 novelle*, written between 1385 and 1387; and Franco Sachetti's *Trecentonovelle*, dating between 1388 and 1395. Two more Italian collections followed in the fifteenth century and another two in the sixteenth. In the first half of the fourteenth century in Spain, there was Juan Ruiz, the Archpriest of Hita's *Libro de Buen Amor*. The list is merely illustrative, not exhaustive.

England is very much a part of this movement, and Chaucer plays a leading role. Within the space of two decades, there came the *Legend of Good Women*, the *Monk's Tale* (a collection, though a brief one, whether or not we see it as initially a separate project), the *Canterbury Tales*, and Gower's *Confessio Amantis*. Other collections followed, such as Lydgate's *Fall of Princes*, which, though an amplified translation of Laurence de Premierfait's expanded translation into French of Boccaccio's *De Casibus Virorum Illustrium*, should be placed in the same movement. To it we might add, near the end of the fifteenth century, Caxton's translations of *Reynard the Fox* and *Aesop's Fables* (noting their Continental originals as two more items), and perhaps Henryson's *Fables*. For England and the Continent, the list could obviously go on.

The collections by Chaucer and Gower in England in the space of about fifteen or twenty years are a remarkable phenomenon. John Burrow has rightly, I believe, identified *narrative* as the characteristic genre of Ricardian poetry: "the voice of narrative prevails. . . . Perhaps no subsequent period is so dominated by the narrative voice." And before considering "something of the subtle literary artistry displayed in Ricardian narrative," he pays tribute to "its simpler qualities of sheer vigour and narrative conviction . . . .They preserve a pristine energy in their narrative as few poets in the Renaissance or after have been able to do."[1] Burrow suggests they owe this to earlier minstrel traditions. This may be largely correct. But the. great harvesting of story, going on over much of western Europe in these centuries, is the larger context in which Ricardian narrative must be placed. The primacy of story is not a local phenomenon. Clearly, story was a matter of the greatest importance. And the *Legend of Good Women* forces this on our attention, with implications that also must be attended to, in the very first statement of its *Prologue:*

> Than mote we to bokes that we fynde,
> Thurgh whiche that olde thinges ben in mynde,
> And to the doctrine of these olde wyse,
> Yeve credence, in every skylful wise,
> That tellen of these olde appreved stories
> Of holynesse, of regnes, of victories,
> Of love, of hate, of other sondry thynges,
> Of whiche I may not maken rehersynges.
> And yf that olde bokes were aweye,
> Yloren were of remembrance the keye[2]   (*LGW*, F 17-28)

If we go back to Chaucer's earlier work, we can find a few comments in a not dissimilar vein—his remarks in the opening of the *Book of the Duchess* on the book of fables which whiled away sleepless hours; his catalogue of "rounynges and of jangles" in the wicker cage of Rumor in the *House of Fame*; his concern for "the olde storie, in Latyn," in *Anelida and Arcite:*

> That elde, which that al can fret and bite,
> As it hath freten mony a noble storie,
> Hath nygh devoured out of oure memorie.[3]

And he tells the tale of Ceys and Alcione in the *Book of the Duchess* and summarizes the Dido-Aeneas story in the *House of Fame* before the more leisurely lyric and expository modes take over in those poems.

But the *Legend* for the first time insists that we attend to "olde appreved stories" that range widely over human experience—love and hate, holiness, reigns, victories. And the *Legend* is Chaucer's first collection of tales told, swiftly and economically, for story's sake: ten in all, if we count "Hypsipyle and Medea" as two tales, and originally the plan seems to have been for the *Legend* to be at least twice as long as what we have. For this fact alone the *Legend* deserve the critics' attention.

Few works, however, have been more badly served by criticism. The canard, sent out into the world by Skeat at the very beginning of modern Chaucer studies, and supported by Lounsbury, Tatlock, and Root, that the *Legend* bored its author almost before he began it, has paralyzed criticism of the *Legend* for eighty years.[4] The enormously greater variety, artistic success, and popularity of the *Canterbury Tales* in the twentieth century has seemed to corroborate those early scholars' judgment: that his boredom made him turn from the *Legend* to the Canterbury project. The truth of the matter, however, is exactly opposite: it is precisely because the project begun in the *Legend* fascinated Chaucer that he began the *Canterbury Tales*. That is, the telling of a series of tales proved to be so satisfying an experience that he spent the remainder of his life doing more of the same. He altered the frame device and expanded the range of tales, but essentially the *Canterbury Tales* continues what he first does in the *Legend*. If we can rid ourselves of the critical misconceptions about the *Legend*, perhaps we can begin to see it for what it is.

What does Chaucer do in the *Legend*? He tells stories. This seems so obvious that it is hardly worth mentioning, but it is what is most important about the *Legend* and most worth examination. It places the

Legend, and Chaucer, in that great stream of storytelling that is a major fact of Western literature in the fourteenth century and for two centuries to follow. When we look at them as stories, what do we see? Here his older friend, Gower, is very helpful, for apparently he was doing exactly the same thing at almost precisely the same moment. We do not know whether Gower's example inspired Chaucer, or whether Gower advised him in his undertaking, or whether they started independently of one another and, one would guess, compared what they were doing as they worked away. But to look at the stories in the *Confessio* and the stories in the *Legend*, side by side as it were, is very instructive. They possess many elements in common, elements we must assume their authors wished and worked for. Many of these common elements, however, in Chaucer are the very qualities for which the *Legend* is belittled.

Most peripheral for our examination is the fact that these stories have a point: in Gower they are tied to a rather elaborate moral scheme which Gower takes seriously; in the *Legend* they are tied to a simple value scheme—women are true in love; men are usually false—which Chaucer takes lightly. For a story to have a moral, an explicitly stated moral, that is, is a fatal weakness in the eyes of modern critics. It is better for a story to have a point than not to have one, and a moral is a particular kind of point. When the point or moral of a story is clearly spelled out at the beginning (as is true of both the *Confessio* and the *Legend*), a specific advantage accrues: the reader or listener can concentrate more on the story, on the sequence of events. (Further, a particular pleasure or satisfaction is opened up—not in discovering the point, as in so much modern narrative, but in seeing how the story does in fact demonstrate or work out the purpose, the moral lesson, claimed for it.)

A more important characteristic shared by the tales that make up the *Legend* and the *Confessio* is the easy, unimpeded succession of events. The key word is "unimpeded." Nothing seems easier, but it is not so easy to achieve. The narrator must never linger, however great the temptation, in introducing a character, describing a scene, or reporting speech.

Gower's story of "Paulus and Mundus" in Book I of the *Confessio*[5] is told to illustrate the sin of hypocrisy. In Rome a duke, Mundus, lusts after a beautiful married woman, Paulina, but his wooing is in vain. By means of gifts, he persuades two priests of the temple of Isis to tell Paulina that because of her chastity the god Anubis is in love with her and has prepared a room in the temple so that he may come to her. She informs her husband, who bids her submit to the god, and so she obeys.

In the temple during the night, Mundus, arrayed like a god, emerges from a secret closet, persuades her that the child he will beget upon her will be worshiped, and seduces her. In the morning, returning home, Paulina meets Mundus, who informs her that he has been Anubis' lieutenant in her bed. Overwhelmed with horror and grief, she tells her husband. He vows revenge, consults his friends, and on their advice takes his complaint to the king. The two priests are executed and Mundus is exiled.

The tale verges on the bizarre, but nevertheless it presents a variety of possibilities for expanded treatment. It raises questions of character and psychology—of Paulina in particular, but also of Mundus. Paulina's reactions on hearing the message from the priests, her reactions in the temple that night, her reactions after she learns the truth would seem too dramatic to ignore. What of the priests? How readily did they consent to this act of profanation? What kind of person was the husband that he should agree, and what were his reactions? None of these considerations is relevant for Gower, who tells the tale in 300 lines. Paulina's character is handled thus: she "was to every mannes sihte Of al the Cite the faireste, And as men seiden, ek the beste" (I, 766-68). Her beauty is described summarily: "This wif, which in hire lustes grene Was fair and freissh and tendre of age" (I, 778-79). When the priests tell her she is the chosen of a god:

> Glade was hire innocence tho
> Of suche wordes as sche herde,
> With humble chiere and thus answerde,
> And seide that the goddes wille
> Sche was al redy to fulfille,
> That be hire housebondes leve
> Sche wolde in Ysis temple at eve
> Upon hire goddes grace abide,
> To serven him the nyhtes tide. (*CA* I, 852-60)

To our taste this may seem a scandalous denial of artistic responsibilities. We must assume., however, that Gower was doing precisely what he wanted to do and what his audience wanted him to do. The priests leave her, she goes home, and her husband bids her obey. One unit of action follows another without pause. Eighteen lines after the priests have given Paulina their awesome news, it is night and she has gone to the temple. The events are everything. Characterization, reaction, scene (no dialogue between husband and wife on this occasion), description are as nothing. It is the story alone that matters.

Two hundred years later, in Shakespeare's day, we must remember, Gower was still a storyteller whose name counted. We must acknowledge the power, the appeal of bald story.

In the *Legend*, we find the same sort of simple narration. If we look at the first legend, "Cleopatra," we are told a Roman senator named Anthony was sent out to conquer kingdoms and gain honor for Rome. At first he prospered. But Fortune was against him: he rebelled and came into conflict against Rome; wanting "another wyf," he was false to Caesar's sister, and came into conflict with Caesar himself. For the love of Cleopatra, he set the world at no value:

> Hym roughte nat in armes for to sterve
> In the defence of hyre and of hire ryght. (*LGW* 605-06)

Antony is characterized only by his possession of the chivalric virtues, Cleopatra only by the quality of beauty:

> He was, of persone and of gentillesse,
> And of discrecioun and hardynesse,
> Worthi to any wyght that liven may;
> And she was fayre as is the rose in May. (*LGW* 610-13)

After their marriage, Octavius sets out to destroy him "With stoute Romeyns, crewel as lyoun," (627) and Antony and Cleopatra go to meet him, "His wif and he, and al his ost, forth wente To shipe anon, no lengere they ne stente . . . " (632-33). The splendid sea fight, one of the few familiar passages in the *Legend*, follows. There is no betrayal; Antony simply loses the battle:

> Tyl at the laste, as every thyng hath ende,
> Antony is schent, and put hym to the flyghte,
> And al his folk to-go, that best go myghte.
> Fleth ek the queen, with al hire purpre sayl . . .
>   (*LGW* 651-54)

Antony sees his cause is lost and kills himself in despair. There are no complexities of motive or feeling and there is no death scene:

> "Allas," quod he, "the day that I was born!
> My worshipe in this day thus have I lorn."
> And for dispeyr out of his wit he sterte,
> And rof hymself anon thourghout the herte,

Or that he ferther wente out of the place. (*LGW* 658-62)

The remaining 40 lines of this poem of 120 lines are given over to Cleopatra's dedicated love for the dead Antony, which is the point of the narrative:

> But herkeneth, ye that speken of kyndenesse,
> Ye men that falsly swereth many an oth
> That ye wol deye, if that youre love be wroth,
> Here may ye sen of wemen which a trouthe! (*LGW* 665-68)

Cleopatra has workmen build a shrine of rubies and precious stones and has Antony's body embalmed and placed in the shrine. Next to it a pit is dug and filled with snakes, "all the serpentes that she myghte have, She putte hem in that grave." In fifteen lines, she explains that she had made an oath to experience whatever Antony did, whether weal or woe, and to that oath she is true:

> "And thilke covenant, whil me lasteth breth,
> I wol fulfille; and that shal ben wel sene,
> Was nevere unto hire love a trewer quene." (*LGW* 693-95)

Whereupon, "with ful good herte" she goes naked into the pit of adders. "And she hire deth receyveth with good cheere, For love of Antony that was hire so dere" (700-701).

I have deliberately chosen the first and probably the weakest of the legends.[6] Much is wrong with Chaucer's "Cleopatra," but it does what it sets out to do: One, it makes its point. Two, it tells a story expeditiously—from this point of view the famous sea battle may be a mistake. Three, it takes us into a momentous world: a great Roman rebels and incurs Caesar's enmity for love of a queen, whom he marries. Caesar comes to destroy him. In despair, the Roman kills himself. The queen buries him in a splendid tomb and, true till death, walks naked into a pit of serpents. We can read the newspapers a long time before we ever come across such story elements: power and kingdom lost, great generals and an Egyptian queen, exotic lands and an exotic death.

"But, but," you are spluttering, "what about the big scene, what did Antony feel and say before he died, where's the serpent of old Nile?" The questions are irrelevant. The story and its point are what matter. If the story moves a bit awkwardly—Chaucer spends too much time in some places, not enough in others—that is because what he does is not all that easy to do. Chaucer's tale does not have quite enough meat on its bones, though the brief recording of a story is a perfectly legitimate narrative activity—Gower himself often does just that and no more. It is a legitimate activity because until we have the story *in outline, at least,* we have nothing.

The famous ballade that appears in both *Prologues* to the *Legend* will illustrate the point. It consists of a litany of names: Absolon, Esther, Jonathas, Penelope, Marcia Cato, Isolde, Helen, Alceste, Lavinia, Lucrece, Polixena, Cleopatra, Thisbe, Hero, Dido, Laodamia, Phyllis, Demophon, Canace, Hypsipyle, Hypermnestra, Ariadne. Some names are identified by a phrase—"Phillis, hangynge for thy Demophon"—but many are not. Let us match this catalogue against another: Mabel, Patricia, Sally, Irma, Wilma, Audrey, Caroline. This second list has no resonances, echoes, or dramatic value (as the first list does), because there are no stories, or at least none that are generally known. The legends of Mabel, of Audrey, of Wilma have never existed, or if they have they are forever lost. For every name on the first list there is a story which even in fragmentary form flashes across the memory and illuminates the name. Without the story there is nothing: without the rape of Paris and the siege, betrayal, and fall of Troy, Helen is only another name.

What is the appeal of bare story, we may ask? As we all know, it almost always entertains. It entertains first because something happened, that is, it came to pass, it is an event. Events are the substance of life, of experience, and even of dream. We do not dream lyrics (except in the rarest instances); we do not dream essays or literary criticism or footnotes to scholarly articles. We dream events, however bizarre. Though life is something more, or something less, than constant events—one must allow for sleep and daydream and vacancy, though these too can be catalogued as events—events give our life such framework as it may possess. "That was the year that John was born, that we went to the mountains, that we bought our first car." The reality external to myself that is closest to myself is a human event, a human action, for of such happenings my own life is made, and though the event happened to you, or to him, it might have happened to me. Since story is reported or remembered events, I can identify with it. In the abstract, events form interchangeable modules. Particular reported events are part of the life of Dido, of Isolde, of Esther, but they might have been a part of mine. Every story is in some degree my story.

Paradoxically, however, story entertains also because the modules in a story have a more patterned arrangement than those ordinarily in my life. This patterned arrangement consequently fixes the attention, focuses and heightens it. Story diverts the mind from worry, from boredom, from blankness (i.e., from reality) by the simple device of setting the situation on a sequential track. By saying *A* (an event) we promise to say *B* (a related event), and our attention is directed to watch and wait for *B*, and then for *C*. Meanwhile we can forget our own lives in which ordinarily *A* (an event) is followed by *T* (a totally unrelated event)—or by *b* (a related event but of such little consequence as to give no sense of pattern and to arouse no further expectations).

Story has another quality as well. It is a remembered action. It is an action, an event sufficiently out of the ordinary to make it memorable, remembered, and so repeated. Ordinary lives are not memorable in the events that compose them. We forget much of our own history; people listen with reluctance to most of what we tell them of it; and they forget most or all of what they have heard. But what happened to Cleopatra, a queen who died for love of a great Roman who lost a great battle, and died by letting snakes poison her, or what happened to Paulina, who was seduced by a Roman duke in the guise of a god, is worth remembering. If we see the appeal as feeding a hunger for sensationalism and nothing more, we are mistaken. The merely sensational explodes and dies. These are *remembered* events. When we hear them we acquire a dimension beyond our mortality. We are linked with others who have heard the story in the past and we share a human history. If extraordinary human events are not to be remembered, then all of human life is for naught. The memorable event makes an assertion about human experience.

Story is memorable also because it has significance. We search the events of our own lives for meanings, often in vain. We search the world of story as an additional body of data with more hope, looking for significance. The fact that here are events worth remembering suggests that they are much more likely to be meaningful. If a moral is already attached, then they are certifiably significant. Story apparently satisfied some of the same need for guidance, for clues to the conduct of life, in the late Middle Ages, that the proverb did. In times of social change and uncertainty, fable may have had social utility.

It is possible, I believe, to justify the telling of relatively simple stories, such as we have in the *Legend*. They must have events, sequence, memorability, meaning—but above all, events, action. The art of such storytelling is not our subject. What the *Legend* reveals, if we allow it its proper voice and weight, is the importance of story for Chaucer. He gives us there what he set out to give us, not quasi-novels, truncated *Troilus and Criseyde's*, failed *Knight's Tales*, but stories.

They are not very complex, but complexity is not essential to a tale, indeed not always desirable. Simplicity is more often a virtue.

A more or less complex vision of experience may develop, as one simple narrative after another is unfolded. The sequence of tales in the *Confessio Amantis* creates a somewhat rigid but articulated and elaborate moral system—there by implication even if the explicit moral connective tissue were to be removed. Although the *Legend* is committed to an apparently simple statement about love (women are always faithful; men are usually false), the stories actually create, I believe, a sense of the variety and violence of love, its capacity to evolve in powerful and unexpected forms. Whatever the view of love, it is fundamentally an excuse for Chaucer to tell stories.

So also is the device of the *Canterbury Tales* an excuse for telling stories. This is the conclusion implied by the *Legend*. We have been talking so long about Chaucer's seeking for a satisfactory frame device, that we have come to think the frame the most important element in his final art. The evidence, however, suggests that the frame is important only as a way of telling stories. The device of the *Legend* enabled Chaucer to tell a number of stories of one kind, the device of the *Monk's Tale* enabled him to tell a number of stories of another kind, and the device of the *Canterbury Tales* enabled him to tell stories of all kinds.

Interesting implications flow from this overwhelming concern with storytelling in the last fourteen years of Chaucer's life. The view that the stories told in the *Canterbury Tales* illustrate the character of the teller or are only projections of the personality or the psychology of the teller[7] assumes, to my mind, an interest in psychology alien to fourteenth-century attitudes and without foundation in fourteenth-century culture. It certainly goes counter to the total preoccupation with the story that we see in Chaucer's last years. The pilgrims are there to make the stories possible; the stories are not there to make the pilgrims possible. The *Legend* is important evidence that story comes first.

The passion of so many men of talent and genius in the last centuries of the Middle Ages for casting their nets among the teeming schools of folk tale, jest, exemplum, legend, myth, history, and narrative of any form is a phenomenon we cannot ignore. As a product of their passion, the *Legend* demands our attention as story. We cannot question that Chaucer progressed to more complex treatment of story in the *Canterbury Tales*, but we should not ignore or condemn what he began with. "*Whilom*—once upon a time—" the master storyteller must begin by responding himself to the magnetic power of simple tale. The *Legend of Good Women* has that distinction.

NOTES

1. J. A. Burrow, *Ricardian Poetry: Chaucer, Gower, Langland and the Gawain Poet* (London: Routledge & Kegan Paul, 1971), pp. 47, 52.

2. *The Works of Geoffrey Chaucer,* ed. F.N. Robinson, 2nd ed. (Boston: Houghton Mifflin, 1957). All quotations are from this edition.

3. *Book of the Duchess*, 44-59; *House of Fame*, 1960; *Anelida and Arcite*, 10, 12-14.

4. I have reviewed these opinions and presented an extended counterargument in "The Legend of the *Legend of Good Women*," *Chaucer Review*, 1 (1966),110-33; and somewhat more briefly in *Chaucer and The Legend of Good Women* (Cambridge, Mass.: Harvard Univ. Press, 1972), pp. 189-210.

5. *The English Works of John Gower*, ed. G.C. Macaulay (Oxford: Clarendon Press, 1900), Vol. 1; also in *EETS*, es 81 (London, 1900).

6. A more detailed discussion in *Chaucer and the Legend of Good Women*, pp. 37-46.

7. The most extended treatment of this point of view is in R.M. Lumiansky, *Of Sondry Folk: The Dramatic Principle in the Canterbury Tales* (Austin: Univ. of Texas Press, 1964), passim.

CHAUCER'S CLASSICAL LEGENDARY

by Lisa J. Kiser

For as long as the *Legend of Good Women* has been the subject of modern study, critics have found the poem engaging largely because of its Prologue, which includes Chaucer's witty handling of the God of Love and his self-effacing narrator, who is characterized more humorously than any of the poet's previous self-portraits. But few critics have discussed the legends themselves as meaningful Chaucerian works. As even a cursory glance at the *Legend*'s relatively short bibliography will show, the bulk of the criticism concerns the Prologue—its relationship to French sources, its subject matter, and its possibly topical origins. But few critics have discussed the legends themselves, and when they have, the discussion has been limited to the diversity of Chaucer's source material and to the ways in which he altered it to conform to the restrictions he was given in the Prologue with regard to plot. Indeed, a common view of the legends, sometimes stated and often implied, is that Chaucer grew tired of the legendary because its subject matter was not his own and because the idea of writing a palinode for the *Troilus* and the *Romaunt of the Rose* (which the Prologue suggests) was sufficiently clear and humorous without the actual task being carried out.

Another problem is that for modern readers the legends are simply not amusing. After the high comedy of the Prologue, the legends are likely to have the same effect that the Monk's tragedies in the *Canterbury Tales* have on us and the pilgrims: we sigh with relief to see that the storytelling ends before the author's plan has reached completion. To be sure, by the time he gets to his seventh legend, Chaucer himself is telling us how tedious his penance is turning out to be. In the *Philomela*, he acknowledges that his brief treatment of certain elements of the story is the result of boredom alone: "For I am wery of hym for to telle" (2258). And in the *Phyllis* his impatience with his task is openly admitted:

> But, for I am agroted herebyforn
> To wryte of hern that ben in love forsworn,

> And ek to haste me in my legende,
> (Which to performe God me grace sende!)
> Therfore I passe shortly in this wyse. [2454-58]

These lines (and others like them) constitute what many critics have
seen as evidence that Chaucer was in actuality bored by his legendary
and that therefore the only proper response to it is to share the poet's
impatience.[1] But this view unfortunately confuses the fictional stance
of Chaucer's narrator (who is tired of having to do penance for a
ridiculous God of Love) with what Chaucer the poet actually manages
to accomplish in his individual legends-despite his narrator's professed
boredom and annoyance with the task. To confuse the narrator's
attitude toward these narratives with Chaucer's own views about them
is, I would argue, as bad a mistake as to confuse the narrator with the
poet himself in any other Chaucerian work. The narrator of the *Legend*
is indeed bored with having to say the same nice things about the ladies
whose stories he is working with—and we, like him, see the
foolishness of the project. But the real Chaucer is not wasting time
while writing his stories. Although the legendary is self-consciously
"bad art," as a parody it is quite carefully constructed.

First, Chaucer means for us to recognize and appreciate his
dextrous (and very funny) avoidance of narrative material that might
contradict the legendary's commissioned goal—to tell of "good
women." Indeed, the legendary is full of what John Fyler has recently
called "the hidden jokes of a translator,"[2] all of which are constructed
to show the devastating results of an artist's unfaithful treatment of
source material. By certain obvious deletions from his *auctores*' texts,
Chaucer is able to show exactly how the literary preferences of the God
of Love force the poet to abuse classical works. The censorship
advocated by the God of Love makes necessary a massive rewriting of
the classics. The comedy here, depending as it does on familiarity with
Chaucer's sources, was certainly not lost on the poet's learned
contemporaries. Moreover, adding to the comedy he generates by
abusing his sources, Chaucer also effectively parodies the exemplum
form in his legendary, that form which, he believed, had so
inadequately prepared readers for an understanding of his own works.

But in addition to the legendary's broadly comic purposes, its
narratives, it should be noted, also raise many serious issues. Like
Chaucer's other "comic" works, these legends are complex enough to
give the poet space to carry on meaningful deliberation about what he
is doing and why. Critics seem not to have noticed what are surely
some of Chaucer's reasons for writing these legends to begin with—an

interest in clarifying his dislike for certain attitudes among poets and readers toward classical literature, a desire to state with certainty that the subjects of classical poetry are in fact useful to Christian readers even in unrevised form, and a wish to experiment with the medieval practice of "retelling," that complex activity that involves borrowing the "matter" of others to fill a "form" of one's own. This chapter, then, will explore the legends both in the context of the issues raised in the Prologue and as narratives that to some extent stand alone, able to be read and judged as independent works. Although many of the individual legends merely elaborate cleverly on the understated issues raised in the Prologue, others express new, quite distinct insights into Chaucer's awareness of the problems of translation, the complexities of morality, and the fluidity of form.

Any examination of Chaucer's legends must begin with the God of Love because he is the one whose taste informs the entire project. That he wants exempla from Chaucer's pen is made clear, as we saw in Chapter 3, by his specifications for the legendary's form and purpose. He wants tales about good women, told in a manner that stresses "corn," not "draff " (G 311-12); he expects the stories to apply to people's lives so that they will modify their "sinful" behavior; and he requires the tales to be brief:

> "I wot wel that thou maist nat al yt ryme,
> That swiche lovers diden in hire tyme;
> It were to long to reden and to here.
> Suffiseth me thou make in this manere,
> That thou reherce of al hir lyf the grete,
> After thise olde auctours lysten for to trete.
> For whoso shal so many a storye telle,
> Sey shortly, or he shal to longe dwelle." [F 570-77]

Much of the comedy of the legendary results directly from Chaucer's straining to meet these particular requirements of the exemplum form. His fulfillment of the God of Love's chosen moral theme is obvious; we get good women and bad men. His attempt to make his narratives mirrors of or commentaries on life is visible in the facile moral applications he appends to all but two of his stories. Seven of the narratives contain passages that try, quite clumsily, to relate the stories to their readers' lives. In *Cleopatra*, for example, Chaucer writes:

> But herkeneth, ye that speken of kyndenesse,
> Ye men that falsly sweren many an oth

318   *Lisa J. Kiser*

> That ye wol deye, if that youre love be wroth,
> Here may ye sen of wemen which a trouthe! [665-68]

And in *Hypsipyle*, he addresses his audience with the express purpose of drawing connections between contemporary falseness in love and that which is exemplified by Jason:

> But in this hous if any fals lovere be,
> Ryght as hymself now doth, ryght so dide he,
> With feynynge, and with every subtil dede. [1554-56]

Other direct statements of applicability occur in *Thisbe* (908-11), *Dido* (1254-63), *Lucrece* (1874-85), *Philomela* (2383-93), and *Phyllis* (2559-61). With these remarks, Chaucer the moralist and preacher makes his exempla useful to badly behaved listeners, pointing them to the purpose of his art with clear, unmistakable directions.

With regard to the legends' brevity, the most obvious characteristic of the exemplum, we need only remark that nearly every piece of criticism on these narratives acknowledges their succinctness. Not all critics, however, have seen the legends' brevity as parodic, possibly because the Monk's tragedies, written later for the *Canterbury Tales,* have so improved on the joke that the legends, in comparison, do not seem amusing. Moreover, critics frequently note that brevity. is not inherently funny, but is (and was) a valuable device for poets; Robert Worth Frank has successfully described its usefulness to medieval poets in his chapter on the legends' use of *occupatio*, for example.[3] To be sure, Chaucer and other medieval poets often used *brevitas, occupatio, abbreviatio,* and other related rhetorical devices with serious purpose, to intensify or otherwise stress some point without unnecessary prolixity. These devices were indeed valuable in many contexts, for they enabled an author to suggest richness of detail without dwelling on it, or to eliminate parts of a source narrative which might not be relevant to his purpose. Thus in an age whose aesthetic was based in part on the utility and pleasure that could be created by retelling old tales, strategies designed to alter or shorten narrative material were necessary to storytellers, whose purposes and intentions might differ from those of the original authors. Obviously, it is not this general function of *brevitas* that Chaucer parodies in the *Legend.* Rather, he parodies the tendency of writers who through *brevitas* "falsen their matere," with the result that justice is not done to the complexities of morality and character in the original source.

We must not forget that in addition to being commanded to be brief, Chaucer is also asked to follow his "olde auctours" (F 575) in his legends, which means that he is not to depart in noticeable ways from the facts he chooses to narrate from his sources. This restriction, coupled with *brevitas* and the preformed moral conclusion that he is given for his legendary—that women are good—can result only in disaster. *Brevitas* turns into something more like lying, for Chaucer is forced to employ it as a device to mask those details in his sources which would complicate our moral judgments of these women and their deeds and would render the narratives useless as exempla. The legends of Cleopatra and Medea are the most obvious examples of this sort of dishonest selectivity which, as readers have noticed, actually succeeds in transforming these ladies of bad reputation into paragons of goodness. These two legends radically misrepresent their sources largely by means of *abbreviatio*; as scholars have pointed out, opinion in the Middle Ages concerning these women was generally that they were stock examples of satanic lust, unfaithfulness, and other assorted vices; Medea was even considered a murderer.[4] By simple elimination of detail and frequent use of occupation Chaucer can turn the bad into good while creating the illusion of following his "auctours." More destructive, perhaps, are the subtler effects of *abbreviatio* on the legendary's development of its male characters. One of Chaucer's most typical editorial practices is to avoid developing male characters enough to clarify their motivations for betrayal, and then, by *amplificatio*, to expand on the women's pitiful states.

I have limited my discussion thus far in this chapter to the three general characteristics of the exemplum form that Chaucer parodies in his legendary—its explicit morality, its applicability to life, and its brevity. Chaucer's legendary, however, is constructed to conform to a particular kind of exemplum, that is, the saint's life. As a subtype of the exemplum, hagiography usually shares with other exemplary narratives the three characteristics just mentioned.[5] Its moral purpose is, of course, beyond dispute; saints' lives were plainly designed to represent the struggle between good and evil. Despite the great variety of the individual Christian narratives within it, the genre always has—at bottom—this purpose.[6] Its applicability to life is also commonly stressed; from the narrative usually considered to be the prototype of European saints' legends, Athanasius's *Life of Anthony*, to the late medieval *specula* containing large numbers of lives, authors and compilers routinely expressed the usefulness of their narratives as models of behavior.[7] Brevity, too, was a common feature of the saints' lives, especially when more than one was collected into a legendary or when a legend appeared with exempla of other kinds to form a compendium.[8]

Another characteristic typical of hagiographical narratives is a claim of historical veracity, a feature that Chaucer mimics in his legendary. In the clearest example, Chaucer writes of Cleopatra's story that "this is storyal soth, it is no fable" (702). However, he also suggests the historicity of other legends by mentioning emperors and kings whose reigns were contemporaneous with the ladies' lives and by having the God of Love in the Prologue talk about classical literary women as if they really existed. The women "in that tyde," the deity remarks, were far truer than men "in this world" (G 302-4). These appeals to history are often comic because of the distortion in some of the narratives of the historical truth. *Cleopatra*, in fact, which includes the strongest assertion of historical validity, is one of the least faithful retellings of a classical source in the entire collection.

The most important feature of Chaucer's legendary, however, is its careless disregard for the differences in subject matter between hagiography and classical literature. The stories in the *Legend* combine pagan erotic love and Christian *caritas* in a facile union that corresponds to the God of Love's own artificial synthesis. As we might expect, the results are appalling,and little justice is done to either of the worlds being represented. Chaucer's classical sources are cheapened by his forcing them into an alien hagiographic pattern,[10] and the spirit of hagiography is profoundly violated by Chaucer's implicit suggestion in these stories that pagan women who die for love are somehow morally comparable to saints dying for the love of God. In fact, in many of the most well-known saint's lives, saints become martyrs by dying at the hands of pagans, that is, *because* of the antipathy between the Christian and pagan cultures. Clearly, in Chaucer's mind, the solution to the problem of how Christian artists should use classical material does not include the wholesale adoption of a hagiographical point of view. The idea of "Cupid's martyrs," the central conception of Chaucer's legendary, is an extreme and finally unworkable one for a serious artist.

To confirm the perversity of this sort of union, even in the opinion of medieval writers who were actively seeking new syntheses of pagan and Christian topics, we need only to turn to Boccaccio, whose *De claris mulieribus* is quite probably one of Chaucer's medieval sources. Boccaccio did not include any Christian saints in his collection because he did not think they were appropriate in the company of pagans. In his preface he writes, "It seemed that they could not very well be placed side by side and that they did not strive for the same goal."[11] To Boccaccio, the natural virtue of pagans is somehow different from

Christian virtue, and the two must not be confused, or even combined in the same exemplary collection. Furthermore, he reminds us that the virtues of Christian saints had already been described in books reserved for them alone:

> . . . not only do Christian women, resplendent in the true, eternal light, live on, illustrious in their deserved immortality, but we know that their virginity, purity, saintliness, and invincible firmness in overcoming carnal desire and the punishments of tyrants have been described in special books, as their merits required.[12]

Though the lives of the saints may have been the generic inspiration for Boccaccio's collection of exempla, he is nevertheless careful to draw a distinction between his own work and the "special books" devoted to saints. To him, saints and classical women were simply not alike.[13]

Although Chaucer's comic project in the *Legend* is different from Boccaccio's serious one in *De claris mulieribus*, the two authors were faced with the same problem—how to retell the lives of classical women in such a way as to make them useful to Christian readers as "examples" of behavior. Boccaccio's solution to this problem was to tell, quite plainly, the stories of natural virtue to be found in classical texts. He did not attempt to introduce the conceptions of hagiography into his collection, beyond the simple idea of making his stories roughly conform—in imitative purpose—to the numerous collections of the lives of female saints. But Chaucer's project is much more difficult, because he has to ignore the incompatibility of the two narrative types in making saints out of classical women, including classical women who were enthralled in what is, from a Christian point of view, an unredeeming passion.

Only Chaucer's *Legend of Lucrece* is, in some ways, an exceptional case. The poet did not have to alter its plot much, because Lucretia was, quite literally, a martyr for chastity, exhibiting (though only superficially, as we shall see) the same virtue that we find in so many female saints. Lucretia may have been, in fact, the most "canonical" of Chaucer's ladies, having survived, good reputation intact, the scrutiny of Jerome and other Christian authorities.[14] But for Augustine, whom Chaucer's narrator unwisely names in his opening lines, Lucretia's "virtue" was actually a crime, for in killing herself, she was killing an innocent victim. As for the motive behind her suicide, Augustine remarks that it was obviously not the "love of purity," but the "overwhelming burden of her shame." Thus, he concludes, there is a significant difference between the "true sanctity" of Christian martyrs and the illusory virtue of Lucretia.[15] This problem raised by Augustine does not interfere with Chaucer's enterprise, however. The narrator simply ignores the substance of Augustine's lengthy commentary on Lucretia's case and attributes to him a feeling of "gret compassioun" (1690) for her. He then introduces a theme common to hagiography—commemoration—by remarking that his story is being told "to preyse and drawe to memorye" (1685) the event in her life which resulted in her "martyrdom."[16]

Chaucer's handling of Lucrece's rape and subsequent death is reminiscent of hagiography in other ways as well. One of his only additions to this story's plot is Lucrece's swoon, which occurs during her rape, and which Chaucer describes as deep and deathlike:

> She loste bothe at ones wit and breth,
> And in a swogh she lay, and wex so ded,
> Men myghte smyten of hire arm or hed;
> She feleth no thyng, neyther foul ne fayr. [1815-18]

Lucrece's swoon serves several purposes. First, it renders her oblivious to Tarquin's violence, sparing her the conscious experience of (and, of course, complicity in) such an outrage. it is intended, perhaps, to resemble the otherworldly states in which God allows His beloved saints miraculously to endure physical suffering (in fires that do not burn them, in hot baths that do not scorch, etc.).[17] Second, it worsens Tarquin's character since it suggests to us that his desire for Lucrece has, as its object, what is most "lifeless" about her—her mere physical form. And third, it is a primitive example of the typological structure sometimes used in hagiographic narratives in that it "prefigures" Lucrece's real death.[18]

Finally, Lucrece's story is fairly easy to force into the hagiographical mold since her own compatriots venerated her for her virtue; as Chaucer writes, she was "holden there / A seynt, and ever hir day yhalwed dere" (1870-71). With these lines, the narrator slyly introduces the terminology he needs to make the Christian parallel clear. Moreover, her corpse, carried through the streets to give witness to the spreading story of her "martyrdom," is surely meant to recall the relics of a Christian saint, circulated with a legend, so that men "may see and here" (1867) of miraculous forebearance and power in the face of great suffering.

These hagiographic devices in Lucrece's tale, coupled with the digression (1759-74) that makes Tarquin fully equal in lustful power to the sexually obsessed pursuers of female saints,[19] by no means confer upon her any easy canonization, however. As hard as our narrator may work to make Lucrece fit the mold of a chaste Christian, she is still saintly only by the standards of her own pagan culture, dying, as Augustine says, not for Christian truth but through shame over the result of someone's violent and lustful desire. Tarquin's character, too, is odd in the extreme, for Chaucer has permitted him to display the tender longings of a stricken courtly lover, even though these details do not fit the purpose of hagiographic legend. The lustful pursuers of female saints should never be allowed to show poignant emotion; such a display conflicts with the moral clarity that such tales are designed to convey. Thus Chaucer's attempt to equate Lucrece's life with that of a saint results in an obviously contrived piece of literary deception that violates the generic specifications of both hagiography and courtly narrative. The story also violates its own professed interest in the strict correlation of "word" and "dede" (1706-7), "contenaunce" and "herte" (1738-39). Chaucer's praise of Lucrece for having beauty "by no craft . . . feyned" (1749) does not seem to deter him from feigning the beauty of sainthood for her. And finally, if we can trust Chaucer's words in the Prologue to his own life of St. Cecilia, the writing of saints' lives is in part a valid method of preventing idleness, a sin with which the tale of Lucrece is concerned. Both Lucrece and Chaucer work to deter that sin; she spins, while he writes. But one must finally question the validity of Chaucer's labor here, for it can hardly be described as "leveful bisynesse," as the Second Nun describes it. He certainly meant for us to notice Lucrece's simple but productive task and to contrast it with his own more complex, more directly "Christian" one which is, however, ultimately idleness.

Another legend that betrays Chaucer's hagiographic adjustments is the *Legend of Cleopatra*. He easily conveys her "truth in love" and other virtues by simply suppressing the historical facts of her seduction and manipulation of Antony and by ignoring her unseemly political life. Her qualifications for "sainthood" are more difficult to establish, though, and Chaucer finally has to alter several details of her biography to make her life conform to a hagiographical pattern. Chaucer's most original contribution to the story of Cleopatra is, of course, his rendering of her death. In all of the poet's sources, Cleopatra's suicide was the result of her placing an adder at her breast, but in Chaucer's version of her story, she dies in a snake pit, a radical departure from tradition and one whose purpose is not immediately apparent. Yet if one recalls that saints' lives often display reenactments of the life of their figural leader Christ, then one can profitably interpret Cleopatra's descent into the snake pit as an event intended to echo one of the most important incidents from the life of Christ, his descent into hell. Similarly, this event recapitulates Alceste's own descent into the underworld. She is to be seen, of course, as the model for the lives of other classical ladies (F 542, G 532), a notion that the narrator of the legendary takes literally as he constructs his martyrology of love.

Cleopatra's life, like Christ's and Alceste's, has a self-sacrificial theme, but not, in its original version, a trip into hell. To make up for this inadequacy, Chaucer creates a miniature snake-filled "underworld" to receive his heroine so that her life can approximate—at least in a general way—the prototypical lives of her figural models.[20] Unfortunately, however, this clever imitation of hagiographical patterning does not make Cleopatra any more saintlike than her original story did, for though she now descends into hell, it is a hell she painstakingly constructs for herself. In digging her snake pit, Cleopatra seems almost aware that her damnation is self-imposed:

> Among the serpents in the pit she sterte,
> And there she ches to have hire buryinge.
> Anon the nadderes gonne hire for to stynge,
> And she hire deth receyveth with good cheere,
> For love of Antony that was hire so dere. [697-701]

We have here only a poor imitation of a saint. Cleopatra willingly undergoes torture and martyrdom, yet instead of having them thrust upon her, she willfully chooses them as her fate, proving only that she is her own persecutor. Not able to approximate the true tragedy of Christ's and Alceste's self-sacrifice, descent, and subsequent resurrection, Cleopatra remains in the snake-filled hell of her own devising, dying not for a noble cause, but, instead, in vain. This legend, the shortest and most elliptical of all, is perhaps Chaucer's best statement about the vanity of his task. Though this pagan life can be supplied with formal correspondences to Christian patterns, ultimately the relationship remains superficial. Even the expensive "shrine" Cleopatra creates to keep Antony's sacred memory alive among the Egyptians is an empty mockery of the precious jewel-studded reliquaries for the remains of saints.[21] Cleopatra's pathetic attempt to canonize Antony resembles Chaucer's own efforts to adorn his worldly tales with the superficial glitter of holy rhetoric or to make them conform to sacred plots.

The unfinished *Hypermnestra* shares with Cleopatra several incidents that schematically retrace Alceste's exemplary life-love for a husband, self-sacrifice in order to save him, and descent into "hell." Hypermnestra's fatal act was to disobey her father's command by sparing the life of her husband Lynceus. As a result of this noble deed, she is caught and "fetered in prysoun," where, the narrator wants us to believe, she eventually dies. If the fetters and the prison are meant to suggest the confinement of souls in hell, then Hypermnestra is reliving the tragedy of Alceste. She is destined to be a "sacrifice" from the moment she is married; indeed, Chaucer's description of her wedding festivities (which departs from all of his sources) is frightening rather than joyful in its detail:

> The torches brennen, and the laumpes bryghte;
> The sacryfices ben ful redy dighte;
> Th'encens out of the fyre reketh sote;
> The flour, the lef is rent up by the rote
> To maken garlondes and crounes hye. [2610-14]

The burning torches, the fire, the "sacryfices," and the uprooted flowers all suggest the hell Hypermnestra was destined to occupy.

But Hypermnestra's destiny, her puppetlike existence which is controlled by the stars, is also exactly what makes her unlike Alceste. In this story, Chaucer's major departure from his sources is his addition of detailed astrological lore.[21] Hypermnestra is given beauty by Venus, "trouthe" by Jupiter, and her visit to prison by Saturn. Her whole character is molded from above:

> The Wirdes, that we clepen Destine,
> Hath shapen hire that she mot nedes be
> Pyëtous, sad, wis, and trewe as stel,
> As to these wemen it acordeth wel. [2580-83]

In other words, Hypermnestra's heroic act of charity is really not her own choice at all. Both her self-sacrifice and her punishment were written in the stars, and she merely acted out the tragic role that was forced upon her. This fact makes her less morally admirable than Alceste, who chose to die without the help of any astrological planning, making her decision truly charitable and worthy of reward. Had Hypermnestra been the author of her own destiny as was Alceste, then, in Chaucer's own words, "of the shef she sholde be the corn" (2579). But like the uprooted flowers at the wedding feast, she withers before she can bear fruit.

Even though Chaucer's story is incomplete, it is clear that he did not intend to end it with less tragedy than any of the other legends. Hypermnestra's husband leaves the court without her, and the tale comes to an abrupt halt just as she is locked in prison. Closely following Ovid's account in the *Heroides*, Chaucer chooses not to lighten Hypermnestra's grief or mention her later reward, as does Boccaccio in *De claris mulieribus*, in which she becomes Lynceus's queen after the wicked Danaus is killed. Chaucer is thus able to maintain some resemblance between this plot and that of Alceste's tragic biography—without, of course, the triumphant resurrection that distinguishes Alceste from the "saints" that imitate her. But as in *Cleopatra*, Chaucer finally shows us that the heroine only superficially approximates the virtue of Alceste. The implication, again, is that recording only the misleading and artificial resemblances between two very different human lives does little justice to the complexity of either. In order to force Hypermnestra into Alceste's mold, her life must be radically simplified, emptied of articulate motives, and, with the worst insult of all, deprived of a happy ending.

These first three legends I have discussed overtly display Chaucer's crafty reshaping of classical fiction to fit the moral hagiographic form that the God of Love will like and deem superior to any other possible forms that these ladies' stories can take.[23] In so doing Chaucer suppresses parts of the ladies' lives to make them more virtuous and alters their biographies to fit the preconceived shape of Alceste's prototypical life. But Chaucer tells us in other ways both that he is painfully aware of the literary assumptions that his penance must reflect and that he is conscious of the processes necessary to this task. For example, several passages in the legendary, particularly in the *Legend of Philomela* and the *Legend of Medea*, reveal that Chaucer is aware of his manipulation of "matter" and "form."

Chaucer opens the story of Philomela with some lines addressed to God who, as "yevere of the formes," carried in his mind the "idea" of the world before he undertook its actual construction:

> Thow yevere of the formes, that hast wrought
> This fayre world, and bar it in thy thought
> Eternaly, er thow thy werk began. . . . [2228-30]

Karl Young has suggested that Chaucer derived these opening lines from one of the many *accessus* that were so often added to Ovid's works in the Middle Ages as "critical introductions" to aid the reader in his quest for moral edification.[24] But this passage about the giver of forms also describes the task of the human creator, the artist who must hold within his mind, as Geoffrey of Vinsauf relates, the plan of his "edifice" before he carries out its construction.[25] Quoted by Pandarus in *Troiluis and Criseyde*, this metaphor succinctly expresses the care with which any artist must plan the project he has chosen; from the beginning, he must have mental control over the varied details that will make up his finished product.

Philomela herself vividly enacts the role of the giver of forms in this legend. After Tereus cuts out her tongue to prevent her from spreading the story of his violent deeds, she weaves her tragedy into a tapestry to tell what actually happened. And though this truth must be told indirectly, Philomela's translation of it does not appear to have diminished its horror, for Procne, when seeing it, "no word she spak, for sorwe and ek for rage" (2374). Here, truth clearly finds effective expression in art. In fact, one might judge Philomela a much better "translator" than Chaucer himself in this legendary, for she is weaving true experience into art without the kind of falsification Chaucer uses in giving form to his ladies' lives. Yet her skill as a narrative artist cannot, of course, make her a Christian saint. She, like the other ladies, still falls short of fulfilling the requirements of a perfectly realized Christian life.

The *Legend of Medea*, like the *Philomela*, also defines its heroine as a "giver of forms." Only two lines into her narrative, Chaucer writes:

> As mater apetiteth forme alwey,
> And from forme into forme it passen may,
> Or as a welle that were botomles,
> Ryght so can false Jason have no pes.[26] [1582-85]

Written in reference to Jason's insatiable desire, these lines suggest that he searches insistently for something to lend form to his base longings, just as the chaotic "matter" of the medieval philosophers constantly "apetiteth" new existence.[27] In literary terms, this passage reminds us that the basic stories of history and past fiction may pass from "forme into forme"; they are not limited to a single, inviolable shape. But the irony here is that Jason's indiscriminate shape changing constitutes little more than deception. Both Hypsipyle and Medea become the unfortunate victims of Jason's endless quest for "form." He is an experienced deceiver who, by "the art and craft" (1607) of love, leads the innocent into believing that his "farced" words are true. Like the fowler of Chaucer's Prologue (F 130-39, G 118-26), Jason is a master of sophistry. He is the legendary's example of a lying poet, whose fictions ensnare those who attend to them. Appropriately, he is compared twice to a wily hunter:

> For evere as tendre a capoun et the fox,
> Thow he be fals and hath the foul betrayed,
> As shal the good-man that therfore hath payed. [1389-91]

> Thow madest thy recleymyng and thy lures
> To ladyes of thy statly aparaunce,
> And of thy wordes, farced with plesaunce,
> And of thy feyned trouthe and thy manere,
> With thyn obeÿsaunce and humble cheere,
> And with thy contrefeted peyne and wo. [1371-76]

Jason's trickery is possible because of his verbal skills and his ability to counterfeit the truth. In one of Chaucer's original passages in *Hypsipyle*, we find Jason and Hercules acting as coconspirators in the creation of a fiction intended to "bedote" Hypsipyle into marriage:

> This Ercules hath so this Jason preysed
> That to the sonne he hath hym up areysed,
> That half so trewe a man there nas of love
> Under the cope of heven that is above;
> And he was wis, hardy, secre, and ryche. [1524-28]

It is just this kind of dissemblance that causes both Hypsipyle and Medea to fall victim to the beastly desires of the man who pursues them. They are moved by the fictions they too easily believe, especially the false representations of Jason's character which make any accurate judgment of him impossible. It would not be far from the truth to say that Chaucer's role as "misrepresenter" in this legendary is much like that of the deceitful Jason. Both use their artistry to distort complex human characters into mere blueprints of "goodness" and "faithfulness" in love. Just as Jason profits from the innocence of these credulous women, moving from them to "yit the thridde wif anon" (1660), so too Chaucer exploits these ladies (and the men) by regarding their lives as disorderly matter on which to impose his own prearranged form. Considerably simplified in Chaucer's versions, each of these ladies' lives is deprived of any distinctive detail that could make them more than simply items in the list of "good women" they now comprise. Chaucer, the bad translator, has done to all these women what Jason did to Hypsipyle—he "tok of hir substaunce / What so hym leste, unto his purveyaunce" (1560-61).

In *Ariadne*, Chaucer again modifies the details of his sources to emphasize similarities, as a saint's life might, between his characters and exemplary models. This time, however, the males are the center of attention as Chaucer strives to show parallels between the experience of Theseus, who escapes the labyrinth, and that of Admetus (Alceste's husband), who is saved from death and eternal confinement in the underworld. Aiding Chaucer in this task was a medieval tradition in which the story of Theseus's adventures in Crete was allegorically interpreted as a Christian's escape from damnation and the jaws of the fiend. The opening line of *Ariadne*, "Juge infernal, Mynos, of Crete kyng" (1886), follows Boccaccio in assigning to Minos the role of judge of the lower world, thus implicating him in the drama of Theseus's struggle against potential damnation.[28] But Chaucer further strengthens the comparison of the labyrinth and the underworld by describing Theseus as damned (1953, 2030), the labyrinth as a "prysoun, ther he shal descende" (1997), and most appropriately, the Minotaur as the "fend" (1996), this last detail suggesting an allegory in keeping with Pierre Bersuire's interpretation of the Minotaur as, among other things, "*diabolum*."[29]

Chaucer, of course, does not intend his narrative to be allegorized in any way. He includes these details merely to underscore the parallels between Ariadne and Alceste, both of whom can now be viewed as saviors, since their actions preserve men from the perils of hell. In most medieval tellings of this story, Theseus escapes the labyrinth and kills the Minotaur with the aid of Dedalus, who, as maker of the maze, suggests the string and the wax as a means of escaping it.[30] In Chaucer's version, however, Dedalus is not even mentioned by name, and his role as keeper of the maze is replaced with a nameless "gaylor," whose function in the story is minimal. In Chaucer's telling, it is Ariadne who takes pity on Theseus and with the aid of her sister Phedra explains to him the best means of escape:

> And by the techynge of this Adryane
> He overcom this beste, and was his bane;
> And out he cometh by the clewe agayn
> Ful prively, whan he this beste hath slayn. [2146-49]

Furthermore, Ariadne's crown, later made part of a constellation, serves conveniently as an imitation of Alceste's crown of martyrdom

and complete stellification. We have in Ariadne, then, another lesser
Alceste.

As in many of the other legends, however, the heroine's
misfortunes are in some ways ironic. The labyrinth, conventionally a
metaphor for the intricacies of art,[31] may have brought about the
salvation of Theseus, but for poor Ariadne, its halls seem to symbolize
the lies that caused her undoing. Misled by Theseus's false promises
and the hidden snares of his artful love talk, Ariadne ends up alone on a
wilderness island, inhabited, like the labyrinth, with "bestes wilde."
Wondering which way to go, she wanders about, painfully realizing
that her former ability to give advice on how to escape tricky snares is
now gone:

> "Allas! where shal I, wreche wight, become?
> For thogh so be that ship or boot here come,
> Hom to my contre dar I nat for drede.
> I can myselven in this cas nat rede." [2214-17]

Now in her own labyrinth, Ariadne must be rescued through someone
else's compassion, just as Theseus was rescued by her own:

> The goddes han hire holpen for pite,
> And in the signe of Taurus men may se
> The stones of hire corone shyne clere. [2222-24][32]

Thus in *Ariadne*, as in other legends, we can see images, phrases,
allusions to Alceste, and other embellishments that are designed to call
attention to the poet's self-reflexive "making."

In this legendary, which has as one of its purposes the
condemnation of men as one-sided villains in matters of love, the
Legend of Thisbe, our next subject, comes as a surprise. It is an unusual
choice for inclusion in a collection of stories intended to extol women's
constancy and virtue in the face of men's deceits. This story differs
markedly from the other narratives in the *Legend* in that it concerns the
tragic deaths of two faithful lovers instead of just one, both of whom
die for their love. Furthermore, the story does not contribute much to
the legendary's hagiographical scheme because Thisbe's experiences
are not made to conform to Alceste's, nor is Pyramus drawn in such a
way as to remind us of Admetus's own close escape from death. And
finally, Thisbe's name is not often included among standard medieval
catalogues of exemplary female sufferers. Though her story was told
with as much frequency as the others, she does not seem to be a regular

member of conventional lists designed to memorialize the names of classical women who suffered in love. Unlike Cleopatra, Dido, Hypsipyle, Medea, Lucretia, Ariadne, Philomela, Phyllis, and Hypermnestra, Thisbe is not an automatic candidate for commemoration, because she does not illustrate the premise that women are more frequently victimized by their partners than are men. In fact, Chaucer has to moralize this narrative awkwardly after he has told it, in hopes of making it appropriate to his project. First, Thisbe herself is given a clumsy death speech, meant to help her turn her particular misfortune into an exemplum of universal female worthiness, a speech that ends by suggesting that the sole reason for her suicide is to further women's reputations as true lovers:

> "But God forbede but a woman can
> Ben as trewe in lovynge as a man!
> And for my part, I shal anon it kythe." [910-12]

Second, the narrator concludes his version of the story by pointing out once again that Thisbe has competed well with any virtuous man: "A woman dar and can as wel as he " (923).

These strained moralizations help make Thisbe's story comply with the formulaic theme Chaucer is seeking to convey in this legendary. Still, this story describes an exceptionally virtuous man, one who dies perhaps more nobly and for a better reason than Thisbe. Chaucer does not alter his portrait of Pyramus to make him diabolical, as he does many of the other male portraits in his legendary, and he does little to suppress Pyramus's central importance in this narrative. In fact, he calls attention to his virtue in the following lines:

> Of trewe men I fynde but fewe mo
> In alle my bokes, save this Piramus,
> And therfore have I spoken of hym thus.
> For it is deynte to us men to fynde
> A man that can in love been trewe and kynde. [917-21]

Clearly, Pyramus stands nearly alone as an example of masculine truth in love. Though such are few, however, readers familiar with Chaucer's own corpus would immediately think of another, equally true man—Troilus, whom Chaucer extolled earlier in his career as a man deserving poetic treatment because of his steadfast (and tragic) love. In fact, the *Legend of Thisbe* can be read profitably with *Troilus and Criseyde* in mind, because the story of Pyramus and Thisbe appears to have been chosen for this collection precisely because it contains similarities in theme to the poet's earlier treatment of love and its attendant misfortunes. Indeed, it is possible to see the *Legend of Thisbe* as a diminutive *Troilus and Criseyde* in theme, a retelling of that poem intended to allow readers like the God of Love further opportunity to understand its issues.

The two works have many similarities of plot—forced separation, illicit love, secret meetings, mistaken "deaths," and misread signs, to name a few. They also share a theme—that misfortune and tragedy can occur in love despite the essential blamelessness of the lovers. And because the God of Love has erred in his reading of the *Troilus* by forcing blame on Criseyde, thus missing the poem's philosophical tragedy, Chaucer cleverly demonstrates the limitations of this reading by telling what is very nearly the same story but with one significant difference—Pyramus is given a "true Criseyde." In other words, the *Legend of Thisbe* relates a tragedy in which no single character can be blamed for the misfortunes that occur. Yet in this "retelling" of the *Troilus*, we learn that the tragic consequence of earthly love is still the same with or without a culpable character; in fact, one might say that it is greater, for love causes the downfall of two lovers rather than one.

Thisbe, then, is a corrective to the God of Love's reading of the *Troilus* in several ways. It suggests that poems like the *Troilus* ought to be read not simply as exempla, as some readers had supposed. Tragedy can occur despite the "goodness" the God of Love demands from his stories. Simple accidents, such as Thisbe's loss of her veil and the complex workings of Fortune and free will in the *Troilus*, are often prime causes of earthly tragedy in love. Even faithful lovers can meet disastrous ends; two "goods" can result in a "bad." Both the *Troilus* and *Thisbe* illustrate the limitations of a narrowly moral reading of human affairs, which are complicated not only by chance and circumstance, but also, as Chaucer shows, by faulty human perception such as Pyramus's belief that blood on a wimple means his lady's death[33] or Troilus's belief that his beloved lady is the sacred shrine of a true religion.

The *Legend of Thisbe* is recognized as one of Chaucer's most literal renderings of an Ovidian text.[33] He has faithfully preserved Ovid's original, including some of the Roman poet's exaggerated rhetorical flourishes, such as the ghastly image of Pyramus's blood spurting out as if it were water from a broken conduit (851-52). In other words, with this legend Chaucer is playing the role of translator rather than devious falsifier of others' truths. With the exception of his appended moralizations (which do little to alter the significance of

Ovid's own story), Chaucer has remained faithful to his source. Thus the *Legend of Thisbe*, while ostensibly fulfilling the requirements of the God of Love's project, nevertheless simultaneously undermines the validity of the regulations he has imposed upon the narrator's literary enterprise. Moreover, if he approves this narrative, the God of Love unknowingly admits that his judgment of the *Troilus* has been inadequate and that his sole assumption regarding human love (that tragedy in love occurs because of an unfaithful partner) ignores the wide range of human experience that literature can reflect. Chaucer's decision to include *Thisbe* and, on top of that, to translate it accurately, constitutes rebellion against the doctrines he knows are unwise.

Like *Thisbe*, the *Legend of Phyllis* contains much close translation from Ovid's *Heroides*. Chaucer's brief summary of her story repeats the now familiar pattern of betrayal, as well as the hagiographical device of recalling Alceste's precedent with the lines that describe Phyllis as "fayrer on to sene / Than is the flour ageyn the bryghte sonne" (2425-26). This summary is handled with great dispatch to leave space for her long letter, whose eloquence proves her a capable narrator of her own misfortunes. The narrator mentions that he regretfully cannot include this letter in its entirety because of the God of Love's demand for brevity:

> But al hire letter wryten I ne may
> By order, for it were to me a charge;
> Hire letter was ryght long and therto large.
> But here and ther in rym I have it layd,
> There as me thoughte that she wel hath sayd. [2513-17]

But despite his radical shortening of Ovid's original, Chaucer has nevertheless managed to let Phyllis's voice dominate her own legend.[35] In this sense, as he himself might be humorously boasting in the last lines of this story, he is a faithful man (both to Phyllis and to Ovid), clearly more trustworthy than the poetic villains who may have neglected her pain in their works, or may have exalted her deceiver Demophoon for his other adventures:

> Be war, ye wemen, of youre subtyl fo,
> Syn yit this day men may ensaumple se;
> And trusteth, as in love, no man but me. [2559-61]

Chaucer, though unable to prove his fidelity as an actual lover, is nevertheless faithful to the classical female lovers (if not always to the

facts of their lives) this collection is designed to serve. And as a mark
of his loyalty to Phyllis, he echoes her last wish—that Demophoon's
betrayal of her be described truthfully in future accounts of his life:

> And whan thyne olde auncestres peynted be,
> In which men may here worthynesse se,
> Thanne preye I God thow peynted be also
> That folk may rede, forby as they go,
> "Lo! this is he, that with his flaterye
> Bytraised hath and don hire vilenye
> That was his trewe love in thought and dede!"   [2536-42]

Phyllis's concern with the preservation of truth in all subsequent
records of Demophoon's illustrious and heroic family brings us to one
of Chaucer's own major concerns in the *Legend of Good Women* as a
whole. In writing these legends, he has been keenly aware of how easy
it is for a poet to magnify or diminish a human reputation simply by
exercising poetic legerdemain. Moreover, he realizes that there is
nothing mystical about poets creating illusions of truth; doing so
merely involves the use of everyday literary skills such as cutting,
expanding, editing, moralizing, or choosing the right authorities on
which to base one's tale. Thus the stability of literary fame is
theoretically always in question, since one's fate depends solely on the
vacillating and unpredictable decisions of poets. Criseyde's painful
realization of this fact resulted in her fear that she would be condemned
in subsequent versions of her story, a fate that actually came to pass in
the works of Henryson and Shakespeare. Like Criseyde, Phyllis realizes
that her literary future is likely to hold a far worse betrayal of her than
could be caused by any unfaithful man.

Chaucer's deepest involvement with this issue occurs in the *House
of Fame*, a work very pertinent to the *Legend* because in it we see two
conflicting versions of a story. In the *House of Fame*, Virgil's *Aeneid*
and Ovid's *Heroides* vie for the honor of transmitting to posterity the
love story of Aeneas and Dido. Only Virgil's account of this story
seems to appear on the glorious walls of Venus's temple, but by the
time the narrator has finished describing the love affair as it appears
there, he has managed to introduce, in some detail, the Ovidian
perspective as well. The result is a ludicrous, hybrid version of the
Dido/Aeneas story which manifests radical inconsistencies in point of
view, as might be expected from such a hasty amalgam of two poets
with very different sympathies. Virgil's Aeneas appears as a
responsible hero, Ovid's as a thoughtless deceiver, and both of these

judgments get equal transmission in the *House of Fame*, thus allowing little possibility of arriving at objective truth in this matter.

However comic this mixed rendition of the story may seem, there is something to be said for Chaucer's conscious desire to record a side of the story that did not have an epic tradition to help secure its survival—namely, the Ovidian perspective that favors Dido's emotional tragedy in the face of Aeneas's departure from her. Ovid's partiality to Dido, when combined with Virgil's whole-hearted approval of his hero, makes for an inorganic and confusing narrative, but one that nevertheless succeeds in achieving a measure of fairness uncharacteristic of any previous version of the story. Chaucer, then, sets himself up as the Ovidian challenger of Virgil's one-sided case, working not to destroy what Virgil had left to posterity but simply to provide an alternative to it. With this in mind, the *House of Fame*'s narrator alludes to the tragedies of other ladies whom Ovid had rescued from literary neglect, including some of those who appear in Chaucer's legendary, such as Phyllis, Hypsipyle, Medea, and Ariadne.[36]

There is an important difference, however, between the ways in which these two works represent the classical people with whom they are concerned. In the *House of Fame*, Virgil never gets completely upstaged by the silly, impassioned narrator who introduces Ovid's viewpoint; after all, it is Virgil's account—not Ovid's—which was chosen by Venus to adorn her walls for eternity. Thus Aeneas is not likely to lose his reputation as a flawless hero merely because of the alternative opinion offered by the narrator as he scans the images about him. But in the *Legend of Good Women*, Aeneas is not shown the courtesy of fair representation (even though he is given equal time), nor are any of the other men, many of whom deserve much better treatment than they receive in the *Legend*'s short summaries. Demophoon, for example, is badly misrepresented, for in many versions of his affair with Phyllis, he returns to her after a delay, only to find that she hanged herself prematurely.[37] Therefore she only *imagined* that he was false, because he was unable to honor the prearranged date of his homecoming. This accident, of course, in no way lessens Phyllis's tragedy; she is as convinced as other ladies whose betrayals were real that she is a victim of deceit and dishonesty. She is therefore justified in desiring an honest appraisal of her fidelity to her lover, which she showed in "thought and deed." But Demophoon clearly suffers in Chaucer's (and Ovid's) hands, and one is inclined to ponder the terrible misunderstanding that might have been perpetuated if Phyllis's last wish—to see Demophoon permanently drawn as a villain—had been honored by all artists everywhere. In other words, the full artistic accommodation of one viewpoint often entails the conscious neglect of another. Thus we see that the Chaucer who is so faithful to the women in this legendary is at the same time the faithless betrayer of its men. Such is the travesty the ignorant God of Love has made of Chaucer's art in his demand that it be rid of the so-called chaff of honesty, fairness, and perspicacity. For once a literary artist is handed a set of predetermined conclusions regarding human culpability, he has no choice in the course of his narrative but to commit the injustices necessary to lead him there. In an age of moralized exempla, when literary appetites demand gratification in the form of a simple dialectic, an artist must work hard to make his stories confirm the expectations that await them, even if it means he must deface the images chosen by Fame to adorn the walls of Venus's temple.

Chaucer's awareness that he is contradicting traditional opinion is nowhere more evident than in the *Legend of Dido*. Chaucer opens his narrative by praising Virgil and by announcing the *Aeneid* as the story's main source:

> Glorye and honour, Viro Mantoan,
> Be to thy name! and I shal, as I can,
> Folwe thy lanterne, as thow gost byforn,
> How Eneas to Dido was forsworn. [924-27]

But as in the *House of Fame*, the poet plans to introduce Ovidian elements into this Virgilian tale:

> In Naso and Eneydos wol I take
> The tenor, and the grete effectes make. [928-29]

To synthesize these two versions of the story, however, Chaucer must make some important changes in Virgil's text, one of which occurs in the scene describing the temple in which Dido and Aeneas first meet. In the *Aeneid,* the hero finds pictures painted on the temple walls which recall to him his suffering and fortitude in the Trojan War (1.456-63). He remarks to one of his companions that these pictures, powerful in their evocation of Trojan heroism, could ensure them a measure of safety in their travels because they present such a moving account of the losses of war that people will honor or pity the men shown there. Chaucer's re-creation of this scene involves some very subtle changes in its significance. Most important, he has altered the effect these images have on Aeneas, making them convey shame to him rather than glorious fortitude:[38]

And whan this Eneas and Achates
Hadden in this temple ben overal,
Thanne founde they, depeynted on a wal,
How Troye and al the lond destroyed was.
"Allas, that I was born!" quod Eneas;
"Thourghout the world oure shame is kid so wyde,
Now it is peynted upon every syde.
We, that weren in prosperite,
Been now desclandered, and in swich degre,
No lenger for to lyven I ne kepe." [1023-32]

Whatever Aeneas's reaction might imply about what the images on the
wall actually depict, it is clear that what he sees there somehow causes
him shame. Aeneas judges this particular account of the Trojan story as
nothing but slander, suggesting either that the creator of these images
was lying or that he told the true story in such a way as to misrepresent
Aeneas and his fellow soldiers. The "desclandered" Trojans, with good
reputations lost, are now permanently enshrined in the cultural memory
as disgraceful losers.

In making this change, Chaucer demonstrates the awesome control
artists have over human destiny and reputation. Moreover, through
changing the pictures on the wall, he cleverly depicts his own
adjustments of Virgil's historical truth: what Aeneas sees on the wall is
exactly what the readers of this slanderous legend will see—a shameful
betrayer instead of a hero. And ironically, both Aeneas's concern for
his good reputation and his willingness to die because of its loss are
actually Dido's feelings about herself, if we are to believe the *Heroides*,
the *Aeneid*, and Chaucer's *House of Fame*:

"O, wel-away that I was born!
For thorgh yow is my name lorn,
And alle myn actes red and songe
Over al thys lond, on every tonge." [*House of Fame*, 345-48]

In this legend, Chaucer has obviously reversed the positions of Dido
and Aeneas relative to Fame, keeping Virgil's story intact only where it
does not conflict with Ovid's sympathy for Dido. He can faithfully
reproduce Virgil's "images on the wall," if you will, until they interfere
with the legend's moral purpose, at which time it becomes necessary to
deviate from his principal "auctour" and make Dido the one whom
Fame has chosen to patronize:

> ... she was holden of alle queenes flour,
> Of gentillesse, of fredom, of beaute;
> That wel was hym that myghte hire ones se;
> Of kynges and of lordes so desyred,
> That al the world hire beaute hadde yfyred;
> She stod so wel in every wightes grace. [1009-14]

This expansive praise for Dido is not in itself a radical departure from Virgil, but when Chaucer implies that the Trojan lords seek her help solely *because* of her fame ("Swich renoun was there sprongen of hire goodnesse" [1054]), then he is obviously stretching Virgil's text.

Chaucer exhibits another tendency in the *Legend of Dido* which must be briefly noted. He is extremely reluctant to include in his version any of Virgil's accounts of supernatural interference, especially when that interference somehow affects the relationship between the two main characters. For example, he is unwilling to blame Venus and Cupid for initiating Dido's love for Aeneas:

> But natheles, oure autour telleth us,
> That Cupido, that is the god of love,
> At preyere of his moder hye above,
> Hadde the liknesse of the child ytake,
> This noble queen enamored to make
> On Eneas; but, as of that scripture,
> Be as be may, I take of it no cure. [1139-45]

Similarly, the storm that forces them into a cave together is a natural event in Chaucer's version but a contrivance plotted by Juno and Venus in the *Aeneid*.[39] Jove's connection with Iarbas is never mentioned by Chaucer, nor does he place much faith in Virgil's account of Aeneas's entering the temple at Carthage hidden in a cloud:

> I can nat seyn if that it be possible,
> But Venus hadde hym maked invysible—
> Thus seyth the bok, withouten any les. [1020-22]

Finally, Chaucer entirely omits Virgil's long description of Mercury's appearance before Aeneas to deliver the message that the hero must leave for Italy (*Aen.* 4.238-78). In its place, Chaucer has Aeneas pretend that he learned all this in a dream—a notoriously unreliable source of information even if we could be certain that the now bored

Aeneas was not simply making it up to deceive his newfound queen. It becomes clear that all of these curious alterations Chaucer made in his Virgilian text contribute to a single intention: by banishing supernatural interference in the lives of his characters, Chaucer is better able to assign blame to them and thus to make the moral judgment we have come to expect, that Aeneas is an unmercifully evil man who has full control over his own sinful behavior.

The *Legend of Dido* is certainly a coherent narrative, unlike the *House of Fame*'s version of this same love story, but readers hardly need anyone to point out to them what Chaucer has sacrificed to achieve that coherence. He has worked hard at the task of blackening Aeneas's reputation, largely by subtle revision of those Virgilian episodes that are in conflict with his intended purpose. Yet at the same time, he has retained a degree of fidelity to his sources, since he cannot be accused of independently creating any of this narrative's episodes. Even with such clever appropriation of the personae of two classical poets—Virgil and Ovid—Chaucer has nonetheless managed to tell a tale that is distinctly anomalous in its tone and significance. This legend, like others in the collection, brilliantly parodies the unfortunate results of so many medieval retellings of classical stories, especially those that are told to fit a prearranged context or to confirm some a priori system of morality. To be sure, the practice of making saints out of pagan lovers is a greatly exaggerated example of literary falsification, yet it is close enough to actual medieval practice to be classified as parody.

The God of Love is certainly justified in wishing to glorify ancient achievements, especially Alceste's, that have the power to teach us about the depth and truth of human love. But in demanding that she be set up as the "calendier," or model, for all the other ladies, he is grossly unfair. His directive to the poet, that

> ". . . of Alceste shulde thy wrytynge be,
> Syn that thow wost that calendier is she
> Of goodnesse. . . ."[40] [G 532-34]

suggests a plan that is bound to fail, because with Alceste as the standard by which feminine truth in love is to be measured, the other ladies, as good as they are, can only suffer in comparison to her life of perfect charity. Although the ladies' lives are written to conform to her archetypal example, we must always realize the major differences between them and Alceste. Chaucer's "good women" vainly sacrificed themselves for unworthy causes, and because suicide resulting from

despair does not deserve resurrection, they were not given life again by
a herculean judge. The men they "saved" or died for were not devoted
husbands like Alceste's Admetus, but, as Chaucer's legends would
have it, merely fickle lovers whose motives were suspect from the start.
Finally, many of the ladies had biographies badly in need of editing by
anyone seeking to redeem them from charges of general moral
turpitude. They are, without question, far inferior to Alceste if one
wishes to measure them by a Christian standard of morality. For these
and other reasons, the project of the legendary, designed specifically to
please the God of Love, disproves his assumptions once it is carried
out. His desire to have literature that is simple, unambiguous in its
moral force, and part of an endless repetition of the same witless
themes results in a "hagiographical classicism" that is patently
unworkable. On top of that, his requirement that Christian charity and
pagan eros be reconciled forces Chaucer to produce a "martyrology of
love" that does little more than violate the true character of his sources.

Oddly enough, the ladies whose stories are told in this poem do not
sustain the kinds of injuries we might expect of participants (and
victims) in this typical Chaucerian mockery. The poet often seems quite
moved by their predicaments, conveying in some instances true
compassion and sympathy. In this regard, Chaucer is imitating Ovid,
especially the sophisticated narrator so visible in the *Heroides*, where
the poet's ludicrous bombast and brilliant rhetorical parody are mixed
with unmistakable tenderness and pity for the female victims he
describes. Like Ovid, Chaucer finds his target solely in the literary
forms and techniques that traditionally serve as vehicles for human
experiences, not in the characters who represent those experiences.[41]
We must bear in mind that throughout his legendary, Chaucer is
attacking narrative strategies, not saints or classical lovers. The ladies
of antiquity are not sacrificed at the God of Love's altar, even though
their lives fall short of Alceste's ideal model. By telling their stories in
many of Ovid's own sympathetic words, Chaucer has taken it upon
himself to reward the women with the literary afterlife they all deserve.
And as for the men, whose good reputations were never in question
before the God of Love asked Chaucer to blacken them in his penance,
they do not suffer an enduring wound either. Chaucer's gross betrayal
of them in this poem is so obviously what makes the legendary "bad
art" that readers are never in danger of taking seriously its views on
male culpability. For, as the *Troilus* tells us, blame is not what art is all
about.

NOTES

1. See [Robert Worth] Frank [Jr.], [*Chaucer and the Legend of Good Women*. Cambridge, Mass.: Harvard Univ. Press, 1972] pp. 189-96, for an excellent summary of this critical view.

2. [John M. Fyler] *Chaucer and Ovid* [New Haven, Conn.: Yale Univ. Press, 1979], p. 104. See also [H.C.] Goddard, "Chaucer's *Legend of Good Women*, II," [*JEGP*, 8 (1909), 47-111] pp. 60-86, for a lively commentary on Chaucer's abuse of his sources in the legendary.

3. *Chaucer and the Legend of Good Women*, pp. 199-204. See also Fyler, pp. 99-100.

4. On Cleopatra's medieval reputation, see Beverly Taylor, "The Medieval Cleopatra: The Classical and Medieval Tradition of Chaucer's *Legend of Cleopatra*," *Journal of Mediaeval and Renaissance Studies*, 7 (1977), 249-69. On Medea, see Frank, pp. 83-84; Goddard, pp. 76-77; and Robert K. Root, "Chaucer's *Legend of Medea*," *PMLA*, 24 (1909), 124-53.

5. Not every saint's life exhibits all three characteristics of the exemplum form; there are, for example, some very long legends. Moreover, not every legend is intended as a model for behavior; Chaucer's legend of Cecilia is a good example. But in spite of the exceptions, most saints' legends were considered to be exempla and were gathered into collections together with other narratives to form exemplary *specula*. For corroboration of this point, see [Joseph Albert] Mosher [*The Exemplum in the Early Religious and Didactic Literature of England*. New York: Columbia Univ. Press, 1911], p. 74n.: "These legendary lives of holy men and women and the Virgin furnished more exempla than any other class of material. In a sense, a saint's life or a collection of saints' lives constituted a sort of example-book." [J.-Th.] Welter, in *L'Exemplum* [*dans la littérature religieuse et didactique du moyen age*. Paris: Occitania, 1927], also categorizes saints' lives as exempla, as does [G.R.] Owst [*Literature and the Pulpit in Medieval England*. 2d ed. 1933; rpt. Oxford: Blackwell, 1961], pp. 123-35.

6. 'On the struggle between good and evil in saints' legends, see Theodor Wolpers, *Die Englische Heiligenlegende des Mittelalters* (Tübingen: Max Niemeyer, 1964), pp. 28-30. See also Alexandra Hennessey Olsen, "'*De Historiis Sanctorum*': A Generic Study of Hagiography," *Genre*, 13 (1980), 415-25; Charles W. Jones, *Saints' Lives and Chronicles in Early England* (Ithaca, N.Y.: Cornell Univ. Press, 1947), p. 73; and Rosemary Woolf, "Saints' Lives," in *Continuations and Beginnings: Studies in Old English Literature*, ed. E.G. Stanley (London: Thomas Nelson, 1966), p. 41.

7. See Owst, pp. 123-24, 134-35. Indeed, Owst sees imitation as the "chief object" of the saint's life. In Athanasius's *Life of Anthony*, the author twice mentions Anthony's value as a model, once in the Prologue and once in the Conclusion. See also [Jacobus de Voraigne] the *Golden Legend* [Trans. Granger Ryan and Helmut Ripperger. 1941; rpt. New York: Arno Press, 1969], p. 645: "[The Martyrs] are given to us as models for combat," and Jaroslav Pelikan, *The Growth of Medieval Theology (600-1300)* (Chicago: Univ. of Chicago Press, 1978), p. 125.

8. See Wolpers, pp. 13, 33; Olsen, p. 411; the *Golden Legend*, p. 687; and Ernst Robert Curtius, *European Literature and the Latin Middle Ages*, trans. Willard R. Trask (1953; rpt. New York: Harper and Row, 1963), p. 160.

9. On the "historicity" of saints' lives, see Owst, pp. 125-26, where he quotes from a fourteenth-century manuscript as showing this typical claim: "This is no fabull that I sey you." See also Olsen, p. 417; William Nelson, *Fact or Fiction: The Dilemma of the Renaissance Storyteller* (Cambridge, Mass.: Harvard Univ. Press, 1973), pp. 23-24; and Hippolyte Delehaye, *The Legends of the Saints: An Introduction to Hagiography*, trans. V.M. Crawford (1907; rpt. South Bend, Ind.: Univ. of Notre Dame Press, 1961), p. 9, pp. 65-69.

10. On the single "pattern" of Christ's life as it is demonstrated in saints' lives, see Olsen, p. 411, who reminds us of Gregory of Tours's comment: "And it is asked by many whether we should say the Life of the saints, or the Lives." See also Pelikan, p. 174.

11. *Concerning Famous Women*, trans. Guido A. Guarino (New Brunswick, N.J.: Rutgers Univ. Press, 1963), p. xxxviii.

12. *Concerning Famous Women*, p. xxxix.

13. Boccaccio's translator, Guido A. Guarino, writes: "He did not write of saints and martyrs simply because he was not drawn to them, while classical antiquity held him enthralled with its charms" (*Concerning Famous Women*, p. xxv). The issue is probably more complicated than Guarino suggests.

14. For Jerome's approval of her, see *Adversus Jovinianum* 1.46 (*PL* 23, col. 287). Also see Odo of Cluny's *Collationum libri tres*, *PL* 133, col. 557. For examples of the medieval view of Lucretia's story, see *Gesta Romanorum*, trans. Charles Swan and revised by Wynnard Hooper (London: Bohn's Antiquarian Library, 1891), p. 239; *Le Ménagier de Paris*, trans. Eileen Power (London: Routledge and Sons, 1928), pp. 101- 5; and the *Romance of the Rose*, ll. 8608ff. Some of Chaucer's alterations of the original story are discussed by Frank, pp.

93-110, and by Edgar Finley Shannon, *Chaucer and the Roman Poets* (Cambridge, Mass.: Harvard Univ. Press, 1929), pp. 220-28.

15. *The City of God* 1.19. See also John S.P. Tatlock, "Chaucer and the *Legenda Aurea*," *MLN*, 45 (1930), 296-98.

16. See Owst, pp. 123, 125-56, who quotes two typical examples of hagiography being called a means of "blessid commemoraciouns" and a form of "remembrance."

17. See, for example, the *Golden Legend*, pp.593, 632, 695; and *The South English Legendary* 1, ed. Charlotte D'Evelyn and Anna Mill, EETS e.s. (London: Oxford Univ. Press, 1956), pp. 63-64, ll. 41-45, 56-60.

18. Compare, for example, the "foreshadowings" of death in the life of St. Martha, *Golden Legend*, p. 393.

19. See,. for example, the *Golden Legend*, pp. 52, 540, 552, 571, and *The South English Legendary* 1, p. 19, ll. 8-16; p. 293, ll. 43-50; and 2, p. 586, ll. 5-8.

20. John S.P. Tatlock, "Notes on Chaucer: Earlier or Minor Poems," *MLN*, 29 (1914), 99n, also speculates on this snake pit and its relationship to Hell.

21. The analogy of the reliquary may have been intended by Chaucer. In *The Sacred Shrine* [Boston: Beacon Press, 1957], [Yrjö] Hirn observes that it was a common practice in the late medieval period "to use heathen works of art as coverings for Christian relics. Crusaders and pilgrims brought with them relics lying in costly cases and receptacles which they had procured in the East. . . . The same liberality was shown with regard to the profane art of the European nations. As the Church on the whole rejected nothing—whether old folk legends or heathen customs or motives or artistic decoration—so too it gave house-room to gems, receptacles, and implements. Worldly objects were transformed into holy shrines" (p. 53).

22. Hypermnestra's nativity is described by Frank, pp. 160-61, and Fyler, p. 107, who has a view very similar to mine of this legend's irony.

23. Delehaye notes that hagiographers commonly altered their sources or added to them in order to make their heroes and heroines appear in the best light possible. See *Legends of the Saints*, pp. 68-69. Some of Chaucer's methods in the *Legend* are comparable.

24. "Chaucer's Appeal to the Platonic Deity," *Speculum*, 19 (1944), 1-13. On the *accessus* tradition, see Edwin A. Quain, "The Medieval *Accessus ad Auctores*," *Traditio*, 3 (1945), 215-64. For typical *accessus*, see those written by Bernard of Utrecht and Conrad of

Hirsau which have been edited by R.B.C. Huygens, *Accessus ad Auctores* (Leiden: E.J. Brill, 1970).

25. *Poetria nova* 40-48 and *Troilus and Criseyde* 1.1065-69.

26. These lines are from Guido delle Colonna's *Historia Destructionis Troiae*, the modern edition edited and translated by Nathaniel E. Griffin, Medieval Academy of America Publication 26 (Cambridge, Mass.: Mediaeval Academy, 1936), p. 17.

27. For a short history of the philosophy of matter and form, see [Gordon] Leff [*Medieval Thought*. Baltimore: Penguin Books, 1958], pp. 49, 70, 118, 120-23, 152-64, 185-89, 193, 211, 217. Before Aquinas, medieval thinkers in general believed that form gave being to substance and was closely connected to the "ideas" that lay in God's mind. Our knowledge of things derived ultimately from our observations of these "forms." Matter itself was recalcitrant and confused and could not exist without a "form" in which to be contained. Aquinas's revision of this Platonic scheme was to allow matter a more independent and important place in theories of existence. To Aquinas, matter was a "principle of individuation" by which things were made distinct from one another. On the early application of these ideas to rhetorical theory, see Boethius's *De differentiis topicis* 4, cited in John O. Ward's "From Antiquity to the Renaissance: Glosses and Commentaries on Cicero's *Rhetorica*," in *Medieval Eloquence*, ed. James J. Murphy (Berkeley: Univ. of California Press, 1978), p. 43-44, 50.

28. See [F.N.] Robinson [ed., *The Works of Geoffrey Chaucer* 2nd Ed. Boston: Houghton Mifflin, 1957], p. 851n.

29. See Pierre Bersuire's *Reductium Morale* 15, reprinted as *Metamorphosis Ovidiana Moraliter . . . Explanata*, 1509; facsim., intro. Stephen Orgel (New York: Garland, 1979), 8.63. Also see *Gesta Romanorum* 63, p. 112, which tells essentially the same story, interpreting the beast as the devil.

30. Sanford Brown Meech, in "Chaucer and an Italian Translation of the *Heroides*," *PMLA*, 40 (1930), 110-28, points out that most medieval and some classical discussions of this story name Dedalus as Theseus's helper. Ovid, in the *Heroides*, is the exception.

31. On the image of the labyrinth and its relation to art, see Frank, p. 132. See also Donald R. Howard, *The Idea of the Canterbury Tales* (Berkeley: Univ. of California Press, 1976), pp. 326-32, where the figure of the labyrinth is discussed as it appears in Chaucer's other works. It is also possible that the title of Eberhard the German's art of poetry, *Laborintus*, suggests this connection. And finally, in the fifteenth century, Gavin Douglas suggests this connection in his

Prologue to the third book of the *Aeneid*, ed. David F.C. Coldwell, Scottish Text Society, no. 25 (Edinburgh: Blackwood and Sons, 1957), ll. 10-16. Perhaps the connection between the labyrinth and art was implied in the word *involucrum*, the term most frequently used by mythographers and others to describe the enigmas of myth and fable, especially those fables whose meaning is deliberately concealed by their authors. On the term *involucrum* see Brian Stock, *Myth and Science in the Twelfth Century: A Study of Bernard Silvester* (Princeton, N.J.: Princeton Univ. Press, 1972), pp. 48-62. Also see M.-D. Chenu, "*Involucrum*: Le mythe selon les théologiens médiévaux" *AHDLMA*, 22 (1956), 75-79, and H. Brinkmann, "Verhüllung (*Integumentum*) als literarische Darstellungsform im Mittelalter," *Miscellanea Medievalia* 8, *Der Begriff der Repraesentatio im Mittelalter* (Berlin, 1971), pp. 314-39. Finally, Boccaccio's labyrinth, the labyrinth of love in his *Carbaccio*, trans. Anthony K. Cassell (Urbana: Univ. of Illinois Press, 1975), pp. 6, 7, 10, 14, may be useful in the interpretation of Chaucer's *Ariadne*.

32. Ariadne's crown is mentioned in Bernard Silvester's *De Mundi Universitate* (see [Winthrop] Wetherbee's translation [*Platonism and Poetry in the Twelfth Century*. Princeton, N.J.: Princeton Univ. Press, 1972], p. 77), as well as in several other classical and medieval works, including Dante's *Paradiso* (13.1-30). See *TLL*, [*Thesaurus Linguae Latinae*. Leipzig, 1806-9] s.v. *corona*, 3.B.2.b, for citations.

33. In Stephen Scrope's *The Epistle of Othea*, ed. Curt F. Bühler, EETS e.s. 264 (Oxford: Oxford Univ. Press, 1970), pp. 49-51, the Pyramus and Thisbe story is moralized as a warning to its readers to beware of misinterpreting evidence as Pyramus did.

34. See [Edgar F.] Shannon, *Chaucer and the Roman Poets* [Cambridge, Mass.: Harvard Univ. Press, 1929], p. 190.

35. Gavin Douglas, in the *Palice of Honour* 2.808-25, suggests strongly that the ladies of Ovid's epistles are themselves capable poets. About them he writes, "I had greit wonder of thay Ladyis seir, / Quhils in that airt micht have na compeir; / Of castis quent, Rethorik colouris fine, / Sa Poeit like in subtell fair maneir / And eloquent firme cadence Regulair" (*The Shorter Poems of Gavin Douglas*, ed. Priscilla J. Bawcutt, Scottish Text Society, ser. 4, no. 3 [Edinburgh: Blackwood and Sons, 1967]).

36. See the *House of Fame* 388-426, and Fyler, pp. 32-41 and 111-13, for the Chaucerian conflicts between Virgil and Ovid.

37. In Gower's *Confessio Amantis*, Demophoon forgets about Phyllis, but later repents his forgetfulness and returns to find her dead (4.874-78). Boccaccio, however, in the *Genealogia*, mentions

Demophoon's later return but does not say that he was guilty of any neglect.

38. R.W. Frank has also observed this alteration, but he draws a different conclusion from it. See *Chaucer and the Legend of Good Women*, p. 74.

39. On the natural storm, see Shannon, p. 203. Fyler has also commented on Chaucer's editing out of supernatural elements, and he draws conclusions similar to mine. See *Chaucer and Ovid*, pp. 112-13.

40. The F version is slightly different: "And wost so wel that kalendar ys shee / To any woman that wol lover bee" (F 542-43).

41. The Ovidian and the Chaucerian narrators share several features that are instructive to compare. Howard Jacobson, in *Ovid's Heroides* (Princeton, NJ.: Princeton Univ. Press, 1974), has shown, for example, that the *Heroides* are in some ways narratives that experiment with the "reductionist tendency" of individuals to view history from a single perspective (pp. 353-54). He also describes Ovid's interest in the "archetypal structure" of myth, the recurrent patterns that appear in the subject matter he treated (pp. 376-80). For other relationships between Chaucer and Ovid as narrators, Fyler's *Chaucer and Ovid* is the most thorough and expert study. For Ovid's interest in "parallelism" and "repetition" in literature, see also Brooks Otis, *Ovid as an Epic Poet* (Cambridge, Mass.: Harvard Univ. Press, 1970).

"THE NAKED TEXT IN ENGLISH TO DECLARE": THE *LEGEND OF GOOD WOMEN*

by Carolyn Dinshaw

Criseyde was right. Having transferred her "trouthe" from Troilus to Diomede, she predicted the outrage of "wommen" as they read and hear her story, the tale of the treacherous female who is "slydynge of corage." She knew that "thise bokes" would represent her only as unfaithful to the steadfast Troilus, would castigate or turn away from her in drawing their moral conclusions, and that "wommen" would be schooled by these books.[1] As we have seen, the narrator of *Troilus and Criseyde*—that "litel bok"—has dealt with her, finally, in just this manner: like the rest of the masculine readers in and of the poem, he finally rejects unsatisfying involvement with the female character and closes off the tale by getting rid of the troubling feminine.

Even the narrator himself recognizes, toward the end of his poem, that women in his audience might take offense at his choice to write of an unworthy, guilty woman. But this recognition does not mitigate his final antifeminist gesture; in fact, his apologetic lines reinscribe the authority and veracity of the essentially antifeminist tradition of representing Criseyde, as he beseeches

> every lady bright of hewe,
> And every gentil womrnan, what she be,
> That al be that Criseyde was untrewe,
> That for that gilt she be nat wroth with me.
> Ye may hire gilt in other bokes se;
> And gladlier I wol write, yif yow leste,
> Penolopeës trouthe and good Alceste. (5.1772-78)

The narrator maintains that he would rather write of Penelope and Alceste.[2] Of course he would; for this would give him the opportunity apparently to appease "every gentil womman" while still reading like a man.

In fact, if it is "ladies" (and their advocates) in the courtly audience who call out for stories of simply good women—who call out for an antidote to *Troilus and Criseyde* and the *Roman de la rose*—they, too, are reading like men. It is Criseyde who intimates a knowledge of such a phenomenon. She not only laments that "wommen" will hate her because they will have read authoritative (masculine) versions of her story (their view is thus immasculated, as we saw in the last chapter); she also implicitly acknowledges that what men would have her read is very different from what she does read. When Pandarus bursts into her parlor at the beginning of book 2, as we've seen, he interrupts her reading of a romance of Thebes in the company of several of her women; when he insists that she put that book away, she says that, as widow, she *should* be sitting in a cave, dutifully reading saints' lives. As opposed to the romance, a form associated with the feminine, saints' lives are uniform, unambiguous narratives-perfect for immasculated readers, A "Seintes Legende of Cupide" (as the Man of Law will later call it [*CT* 2:6o-6i]) is exactly what the narrator's audience of immasculated readers—represented in the Prologue to the *Legend of Good Women* by the God of Love and Alceste—demands: after the threat of disorder and unfulfillment that the feminine poses in *Troilus and Criseyde*, they want unproblematic fables of faithful women repeated over and over.

The narrator is indeed willing to comply. His self-defense in the Prologue is brief, and he expresses gratitude to Alceste for her intercession and imposition of the light penance of writing a legend of good women. After the disappointments of pagan letter and female character, he wants his females simple, stable, and orderly. He again narrates pagan fables and again positions himself as masculine lover, as we'll see; but this time he immediately strips and cleans up that alien woman, as he did only *after* being seduced by her in *Troilus and Criseyde*. This time he refuses to become vicariously, erotically involved in the act of *translatio*; this time he rigorously chastens the letter and controls the slippery feminine.

Chaucer thus continues in the *Legend of Good Women* to analyze readers' responses of flight into security and control in gendered terms, as, specifically, a masculine—or immasculated—flight from the threateningly mobile, "slydynge" feminine "corage." If, as seems likely, this palinode was indeed written in response to discussion at court of his works, Chaucer's analysis reveals the reductiveness and unhappy social implications not only of an abstract notion of totalizing reading and literary history but of the demands for simplicity and closure made by his own audience. As we'll see at last, the *Legend of Good Women* makes clear that it is not just the feminine "corage"—the fable, the female character—that suffers under such restraint.

Constraining the feminine takes its toll on the masculine as well—on the moral "spirit" of the fables and on the male characters. Indeed, it stops literature itself.[3]

1

If *Troilus and Criseyde* is thoroughly but implicitly preoccupied with reading, the Prologue to the *Legend of Good Women* is directly and explicitly about readers' (and listeners') responses to Chaucer's works. Chaucer's later revisions of the F Prologue in the G Prologue (the version I shall focus on) make literary concerns even more central.[4] The Prologue stages a heated confrontation between the narrator—fictionalized image of the real poet—and his audience, disgruntled with his having translated *Troilus and Criseyde* and the *Roman de la rose*. Contemporary witnesses suggest that medieval readers were deeply unsettled by both the *Rose* and *Troilus and Criseyde*. Since response to the latter is my concern here, I'll not document the vast evidence of upset over the *Rose*; suffice it to note that the whole *querelle* (dating from 1399 to about 1402) evinces high-level agitation over the *Rose*'s representation of women.[5] Several medieval responses to *Troilus and Criseyde* in fact reenact the masculine response as we have seen it represented in the poem itself: after reading the work Henryson felt the need to finish off the narrative by finishing off Criseyde, making his moral point loud and clear. And an anonymous fifteenth-century reader of the poem, a male cleric instructing women religious—a man teaching women, implicitly, how to read—felt a similar need for moral disambiguation and closure of the poem.[6] If then, Queen Anne herself demanded a palinode for these poems (as an enduring but unlikely notion would have it), she was responding precisely as other readers in and of *Troilus and Criseyde* responded.[7] Alceste and the God of Love—fictional (and perhaps rather exaggerated) representations of Chaucer's real readers—articulate this immasculated courtly response; wanting to hear only of good women, simply refusing to hear of any other kind, they chide the narrator: "Why noldest thow han writen of Alceste, / And laten Criseide ben aslepe and reste?" asks the God of Love (G:530-31).

The narrator's unsettling confrontation with his public takes place in a dream vision. Chaucer's choice to return to the courtly dream-vision form after *Troilus and Criseyde* has puzzled critics, but it seems to me that this courtly form as Chaucer has developed it is well suited to a critique of masculine reading and literary history. The courtly genre alone serves him well: from what we saw of "courtly love" in

Troilus and Criseyde (its use as a cover for the patriarchal exchange of women, which denies women independent desire) we can infer a fundamentally patriarchal intent under the courtly setting of this Prologue as well. Chaucer typically uses dream visions to explore the dreamer-narrator's imaginative response to a text that is narrated in the frame: in *Book of the Duchess* it is Ovid's tale of Ceyx and Alcione that appears in the frame; in *Parliament of Fowls* it is the *Somnium Scipionis*; and in *House of Fame* the *Aeneid* appears in the dream. In the Prologue to the *Legend of Good Women* Chaucer explores not only response to *Troilus and Criseyde* and the *Rose* in the dream but response to the whole authoritative, monolithic tradition of "olde bokes," introduced by the narrator in the frame's first twenty-eight lines. The problems of representation in *Troilus and Criseyde* and the *Rose* are problems in all "olde bokes"; the credibility of literary tradition and, indeed, the monumental structure of "authoritees" itself (83), so anxiously advanced by the narrator at the beginning of the poem (he haltingly explains why he even brought the subject up: "But wherfore that I spak, to yeve credence / To bokes olde and don hem reverence, / Is for men shulde autoritees beleve . . ." [81-83]), are implicated in the dream confrontation between the poet and his audience.

The dream-vision setting, further, encourages us to read these characters as parts of the narrator's own mind. Just as we can understand the Black Knight and the dreamer in the *Book of the Duchess* as figures who work through a grief like the narrator's own,[8] we can read the God of Love and Alceste as reifications of the narrator's uneasiness about the reception and understanding—the afterlife—of his works. They have value as figures both exterior and interior to the narrator's own psyche, and his interactions with them in the dream indicate the way the narrator will find resolution of the issues opened up by the end of *Troilus and Criseyde*. Cupid gives voice to the essential dilemma of the narrator after *Troilus and Criseyde*: if one begins to become aware, as he does via women in his audience, that authoritative tradition proceeds by defaming women, how would one be able to write a poem or construct a literary tradition that is *not* misogynistic in theme and/or structure? Alceste's representation in the Prologue suggests that the problem can be articulated; however, a positive solution is far from imminent.

The dream opens by figuring the narrator in an uneasy position.[9] He finds himself in a meadow straight out of the *Parliament of Fowls*—apparently beautiful, but the scene of erotic dissension and problematic closure, deferred resolution. Although we are told that the birds choose their mates and consummate their desire in this lovely setting beyond compare, we are also told, as John Fyler notes, that the delightful meadow isn't always like this: the baleful season winter has just departed.[10] The narrator listens to the sound of the birds and hears a lark proclaim the arrival of the God of Love, with Alceste, clothed "al in grene" (174), and a huge crowd of women: it is a sight that astonishes (164). After the women sing a *balade,* they arrange themselves perfectly in order and "nat a word was spoken in that place / The mountance of a furlong-wey of space" (232-33). A very long silence ensues. The narrator hides near a hillside, keeping "as stille as any ston" (236), only to be discovered and berated by the God of Love. On the basis of the narrator's literary endeavors, the God sets his worth at less than a worm's.

Cupid's objections are twofold: he claims that by translating the *Roman de la rose,* Guillaume de Lorris' and Jean de Meun's "heresye," the narrator has made "wise folk fro me withdrawe" (257) and that by writing *Troilus and Criseyde,* he has been intent on "shewynge how that wemen han don mis" (266). These objections are of course interrelated: by demonstrating in the *Rose* that "he nys but a verray propre fol / That loveth paramours to harde and hote" (259-60), the narrator has, in the God's opinion, turned readers' attention away from worthy women. It is upon this alleged defamation of women that the God focuses his remonstrations:

> Why noldest thow as wel [han] seyd goodnesse
> Of wemen, as thow hast seyd wikednesse?
> Was there no good matere in thy mynde,
> Ne in all thy bokes ne coudest thow nat fynde
> Som story of wernen that were goode and trewe? (268-72)

The narrator's mistake, according to Cupid, is in his ill-advised choice of bad "matere"; and the rectification of this mistake, Cupid advises, lies in the proper choice of stories of good, true women.[11] There is a long literary tradition, he claims, of just such stories of women true in love: "al the world of autours," including "Valerye, Titus[,] . . . Claudyan[,] . . . Jerome[,] . . . Ovyde[,] . . . Vincent" (280-310), write them. The fact that he can reasonably appeal to the notorious "Jerome" and "Valerye" here—they do contain images of women true in loving—is not merely "ironic"; it is a symptom of the antifeminism inherent in the act of totalizing, of the misogyny that closure enacts. The God of Love would turn away from the literature that threatens his order and embrace totality, would embrace the "world of autours' that celebrates a single, uncomplicated, unwavering image. He elides the "draf," the bad woman, and advances an ideal that immobilizes woman, effectively kills her off. And further, he makes that immobility her choice. As he tells the narrator,

> For to hyre love were they so trewe
> That, rathere than they wolde take a newe,
> They chose to be ded in sondry wyse,
> And deiden, as the story wol devyse. (288-91)

Shaking with masculine ire, Cupid claims that the narrator will repent the errors of his ways. At this moment Alceste intervenes—Alceste, who has been cited in desperation—by Troilus as an exemplary true woman, Alceste, who is extolled by the narrator in this Prologue as "calandier" of "goodnesse . . . and . . . wifhod" (533-35). She urges the god to allow the narrator a chance to reply to these accusations, insisting that a good ruler should not be an overbearing 'tyraunt" (357). In her insistence that both sides of the story be heard and in her advancing *various* hypotheses or possible answers to the god's objections, she may be said to be responding *not* like a man; and because she does this while interceding between two men at odds with one another—that is, she is at this moment in the paradigmatic position of woman in patriarchal social structure—we might suggest that this response is a response not just *like* but *as* a woman.

But the penance she orders the narrator to perform is in fact an entirely totalizing literary activity. She orders him to compose a series of legends that repeatedly represent women as nothing but steadfast in love and that consequently must represent men as fickle and faithless.

> Thow shalt, whil that thow livest, yer by yere,
> The moste partye of thy tyme spende
> In makynge of a gloryous legende
> Of goode women, maydenes and wyves,
> That were trewe in lovynge al here lyves;
> And telle of false men that hem betrayen,
> That al here lyf ne don nat but assayen
> How manye wemen they may don a shame;
> For in youre world that is now holden game. (471-79)

The legends in *Legend of Good Women,* as we have them in all their flatness and reductiveness, are indeed what Alceste ordered: "trewe" women, "false" men, and a "game" played over and over in which women are the inevitable losers. Compelled to right the balance of misogynist literary tradition, she commissions a very long work dedicated only to positive images of women; but her plan ensures a work peopled by caricatures. Her totalizing vision severely limits the feminine—the female character, the letter itself—and in so doing it finally and necessarily constrains the masculine—the male character, the moral spirit of these fables—as well.

The figure of Alceste seems itself a concentrated locus of the narrator's conflicting impulses. She is beautiful, full of grace, virtue, wisdom. But perhaps there's something slightly unsettling about this female, too. Her critical reputation might itself serve as a testament to a certain ambivalence in her representation. A long series of critics has seen Alceste as an unspotted, ideal lady whose poetic valence includes daisies, the Virgin Mary, the sun, the transcendent powers of the imagination, effective metaphoric language. Others, though, have pointed to inconsistencies in her representation that make her laughable, the butt of satire, or have characterized her behavior as aggressive and peremptory.[12] The narrator's representation of her is indeed double. He praises her in ways that recall the Blessed Virgin (wearing a crown of pearls, she acts as an intercessor for the poet). In her going down to Hell in an act of self-sacrifice, and in her association with the sun and resurrection, she is associated, further, with Christ himself. Moreover, she's wise: she instructs the God of Love in the duties and the merciful spirit of an earthly governor. She is acquainted with the narrator's whole oeuvre, from his earliest productions ("Orygenes upon the Maudeleyne") to his latest works, including even obscure and ephemeral ones: she recalls "al the love of Palamon and Arcite / Of Thebes, thogh the storye is knowen lite; / And many an ympne for your halydayes, / That highten balades, roundeles, vyrelayes" (408-11). And she knows enough about the circumstances of courtly literary production to attempt a defense of him—enough, perhaps, even to make a little fun of him: in addition to the above virtues, perhaps she even has a sense of humor. In her lighthearted intercession, she is responding as a woman, breaking up, dispersing the lugubrious seriousness of masculine conflict and desire for closure.

But if she's not "slydynge of corage," she is nonetheless physically shifting and changeable, having been metamorphosed into flower and star. (Chaucer in fact created these myths of metamorphosis and stellification for her.) She knows *all* of the narrator's works, major and minor—more, perhaps, than are even in his own "remembraunce" (as Chaucer will express it later in the Retractions)—and she abruptly ends his self-defense (his "arguynge") even after she has pointedly instructed the God of Love to hear whether he can "replye / Ageyns these poynts" (319-20). One critic has shuddered at this "fierc[e] rebuk[e],"[13] The narrator himself praises her mercy, praises her generosity in imposing a light penance; but he does in fact have this disturbing female under control. In his dream he both represents the independent, forceful woman, so troubling in *Troilus and Criseyde*, and neutralizes her power. He has Alceste ask for simplistic stories of women constantly duped and betrayed. The narrator gets what he wants—a long series of passive women—and adds credibility to it by having a *woman* ask for it. In this masculine fantasy, woman herself authorizes the antifeminist work.[14] But antifeminism is not, finally, man's best friend: a totalizing vision such as Alceste's not only silences women and constrains the letter but makes every man in the text unspeakable and, at last, unspeaking.

2

Alceste orders the narrator to spend most of the rest of his life making a "gloryous legende / Of goode women, maydenes and wyves" (473-74). The penitential writing of such a "legende" is, as we've seen, exactly suited to the narrator's masculine desire. Fed up with the feminine in *Troilus and Criseyde*, wanting unproblematic tales and subdued, predictable female characters, he again takes up with an alien woman; but this time he shaves her head, pares her nails, strips off her garments of captivity. He edits his pagan tales—tales of "hethene" women, as Cupid says (299)—to conform to a single, closed, secure, and comforting narrative model. He pares down the tales so drastically, refusing to be engaged by the narratives, that no possible textual seduction can take place. And it is the form of hagiographic narrative, the saint's life, that allows the narrator to manipulate the feminine letter of the classical text and to enervate traditionally aggressive, passionate, even dangerous female characters like Cleopatra, Medea, Philomela, and Procne, and, equally unnerving, women capable of independent moral judgment and action, women like Lucrece, Hypsipyle, and Hypermnestra.

Let us consider the form of the saint's life for a moment, to see how it provides the narrator with so precise a narrative tool for control of the feminine. The similarity among saints' lives that so strikes modern readers is in fact a defining feature of the form.[15] Saints' lives not only *seem* all the same to readers, they very frequently *are* the same: the *Life of Saint Hubert*, the *Life of Saint Arnold of Metz*, and the *Life of Saint Lambert*, for example, contain several parts in common;

and the Life of *Saint Remaclus* is entirely an imitation of the *Life of Saint Lambert*.[16] A life is written to witness the sanctitude of its subject, and, to that end, particular details of everyday life are often pared out; hagiographic conventions and topoi are invoked; and heavy, often verbatim borrowing from other written lives is routine. Hagiographers considered it perfectly credible to attribute the same miracles to saints in entirely different centuries. A pattern with its themes and motifs is clearly followed in the process of saintly "mythmaking," as Weinstein and Bell put it.[17] The fact that individual saints' lives do differ in purpose from one another, having been written in various forms and for various audiences, should not obscure the theory of the genre: it is *based on* a principle of imitation.[18] Agnellus of Ravenna explains his practice of composing the history of the bishops of Ravenna, by remarking that when he could not find material about particular bishops, he *made up* lives for them, on the principle that all things are common in the communion of saints.

> Wherever I found material they [the brothers of the see] were sure about, I have presented it to you; and anything I have heard from the elderly graybeards, I have not withheld from you. Where I could not uncover a story or determine what kind of a life they led, either from the most aged or from inscriptions or from any other source, to avoid a blank space in my list of holy pontiffs in proper order according to their ordination to the see one after another, I have, with the assistance of God through your prayers, made up a life for them. And I believe no deception is involved, for they were chaste and almsgiving preachers and procurers of men's souls for God.[19]

This is an echo of Gregory of Tours' oft-cited conclusion that

> it is better to talk about the *life* of the fathers than the *lives*, because, though there may be some difference in their merits and virtues, yet the life of one body nourished them all in the world. (My emphasis)[20]

Differences in "merits and virtues" are minimized; references to particular times, dates, and places are systematically eliminated (as in Bede's *Life of Saint Cuthbert*); the conventional "One Life" of the saint emerges as definitive.

In the history of the legend of Saint Marciana we can in fact observe the emergence of just such a conventional hagiographic narrative. In a telling retelling of the *Acta* of the martyr, the author of a hymn in her honor turns a detail in the spare prose narrative into a wondrous sign of sanctitude. According to the prose *Acta*, a lion was released into in amphitheater in order to devour the Christian maiden (during the persecution of Diocletian and his successors), but after smelling her, did her no harm: "Martyris corpus odoratus eam ultra non contigit" ("Having smelled the body of the martyr, he bothered her no further"). The later author of the hymn undertakes to explain why the lion didn't harm her: exploiting, perhaps, the phonological similarity between *odoratus* and *adoratus*, he proclaims:

> Leo percurrit percitus
> Adoraturus veniens
> Non comesturus virginem.[21]

In the latter version the saint's body *odor* has thus been interpreted as miraculous and becomes the cause of a leonine act of *ador*ation—a convention in hagiographic narrative.

The Christian saint's life, of course, demands the recognition of the *constitutive* imperfection—the all-too-human odors—of the body. "When I am weak, then I am strong": Saint Antony's asceticism recognizes his own imperfection and leads him, paradoxically, to perfection.[22] On the level of narrative form, however, paradox or contradiction do not enter in. The soothing regularity and repetition of the canonical saints' lives is intended to bring about in the reader a recognition of—even a participation in—the unified community of the blessed.[23]

But the narrator of the *Legend of Good Women* uses the form defensively. To protect himself from complications—from the dissatisfactions of involvement with the feminine—he reduces or omits entirely details that would distress or vex his working definition of the "good woman." Having been seduced by the unfaithful, ultimately unfruitful feminine in *Troilus and Criseyde*, the narrator uses the form of hagiographic narrative like "niter" on the alien woman's body that Jerome speaks of (in letter 66), to eliminate any disturbing odors in the lives of his heroines—to eliminate anything in the narratives of these women that threatens to upset or undermine patriarchal order. But he so severely reduces the letter that he does not produce a text that invites the mimetic participation of the reader. Indeed, his strategy for controlling his material, as he cuts and pares and scrubs, is to make it downright boring.

3

Passive women, weak martyrs of love, thus populate the *Legend*, and we witness in these tales not only the suppression of female characters in the making of individual narratives but the appropriative, and exclusionary processes of masculine literary tradition in its entirety. John Fyler and Elaine Hansen, in their excellent discussions, demonstrate the narrator's individual choices in detail: Cleopatra's infidelities, for example, are glossed over; Medea's grisly revenge is only vaguely mentioned; Phyllis' angry words of recrimination are softened.[24] Virtuous acts, strong expressions of will, are omitted as well: Dido's vow to be true to Sichaeus is not mentioned; Hypsipyle's helping her father escape the murderous Lemnian women is elided; and the uniqueness of Hypermnestra's refusal to murder her husband is not evident in the narrator's redaction. As the heroines lose their individuality in the series of legends, they come to seem increasingly passive, until we reach the final image in the series: Hypermnestra, in flight from her father, finally just *sits down* in abandonment and defeat (2720-22). Expressions of violence, recrimination, and revenge are softened or, more often, elided altogether; the ugly fates of many of the women are mollified; the violent rupture of death, the sudden shock of metamorphosis are lessened as Philomela and Procne are simply left sobbing in each other's arms, Hypsipyle pines away for Jason and finally expires, Medea merely fades from the picture.

These enervated, passive heroines, put into unfamiliar situations and strange places by men, don't have even basic motor control of their own bodies: they quake, shake, tremble for dread. Philomela "quok for fere, pale and pitously" (2317); Hypermnestra "quok as doth the lef of aspe grene. / Ded wex hire hew . . . / dredfully she quaketh" (2648-49, 2680). The narrator's version of the *Legend of Lucrece* indeed exaggerates her physical loss of control: it is the one of the few redactions in which she actually loses consciousness.[25] About to be raped by Tarquin, she

> loste bothe at ones wit and breth,
> And in a swogh she lay, and wex so ded

Men myghte smyten of hire arm or hed. (1815-17)

Men literally do divide up women's bodies and separate their bodies
from their spirits: Philomela's tongue, for example, is carved out of her
mouth. The narrator revises a passage from Ovid's treatment of
Hypermnestra to emphasize her dissociation from her own body:
Hypermnestra looks at her hands, which are forced by her father to
carry a knife, and remarks on their incongruity with the rest of her
being:

> Allas! and shal myne hondes blody be?
> I am a mayde, and, as by my nature,
> And bi my semblaunt and by my vesture,
> Myne handes ben nat shapen for a knyf. (2689-92.)

The narrator, similarly, picks up and expresses Ovid's sense of the
violated Lucrece as separated from herself: Lucrece, whose
"contenaunce is to hire herte dygne, / For they acorde bothe in dede and
sygne" (1738-39), is deprived by rape of that pure accord of body and
heart; her "herte" is still "so wyfly and so trewe" (1843), but her bodily
appearance is deathly (1829-34). Indeed, it is only in death that she is
able to try to regain that accord:

> And as she fel adoun, she kaste hir lok,
> And of hir clothes yet she hede tok.
> For in hir fallynge yet she had a care,
> Lest that hir fet or suche thyng lay bare;
> So wel she loved clennesse and eke trouthe. (1856-60)

In the death of the female body, in its un-quickening, the narrator
allows the woman to be significant, to signify. Good women gain their
identity—become significant—only by dying; as the God of Love says,
good women *are* good women because they "chose to be ded in sondry
wyse" (290). In killing herself—an act regarded by Augustine[26] as in
fact the sin of murder—the good woman takes her only strong action,
constitutes herself. Thisbe, in her final words, explicitly offers her dead
body as sign of woman's "trouthe":

> "But God forbede but a woman can
> Ben as trewe in lovynge as a man!
> And for my part, I shal anon it kythe."
> And with that word his swerd she tok as swythe,
> That warm was of hire loves blod, and hot,
> And to the herte she hireselven smot. (910-15)

Hypsipyle keeps herself chaste and joyless, and finally dies for love of
the absent Jason, "as for his wif" (1577): she dies because, to be his
good wife, she must. Phyllis tells Demophon that soon he will be able
to see her floating in Athens' harbor, her body the ironic image of his
own stony hardness:

> My body mote ye se withinne a while,
> Ryght in the haven of Athenes fletynge,
> Withoute sepulture and buryinge,
> Thogh ye ben harder than is any ston. (2551-54)

Lucrece, laid out on her bier, offers a publicly legible sign, in death, of
woman's "trouthe": Brutus

> openly let cary her on a bere
> Thurgh al the toun, that men may see and here
> The horryble dede of hir oppressyoun. (1866-68)

It is, of course, an index of the patriarchal context of this text that the
self-defining or self-signifying act—the only strong act of the
heroines—is a sin, and is, furthermore, both overdetermined by men's
actions and completely self-destructive, "The death of a beautiful
woman is, unquestionably, the most poetical topic in the world,"
according to Edgar Allan Poe in *The Philosophy of Composition*, and to
the narrator of the *Legend of Good Women* before him.[27] Criseyde's
"corage" may threateningly "slyde," but the narrator fixes Lucrece
firmly to her bier.

Even as Lucrece's body makes it known, Brutus openly tells her
tale to the town of Rome. The female body as sign of "trouthe" is still
supplemented, explained by a man, and it is perhaps this condition that
allows Lucrece in particular to be canonized ("she was holden there / A

seynt" [1870-71]). The idea of masculine appropriation of feminine story, or feminine wit and knowledge, comes up also in the legend of Medea, wherein Jason is "taught" by Medea how to win the fleece; he "gat hym a name ryght as a conqueror, / Ryght thourgh the sleyghte of hire enchauntement" (1649-50). Medea's magic arts may have been suspect as wisdom or truth, but they win Jason glory. Similarly, Phaedra, in the *Legend of Ariadne*, solves the puzzle of the labyrinth for Theseus. As the series of legends goes on, as the heroines get more passive and the narrator more restive, masculine appropriation of the feminine becomes more obvious, and processes of masculine literary tradition become more and more explicit. I want to focus now on the last four tales in the series of legends to see how they in fact reveal the workings of patriarchal literary history.

Such workings are delineated precisely in the *Legend of Ariadne*. Feminine knowledge, truth, wisdom are represented by the "clewe of twyn" Ariadne (prompted by Phaedra) gives to Theseus as a solution to the problem of the labyrinth. For this solution, Theseus promises that he, will not "twynne" from her (2029-40). But he does, of course, and the *Legend of Ariadne* is yet another demonstration of masculine perfidy, made worse perhaps than others in the series because Theseus will father the faithless Demophon, "wiked fruit . . . of a wiked tre" (2395). But *Ariadne* is not only a paradigmatic legend of betrayed love; its central image, the labyrinth, is one associated by Chaucer and other medieval readers and writers with texts, and, I shall argue, with the female body. The *Legend of Ariadne* offers an image of gendered reading as well as of betrayed love.

A labyrinth was known in the Middle Ages as both a literal and a figurative maze. Isidore enumerates and describes the four classical labyrinths in his *Etymologies*, as do writers through the medieval period. Boethius exploits the figurative meaning: in Chaucer's translation, the prisoner addresses Lady Philosophy:

> "Scornestow me," quod I, "or elles, pleyestow or disseyvistow me, that hast so woven me with thi resouns the hous of Didalus, so entrelaced that it is unable to ben unlaced, thow that otherwhile entrist ther thow issist, and other while issist ther thow entrest?" (Bk. 3, pr. 12)

A labyrinth is an argument wherein one can get lost; in Trevisa's translation of Higden's *Polychronicon* it is the complex "matir" of the book; it is also the name of the mark made by a perplexed reader in the margin of a difficult text.[28] Chaucer himself makes the connection of labyrinth and text specific and constitutive in *House of Fame*: the narrator comments that the House of Rumour, where all literature originates, is even more intricately—"queyntelych"—wrought than is Daedalus' labyrinth (1918-23).[29]

That charged word, "queynte," reappears in *Ariadne* in Phaedra's description of the labyrinth:

> And for the hous is krynkeled to and fro,
> And hath so queynte weyes for to go—
> For it is shapen as the mase is wrought—
> Therto have I a remedye in my thought. (2012-15)

Sheila Delany has recently drawn attention to the obscene punning that pervades the *Legend of Good Women*, citing as one loaded locus Phaedra's long speech here ("Lat us wel taste hym at his herte-rote, / That if so be that he a wepen have / . . . / And we shul make hym balles ek also" [1993-94, 2003)[30] The references to male sex organs are obvious; but I suggest that there is, in addition, in this legend a specific association of the labyrinth with female sexuality and the female body. This association (which Delany observes in passing) is dependent not only on the remark that Theseus will have room in the labyrinth 'to welde an ax, or swerd, or staf, or knyf' (2000), this line running through the repertoire of euphemisms for penis. The description of the labyrinth, with its "krynkeled" walls (in Trevisa's translation of the *Polychronicon* it is "wrynkyngliche i-wroght")[31] housing a "monstre" (1991), a "fend" (1996), accords with the strident vocabulary of antifeminist literature's descriptions of women. To cite one example among many, Walter Map ("Valerius") tells "Rufinus" (in *De nugis curialium* 4.3) that woman is a monster, polluted and stinking.[32] The association of woman with the "fend" is well known and deployed, as we shall see, by Chaucer's Man of Law. Images of monstrous females—wrinkled, reeking, sagging, dripping—populate Le Jaloux's tirade in the *Roman de la rose*. Further on, sexual intercourse in the *Rose* is associated with seductive bypaths ("queynte weyes" of the labyrinth), turnings and twistings of the straight way. And such turnings and twistings are identified as "il laberinto d'Amore" in Boccaccio's late dream vision, *Il Corbaccio*, a treatise that seethes with images of monstrous females.[33]

Woman has the "clewe" to the labyrinth; she knows the secrets not only of her own body (which knowledge is a source of fury and suspicion to Le Jaloux) but also of the labyrinth that is a text. Woman's body is associated with the truth of the text here—an association also suggested by the image of the allegorical text as veiled female body in Macrobius, Jerome, Richard of Bury. But as is also suggested by that image—as I discussed it in the Introduction—*femina* is assimilated to the superfluous surface as well; and here, as labyrinth, she is something to be *passed through*. It is thus no coincidence that in the *Legend of Ariadne* her "remedye" becomes "*His* wepne, *his* clewe, *his* thyng" (2140), where "wepne" and "thyng" are established euphemisms for the penis and, between them, as Delany also suggests, "clewe" becomes one, too. The hermeneutic value of *femina* thus shifts from truth—from spirit—to carnal letter; the spirit of the text assumes a concomitant masculine value.

The "clywe of twyn," then, passes into masculine hands. Theseus, in return, promises never to "twynne" from Ariadne. "Twynnen" here means "to divide, to separate," but the Middle English verb can also mean "to multiply by two." "Twinning" is in fact an important function in *Ariadne* and in the patriarchal tradition that is demonstrated on a small scale by the *Legend of Good Women*. Multiplication occurs as good women are multiplied into what appears to be a potentially endless series (note that even within *Ariadne*, Nisus' daughter is made into another good woman, despite her treachery to father and country;[34] Phaedra's role is also enlarged from the sources). But division seems to be the dominant function. Women are divided from their men (Theseus does, after all, "twynne" from Ariadne, as do all the rest of the men from their women), and women are divided from one another as well: Theseus runs off with Ariadne's sister; Tereus, in another legend, imprisons Philomela, Procne's sister. This separation of women from women is necessary to the perpetuation of a misogynist literary tradition, and it is what Criseyde implicitly understands as the inevitable result of women's reading authoritative "bokes." Although there is filiation ("twyn") among the men in the *Legend of Good*

Women—Tarquin and Tarquin, Jr.; Theseus and Demophon; Danao and Lyno—there is and must be no society of women in which women can teach one another.[35] Sisters are divided up, and any communication of ethics or mores is cut off by the narrator: Dido complains to "hire syster Anne," but the narrator, in a hurry to finish up the tale, hastily excuses himself, "I may nat wryte, / So gret a routhe I have it for t'endite" (1344-45). No wonder women in the *Legend of Good Women* are not trainable: the narrator may chide "sely wemen, ful of innocence" for their credulity ("Have ye swych routhe upon hyre feyned wo, / And han swich olde ensaumples yow beforn? / Se ye nat alle how they ben forsworn?" [1257-59]),but lack of their own tradition prevents women in the legends from seeing and learning. Divided from men, divided from women, divided from themselves (as the examples of Hypermnestra and Lucrece have shown), they can only try to regain themselves, paradoxically, in death or metamorphosis.

"Twyn" becomes "twynne"; Ariadne's "thred" (2018) becomes, in the next legend, Philomela's "cloth." The *Legend of Ariadne* parabolically articulates principles of a male-centered tradition as it shows the appropriation of the truth of the text and demonstrates the necessary separation of women from each other. The *Legend of Philomela* elaborates on these patriarchal literary techniques. Philomela is a prime example of a woman denied the "proper" means of making meaning, signifying: Ariadne wanders around the island, able only to produce an echo from the hollow rocks, but Philomela's very *glossa* is removed by Tereus. To make this woman's limitations in the signifying project of literary tradition even more obvious, the narrator specifies that "She coude eek rede and wel ynow endyte, / but with a *penne* coude she nat wryte" (2356-57; my emphasis). She can, however, weave letters, and she creates a *textus* whose motive and theme are the violation and silencing of a woman.[36] This is a story that doesn't get told by the tongue or pen; it is the story of the origin of the narrative tradition of which the *Legend of Good Women* is an exemplar. To know narrative origins is, as we've seen in the case of Criseyde at the beginning of book 2, denied the female because such knowledge is potentially disruptive of linear masculine order; in the *Legend of Philomela* the silenced woman's story remains between the two sisters, in prison, weeping in each other's arms.

We might pause for a moment here to recall that the Philomela legend figures in *Troilus and Criseyde* at several critical moments. At the beginning of book 2, at the moment when the love affair of Troilus and Criseyde is about to begin, the narrator alludes to the tale, Pandarus, having tossed and turned all night in the throes of unrequited love,[37] is roused by the song of a swallow:

> The swalowe Proigne, with a sorowful lay,
> Whan morwen com, gan make hire waymentynge
> Whi she forshapen was; and ever lay
> Pandare abedde, half in a slomberynge,
> Til she so neigh hym made hire cheterynge
> How Tereus gan forth hire suster take,
> That with the noyse of hire he gan awake. (2.64-70)

Awakened by the story of Tereus' rape of Philomela, Pandarus gets up and dressed, "Remembryng hym his erand was to doone / From Troilus, and ek his grete emprise" (72-73). In this narrative whose background is a war begun with a rape, Procne, the betrayed sister, sings a "lay" of rape that reminds Pandarus to begin the wooing of Criseyde. Pandarus, as we have seen in the previous chapter, is a character who understands most thoroughly the patriarchal necessity of the exchange of women—in Troy as in every patriarchal society—of which rape is but the most violent acting-out.[38]

The story of Philomela in fact haunts *Troilus and Criseyde:* after she has heard Pandarus' profession of Troilus' love and has heard Antigone's song of love, Criseyde is lulled to sleep by a bird's song:

> A nyghtyngale, upon a cedre grene,
> Under the chambre wal ther as she ley,
> Ful loude song ayein the moone shene,
> Peraunter in his briddes wise a lay
> Of love, that made hire herte fressh and gay. (2.918-22)

Criseyde falls asleep, only to dream that an eagle violently (though without pain to her) rips open her breast and exchanges her heart for his. When, in book 3, she herself "Opned hire herte" to Troilus, she is likened to a "newe abaysed nyghtyngale" (3.1233-39).

The story of Philomela is thus deeply implicated in the motive of this narrative: it appears, but only indirectly, at crucial moments of the affair's inception and consummation.[39] The wooing and winning of Criseyde is not a rape in any simple sense; Criseyde does not consistently resist, emotionally or physically, the development of the affair. She finally states the fact of her complicity baldly when Troilus orders her to yield: 'Ne hadde I er now, my swete herte deere, / Ben yold, ywis, I were now nought heere!" (3.1210-11). But on another level, there's a rape going on: it's a figurative violation of Criseyde by literary tradition—a future violation, of which she herself is aware when, in book 5, she bewails her future literary reputation. Tradition will record *only* her infidelity. And if the exchange of women, always potentially a rape because it proceeds regardless of women's independent desires, structures the workings of Troy, as we've seen, it also describes the workings of literary history as they are alluded to at the end of *Troilus and Criseyde*: the feminine body of the text, enjoined to "kis the steppes" of the great male *auctores*, can itself be violated in the process of scribal transmission (5.1786-98). The careless scribe is, we recall in "Adam Scriveyn," blamed for his "rape" (7).

Some alternative to such a tradition of patriarchal literary history and representation is explicitly wished for in the *Legend of Phyllis*, following Philomela. *Phyllis* is, in plot outline, one of the sparest of the lot: Demophon arrives, weak and weary, on Phyllis' island; she nurses and weds him; he leaves and doesn't come back. Phyllis laments her loss, laments her beguilement ("How coude ye wepe so by craft?" she writes the absent Demophon, and prays to God that Demophon get no more glory than that of having betrayed a "sely mayde":

> And whan thyne olde auncestres peynted be,
> In which men may here worthynesse se,
> Thanne preye I God thow peynted be also
> That folk may rede forby as they go,
> "Lo! this is he, that with his flaterye
> Bytraised hath and don hire vilenye
> That was his trowe love in thought and deed!" (2536-42)

In such a depiction, she continues, the viewer would be able to discern Demophon's relation to Theseus, "For he begiled Adriane, ywis, / With swich an art and with swich subtilte / As thow thyselven hast begyled me" (2545-47). What Phyllis prays for here resembles the revision of patriarchal tradition the Wife of Bath calls out for, a reversal revealing *men's* "wikkednesse" and "vilenye":

> By God, if wommen hadde writen stories,
> As clerkes han withinne hire oratories,
> They wolde han writen of men moore wikkednesse
> Than al the mark of Adam may redresse. (3:693-96)

But women *didn't* write the "stories," and the narrator of the *Legend of Good Women* will report only what he considers well put by Phyllis in her letter to her false lover: "Here and ther in rym I have it layd, / There as me thoughte that she wel hath sayd" (2516-17). Both Phyllis' prayer and the Wife's exclamation remain in the conditional; the only means of Phyllis' entering into patriarchal signifying activity —let alone changing it—is through death: she warns Demophon that she will make of her dead body a sign of her "trouthe" to him (2551-53). Phyllis does kill herself, at last, but not by drowning; instead, a "corde" (like "twyn") cuts off her breath, stopping her *glossa* forever.

What follows *Phyllis* is in effect a tale that is not told. The *Legend of Hypermnestra* is not finished, but it is not simply because of its lack of explicit "conclusioun" (2723) that there is a story left untold. The tale of Hypermnestra and her no-good husband follows the profile of all the legends, and its unspoken conclusion need hardly be drawn for the reader to be able to formulate it. But the tale of Hypermnestra and her *father* remains unexplored, a tale of "abhomynacion" (to use the Man of Law's term) unspoken. Hypermnestra's victimization is double, but the narrator's narrative model doesn't allow him to acknowledge that, as Anne Middleton puts it, "incestuous rape, threatened if not performed, activates the plot,"[40] Patriarchal ideology, the mechanism by which he manipulates his narratives, will not allow the explicit recognition of father-daughter incest, for incest, as we shall see in detail in the *Man of law's Tale*, violates patriarchy's necessary structure of the circulation—the exchange—of women between men. But incest is certainly implicit here: Hypermnestra's father, on her wedding night, summons her, looking on her with "glad chere" and telling her, "So nygh myn herte nevere thyng ne com / As thow, myn Ypermystre,

doughter dere" (2631-32). He orders her to obey his will, then whips
out his "knyf, as rasour kene"—we recall all the euphemisms for
Theseus' "wepen"—to force her to kill her new husband, whom her
father has dreamt will be his "bane." Hypermnestra disobeys her father
by warning her husband and trying to escape with him, but Lyno, in a
hurry, leaves her in the dust to be caught and incarcerated. At this point
the narrator breaks off the legend. Hypermnestra's victimization is in
fact not double—by father and husband—but triple: having become
bored with her, the narrator cuts off her story.

Terminally bored, the narrator finally quits. He is bored not just
with the tale of Hypermnestra but with the whole series of legends of
good women and false men. His weariness grows from legend to
legend: he has registered masculine perfidy over and over. As he begins
the tale of Tereus' outrage, for example, he plans "But shortly of this
story for to passe, / For I am wery of hym for to telle" (2257-58). It's
the same old story; there is little need to go into detail about
Demophon, for another example, because the narrator has already in
effect told the tale while speaking of Theseus:

> Me lyste nat vouche-sauf on hym to swynke,
> Ne spende on hym a penne ful of ynke,
> For fals in love was he, ryght as his syre. (2490-92)

The tale of the betrayed is, similarly, always the same: the narrator has
told it again and again, and by the time he gets to Phyllis the
redundancy is almost overwhelming:

> But, for I am agroted herebyforn
> To wryte of hem that ben in love forsworn,
> And ek to haste me in my legende,
> (Which to perform God me grace sende)
> Therfore I passe shortly in this wyse. (2454-58)

The women's words, in their letters to their false men, are always the
same, and the narrator hints that they are not very interesting to begin
with. I have already mentioned the narrator's editing Phyllis' letter,
with his indirect suggestion that the whole is tedious stuff:

Hire letter was ryght long and therto large.
But here and ther in rym I have it layd,
There as me thoughte that she wel hath sayd.   (2515-17)

The other letters—by Dido, Hypsipyle, Medea, Ariadne—are
mentioned only to be omitted: "It is so long, it were an hevy thyng" to
report it (2219); it is "to longe to wryten and to sen" (1565); "as now to
long for me to wryte" (1679); "Rede Ovyde, and in hym he shal it
fynde" (1367).[41]

The narrator's weariness with the fables links him in fact to the
betrayers who tire of and leave their women. The narrator has, of
course, enlisted the trust of amorous ladies in his audience by alleging
his faithfulness in love: "trusteth, as in love, no man but me" (2561).[42]
Aeneas, in contrast, departs because he has wearied of Dido:

This Eneas, that hath so depe yswore,
Is wery of his craft withinne a throwe;
The hote ernest is al overblowe.   (1285-87)

Demophon, second-generation womanizer, arrives in Phyllis' land,
tellingly "Wayk, and ek wery, and his folk forpyned / Of werynesse"
(2427-29). Jason and his men, similarly, arrive at Lemnon, Hypsipyle's
land, ready to "pleye" because they are "wery" of the sea-voyage
(1492-96). Theseus even feigns weariness for his own erotic purposes:
sailing from Crete with Ariadne and Phaedra, he stops along the way on
an island, saying "that on the lond he moste hym reste" (2168). Ariadne
falls asleep, with true "werynesse atake" (2182); Theseus'
"werynesse," however, proves to have been a mere convenience: he
energetically sails away with Phaedra while Ariadne slumbers. But as
inevitably as do the lovers, the narrator wearies of his "craft": they
abruptly leave their women, with little or no explanation, moving on to
the next victim (Jason, for example, moves on to "yit the thridde wif
anon" [1660]); the narrator passes "shortly" on to the next story,
protesting that the rest is "to long" (1679), or is "no charge for to telle"
(2383).

Stripped, clipped, and scrubbed, his pagan source texts are like
female bodies in narrator's masculine hands. As he promised, he indeed
delivers the "naked text" (86) of the legends. His *translatio* this time is

not the record of his seduction but is, rather, a record of his continual exercise of control over the feminine. He domesticates the alien woman—marries her, settles her down in his household; he produces a dull text and wearies of it. His weariness, unlike Ariadne's exhaustion, is powerful: it is a specifically masculine defense against the feminine.[43] The narrator's excising of the women's acts of honor and virtue, or recrimination and revenge—his rendering of all the fables as "the same old story"—constitutes this masculine narrative strategy of weariness: he makes his heroines and the fables boring because they would otherwise terrify. Philomela and Procne dully and passively dissolve in tears; better narrate this than recount the horrifying Bacchanalian revels, the killing and cooking of Itys, the thrusting of the son's bloody head in Tereus' face, the disorienting shock of metamorphosis. This is, again, an ideological strategy designed to provide comfort and rest, functioning the same way we have seen the Epilogue to *Troilus and Criseyde* functioning. There *is* something soothing and reassuring about the repetition of a single narrative pattern over and over, as the example of saints' lives demonstrates; but here, the specifically gendered defensive function of that reassurance and security is apparent in the masculine associations of the totalizing gesture. Woman's story—the letter—becomes dull, a formula. The female character is reduced to a never-varying caricature.

As is the male character. The men of the *Legend of Good Women* are as undifferentiated and unsavory in their villainy as the women are in their victimization. Men are, of course, the motivating agents of the narratives: every legend, with the exception of the *Legend of Thisbe*, as Peter L. Allen observes, begins with the introduction of a male character, usually with a vehement excoriation of his vile nature and acts.[44] The narrator at points even admits that he talks about women so that he can talk about men: he tells the tale of Ariadne "for to clepe ageyn unto memorye / Of Theseus the grete untrouthe of love" (1889-90), and, similarly, brings up Phyllis "for this ende . . . / To tellen yow of false Demophon" (2397-98). Simple statistics reveal the narrative dominance of men over women: men are named much more frequently than are women (for example, Jason is named thirty-five times, while Hypsipyle and Medea a total of seven times).[45] And the proportions of several of the legends betray the narrator's greater interest in sea battles (the *Legend of Cleopatra*) or the challenge of the Golden Fleece (the

Legend of Hypsipyle) than in his heroines. Even as these women die, violated, betrayed, and abandoned, their men characteristically skip out, as Allen also remarks, escaping without harm. It can't be denied that the motive power of this series is masculine.

But the male characters are unvarying, nothing but opportunistic scoundrels in love, and the "moralitee" of each fable is a truism. The, techniques of reading like a man—imposing a single pattern, insisting on reducing complexity to produce a whole, monolithic structure, thus constraining the feminine—are reductive of *all* human experience, just as we saw in *Troilus and Criseyde*. And although closure in the Epilogue to that poem proved satisfying to the narrator, in the *Legend of Good Women* reductiveness is, finally, shown to be profoundly narrow and unsatisfying. The narrator, defending himself against the mobile feminine, becomes himself bored, idle, torpid, *silent*. It's clear from the abandoned series of legends that reading like a man leads to no literary activity at all. If the Second Nun tells *her* legend of a saint—Cecilia—in order to stave off "ydelnesse"—purposeless talk or sterile silence—the narrator of the *Legend of Good Women* approaches, rather, the condition of the idle in the *Inferno*, who can't even speak whole words. You can't found a tradition on the constraining of the feminine, Chaucer suggests here, because it will eventually silence men, too. The Man of Law, who picks up directly where the narrator of *Hypermnestra* leaves off, finds plenty *not* to talk about.

NOTES

1. As E.T. Donaldson comments on Criseyde's literary history, "From Benoît de Sainte Maure, who invented her, up to Dryden, who destroyed her by making her faithful, the Cressid figure had only a single raison d'être, her infidelity" ("Cressid False, Criseyde Untrue: An Ambiguity Revisited," in *Poetic Traditions of the English Renaissance*, ed. Maynard Mack and George deForest Lord [New Haven, Conn.: Yale Univ. Press, 1982], p. 68). See also Gretchen Mieszkowski, "The Reputation of Criseyde, 1155-1500," *Transactions of the Connecticut Academy of Arts and Sciences* 43 (1971): 71-153.

2. For a discussion of male authorial apologies to female readers that cites the *Legend* in making this point, see Susan Schibanoff,

"Taking the Gold Out of Egypt: The Art of Reading as a Woman," in *Gender and Reading: Essays on Readers, Texts, and Contexts*, ed. Elizabeth A. Flynn and Patrocinio P. Schweickart (Baltimore: Johns Hopkins Univ. Press, 1986), pp. 83-106. Schibanoff analyzes the "immasculation" of woman's literary response, as I do here.

3. I wish to acknowledge a general indebtedness in my reading of the *Legend of Good Women* to Elaine Hansen, "Irony and the Antifeminist Narrator in Chaucer's *Legend of Good Women*," *JEGP* 82 (1983): 11-31, and John M. Fyler, "The *Legend of Good Women*: Palinode and Procrustean Bed," chapter 4 of his *Chaucer and Ovid* (New Haven, Conn.: Yale Univ. Press, 1979), pp. 96-123.

4. The F version (formerly called B) is found in Bodleian MS. Fairfax 16 and ten other manuscripts; the G version (formerly A) is extant in a single manuscript, Cambridge MS. Gg. 4.27. There has been considerable debate over the causes and chronology of the two versions, and the questions are still open; but critics generally agree these days that G is Chaucer's revision, made about eight years later, of the original F. If F dates from 1386-88, G dates subsequently from 1394-96—about the time, as Alfred David suggests, Chaucer must have been working on those other poems having to do with antifeminist thought, the Prologue to the *Wife of Bath's Tale* and the *Merchant's Tale*; see *The Strumpet Muse* (Bloomington: Indiana Univ. Press, 1976), p. 50.

5. See Eric Hicks, ed., *Le Débat sur "Le Roman de la rose"* (Paris: Champion, 1977) for the dossier of the *querelle*. John Fleming, "Hoccleve's 'Letter of Cupid' and the 'Quarrel' over the *Roman de la Rose*" (*Medium Aevum* 40 [1971]: 21-40), focuses on changing styles of reading the *Rose*; Christine de Pizan comes off rather badly in this analysis. It is interesting indeed to note Christine's totalizing, ideological techniques of reading as she argues against what she perceives as Jean de Meun's antifeminism: she alleges that Jean was simply untruthful in his excessive and impetuous defamation of women; even if some of these negative images were true, Christine goes on to say, they shouldn't be represented. The letter of the *Rose*, she argues, is not unambiguous, as it should be, and its female characters are not worthy of attention, let alone imitation. See Christine's letters to Jean de Montreuil (c. 1401) and Pierre Col (2 October 1402). In her revisionist feminist project, then, Christine would

nevertheless keep the dangerous feminine in line. This accords with the admixture of revisionist and conservative social vision in Christine's work, especially *Le Livre de la cité des dames*. For a discussion of that admixture, see Sheila Delany, "Rewriting Woman Good: Gender and the Anxiety of Influence in Two Late-Medieval Texts," in *Chaucer in the Eighties*, ed. Julian N. Wasserman and Robert J. Blanch (Syracuse, N.Y.: Syracuse Univ. Press, 1986), pp. 75-92.

6. See Lee W. Patterson, "Ambiguity and Interpretation: A Fifteenth-Century Reading of *Troilus and Criseyde*" (*Speculum* 54 [1979]: 297- 330), slightly revised as chapter 4 of *Negotiating the Past: The Historical Understanding of Medieval Literature* (Madison: Univ. of Wisconsin Press, 1987).

7. A passage in the early version of the Prologue to the *Legend* suggests that it was royally commissioned: Alceste instructs the narrator, "And whan this book ys maad, yive it the quene, / On my byhalf, at Eltham or at Sheene" (F: 496-97). The idea of a royal *command* seems to modern scholars to be a fiction, but it proved immediately useful and satisfying nonetheless: Lydgate mentions it in his notice of *Legend of Good Women* in the *Fall of Princes*: "This poete wrot, at request off the queen, / A legende off parfit hoolynesse, / Off Goode Women to fynde out nynteen / That dede excelle in bounte and fairnesse" *(Lydgate's Fall of Princes*, ed. Henry Bergen, EETS e.s. 121 [London: Oxford Univ. Press, 1924], 1.330-33). Discussions of the occasional nature of the poem dominated the scholarship in the late nineteenth century and early twentieth century; there seems to be a general sense these days that the poem did arise from some discussion at court. See Alfred David, "The Man of Law vs. Chaucer: A Case in Poetics" (*PMLA* 82 [1967]: 217-25), for the suggestion that the God of Love is "repeating objections to Chaucer's works made either seriously or in jest by members of his circle who thought that they knew best what he should write about" (p. 219). In the Prologue to the *Legend of Good Women*, according to David, "Chaucer is dramatizing the difficulties of a poet who writes for a small and opinionated audience" (p. 219). See also Robert B. Burlin, *Chaucerian Fiction* (Princeton, N.J.: Princeton Univ. Press, 1977), p. 34. As John M. Fyler comments in his *Chaucer and Ovid* (New Haven, Conn.: Yale Univ. Press, 1979), there is no way to know whether the *Legend of Good Women* resulted from adverse reaction to *Troilus and Criseyde*; he doesn't believe,

however, that Chaucer's "penance" can be regarded as at all serious (p. 97).

8. For such an analysis of the *Book of the Duchess*, see D.W. Robertson, Jr., and B.F. Huppé, *Fruyt and Chaf* (Princeton, N.J.: Princeton Univ. Press, 1963), ch. 2.

9. H. Marshall Leicester, Jr., in "Dreaming and Writing: Temporality and Narrative in the Prologue to the *Legend of Good Women*," a talk presented at the 1984 Modern Language Association convention, analyzed the implications of this uncomfortable setting in a reading of the Prologue that stressed its dark, menacing aspects.

10. John M. Fyler, *Chaucer and Ovid*, p. 120.

11. Cupid's basic literary abilities are routinely assailed by critics. I take his objections to the narrator's works seriously and see that he is, in a sense, a paradigmatic reader: he is not incapable, or simpleminded, but is a particularly, defensively totalizing reader, a masculine reader. For analyses of the God of Love that see him as simpleminded or frivolous, see David, "The Man of Law vs. Chaucer"; Lisa J. Kiser, *Telling Classical Tales* (Ithaca, N.Y.: Cornell Univ. Press, 1983), pp. 62-70; and Fyler, *Chaucer and Ovid*, pp. 96-123. It should be pointed out, however, that Cupid's taste for stories (his emphasis on plot, not style or treatment) does not alone brand him as a shallow or bad reader; it is shared by late-medieval writers in all genres, and his emphasis on the narrator's choice of material as the most important step in the process of writing reflects the traditional and rhetorical nature of medieval literary composition. See J.A. Burrow, *Ricardian Poetry: Chaucer, Gower, Langland, and the Gawain-Poet* (New Haven, Conn.. Yale Univ. Press, 1971), pp. 47-92; and Robert Worth Frank, *Chaucer and the "Legend of Good Women"* (Cambridge, Mass.: Harvard Univ. Press, 1972), pp. 30- 36, 185-87. J.L. Lowes, in "Chaucer and the *Ovide moralisé*" (*PMLA* 33 [1918]: 318), suggests that Chaucer takes over from the *Ovide moralisé* "details which enhance the vividness and clarify the motivation of the narrative" (speaking in particular of the *Legend of Philomela*).

It's also important to note that Cupid's specific objection to the *Rose*—that in it, of myne olde servauntes thow mysseyest,

. . . .

And lettest folk to han devocyoun
To serven me, and holdest it folye
To truste on me

(Prologue to the *Legend of Good Women*, G version, ll. 249-53)

—has been the thesis of a wide range of recent studies of the poem, from John V. Fleming's Robertsonian readings to Thomas D. Hill's discussion of the sterility of narcissistic courtly love. See, for example, Fleming's most recent book, *Reason and the Lover* (Princeton, N.J.: Princeton Univ. Press, 1984), as well as his earlier *Roman de la Rose: A Study in Allegory and Iconography* (Princeton, N.J.: Princeton Univ. Press, 1969); Hill, "Narcissus, Pygmalion, and the Castration of Saturn: Two Mythological Themes in the *Roman de la Rose,*" 71 (1974): 404-26; Daniel Poirion, *Le Roman de la rose* (Paris: Hatier, 1973); Paul Zumthor, "Récit et anti-récit: *Le Roman de la rose,*" in his *Langue, texte, énigme* (Paris: Seuil, 1975); and R. Howard Bloch, *Etymologies and Genealogies: A Literary Anthropology of the French Middle Ages* (Chicago: Univ. of Chicago Press, 1983), pp. 137-41.

12. For an analysis that suggests all of these positive values, see Kiser, *Telling Classical Tales*, the most recent of idealistic readings of Alceste. Burlin's *Chaucerian Fiction*, pp. 33-44, provides a complement. On the other side, H.C. Goddard, "Chaucer's *Legend of Good Women,*" (*JEGP* 7 [1908]: 87-129), reads Alceste as a comic figure, the butt of the poem's irony. Alfred David, in *The Strumpet Muse*, p. 46, recognizes both her ideal saintliness and her more aggressive actions but finds that the latter comfortingly humanizes the former. Delany ("Rewriting Woman Good," pp. 83-84) comments on Alceste as a "deeply ambiguous figure." A certain doubleness is suggested by Alceste's textual reputation itself: her powerful spiritual value in F is reduced considerably in G. See D. D. Griffith, "An Interpretation of Chaucer's *Legend of Good Women,*" in *The Manly Anniversary Studies in Language and Literature* (Chicago: Univ. of Chicago Press, 1923).

13. As A.C. Spearing has pointed out in his *Medieval Dream-Poetry* (Cambridge: Cambridge Univ. Press, 1976), Alceste's "abrupt

treatment" of the narrator here is similar to treatment of the narrator in Chaucer's earlier dream visions: he is "fiercely rebuked by the authoritative figure who confronts him" (p. 106).

14. Elaine Tuttle Hansen, in "Irony and the Antifeminist Narrator in Chaucer's *Legend of Good Women*" (*JEGP* 82 [1983]: 19), makes a related point in a different context, and quotes Eve Kosofsky Sedgwick on Dickens and Thackeray (from a paper read at the Mid-Atlantic Regional Meeting of the National Women's Studies Association, March 1980):

> "There is an unspoken rule of propaganda . . . that goes like this: whenever an ideological judgment against a woman is so crushingly cruel that even the institutions of the society cannot bring themselves to pronounce it—for instance, that a mother must give up her child, or that a wife must die to further her husband's moral growth—in those cases it is the woman herself who is forced to pronounce and justify the sentence."

15. Hippolyte Delehaye was the first to recognize and stress the conventionality of the form; see *Les Légendes hagiographiques*, 2d ed. (Brussels: Société des Bollandistes, 1906), and *Cinq leçons sur la méthode hagiographique* (Brussels: Société des Bollandistes, 1934). For an example of this conventionality, Charles W. Jones notes in his *Saints' Lives and Chronicles in Early England* (Ithaca, N.Y.: Cornell Univ. Press, 1947), p. 54, that Bede, in his *Life of Saint Cuthbert*, systematically eliminated all references to particular times, dates, and places. Donald Weinstein and Rudolph M. Bell, in *Saints and Society: The Two Worlds of Western Christendom, 1000-1700* (Chicago: Univ. of Chicago Press, 1982), provide a sociological analysis of this conventionality, well summarized in their quotation of the French sociologist Pierre Delooz:

> "The reputation of sanctity is the collective mental representation of someone as a saint, whether based on a knowledge of facts that have *really* happened, or whether based on facts that have been at least in part *constructed* if not entirely imagined. But in truth, all saints, more or less, appear to be constructed in the sense that being necessarily saints in consequence of a reputation created by others and a role that

others expect of them, they are remodelled to correspond to collective mental representations." (p. 9)

In regard to the conventionality of saints' lives, I have also benefitted from the studies by James W. Earl, "Typology and Iconographic Style in Early Medieval Hagiography," *Studies in the Literary Imagination*, 8 (1975): 15-46, and David L. Jeffrey, "English Saints' Plays," in *Medieval Drama*, ed. Neville Denny, Stratford-upon-Avon Studies 16 (London: Arnold Press, 1973), pp. 69-89.

16. Delehaye, *Les Légendes hagiographiques*, p. 115.

17. Weinstein and Bell, *Saints and Society*, p. 13.

18. Alexandra Hennessy Olsen, in "'De Historiis Sanctorum': A Generic Study of Hagiography" (*Genre* 13 [1980]: 407-29), defends the varieties within the genre against what she feels are reductionist readings of saints' lives. Her point is well taken, but there does exist a theory of imitation, abundantly enunciated in the documents, that is powerful in the Middle Ages. See Weinstein and Bell, *Saints and Society*, "Introduction: The Historian and the Hagiographer," for a discussion of the relation between two kinds of *vitae*, one which confines itself "to delineating the pattern of virtues" in order to demonstrate the saint's participation in the unified community of saints, and one which "departs from the routine pattern" and details the secular aspects of the saint's life (pp. 13-14). I am concerned with the first kind—what Weinstein and Bell call the "official" view—that clearly sets out a "routine pattern" or form, from which the second kind of *vita* is understood to deviate.

19. Et ubi inveni, quid illi certius fecerunt, vestris aspectibus allata sunt, et quod per seniores et longaevos audivi, vestris oculis non defraudavi; et ubi istoriam non inveni, aut qualiter eorum vita fuisset, nec per annosos et vetustos homines, neque per haedificationem, neque per quamlibet auctoritatem, ne intervallum sanctorum pontificum fieret, secundum ordinem, quomodo unus post alium hanc sedem optinuerunt, vestris orationibus me Deo adiuvante, illorum vitam composui, et credo non mentitum esse, quia et hortatores fuerunt castique et elemosinarii et Deo animas hominum adquisitores.

(Agnellus of Ravenna, *Agnelli Liber pontificalis ecclesiae Ravennatis,*19.32, in MGH, Scriptores rerum langobardicarum et italicarum saec. VI-IX, p. 297; trans. Jones, *Saints' Lives and Chronicles*, p. 63)

"All things are common in the communion of saints," as Reginald of Canterbury, cited by Jones (p. 61), puts it. Reginald wrote a *Life of Saint Malchus*, in whose preface he states that since Malchus was just, holy, loved by God, and full of the spirit of all the just, Reginald did not deviate from the truth in ascribing *any* miracle to him. See Reginald of Canterbury, *The Vita Sancti Malchi of Reginald of Canterbury*, ed. Levi R. Lind (Urbana: Univ. of Illinois Press, 1942), pp. 40-41.

20.   Unde manifestum est, melius dici vitam patrum quam vitas, quia, cum sit diversitas meritorum virtutumque, una tamen omnes vita corporis alit in mundo.

(Gregory of Tours, *Gregorii episcopi Turonensis Liber vitae patrum*, ed. Bruno Krusch, in MGH, Scriptores rerum merovingicarum, vol. 1, pp. 662-63; trans. Jones, *Saints' Lives and Chronicles*, p. 62)

21.   The lion, agitated, ran,
Coming toward her, intending to adore,
Not to eat, the virgin.

Delehaye, *Les Légendes hagiographiques*, p. 90, recounts this transformation, though he seems to favor scribal error over deliberate interpretation as an explanation of it. For the dossier of the saint, see *Acta sanctorum*, January, 1: 568-69. There has been considerable disagreement about the date and location of her martyrdom and the authority of the documentation. There may, in fact, be two saints Marciana, one from Caesaria (whose feast is January 9) and one from Toledo (July 12): see *Bibliotheca hagiographica latina*, ed. Société des Bollandistes (Brussels: Société des Bollandistes, 1900-1901), pp. 780-81; and *Acta sanctorum*, July, 3: 233-34. See also *Analecta bollandiana* 24 (1905): 261-64; 58 (1940): 80-81; and 59 (1951): 305, for additional discussion of manuscript authority. (Hippolyte Delehaye, in his *Origines du culte des martyrs* [(Brussels: Société des Bollandistes, 1933), p. 391], suggests that the *Acta* of the saints of Mauritania should not be neglected, even though the manuscripts are not "des textes de premier choix.")

22. Athanasius, *The Life of Antony*, trans. Robert C. Gregg (New York: Paulist Press, 1980), p. 36.

23. Readers were encouraged to venerate the saints, to wonder at the miracles, to pray and ask for intercession, and to emulate the saints. This emulation was often the simple following of the moral example of the saint. See Earl, "Typology and Iconographic Style," p. 36. But in at least two cases it took the form of actual repetition of the actions of the saint. In book 8 of the *Confessions*, Saint Augustine, moved by the story of the life of Saint Antony, who received a divine injunction from the Word of God, takes up his Bible and opens it to receive his own divine injunction. As John Freccero has noticed, Augustine then hands his Bible to Alypius, "thereby suggesting that his own text is to be applied metaleptically to the reader himself as part of the continual unfolding of God's Word in time" ("The Fig Tree and the Laurel: Petrarch's Poetics," *Diacritics* 5 [1975]: 37). And Petrarch, failed saint, exploited this pattern of reader's repetition by opening his volume of Augustine's *Confessions* atop Mount Ventoux. The reader's response to the saint's life—an *imitatio* of an *imitatio*—makes him a part of the great pattern of prefiguration and fulfillment that is scriptural history.

24. For Chaucer's use of his sources (which include Ovid, *Heroides*, *Metamorphoses*, *Fasti*; Boccaccio, *De claris mulieribus*; Virgil, *Aeneid*; Guido delle Colonne, *Historia destructionis Troiae),* see Fyler, *Chaucer and Ovid*, and Hansen, "Irony and the Antifeminist Narrator." Eleanor Winsor Leach, who earlier analyzed the *Legend* in "A Study in the Sources and Rhetoric of Chaucer's *Legend of Good Women* and Ovid's *Heroides* (Ph.D. diss., Yale University, 1963), writes in a more recent essay that the narrator does not merely "shape" the legends by applying principles of abbreviation and expansion (as she had argued earlier); he poetically "disfigure[s]" them. This shift in sensibility accompanies a shift in her sense that the poem is not only about rhetoric but about women. See Eleanor Winsor Leach, "Morwe of May: A Season of Feminine Ambiguity," in *Acts of Interpretation: The Text in Its Contexts, 700-1600*, ed. Mary J. Carruthers and Elizabeth D. Kirk (Norman, Okla.: Pilgrim Books, 1982.), pp. 299-310.

25. In this way the narrator seems to be taking sides in the vexed question of Lucrece's culpability in the rape itself and in killing herself afterward. Unconscious, she couldn't possibly have consented to the rape, as she does in Livy—a fact which was to bother later redactors.

See Ian Donaldson, *The Rapes of Lucretia: A Myth and Its Transformations* (Oxford: Clarendon, 1982), esp. 69-70.

26. See Augustine, *De civitate Dei*, 1. 19-22, CC 47 [Turnhout: Brepols, 1955], pp. 20-24). On female suicide as an act of signification, see Margaret Higonnet, "Speaking Silences: Women's Suicide," in *The Female Body in Western Culture: Contemporary Perspectives*, ed. Susan Rubin Suleiman (Cambridge, Mass.: Harvard Univ. Press, 1986), pp. 68-83.

27. Poe's *Philosophy of Composition* is quoted as an epigraph to Higonnet, "Speaking Silences," p. 68.

28. *Polychronicon Ranulphi Higden, Monechi Cestrensis, Together with the English Translations of John Trvisa and of an Unknown Writer of the Fifteenth Century* 1.1.7, ed. Churchill Babington, Rolls Series (London: Longman, 1865), 1:9; C. Du Cange, *Glossarium mediae et infimae latinitatis* (Paris: Firmin Didot, 1840-1860; rpt. Graz, 1954), s.v. "labyrinthus."

29. Donald R. Howard, in his *Idea of the "Canterbury Tales"* ([Berkeley and Los Angeles: Univ. of California Press, 1976], pp. 326-32), analyzes Chaucer's association of labyrinth with text. J. Hillis Miller, "Ariadne's Thread: Repetition and the Narrative Line" (*Critical Inquiry* 3 [1976]: 57-77), analyzes the text (generic, timeless text; no claims of historical specificity are made) as labyrinth. For a provocative critique of this text-as-labyrinth analysis that takes the gender of critic and text into account and forces questions about masculine appropriation of the feminine, see Nancy K. Miller, "Arachnologies: The Woman, The Text, and the Critic," in *The Poetics of Gender*, ed. Nancy K. Miller (New York: Columbia Univ. Press, 1986), pp. 270-95. Miller's reading of the Ariadne legend as "a parable of women's writing" (p. 286) inspired my analysis here.

30. Sheila Delany, "The Logic of Obscenity in Chaucer's *Legend of Good Women*," *Florilegium* 7 (1985): 189-205.

31. *Polychronicon Ranulphi Higden*, 1.30; ed. Babington, 1:313.

32. Walter Map, *De nugis curialium; Courtier's Trifles*, ed. M.R. James, rev. C.N.L. Brooke and R.A.B. Mynors (Oxford: Clarendon, 1983), pp. 288-311; quotation on p. 291.

33. Giovanni Boccaccio, *Il Corbaccio*, ed. Tauno Nurmela, Suomalaisen Tiedakatemian Toimituksia, Annales Academiae

Scientiarum Fennicae, ser. B, no. 146 (Helsinki: Academiae Scientiarium Fennicae 1968), p. 52; an English translation, *The Corbaccio*, has been made by Anthony K. Cassell (Urbana: Univ. of Illinois Press, 1975). Kiser cites Boccaccio's text in her note on labyrinths (*Telling Classical Tales*, p. 117, n. 31).

34. See Sanford Brown Meech, "Chaucer and the *Ovide moralisé*: A Further Study," *PMLA* 46 (1931): 182-204, esp. 187.

35. Le Jaloux, in the *Roman de la rose* (ed. Félix Lecoy, CFMA 95 [Paris: Honoré Champion, 1970], vv. 9283-9330), yells to his profligate, unruly wife that it's like mother, like daughter; to avoid women's handing down the tricks of the trade of being uncontrollable wives, he implies, men clearly ought to keep women apart.

36. Philomela has been taken as an emblem of the female writer by recent feminist critics: see, for example, Cheryl Walker, *The Nightingale's Burden: Women Poets and American Culture before 1900* (Bloomington: Indiana Univ. Press, 1982); and Jane Marcus, "Liberty, Sorority, Misogyny," in *The Representation of Women in Fiction*, ed. Carolyn G. Heilbrun and Margaret R. Higonnet, Selected Papers of the English Institute, 1981, n.s. 7 (Baltimore: Johns Hopkins Univ. Press, 1983), pp. 60-97. Walker (pp. 21-22) argues against Geoffrey Hartman's use of the legend to describe a genderless voice; see his essay, "The Voice of the Shuttle," in *Beyond Formalism* (New Haven, Conn.: Yale Univ. Press, 1970), pp. 337-55. Walker contends that the legend has a particular, gendered value: the figure of the poet, after all, is a raped woman whose tongue has been cut out. For another comment on Hartman's essay and a strong analysis of the Philomela legend, see Patricia Klindienst Joplin, "The Voice of the Shuttle Is Ours," *Stanford Literature Review 1* (1984): 25-53.

37. See my discussion of Pandarus as "courtly lover" in the previous chapter. I contend that his obscure, unrequited love is but a fiction, an obfuscation of his fundamental engagement in the exchange of women (which structure precludes any sense of a woman as uniquely desirable).

38. As Gayle Rubin notes in "The Traffic in Women: Notes on the 'Political Economy' of Sex" (in *Toward an Anthropology of Women*, ed. R.R. Reiter [New York: Monthly Review Press, 1975], p. 182), the woman traded had best conform her desire to the man in possession of

her in the patriarchal social structure which regards women as objects to be traded. The resistant raped woman is one who presumably does not consider herself the possession of the man attempting to take her, and consequently does not docilely conform her desire.

39. It is no surprise, then (although Frank, p. 139, alludes to a possible "mystery" here), that the Philomela legend should be both treated in the palinode for *Troilus and Criseyde* and elided in lists of the legends: in the Man of Law's Introduction, in the "Cronycle made by Chaucier," and in the Prologue's Balade, no mention of Philomela is made. (The Man of Law also omits Cleopatra, and the Balade omits Medea.) For the "Cronycle," a nine-stanza summary of the *Legend of Good Women* in MS. Ashmole 59, fol. 38v. (copied between 1447 and 1456), see *Odd Texts of Chaucer's Minor Poems*, ed. F.J. Furnivall, Chaucer Society, 1st ser., nos. 23, 60 (London: Trübner, 1868-80).

40. Anne Middleton, 'The *Physician's Tale* and Love's Martyrs: 'Ensamples mo than ten' as a Method in the *Canterbury Tales*," *ChauR* 8 (1973): 29. As far as I know, Middleton is the only critic who has noted this in the *Legend of Hypermnestra*. Pat Trefzger Overbeck, in "Chaucer's Good Woman" (*ChauR* 2 [1967]: 78), comments on the familial situations of the heroines but links these to the women's rejection of authority.

41. There is, as Robert Worth Frank argues in *Chaucer and the "Legend of Good Women*," plenty of *occupatio* and *abbreviatio* in the *Legend*. Phrases such as "And shortly, lest this tale be to long" (2675), "But shortly to the ende I telle shal" (2221), "But now to purpos; in the story I rede" (1825), "Now to th'effect, now to the fruyt of al" (1160), "Who coude wryte which a dedly cheere / Hath Thisbe now" (869-70), do not, *in themselves*, indicate boredom or weariness; Frank contends that they are necessary devices for responsibly pruning sources to form compressed and specific narratives. But there is another agenda motivating the narrator's constantly visible shaping hand. Combined with the protestations of weariness, these rhetorical interjections, I argue, serve to characterize a narrator who simply refuses to go into the more complicated—the difficult, the hard to interpret—aspects of his stories of "good women." He turns away, that is, from the feminine as it threatens to disrupt the patriarchal project that would constrain it. Countering the legend of Chaucer's boredom, Frank argues firmly that

Chaucer was far from bored when writing the *Legend of Good Women*. And I agree: Chaucer was busy depicting sheer boredom, utter weariness in his narrator, and revealing it as a specifically masculine defense against the feminine. Elaine Tuttle Hansen, in "Irony and the Antifeminist Narrator," makes a similar claim about the narrator's boredom: it is, she writes, "undisguised" (p. 29), and it must be distinguished from Chaucer's motives.

42. Peter L. Allen discussed such implications of this line in "'And trusteth, as in love, no man but me': Irony and the Narrator in *The Legend of Good Women*," a talk presented at the Nineteenth International Congress on Medieval Studies, The Medieval Institute, Western Michigan University, Kalamazoo, in May 1984, later expanded into "Reading Chaucer's Good Women," *ChauR* 21 (1987): 419-34.

43. Boredom—the flip side of aggression, as modern psychologists suggest—is an affect in itself. For a thorough discussion and extensive bibliography on boredom, see Franz R. Goetzl, "Root of Discontent and Aggression," in *Boredom: Root of Discontent and Aggression*, ed. Franz R. Goetzl (Berkeley, Calif.: Grizzly Peak Press, 1975), pp. 55-109. For a brilliant analysis of the boring in Trollope that has influenced my discussion here of *Legend of Good Women*, see D.A. Miner, 'The Novel as Usual: Trollope's *Barchester Towers*," in *Sex, Politics, and Science in the Nineteenth-Century Novel*, ed. Ruth Bernard Yeazell, Selected Papers from the English Institute, 1983-84, n.s., no. 10 (Baltimore: Johns Hopkins Univ. Press, 1986), pp. 1-38.

44. Allen, "Reading Chaucer's Good Women," p. 429.

45. Ibid.

VI. THE SHORT POEMS

The Riverside edition presents a gathering of twenty-three "Short Poems" (attributed to Chaucer with varying degrees of confidence) plus the fragmentary "Anelida and Arcite" (which is placed between *The House of Fame* and *The Parliament of Fowls* on the basis of its putative chronology). Numerous questions about the exact count, authenticity, and chronology of Chaucer's shorter poems remain unresolved. Literary critics who subsequently wish to cite this or that particular verse as Chaucer's own must often do so with highly conditional and awkward phrasing—a clumsiness also familiar to any Chaucerian quoting from *Boece* or the *Romaunt*. And the literary merit attributed to what may or may not be a genuine Chaucerian piece is as often equally unstable—or neglected. Alternatively, there is no reason to doubt that "many a song and many a leccherous lay" by Chaucer (*CT* 10. 108) has been lost or, at least, misfiled.

Thirty years ago, in the first issue of *The Chaucer Review*, Edmund Reiss felt it necessary to "dust off the cobwebs" regarding Chaucer's lyric accomplishments. Relatively few Chaucerians have disturbed the dust since then, however. Throughout the 1960's and 70's, *the lyric* as a genre may have dominated the attention of New Critics, but Chaucerians then as now paid much more attention to Chaucer's narratives. The designation "Short Poems" serves best as a critical confession that it is often quite impossible to maintain any clear distinction between *narrative* and *lyric* when reading such poems as "The Complaint of Mars" or "The Complaint of Venus" or "Anelida and Arcite." Indeed, perhaps any poem that Chaucer originally intended for actual performance should be categorized as *dramatic* instead.

Furthermore, our book-based need to gather Chaucer's "Short Poems" together as such hardly justifies exclusion of his intercalated or embedded lyrics as part of the same consideration, since they may very well have originally been presented as stand-alone songs. Any putative genre boundary between Chaucer's dream-visions in particular and his lyrical interludes often seems to have been extremely blurry to Chaucer himself. The rehearser of "The Complaint of Mars" implies that this lyric could possibly be incorporated into a dream vision context when he professes that he will sing "in briddes wise" (23) to "yow al awake"

(15). The difficult second stanza of "A Complaint to His Lady" likewise suggests that this complaint could act as a monologue in an insomniac's vision. Rossell Hope Robbins speculated that some of Chaucer's dream visions may have actually grown from such lyric kernels (in Rowland's *Companion*, p. 388). And Stephen Knight in *Rymyng Craftily* (1973) has demonstrated that "Anelida and Arcite" (in addition to serving as a sort of lyric overture to the Knight's tale) has close stylistic affinities to the tercel's complaint in the *Parliament of Fowls*.

Source studies and the comparative analyses generated thereby have proven especially fruitful for appreciation of Chaucer's short poems. Jean Froissart, Oton de Grandson, and especially Guillaume de Machaut are generally recognized as the most proximate and significant French influences on Chaucer's emergence as an English lyricist. Indeed, it is more proper and precise to use an assortment of Middle English (originally French) terms in lieu of the label *lyric*, including: complaint, rondel, ballade, carol, virelay, dittee, and even priere. Most of these terms convey some sense of performance, either song or public recitation—except for "envoy" when it designates an entire poem meant to be "sent" and then read silently by some individual recipient.

Relatively speaking, Chaucer's lyric "I" has not been so fully discussed as his narrative poses. Where some readers wish to hear first-person (and as such autobiographically reliable) declarations, others insist on interposing the interpretive distance of a fully fictionalized impersonation. Purely aesthetic responses to Chaucer's lyrics *qua* verbal icons have hardly been too enthusiastic. In 1968, Rossell Hope Robbins remarked that "Chaucer's lyrics are minor not only in comparison with his great works; they're just minor poems" (in Rowland's *Companion*, p. 380). Ten years later, Robbins felt no need to retract this opinion; indeed, he prophesied that "Articles about the lyrics will routinely continue to appear, but I doubt any kind of critical approach will elevate these little poems into the masterpieces of the criticasters." "Short" is decreed synonymous with "little," as is "occasional" with "run-of-the-mill" (*Companion*, p. 396), and this dismissive bias still remains very prevalent among Chaucerians. Yet, Robbins also affirmed that Chaucer's "formal, conventional lyrics" contributed to his major influence on the fifteenth century. Chaucer is *the* start of the modern English lyric's literary history (*Companion*, p. 383). And V.J. Scattergood's analyses of Chaucer's short poems recurrently offer extraordinarily positive and provocative appreciations of these much neglected compositions.

Study of the manuscript and early print records of Chaucer's compositions often gives a quite different perspective as to what Chaucer's contemporaries and most proximate readers considered his *best* work. Julia Boffey has detailed the significance of "The Reputation and Circulation of Chaucer's Lyrics in the Fifteenth Century" (1993). Whatever implications Chaucer's "Complaint of Venus," "Complaint of Mars," "Anelida and Arcite," "Complaint to Pity," "Complaint to his Lady," "Complaint d'Amours," and "A Balade of Complaint" may have for determining the increasingly elusive significance of a courtly love tradition in fourteenth-century England, these poems have all generally proven more accessible to modern sensibilities than the "A.B.C." precisely because they are "secular rather than religious" (Minnis' *Guide*, p. 465). The high style and apparently high seriousness with which Chaucer begins "Anelida and Arcite" is remarkable, extraordinary, atypical and so, some think, very "un-Chaucerian." Chaucer's failure to finish "Anelida and Arcite" also contributes to the impression that he felt uncomfortable inheriting the vatic mantel of a Virgil or Dante.

Chaucer's amorous complaints (from which, of course, must be excluded the "Complaint To His Purse") all maintain a sincere intensity. Such tonal consistency is not, however, evident in the group of poems that Scattergood calls Chaucer's "Love Lyrics"—those lyrics which directly address a lady. "Womanly Noblesse" sounds almost like a Marian hymn, but "To Rosemounde" (actually a burlesque about Rosemounde) subverts the same quasi-idolatrous idiom. "Merciless Beute" and "Against Women Unconstant" translate the tone and occasion of complaint into *ad feminam* insult.

In his discussion of a final sub-category of Chaucer's short poems, the "Philosophical and Political Lyrics," Scattergood demonstrates the interpretive fruitfulness of historicism as a critical method. Who was Bukton? What court scandal does the "Complaint of Mars" both mask and disclose? Provenance questions preclude certainty regarding the interpretive contexts to be attributed to many of Chaucer's short poems. This instability must be especially confessed whenever "Chaucer's own voice" is attributed to a lyric like "Gentillesse" in order to de-mask the Loathly Lady's comments on the same topic in the Wife of Bath's tale and to determine thereby Chaucer's own politics.

It is tempting to attempt some distinction between the macro-history that contextualizes Chaucer's public or laureate pronouncements (*e.g.*, "Gentilesse," "The Former Age," "Lak of Stedfastness," and perhaps even "Proverbs") from the micro-history frequently assumed to occasion Chaucer's more familiar or collegial or private lyrics (*e.g.*, the envoys "à Bukton" and "à Scogan," "Truth," and the "Wordes Unto Adam"). However, several of the laureate poems seem motivated by Chaucer's political or philosophical or financial and so very domestic circumstances. Furthermore, even Chaucer's most nonce lyrics, those intended solely as "sophisticated fun for poet and a knowledgeable audience" (*Companion*, p. 384), voice universal and timeless convictions. Chaucer's lyrical use of aphorism and conventional wisdom, therefore, challenges many modern preconceptions regarding the lyric poet's highly individuated point of view.

Defining the *you* (or *thou*) of each of Chaucer's short poems demands no less attention than each *I.* Though not specifically addressing the "short poems" as a subset of Chaucer's career *per se*, Richard Firth Green's frequently cited essay (1982) reprinted below assesses the documentary evidence regarding the presence (or absence) of noblewomen in the Ricardian court. Green also suggests several critical implications that accrue to this highly speculative but mandatory consideration of the original reception contexts attributable to all of Chaucer's extant texts. As samples for the study of Chaucer's formal versecraft and his place in the history of English prosody, the short poems are no less challenging bits of evidence. In his "Natural Music in 1400" (1991), reprinted below, James I. Wimsatt offers an extremely detailed and perceptive study of the formal challenges facing Chaucer as a translator. The now questionable custom of applauding Father Chaucer as inventor of both rime royal and the pentameter couplet has somewhat distracted attention from analysis of his real significance as the "grand translateur" (both importer and adapter) of regular forms "Syth rym in Englissh hath such skarsete" ("The Complaint of Venus," 80). Chaucer's short poems offer several self-conscious experiments in the creative process that helped define stylistic *equivalence* in English for the next century and that, therefore, can claim grand-paternity to Surrey's blank verse and the English sonnet. But designating Chaucer "the Father of English Poetry" entails more than simply a formal acknowledgment of his formalist innovations. And Lee Patterson's first chapter from *Chaucer and the Subject of History* (1991) interprets the inherent doubleness of "Anelida and Arcite" as exemplary of the progress of Chaucer's career from court poet to the primogenitor of English literariness.

WOMEN IN CHAUCER'S AUDIENCE

by Richard Firth Green

When we speak of Chaucer's audience we will probably mean one of two things. Since it is quite clear that most, if not all, of Chaucer's works were intended for oral presentation, we may use the term (as we do when we speak of Shakespeare's audience) to refer to the actual group of people who witnessed their first performance (and thus draw a useful distinction between Chaucer's original audience and his readership). On the other hand, because Chaucer wrote for readers as well as hearers, he is forced, in Walter Ong's words, to "construct in his imagination ... an audience cast in some sort of role,"[1] and this audience (the audience within the poetry, fictional and universal, not historical and localized—what Paul Strohm refers to as his implied audience) exerts a far stronger hold over our imaginations. As Dieter Mehl has written, "we may discover which people Chaucer actually read to or who first read his works, but our own understanding and experience of Chaucer is largely directed by the fictional audience suggested by the poems, an audience with which every reader is invited to identify himself."[2] Mehl is unquestionably right in saying that "we take too limited a view of the kind of poetry [Chaucer] intended if we think of his audience only in terms of a well-defined group on one or two particular occasions,"[3] but nevertheless, as Ian Watt for instance showed in his study of the rise of the novel, knowledge of the historical group addressed by the author in the first instance can add greatly to our understanding of his work, even if it affects our reading of him only at second hand.

I have spoken of these two audiences as if they are easily distinguished, but in practice of course this is far from being the case. The point at which oral performance and literary production meet produces a particularly complex relationship between the two audiences, a relationship which, as Paul Zumthor has shown in the case of the *rhetoriqueurs*, is open to the most subtle critical analysis.[4] My point is simpler; I wish to examine one of the ways in which the imaginative appeal of the implied audience may have distorted our understanding of the actual historical one, and to suggest how a historical revaluation may affect our critical perspective on the poems themselves.

Anne Middleton has written of the way in which Ricardian public poetry "speaks 'as if' to the entire community—as a whole, and all at once rather than severally—rather than 'as if' to a coterie or patron."[5] The point is well made, and helps to explain why, though we may safely surmise that Chaucer's poems were first performed before a fairly small group of courtiers (there is no direct proof of this, but a great deal of circumstantial evidence), our sense of such an audience is far from clear from the texts themselves. Edmund Reiss's recent attempt to characterize it from internal evidence is stimulating but, as should by now be clear, methodologically open to question,[6] creating what Paull Baum might have regarded as yet another scholarly fiction.[7] Paul Strohm is on safer ground when he draws on external evidence to characterize Chaucer's principal public, a public he finds amongst "the lesser gentry—the knights, esquires, and women of equivalent rank, and especially those closely connected with the court."[8] In all but one respect I find myself in general agreement with his characterization, but when he includes "women of equivalent rank" I cannot help wondering whether Strohm has not been listening to that voice speaking " 'as if' to the entire community."

Let us begin with a recent social historian who has not been distracted by that voice. "Women made up a minute proportion of the total household," writes Mark Girouard; and a little later: "it is hard to believe that the majority of the household were totally celibate, but the whereabouts of its women, licit or illicit, remains mysterious."[9] To most readers of Chaucer, I imagine, these words will come as something of a surprise; many of us continue to envisage Chaucer's courtly audience much as the illuminator of Corpus Christi 61 had done, despite the warnings of Salter and Pearsall. Surely Richard II's household contained lords and ladies, esquires and damsels, serving men and waiting women, if not in equal proportions, at least with both sexes sufficiently represented for easy social intercourse between them to be common? Yet when we turn to the *Liber Niger* of Edward IV, the fullest account of a late medieval royal household to survive in England, we find not one female servant—not a single equivalent of the cooks, chamber maids, and tweenies, without whom the Victorian household would have ground to a halt. Men looked after the king's clothes, dressed and undressed him, made his bed, and cleaned his chamber; men served his meat, poured his wine, washed his hands, and cooked his food; not only did men look after his horses and his hawks, they did his laundry and washed his dishes. Many of his more important servants were allowed to keep (male) servants of their own at court at the king's expense, but the *Liber Niger* says nothing of their wives. Perhaps, however, this silence is significant, for an earlier ordinance, the Ordinance of York of 1318, is quite specific: "null de la mesnee le roy, de quele condicioun qil soit, tenust sa femme a la court, ne nulle part dehors suyant la court, chiualer ou clerc, sergeant, esquier, charetter, ou somere, garceouns ou page."[10] There are two exceptions: women entitled in the crowner's roll in the marshalsea (it is not clear who these might be—perhaps laundresses and suchlike), and "tels femmez qi sount en chief ov le roi" (it would have been a rash steward who would have tried to banish the likes of Alice Perrers from court). The Ordinance of York does in fact give us a glimpse of the household's "illicit" womenfolk: "femmes de fol vie" who follow the court are to be expelled for a first offence, and for a subsequent one to be marked on the forehead with hot wax. This attempt to maintain a state of secular celibacy in the household is also reflected in an ordinance of Philippe le Bel's queen, Jeanne de Navarre (1286): "il est ordené que nus chevalier, ne autres, ne gira avec sa femme en l'Ostel ma dame."[11]

Of course queens had female servants, but we may be surprised to discover how few of them there were. The Ordinance of 1445 for instance specifies two "dames" (each with her own "dauncell" to serve her), six "dauncelles," two "chambrers" (presumably female), and two "lauenders"—a total of fourteen in all.[12] That this figure was not unrealistic is confirmed by two sets of domestic accounts which have survived for fifteenth-century queens: Margaret of Anjou in 1452/3 paid the salaries of sixteen women in her service (not all of whom would have been serving at any one time), and Elizabeth Woodville in 1466/7 paid for fourteen.[13] Moreover, even in the queen's household male servants would have been far more numerous; in the accounts of Margaret of Anjou just referred to, for instance, there are a hundred of them. On great feast days or for ceremonial occasions the number of women attached to the queen's household would be swollen by the arrival of great ladies with their own *dames* and *damoiselles*: thus for the Christmas festivities, 1368, Queen Philippa's retinue contained thirty-two women, and at Philippa's funeral a year later fifty-one women were allowed mourning livery.[14] At the height of her power, the entourage of Queen Isabel of Bavaria contained only fifteen or so female attendants (others were employed in the satellite households of her young children), and, as Maurice Rey points out, "c'était seulement en des circonstances extraordinaires, fêtes ou cérémonies, qu' [elle] se trouvait environnée de cortège brillant des grandes dames du royaume

suivies des femmes des principaux administrateurs et des Parisiennes
les plus distinguées."[15]

Except for high-days and holidays, then, the number of women to
have been found in Anne of Bohemia's retinue would probably have
been less than twenty (and fewer yet in the case of Isabelle of France,
who was still a minor). Moreover, the queen's household did not
inevitably accompany the king's (though perhaps it did so more
frequently than usual under Richard II, reputedly a somewhat uxorious
king). Even when both households were residing in the same place they
were generally kept separate. They would, for instance, have taken
meals in different chambers, and informal social interchange between
them seems to have been infrequent enough to have been worth
remarking upon. Thus, when Edward IV's friend Louis de Bruges, lord
of Gruthuyse, visited him in 1472, a herald reports:

> When they had sopte, my lord chamberleyn had hym againe to
> ye Kinges chamber, and incontinent the Kinge had hym to y^e
> quenes chamber, wher she sat plainge w^t her ladyes at the
> morteaulx, and some of her ladyes and gentlewomen at the
> Closheys of yvery and Daunsing, And some at dyuers other
> games accordinge. The whiche sight was full plesant to them.
> Also ye Kinge daunsed w^t my lady Elizabethe, his eldest
> doughter. That done, the night passed ouer, they wente to his
> chamber. The lord Gruthuse took leue, and my lorde
> Chamberleyn w^t dyuers other nobles accompanied hym to his
> chamber, where they departed for that night.[16]

The number of queen's damsels who married esquires in the king's
household (not to mention those like Alice Perrers and Agnes
Launcekron, whose aspirations were higher if less regular) suggests
that the two retinues must have mingled (four of Elizabeth Woodville's
domicellae in 1466/7 were married to king's esquires, and Hulbert lists
several esquires other than Chaucer who had found wives among the
queen's servants);[17] nevertheless, in the normal run of things the king
would have gone about his business surrounded by his own (male)
servants, and only exceptionally would his entourage have included his
consort and her ladies. If, then, in calling Chaucer a court poet, we
mean that he would have read his poems aloud after supper in the
king's chamber or hall (as Froissart had read *Meliador* to the Count of
Foix), we must think of him reading to an audience which was
primarily, if not exclusively, male.

We should not imagine that a masculine audience might have had
no great interest in love poetry (at the Count of Foix's castle Froissart
found "en la sale et es chambres et en la court chevaliers et escuiers
d'onneur aler et marcher, et d'armes et d'amours les oioit on parler"),[18]
and it is in fact very interesting to read some of Chaucer's verse with
such an audience in mind. We might, for instance, consider *the
questions d'amour* which he addresses to his audience:

> But now to yow, ye loveres that ben here,
> Was Troilus nought in a kankedort? (*Troilus,* II, 1751-52)

> Yow loveres axe I now this questioun:
> Who hath the worse, Arcite or Palamoun? (*KnT*, 1347-48)

> Lordynges, this question, thanne, wol I aske now,
> Which was the mooste fre, as thynketh yow? (*FranklT*, 1621-
> 22).[19]

In every case, it is the masculine view which is elicited: we are asked to
consider Troilus (not Criseyde), Palamon and Arcite (not Emily),
Arveragus, Aurelius, and the clerk (not Dorigen). As T.C. Rumble has
written, "in Poitiers or Troyes the question posed at the end of
Chaucer's *Franklin's Tale* would no doubt have been debated long and
enthusiastically, though surely there it would have been seen
immediately that the Franklin's *demande* excludes the one person best
qualified to be judged 'mooste fre.'"[20] What, moreover, might we
conclude about the makeup of Chaucer's audience from an aside such
as the Knight's: "For wommen, as to speken in commune, / Thei
folwen alle the favour of Fortune" (*KnT*, 2681-82)—to say nothing of
the smoking-room sallies of the Nun's Priest? Chaucer is of course too
generous a poet to be stereotyped by Huizinga's generalization:
"medieval literature shows little true pity for women, little compassion
for her weakness and the dangers and pains which love has in store for
her" (his treatment of Criseyde, for instance, rises above mere social
posturing), but he is nevertheless writing within an erotic culture
which, as Huizinga puts it, "even when it dons an idealistic guise . . . is
altogether saturated with male egotism."[21] Undoubtedly such a culture
was shaped by the predominantly male aura of the courts in which it
flourished.

I do not want to overstate my case. The probability that there were
some women, albeit in rather small numbers and perhaps only
occasionally, in Chaucer's audience seems high. Direct addresses to

women, although far less common than those to men, are not difficult
to find in his work; some of these, like the Clerk's envoy to
"archewyves," or the Physician's advice to "maistresses . . . that lordes
doghtres han in governaunce," seem to be directed to an implied
audience, as does the injunction that "every lady bright of hewe" look
charitably on the portrait of Criseyde (*Troilus*, V, 1772-74), or that
queens, duchesses, and ladies sympathize with Constance's plight
(*MLT*, 652-54); other cases (such as the "yonge fresshe folkes, he or
she") are less clear. What for instance are we to make of the Clerk's
question: "But now of wommen wolde I axen fayne / If thise assayes
myghte nat suffise?" (*ClT*, 696-97)? Is Chaucer here addressing a
specific or a general audience? Or what of the ending of the *Legend of
Phyllis*:

> Be war, ye wemen, of youre subtyl fo,
> Syn yit this day men may ensaumple se;
> And trusteth, as in love, no man but me. (*LGW*, 2659-61)

Would such a joke be more effective before a mixed audience or not?

There is one further aspect of this whole question which I should
like to touch on briefly. Though the number of women at Richard II's
court was probably proportionately very small, it was undoubtedly
larger than at earlier periods. Gervase Mathew has claimed that "the
presence of women of influence and standing" was one of the factors
that distinguished the new international court culture which first
flowered in England at the end of the fourteenth century.[22] Though I
believe he exaggerates their importance at this period, he is
undoubtedly right that their presence was a novelty. A celebrated
petition presented to parliament in 1397 by Thomas Haxey complains,
among other things, of "le grant & excessive charge de l'hostel du roy"
caused by "la multitude d'evesques, qui ont seigneuries, & sont
avancez par le roy, & leur meignee; & aussi de pluseurs dames & leur
meignee qui demuront en l'ostel du roy, & sont a ses costages."[23] Now,
it is quite clear from this that the presence of "pluseurs dames" in the
household was an innovation (an unwelcome one to those whose taxes
supported the royal entourage); otherwise Haxey would not have dared
raise the matter- though predictably Richard was outraged by this
attack on his prerogative ("les communes firent en ce grant offense &
encontre sa regalie, & sa roiale mageste, & la liberte de lui & de ses
honorables progenitours"). It is less clear what Haxey means by
"pluseurs"; the "multitude" of bishops could hardly have numbered
more than seventeen (the total number of sees in England at the time);

all we can reasonably say of the "many" ladies is that there were more of them than there had been in the past.

There are other indications that the female presence at court was becoming more marked throughout the late Middle Ages. We have already seen that the injunction in the Ordinance of York against servants bringing their wives to court is not repeated in later household ordinances (a significant omission, perhaps, in view of the derivative nature of such ordinances). Christine de Pisan, in her advice to a young princess in the *Livre des Trois Vertus*, says of the choice of male servants, "et se ilz sont mariez tant mieulz vault et par especial ceulx qui la seruiront a table et qui plus frequenteront enuiron elle et ses femmes, et se il eschiet est bien seant que leurs femmes demeurent semblablement a court,"[24] so perhaps such an arrangement was becoming more possible in the king's court as well. The most splendid of all the fifteenth-century northern European courts, that of the Burgundian duke Charles the Bold, seems to have contained a great number of women, since Olivier de la Marche, writing in 1473, estimates their cost to the duke at forty thousand pounds a year (only a tenth of what was paid to male members of the court but still an enormous sum): "et au regard de l'estat des dames et de leur pencion, je n'en fay grant mention, combien que se soit en frait pour le prince plus de quarante mille livres par an."[25]

I should like to conclude by tentatively linking the increasing presence and importance of women at court after the middle of the fourteenth century with the decline of one of the liveliest of thirteenth-century genres, the *fabliau*. This is not wholeheartedly to endorse Nykrog's view of the fabliau as a courtly genre (the limitations of this position have recently been demonstrated by Muscatine)—merely to suggest that courtly standards of decorum may have set limits on literary indecency which would have filtered through to other levels of society (Muscatine himself seems willing to countenance such a view).[26] Might not the growing number of women at court have helped establish these standards, and the difficulties of performing before a mixed audience explain why the fabliau seems to have fallen out of favor in France after Jean de Condé's time? Muscatine has distinguished among the fabliaux a group of four "anti-prudery" poems,[27] and it is worth noting that the butts of all four are women. Jean de Meun's remark about earthy words similarly links prudery with feminine sensibility: "Se fames nes nomment en France / Ce n'est fors de acoustumance" (7131-32). In the early fifteenth century Christine de Pisan duly rises to his bait. There is nothing surprising, then, in the Merchant's apology:

> Ladyes, I prey yow that ye be not wrooth;
> I kan nat glose, I am a rude man—
> And sodeynly anon this Damyan
> Gan pullen up the smok, and in he throng.
>
> (*MerchT* 2350-53)

If I am right that Haxey's petition indicates that the English did not follow the French fashion of bringing ladies to court in significant numbers until the final years of the fourteenth century, then perhaps we have in part this conservatism to thank for the legacy of the Miller and the Reeve.[28]

NOTES

1. "The Writer's Audience is Always a Fiction," *PMLA*, 90 (1975), 12.

2. "Chaucer's Audience," *Leeds Studies in English*, 10 (1978), 60.

3. "The Audience of Chaucer's *Troilus and Criseyde*," in *Chaucer and Middle English Studies in Honour of Rossell Hope Robbins*, ed. Beryl Rowland (Kent, Ohio: Kent State Univ. Press, 1974), p. 173.

4. "From Hi(story) to Poem, or the Paths of Pun," *NLH*, 10 (1979), 238-43.

5. "The Idea of Public Poetry in the Reign of Richard II," *Speculum*, 53 (1978), 98.

6. "Chaucer and his Audience," *ChauR*, 14 (1980), 390-402.

7. *Chaucer: A Critical Appreciation* (Durham: Duke Univ. Press, 1958), p. 204.

8. "Chaucer's Audience," *Literature & History,* 5 (1977), 3 1.

9. *Life in the English Country House* (1978; Harmondsworth: Penguin Books, 1980), p. 27.

10. T.F. Tout, *The Place of the Reign of Edward II in English History*, 2nd ed. (Manchester: Manchester Univ. Press, 1936), p. 280.

11. M.L. Douët-d'Arcq, *Comptes de l'hotel des rois de France aux XIV^c et XV^c siècles* (Paris: Soc. de l'hist. de France, 1865), p. xii.

12. A.R. Myers, *The Household of Edward IV* (Manchester: Manchester Univ. Press, 1959), p. 72.

13. A.R. Myers, "The Household of Queen Margaret of Anjou, 1452-3," *BJRL*, 40 (1957/58), 404-06; and "The Household of Elizabeth of Woodville, 1466-7," *BJRL*, 50 (1967/68), 451-53.

14. Martin M. Crow and Clair C. Olson, *Chaucer Life-Records* (Oxford: Clarendon Press, 1966), pp. 94-100 (and see p. 84).

15. Maurice Rey, *Les finances royales sous Charles VI: les causes du déficit, 1388-1413* (Paris: S.E.V.P.E.N., 1965), p. 192.

16. C.L. Kingsford, *English Historical Literature in the Fifteenth Century* (1913; repr. New York: Burt Franklin, 1972), p. 386.

17. J.R. Hulbert, *Chaucer's Official Life* (1912; repr. New York: Phaeton Press, 1970), p. 42.

18. *Voyage en Béarn*, ed. A.H. Diverres (Manchester: Manchester Univ. Press, 1953), p. 68.

19. These and subsequent references are to *The Works of Geoffrey Chaucer*, ed. F.N. Robinson, 2nd ed. (Boston: Houghton Mifflin, 1957).

20. *The Breton Lay in Middle English* (Detroit: Wayne State Univ. Press, 1965), p. xxi.

21. J. Huizinga, *The Waning of the Middle Ages*, tr. F. Hopman (London: Edward Arnold, 1924), p. 114.

22. *The Court of Richard II* (London: John Murray, 1968), p. 1.

23. *Rotuli Parliamentorum* (London, 1783), III, 339.

24. Bodley, MS. Fr.d.5, f.38v [Ch. 24].

25. *L'estate de la maison du duc Charles de Bourgoingne*, in *Mémoires d'Olivier de la Marche*, IV, ed. H. Beaune and J. d'Arbaumont (Paris: Soc. de l'hist. de France, 1887), p. 11 (some MSS, however, read *écus* for *livres*—perhaps a more likely sum).

26. "The Social Background of the Old French Fabliaux," *Genre*, 9 (1976), 1-19; and "Courtly Literature and Vulgar Language," in *Court and Poet*, ed. Glyn S. Burgess (Liverpool: Francis Cairns, 1980), pp. 1-19.

27. "Courtly Literature," pp. 13-15.

28. This paper, written for delivery at the Third International New Chaucer Society Conference, is intentionally speculative; if it merits publication at all, it is as a stimulus to further investigation, and no one would be less surprised than myself if such investigation were to prove its conclusions nugatory. I should like to take this opportunity to express my thanks to Dr. Marie Borroff, with whom I discussed this paper at an early stage and several of whose suggestions I have followed up with profit.

"THIRLED WITH THE POYNT OF REMEMBRAUNCE": THE THEBAN WRITING OF *ANELIDA AND ARCITE*

by Lee Patterson

"I don't like the kind of double-minded feeling I have about this thing."

The social meaning of Chaucer's poetry—the institutional context from which it derived, the audience to which it was addressed, above all the class values it expresses—has been and remains an open question.[1] For the most part fifteenth-century poets valued Chaucer as a source of the kind of writing admired in aristocratic circles: as the learned expositor of "fructuous sentence" and the eloquent celebrant of *fine amor*, Chaucer provided the texts they imitated, rewrote, and sometimes simply rehearsed.[2] At the same time, however, the wide-ranging provenance and often modest format of the sixty or so fifteenth-century manuscripts of the *Canterbury Tales* argue for an appeal to less highly placed readers.[3] These two versions of Chaucer—the courtly versus the popular—have similarly dominated modern scholarship from its nineteenth-century beginnings. One strain of criticism has seen Chaucer as a royal favorite who promoted noble values: according to one Victorian commentator, Chaucer was a celebrant of "chivalrous love"who was "careful to remember that he was writing for a courtly audience, studious to guard against giving offense to the chivalrous mind."[4] On the other hand was the more romantic view that "it was in Chaucer that the literary spirit of the English people, vigorous, simple, and truthful, found its voice. . . . The sympathies of Chaucer are not those of coteries and courts, they are with common and universal feelings."[5]

Twentieth-century critical opinion has on the whole been organized by a similar dichotomy. One position, vigorously prosecuted throughout the century although still a distinct minority, holds that Chaucer's poetry is essentially and often explicitly confirmatory of established medieval values and institutions, including those of the court within which he came to maturity and whose patronage provided him with his livelihood.[6] The other, majority position is that Chaucer is not a spokesman for any opinions at all, much less those of the court.

On the contrary, to the liberalism that has held sway in the university for most of this century, Chaucer's poetry richly expresses the "common and universal" values with which literature has always concerned itself. To immure him within the court and to understand his poetry as in consequence ideologically constrained is not merely to subject subtle and searching poetry to crassly reductive readings; it is also, since literature is by definition a disinterested discourse, to deny to the father of English poetry his legitimate title.

The view promoted in this book is that these opposed positions are at once right and wrong. That Chaucer was at least until the initiation of the *Canterbury Tales* a court poet can hardly be disputed; that he found this condition uncomfortable and constraining is also clear, especially in light of poems like the *House of Fame* and the *Legend of Good Women*. But even given a desire to break away from the confining conditions of court production, what were the alternative discourses available to him and how were they to be exploited? *Anelida and Arcite* and *Troilus and Criseyde* bespeak Chaucer's efforts to expand the cultic language of the court beyond its prescribed limits, thus examining and implicitly challenging the largest presuppositions of aristocratic culture. The *Canterbury Tales*, on the other hand, register the process by which he forged a way of writing that was at once oppositional and nonpolitical. In effect, the course of his career shows a writer of coterie verse expressing values that now seem quintessentially literary, and it traces the route by which a court poet came to be the father of English poetry.

I

The development of a court poetry—a poetry, that is, specifically of the court and not merely a "courtly" poetry expressive of aristocratic values in general—is a relatively late phenomenon in England.[7] To be sure, the twelfth-century court of Henry II supported a highly developed literary culture that included vernacular writers such as Benoît de Sainte-Maure, the author of the *Roman d'Eneas*, Wace, probably Marie de France, and perhaps even the young Chrétien de Troyes—not to speak of a large number of Latin writers.[8] But not only was this an exclusively French- speaking court but also one that stands in lonely eminence in relation to the next century and a half. While there are of course numerous examples of aristocratic and royal patronage throughout this period, they are isolated instances rather than parts of a coordinated program of cultural development and ideological promotion. Only in the second half of the reign of Edward III—beginning, that is, about the 1360s—does there develop an extensive and sophisticated literary culture centered on and fostered by the court and serving to articulate a court ideology. [9] And in part—perhaps in large part—this is a function of certain structural changes in the role of the royal household. In the latter years of the reign of Edward III and throughout that of Richard II there was not only a gradual concentration of the business of government in the *camera regis*, but the royal household came to function less as the focus of the aristocratic community as a whole than as the king's *privata familia*.[10] And under Richard, this concentration of power in the court, and the parallel development of a specifically courtier nobility, became a matter of royal policy.[11]

The first sign of a *literary* court culture in England is the presence of Jean Froissart at the court of Edward III: a Hainaulter, he entered the service of Queen Philippa in 1361 and remained in England until about 1369.[12] In the first book of the *Chroniques* Froissart describes himself as one of the queen's "clers et familiers," and he later memorialized Philippa as one "à laquelle en ma jeunesse je fus clerc et la servoie de beaulx dittier et traités amoureux."[13] The next sign is the emergence of Geoffrey Chaucer, whose *Book of the Duchess*, written to commemorate the death of Blanche of Lancaster in 1368, drew upon Froissart's poetry, as well as that of his more prominent French colleague Guillaume de Machaut, and was in turn imitated by Froissart himself.[14]

That Chaucer, a king's esquire in the households of both Edward III and Richard II, was very much a court poet—at least until he began writing the *Canterbury Tales* in the late 1380s—is clear from the poetry itself. The *Book of the Duchess* was written for John of Gaunt, in the absence of the Black Prince the most powerful member of the royal family in England and a man deeply involved in royal and metropolitan affairs in the period around 1370. The *Parliament of Fowls* also reflects royal interests in its reference to the negotiations for the marriage of Richard and Anne of Bohemia in 1380.[15] So too *Troilus and Criseyde*, the preeminent courtly poem of the English Middle Ages, is also a specifically *court* poem: it not only includes a royalist commentary on the Wonderful Parliament of 1386 but speaks in other, subtler ways to the dilemma of the Ricardian monarchy in the 1380s.[16] There are as well the short poems—two balades, four complaints, eight epistles, and the delicate "ABC"—that presuppose for their audience "a circle of gentlemen and clerks" derived from if not always located within the royal household.[17] Hence Chaucerians have reasonably assumed that

the "many a song and many a leccherous lay" (X, 1087) to which
Chaucer refers in the Retractions appended to the *Parson's Tale*
designate the kind of occasional lyrics that were routinely produced at
court, poems written to provide "intellectual and social diversion and
amorous dalliance among a minuscule élite group," in the words of
Rossell Hope Robbins.[18] In Gower's *Confessio amantis* Venus
describes Chaucer as "mi disciple and mi poete" and says that "in the
floure of his youthe" he wrote so many "ditees and . . . songes glade, / . . .
for mi sake" that "the land fulfild [was] overal": that we now have only a
few of these poems indicates not the size of Chaucer's production but
only the fragility of so ephemeral a product.[19]

If Chaucer wrote poetry both about and for the court, it derived not
from a native tradition of courtly lyricism—there was virtually
none—but instead from contemporary French writing, the writing that
Froissart no doubt first introduced into the royal court.[20] As Robbins
has said, "What separated Chaucer . . . from other comparable poets
living in regional courts of the great nobles (the Warwicks, the
Mortimers, the Bohuns, the Beauchamps, the Percys) is that Chaucer
went to the currently fashionable *dits amoureux* [of Machaut and
Froissart] for his models, and not to the old-fashioned French romances
(as did the author of *Sir Gawain and the Green Knight*)."[21] Certainly
we could overestimate this division—Elizabeth Salter has well shown
how cosmopolitan tastes were throughout England—but it is real
nonetheless and suggests that the late Edwardian and Ricardian courts
were developing a distinctively royal literary style.[22]

Chaucer's court poetry, both the largely vanished "ditees and
songes glade" and the extant longer poems, are examples of what he
and his contemporaries called *makyng*.[23] That is, they were poems
designed above all to serve the recreative needs of the court. The *maker*
provided the materials of courtly diversion, the texts that were not
merely the occasion for courtly conversation (as is clearly envisaged,
for instance, by the *demande d'amour*) but both provided paradigms for
and constituted that conversations.[24] It is from the world of what the
Gawain-poet called "luf-talkyng" that these texts arise and to which
they refer: they are surviving fragments of an ephemeral social activity.
In this sense, *makyng* was defined as a purely aesthetic practice.
Constantly drawing attention to its technical intricacy, basing its
generic distinctions on prosody rather than content, and deploying a
polysemous discourse of riddles, *doubles entendres,* allegory, and
allusion, *makyng* explored the potentialities inherent in language as
both a signifying and a phonetic system. As Robert Guiette has said, it
is a "jeu des formes," a practice that aspires to pure aestheticism.[25] And

the total effect is to create what Paul Zumthor has suggestively called a cultural *hortus conclusus*, a site where an aristocratic "culte égocentrique" can find an unconstrained fulfillment denied it in the threatening world of late fourteenth-century history.[26]

Yet of course the aesthetic is in no sense outside ideology, nor can history be so willfully set aside. The aristocratic privileging of play served itself as an important marker of social identity, declaring the nobility to be, as a class, released from the penance of both labor and prayer. And the aestheticization of life, of which the formalism of *makyng* was simply one aspect, was central to the ideological project of class self-definition and self-legitimization in which late medieval aristocratic culture was ceaselessly engaged. Just as its cuisine transformed food into art, just as its fashion transformed the body into a visual display, so the *makyng* of the court transformed words into elegant discursive artifice.[27] What the courtly *maker* taught was, again in the words of the *Gawain*-poet, "the teccheles termes of talkyng *noble*." The obsessive focus upon love that characterizes this verse supports this project as well, not just by demonstrating over and over again that "pitee renneth soone in *gentil* herte," but by fashioning the turbulence of erotic feeling into the elegant artifice of lyric. As Derek Pearsall has said of the complaint, perhaps the most quintessentially courtly of lyric forms, "There is no movement, no action, only the lover and his mistress for ever frozen into ritual gestures of beseeching and disdain."[28] Like the other kinds of fetishized objects with which the aristocratic world adorned itself (tapestries, jewelry, books), the complaint beautifully stages, over and over again, a reified extravagance, a petrified excess. In Anne Middleton's words, it serves a "socially or cultically reaffirmative function," and Zumthor has shown how the "register" of the *grand chant courtois* articulates the shared assumptions that bind together poet and audience.[29] It constructs, objectifies, and beautifies—but declines to analyze or understand—courtly subjectivity, just as the books in which these texts were inscribed were themselves objects placed in the service of ostentatious self-display.[30] Correspondingly, the task of the *maker* was to provide the aristocracy with languages, pastimes, modes of feeling, and objects that confirmed their nobility. Social historians have shown that in the late fourteenth century the English aristocracy was seeking, under the pressure of far-reaching economic changes, to transform itself from a loosely organized and permeable class into a hereditary caste defined by a highly distinctive life-style.[31] The *aesthetic* transformations accomplished by courtly *makyng* served a crucial ideological function in fulfilling this purpose.

This writing served other ideological functions as well. For if it entertained court servants, it also trained them: it provided what *la belle dame sans merci* called a "school" of "fayr langage," teaching its students to "parler mignon" (Christine de Pisan's wonderful phrase).[32] From the time of its medieval beginnings in the eleventh century, courtliness made verbal facility a central value: *facetus* is virtually a synonym for *curialis*, and it means both "elegant" and "clever," both "refined" and "witty."[33] According to another medieval definition, a man who is *facetus* is one who can get what he wants out of words, whether it be a subtle meaning or a desired effect.[34] And if to be courtly is to be adroit with words, the riddles, acrostics, *jeux partis*, and *demandes d'amour* that are preserved, either intact or in allusion, are evidence of the assiduity with which this talent was practiced and displayed.[35]

A correlative talent is the capacity to interpret, to be able to read the elegantly metaphoric and topically allusive language of the court poem. According to Thomas Usk, an ill-fated sergeant-of-arms in Richard's court, Love teaches her servants "to endyten letters of rethorike in queynt understondinges," and in the *Prison amoureuse*, Froissart explains that a courtly poem is "a gloss of something which cannot or must not be openly stated."[36] In the *Livre messire Ode*, written by Oton de Grandson while at the Ricardian court in the 1370s and 1380s, the narrator overhears a lover grieving for the loss of his sparrowhawk but fails to understand that he is speaking "par poetrie" and really means his lady.[37] In the *Book of the Duchess* Chaucer had already used the same device but had laid bare the social meaning it contains: his narrator's inability to understand the Black Knight's metaphor of the chess game is a sign of his social inferiority. It is this interpretive alertness, even suspicion, that led Puttenham in the sixteenth century to call the trope of allegory—"which is when we speake one thing and thinke another"—"the Courtly figure," one known not only to "euery common Courtier, but also [to] the grauest Counsellour."[38] Court poetry, in other words, is not simply a form of entertainment but a social practice, the means by which courtiers both learned and displayed the talents needed for success.

As literary historians have shown, court writing was in no sense the preserve of a special group of professional poets.[39] In fact, the demise of the minstrel in the late fourteenth century represents not merely the shift from one kind of taste to another but the deprofessionalization of writing per se. No longer was literary activity confined to a particular group of specially trained men but became instead the preserve of the court as a whole. Hence the fact that not only do none of the large number of documents that record Chaucer's career refer to him as a writer, but that his career was probably not advanced by his literary activity.[40] To have acknowledged that Chaucer could do something special that other members of the court could not would have been to undermine the socially legitimizing function of courtly *makyng*, According to Deschamps' *Art de dictier*, there are two kinds of music: a "musique artificiele" played on instruments by "le plus rude homme du monde," and a "musique naturelle," the harmony of verse ("une musique de bouche en proferant paroules metrifiées") inspired by the "amorous desire to praise ladies" that inhabits gentle hearts.[41] In fact, a great many courtiers did write poetry: we have the names and some of the poems of over a dozen noble *makers* from late medieval England, as well as the rather bizarre fact that Richard II wanted his epitaph to compare him to Homer.[42] Indeed, one of the tasks of the professional poet (if the title be admitted at all) was to collaborate with the patron in the production of the courtly text. Froissart's *Prison amoureuse*, for instance, records the way in which the poet instructed his patron, Wenceslas of Brabant, in the art of *makyng*, and both this text and the later *Meliador* contain poems by both authors.[43] The same is true of Machaut's *Fonteinne amoureuse*, which describes the departure of Jean, duc de Berri, into exile and incorporates several of his laments. Indeed, it is possible that the rather inept lyrics ascribed to the grieving Black Knight in the *Book of the Duchess* really were written by John of Gaunt.

This expansion of literariness to include the court as a whole also helps to account for a pronounced generic shift in the literary system of fourteenth-century England. Romances and histories, almost entirely in prose, continued to be copied and read, as library lists and manuscript survivals demonstrate. But the literature of fashion produced within the court—excluding, that is, works of instruction—was almost exclusively lyric. This category includes not only lyrics per se, the many "compleyntis, baladis, roundelis, virelais" that Lydgate ascribed to Chaucer and that must have been written by other courtly versifiers in the hundreds, but also the new genre of the *dits amoureux* produced by Machaut and Froissart.[44] For all their apparently narrative form, these works are in fact sets of lyric performances enclosed within a narrative frame: they provide lyrics with a context that is, in their usual, freestanding state, only implied. The *Book of the Duchess*, largely derived from the *dits amoureux*, is the first poem to transfer this form into English; and while there are no Chaucerian poems that fully replicate French models, we can recognize in the roundel of the *Parliament of Fowls*, in the complaint of *Anelida and Arcite*, in the balade of the *Prologue* to the *Legend of Good Women*, and above all in the many lyric moments, both celebratory and lamenting, of *Troilus and Criseyde*, the overwhelming pressure of the lyric impulse.[45]

While Chaucer is the first English court poet, if not the first in England, his own relation to this kind of writing was deeply problematic. On the one hand, as the fifteenth-century rewriting of his poetry shows, he provided the materials for courtly writing for several generations of successors. As John Stevens has said, "Chaucer was, above all, the Articulate Lover, the 'well of eloquence,' the master of the language of the heart. To read *The Knight's Tale* or *Anelida and Arcite* was a sentimental education," and the courtier wrote his poems "out of *Troilus and Criseyde*, the great poem in which he could study and find how 'most felyngly' to speak of love."[46] Nor was it only lovers who recognized in *Troilus and Criseyde* the authentic language of the court: in the fifteenth century a courtier poet included Pandarus's warnings to Criseyde about the dangers of unbridled speech (3, 302-22) in a poem on the dangers of truth-telling and the burdens of service at court.[47] Yet the *Prologue* to the *Legend of Good Women* shows that Chaucer found the court to be deeply unsatisfactory as a place both to write and to be read. Here an irascible God of Love (with unmistakable affinities to Richard II) reads the complex contextualization of eroticism accomplished by the *Troilus* as a simplistic attack on love per se. Insisting upon turning all cultural products to the task of self-legitimization, the patron seeks to govern both the production and the reception of the text, insisting that it signify a monolithic, self-identical meaning, that it rehearse and celebrate but never analyze much less criticize court values.[48] This is an absolutism that the poem resists through its own incomplete submission both to the patron's commission and to its source texts, and then ironically restages in the tyranny to which its saintly heroines are subjected. In short, for all the linguistic playfulness and apparent recreative freedom claimed by courtly *makyng*, it is represented in the *Legend of Good Women* as ideologically and discursively imprisoning.

Moreover, the *House of Fame* presents a trenchant commentary on both the vagaries of service in the prince's court and its effect on literary ambition.[49] In Fame's court writers become mere agents of the powerful: whether they are "mynstralles / And gestiours that tellen tales" (1197-98) or the great *auctores* of antiquity, their mutual task is simply to bear up the fame of the mighty. In this world, even the greatest of poets are simply propagandists. After listing the classical poets from Homer to Claudian, Chaucer sadly and dismissively comments that Fame's court is as full "of hem that writen olde gestes /

As ben on treës rokes nestes" (1515-16): they are little better than the "pursevauntes and heraudes / That crien ryche folkes laudes" (1321-22). Set against this dismissive recognition, however, is the poem's invocation, in its structure and patterns of allusion, of the vast cultural ambitions and achievement of Dante. These are ambitions Chaucer comes to share: recent critics have well shown how both the *House of Fame* and, especially, *Troilus and Criseyde*, bespeak the poet's heroic desire to forge a vernacular literary tradition equivalent to those of classical Rome and *trecento* Italy.[50] If, as A.C. Spearing has said, Chaucer was "the father of English poetry in the sense that before him there was no such thing as an *idea* of English poetry," this was an idea derived in large part from the example of the antique poets and Dante.[51]

It was, in sum, by means of what he called *poetrye*—the writings of the ancients and of their *trecento* inheritors, Dante, Petrarch, and the unacknowledged but all the more ubiquitous Boccaccio—that Chaucer prised himself loose from an imprisoning court ideology. According to a familiar ratio, Chaucer sought to be modern through a return to antiquity; by establishing a relation to a recuperated past he projected himself into a new future. The distinction between courtly *makyng* and the *poetrye* of the ancients and of their imitators was, as Glending Olson has shown, ubiquitous within Chaucer's literary world, and one that he himself maintains rigorously throughout his work.[52] Yet as he makes explicit at the conclusion of the *Troilus*, and as is implicit throughout, he cannot quite conceive of himself as a poet:

> Go, litel bok, go, litel myn tragedye,
> Ther God thi makere yet, er that he dye,
> So sende mygt to make in som comedye!
> But litel book, no makyng thow n'envie,
> But subgit be to alle poesye;
> And kis the steppes where as thow seest pace
> Virgile, Ovide, Omer, Lucan, and Stace. (5, 1786-92)

In the final line Chaucer reconstitutes Dante's "bella scola" of *Inferno* 4, with the significant substitution of the epic Statius for Horace the satirist—a Statius who plays a crucial role in Chaucer's attempt to write a more than courtly poetry in both the *Troilus* and in *Anelida and Arcite*. But far from allowing himself to be incorporated within this group as an equal, as had Dante, Chaucer remains "subject," a petitioner whose humble posture reinvokes the courtly configuration of dominance and submission that Dante's vision of humanistic fellowship—"each shares with me the name [of poet]," says Dante's

Virgil—had supplanted. Even the form in which the *maker* imagines his relation to *poetrye* figures his distance from it.[53]

Moreover, although Chaucer's initial impulse toward classicism clearly derived from the Italian humanists—there is hardly an ancient text that he does not approach through their mediation—the relation he establishes to antiquity is in fact far different. Rather than seeking to recuperate antiquity in its otherness, an otherness that can then provide the terms by which a modern or Renaissance self can define itself, Chaucer is persistently, even painfully aware of the affiliations that bind together past and present into a seamless and finally inescapable web. Similarly, while the humanist conception of the poet offers the court *maker* an opportunity to establish a secure professional identity within a posture of cultural superiority, its grandiose claims seem to have struck Chaucer as both intimidating and foolish. In the *House of Fame* he both attacks the tradition of visionary poetry and questions his own fitness as a *vates*; presents the classical poets as points of stability within a chaotic literary tradition who are nonetheless victimized by demeaning acts of appropriation; and dismisses the very idea of fame while unmistakably asserting his own superior virtue. But the classics do provide Chaucer with two things: first, a form of writing that allows for meaningfulness—for interpretability—while resisting the preemptive hermeneutics of allegorical exegesis; and second, a prospect upon life that is capacious and synoptic but not dismissively transcendental—in other words, a historiography. For Chaucer, as for many other medieval readers, the classical poets, and especially Virgil and Statius, were essentially historians; and they provided him with a historical vision that allowed him to step outside the suffocating narcissism of court *makyng* and to recognize the mutual interdependence of subjectivity and history.[54] And yet this effort at escape was incomplete: the failure of classical history, and of the poets who are its historians, to provide an escape from history is, as we shall see, a large part of the topic of both the *Troilus* and the *Knight's Tale*.

It is also the topic of *Anelida and Arcite*. Here a series of terms derived from the lexicon of court poetry—especially "doublenesse," "newefangelnesse," and "trouthe"—are stretched beyond their usual meaning in order to encompass a far larger reference. And the court form of complaint is here rewritten so as to function not just as an aesthetic object but as an occasion to explore the relation of language to the speaking subject. In this apparently modest and little read poem, in other words, we can begin to see the way in which Chaucer began to use the idea of history, and specifically classical history, to transform himself from a court maker into a European poet.

II

The poem is entitled in the manuscripts "The Compleynt of Feire Anelida and Fals Arcite"—a title that misleadingly attempts to fit into a familiar courtly category a poem that in fact asserts an almost *sui generis* idiosyncracy.[55] For a number of reasons the poem is no critical favorite.[56] It is radically, almost self-destructively segmented, being composed of what appear to be two distinct fragments: first are ten rhyme royal stanzas that invoke Mars, introduce Theseus, and recapitulate the story of the Seven against Thebes; then follows a wholly amorous account of a love affair between the two protagonists, an account that itself falls into two parts, a 140-line narrative of love won and then betrayed, and Anelida's 140-line complaint in an elaborate French rhyme scheme. This second, two-part romantic fragment bears apparently no relation to the epic opening, a discontinuity that critics have usually explained by pleading incompletion. But while four of the thirteen witnesses to the text do append a stanza that promises more to come, this addition is almost certainly scribal, while the explanation of incompletion is in any case a desperate remedy that begs the questions the poem poses.[57] Indeed, the reduplicative structure of the poem as we have it—an opening 70 lines that are then doubled into a 140-line segment that is then itself in turn replicated by another 140 lines—is itself thematically expressive; and despite its peculiarity the poem is in fact a recognizable kind of Chaucerian writing. It is a miniaturized conjunction of epic and romance as they are articulated, in more fully amplified forms, in *Troilus and Criseyde* and the *Knight's Tale*; and its closest analogue in the Chaucerian canon is the so-called "Broche of Thebes," a diminutive poem with similarly divided loyalties that literally fell apart in the fifteenth century, becoming the poems we now know as the "Complaint of Mars" and the "Complaint of Venus."[58] These four poems are structured, in typically Chaucerian fashion, according to a series of oppositions: love is juxtaposed with war as both astrologized mythography (Venus and Mars) and genre (romance and epic); a transcendental rationality conceived in Boethian terms is set against the irreducible specificity of individual experience; and above all, the discourse of contemporary courtly *makyng* is set within a classical context derived primarily from Virgil, Ovid, and Statius, with Dante, Petrarch, and Boccaccio as mediatory figures. The result are poems that explore the relation of past to present as both cultural and psychological events: the cultural project of classicism is inflected into the psychology of a lover's memory, and the recovery of antiquity is

enacted in terms of the drama of loss and reparation staged by the
amorous complaint.

As I have suggested, *Anelida and Arcite* is double in both
inspiration and structure. Establishing at the outset a literary context
that is martial in tone, narrative in form, and male in ideology, it then
modulates into a venerean world of amorousness that culminates in a
highly aestheticized female lyricism. Chaucer ascribes these two
elements of his poem to two different sources: "First folowe I Stace,
and after him Corynne" (21). The *Thebaid* is a powerful if significantly
obscured presence throughout the first ten stanzas, but we cannot be
sure even whom Chaucer means by Corinna: he may be thinking of the
Theban poetess of that name, or a feminine Ovidian voice with links to
the *puella* of the *Amores*, or both.[59] But whoever she is, she functions
as both an alternative and a counterpart to Statius, enforcing the
differences between the poem's two parts but suggesting as well a
complementary relationship. We are thus encouraged to read this
female romanticism as both a modern graft onto an antique epic and as
a coherent part of the poem as a whole, a gloss that constitutes as well
as interprets the text. It is at once superior to the epic history it
explicates and yet absorbed by and made one with it. And the
ambiguous relationship between these two literary elements typifies the
ambivalence that inhabits Chaucer's thought about the relationship of
both the classical past to the medieval present and of the epic world of
history to the romantic world of love. On the one hand, the erotic is an
organon to explain the historical: just as the failed love of Troilus and
Criseyde can presumably teach us about the failure of Troy, so can
Theban compulsions be explicated by reference to Anelida and Arcite.
But conversely, the historical is a determinant of the erotic and the past
of the present: historical precedents impose dark coercions upon young
lovers seeking to escape a similar fate, and the local enclave of love is
subsumed by the tangled world of history it seeks to explicate. Hence
we are forced to acknowledge that a linear model of cause and effect
(love engenders war, war dooms love) must be replaced by a model of
equivalence, in which love equals war. And the ultimate cause—the
origin—must either lie somewhere else or, more likely, be itself
subsumed within the pattern of replication.

The terms in which Thebanness is represented in *Anelida and
Arcite* are suggested by the Muse to whom the poet calls for inspiration.
Ignoring epic Calliope and lyric Erato, Chaucer here invokes
Polyhymnia (15). Literally the muse of many songs, Polyhymnia was in
the classical period given responsibility for the mimic arts, while
medieval mythographers ascribed to her the *Magna memoria* necessary

for an poetry; in this poem she sings with "vois memorial in the shade, / Under the laurer which that may not fade" (18-19).[60] *Anelida and Arcite* is an explicitly memorial poem, seeking to preserve an "olde storie" (10) that "elde . . . Hath nygh devoured out of oure memorie" (12-14). Moreover, when Anelida turns to "write" her "compleynynge" (208-9), she is impelled by what she calls "the poynt of remembraunce"—a phrase that is in the first instance a recollection of Dante, and then of itself, serving the complaint as both its opening and closing lines (211, 350). Indeed, the poem witnesses to and represents the workings of a memory that is at once compulsive and incomplete. Both Anelida's complaint and the poem in which it is embedded are ostentatiously and deliberately incomplete; each represents a consciousness *in medias res*, burdened with a multiplicitous past but incapable of being subordinated to a controlling understanding that would allow for a satisfactory closure. *Anelida and Arcite* articulates a form of consciousness that remembers everything yet understands nothing, that recapitulates an unforgettable past by unwittingly reliving it in the present, that finds no ending because it is unable to grasp its beginning.

Most tellingly, this disturbed mnemonics is represented in the poem in terms not only of the abandoned lady and her false lover but also of the recording poet: in effect, it is allowed to define Chaucerian literary modernity itself. While Chaucer engages in a continuous and respectful recourse to his predecessors, he is simultaneously aware that such recourse is typical of all literary production, including theirs; and his scepticism about his own achievements, implicit in the diminutive and even dismissive self-representations that pervade his work, extends to a larger scepticism about the availability of a legitimizing originality. On the one hand, the modern poet is in danger of becoming nothing more than an impersonator standing at an alienating distance from the sources of Western writing; on the other hand, those very sources are of uncertain reliability.

III

The poem establishes the thematic opposition between Anelida and Arcite in the apparently straightforward and unqualified terms of her singleness of purpose set against his duplicity She is "pleyn" (116) while he is "double in love and no thing pleyn" (87); her "entent" is set wholly "upon trouthe" (132) While he is "fals" and "feyned" (97 and passim).[61] But while the narrative is posited upon Anelida's moral integrity, it simultaneously reveals her love to be almost literally self-divisive. Compulsively thinking of Arcite, Anelida barely attends to her food (134-35); lying in bed, "on him she thoghte alwey" (137); "when that he was absent any throwe, / Anon her thoghte her herte brast *a-two*" (93-94). And having thus warred against herself in a futile effort to become wholly at one with her lover, Anelida reacts to her abandonment with a violence that brings her to the edge of self-extinction:

> She wepith, waileth, swowneth pitously;
> To grounde ded she falleth as a ston;
> Craumpyssheth her lymes crokedly;
> She speketh as her wit were al agon;
> Other colour then asshen hath she noon;
> Non other word speketh she, moche or lyte,
> But 'Merci, cruel herte myn, Arcite!" (169-75)

This is a scene that mixes pathos with horror and invites sympathy while insisting upon judgment. If Anelida is betrayed by Arcite, she is also self-betrayed; and when Arcite unjustly accuses her of duplicity—he swears that "he coude her doublenesse espie, / And al was falsnes that she to him mente" (159-60)—we recognize that beneath the literal falsehood lies a metaphoric truth. Divided against herself first in her love and then in her grief, Anelida surrenders herself to a necessarily interminable process of self-destruction. As she herself says in her subsequent complaint, "For thus ferforth have I my deth [y]-soght? / Myself I mordre with my privy thoght" (290-91).[62]

The extent of Anelida's self-division is made vivid by the way in which the complaint aspires to the self-possession of understanding—to recollection as self-collection, in the Augustinian sense—and yet falls far short.[63] Anelida begins in the confident voice of the moralist: the *sententia* she seeks to demonstrate is the sad lesson that "whoso trewest is, hit shal hir rewe" (217), and the illustrative *exemplum* is the speaker herself. "I wot myself as wel as any wight" (220), she says, meaning three things: she knows the lesson herself, she knows herself as well as anyone else knows her, and she knows herself as well as anyone else knows herself or himself. But these ambitious claims are undone by the rest of the complaint, which shows Anelida as still possessed by the very experience she seeks to understand. Far from standing outside her experience and looking back upon it, she remains wholly absorbed within it. "That I have seid, be seid for evermore!" (246), she bravely asserts, yet she is referring not to the moralizing *sententia* that would seek to categorize and so dismiss the past as a grievous if instructive mistake but to her earlier and foolish commitment to a faithless lover. The complaint is baffled at every turn, and by composing it as a letter for Arcite she acknowledges her self-chosen imprisonment. "I wil ben ay ther I was ones bounde" (245), she says, using an amorous metaphor that also has powerful, if here unacknowledged, Boethian implications.[64] While the mood of the complaint is largely interrogative, only once do the questions rise to the level of philosophical inquiry: "Almyghty God, of trouthe sovereyn, / Wher is the trouthe of man? Who hath hit slayn?" (311-12). But no answer is forthcoming, and Anelida's questioning remains merely rhetorical: "Who may avaunte her beter of hevynesse / Then I?" (296-97); "Shall I preye or elles pleyne?" (282); "Allas! Wher is become your gentilesse. (247); "My swete foo, why do ye so, for shame?" (272). The very possibility of enlightenment is preempted by the anxiety of the fearful lover: 'Now merci, swete, yf I mysseye! / Have I seyd oght amys, I preye?" (317-18).[65]

The final stanza of the complaint opens with a brave effort at conclusiveness: "Then ende I thus, sith I may do no more, / I yeve it up for now and evermore" (342-43). But what is being abandoned is not her love for the faithless and unworthy Arcite but her attempt to understand that love: "But me to rede out of this drede, or guye, / Ne may my wit, so weyk is hit, not streche" (340-41). Anelida will never "leme of love the lore" (345), neither an *ars amatoria* nor the wisdom that unhappy love might teach. Hence she misunderstands the genre of the *Chauntepleure*, taking it to be not a moralizing poem that instructs one in the falseness of a passing world but rather as a vehicle for expressing, and reenacting, the turmoil of uninstructed emotion.[66] In attempting to understand her past, Anelida has revealed how powerfully present it is; trying to append a dismissive *explicit*, she finds herself hopelessly implicated. The conclusion to the complaint is thus appropriately inconclusive. The last line—"thirled with the poynt of remembraunce" (350)—exactly replicates the first (211): memory encapsulates the complaint as it engrosses the speaker, and her ending returns her to her beginning in an endless cycle of repetition. This is surely why the complaint is, as Skeat long ago noted, formally circular: the first six stanzas are exactly matched, in content as well as form, by the last six.[67] Lacking a fixed perspective outside her experience from which to understand it, Anelida is condemned to repeat it.

The final stanza of the complaint also contains an allusion to another famous complaint that serves to raise larger questions about the

shape of literary history as a whole, and about the position of the
medieval poet within this history:

> But as the swan, I have herd seyd ful yore,
> Ayeins his deth shal singen his penaunce,
> So singe I here my destinee or chaunce. (346-48)

This is a citation of Dido's epistle in the *Heroides*, and by alluding to it
here Chaucer invokes both the specific text that ultimately underwrites
the amorous elements of *Anelida and Arcite* and the classical genre
upon which he modeled the epistolary complaints that appear
throughout his work.[68] Both Anelida's complaint and the poem as a
whole are pervaded with echoes of Dido's epistle, and there is a deep
affinity of purpose between the two texts: both are largely interrogative
efforts to achieve a self-understanding that will emancipate the speaker
from the corrosive ambivalence of her feelings, and both come
ultimately to naught.[69] There are as well obvious affinities between
"quene Anelida" (47) and *Dido regina*.[70] Both are royal, both exiles,
both in love with a man who represents a great political hegemony
(Thebes, Rome) and yet proves to be "fals" (*perfidus*), and false in
ways that are, as we shall see oddly similar.

By invoking Dido here Chaucer establishes a curious but telling
chronological disjunction. In terms of the fictive time of her complaint,
Anelida speaks now as Dido will come to speak later, a priority that is
stressed by having Anelida *close* with the image of the swan song with
which Dido will "later" *begin*. But in terms of the time of literary
history, priority goes to Dido: the image of the swan song is originally
hers. The effect of this temporal amalgamation is thus not to adjudicate
originality but to challenge the very concept of an origin. Complaint is
a form of speech that transgresses the usual temporal categories, both in
the individual sense that it elides temporal divisions—before and after,
then and now, past and present are distinctions the plaintive voice
refuses to observe—and in the general sense that it is always with us:
Anelida speaks in Thebes as Dido speaks in Carthage and, as the
elaborately contemporary rhyme scheme of her complaint reminds us,
as women still speak in the courts of Chaucer's England.[71] The swan
song of complaint is thus both always original and already belated: a
first utterance that breaks a lifelong silence, it issues forth at the point
of extinction and bespeaks a helplessness before the temporality that
has inflicted a mortal wound. This is what it means, then, to speak
while "thirled with the poynt of remembraunce." Apparently "pleyn,"
Anelida's "compleynynge" is an echoic doubling that turns back upon

itself not only formally and psychologically but also temporally. As with Anelida's self-division, Arcite's duplicity—"he was double in love and no thing pleyn" (87)—is an erotic disorder with an Ovidian aetiology. His "falsnes" mimics the Ovidian Aeneas's perfidiousness, and his restless questing after "another lady" (144) parallels Aeneas's attraction to an always beckoning *alter amor* (17).[72] "Put by your wanderings," Dido urges Aeneas, and her phrase—*ambage remissa* (149)—points as well to the evasive circumlocutions with which he first won her love and has now rejected it. Whether the goal be empire or love, the questing impulse remains the same, and both Aeneas and Arcite are insatiable, satisfied only with dissatisfaction. *Facta fugis, facienda petis* (13), Dido accuses Aeneas: "You flee what has been done; what is to be done, you seek." If for Ovid the characteristically feminine erotic disorder is endless pining, the masculine counterpart is endless discontent.[73] As the *Amores* explore in detail, the elaborate system of impediments and frustrations that typifies Ovidian eroticism, and that Chaucer here and elsewhere calls "daunger" (186, 195), is established for no other reason than to forestall the disappointment of full possession. As Ovid says to an inattentive rival, "If you feel no need of guarding your love for yourself, you fool, see that you guard her for me, that I may desire her the more! What is permitted is unwanted, but what is forbidden burns all the more sharply."[74]

Chaucer's term for this discontent, in this poem and elsewhere, is "newefangelnesse" (141), a condition that "naturally" afflicts men:

> The kynde of mannes herte is to delyte
> In thing that straunge is, also God me save!
> For what he may not gete, that wolde he have. (201-3)

Although this condition, like Anelida's "languisshing" (178), can be adequately glossed by reference to Ovidian texts, Chaucer in fact thinks of it in larger, philosophical terms. This is suggested in part by the anachronistic reference to Lamech, "the firste fader that began / To loven two, and was in bigamye" (152-53); the biblical Lamech is not only a bigamist but a homicide, a self-confessed member of the fratricidal race of Cain—a scriptural analogue, as it were, to the Thebans of classical mythology.[75] Evidently more is at issue than Ovidian wit would suggest, and this allusion begins to invoke the darker passions that lie behind Arcite's eroticism.

We can locate the center of Chaucer's concern by collating the new-fangledness of *Anelida and Arcite* with cognate texts from elsewhere in Chaucer's poetry. Most directly relevant is the complaint of the falcon in the *Squire's Tale*, a complaint that echoes *Anelida and Arcite* in a number of other instances as well.[76] In explaining the tercelet's infidelity, the falcon has recourse to a Boethian allusion:

> I trowe he hadde thilke text in mynde,
> That 'alle thynge, repeirynge to his kynde,
> Gladeth hymself;' thus seyn men, as I gesse.
> Men loven of propre kynde newefangelnesse,
> As briddes doon that men in cages fede. (607-11)

Even if a bird is fed on delicacies, continues the falcon, it will prefer worms, "So newefangel been they of hire mete, / And loven novelties of proper kynde" (618-19). In the *Manciple's Tale* the same *exemplum* reappears, again designed to show that "flessh is . . . newefangel" and that men "konne in nothyng han plesaunce / That sowneth into vertu any while" (193-95).[77]

Both of these cognate texts are in the first instance comic and even frivolous: the falcon's objection to her avian lover is that he has, unsurprisingly, behaved just like a bird, while the Manciple's allusion is part of a complex set of evasive insults. But in both instances a serious question is at issue: by what means can the natural man be redeemed? In the *Squire's Tale* it is the redemptive powers of culture—what the Squire calls "gentilesse"—that are tested and found wanting, while the vividness with which the Manciple's classical fable represents the corruptions of the flesh preempts any possibility of social redemption and thus provides a fitting preparation for the Parson's terminal Christian prescriptions. Moreover, the seriousness of all three of these Chaucerian meditations on the newfangledness of sexual infidelity becomes clear when we invoke the Boethian subtext that lies behind them. This is meter ii of Book 3, which describes how Nature "restreyneth alle thynges by a boond that may nat be unbownde" (3, ii, 6-7). Boethius gives several examples of this binding: tamed lions that become wild again upon tasting blood, the caged bird that scorns the luxurious food of its captivity and sings always of the shadowed wood, the bent bough that springs upright when released, the westering sun that returns to its orient source. These natural bindings are small instances of the cosmic binding that orders the universe as a whole. "Alle thynges seken ayen to hir propre cours [*recursus*]," says Boethius in the same meter, "and alle thynges rejoysen hem of hir retornyng ayen to hir nature" (39-42). Just as it is right for the bird to return to the wood, so the proper course for man is to return to his heavenly origins. This is a homecoming that is to be accomplished through a philosophical pedagogy that will enable man to gaze once again upon that "clere welle of good' (3, xii, 1-2) that is itself both "the begynnynge of alle thinges" (3, 10, 100) and the "oon ende of blisfulnesse" (3, 2, 8). To possess this knowledge is to enjoy "the ferme stablenesse of perdurable duellynge" (3, 11, 185-86), what Boethius elsewhere calls "the ende of alle thinges that ben to desire, beyonde the whiche ende ther nys no thing to desire" (4, 2, 165-67).

Man is impelled on this quest for stability by a force that Boethius metaphorically designates "ayen-ledynge fyer" or *ignis revertus* (3, ix, 38) and, in more philosophical language, *intentio naturalis* or "naturel entencioun" (3, 11,154-55). This intention is a kind of love. Boethius calls it *caritas,* a word Chaucer translates with the doublet "this charite and this love" (3, 11, 175-76). It represents at the level of subjectivity the force that governs the recursive action that characterizes being as a whole: all things are "constreynede . . . into roundnesses" and "comen . . . eftsones ayein, by love retorned [*converso . . . amore*], to the cause that hath yeven hem beinge" (4, iv, 56-59). And at the level of ethics it is the love that "halt togidres peples joyned with an holy boond, and knytteth sacrement of mariages of chaste loves" (2, viii, 21-23). Its opposite is what Boethius calls the "willeful moevynges of the soule" (3, 11, 153-54) that deflect men into "myswandrynge errour [and] mysledeth hem into false goodes" (3, 2, 24-25). It is above all else that regressive Ovidian love that possesses Orpheus, in Boethius's most famous meter, and that persuades him to turn his eyes backward, in an infernal parody of the authentic recursive gaze, upon the doomed Eurydice.

Chaucer's depiction of the "newefangelnesse" of Arcite's erotic restlessness invokes this kind of Boethian critique. Willfully rejecting Anelida's chaste love, Arcite rejects as well a fully human nature that ineluctably tends toward the true end of things, aligning himself instead with a less than human self that "delyte[th] / In thing that straunge is" (201-2). Hence he is throughout the poem subjected to metaphors drawn from the animal world. He behaves "ryght as an hors, that can both bite and pleyne" (157); "His newe lady holdeth him so narowe / Up by the bridil, at the staves ende" (183-84); and in following her "he is caught up in another les" (233). Anelida herself completes this pattern of judgment with a final, plaintive question that returns us to the Boethian passage from which we began: "Is that a tame best that is ay feyn / To fleen away when he is lest agast?" (315-16). It is this self-division, between a truly human nature and a less than human hankering after the unavailable and the forbidden, that most profoundly defines Arcite as "double in love" (87) and that links him to the ironically self-divided lady whom he seeks to abandon. What also links him to Anelida is his disordered memory, for his negligence of his lady is a sign of a larger forgetfulness. Arcite is one of those who has, in Lady Philosophy's words, "foryeten hymselve" (1, 2, 22): he no longer "remembre[s] of what cuntre" he is born (1, 5, 16-17) nor "remembres . . . what is the ende of thynges, and whider that the entencion of alle kynde tendeth" (1, 6, 37-39). "Drerynesse hath dulled my memorie" (1, 6, 41), says the prisoner in the *Consolation*, and the philosophical understanding to which the dialogue with Philosophy is devoted is defined as a process of remembering or anamnesis. Man, says Lady Philosophy, "alwey rercheth and seketh the sovereyne good, al be it so with a dyrkyd memorie; but he not by whiche path, ryght as a dronke man not nat by whiche path he may retourne hom to his hous" (3, 2, 83-88)—a passage that is later cited by the Arcite of the *Knight's Tale* (1260-67). Just as Anelida's obsessive memory forecloses her future, so does Arcite's darkened memory keep him wandering in quest of a "suffisaunce" that was once his but that he has now abandoned. And as Arcite is alienated from his true origin so is Anelida denied access to a transcendent end: together they are condemned to an endless repetitiveness that stands as a sad parody of the authentic recursions of Boethianism.

In soliciting a Boethian reading of its lovers, *Anelida and Arcite* prefigures the more extensive Boethianism of "The Complaint of Mars," *Troilus and Criseyde* and the *Knight's Tale*. What is important for interpretive purposes, however, is that such a reading opens a prospect upon the complex affiliations that Chaucer establishes throughout his work among Boethian philosophy, Ovidian love, and Thebanness. In exploring these affiliations we shall come to understand how insecurely grounded is the interpretive authority we are encouraged to cede to Boethianism. For if Thebanness stands as the other that Boethianism suppresses, this is because its configurations provide a dark mirroring of Boethian idealism that raise disquieting and finally unanswerable questions. The Theban story is itself about disordered memory and fatal repetition, about the tyranny of a past that is both forgotten and obsessively remembered, and about the recursive patterns into which history falls.

In its fullest form, the story begins with acts of sexual violence—the abduction of Europa by Jove—and paternal tyranny: Agenor unfairly commands Cadmus either to recover his sister Europa or go into permanent exile, a command that in the *Metamorphoses* Ovid designates as *pius et sceleratus eodem* (3, 5). Necessarily failing in his quest, Cadmus wanders in exile until Apollo leads him to Boeotia where he is to found Thebes. But this originary act, despite its divine superintendence, is both flawed in itself and proleptic of the disasters to follow: slaying a serpent sacred to Mars, Cadmus is told that he will himself end his days as a serpent, and when he sows the serpent's teeth there spring up warriors who engage in fratricidal slaughter. Born from the earth, these first Thebans now return to it; in Ovid's phrase (which Chaucer remembered when writing the *Pardoner's Tale*), they beat on the warm breast of their mother for reentry: *tepido plangebant pectora matrem* (3,126). Here is the central, recursive act of Theban history, the first instance of a chthonic return that is then endlessly repeated.

The details of this recursion are articulated in the history of "the broche of Thebes" to which Chaucer alludes in the "Complaint of Mars." The brooch is itself a sign of illicit sexuality: it is made by Vulcan as a bitter wedding gift for Harmonia, the daughter of Mars and Venus, when she marries Cadmus—a marriage that causes their exile from their city and transformation into the originary serpents. The next owner is Semele, struck by Jove's lightning; then Agave, driven mad by the Furies; then Jocasta; then Argia, wife of Polynices, who gives it to Euripyle if she will reveal the hiding place of her husband Amphiauraus so that he may become one of the seven against Thebes, an act of betrayal that issues in his all-too-Theban engulfment in the earth. When Euripyle is then murdered by her vengeful son Alcmaeon, Ovid tellingly designates the crime as *pius et sceleratus eodem* (9, 408), the same phrase he had earlier applied to Agenor's exile of Cadmus at the beginning of Theban history. The final owner of the brooch is Orestes, whom it incites to repeat an identical act of filial vengeance against *his* mother, Clytaemnestra.[79] Like the boar that becomes the heraldic device of the Theban family of Tydeus in the *Troilus*, the brooch is an object of desire whose possession is inevitably fatal; as Chaucer's Mars says in his complaint, its owner has "al his desir and therwith al myschaunce" (241).[80] It arouses emotions that are in the first instance erotic (Harmonia, Semele, Agave, Jocasta) but that entail deadly consequences, and it functions in a context in which the venerean and the martial are in a continual process of mutual subversion, in which amorousness and violence are metamorphosed and finally fused, whether as internecine vengeance or romantic betrayal. Descending down through the Theban line—*longa est series*, says Statius (2, 267; cf. 1, 7)—the brooch metonymically represents the primal polymorphousness of Theban emotions and the self-destructive regressiveness that results from submitting to a self unknown.

At the center of Theban history is Oedipus, the tragic figure who encapsulates the Theban fate with terrifying economy. The profound circularity of Thebanness, its inability ever to diverge from the reversionary shape ordained in and by its beginning, is reflected in the details of Oedipus's life as the Middle Ages reconstructed them. At once malevolent and pitiable, Oedipus becomes both agent and victim of the self-imposed genocide that decimates Thebes. As a son he kills his father Laius—one medieval text has him say that he "struck iron through my father's loins"—and as a father he reenacts his primal crime by cursing his sons with what the same text has him describe as "the sword of my tongue."[81] Similarly, he reenacts the return of the dragon- warriors to their mother earth in his incest with Jocasta: his union with his mother is described by both Statius and Seneca as a *revolutus in ortus*.[82] Even the smallest details of his life express the compulsions of repetition and circularity: exiled as an infant to Mount Cithaeron by his father, he is in his old age exiled there once again by Creon, and the riddle that marks him as extraordinary presents his life, and all life, as inescapably replicating. In the *Roman de Thèbes* and its prose adjuncts the riddle is itself given a duplicative form: "I have heard tell of a beast," says the Sphinx, "that when it first wishes to walk on the ground it goes on four feet like a bear; and then comes a time when it has no need of the fourth foot and it moves with great speed on three; and when it has greater strength it stands and goes on two feet; and then it has need of three, and then four. Friend, tell me if you have ever seen such a beast?"[83] Man is the beast, and whether he is figured as a bear or, as in the *Troilus*, as a boar, it is his irredeemable animality that lies at the heart of Theban history, just as it lies at the center of Arcite's Theban consciousness in *Anelida and Arcite*.

Thebanness is a fatal doubling of the self that issues in a replicating history that preempts a linear or developmental progress. Theban history in its pure form has neither origin nor end but only a single, infinitely repeatable moment of illicit eroticism and fratricidal rivalry—love and war locked together in a perverse fatality. In its circular recursions moreover, it stands as a dark echo of the idealistic *recursus* of Boethianism, a specular impersonation that destabilizes the interpretive authority with which the *Consolation* is usually invested. Like the Theban dragon-warriors and their Oedipal descendants, the Boethian philosopher is also engaged in a *revolutus in ortus*, a return to the *fons et origo* from which all being descends. For Boethius this origin is celestial: as Chaucer's most securely Boethian poem advises its readers, "Know thy contree, look up, thank God of al; / Hold the heye wey and lat thy gost thee lede."[84] But the lesson about origins that the Theban legend teaches is epitomized in a phrase from the *Thebaid: crudelis pater vincit*. Whether personified as father Oedipus or the dragon-warriors' mother earth, the parent ineluctably calls the Theban back, either temporally by enacting the past or spatially by reentering the earth, the chthonic source of life. According to Boethius's Platonic rationalism, moral failure is a function of intellectual error: an undiverted *intentio naturalis* directs us to the "good [that] is the fyn of alle thinges" (3, 2, 230), and it is only "myswandrynge errour [that] mysledeth [men] into false goodes" (3, 2, 23-25; cf. 3, 3, 6-8). Boethian *caritas* is an *amor conversus* that irresistibly returns us to the divine origin. But the *amor* that motivates the Theban, however well intentioned, has a twofold character (*pius et sceleratus eodem*)that leads him inevitably to disaster. The Theban legend harshly argues that the natural self is by definition ill-behaved and self-defeating, an unconstrained appetitiveness that bespeaks not a transcendent origin but one that is primordial and earthbound.

IV

This Theban economy has a powerful relevance as well to a poet like Chaucer, whose own habits of literary recall witness to a dynamic strikingly similar to that articulated by Theban history. If we return now to *Anelida and Arcite* in order to examine the intertextual relations that inform it, we can begin to understand the way in which Chaucer's poetics of memory stand as a compositional version of Thebanness. An important instance is Anelida's echoed phrase, "the poynt of remembraunce" (211, 350)—a phrase that derives from *Purgatorio* 12, where Dante and Virgil tread upon the figured pavement of the cornice of pride. This is the terrace where the "gran tumor" (*Purg.* 11, 119) of Dante's own artistic pride is put down by a discussion of the fruitless rivalry between artistic generations. The divine images with which the cornice is adorned are compared with the sculptured paving stones that cover the tombs set into the floor of the church nave: "In order that there be memory of them, the stones in the church floor over the buried dead bear figured what they were before: wherefore many a time men weep for them there at the prick of the memory [*la punctura de la rimembranza*] that spurs only the faithful."[85] Bearing an artistic refiguring of the original that lies within, the sculptured stones are memorial images that spur the pious with the *punctura de la rimembranza*. Chaucer's own poem is a similar act of piety toward his dead poetic precursors: Corinna, Ovid, Statius, Dante himself, even the stubbornly unacknowledged Boccaccio. As with Anelida's lament over the departed Arcite, the poem testifies to the presence of those who are

absent, and Chaucer presents himself, here as elsewhere, as a merely
curatorial figure. He is the scribe who will "*endyte* / This olde storie"
(9-10) and will loyally "folowe" (21) in the footsteps of Statius and
Corinna. But the poem itself refuses to endorse even the possibility of
such an unmediated access to the past. For it argues throughout, and
especially in the first ten stanzas, that the foundations of the poet's
literary heritage are only fitfully available in their original and
authentic form, and that he must instead make do with artful
refigurings, modern rewritings that stand always at some distance from
the original.[86]

Such an understanding of the poetic past is implicit in the enigma
of Corinna, whether she be the Theban *tenuis Corinna* (artful Corinna)
of Statius's *Silvae*, who could have been at most only a name to
Chaucer, or the Roman *versuta Corinna* (well-versed Corinna), who is
implied throughout Ovid's *Amores* but, represented only as the figure
of the poet's desire, has herself no voice.[87] Whoever she is, the name
signifies a presence that devouring time has taken away, leaving behind
only a verbal image. Time has likewise but differently distanced the
poem's other announced source: Statius's *Thebaid* is everywhere
present in the first ten stanzas, but present in a way that insists upon
distance. For what a close comparison of these ten stanzas with the
Thebaid reveals is that Statius appears in the poem only accompanied
by his belated imitator Boccaccio, whose own version of the master's
poem—the *Teseida*—permeates these lines. If we start with the three
opening stanzas, we find them to be a rewriting of the comparable
opening stanzas of the *Teseida*, itself a rewriting of the *Thebaid*. They
are, moreover, a rewriting with a difference, for they both reverse the
order of Boccaccio's stanzas—1, 2 and 3 here become 3, 2 and 1—and
in one crucial point flatly contradict them. Whereas Boccaccio says that
the *storia antiqua* he will tell has never been told by a Latin author,
Chaucer assures us that he found the "olde storie" precisely "in Latin"
(10).[88] Contravening his authority in order to invoke an authority,
Chaucer uses the same gesture both to demonstrate and to deny his own
originality; and he implies that it is not pious accuracy that
characterizes the relation of follower to precursor but deformation and
even reversal.

The next three stanzas of *Anelida and Arcite*, however, do return
us directly to a Theban master source in Statius's *Thebaid*: describing
the return of Theseus from the conquest of Hyppolyta, they begin by
closely translating sixteen lines from Statius's last book (12, 519-35).[89]
But before they finish they again veer off into the *Teseida* by invoking
the non-Statian Emily and establishing the terms of Boccaccio's story

(38-42). When Statius does appear, then, and even here in what are close to his own words, it is in service to Boccaccio, the imitator from whom he seems never to be quite free. Then in the seventh stanza Chaucer begins a final effort to return to the original version of the Theban story: leaving Theseus "in his weye rydynge" (46) toward Athens, the poet doubles back to the chronologically prior Theban War of which Statius is the chronicler, describing both his rhetorical turn and the Theban matter itself with the provocative phrase, "the slye wey."[90] But this return to the origin is also predictably thwarted: when in stanzas 8-10 the story of the Theban War is summarized, it appears in a précis drawn not from the *Thebaid* but from the unavoidable *Teseida*. The Theban matter cannot, it seems, be represented in its original Statian form; just as classical texts are encrusted with medieval glosses, so does Statius come to Chaucer embedded within a Boccaccian context.

Nor should we assume that the difference between original and imitation is so radical as to guarantee their distinction. However unlike the *Thebaid* the *Teseida* may appear to us, it is clear that Boccaccio intended his poem to be a vernacular recreation of the classical epic. Divided into twelve books and containing, in some manuscripts at least, the identical number of lines as the *Aeneid*, the *Teseida* deploys elaborate mythographical and even archaeological allusions, articulates sentiments and values appropriate to the pre-Christian past, and appends to its classicized text a medieval gloss. Even as it draws heavily upon the vernacular *romanzi* of contemporary Italy, it locates medieval forms in the service of a classicizing project. Unlike *Anelida and Arcite* and the *Knight's Tale*, the *Teseida* declines to acknowledge that its historicist piety may be itself a form of Thebanness. Arcita may be a victim of the Theban curse, but he is the last victim, and his finally selfless love for Emilia makes possible a healing reconciliation with Palemone that lays the past to rest. For Boccaccio, modern love can appease ancient hatreds, and his romantic grafts onto the epic stock are not infected by the original malignity but claim to redeem the whole.[91] But if for Boccaccio the *Teseida* bespeaks a medieval mastery over the classical past, for Chaucer, here as in the *Troilus* and the *Knight's Tale*, antiquity bears a dark, almost atavistic power.

Finally, if it is true that for Chaucer the original Theban voice is confusingly doubled by later echoes—and he seems to have heard not only Statius, Ovid, and Seneca but also the so-called *Histoire ancienne jusqu'à César*, the anonymous authors of the *Roman de Thèbes* and the *Planctus Oedipi*, and Dante—is it any longer possible to speak of an original or authentic story at all?[92] Indeed, what effect does the mysterious Corinna have upon Statius's authority? Can we any longer assume that the poet whom Chaucer in the *House of Fame* identified as a native of Toulouse is himself the original Theban poet?[93] Just as *Anelida and Arcite* is hardly the last word on Thebes, neither surely is the *Thebaid* the first. Statius himself implies as much at the beginning of his own poem: *longa retro series*, he says (1, 7), and whatever starting point is chosen must be arbitrary.[94] Every beginning is *in medias res*, every account a selection, every telling a retelling. Far from being a straightforward linear development, the history of Theban writing is what Chaucer in the *Boece* calls a "replicacioun of wordes" (3, 12, 160-61), and to enter upon it is to broach a labyrinthine way, "so entrelaced that it is unable to ben unlaced" (3, 12, 157). Haunted by a past that is at once sustaining (like a pavement) and galling (like a spur), Theban writing simultaneously salves and reopens the wound caused by "the poynt of remembraunce;" and Chaucer, by invoking Thebes as an early and recurrent locus of his own work, and as a metaphor for his own poetics of memory, sets himself in a relationship with origins so sceptical that it will never receive a final resolution until (which will never happen) the pilgrims arrive at Canterbury.

NOTES

1. The question has been most recently and usefully discussed by Paul Strohm, *Social Chaucer* (Cambridge: Harvard University Press, 1989).

2. The Chaucerian roots of fifteenth-century didacticism are visible in Lydgate's *Fall of Princes,* which although based on a French translation of Boccaccio's *De casibus virorum illustrium* finds its precedent, its characteristic rhyme scheme, and its generic definition (as Lydgate makes clear in Book 5, lines 3118-22) in the *Monk's Tale*; and in Hoccleve's *Regement of Princes, a miroir de prince* analogous to the *Tale of Melibee*. For Chaucer as the source of fifteenth-century amorous verse, see Rossell Hope Robbins, "The Vintner's Son: French Wine in English Bottles," in *Eleanor of Aquitaine: Patron and Politician,* ed. William W. Kibler (Austin: University of Texas Press, 1976), 147-72, and his chapter "The Lyrics," in *A Companion to Chaucer Studies*, ed. Beryl Rowland, rev. ed. (New York: Oxford University Press, 1979), 380-402.

3. It should be noted, however, that the tales chosen for anthologizing in the fifteenth century suggest a conservative attention to moralizing and courtly writing; see Daniel Silvia, "Some Fifteenth-

Century Manuscripts of the *Canterbury Tales*," in *Chaucer and Middle English Studies in Honor of Rossell Hope Robbins*, ed. Beryl Rowland (London: Allen and Unwin, 1974), 153-61, and Paul Strohm, "Chaucer's Fifteenth-Century Audience and the Narrowing of the 'Chaucer Tradition'," *SAC* 4 (1982): 3-32.

4. Derek Brewer, ed., *Chaucer: The Critical Heritage* (London: Routledge and Kegan Paul, 1978), 2:186-87; the passage is from an article by William Minto, professor of logic and English at Aberdeen University, published in the ninth edition of the *Encyclopedia Britannica* (1876).

5. Ibid.,1:3-15; from an anonymous article published in the *Edinburgh Review* in 1837.

6. The latest version of this argument can be found in Paul Olson's *The* Canterbury Tales *and the Good Society* (Princeton: Princeton University Press, 1985). For Olson the *Tales* deal directly with matters under debate in the Ricardian court of the 1380s and 1390s: peace versus war, the nature of kingship, the relation of the monastic orders to secular government, the abuses of the contemporary church, and so on. In effect, Olson's Chaucer is a court apologist, expressing through the *Tales*, as through the earlier poems, opinions that Olson takes to be those of the court. Olson's work is a natural extension of D.W Robertson, Jr.'s, *A Preface to Chaucer* (Princeton: Princeton University Press, 1962). For Robertson's own account of Chaucer as a court poet, see his "The Historical Setting of Chaucer's *Book of the Duchess*," in *Medieval Studies in Honor of Urban Tigner Holmes*, ed. John Mahoney and John Esten Keller (Chapel Hill: University of North Carolina Press, 1965), 169-95; "The Probable Date and Purpose of Chaucer's *Troilus*," *M&H* 13 (1985): 143-71; and "The Probable Date and Purpose of Chaucer's *Knight's Tale*," *SP* 84 (1987): 418-39.

7. The distinction between poetry of the court and courtly poetry is drawn, in somewhat different terms, by Derek Pearsall, *Old English and Middle English Poetry* (London: Routledge and Kegan Paul, 1977), 212.

8. For the literary culture at the court of Henry II, see Walter F. Schirmer and Ulrich Broich, *Studien zum literarischen Patronat im England des 12. Jahrhunderts* (Cologne: Westdeutscher Verlag, 1962); for Chrétien and the author of the *Roman d'Eneas*, see my *Negotiating the Past: The Historical Understanding of Medieval Literature* (Madison: University of Wisconsin Press, 1987), 157-95, and the references cited there (158 n. 4).

9. See Gervase Mathew, *The Court of Richard II* (London: John Murray, 1968).

10. For these developments, see Christopher Given-Wilson, *The Royal Household and the King's Affinity* (New Haven: Yale University Press, 1986).

11. This process is described by Anthony Tuck, *Richard II and the English Nobility* (London: St. Martin's, 1974). For the political meaning of the cultural attitudes of the Ricardian court, see Patricia J. Eberle, "The Politics of Courtly Style in the Court of Richard II," in *The Spirit of the Court: Selected Proceedings of the Fourth Congress of the International Courtly Literature Society*, ed. Glyn S. Burgess and Robert A. Taylor (Cambridge: Brewer, 1985), 168-78.

12. In a later poem, Froissart says that while in England he wrote poetry not only for the queen but for her daughter, Isabelle de Coucy, and daughter-in-law, Blanche of Lancaster; for Humphrey of Bohun, the Earl of Hereford; for John Hastings, the Earl of Pembroke; for Lord Edward Despenser; and for a number of French knights then in England: Anthime Fourrier, ed., *Le joli buisson de jonece* (Geneva: Droz, 1975), lines 230- 373. We also know that he sent a balade to Philippa, the eldest daughter of Henry of Lancaster: see Elizabeth Salter, *Fourteenth-Century English Poetry: Contexts and Readings* (Oxford: Clarendon Press, 1983), 62-63.

13. These passages are cited by Peter F. Dembowski, *Jean Froissart and his* Meliador: *Context, Craft, and Sense* (Lexington: French Forum, 1983), 43, 163 n. 43. Dembowski calls these years at the English court "without doubt the period of [Froissart's] most intense poetic activity. It was then that he composed the greater number of his lyric poems and much of his other poetic output. There is no doubt that Froissart flourished in those years as a court poet and, at the same time, underwent a period of preparation and apprenticeship for his future profession as a chronicler" (42-43).

14. For Chaucer's borrowings from Froissart's *Paradys d'Amour*, see Barry A. Windeatt, ed. and trans., *Chaucer's Dream Poetry: Sources and Analogues* (Cambridge: Brewer, 1982), 41-57; for the reverse process, see James I. Wimsatt, "The *Dit dou Bleu Chevalier*: Froissart's Imitation of Chaucer," *MS* 34 (1972): 388-400.

15. See Larry D. Benson, "The Occasion of the *Parliament of Fowls*," in The Wisdom of *Poetry: Essays in Early English Literature in Honor of Morton W. Bloomfield*, ed. Larry D. Benson and Siegfried Wenzel (Kalamazoo: Institute for Medieval Studies, 1982), 123-44.

16. See below, chapter 2, 155-62.

17. See R.T. Lenaghan, "Chaucer's Circle of Gentlemen and Clerks," *ChR* 18 (1983-84): 155-60; Paul Strohm, "Chaucer's

Audience," *L&H* 5 (1977): 26-41; Derek Pearsall, *"The Troilus* Frontispiece and Chaucer's Audience," *YES* 7 (1977): 68-74.

18. Rossell Hope Robbins, "The Structure of Longer Middle English Court Poems," in *Chaucerian Problems and Perspectives: Essays Presented to Paul E. Beichner,* ed. Edward Vasta and Zacharias P. Thundy (Notre Dame: University of Notre Dame Press, 1979), 245. See also Robbins's "The Middle English Court Love Lyric," in *The Interpretation of Medieval Lyric,* ed. W.T.H. Jackson (New York: Columbia University Press, 1980), 205-32.

19. John Gower, *Confessio amantis* 8:*2942-47, in G.C. Macauley, *The Complete Works of John Gower* (London: Clarendon Press, 1900), 2:466.

20. The absence of a native tradition is well illustrated by the courtly lyrics of Harley 2253, which represent virtually the only pre-Chaucerian body of love lyric in English: these are courtly poems written without a court to sustain them, a situation reflected in a series of odd incongruities, as Derek Pearsall has shown (*Old English and Middle English Poetry,* 128).

21. Rossell Hope Robbins, "Geoffroi Chaucier, Poète Français, Father of English Poetry," *ChR* 13 (1978-79), 106; see also Robbins's "Chaucer and the Lyric Tradition," *Poetica* 15/16 (1983): 107-27, and "The Vintner's Son."

22. Salter, *Fourteenth-Century English Poetry,* 52.-85.

23. See the seminal article by Glending Olson, "Making and Poetry in the Age of Chaucer," *CL* 31 (1979): 272-90.

24. See John Stevens, *Music and Poetry in the Early Tudor Court* (London: Methuen, 1961), 147-232, Daniel Poirion, *Le poète et le prince* (Paris: Presses universitaires de France, 1965), 59-139, Richard Firth Green, *Poets and Princepleasers: Literatureand the English Court in the Later Middle Ages* (Toronto: University of Toronto Press, 1980), and Glending Olson, "Toward a Poetics of the Late Medieval Court Lyric," in *Vernacular Poetics in the Middle Ages,* ed. Lois Ebin (Kalamazoo: Medieval Institute Publications, 1984), 227-48.

25. Robert Guiette, "D'une poésie formelle en France en Moyen Age," *Romanica Gandensia* 8 (1960), 17; see also Roger Dragonetti, *La technique poètique des trouvères dans la chanson courtoise* (Bruges: De Tempel, 1960).

26. Paul Zumthor, *Essai de poétique médiévale* (Paris: Seuil, 1972), 243, 267. The social and economic constraints to which the late medieval English nobility were subjected are described in relation to the *Knight's Tale* in chapter 3.

27. For the importance of cuisine and fashion in the late medieval court, see Mathew, *Court of Richard II*, 23-31.

28. Derek Pearsall, *John Lydgate* (London: Routledge and Kegan Paul, 1970), 92-93.

29. Anne Middleton, "Chaucer's 'New Men' and the Good of Poetry," in *Literature and Society*, ed. Edward W. Said (Baltimore: Johns Hopkins University Press, 1980), 32; Zumthor, *Essai de poétique*, 239- 40. As Zumthor says, the *grand chant courtois* "tend à la fois à convaincre l'auditeur d'une manière 'nouvelle,' inattendue, de quelque chose que, en un certain sens, il ignorait; et a manifester les conclusions inéluctables de quelque chose qu'en un autre sens il savait déjà. D'où une oscillation incessante entre information et redondance" (239).

30. When Froissart presented a copy of his poems to Richard II, he tells us that the king "opened it and looked inside and it pleased him greatly. Well it might, for it was illuminated, nicely written and illustrated, with a cover of crimson velvet with ten studs of silver gilt and golden roses in the middle and two large gilded clasps richly worked at their centres with rose-trees" (cited by Green, *Poets and Princepleasers*, 64). What Richard valued was the book as an object of beauty rather than as a source of understanding. As Green says, "Books were regarded as an important part of the prince's assets, able to take their place alongside the more predictable items in the aristocratic showcase" (60). And Mathew argues that "a court fashion in *objets de luxe* may best explain some of the new developments in book production and illustration" in the later fourteenth century (*Court of Richard II*, 39).

31. For a summary of these transformations, see Chris Given-Wilson, *The English Nobility in the Late Middle Ages* (London: Routledge and Kegan Paul, 1987). The difference between class and caste is succinctly described by Edmund Leach, "Caste, Class and Slavery: The Taxonomic Problem," in *Caste and Race: Comparative Approaches*, ed. Anthony de Reuck and Julie Knight (Boston: Little, Brown, 1966): "A 'ruling class' may be defined as a *caste* when the fact of class endogamy is strikingly obvious and when the inheritance of privilege has become narrowly restricted to members of that 'caste' in perpetuity. This kind of situation is likely to arise when the ruling group is distinguished from the inferior group or groups by *wide* differences of standard of living or by other easily recognizable labels" (9).

32. For the first two phrases, see Walter W. Skeat, ed., "La Belle Dame Sans Merci," *Chaucerian and Other Pieces*, Supplement to the

Complete Works of Geoffrey Chaucer, vol. 7 (Oxford: Oxford University Press, 1897), lines 328-29 (309); for "parler mignon," see Christine de Pisan, *Cent ballades d'amant et de dame*, ed. Jacqueline Cerquiglini (Paris: Union Générale d'Editions, 1982), poem 8, line 11 (39).

33. See C. Stephen Jaeger, *The Origins of Courtliness: Civilizing Trends and the Formation of Courtly Ideals 939-1210* (Philadelphia: University of Pennsylvania Press, 1985), 162-68; on the meaning of *facetus*, see Alison Goddard Elliott's introduction to her translation of "The *Facetus*: or, The Art of Courtly Living," *Allegorica* 2 (1977): 27-57.

34. This definition is given by Donatus in his commentary on Terence's *Eunuchus*, cited by Laura Kendrick, *The Game of Love: Troubadour Wordplay* (Berkeley: University of California Press, 1988), 53.

35. Stevens, *Music and Poetry*, 163; Part I of the *Knight's Tale* itself provides the occasion for a *demande d'amour*, as do the *Franklin's Tale* and the debate among the noble suitors in the *Parliament of Fowls*. Apparently *demandes* were not always as highminded as these instances: for a collection of *demandes* that turn on racy *doubles entendres* and so require fast-paced verbal banter rather than lofty eloquence, see Eustache Deschamps, *Oeuvres complètes*, ed. Gaston Raynaud, SATF (Paris: Firmin-Didot, 1893), 8:112-25. For examples of linguistically playful poems in English, see Rossell Hope Robbins, ed., *Secular Lyrics of the XIVth and XVth Centuries*, 2d ed. (Oxford: Clarendon Press, 1955), poems numbers 172, 173, and 177.

36. Thomas Usk, "Testament of Love," in Skeat, ed., *Chaucerian and Other Pieces*, 12; for Froissart, see William W. Kibler, "Poet and Patron: Froissart's *Prison amoureuse*," *L'Esprit Créateur* 18 (1972), 38.

37. *Le livre messire Ode*, in Arthur Piaget, *Oton de Grandson, sa vie et ses poésies* (Lausanne: Librairie Payot, 1941), line 1478 (439).

38. George Puttenham, *The Arte of English Poesie* (London: Richard Field, 1589 [printed in facsimile: London: Scolar Press, 1968]), 155.

39. See especially Green, *Poets and Princepleasers*, 101-34.

40. See J.R. Hulbert, *Chaucer's Official Life* (Menasha: Collegiate Publishing, 1912).

41. Green, *Poets and Princepleasers*, 107; Glending Olson, "Descharnps' *Art de dictier* and Chaucer's Literary Environment," *Speculum* 48 (1973): 714-23.

42. A list of English aristocratic poets of the late fourteenth and fifteenth centuries (compiled largely from Green's discussion) includes John Montagu, earl of Salisbury; Edward Plantagenet, second duke of York; Richard Beauchamp, earl of Warwick; William de la Pole, duke of Suffolk; John Tiptoft, earl of Worcester; Anthony Woodville, Earl Rivers; Sir Richard Roos; and of course Sir John Clanvowe. As K.B. McFarlane has said, "In what other century has the peerage been so active in literature?" (*The Nobility of Later Medieval England* [Oxford: Clarendon Press, 1973], 242). Non-English noble *littérateurs* include Marshall Boucicaut and his friends, like the Duc de Berri, who composed the *Livre de cents ballades*; James I of Scotland; René of Anjou and his son, Jean, Duc de Calabre; Wenceslas de Brabant; Charles d'Orléans; and Jean II, Duc de Bourbon.

43. See Kibler, "Poet and Patron," 32-46, and Dembowski, *Jean Froissart*.

44. According to Robbins, "The Middle English Court Love Lyric," there survive perhaps three hundred love lyrics and thirty "love aunters," by which he means poems such as Lydgate's *Temple of Glass*, *The Flour and the Leaf*, and *The Court of Love* (207).

45. The influence of the *dits amoureux* on Chaucer has been most vigorously argued by Robbins, "Chaucer and the Lyric Tradition," and "The Vintner's Son;" and by James I. Wimsatt, *Chaucer and the French Love Poets* (Chapel Hill: University of North Carolina Press, 1968). For the lyric presence in the *Troilus*, see James I. Wimsatt, "The French Lyric Element in *Troilus and Criseyde*," *YES* 15 (1985): 18-32. For an argument that Chaucer's poetry develops out of these lyric moments, see W.A. Davenport, *Chaucer: Complaint and Narrative* (Cambridge: Brewer, 1988).

46. Stevens, *Music and Poetry*, 213.

47. The poem is printed by Frederick J. Furnivall, ed., *Odd Texts of Chaucer's Minor Poems*, Chaucer Society, 1st series, nos. 23, 60 (London: Trübner, 1868-80), xi-xii. As Gervase Mathew argues, Pandarus should not be "misconceived as a comic character; he is an experienced English courtier of the late fourteenth century, . . . a man of cultivated sensibility, facilely expressed emotions and quick strategems—all qualities then prized" (*Court of Richard II*, 68).

48. For a well-documented account of Richard's "high-handed notions of regality," see George B. Stow, "Chronicles versus Records: The Character of Richard II," in *Documenting the Past: Essays in Medieval History Presented to George Peddy Cuttino*, ed. J.S. Hamilton and Patricia J. Bradley (Woodbridge: Boydell, 1989), 155-76.

49. See Laura Kendrick, "Fame's Fabrication," in *Studies in the Age of Chaucer Proceedings, 1, 1984: Reconstructing Chaucer*, ed. Paul Strohm and Thomas Heffernan (Knoxville: New Chaucer Society, 1985), 135-48. See also below, 197.

50. See Winthrop Wetherbee, *Chaucer and the Poets. An Essay on Troilus and Criseyde* (Ithaca: Cornell University Press, 1984); on the *House of Fame*, see Karla Taylor, *Chaucer Reads the* Divine Comedy (Stanford: Stanford University Press, 1989), 20-49.

51. A.C. Spearing, *Medieval to Renaissance in English Poetry* (Cambridge: Cambridge University Press, 1985), 34. For the importance of Dante, see Piero Boitani, "What Dante Meant to Chaucer," in *Chaucer and the Italian Trecento*, ed. Piero Boitani (Cambridge: Cambridge University Press, 1983), 115-39, David Wallace, "Chaucer's Continental Inheritance: The Early Poems and *Troilus and Criseyde*," in *The Cambridge Chaucer Companion*, ed. Piero Boitani and Jill Mann (Cambridge: Cambridge University Press, 1986), 19-39, and Salter, *Fourteenth-Century English Poetry*, 123.

52. See note 23.

53. In the *Vita nuova* Dante had already asserted that vernacular versifiers were equal in status to the classical poets: "It is only recently that the first poets appeared who wrote in the vernacular; I call them 'poets' for to compose rhymed verse in the vernacular is more or less the same as to compose poetry in Latin using classical meters" (trans. Mark Musa [Bloomington: Indiana University Press, 1973], 54. For the role of the *trecento* poets in mediating Chaucer's access to the classics, see Charles Muscatine, *Poetry and Crisis in The Age of Chaucer* (Notre Dame: University of Notre Dame Press, 1972), 118-28.

54. As Wetherbee well says, "It is clear that one of the things [Chaucer] valued most highly in the *poetae* was their ability to link the enactment of historical change with the most complex kinds of human experience" (*Chaucer and the Poets*, 27).

55. For the title, and other textual information, see Eleanor Prescott Hammond, *Chaucer: A Bibliographical Manual* (New York: Macmillan, 1908), 355-58. A.S.G. Edwards, "The Unity and Authenticity of *Anelida and Arcite*: The Evidence of the Manuscripts," *SB* 41 (1988): 177-88, has questioned Chaucer's authorship of the entire poem, and especially lines 1-120 and 351-57 (the final stanza). But Lydgate's attribution of the "compleynt" of "Anneleyda and of fals Arcite" to Chaucer in the Prologue to the *Fall of Princes* (lines 320-21), and his allusion to the poem in the *Siege of Thebes* (see below, note 86), provides at least some external attribution other than that ambiguously inscribed on the manuscripts. Furthermore, the present

discussion means to demonstrate the unity of the poem (less the final stanza), its poetic sophistication, and above all its profoundly Chaucerian character.

56. The almost entirely dismissive criticism to which the poem has been subjected is surveyed by Russell A. Peck, *Chaucer's Lyrics and Anelida and Arcite: An Annotated Bibliography (1900-1980)* (Toronto: University of Toronto Press, 1983).

57. John Norton-Smith persuasively argued the scribal nature of this final stanza in "Chaucer's *Anelida and Arcite*," in Peter Heyworth, ed., *Medieval Studies for J.A.W. Bennett* (Oxford: Clarendon Press, 1981), 81-99; see also Edwards, "Unity and Authenticity," 181.

58. That these two poems are probably one has been argued by Rodney Merrill, "Chaucer's *Broche of Thebes*: The Unity of *The Complaint of Mars* and *The Complaint of Venus*," *Literary Monographs* 5 (1973): 3- 61.

59. Edgar F. Shannon, *Chaucer and the Roman Poets* (Cambridge: Harvard University Press, 1929), claims that "Corinna" was a name commonly applied to Ovid's *Amores* (15-47); but Douglas Bush, "Chaucer's 'Corinne,'" *Speculum* 4 (1929): 106-8, refutes this claim and argues that the Theban poetess is not only an appropriate but a likely referent. In support Bush cites Lydgate's inclusion of Statius and "Corrynne" in a list of poets in the *Troy Book* and suggests that Chaucer "met the name of Corinna in some such list" (107). But what list? Lydgate's authority for the name is doubtless Chaucer himself, and lists of the seven or nine great poets of the classical world seem not to include Corinna; see Servius's commentary on *Aeneid* 1, 12, and *Eclogues* 7, 21; and Quintilian, *Institutio oratoria* 10, 1. Greek sources do list her (see Vincent Dimarco's headnote in the *Riverside Chaucer*, 991), but Chaucer could not have known these. Not even Vincent of Beauvais seems to have heard of her, and while Statius mentions her in Eclogue 3 of the fifth *Silvae* (line 158), there is no evidence that the *Silvae* were read in the Middle Ages between the ninth century and 1416, when the text was rediscovered at St. Gallen. She is also mentioned in Propertius, *Elegies* 2, 3, 21, a text Chaucer might possibly have read; but Propertius's reference is glancing and makes no reference to Thebes. For Chaucer to know the very obscure fact that Corinna was a Theban poetess—and the context of the reference here makes it almost certain that he did—argues for an intense and persistent interest in the Theban story.

60. For the medieval Polyhymnia, see, for example, Fulgentius, *Mythologicon*, ed. August van Staveren, *Auctores Mythographi Latini* (Amsterdam: Wetstenium and Smith, 1742), 1, 14: "Πολύμνια . . . id

est multam memoriam faciens dicimus; quasi per capacitatem est memoria necessaria" (643). Thomas Walsingham's *De archana deorum*, ed. Robert A. van Kluyve (Durham: Duke University Press, 1968), written about 1400, cites the same definition, and adds that Polyhymnia is Saturn's Muse (16-17). Norton-Smith, "Chaucer's *Anelida and Arcite,*" also makes this identification, and cites (unconvincingly, to my mind) Boccaccio's commentary on Dante and the *Genealogie* as Chaucer's probable sources for the information (92-93).

61. In *his* Theban poem, the *Siege of Thebes*, Lydgate understands doubleness neither amorously nor metaphysically but as moral and hence political instability: the cause of the Theban war is the "doublenesse of Ethiocles" (1778), which is elaborately contrasted to truth (1747-59); ed. Axel Erdmann, EETS, ES 108 (London: Kegan Paul, 1911).

62. If we accept the suggestion of Boyd Ashby Wise, *The Influence of Statius upon Chaucer* (Baltimore: J.H. Furst, 1911), 70 n. 1, that Anelida's designation as "the quene of Ermony" (71-72) is meant to recall Harmonia, the daughter of Mars and Venus, rather than Armenia, then we can see that her career in the poem traces a movement from an original if unstable unity to a characteristically Theban discord. In this connection, it is relevant to recall that it was for Harmonia that Vulcan made the fatal Brooch of Thebes as a wedding gift for her marriage to Cadmus, as Chaucer points out in the "Complaint of Mars." Anelida is in this case the outsider who is undone by Theban divisiveness: Creon forces "the gentils of that regioun / To ben his frendes and dwellen in the toun," one of whom is "Anelida, the quene / Of Ermony" (68-72). Given the implied geography of the poem, Harmonia would seem to fit better than Armenia and is certainly a *durior lectio*. In the copy of Clanvowe's *Boke of Cupide* preserved in Bodleian MS Fairfax 16, "harmony" is spelled "ermonye" (ed. V.J. Scattergood [Cambridge: Brewer, 1975], line 83).

63. Augustine presents the recollection of autobiography as a re-collecting of a self dispersed among earthly pleasures by sin; see, for example, *Confessions* 2, 1, with its punning on *recolo* and *colligo;* and 10, 11, which connects *cogo* and *cogito*.

64. For the Boethianism of the term, see Stephen Barney, "Troilus Bound," *Speculum* 47 (1972): 445-58.

65. The strikingly interrogative mood of Anelida's complaint is created by the fact that a fifth of its lines are questions: 238-40, 247-52, 253-54, 272, 273-74, 275-77, 281-82, 283, 296-97, 299, 301, 311-12, 315-16, 318. Yet none of these questions actually anticipates an

answer, and they serve merely to express the bafflement and emotional turmoil of the amorous complaint. For a discussion of questioning as a stylistic element of the French complaint, see Charles Muscatine, *Chaucer and the French Tradition* (Berkeley: University of California Press, 1957), 24-25, and the earlier studies cited there.

66. Anelida says, "I fare as doth the song of *Chaunte-pleure*, / For now I pleyne and now I pleye" (320-21). But as Skeat, *The Works of Geoffrey Chaucer* (Oxford: Clarendon Press, 1894), points out in his note to these lines, according to Godefroy the *Chaunte-pleure* "was addressed to those who sing in this world and will weep in the next. Hence also the word was particularly used to signify any complaint or lament, or a chant at the burial service" (1:537).

67. Ibid., 536 (note to line 220).

68. For the swan image, see *Heroides* 7, 1-2; Chaucer also cites the lines at the end of the Legend of Dido in the *Legend of Good Women*:

> "Ryght so," quod she, "as that the white swan
> Ayens his deth begynnyth for to synge,
> Right so to you make I my compleynynge." (1355-57)

Both Shannon (*Chaucer and the Roman Poets*) and Nancy Dean ('Chaucer's *Complaint*, A Genre Descended from the *Heroides*," *CL* 19 [1967]: 1-27) argue that Chaucer's insistence upon the specificity of the narrative setting, and his incorporation of details of that setting into the lyric complaint, mark his complaints as Ovidian. In "Guillaume de Machaut and Chaucer's Love Lyrics,' *MAE* 47 (1978): 66-87, James I. Wimsatt argues on the contrary that Anelida's complaint is derived from Machaut's *chant royal*, "Amis, je t'ay tant amé et cheri" (no. 254 in *Poésies Lyriques*, ed. V. Chichmaref, SATF [Paris: H. Champion, 1909], 1:223-24). But a comparison of the two texts does not, in my view, support his claims. In an earlier article, *"Anelida and Arcite*: A Narrative of Complaint and Comfort," *ChR* 5 (1970-71): 1-8, Wimsatt assimilates the poem to the pattern of the French *dits amoureux* and suggests that it would have fulfilled this pattern more fully had it been completed. But it is exactly the variation from the pattern that is important.

69. As well as the swan image, for specific Ovidian allusions, compare *Anelida*, 134-37 and 256-58 to *Heroides* 7, 25-26 and 64, 76, 195, respectively; for more general analogies between the emotional condition described by Anelida and Dido, see, for example, *Heroides* 7, 6, and 168. The interrogative nature of *Heroides* 7 is suggested by the eighteen questions that Dido poses in the course of the poem, fifteen of

them in the first half (see lines 7-8, 9-10, 11-12, 15, 16, 19-20, 21-22, 41, 45, 53-54, 66, 71-72, 77, 78, and 83; the other three are lines 125, 141-42, and 164). Aware of her responsibility for her own condition (see lines 23-24, 33, 85-86, 97-98 and 104), of her own self-delusions (35), and of the complexity of her feelings (29-30), Dido struggles toward self-understanding in the course of her complaint but finally remains baffled. It is that struggle, however, that distinguishes the classical complaint, both in the *Heroides* and in *Aeneid* 4, from its French descendent, which seeks above all to encase a static emotional posture in the beautifully wrought reliquary of its ritualistic language. The point is that *Anelida and Arcite* represents Chaucer's attempt to explicate the continuities between the antique past and the modern present.

70. Ovid's Dido never, it is true, refers to herself as a queen; but *Aeneid* 4 is structured by the repeated invocation of her title: see lines 1, 296, and 504. Interestingly enough, one of the manuscripts of the *Anelida and Arcite* (Longleat 258, a Shirley manuscript) gives as the title *Balade of Anelyda Quene of Cartage* (see DiMarco's textual notes in the *Riverside Chaucer*, 1144). It may even be that Anelida's name is a compilation of elements of the three female names of *Heroides* 7—*An*na, *El*issa, and D*ido*.

71. In "*Anelida and Arcite*: A Narrative of Complaint and Comfort," Wimsatt points out that a generic "feature [of the complaint] which Machaut evidently tried to establish is the use of different rhyme-endings for each stanza; in the *Remède de Fortune* the poet states explicitly that a complaint is a poem with 'sad matter and many different rhymes'. . . . In the complaint of the later *Fonteinne amoureuse*, as the lover boasts, there are a hundred different rhymes without one repetition" (5-6). In contemporary French poetry there are stanzas very like Chaucer's elaborate *aabaabbab*, such as Deschamps's *Complainte pour la religieuse Marguerite* (*aabaabbabaa*) and the Sénéchal d'Eu's *Complainte pour sa femme* (*aabaabbabba*). Indeed, subsequent literary history suggests that Chaucer's example in the *Anelida* did in fact succeed in establishing the complex metrics and rhyme scheme of Anelida's complaint as a generic norm for his fifteenth-century Scots disciples. The *Anelida* stanza was used by Gavin Douglas for Parts 1 and 2 of *The Palice of Honour* and for the Prologue to Book 3 of the *Aeneid*, and by Dunbar in *The Golden Targe*. It was used as well in three poems found in MS Arch. Selden B.24: "The Quare of Jelusy," "The Lay of Sorrow," and "The Lufaris Complaynt." But its most brilliant use was by Henryson for Cresseid's complaint in *The Testament of Cresseid*, a poem that both anatomizes

the workings of retrospection as erotic yearning, penitential regret, and literary indebtedness and stresses the inadequacy of complaint as a vehicle for self-understanding.

72. Ovid stresses the compulsive and impersonal nature of Aeneas's desire by having Dido use the word *alter* five times in order to designate the object to which that desire is directed—as if the precise goal did not matter as long as it were other than that which he now has: see lines 14 (twice), 17 (twice), and 18.

73. Chaucer explores male dissatisfaction at length in the *Legend of Good Women*, and nowhere more extensively than in the account of another questing deceiver, Jason. In the "Legend of Medea" he describes Jason as "of love devourer and dragoun" (1581; and see 1369):

> As mater apetiteth forme alwey,
> And from forme into forme it passen may,
> Or as a welle that were botomles,
> Ryght so can false Jason have no pes. (1582-85)

Derived from Guido delle Colonne's *Historia destructionis Troiae*, these lines represent male desire not as surplus or excess but as lack or inadequacy, as loss rather than endowment. It is perhaps appropriate, then, that Jason's third wife (after Hypsiplye and Medea) is Creusa, the daughter of Creon of Thebes—a name that locates Jason within the economy of Theban recursion and that also links him with that other adventurer, Aeneas.

74. *Amores* 2, 19, 1-3; for instances of similar statements, see: 1,5 , 2,5, 2,19, 3,4, 3,14.

75. See Genesis 4:19-24.

76. See the note to line 105 in the *Riverside Chaucer*, citing earlier suggestions by Skeat and Tupper. These analogies suggest that if the *Knight's Tale* is a mature rewriting of *Anelida and Arcite*, then the *Squire's Tale* is a satiric version.

77. This image of the bird-in-the-cage, derived from Boethius, reappears in a submerged form and with a sharply different valence in the *Miller's Tale*: Alisoun, who sings "as loude and yerne / As any swalwe sittynge on a berne" (3256-57), is kept by her jealous husband "narwe in cage" (3224) but of course manages to escape.

78. "And if so be that the Muse and the doctrine of Plato syngeth soth, al that every wyght leerneth, he ne doth no thing elles thanne but recordeth, as men recorden thinges that ben foryeten" (3, xi, 43-47).

79. The fullest medieval survey of the genealogy of the Brooch is provided by the Second Vatican Mythographer; see Georg Bode, ed., *Scriptores rerum mythicarum latini tres romae* (Celle: Schulze, 1834),

1:101. A modern account is offered by Neil C. Hultin, "Anti-Courtly Elements in Chaucer's *Complaint of Mars*," *AnM* 9 (1968): 58-75.

80. The device of the boar signifies the Calydonian boar killed by Meleager and then given by him to Atalanta as a love gift, an act that enraged his uncles and led to the family feud in which the nephew slaughtered his uncles and was, in revenge, consigned to death by his own mother. The story is told in a compressed form by Cassandra as an explication of Troilus's dream (5, 1471-84)

81. These are two lines from the so-called *Planctus Oedipi*, an eighty- four-line poem that survives in at least twelve manuscripts, both by itself and with the *Thebaid*. I have here translated lines 30 ["vibrans ferrum per patris ilia"] and 79 ["ut gladium linguam exacui"] from the transcription of Berlin lat. 34, fol. 113, printed by Edélestand du Méril, *Poésies inédites du moyen âge* (Paris: Franck, 1854), 310-13.

82. Seneca, *Oedipus*, line 238, and see also lines 638-39; Statius, *Thebaid* 1, 235.

83. Leopold Constans, ed., *Roman de Thèbes*, SATF (Paris: H. Champion, 1890), lines 28-91. The same circularity is stressed by the Second Vatican Mythographer: "quod primo quatuor, deinde tribus, deinde duobus, deinde tribus, deinde quatuor graditur pedibus?" (Bode, ed., 1:150-51). It is also prominent in Lydgate's version in the *Siege of Thebes*, who sums up the Oedipal condition as one of return to mother earth: "And fynaly this the trouthe pleyn, / he retourneth kyndely ageyn / To the matere which that he kam fro"; "And for he may no whyle here soiourne, / To erthe ageyn he most in hast retourne, / Which he kam fro, he may it not remewe" (Erdmann, lines 673-75, 723-25). This Oedipal return to mother earth is also figured by Chaucer in the Old Man of the *Pardoner's Tale*: see below, chapter 8. In "Oedipus in the Middle Ages," *Antike und Abendland* 22 (1976): 140-55, Lowell Edmunds points out that "in the ancient sources the riddle is always simpler: first four, then three, then two feet" (144 n. 15).

84. "Truth," 19-20; in the *Riverside Chaucer*, 653.

85. Come, perché di lor memoria sia,
   sovra i sepolti le tombe terragne
   portan segnato quel ch'elli eran pria,
      onde lì molte volte si ripiagne
   per la punctura de la rimembranza,
   che solo a' pïi dà de la calcagne. (*Purg.* 12, 16-21)

86. Lydgate cited this Chaucerian phrase in the *Siege of Thebes*: Cupid's arrow stakes the lovers (Polymyte and Argyve, and Tideus and Deyfyle) with "the poynt of remembraunce, / which may not lightly raced ben away" (Erdmann, lines 1487-89).

87. In *Silvae* 5, Eclogue 3, Statius refers to "the hidden thought of subtle Corinna" (*tenuisque arcana Corinnae* [158]); the girl to whom Ovid addresses most of the *Amores* is referred to in 21, 19 as "Corinna the artful" or, more literally, "well-versed Corinna" (*versuta Corinna*). On the problems of assigning a Statian source to Chaucer's use of the name, see above, note 59.

88. This is Boccaccio's account of the genesis of the *Teseida*, ed. Mario Marti, *Opere Minori in Volgare* (Milan: Rizzoli, 1970), 2:257:

> E' m'é venuto in voglia con pietosa
> rima di scrivere una istoria antica,
> tanto negli anni riposta e nascosa
> che latino autor non par ne dica,
> per quel ch'io senta, in libro alcuna cosa. (1, 2)

"The desire has come to me to set down in plaintive verse an ancient tale, set aside and left long undisclosed over the years, so that no Latin author appears to have recounted it in any book, as far as I know" (*The Book of Theseus*, trans. Bernadette Marie McCoy [New York: Medieval Text Association, 1974], 20). In his gloss to this passage, Boccaccio makes it clear that he is claiming not originality for the *Teseida* but a more profound form of authenticity than would be the case if his source were Latin: "Non è stata di greco translata in latino" (662)—"It has not been translated from Greek into Latin" (47). By returning to an original Greek account, Boccaccio is claiming an authenticity comparable to Dares's or Dictys's accounts of the Trojan War (both of which were originally written in Greek although known to the Middle Ages in Latin translations).

89. Chaucer's rewriting of Statius's lines is preceded in the manuscripts of the *Anelida* by a citation of *Thebaid* 12, 519-21, the same lines as several of the manuscripts of the *Canterbury Tales* include at the start of the *Knight's Tale*. In terms of the chronology of the events, the *Anelida* takes place before the *Knight's Tale*, and few scholars have doubted that it also stands earlier in Chaucer's career; but the precise nature of the relationship remains obscure.

90. Chaucer leaves Theseus riding towards Athens:

> And founde I wol in shortly for to bringe
> *The slye wey* of that I gan to write,
> Of quene Anelida and fals Arcite. (47-49)

The striking phrase is elliptical, referring both to the means by which the subject matter of the poem will be introduced and that subject matter itself, "the slye wey" with which Arcite dealt with Anelida. The ambiguity thus serves to correlate Arcite's Theban action with Chaucer's Theban writing, not only suggesting that doubleness pervades both but demonstrating its workings through the lexical instability of a double meaning.

91. That this redemptiveness is to be understood as working in both individual and collective ways is clear from the poem's concluding movements. As Arcita lies dying, he prays that he not be consigned to a place among the other Theban damned since he has always sought, even if unsuccessfully, to evade the Theban fate (10, 96-99); the subsequent account of his ascent through the spheres (the source for Troilus's ascent at the end of *Troilus and Criseyde*), and of his enlightenment about "la vanitate / . . . dell'umane genti" (11, 3), shows that his prayer has been answered. Then when the question of marrying Emilia is suggested to Palemone, he demurs on the grounds that he is "the sole heir of the great infamies of my ancestors" (12, 24 [trans. McCoy, 317]), but is dissuaded by Teseo. The elaborate account of the wedding with which the poem then concludes affirms the rightness of the reconciliations that consolidates: modern love redeems ancient wickedness.

92. For the *Roman de Thèbes*, see Wise, *Influence of Statius*, 116-37. For the *Histoire ancienne*, see Paul Meyer, "Les premières compilations françaises d'histoire ancienne," *Romania* 14 (1885): 36-76; this text included prose versions of the *romans d'antiquité*: see Guy Raynaud de Lage, "Les romans antiques dans l'*Histoire ancienne jusqu'à César*," *Moyen Age* 63 (1957): 267-309. In the Middle Ages the *Histoire* was known as, among other things, the *Livre des histoires*, the *Trésor des ystoires*, and the *Livre d'Orose* (since it adopted Orosius's chronology). For an edition, see the version ascribed to C. de Seissel and entitled *Le premier volume de Oroze*, 3 vols. (Paris: A. Verard, 1509). There is no evidence that Chaucer actually read Seneca's *Oedipus* (although see Skeat's note to the *Parliament of Fowls*, line 176); but it was known throughout the Middle Ages, and Nicholas Trevet, whose *Chronique* and whose commentary on Boethius's *Consolation* Chaucer did read, wrote a commentary on it and other Senecan plays. Several manuscripts of the *Thebaid* include the *Planctus Oedipi*, so it was certainly available to Chaucer; see Edmunds, "Oedipus in the Middle Ages," and Paul M. Clogan, "The *Planctus* of Oedipus: Text and Comment," *M&H* 1 (1970): 233-39.

93. *House of Fame*, 1460. Statius identified himself as a native of Naples, but the Middle Ages assigned him to Toulouse: see Charles Singleton's note to *Purgatorio* 21, 89.

94. Statius, for example, begins the story with the struggle between Eteocles and Polynices, while the *Roman de Thèbes* goes back to Oedipus's killing of Laius (see *Troilus and Criseyde*, 2, 100-l03).

NATURAL MUSIC IN 1400

by James I. Wimsatt

It suits the Procrustean tradition of literary historians, who like to divide materials into time segments of one century, that the deaths of Chaucer and Richard II neatly close off the great age of Ricardian poetry in 1400. Langland and the Gawain Poet had disappeared by the end of the century, and if Gower lived on into the fifteenth century (until 1408) it was only for a few less productive years, which can be safely ignored. So also in France the major disciples of Machaut—Froissart (died c 1404), Granson (1397), and Deschamps (c 1406)—faded from view near the turn of the century. Moreover, the founding of the French Cour amoureuse, a significant sign of the times,[1] took place in 1400. This is all to say that facts as well as the appeal of round numbers justify our focusing on the year 1400 in this concluding chapter.

In the course of the fourteenth century the poetry of the formes fixes evolved perceptibly. After Machaut the most prominent writers no longer provided music for their texts, but many poet-musicians remained active.[2] More of the nobility, and perhaps more of the townspeople, took part in verse composition. The forms themselves changed; only in relative terms were they 'fixed.' Ballades became much longer with stanzas of eight or ten decasyllabic lines, and often with substantial envoys; the rondeau form, increasingly popular, became diversified and generally longer; and by 1400 the lay and the virelay were moribund. Such are some obvious features in the evolution. However, my purpose is not to review and forecast the broad development of Middle French poetry, most of which became tangential to Chaucer's work in the last decade of his life. Instead, I will concentrate on two limited questions about developments that particularly concern Chaucer at the end of his career. One question is retrospective, having to do with the relationship of the puys and the courts as far as we can follow that shadowy history from the late thirteenth century to 1400. The other looks forward, and probes the essence of Chaucer's 'natural music'; it asks how successful Chaucer was in overcoming the great barrier of his Germanic stress language in translating the French natural music into English, and to what degree he then was able to pass along his version of that music to subsequent English poets.

THE COURT AND THE PUY

Since the available information about the medieval civic literary societies, the puys,[3] is fragmentary, and since no comprehensive study has been made, the common understanding of them is based more on impression than on fact. Because they are said to have been middleclass, the membership is readily imagined to be Philistine; because the intentions were outspokenly religious and moral, the verse is assumed to be unpoetic; and because certain aspects of the practices imitate the court—a prince presides, a lyric is 'crowned,' its author becomes 'king'—the writers are thought to be epigones of the court poets. All of these assumptions were no doubt true some times in some places; like most medieval social phenomena, the puys were quite varied from one group to another. Nevertheless, in the fourteenth century eminent and highly cultivated men took part in the concours, the poetry that we know to have emanated from the puys is not notably inferior to the common run of the 'courtly,' and the puy writers were often the same as the court writers. Indeed, instead of battening on the court tradition, the puys through the fourteenth century seem to have been a source of nourishment and strength for court poetry, and the century ended with the court groups openly imitating the 'bourgeois' literary societies. The formes fixes mode in part shared Chaucer's middle-class origins in the city, and it retained its ties there.

We may connect the very beginnings of the formes fixes with the puys. The oldest body of extant lyrics that clearly belongs to the mode was composed by the original and versatile genius Adam de la Halle. His *Jeu de la feuillée*, itself perhaps written for a concours, strongly suggests that he wrote such lyrics for the puy at Arras. Thanks in part to Adam, we know more about the organization in Arras than any other of its kind. An important aspect of the puy there—and of puys elsewhere, it seems—is that it brought together a diverse group of devotees on a relatively equal footing. Scholars have seen this social inclusiveness as serving importantly to elevate the status of the minstrels.[4]

One evidence of the democratic nature of the puys may be found in Gilles li Muisis' list, compiled in 1351, of prominent poets of the day. As I noted in chapter 2, li Muisis names Jean de le Mote third among prominent poet-musicians of his time, after Philippe de Vitry and

Guillaume de Machaut. The fourth and final writer he lists is a talented illiterate who is a puy poet, probably a participant with Abbot Gilles himself in the concours at Tournai:

> Collart Hobiert n'oublieray,
> Avoec Jehan le metterai,
> S'il n'est letrés, s'est boins fasières;
> Esprouvés est par lies chières
> Es puis l'a-on l'à couronnet
> Ou l'estrivet capiel donnet.[5]

I will not forget Colard Aubert. I will put him with Jean [de le Mote]. Though he is not educated, he writes good poems; that is proven by the joyful faces in the puys where he has been crowned or awarded the contested garland.

The four poets whom Gilles mentions occupied various rungs on the social ladder: Vitry was a bishop, Machaut a canon at Reims, le Mote a clerk at Hainault, and Colard Aubert evidently an unlettered townsman, perhaps a professional minstrel. The good abbot lists these writers according to social rank, the highest first, but he nevertheless puts them all together in the world of verse. All four, together with Gilles himself, could have comfortably come together in the puy.

Prominent churchmen and distinguished citizens supported and participated in the puys. One of the few extant records of the London society records a substantial gift from Henry le Waleys, an outstanding citizen who was several times mayor, to support the chaplain of the society. The chief surviving London record is a set of regulations from the late thirteenth century, providing as complete a description as we have of a northern European puy. The rules direct that meetings be held once a year for a fine spectrum of reasons: for the honour of God, the Blessed Virgin, the saints, the king, and the barons, 'for the increasing of loyal love,' for the renown of London, 'and to the end that mirthfulness, peace, honesty, joyousness, gaiety, and good love without end may be maintained.' The pious and patriotic aspect of the purposes clearly did not rule out ardent poetic activity. While there were charitable and religious functions, the poetic and musical ends were paramount. At the meetings songs were to be submitted that praised 'the becoming pleasaunce of virtuous ladies.' The 'prince of the puy,' elected yearly, was to 'crown' the best song at the great annual feast.[6] We do not know how long the London society lasted, but if it endured a century, Chaucer and associates like Froissart and Gower, and the knight Granson too, could have belonged.[7]

The puys probably had most effect on Chaucer through their influence on the Continental poets with whom he associated. There is a good chance that Froissart began his poetic career in meetings of the puy at Valenciennes. He remained proud of his accomplishments at the concours, particularly of his victories; the manuscripts retain records of the crowning of five of his chansons: 'Canchon Amoureuse Couronnee a Valenchienes,' 'Canchon Amoureuse Couronnee a Abbeville,' 'Chançon Royale Sote Couronnee a Lille,' 'Serventois de Nostre Dame Couronnés a Valenchiennes' (twice).[8] As I have already suggested, his pastourelles probably represent adaptations of a puy genre to court purposes, providing a good example of how the court might draw strength from the presumably imitative organization. Jean de le Mote too publicized his puy experience. Towards the beginning of *Regret Guillaume*, written for Queen Philippa on the death of her father—a thoroughly courtly occasion—the dreamer muses over a poem that he wants to take to a puy;[9] no doubt le Mote had in mind a concours at Valenciennes. Even Machaut, though he came from outside the area where the puys flourished and was always associated with the courts, probably participated as a guest at more than one concours. Of his chants royaux, five have envoys addressed to 'Prince,' one requesting explicitly that his work be crowned: 'Prince, veuillez d'un chapel de soucie . . . Moy et mon chant, s'il vous plaist coronner' / 'Prince, please crown me and my lyric with a wreath of marigold.'[10]

Machaut's participation seems unlikely only if we wrongly think of the puys as organizations of equivocal social status. It is true that poetic activity appropriate in the courts is sometimes distinguished from' that appropriate to the puys, but this need not be taken as denigration. In the *Art de dictier*, addressed to a great lord, Deschamps refrains from describing the serventois in detail 'because this is a form which pertains to the *puis d'amours*, and noblemen do not usually compose them.'[11] A sense that Deschamps is disdainfully dismissing the puys is misleading, for elsewhere in the treatise he uses their proceedings to make an important point. In illustrating the distinction between 'musique naturelle' and 'musique artificielle,' he describes the poet's carrying his original verse to the prince at a concourse where he recites it from memory; this, Deschamps says, is known as 'en disant.' After the recitation, the poet must also sing it to the prince.[12] Thus, while we see Deschamps assuming that noblemen will not participate in the puys (a restriction that probably applied only to the highest nobility), and that certain forms are peculiar to them, his use of puy practice as example and model shows serious respect for the societies. Deschamps had good personal reason to think well of the puys. One gathers from envoys in his poems, as one might guess from his knowledgeable depiction in the *Art de dictier*, that he himself participated in the concours.[13]

Throughout the fourteenth century, puys flourished in the major French-speaking cities closest to England: Amiens, Tournai, Abbeville, Lille, Dieppe, Valenciennes. The poetic skill which Jean de le Mote and Jean Froissart brought to England no doubt reflected extensive experience in these societies which provided them opportunities to learn the conventions, to associate with the prosperous and cultivated men of the cities, and to popularize the performance and composition of the formes fixes. In the puys the forms of the crowned poems generally were five-stanza chants or related types, no longer favoured in the courts; however, the main court form, the ballade, was also popular in the societies, and all of the forms were practised there.[14] All evidence indicates that the puys were both influential and prestigious. Three unmistakable adaptations of their practices in court literature provide important evidence: an episode of le Mote's *Parfait du paon*, the court literary activity evoked in the *Cent ballades*, and the 'Charte de la Cour d'Amour.'

In Jean de le Mote's Alexander romance the *Parfait du paon* there is a long interlude, described in chapter 2, in which the court games depicted reflect two traditions: the fictive tradition that represents the posing and judging of demandes d'amour, and the social tradition by which poetic contests are held in the puys. In the interlude of the *Parfait*, after some questions of love are arbitrated, Alexander and three of his peers, together with the four daughters of the pagan King Melidus, present ballades in turn to be judged by prominent figures in their audience. After the merits of each poem are deliberated one of them is selected to be crowned. Le Mote, experienced in court ways, is not simply naive or confused in having his fictional court imitate the puy. For him and his audience the procedures of the civic literary societies provide an attractive and wholly respectable model for the court to follow.

Another work that combines the traditions of the demande d'amour and the puy is the *Cent ballades* (c 1390),[15] which represents better than any other single text the state of formes fixes poetry at the end of the century. Froissart's long poems had incorporated increasing numbers of lyric set pieces, and Granson's *Livre Messire Ode* is preponderantly made up of them, to the point that narrative episodes are presented in the lyric pieces as well as in the connecting couplets.

The *Cent ballades*, composed by Jean le Seneschal and three other noblemen, carries the poetic development to its logical end: the whole poem, both the narrative and lyric elements, is presented in a hundred sequential ballades of varying versification. The story is of a pensive young lover who goes riding; he encounters an old knight who in a long series of ballades counsels him on the necessity of loyalty in love. The second half of the work offers a contrasting lesson in a second set of ballades. A lively young lady, who is part of a group of young people that the lover encounters, argues for the delights of playing the field. Obviously, a *demande d'amour* is propounded here. Must a young lover remain faithful to one person, or is it preferable to divide one's amorous attentions among many?

Having listened to the arguments on both sides, the lover, a surrogate of the major author, Jean le Seneschal, returns to the château, where he consults with his three collaborators on the question whether loyalty or changeability is better in love. All four decide in favour of loyalty, but in the hundredth and last ballade they make a plea to each 'amoureux' to compose a ballade setting forth his opinion. In the thirteen ballades that follow the hundred, thirteen different noblemen offer their 'responses,' enunciating various solutions. In total the work involves the collaboration of seventeen Frenchmen of high rank, and it shows vividly the increasing participation by the courtiers themselves in the composition of poetry. For the first sixty years of the fourteenth century, the nobility produced few of the lyrics that have come down to us. In the last forty years of the century, though, the amount of their verse increased: a substantial number of texts by Wenceslas of Luxembourg, Oton de Granson, and Jean de Garencières, the chamberlain of Louis d'Orléans, have survived.

The appearance of these poets, along with the seventeen noble participants in the *Cent ballades*, shows that by century's end much of the French nobility was actively writing verse. The editor of the *Cent ballades* projects one or more 'concours poétiques' in Avignon in November 1390, when the creators of the *Cent ballades* might have presented the work and the respondents delivered their ballades.[16] Though no actual crown was offered, the call for responses in the last ballade emphasizes the competitive aspect; it is to be a contest to compose the *best* response: 'faire věoir / . . . Par vo dit, le *plus* eüreux / Conseil, dont amant main et soir / Peut *miex* manoir, / Qui *plus* le fait d'amours joieux' / 'To make clear in your poem the *most* effective counsel by which a lover can *best* maintain himself night and day, which makes him the *most* joyful in love' (c 31-6). The coming together of the *Cent ballades* poets to produce a large set of ballades on a subject of love was inspired by the practices of the puy. Instead of ignoring or patronizing the civic societies, these courtiers found a model in their practice.

The most patent courtly imitation of the puys is found in the charter of 1400 of the Cour amoureuse, attributed to Charles VI, which sets up an elaborate court with three grand conservators, eleven ordinary conservators, a 'Prince d'amour,' twenty-four ministers, and so on.[17] Ostensibly it imitates literary courts of love and governmental organizations, but the most basic model for the charter, as is amply confirmed by the prescribed procedures, is the tradition of the puys.[18] The ceremonies and feasts all partake of concours: each month there is to be a 'feste de puy d'Amours,' and on Valentine's Day a great celebration with specially composed ballades for which prizes are awarded; in May there is to be another special 'puy.' As is traditional in the puys, refrains are assigned for the ballade contests, crowns are awarded, and the feast-days of the Virgin are observed. Also following the model of the puys, a moral purpose is asserted. The court, the charter declares, is founded on the virtues of humility and loyalty to promote 'the honour, praise, and commendation of all ladies'; severe penalties are prescribed for anyone doing anything to the dispraise of womanhood. The conception of the court evidently was in part the fantasy of Isabelle of Bavaria and her entourage;[19] notwithstanding, the documents witness the strong influence of the civic puys on the literary ideas of the nobility.

The numerous membership list of the Cour amoureuse was not confined to the nobility; names from the bourgeosie, especially from the north of France, appear on the rolls.[20] Among other members are nine of the participants in the *Cent ballades*. Also named in Eustache Deschamps, 'hussier d'armes du roy et bailli de Senlis,' who is one of the 'auditeurs.' Shortly after the charter of the court appeared in 1400, Deschamps, assuming the guise of 'prince de haulte eloquence,' burlesqued it in two poems.[21] In the shorter of the two, a ballade that summarizes the longer work, he calls for a parliament to be held each May at 'Lens en Artois.' He summons several of his friends by name, the purpose being, as the refrain declares, 'Pour compte de ses bourdes rendre' / 'To give an account of one's jokes.' He who brags the best is to be 'crowned like a king' (26). At other times Deschamps freely invented strange societies and orders,[22] so we need not assign great significance to the burlesque. Whatever wry commentary on Queen Isabelle's society his poems constitute, both they and the Cour amoureuse provide further testimony of influence and seminal power flowing from puy to court rather than from court to puy.

The poetry of the courts, then, was substantially affected by the puys. Instead of disdaining the civic organizations as upstart imitators, the courts willingly adopted their customs. The professional writers active in the courts often had extensive experience in the concours and they paraded their affiliations rather than attempting to conceal them. The increasing involvement by the French nobility in the poetry, which reached its apogee in the poetry of Charles d'Orléans, thus implies their participation in an activity with origins in the guildhalls as well as in the castles. If one seeks specific effects on the lyrics themselves, the puy influence may be seen in what happens to the forms: the prescriptiveness, the tendency for the stanzaic units to become longer, the use of envoys in ballades, even the divorce of the words from the music. Or one may see it in the moral tenor of the work: the earnest ethical purposes, the absence of references to physical acts of love.

As we have traced the course of formes fixes poetry through the fourteenth century, the poets have appeared as functionaries of the court, producing verse that has its sources in the life and aspirations of the nobility. From the vantage-point of the *Cent ballades* and the Cour amoureuse in 1400, however, we can see that the civic puys played a part in the work. The consequences for Chaucer's poetry are important. We recognize that even the French component in his oeuvre has a non-courtly element. There is a chance that he participated in puys in London or France and learned their practices, and we know that he had important associations with poets experienced in the puys, notably le Mote and Froissart. What is more, many of the texts that he found in the courts were born in the concours or affected by poems that were. The lyrics he heard when he came into the service of the Countess of Clarence were not as foreign to his natal class as one might imagine. The civic societies that Chaucer's and Froissart's fathers and uncles might have belonged to played a part in the tradition along with the courts of the Valois and Plantagenets.

There is no evidence of imitation of the puys by the nobility in England comparable to that shown in France by the *Cent ballades* or the Cour amoureuse. To be sure, men of rank had become conspicuously involved in poetic activity; Sir Thomas Clanvowe and Sir John Montague, Earl of Salisbury, for instance, were probably composing love lyrics in the conventional forms at the end of the century. But the decline of the French language in England, the general absence of puys in the cities, and the powerful example of Chaucer's long poems dictated that as the new century opened poetic activity in England would be gradually diverted. Chaucer himself composed several ballades and ballade envoys which seem to date from the 1390s, but he was mainly busy with the *Canterbury Tales*. Nevertheless, even as there remain echoes of the Middle French lyrics in the *Tales*, so also we find in them intimations of both the court-of-love games and the puys. The demande d'amour is a feature both of the 'Knight's Tale' and the 'Franklin's Tale.' And in the Host's proposal at the end of the 'General Prologue,' which sets up a poetic competition between various citizens with the best performance to be recognized and rewarded at a dinner, the model of the concours may well have some part.[23] Nevertheless, the congruency between a concours and the assemblage of pilgrims in the *Tales* is on most counts tenuous. The major implications of puy influence are for the court poetry itself and Chaucer's stanzaic poetry. A question with a different orientation, looking not to origins but to effects, concerns the degree to which Chaucer was successful in adapting the Middle French 'natural music' to the English language, whose patterns of intonation are quite different from the French.

NATURAL MUSIC IN ENGLISH

In concluding his impressive essay 'The "Music" of the Lyric: Machaut, Deschamps, Chaucer,'[24] John Stevens applies his thoughtful understanding of the problems of rhythm and meter to the very question I want to deal with in this final section: how successful was Chaucer in translating the rhythmical character of the French lyric into English? The discussion in chapter 1 shows that Chaucer's stanzaic poetry absorbs much of the French mode, including important prosodic features, and the remainder of the book establishes a broad relationship between the formes fixes tradition and the English poet and his work; however, it has not confronted the narrower but important question of how effectively Chaucer overcame the difference between the relatively unstressed French language and the strongly stressed English in adapting the natural music to his verse. Any positive answer to the question, furthermore, evokes the broader and even more vexed question of whether this 'music' lived on after him in English poetry. Deschamps' description of the performance of natural music gives us an idea of the qualities which the poets prized and strove for:

> Et ja soit ce que ceste musique naturele se face de volunté amoureuse a la louenge des dames . . . et que les faiseurs d'icelle ne saichent pas communement la musique artificiele ne donner chant par art de notes a ce qu'ilz font, toutesvoies

est appellee musique ceste science naturele, pour ce que les
diz et chançons par eulz faiz ou les livres metrifiez se lisent de
bouche, et proferent par voix non chantable, tant que les
douces paroles ainsis faictes et recordees par voix plaisent aux
escoutans que les oyent, si que au *Puy d'amours* anciennement
et encores est accoustemez en pluseurs villes et citez des pais
et royaumes du monde.[25]

And although this natural music is made by an amorous
disposition for the praise of ladies . . . and although the makers
of it commonly do not understand artificial music or how to
compose musical notation for their verse, still this natural
knowledge is called music because they read orally the dits
and chansons and verse-books that they have written,
presenting them without singing, so that the sweet words
which they compose and recite aloud please those who hear
them, as has been done of old at the puys d'amours, and still is
done in many towns and cities of the countries and kingdoms
of the world.

The quality of 'sweetness' or 'pleasingness' particularly characterizes
both kinds of music for Deschamps. He speaks of 'la douceur tant du
chant comme des paroles qui toutes sont prononcees et pointoyees par
douçour de voix et ouverture de bouche' / 'the sweetness of the melody
as much as of the words which are all pronounced and accented
[separated ?] by the sweetness of the voice and the opening of the
mouth.[26]

Stevens offers his conclusions about Chaucer's adherence to
French musique naturele only tentatively. For him the question of stress
is central, though it is an aspect that Deschamps—dealing with an
unstressed French language—does not consider in his discussion in the
Art de dictier. On the one hand, Stevens finds that many of Chaucer's
effects seem 'sufficiently distant from the suave norm of, say, Machaut
to make us doubt whether he had the sort of *armonia* in mind that the
French poets looked for.' Chaucer's effects are those of 'emphatic
natural speech,' he says, while those of the French are not. In this, he
believes, Chaucer breaks away from 'the ideal of *musique naturele*.'
On the other hand, Stevens believes it likely that, instead of an iambic
model, Chaucer 'took from the main tradition of medieval verse, in
Latin, Italian and above all French, its most distinctive feature—its
measurement of the line by syllables, counted and variously grouped.

Concepts of a metrical foot, of regular binary stress and, I would add, of a tension between rhythm and metre belong to other systems.'[27]

In finding that Chaucer abandons the douceur of Machaut in favour of 'natural speech rhythms,' Stevens nevertheless recognizes that Deschamps' ballade praise of Chaucer's *'douce* melodie' offers a contrary indication. If, as Stevens is inclined to say, the English speech rhythms are incompatible with douceur, then the word applied to Chaucer is inaccurate. But I would offer an obvious alternative explanation, one that would save both Deschamps' 'douce melodie' and Stevens 'English speech rhythms' as accurate descriptions of Chaucer's verse. I suggest that the variations of English speech rhythms from the French intonation, in particular the strong stresses, do not vitiate the douceur that Deschamps has in mind. The single trait Stevens adduces to illustrate Chaucer's deviation from the 'sauve norm' is that of adjacent strong stresses, like 'fréssh fétures' or 'ál béaute'; however, it is mainly in the context of the iambic norm, which Stevens has excluded for Chaucer, that adjacent stresses are unmusical. One might think, then, that the douceur of the *Art de dictier* is minimally affected by stress, that it involves chiefly the features of sound that Deschamps explicitly discusses: the regular number of syllables, the regular size of lines and stanzas, and the nature of the sounds.[28] Adopting a system that takes no account of stress does not obliterate it in the language, of course, but does automatically subordinate it, and it is entirely possible to modify stress in any reading.

With the question of douceur in mind, I would like to look at three partial texts from near the end of the century. The first consists of the two initial stanzas from the eleventh response in the *Cent ballades*, a typical ballade of the 1390s. Monseigneur de La Tremoïlle argues for loyalty and against inconstancy:

> De grant honneur amoureux enrichir
> Ne peut, s'il n'a Loyauté en s'aÿe,
> Et pour ce fay dedens mon cuer florir
> Loyal Amour d'umilité garnie,
> Dont doucement sans Fausseté servie
> Sera la flour non pareille d'onneur,
> De grant beauté, de bonté, de valeur,
> Qui de mon ceur souveraine maistresse
> Est et sera. S'aray dame et seignour:
> *En ciel un Dieu, en terre une deesse.*

En ce me veul tout mon vivant tenir
Sans ressambler la fausse compaignie
De ceulx qui vont prier et requerir
Dames pluseurs, et font par tout amie
A leur pouoir; pour leur grant tricherie
Cil sont vilain, envieux et menteur
Outrecuidex, felon, fol et vanteur;
Tout leur desir a Faux Penser s'adresse.
Tel gent reny; si prens pour le milleur
En ciel un Dieu, en terre une deesse.[29]

The lover cannot grow rich in great honour if he does not have Loyalty to help him, and for this reason I cause to blossom in my heart Loyal Love adorned with Humility, with which I will sweetly serve without Falsity the unmatched flower of honour, of great beauty, of goodness, of worth, who is and will be sovereign mistress of my heart. I will have lady and lord: in Heaven a God, on earth a goddess.

In this I desire to hold fast all my life, without being like the false company of those who pray and petition many ladies, and everywhere have as many lovers as they can. Because of their great trickery they are low, envious, and liars, presumptuous, treacherous, fools, and braggarts; all their desire is directed toward False Thought. I renounce such people, and I take the best way, in heaven a God, on earth a goddess.

The final stanza elaborates the misdeeds of the followers of Faux Semblant, and the envoy returns to a commendation of loyalty. The late-century characteristics of this ballade—the ten-line stanza form and the envoy—make it unsuited to a musical setting, but it remains a good example of natural music. In the whole poem each line has exactly ten syllables (not counting the feminine endings), and in all except one line (2) the caesura falls obviously after the fourth syllable. The four rhyme sounds alternate masculine and feminine, and their consonants are continuants only, what Deschamps calls semi-vowels. There are a substantial number of run-on lines, but the line ends occur at natural points in the syntax and the rhymes, as usual, well define the line units. The sentences are long and complex. While there are more inversions of natural word order than is common in Machaut's lyrics, on the whole these are not awkward. The diction throughout is entirely what one would expect, with numerous repetitions ('amoureux,' 'Amour'; 'Fausseté,' 'faux'; 'Loyauté,' 'loyal,' etc.). Aside from the developments in the form beyond the limits that musical notation set, one would say that the formal features are entirely consistent with the model for 'natural music' that Machaut offered.

For comparison, we might consider a sample of Chaucer's poetry from about the same time,[30] the 'Envoy de Chaucer' which the Clerk presents after his tale, identifying it as a 'song.' I quote the last three of the six stanzas:

> Ye archewyves, stondeth at defense,
> Syn ye be strong as is a greet camaille;
> Ne suffreth nat that men yow doon offense.
> And sklendre wyves, fieble as in bataille,
> Beth egre as is a tygre yond in Ynde,
> Ay clappeth as a mille, I yow consaille.
>
> Ne dreed hem nat; doth hem no reverence,
> For though thyn housbonde armed be in maille,
> The arwes of thy crabbed eloquence
> Shal perce his brest and eek his aventaille.
> In jalousie I rede eek thou hym bynde,
> And thou shalt make hym couche as doth a quaille.
>
> If thou be fair, ther folk been in presence
> Shewe thou thy visage and thyn apparaille;
> If thou be foul, be free of thy dispense,
> To gete thee freendes ay do thy travaille;
> Be ay of chiere as light as leef on lynde,

And lat hym care, and wepe, and wrynge, and waille.
(E 1195-1212)

As with most of the *Canterbury Tales*, the content of the 'Clerk's
Envoy' is quite different from that usual in the French lyrics, and seems
far from douceur. Nevertheless, in its versification it has a close
relationship to the French, and versification is the basic constituent of
natural music.

The decasyllabic *ababcb* stanza form of the piece has no direct
counterpart in the formes fixes, but it resembles common ballade and
rondeau stanzas, and the carrying through of the same rhymes in the six
strophes makes it still closer to the French forms, especially since the
dominant rhymes, *-ence* and *-aille*, are characteristically French. With
their feminine endings, all of the rhymes are extended, and they
combine with the consistent end-stopping to emphasize the line units.
A judicious sounding and muting of the final *-e*'s in one's reading
makes it possible to see every line as having exactly ten syllables. But
the caesura is comparatively irregular. As I analyse the passage, only
ten of the eighteen lines have caesuras at the standard French position,
syllable 4. In six lines the caesura falls right in the middle, at syllable
5.[31] The diction, of course, is not conventional, and there are some
consonant combinations in 'sklendre,' 'clappeth,' and 'crabbed' that
are rough rather than douce.

In this late piece, in sum, this English verse varies substantially
from the standard represented by La Tremoïlle's poem. Chaucer uses
all feminine rhymes rather than an alternation of masculine and
feminine; he allows more leeway in the placement of the caesura; he
has a higher percentage of end-stopped lines; and he generally
abandons conventional diction in favour of colourful battle and animal
imagery. But in his variations, we might see Chaucer offering a
compatible version of the 'natural music' rather than a rejection of the
French. He retains 'the most distinctive feature' of the French, 'its
measurement of the line by syllables, counted and variously grouped.'[32]
Another essential feature of the French metrical effects that Chaucer
uses here is the complex stanzaic unit. He most noticeably differs from
Machaut in his more distinctly segmented syntax. He sets up a two-part
rhythm in the successive lines of each stanza, which he varies or
stretches out for firm closure in the last line: 'if thou be fair / . . . if thou
be foul / . . . By ay of chiere / . . . And lat hym care, / and wepe, and

wrynge, and waille!' The flow is regularly interrupted by the breaks in the syntax and sometimes complicated by the consonant combinations and abutting stresses, but there remains a musical rhythm that justifies the Clerk's calling the envoy a 'song.'

Indeed, if one inspects the examples that Deschamps himself provides in the *Art de dictier* or in the volumes of his short verse, we do not often find the 'sauve norm' of Machaut. A rather different norm seems present, for instance, in one of the best-known and most lyrical of Deschamps' works, a virelay of unusual structure, which the editor entities 'Portrait of a maiden by herself.'[33] A conventional head-to-toe physical description structures the first half, quoted here:

> *Sui je, sui je, sui je belle?*
>
> Il me semble, à mon avis,
> Que j'ay beau front et doulz vix
> Et la bouche vermeillette:
> *Dittes moy se je suis belle.*
>
> J'ay vers yeulx, petis sourcis,
> Le chief blont, le nez traitis,
> Ront menton, blanche gorgette;
> *Sui je, sui je, sui je belle?*
>
> J'ay dur sain et hault assis,
> Lons bras, gresles doys aussis
> Et par le faulz sui greslette;
> *Dittes moy se je suis belle.*
>
> J'ay bonnes rains, ce m'est vis,
> Bon dos, bon cul de Paris,
> Cuisses et gambes bien faictes;
> *Sui ju, sui je, sui je belle?*
>
> J'ay piez rondes et petiz,
> Bien chaussans, et biaux habis,
> Je sui gaye et joliette;
> *Dittes moy se je suis belle.*
> (1-21)

> Am I, am I, am I pretty? It seems to me, I think, that I have a
> lovely forehead and a sweet face and a red mouth; tell me if I
> am pretty.
>   I have   grey eyes, slender eyebrows, blonde hair, straight
> nose, rounded chin, white throat; am I, am I, am I pretty?
>   I have a firm breast set high, long arms, thin fingers also, and
> my waist is slim; tell me if I am pretty.
>   I have good hips, I think, good back, good 'cul de Paris,'
> well-made thighs and legs; am I, am I, am I pretty?
>   I have rounded, small feet, nice shoes, and beautiful dresses,
> I am gay and graceful; tell me if I am pretty.

In the last half of the poem the girl, who is not yet fifteen, tells of her
furs and clothes and brooches, and promises to guard the key of her
treasure. The one who will capture her love will have to be courteous,
well-bred, and brave. If he is these things, she concludes, he will win
his contest (with her).

The short phrases and strong, juxtaposed monosyllables ('doulz
viz,' 'vers yeulx,' 'chief blont') here make the whole quite different
from what we find in Machaut. The lines are almost all end-stopped.
Though they have only seven syllables, most have a strong caesura of
variable position, alternating between the fourth, the third, and even the
second syllable. The sentences, made up of simple phrases and clauses,
are quite brief. In these matters the 'music' of the virelay is much more
like the 'Clerk's Envoy' than the Machaut standard. Notwithstanding, I
believe that one can still see both Chaucer's and Deschamps' poems as
possessing what the Frenchman would call 'douceur.' The distinct
divisions between the lines and within the lines do not make the Clerk's
and the girl's lyrics less song-like, Indeed, the divisions impart a
rhythmic verve to both performances that Machaut's smooth syntax
cannot achieve. At the same time the regularity of the syllable count,
and the organization of the lines in stanzas whose identical structure is
emphasized by extended repeated rhymes, make it possible still to
speak of 'sweetness'—lightness and ease—in the verse. Certainly one
can say that, aside from a few isolated locutions on the 'Clerk's
Envoy,' there is little that is harsh and heavy in either performance.[34]

Musique naturele is represented in the variety of styles of diverse
Middle French writers. Among the contemporaries of Chaucer, the

verse styles of le Mote, Machaut, and Deschamps have notable differences, but their lyrics share the basic features of the mode: a fixed number of syllables to the line with the lines bound together in uniform stanzas by a complex scheme of rhymes, often polysyllabic, and a refrain. Much of Chaucer's stanzaic poetry effectively incorporates and carries over into English the techniques and spirit of this mode, this natural music broadly conceived. All of his verse shows its effects. For the music, Machaut was his main French model, but as in the 'Clerk's Envoy' he also exploited the potential represented in the work of various authors.

It would be rash at this point to claim that Chaucer's verse participates fully in the natural music of the French mode. A consequence of such a claim would be to accept the line and the caesural segment rather than the metrical foot as the basic units of Chaucer's verse. But even if one is not prepared to go that far, it still seems clear that his versification does not accord with Old and Middle English accentual mode, and that the French syllabic model had a crucial effect on it.[35] I believe it is reasonable to maintain, in addition, that whatever conclusion one arrives at on the matter of stress, one can speak of Chaucer's having successfully created a version of the French natural music in English. I therefore want to consider very briefly the extent of the effect of his natural music on subsequent English verse.

In a 1956 essay on the relationship of word and melody—of 'lexis' and 'melos'—in the tradition of English poetry, Northrop Frye made some interesting remarks on the nature and effects of Chaucer's versification. The principle Frye enunciates for musicality in poetry is very different from Deschamps' concept; as a matter of fact, in its assumption of a stress language and variation in the number of syllables, his dictum rules out French poetry. Musicality for Frye entails 'a principle of accentual scansion, a regular recurrence of beats with a variable number of syllables between the beats.'[36] He recognizes that Chaucer did not write this kind of accentual poetry, and therefore by his standards it is unmusical,[37] but he finds that for later writers Chaucer's poetry 'began to sound more like the accentual rum-ram-ruf poets he ridiculed' and thereby became musical. Thus Spenser, in imitating Chaucer, 'begins with accentual experiments but abandons them later for an elaborate unmusical stanza.'[38] Here the opposition of Frye's concept of musical poetry to French 'natural music' is manifest. For it is Spenser's stanza, an expanded version of rime royal with ten-syllable lines and complex rhyme, that imitates the natural music of Chaucer. In using an alexandrine line to close off the stanza, Spenser provides an additional feature that emphasizes the stanzaic unit, as Chaucer, in the 'Clerk's Envoy', stretched out in other ways the last lines of the stanzas ('And lat hym care, and wepe, and wrynge, and waille'). The tradition in which Spenser is working is unbroken from Chaucer's time. Serving to connect the work of the two poets, the Ricardian poet with the Elizabethan, is the tremendous volume of poetry in rime royal and 'Monk's Tale' stanza that was produced through the fifteenth century.

Although I have conducted this discussion as if the technical features of versification are all that enter into the question of natural music, it must be acknowledged that the content of the work, surely has a bearing. In his *Art de dictier* Deschamps could leave questions of content to his examples because the poetry of the formes fixes is virtually all lyric in nature. While it is not all love poetry, it is discontinuous, discursive, and reflective rather than narrative. Accordingly, the content and the treatment of content in *Troilus and Criseyde* make it possible to classify large parts as lyric. By contrast, most of the rime royal of the *Canterbury Tales* cannot be so classified. Similarly, John Lydgate's rime royal *Complaint of the Black Knight* in following Chaucer is quite in the French mode, while his *Fall of Princes*, composed in the 'Monk's Tale' stanza and equally Chaucerian, is clearly not natural music. If the influence of natural music lives in English beyond the fifteenth century, it is in the extensive lyric parts of the *Faerie Queene* and in the ensuing tradition of stanzaic poetry that Spenser fathers. Frye finds that such verse is not musical: 'Spenser and Keats belong to the tradition of unmusical opsis [visual poetry] to which Tennyson also belongs.'[39] Frye's generalizations are compelling: 'Opsis' in vivid colour is surely a quality which the work of these English poets possesses, and which the fourteenth[-]century French poets do not strive for. In *Troilus and Criseyde*, likewise, 'melos' is dominant, at least in the lyric parts. One may question whether 'opsis' and melos' are mutually exclusive, as Frye seems to assume.

The complications and contradictions to which Frye's generalizations lead us are perhaps not resolvable, certainly not in brief compass. It will be better to conclude this study still in contact with a medieval authority, Eustache Deschamps, however unsteady an authority he may sometimes be. In the course of the *Art de dictier*, a treatise that seems highly quixotic and incompletely conceived, Deschamps nevertheless writes several paragraphs about the distinctive lyric poetry of his time (christening it 'natural music') which crystallize its character. His words provide profound insight into the work. At the beginning of his description of natural music, he makes an enigmatic statement which, though one could easily dismiss it as meaningless formula, has intriguing resonances: 'L'autre musique est appellee *naturele* pour ce qu'elle ne puet estre aprinse a nul, se son propre couraige naturelment ne s'i applique'[40] / 'The other music is called *natural* because it cannot be taught to anyone if his heart does not naturally devote itself to it.' The words recall Dante's explanation to Bonagiunta in *Purgatorio* 24 of the dolce stil nuovo. What differentiates our new poetry from the verse of our predecessors, Dante says, is that we listen to what Love says, and then write. His formulation and that of Deschamps suggest that the poets apply a sensibility to composing their verse that contributes an indispensable and ineffable property. Despite the frustrating vagueness of Dante's formulation, it has never been hard to accept that the ineffable enters into his work. Though it may be somewhat harder for a modern reader to accept, the fourteenth-century French poets share with Dante an authentic and profound sense of the lyrical. The natural music of their work at its best also possesses an element of lyric genius, mysterious in origin and ineffable in effect, and Chaucer's work draws an important part of its own genius from it.

NOTES

1. [Daniel] Poirion *Le poète et le prince* [Université de Grenoble Publications de la Faculté des Lettres et Sciences Humaines 35. Paris: Presses Universitaires de France 1965] 37 finds the Cour amoureuse especially important as a reflection of the socio-political developments in France: 'Rien de plus significatif, dans cette perspective [ie, in the perspective of an evolution towards formalism and etiquette] que l'institution de la *Cour d'Amour* le 6 janvier 1400.'
2. For an excellent inclusive treatment of the Middle French poets after Machaut who continued to compose music, see [Nigel] Wilkins

'[The] Post-Machaut Tradition [of Poet-Musicians].' [*Nottingham Medieval Studies* 12 (1968) 40-84]

3. In the documents they are sometimes called 'puys d'amours' and sometimes 'puys-Notre Dame'; accordingly, many of the extant poems that originated in the *puy* celebrate the Virgin, and many the beloved lady. For the origin of the name 'puy' and, various aspects of the organization in Arras, see [Henry] Guy *Essai sur la vie [et les oeuvres du trouvère Adam de la Hale*. Paris: Hachette 1898] xxxiv-lviii.

4. Ibid lvi-lviii; [Edmond] Faral *Les Jongleurs [en France au Moyen Age*. Paris: Champion 1910] 139-42

5. Gilles li Muisis *Poésies [de Gilles li Muisis*. Ed Kervyn de Lettenhove. 2 vols. Louvain: Lefever 1882] I, 89

6. Quoted from [D.W.] Robertson [Jr.] *Chaucer's London* [New York: Wiley 1968] 88

7. [John H.] Fisher *John Gower* [New York: New York University Press 1964] 77-84 advances the reasonable possibility that Gower could have been a member. A similar argument could be made for Chaucer and other contemporaries. Granson, though a knight, probably would have felt no compunction at participating. One of his ballades printed in the *Jardin de Plaisance* has an envoy addressed to 'Prince du puy,' though [Arthur] Piaget [ed.] in *Oton de Grandson [: sa vie et ses poésies*. Mémoires et documents publiés par la Société de la Suisse Romande, 3rd series, vol 1. Lausanne: Payot 1941] 126 thinks the envoy not authentic.

8. [Jean] Froissart [*The] Lyric Poems [of Jehan Froissart*. Ed Rob Roy McGregor Jr. University of North Carolina Studies in Romance Languages and Literatures no 143. Chapel Hill: University of North Carolina Press 1975] 169-203

9. 'En dormant melancolioie / A une cançon amoureuse, / Et par samblance grascieuse / Dis k'a .i. puis le porteroie / Pour couronner, se je pooie' (*Le Regret Guillaume [comte de Hainault*. Ed Auguste Scheler. Louvain: Lefever 1882] 100-3).

10. *Louange* no 7 (Poésies [*lyriques*. Ed Vladimir Chichmaref. 2 vols. 1909. Reprint Geneva: Slatkine 1973] XLVIII) 51-3. Poems addressed simply to 'prince' may or may not be connected with a puy; often the envoy will more specifically designate 'prince du puy.' Machaut's chant royal with the refrain, 'Cuer de marbre couronné d'aymant . . . (*Louange* no 1; *Poésies* CCLIV), which imitates a refrain

of le Mote's (See chapter 2), could well have been designed for a concours at Valenciennes or another locale in le Mote's home area.

11. *Oeuvres [complètes de Eustache Deschamps*. Ed le Marquis de Queux de Saint-Hilaire and Gaston Raynaud. 11 vols. S.A.T.F. Paris: Firmin Didiot 1878-1904] VII, 281

12. Ibid 271. Deschamps' description here is in the service of contrasting the two 'musics'; one assumes that not all presentations had both spoken and sung dimensions.

13. The envoys of a chant royal (*Oeuvres* III, 134, no 326, 46) and of a ballade (VI, 132, no 1180, 31) are addressed to the 'Prince du Pui,' and in a ballade (V, 54, no 872) directed to the 'dus de Poligieras,' who may well be the poet himself, the speaker asks that the 'duke' not depart, but rather that he remember the 'puis d'amours' (20). Many other of Deschamps' poems may be puy productions, especially the five-stanza works; there is a section of ninety-four chants royal (*Oeuvres* III, 1-205) and there are other five-stanza lyrics in other sections of his work. Envoys addressed to 'prince,' of course, may or may not indicate puy poems. [Ernest] Hoepffner [*Eustache*] *Deschamps* [*: Leben und Werke*. Strassburg: Trübner 1904] 128 n4 thinks it very unlikely that Deschamps participated in the puys, while Poirion *Le Poète et le prince* 226-7 believes as I do that he assisted, at least on occasion, at the concours.

14. The fifteenth-century rhetorical treatises that were evidently intended for the instruction of aspiring puy poets describe all the common forms. For the audiences of the treatises, see [Ernest] Langlois [, ed. *Recueil d'arts de*] *Seconde rhétorique* [Paris: Imprimerie Nationale 1902] vi and n2. In the *Art de dictier* Deschamps *Oeuvres* VII 271 imputes to the puy poet 'serventois de Nostre Dame, chançons royeaulx, pastourelles, balades et rondeaulx.'

15. [Gaston] Raynaud [ed. *Les] Cent ballades [: Poème du XIVe siècle composé par Jean le Seneschal avec le collaboration de . . .* S.A.T.F. Paris: Firmin Didot 1905]

16. Ibid xlviii-li

17. See [Charles] Potvin [ed.] '[La Charte de] La Cour d'Amour [de l'année 1401]' [*Bulletin de l'Académie Royale des Sciences, des Lettres, et des Beaux-Arts de Belgique* 3rd Series, vol. 12 (1886) 191-220]; [Arthur] Piaget 'La Cour Amoureuse[, dite de Charles VI.]' [*Romania* 20 (1891) 417-54] and 'Un Manuscrit [de la *Cour amoureuse*

de Charles VI.]'[*Romania* 31 (1902) 597-603] For a summary of the organization of the Cour see Poirion *Le Poète et le prince* 41.

18. See ibid 38-9.

19. See [Theodor] Straub 'Die Gründung [des Pariser Minnehofs von 1400].' [Zeitschrift für romanische Philologie 77 (1961) 1-14]

20. In speaking of the social makeup of the court, Poirion *Le Poète et le prince* 39-40 notes, 'Sans compter les chanoines de Tournai et de Lille qui figurent parmi les *maîtres des requêtes,* on voit parmi les *substituts du procureur général* bourgeois de Tournai encore et d'Amiens.' He notes further that the prince himself presided over a kind of 'confrérie littéraire, celle du *Chapel vert*,' at Tournai and Lille.

21. *Oeuvres* VII, 347-62, nos 1404 and 1405. Poirion *Le Poète et le prince* 223-4 notes that the 'assemblée burlesque' that Deschamps envisions 'semble une exacte parodie de la *cour amoureuse.*'

22. See *Oeuvres* XI, 281-4.

23. The members of the Amiens puy who were crowned in 1389 included lawyers, prosecutors, canons, priests, mercers, tanners, goldsmiths, tavern-keepers, and other merchants. See Poirion *Le Poète et le prince* 39.

24. In [Piero] Boitani and [Anna] Torti [eds.] *Medieval and Pseudo- Medieval Literature* [D.S. Brewer 1984]

25. *Oeuvres* VII, 270-1

26. Ibid 271-2. The appeal to the example of the puys in this passage suggests once more that they had a basic role in the poetic tradition.

27. [John] Stevens '[The] "Music" of the Lyric[: Machaut, Deschamps, Chaucer' [in Boitani and Torti] 127, 129

28. One may feel that the handling of strong stress would be a matter that the French-speaking Deschamps would not be attuned to. Nevertheless, Raynaud's glossary indicates that 'paroles . . . pointoyees' in the above quotation from Deschamps signifies 'accented words.' Other glosses are possible, of course.

29. Raynaud *Cent ballades* 221-2, lines 1-20

30. The Clerk's reference to the Wife of Bath in introducing the Envoy (E 1170) indicates that it was written after Chaucer composed the 'Wife's Prologue,' generally placed in the early 1390s.

31. Of the other two lines, in one the caesura falls at the end of syllable 6, and one at the end of syllable 3. 1 do not believe that we should see in the frequency of the 5/5 syllable division any particular

relationship to the division of lines in the English alliterative verse tradition. In English alliterative verse the first half-line tends to be heavier than the second and in any event stress is the main factor.

32. Stevens '"Music" of the Lyric' 129

33. *Oeuvres* IV, 8-10, no. 554. The text I quote is from [Nigel] Wilkins [ed.] *One Hundred Ballades*[, *Rondeaux and Virelais*. Cambridge: Cambridge University Press 1968] 79-80.

34. The harshness of a few words and phrases of the clerk, like 'crabbed eloquence,' achieves a special humorous effect in part because of the generally light and easy movement of the rest of the envoy.

35. See the essays of [Steven] Guthrie ["Meter and Performance in Machaut and Chaucer"] and [James I.] Wimsatt ["Chaucer and Deschamps' 'Natural Music'"] in [Rebecca A. Baltzer, *et. al.*, eds. *The Union of*] *Words and Music* [*in Medieval Poetry*. Austin: University of Texas Press 1991]. The discussion by Thomas Cable also has general relevance to the problem.

36. [Northrop] Frye 'Introduction' [in *Sound and Poetry*. Ed Northrop Frye. English Institute Essays 1956. New York: Columbia University Press 1957] xvii

37. The presence or lack of musicality for Frye is descriptive; it does not involve a necessary value judgment.

38. Frye 'Introduction' xix. On Chaucer he elaborates that his 'basis is metrical rather than accentual scansion.' By 'metrical' one assumes he does not mean the quantitative standard of classical prosody.

39. Ibid xviii

40. *Oeuvres* VII, 270

THE INTERPRETATION OF DREAMS: CHAUCER'S EARLY POEMS, LITERARY CRITICISM AND LITERARY THEORY

by John M. Ganim

As the previous essays demonstrate, and as William Quinn has asserted in his introduction, scholarship on Chaucer's dream visions and shorter poems comprises an unusually mature and focused body of research. The books and articles in which these essays originally appeared form a sort of history of Chaucer studies, reflecting interest in historical background, source study, exegetical and allegorical interpretation, and formal and narratological analysis as these have variously impressed themselves on Chaucer studies over the past half-century or more. These essential articles represent the tip of an iceberg of research, magisterially summarized and extended by A.J. Minnis' *Oxford Guide to The Shorter Poems* (1995) and by Alfred David in the Variorum edition of *The Minor Poems* (1982). What I want to emphasize here is how the study of Chaucer's shorter works, partly because of the challenge of explaining some of these apparently conventional works to modern readers, has predicted the current and perhaps future state of Chaucer scholarship in general. At the same time, the study of the dream visions and the short poems comprises a test case, again because of the poetry's intractability, for some of the chief approaches to literary criticism over the past half-century.

Before such terms became part of our critical vocabulary, however, studies of the dream visions and lyrics more or less invented before their time the most dynamic directions in current medieval scholarship, including the anthropological contextualization of the New Historicism, the related consideration of texts as performances, and the difficult question of poetic subjectivity, particularly in terms of the position of the male poet in relation to female characters and readers or audiences. That is, Chaucer's early poems have consistently represented a challenge to our critical preconceptions and our sense of literary judgment. Categorized as "minor" works, they have forced us to ask questions, as we have learned minor literatures do, about what constitutes a major work or an officially authorized approach.

Most students and non-specialist readers are attracted to Chaucer's poetry because, its linguistic distance notwithstanding, it is apparently accessible and easy and open. But the dream visions are not easy and open. They are difficult, obscure and inscrutable at times, even as they elicit what we consider to be typically Chaucerian pleasures. They seem, for those reasons and others, more "medieval," and so alert us to another Chaucer than the one who has been canonized in our recent literary history. We may continue to delight in the comic realism of the *Canterbury Tales*, but the dream visions and lyrics offer us very different sorts of effects, such as an interest in moral states, an openness to the vagaries and validity of psychological experience and fantasy. They require a previous knowledge of highly conventional medieval forms or a willingness to engage the premises of those forms. We can if we wish read the dream visions and shorter works as experiments towards the *Canterbury Tales* and *Troilus and Criseyde*, but we can also allow ourselves to learn to read the concerns of these great long works as extensions of what has already been proposed in the dream visions and shorter poems. The early poems support both the "conservative" tradition in Chaucer criticism—an emphasis on the moral, rhetorical and didactic elements in the poetry—and a more recent "radical" movement—a concern with demythologizing and critiquing the moderate Chaucer of institutionalized scholarship and common readers. The early poems and the scholarship surrounding them make Chaucer, whom we often turn to as the most genial and accessible of poets, a difficult writer in the best sense of that term.

The fortunes of the dream visions and shorter poems in the hierarchies of scholarship have, like most other genres and periods, depended on shifts in institutional and critical affinities. When literary study become institutionalized in the university in the middle of the nineteenth century, it was organized according to a philological model, imported largely from the dynamic German research universities, that justified itself by a program of the recovery of language and history (Ganim, 1995 and 1996). Medieval literature held a privileged place in this model because of its antiquity and its place as the origin of written vernaculars. An uncommon number of Chaucer scholars held crucial posts in the then recently founded Modern Language Association and the early academic journals in America published disproportionately on medieval literature (Graff, 1987). Although epics, with their claims to national self-definition, were especially prized, the shorter poems received their due attention, and their tantalizing relation to sources and analogues made them an important reservoir of data. While this scholarly interest continued through the 1920's, from the turn of the century on, critical attention to *The Canterbury Tales* became far more prevalent, perhaps reflecting the hegemony of realism and naturalism in contemporary literature and the agenda of a progressivism strongly tied to the universities. Beginning in the 1920's, the New Criticism, fashioned out of the practical criticism espoused by I.A. Richards (1929) and the intense interest in the details of the poetic line espoused by Pound and Eliot, resulted in a newly important position for decontextualized poems, and a taste for metaphoric difficulty that valued lyric poetry, from the troubadours through the Metaphysicals, above narratives that lent themselves less well to local analysis, such as the dream visions. After the Second World War, New Criticism, despite its often elitist origins, was adapted to the demands of the explosive growth of higher education in the U.S. Translated into an almost industrial model of reading, the New Criticism in America allowed an access to texts to an audience less immersed in the cultural context of high literature, rather than, as Richards first proposed, an audience encumbered by that context. The self-enclosed work of art of the New Critical model, almost like a smoothly functioning engine, was far from the ideal approach to Chaucer's shorter poems, or to Chaucer at all.

By the 1950's, however, modifications to the New Criticism, and competing models of analysis, allowed a new access and interest in these works. A new rhetorical emphasis on questions of audience and narration revitalized Chaucer studies, as an explosion of articles on the Chaucerian narrator demonstrates during the 1950's and 1960's. The strain of anxiety in the post-war years, a counterpoint to American optimism reflected in cinema noir, had a reflection in a new interest in Freud, and the more optimistic 1950's followed with an interest in Jung's psychology of myth, both of which promised, if they did not necessarily deliver, a more open approach to the form and premises of the dream visions. The startling claims for the exegetical interpretation of medieval literature, proposed by D.W. Robertson, Jr. (1962) and his followers, offered one of the first period-based historicist alternatives to the New Criticism, arguing for alterity over access, and allegorical over mimetic or dramatic interpretation. While the battleground of this debate tended to be *Troilus and Criseyde* and inevitably *The Canterbury Tales*, new focus was placed on the dream visions with their apparent debt to allegory, commentary and more didactic forms.

All of these internal debates, however, were dwarfed by the impact of poststructuralist theory, largely imported from France, and cultural studies, largely imported from British universities, on American literary study beginning in the mid-1970's and peaking in the mid-1980's. Phenomenology, deconstruction, semiotics, often synthesized in ways at odds with their original formulation, rapidly changed the discourse of American literary study and the very structure of the discipline, changes lumped together under the category of "theory." In some ways the study of English medieval literature seemed like an island of resistance to these changes; but, in more subtle ways, medieval studies was already organized in ways that suggested an openness to some of the most apparently threatening aspects of the "theory" revolution." The notion that literature should be studied in terms of its system of production and reception rather than as the appreciation of individual masterpieces and authors was consistent with the remaining corpus of most medieval literature. The critique of the humanist conception of the integrated self and its replacement by a decentered subject constructed by often conflicting discourses was hardly a blow to an area of study that had repeatedly been imagined as predating the rise of the individual. Even the New Historicism's conception of a text taking part in the production of cultural meaning had already been predicted in the highly occasional readings of poems such as Chaucer's shorter poetry. Most strikingly, medieval texts, ranging from mystical tracts to *The Legend of Good Women*, that had previously been relegated to the status of curiosity suddenly found themselves at the center of critical attention as a result of feminism's strategic deployment of all of these new developments.

In the late 1950's, and continuing into the early 1960's, the focus of generic attention created a climate that briefly favored forms such as the dream vision. The work of Northrop Frye, with its understanding of allegory and its highly formalized understanding of myth, and a general resurgence of interest in poets like Blake and Spenser who worked in allegorical and quasi-allegorical modes, coincided with a new interest particularly by North American scholars both in the dream visions and the early works, as well as in some of Chaucer's sources such as *The Romance of the Rose*. A subset of this interest is revealed in the turn of psychoanalytically inclined critics towards myth criticism, with its foundation in the works of Jung. Indeed, Jungian archetypes, despite Frye's highly objective presentation of them, underlay the structure of *The Anatomy of Criticism* (1957), the most influential book of criticism of its time. As a result, an interest in literature inspired by or related to dreams developed. Despite some intriguing Jungian takes on Chaucer's *Canterbury Tales*, however, no full-scale Jungian reading of dream visions appeared until Paul Piehler's belated *Visionary Landscape* (1971), which appeared as interest in academic Jungianism began to wane (and as Jungianism became part of popular culture).

The aborted development of a myth criticism that might have drawn attention to the dream visions was probably due to the continuing dominance of the New Criticism. Interestingly, the medievalist who has done most to apply and extend the limits of the New Criticism of Middle English literature, A. C. Spearing, has also been one of the most consistently important interpreters of the dream vision form. In *Criticism and Medieval Poetry* (1964), Spearing demonstrated that part of the power of medieval poetry was generated by the formal and verbal integrity that the New Criticism highly prized; he also argued that the rigid mechanics of New Critical method had to be modified to interpret such poetry. Coalescing in E.T. Donaldson's important essays (from the 1950's and 1960's) on the Chaucerian narrator, interest in the dream visions focused on their apparently incipient experiment with the Chaucerian persona (*Speaking* 1970). If the dream visions did not lend themselves to the formal patterning and exquisite symmetries of high New Critical practice, their principle of unity might lie in the coherent perspective of the Chaucerian narrator.

The role of the narrator in longer works, which in any case frustrated a New Critical practice honed on lyric poetry, was the subject of a book which rivaled Frye's in influence, Wayne Booth's *Rhetoric of Fiction* (1961). Indeed, Booth's focus on the variations of narrative perspective was developed at the same time as Donaldson's earliest studies of the Chaucerian persona. Following Booth, the narrator becomes as much the subject of critical analysis as what was being narrated, and as a result allowed critics to talk about a narrative unity that could be discerned beneath the shifting topics of unruly forms such as the novel. This highly rhetorical understanding of Chaucer's narration received some resistance from scholars such as Bertrand Bronson ("Audience" 1940), who, because of their sense of the importance of Chaucer's presence (Bronson argued that Chaucer actually read to the court and the poems should be regarded in terms of Chaucer's performance), rejected the notion of complex screens between the poet and his audience. By the mid-1960's, Donald R. Howard, himself indebted to Donaldson's thinking, asked for a phenomenological understanding of all a poet's work as an aspect of consciousness, arguing that everywhere behind the various rhetorical manipulations lies "Chaucer the Man" (1965). Howard developed his argument at the same time that he began his biography of Chaucer. At the same time, he turned to the *House of Fame* in an important essay called "Flying through Space" (1975), which read the early poems in terms of their representation of time and space, also categories perhaps influenced by the phenomenology, brought to North America by

Georges Poulet (1956) in one of the first incursions of French theory into American literary practice, still current at Johns Hopkins University in the late 1960's.

The ultimate coherence offered by phenomenology, especially in terms of its celebration of personal subjectivity as a principle of coherence, was one of the targets of post-structuralism and deconstruction. By the 1980's, the "subject" had become enormously complicated, because the "subject" was no longer being defined as a principle of unity. While the possibility of coherence through a narrative presence had been questioned in studies from the 1960's, including Robert Jordan's *Chaucer and the Shape of Creation* (1967) and Robert Payne's *The Key of Remembrance*, both of which emphasized rhetorical structure and patterning over organic unity, Alfred David's *Strumpet Muse* (1976) pointed to the ways in which the narrator dramatized conflicts in Chaucer's own poetic agenda, rather than unified it. David Lawton's *Chaucer's Narrators* (1985), fully aware of the definition of the subject following Lacan and Foucault and of the potential of a heteroglossic voicing following Bakhtin, opened the question of the consistency of the Chaucerian narrator as a principle of unity.

It is this last point, the role of the dreamer or narrator, that provided the great new critical key to the dream visions. Here, too, the impurity of history and biography intrudes on the ideal of uncontaminated interpretation, for the Chaucerian narrator's devices are best understood in terms of the position of a poet in a court composed of his social superiors. This broadly autobiographical understanding of the narrator has always been inescapably linked to the larger question of poetic subjectivity. Indeed, it would seem that Chaucer virtually dramatizes the anxiety of subjectivity within the discourses of class, gender and poetic competition. As Seth Lerer acutely observes (1993), Chaucer himself becomes a figure in the family romance of fifteenth-century poetry, resistance or accession to whom determines the poetic identity of his followers.

With the theoretical and methodological innovations of the past few years, the question of subjectivity has broadened in other directions. Related to the continuing interest in the narrator or persona as subject, approaches loosely associated with the New Historicism, such as those by Seth Lerer and Larry Scanlon (1994), have explored the literal question of the "subject" in relation of royal or aristocratic authority or patronage. The subservient, even abject, posture of the narrator of the early poems, with his—as A.C. Spearing (1993) has noted—oddly voyeuristic relation to experience, has—as Lerer has argued—created a model of subjection as a way of negotiating some agency in terms of the representation of the authorial self or of poetic material or form. The cryptic and what Anne Middleton (1978) called the "coterie" quality of the dream visions has always inspired occasional readings. D.W. Robertson ("Historical" 1965) argued that *The Book of the Duchess* was written as an anniversary memorial for the death of Blanche, Duchess of Lancaster. No one doubts its elegiac quality, but the very specific court context of a specific occasion changes the way we read the poem. Similarly, Larry Benson, in a 1965 essay reprinted above, has argued that the *House of Fame* is an elaborate insult to a representative of the Viscontis in England following the collapse of marriage arrangements for Richard II. These theses are hotly debated; but, stepping back from the question of whether they are proven or not, what is striking is the fact that the dream visions encourage us to imagine a context or setting for their performance. Whatever the validity of these arguments, which owe more to an older historicism than anything resembling the New Historicism, with its debt to post-structuralist historiography and anthropology, they imagine the dream visions working as something other than decoration or entertainment. Part of court culture, the dream visions are imagined as not merely reflecting, but shaping and engaging court politics and court behavior. History is not merely reflected in the text; the text itself intervenes in the historical moment and, more importantly, in memory and memorialization. Whether or not the dream visions are allegorical, they share with allegory the obscure representation of potentially volatile statements and outlooks. Indeed, the anxious and insomniac narrator of the dream visions in some fashion reflects an anxiety not only about the profound issues of death and grief, reputation and memory, nature and sexuality, gender and justice, all variously the subjects of the dream vision poems, but also about the dangers of saying anything at all.

In a less systematic way, the formal difficulty of the dream visions and their resistance to new critical analysis resulted in attempts to describe them that prefigured the wide circulation of M.M. Bakhtin's theories of heteroglossia and the carnivalesque (Bakhtin, 1968 and 1981). Drawing on some of the same literary genres that fed into the drama of the dream vision, Bakhtin sought to write a literary history that would be based on these apparently eccentric forms rather than on authorized models such as epic or tragedy. The efforts to understand the tone of the dream visions, particularly *The House of Fame* and *The Parliament of Foules*, have pointed to Chaucer's reliance on festive forms, his unresolved collocation of many different voices and his satiric inversion of high cultural values. Chaucer himself may have been writing in the tradition of the Menippean satire in *The House of Fame*, one of the chief generic forms cited by Bakhtin in his now widely influential theoretical works. Indeed, the qualities of the early poems that most resemble the "comic" and "realistic" *Canterbury Tales* are precisely those that Bakhtin defines as aspects of the carnivalesque. The New Historicist sense of the text as historical actor, participating in events in the same way that anthropologists have analyzed rituals, and the older traditional historicist readings of the shorter poems as occasional, memorial and commemorative, have also been amplified by new theoretical understandings of performance and performativity. For a number of recent scholars, Chaucer does speak to his audience, he even performs for it, and this performance is central to our understanding of the text, even embedded in it in metaphoric, structural and formal ways. Carl Lindahl, for instance, in *Earnest Games: Folkloric Patterns in the Canterbury Tales* (1987) regards Chaucer on the one hand as if he were an "ethnologist," recording the festivals and celebrations around him, and, on the other, as if he were a participant himself, responding to the pressures of audience and situation. William Quinn (1994) argues that the *Legend* is an unusually performable text, in that it invites, and even requires, us to imagine Chaucer reading it aloud, and also imagining his reading it aloud providing its irony or its emphasis. The *Troilus* or *The Canterbury Tales*, for instance, dramatize their tone textually, but the *Legend*'s intractability comes from precisely its performability, the fact that it awaits a performance to make its narrative tone of voice entirely or even partially clear. Robert Edwards in *The Dream of Chaucer* (1989), a section of which appears above, has pointed to certain dimensions in medieval literary theory that allowed a text to be thought of as performative, "doing" as well as "making" (p. 45).

In one local sense, the identity of the narrator, related both to his relation to Chaucer as a historical person and his negotiation of the difficult class and gender positions I have just summarized, can be regarded as "performed." Indeed, Martin Stevens (1978) had already pointed to the idea of a medieval "performing self" (described by Richard Poirier as an authorial role in American literature) as a model for dealing with the then apparently contradictory definitions of author, narrator, persona and historical person. Since the late 1980's, we have gotten used to thinking about identity as performed, as an extension of the theory of the subject. David Lawton (1985) has come closest to accommodating these developments in his study of *Chaucer's Narrators*, but the questions surrounding the "Chaucer" of the early poems and the lyrics, with their specific allusions to biographical background, can be understood as a strategy of performed identity.

This potentially subversive subjectivity, attempting to create a space for expression by seeming to obey the dictates of authority and tradition, may seem to align the question of the late medieval subject with that of the colonial writer, for instance. Such reversals are no longer possible to dismiss as irony alone, particularly in light of Elaine Tuttle Hansen's *Chaucer and the Fictions of Gender* (1991). Hansen's argument in fact begins with the *Legend of Good Women*. She argues that the Chaucerian persona, as is typical of the male poet apparently fascinated with female characters, in fact appropriates the slippery signification and relative lack of fixity of the feminine other, the aspects of that projection most useful to poetic discourse. Chaucer presents himself and his project as "feminized" while in fact effacing female subjectivity from the works themselves. Instead of critiquing misogyny, as it pretends to do, the *Legend of Good Women* is in some radical sense about men and the poetry they do. Hansen's thesis not only questions the possibility of a feminist Chaucer; it is also an attack on a humanist Chaucer, a Chaucer whose ironic perspective transcends his age and reveals the timeless truths that inhabit his fictions. At the same time, interestingly, Hansen's strategy itself is based on a transhistoricized argument—that the nature of male poetic discourse by definition is self-limited in relation to the representation of its other.

Hansen's argument is evidence of the fact that, despite its stereotype as an obstinately traditional field of study, isolated from the currents of contemporary critical discourse, the study of later medieval English literature over the past two decades has in fact generated a significant body of feminist criticism. Partly because of the centrality of medieval female mystics for the French feminist theorists such as Irigaray and Kristeva, and partly because of the debate on the place of women in medieval religious systems initiated by Carolyn Walker Bynum in *Jesus as Mother* and elsewhere (1982), medieval literary texts have acquired a new importance as agents of rather than reflections of cultural practices. In Chaucer studies alone, one of the most widely influential books of the past decade has been Carolyn Dinshaw's *Chaucer's Sexual Poetics* (1989). In all of these studies, texts like the Wife of Bath's Prologue and Tale and *Troilus and Criseyde* obviously are the chief sites of debate, but it is remarkable how often the shorter poems, especially the *Legend of Good Women* and *The Book of the Duchess*, have been the starting point for these arguments.

An interesting historical sidelight to these developments is that the feud that once wracked medieval English studies in the 1950's and 1960's, that between exegetical criticism of medieval literature and a largely formalist and humanist New Criticism, has more or less been absorbed and transcended at least in feminist scholarship. The searching feminist accounts of this debate by scholars such as Carolyn Dinshaw and Louise Fradenburg (1990) have pointed to a male subjectivity that underlay both approaches and replicated the courtly and clerical misogynies of the Middle Ages themselves. At the risk of revealing a patriarchal fascination with genealogies, I would observe that the authors of most recent feminist studies of Chaucer were trained by scholars who were themselves schooled in or friendly to the apparently conservative exegetical rather than an apparently progressive formalist camp. One reason may have been that these younger feminist scholars had to work through some of the identification with hierarchy and patriarchy that marked high Robertsonianism (though not necessarily Robertson's admirers). But another reason is that the concern with reconstructing a system of poetics, the obsession with allegorical signification and the suspicion of surface meanings (endemic to exegetical criticism) provided an avenue of entry by those schooled in its methods to the revolution in literary study (ushered in by structuralism, post-structuralism and cultural studies) that underlies the discourse of feminist theoretical development. A method of literary analysis once anathematized as hopelessly reactionary may have been the ancestor of a generation of radical feminist medieval scholars. Indeed, one of the most basic moves of feminist criticism has been to read texts as allegories of gender, even though the move is modified by densely textural formalist evidence. Nowhere is this more so than in studies of the short poems. An example of a rigorously theorized feminist reading of *The Book of the Duchess* is Gayle Margherita's chapter in *The Romance of Origins* (1994). In this poem, the origin of poetic speaking, of the possibility of the literary itself, is fantasized as the result of bonding between the two male figures of the poem. At the same time, their bonding is the result of the absent female, whom their reminisces and questions recall, but in recalling create an unstable identification with the lost feminine that must be contained and suppressed.

Because of the enormous investment of medieval studies in intellectual history and in philosophy and theology as the master disciplines of the field, the early poems have always served as a mine of information about Chaucer's learning and his absorption of late medieval intellectual trends. Indeed, the self-proclaimed role of reader and searcher in the persona of the early poems has encouraged a narcissistic reflection of scholarship in the Chaucerian figure of these poems, and by extension of Chaucer. The Chaucer that emerges from the tradition of source study is as much "Chaucer the Scholar" as the hypothetical "Chaucer the Poet," "Chaucer the Narrator" or "Chaucer the Man" of formalist and phenomenological criticism. This is also true of the image of the poet of the *Canterbury Tales* and other writings as we read him through the lens of source study since Lowes. At the same time, certain directions in the scholarship on the shorter poems also suggest a way of considering the poetry of the shorter poems as a certain kind of exploratory thinking on its own. Of course, strands of the New Criticism, especially those closely associated with Yvor Winters, asked for a reading of poetry as subject to logical rigor, and the main branches of the New Criticism read literary discourse as a kind of third way, a form of saying and seeking distinct from that achieved in scientific or positivist thinking. Interestingly, the rise of poststructuralism at least in the U.S, while apparently overturning the dominance of the New Criticism, in fact has sought to read what the New Criticism celebrated in the literary as in fact manifest in the non-literary, as, say, Hayden White (1973) has done with history writing or Clifford Geertz (1974) has done with anthropological writing, though it is interesting to note that their challenge to their own disciplines mounted by White and Geertz began with applying the very tenets of the New Criticism to their materials. But some of the scholarship on the shorter poems posits not this largely deconstructive move, but a sense of poetry as philosophical thinking that more resembles the tradition of Wittgenstein or of Rortian pragmatism, which is not to say that Chaucer becomes a Wittgenstein or a Rorty before his time. Rather, the Chaucer of the early poems becomes a poet interesting in exploring the implications of the belief systems and forms of knowledge available to him and his culture. Sheila Delany's *Chaucer's House of Fame: The Poetics of Skeptical Fideism* (1972; rpt. 1994) after nearly thirty years remains the best study of Chaucer's poem and one of the most frequently cited studies of the early poems because it successfully described a similar aspect of Chaucer's poetic endeavor. Very different studies, by such scholars as Paul Olson (1986) and Russell Peck (1978), have successfully argued that Chaucer's early poems seriously consider the claims of heterodox developments such as radical nominalism or Lollard reform, though without necessarily subscribing to their agendas. Important studies from the later 1970's, such as Alfred David's chapter on the early poems in *The Strumpet Muse* (1976), pointed to the ways in which Chaucer transformed the literary devices of French courtly poetry into tools of philosophical investigation. Judith Ferster's *Chaucer on Interpretation* (1985) dealt with the themes of hermeneutic understanding in Chaucer by focusing on the dream visions and demonstrated that Chaucerian hermeneutics was more than a theme. Jesse Gellrich's *The Idea of the Book in the Middle Ages* (1985) demonstrates that Chaucer concerned himself in the early poems with issues of writing, speech and authority, issues that have become newly important after Derrida. The conception of the poetry of the early poems as a form of philosophy rather than a reflection of it achieves a full-blown demonstration in Robert Edwards' *The Dream of Chaucer* (1989), which reads the dream visions as philosophical explorations of their own material and making, as "critical theory." For Edwards, Chaucer not only reflects but reflects upon and extends medieval aesthetic theory.

Another area where the study of dream visions pioneered an important direction in current scholarship is the topic of memory. Following Francis Yates' controversial reconstruction of *The Art of Memory* (1966), with its emphasis on the spatial quality of memory practice especially in terms of the imaginary memory palace a rhetorician was to project, and its use of striking memory figures with their features and clothing associated with categories of the topic that an orator should remember, Beryl Rowland (1981) argued that the *House of Fame* exhibited many of the features associated with the art of memory. Since then, memory has become one of the chief topics of inquiry of historiography and philosophy, spawning an entire subdiscipline of the history of memory and focusing new attention on thinkers such as Halbwachs who concerned themselves with how memory and memorialization operated in the public sphere. For medievalists, one need go no further than the important study by Mary Carruthers, *The Book of Memory* (1992), which in fact extends and corrects Yates and Rowland.

As Steven Kruger demonstrates in *Dreaming in the Middle Ages* (1992), dreams have a privileged place in medieval thought. Dreams also have a privileged place in modern thought. Psychoanalysis foregrounded the interpretation of dreams as one of its key techniques, as the title of Freud's book famously announces. Although apparently irrational, dreams have their own logic as Freud read them and their own grammar as Lacan read them. There have been surprisingly few approaches to the dream visions informed by psychoanalytic theory. It may well be that the inclusion of medieval dream theory within Chaucer's own dreams precluded the importation of psychoanalytic interpretation. The literary representation of a dream with so many explicit literary sources would seem to "intellectualize" data that according to clinical practice needs to be less mediated. However that may be, the biographically and individually oriented methodology of traditional psychoanalytic interpretation would in any case be a curiosity at this point. Yet there are other questions that psychoanalytic thought has been peculiarly acute at raising, such as those concerning the interconnected themes of memory, loss, mourning, nostalgia and melancholia that so inhabit at least *The Book of the Duchess*. If we regard modern dreams as simultaneously containing fears and desires, we might also ask what fears and desires are relegated to dream visions in the Middle Ages and what desires and anxieties we project onto its literature.

The most searching effort to do so, building on rather than applying Lacan and Deleuze and Guattari and even late Freud, has been Louise Fradenburg's remarkable essay on *The Book of the Duchess* (1990). If we follow Fradenburg, we find ourselves asking hard questions about our own responses to the consolations of literature. The themes and materials of works such as *The Book of the Duchess* and *The Legend of Good Women* raise questions about the limits of sympathy and identification, about our need for closure. Even the metapoetic interpretations of the early poems, that they are about Chaucer searching for a poetic stance and poetic material, interpretations validated by the narrator's own turn to these concerns at the end or the beginnings of the poems, are as much symptomatic as hermeneutic, suggesting our own complicity or surrender to the poetry's forgetting or repressing its own most painful or difficult moments. As I have argued, studies of the early poems have occasioned some of our most searching critiques of current critical practice, and Fradenburg in this essay explores our various historicisms in terms of our own moment's cultural fantasies and anxieties.

It has been clear for some time now that a certain notion of the literary has declined or disappeared. One source of that literariness was the prescriptions of the New Criticism. A poem or a novel or a story had to exhibit a certain kind of unity, one that could be disclosed in the form and style, even the texture of a literary work. Images create meaning not only through their content but through their formal relations with each other. Form is content. Another source of the traditional idea of the literary is the romantic conception of the poet. An author's work could be seen as an expression of his particular vision, a highly individual perspective on the relation of the self to the world. The touch of the poet is equivalent to the aura of the work of art generated by its association with creative genius. There are certain contradictions between these various sorts of literariness, one with a formal and the other with a deeply personal foundation, but they have merged over much of the twentieth century to suggest what a literary work should be and how it should be judged. The theoretical revolutions of the last few decades have called into question these preconceptions, to the degree that the concept of the literary is associated with a certain nostalgia. The positions associated with these revolutions (the death of the author, the privileging of the system of literature over its individual expressions, the collocation of all sorts of texts with those canonized as literary, the study of popular culture) are various and well known, but the result has been a demythologization of the idea of the literary. The result for the early poems, the "minor poems," has been a certain liberation from standards of judgment and modes of understanding that had relegated them to apprentice and experimental status. This revision has been assisted by the remarkable growth of interest in Langland studies and in Middle English prose works, where a new understanding of the relation of the discursive and non-discursive (often in the fictional context of dream and rapture) has been disclosed. Where thirty years ago it was possible to appreciate the poems for what they predicted about the *Troilus* and the *Canterbury Tales*, for how they showed Chaucer's debt to and eventual emancipation from convention, for how they demonstrated the evolution of the Chaucerian narrator and for how they detailed Chaucer's growth as a major poet, it is now possible to understand them in terms of all the categories that the idea of the literary excluded.

Yet we should also be attentive to how works like Chaucer's dream visions reshape rather than reject our understanding of the literary, of what non-discursive texts can accomplish. I am reminded of Maria Rosa Menocal's striking critique (1994) of the rejection of lyric (and the canonical replacement of lyric with narrative) and what we lose through that rejection. In some surprising ways, postmodern priorities have in fact rendered the dream visions more rather than less central, given their dislocations of normative temporal and spatial orientation, their tendency to elicit and then frustrate narrative expectation, and their peculiarly elaborate openings and abrupt conclusions. Yet our newly recovered comfort with their formal qualities should not obscure the fact that the poems deal with urgent obsessions and fears about who will love us, who will mourn us, who will remember us and who will succeed us. These are questions that the early poems address generically and thematically (*The Book of the Duchess* as an elegy and memorial, *The House of Fame* as a satire on the dialectic of fame and literature, *The Parlement of Foules* and its discourse of nature and generation) but which they do not necessarily answer in either medieval or modern terms.

WORKS CITED

(Each article reprinted in this volume provides its own bibliographic references. Below are listed full references for all works cited by John Ganim and myself.)

Allen, Judson Boyce. *The Friar as Critic*. Nashville: Vanderbilt University Press, 1971.

—. *Ethical Poetic of the Later Middle Ages*. Toronto: University of Toronto Press, 1982.

Baird, Lorrayne Y. *A Bibliography of Chaucer, 1964-1973*. Boston: G.K. Hall, 1977.

Baird-Lange, Lorrayne Y., and Hildegard Schnuttgen. *A Bibliography of Chaucer, 1974-1985*. Hamden, Conn.: Archon, 1988.

Baker, Donald. "The *Parliament of Fowls*" in Rowland *Companion*, pp. 428-445.

Bakhtin, M.M. *Rabelais and His World*. Tr. Helene Iswolsky. Cambridge, Mass.: MIT Press, 1968.

—. *The Dialogic Imagination*. Ed. Michael Holquist. Tr. Caryl Emerson and Michael Holquist. Austin: University of Texas Press, 1981.

Battaglia, Salvatore, ed. *Grande dizionario della lingua italiana*. Turin: Unione tipigrafico-editrice torinese, 1998.

Beidler, Peter G. and Martha A. Kalnan, eds. *The Chaucer Review: An Indexed Bibliography of the First Thirty Years (1966-96)*. *Chaucer Review* Vol. 31 No. 2 (1997).

Bennett, J.A.W. *Chaucer's Book of Fame*. Oxford: Clarendon Press, 1968.

Benson, C. David, ed. *Critical Essays on Chaucer's Troilus and Criseyde and His Early Major Poems*. Toronto: University of Toronto Press, 1991.

Benson, Larry *et al.*, eds. *The Riverside Chaucer*, 3rd Ed. Boston: Houghton Mifflin, 1987.

Boffey, Julia. "The Reputation and Circulation of Chaucer's Lyrics in the Fifteenth Century." *Chaucer Review* 28 (1993): 23-40.

Boitani, Piero and Jill Mann, eds. *The Cambridge Chaucer Companion.* Cambridge: Cambridge University Press, 1986.

Booth, Wayne. *The Rhetoric of Fiction.* Chicago: University of Chicago Press, 1961.

Bowers, John M., ed. *The Canterbury Tales: Fifteenth-Century Continuations and Additions.* Kalamazoo, Mich.: Western Michigan University Medieval Institute Publications, 1992.

Brewer, Derek, ed. *Chaucer: The Critical Heritage*, 2 Vols. London: Routledge and Kegan Paul, 1978.

Bronson, Bertrand H. "Chaucer's Art in Relation to His Audience." In *Five Studies in Literature*, University of California Publications in English, 8. Berkeley: University of California Press, 1940. Pp. 1-40.

—. *"The Book of the Duchess* Re-opened." *PMLA* 67 (1952): 863-881.

—. *In Search of Chaucer.* Toronto: University of Toronto Press, 1960.

Brownlee, Marina S., Kevin Brownlee and Stephen G. Nichols, eds. *The New Medievalism.* Baltimore: Johns Hopkins University Press, 1991.

Bynum, Caroline Walker. *Jesus as Mother: Studies in the Spirituality of the High Middle Ages.* Publications of the Center for Medieval and Renaissance Studies, 16. Berkeley: University of California Press, 1982.

Cannon, Christopher. *"Raptus* in the Chaumpaigne Release and a Newly Discovered Document Concerning the Life of Geoffrey Chaucer." *Speculum* 68 (1993): 74-94.

—. "The Myth of Origin and the Making of Chaucer's English." *Speculum* 71 (1996): 646-675.

Carruthers, Mary. *The Book of Memory: A Study of Memory in Mediaeval Culture.* Cambridge Studies in Medieval Literature 10. Cambridge: Cambridge University Press 1992.

Chaucer, Geoffrey. *The Minor Poems: A Variorum Edition of the Works of Geoffrey Chaucer.* Ed. George B. Pace and Alfred David. Vol. 5, Part 1. Norman, Oklahoma: University of Oklahoma Press, 1982.

—. *Riverside Edition*, see Benson (1987).

Coleman, Joyce. *Public Reading and the Reading Public in Late Medieval England and France.* New York: Cambridge University Press, 1996.

Crawford, William R. *Bibliography of Chaucer 1954-1963.* Seattle: University of Washington Press, 1967.

Crow, Martin M. and Clair C. Olson, *Chaucer Life-Records.* Oxford: Clarendon, 1966.

Curtius, Ernst R. *European Literature and the Latin Middle Ages.* Trans. Willard R. Trask. New York: Harper Torchbooks, 1963. Princeton: Princeton University Press, Bollingen Series, 1973.

David, Alfred. *The Strumpet Muse: Art and Morals in Chaucer's Poetry.* Bloomington, Indiana: Indiana University Press, 1976.

Davis, Norman *et al.*, comp. *A Chaucer Glossary.* Oxford: Clarendon Press, 1979.

Delany, Sheila. *Chaucer's House of Fame: The Poetics of Skeptical Fideism.* Chicago, 1972. Rpt. with a new foreword by Michael Near, Gainesville: University of Florida Press, 1994.

—. *The Naked Text: Chaucer's Legend of Good Women.* Berkeley: University of California Press, 1994.

Dinshaw, Carolyn. *Chaucer's Sexual Poetics.* Madison: University of Wisconsin Press, 1989.

Donaldson, E. Talbot. "Chaucer the Pilgrim" *PMLA* 49 (1954): 928-936.

—. *Speaking of Chaucer.* New York: Norton, 1977.

Edwards, Robert. *The Dream of Chaucer.* Durham, North Carolina: Duke University Press, 1989.

Ferster, Judith. *Chaucer on Interpretation.* Cambridge: Cambridge University Press, 1985.

Fisher, John H. "The Lyrics" in Rowland *Companion*, pp. 464-476.

—, ed. *The Complete Poetry and Prose of Geoffrey Chaucer*, 2nd Ed. Fort Worth: Holt, Rinehart and Winston, 1989.

Fradenburg, Louise O. "'Voice Memorial': Loss and Reparation in Chaucer's Poetry," *Exemplaria* II (1990): 169-202.

Frank, Robert W., Jr. *Chaucer and the Legend of Good Women.* Cambridge, Mass.: Harvard University Press, 1972.

Frye, Northrop. *Anatomy of Criticism: Four Essays.* Princeton: Princeton University Press, 1957.

Ganim, John M. *Chaucerian Theatricality.* Princeton: Princeton University Press, 1990.

—. "Medieval Literature as Monster: The Grotesque Before and After Bakhtin," *Exemplaria* 7 (1995): 27-40.

—. "The Myth of Medieval Romance" in *Medievalism and the Modernist Temper*, ed. R. Howard Bloch and Stephen G. Nichols. Baltimore: Johns Hopkins University Press, 1996. Pp. 148-167.

Geertz, Clifford. *The Interpretation of Cultures.* New York: Basic Books, 1974.

Gellrich, Jesse. *The Idea of the Book in the Middle Ages: Language Theory, Mythology and Fiction.* Ithaca: Cornell University Press, 1985.

Glare, P.G.W., ed. *The Oxford Latin Dictionary*. Oxford: Clarendon Press, 1982.

Goddard, H.C. "Chaucer's *Legend of Good Women*." *JEGP* 7 (1908):87- 129; 8 (1909): 47-112.

Godefroy, Frederic, ed. *Dictionnaire de l'ancienne langue francaise*. Paris: F. Vieweg, 1881-1902. Rpt. Vaduz: Kraus, 1965.

Graff, Gerald. *Professing Literature: An Institutional History*. Chicago: University of Chicago Press, 1987.

Griffith, Dudley. *Bibliography of Chaucer: 1908-1953*. Seattle: University of Washington Press, 1955.

Hammond, Eleanor. *Chaucer: A Bibliographic Manual*. New York: Peter Smith, 1908.

Hansen, Elaine Tuttle. *Chaucer and the Fictions of Gender*. Berkeley: University of California Press, 1991.

Howard, Donald R. "Chaucer the Man." *PMLA* 80 (1965): 337-343.

—. "Flying Through Space: Chaucer and Milton." In *Milton and the Line of Vision*. Ed. Joseph Wittreich. Madison: University of Wisconsin Press, 1975. Pp. 3-23

—. *Chaucer: His Life, His Works, His World*. New York: Fawcett Columbine, 1987.

Jordan, Robert M. *Chaucer and the Shape of Creation*. Cambridge, Mass.: Harvard University Press, 1967.

—. *Chaucer's Poetics and the Modern Reader*. Berkeley: University of California Press, 1987.

Kean, P.M. *Chaucer and the Making of English Poetry*, 2 Vols. London: Routledge, 1972.

Kelly, Henry Ansgar. *Chaucer and the Cult of Saint Valentine*. Leiden: Brill, 1986.

Kendrick, Laura. *Chaucerian Play*. Berkeley: University of California Press, 1988.

Kittredge, George L. *Chaucer and His Poetry*. Cambridge, Mass.: Harvard University Press, 1915.

Knight, Stephen. *Ryming Craftily*. Sydney: Angus and Robertson, 1973.

Koff, Leonard M. *Chaucer and the Art of Storytelling*. Berkeley: University of California Press, 1988.

Kreuzer, James R. "The Dreamer in *The Book of the Duchess*." *PMLA* 66 (1951): 543-547.

Kruger, Steven. *Dreaming in the Middle Ages*. Cambridge Studies in Medieval Literature 14. Cambridge: Cambridge University Press, 1992.

Kurath, Hans *et al.*, eds. *The Middle English Dictionary*. Ann Arbor: University of Michigan Press, 1952-.

Lawton, David. *Chaucer's Narrators*. Cambridge: D.S. Brewer, 1985.

Lerer, Seth. *Chaucer and His Readers: Imagining the Author in Late Medieval England*. Princeton: Princeton University Press, 1993.

Lindahl, Carl. *Earnest Games: Folkloric Patterns in the Canterbury Tales*. Bloomington: Indiana University Press, 1987.

Lowes, John L. "Is Chaucer's *Legend of Good Women* a Travesty?" *JEGP* 8 (1909) 513-569.

Mann, Jill. *Chaucer and the Medieval Estates Satire*. Cambridge: Cambridge University Press, 1973.

—. *Geoffrey Chaucer*, Feminist Readings Series. Atlantic Highlands, N.J.: Humanities Press, 1991.

Margherita, Gayle. *The Romance of Origins: Language and Sexual Difference in Middle English Literature*. Philadelphia: University of Pennsylvania Press, 1994.

McCall, John P. *Chaucer Among the Gods*. University Park: Pennsylvania State University Press, 1979.

M.E.D., see Kurath.

Mehl, Dieter. *Geoffrey Chaucer: An Introduction to His Narrative Poetry* 1973; trans. 1986. Cambridge and New York: Cambridge University Press, 1986.

Menocal, Maria Rosa. *Shards of Love: Exile and the Origins of Lyric*. Durham, N.C.: Duke University Press, 1994.

Middleton, Anne. "The Idea of Public Poetry in the Reign of Richard II." *Speculum* 53 (1978): 94-114.

Migne, J.P., ed.*Patrologiae cursus completus: Series latina*, 221 Vols. Paris: J.P. Migne, 1844-65.

Miller, Robert P., ed. *Chaucer: Sources and Backgrounds*. New York: Oxford University Press, 1977.

Minnis, A.J. *Chaucer and Pagan Antiquity*. Cambridge and Totowa, N.J.: D.S. Brewer/Rowman Littlefield, 1982.

—. *Medieval Theory of Authorship*, 2nd Ed. Aldershot: Scolar Press, 1988.

—, with V.J. Scattergood and J.J. Smith. *Oxford Guides to Chaucer: The Shorter Poems*. Oxford: Clarendon, 1995.

Morris, Lynn King. *Chaucer Source and Analogue Criticism*. New York: Garland, 1985.

Muscatine, Charles. *Chaucer and the French Tradition*. Berkeley: University of California Press, 1957.

Nichols, Stephen G., ed. "The New Philology." *Speculum* Vol. 65 No. 1 (January 1990).

Niermeyer, J.F. *Mediae Latinitatis Lexicon Minus*. Leiden: Brill, 1976.

O.E.D., see Simpson.

Oizumi, Akio, ed. *Complete Concordance to the Works of Geoffrey Chaucer*, 12 Vols. programmed by Kunihiro Miki. Hildesheim, New York: Olms Weidmann, 1991-1994.

Olson, Paul. *The Canterbury Tales and the Good Society*. Princeton: Princeton University Press, 1986.

Partner, Nancy F. ed. "Studying Medieval Women: Sex, Gender, Feminism." *Speculum* Vol. 68 No. 2 (April 1993).

Patrolologia, see Migne.

Payne, Robert O. *The Key of Remembrance*. New Haven: Yale University Press for the University of Cincinnati, 1963.

Pearsall, Derek. *The Life of Geoffrey Chaucer*. Oxford: Blackwell, 1992.

Peck, Russell A. "Chaucer and the Nominalist Questions." *Speculum* 53 (1978): 745-760.

—, ed. *Chaucer's Lyrics and "Anelida and Arcite": An Annotated Bibliography 1900-1980*. Toronto; University of Toronto Press, 1983.

Piehler, Paul. *The Visionary Landscape: A Study in Medieval Allegory*. London: Edward Arnold, 1971.

Poulet, Georges. *Studies in Human Time*. Tr. Elliott Coleman. Baltimore: Johns Hopkins University Press, 1956.

Quilligen, Maureen. "Allegory, Allegoresis, and the Deallegorization of Language" in Morton W. Bloomfield, ed. *Allegory, Myth and Symbol*. Cambridge, Mass: Harvard University Press, 1981. Pp. 164-186

Quinn, William A. *Chaucer's Rehersynges: The Performability of the Legend of Good Women*. Washington, D.C.: Catholic University of America Press, 1994.

Reiss, Edmund. "Dusting Off the Cobwebs: A New Look at Chaucer's Lyrics." *Chaucer Review* 1 (1966): 55-65.

Richards, I.A. *Practical Criticism: A Study of Literary Judgment*. New York: Harcourt Brace, 1929.

Robertson, D.W., Jr. *A Preface to Chaucer: Studies in Medieval Perspectives*. Princeton: Princeton University Press, 1962.

—. "The Historical Setting of the *Book of the Duchess*." In *Essays in Medieval Culture*. 1965. Princeton: Princeton University Press, 1980. Pp. 235-56.

—. "The *Book of the Duchess*" in Rowland *Companion*, pp. 403-13.

Robbins, Rossell Hope. "The Lyrics" in Rowland *Companion*, pp. 380-402.

—. "Chaucerian Apocrypha" in Albert E. Hartung, gen ed. *A Manual of Writings in Middle English 1050-1500*, Vol.4. New Haven: Connecticut Academy of Arts and Sciences, 1973. Pp. 1061-1101, 1285-1306.

Robinson, F.N., ed. *The Works of Geoffrey Chaucer*, 2nd Cambridge Ed. Boston: Houghton, 1957.

Rowland, Beryl, ed. *Companion to Chaucer Studies*, Rev. Ed. Oxford: Oxford University Press, 1979.

—. "The Art of Memory and the Art of Poetry in the *House of Fame*." *University of Ottowa Quarterly* 51 (1981): 162-171.

Ruggiers, Paul, "The Unity of Chaucer's *House of Fame*." *Studies in Philology* 50 (1953): 16-29.

—. ed. *Editing Chaucer: The Great Tradition*. Norman: University of Oklahoma Press, 1977.

Russell, J. Stephen. *The English Dream Vision: Anatomy of a Form*. Columbus: The Ohio State University Press, 1988.

Scanlon, Larry. *Narrative, Authority and Power: The Medieval Exemplum and the Chaucerian Tradition*. Cambridge Studies in Medieval Literature, 28. Cambridge: Cambridge University Press, 1994.

Schoeck, Richard J. and Jerome Taylor, eds. *Chaucer Criticism II: Troilus and Criseyde and the Minor Poems*. South Bend, In.: University of Notre Dame Press, 1961.

Seymour, M.C. *A Catalogue of Chaucer's Manuscripts, Vol. I: Works Before The Canterbury Tales*. Aldershot: Scolar Press, 1995.

Shook, Laurence. "The *House of Fame*" in Rowland *Companion*, pp. 414-27.

Simpson, J.A., E.S.C. Weiner *et al.*, eds. *The Oxford English Dictionary*, 2nd Ed. Oxford: Clarendon Press, 1989.

Sklute, Larry. *Virtue of Necessity*. Columbus: The Ohio State University Press, 1984.

Spearing, A.C. *Criticism and Medieval Poetry*. London: Edward Arnold, 1964.

—. *The Medieval Poet as Voyeur: Looking and Listening in Medieval Love Narratives*. Cambridge: Cambridge University Press, 1993.

Spurgeon, Caroline. *Five Hundred Years of Chaucer Criticism and Allusion 1357-1900*, 3 Vols. Cambridge: Cambridge University Press, 1925.

Stevens, Martin. "The Performing Self in Twelfth Century Culture." *Viator* 9 (1978): 193-212.

Tatlock, John S.P. and Arthur G. Kennedy, eds. *A Concordance to the Works of Geoffrey Chaucer and to the Romaunt of the Rose.* Washington, D.C., 1927. Rpt. Gloucester, Mass.: P. Smith, 1963.

Taylor, Andrew. "Anne of Bohemia and the Making of Chaucer." *Studies in the Age of Chaucer* 19 (1997): 95-119.

Thomas, Alfred. *Anne's Bohemia: Czech Literature and Society 1310-1420.* Minneapolis: University of Minnesota Press, 1998

Utley, Francis Lee. *The Crooked Rib.* Columbus, 1944. Rpt. New York: Octagon Books, 1970.

Wallace, David J. "Anne of Bohemia, Queen of England, and Chaucer's Emperice." *Litteraria Pragensia* 5 (1995): 1-16.

—. *Chaucerian Polity.* Stanford: Stanford University Press, 1997.

Wagenknecht, Edward, ed. *Chaucer: Modern Essays in Criticism.* London: Oxford University Press, 1959.

White, Hayden. *Metahistory: The Historical Imagination in Nineteenth Century Europe.* Baltimore: Johns Hopkins University Press, 1973.

Yates, Francis. *The Art of Memory.* Chicago: University of Chicago Press, 1966.

CREDITS

Spearing, A.C. "Chaucer." In *Medieval Dream Poetry*. Cambridge: Cambridge University Press, 1976. Pp. 48-110, 221-224. Copyright © 1976 by Cambridge University Press. Reprinted by permission of Cambridge University Press.

Edwards, Robert R. "The Practice of Theory." In *The Dream of Chaucer*. Durham, N.C.: Duke University Press, 1989. Pp.17-39, 161-163. Copyright ©1989 by Duke University Press. Reprinted by permission of Duke University Press.

Lumiansky, R.M. "The Bereaved Narrator in Chaucer's *The Book of the Duchess*," *Tulane Studies in English* 9 (1959): 5-17. © Reprinted by permission of the publisher.

Huppé, Bernard and D.W. Robertson, Jr. "*The Book of the Duchess*." In *Fruyt and Chaf*. Princeton: Princeton University Press, 1963. Pp.32-100. Copyright © 1963 by Princeton University Press. Reprinted by permission of Princeton University Press.

Hardman, Phillipa. "*The Book of the Duchess* as a Memorial Monument," *The Chaucer Review* 28 (1994): 205-215. Copyright © 1994 by The Pennsylvania State University Press. Reprinted by permission of the The Pennsylvania State University Press.

Payne, Robert O. *The Key of Remembrance*. New Haven, Conn.: Published for the University of Cincinnati, Yale University Press, 1963. Pp. 129-139. Copyright © 1963 by Yale University. Reprinted by permission of Yale University Press.

Delany, Sheila."Chaucer's *House of Fame* and the *Ovide Moralisé*," *Comparative Literature* 20 (1968): 254-264. © Reprinted by permission of the publisher.

Benson, Larry D. "The 'Love Tydynges' in Chaucer's *House of Fame*." In *Chaucer in the Eighties*. Edited by Julian N. Wasserman and Robert

J. Blanch, pp. 3-22. Syracuse, N.Y.: Syracuse University Press, 1986. Copyright © 1986 by Syracuse University Press. Reprinted by permission of Syracuse University Press.

Bronson, Bertrand H. "*The Parlement of Foules* Revisited," *ELH* 15 (1948) 247-260. Copyright © 1948 by The Johns Hopkins University Press. Reprinted by permission of the The Johns Hopkins University Press.

Olson, Paul A."Aristotle's Politics and the Foundations of Human Society," *Studies in the Age of Chaucer* 2 (1980): 53-80. © Reprinted by permission of the publisher.

Aers, David. "*The Parliament of Fowls*: Authority, the Knower and the Known," *The Chaucer Review* 16 (1981):1-17. Copyright © 1981 by The Pennsylvania State University Press. Reprinted by permission of the The Pennsylvania State University Press.

Frank, Robert Worth, Jr. "*The Legend of Good Women*: Some Implications." In Rossell Hope Robbins, ed., *Chaucer at Albany*. New York: Burt Franklin, 1975. Copyright ©1975 by The Pennsylvania State University Press. Reprinted by permission of The Pennsylvania State University Press.

Kiser, Lisa J. *Telling Classical Tales*. Ithaca, N.Y.: Cornell University Press, 1983. Pp. 95-131. Copyright © 1983 by Cornell University Press. Reprinted by permission of Cornell University Press.

Dinshaw, Carolyn. "'The naked text in English to declare': *The Legend of Good Women*." In *Chaucer's Sexual Poetics*. Madison, Wisc.: The University of Wisconsin Press, 1990. Pp. 65-87, 219-229. Copyright © 1990 by The University of Wisconsin Press. Reprinted by permission of The University of Wisconsin Press.

Green, Richard F. "Women in Chaucer's Audience." *The Chaucer Review* 18 (1982): 156-164. Copyright 1982 by The Pennsylvania State University Press. Copyright ©1982 by The Pennsylvania State University Press. Reprinted by permission of The Pennsylvania State University Press.

Patterson, Lee. "'Thirled with the Poynt of Remembraunce': The Theban Writing of *Anelida and Arcite*." In *Chaucer and the Subject of*